CW00816044

HISTORY OF THE

IRISH GUARDS

IN THE SECOND WORLD WAR

HISTORY OF THE
IRISH GUARDS
IN THE SECOND WORLD WAR

BY

MAJOR D. J. L. FITZGERALD, M.C.

With a Foreword by

FIELD-MARSHAL THE VISCOUNT ALEXANDER OF TUNIS
K.G., G.C.B., G.C.M.G., C.S.I., D.S.O., M.C.

The Naval & Military Press Ltd

Published by

The Naval & Military Press Ltd
Unit 5 Riverside, Brambleside
Bellbrook Industrial Estate
Uckfield, East Sussex
TN22 1QQ England

Tel: +44 (0)1825 749494

www.naval-military-press.com
www.nmarchive.com

Dedicated to our
Fallen Comrades

FOREWORD

As a boy my ambition was to become an Irish Guardsman. When I joined the Regiment in 1911, I never thought that nearly forty years on I would be writing a foreword to its history in the Second World War.

I am very proud to write this introduction to a book which will be of great interest, not only to all Irish Guardsmen but to those who appreciate reading of the exploits of a great fighting unit.

The story opens on April 11th, 1940, when the 1st Battalion embarked for Norway, under the command of a splendid officer who had been my Adjutant in the First World War. This early adventure into battle was to prove neither happy nor very successful, and this would seem to be the fate of the British Army at the beginning of every major war. Norway was followed by the disastrous period in Northern France which ended in the evacuation from Dunkirk. No blame can be attached to the gallant men who fought our early battles, in which so many of them gave their lives. In fighting and dying they gave us the time to prepare for the great struggle which lay ahead.

In the fall of 1942 the tide turned. And now there is a very different story to tell. For the first time, we had the equipment and material with which to fight the enemy on equal terms.

After the victory at El Alamein we never looked back. Battles were fought and won in a procession which never ceased until the final surrender of the German Armies brought hostilities to an end in Europe.

In January of 1943, the 1st Battalion joined my 18th Army Group as a part of the British 1st Army. And in this final phase of the North African Campaign they were destined to play a very important part in my plan for the capture of Tunis.

The Bou Massif was a strongly held fortress which flanked our advance. My old Regiment with all the fire and dash it had always displayed in the 1914-18 war, captured this Nazi fortress and held it against repeated attacks by the enemy to regain it.

With my left flank secured the British Army swept into Tunis and the Axis forces of close on a quarter of a million men laid down their arms. The whole of North Africa was now in our hands.

The Irish Guards had played their part in no uncertain manner, but not without grievous losses in fine officers and men. Their gallantry was well recognized in the award of the Victoria Cross to Corporal Kenneally whom I decorated at the end of hostilities.

Later in the following year, the 1st Battalion took an active part at Anzio, where some of the hardest and most bitter fighting of the Italian Campaign was waged. Although this surprise landing behind the enemy's flank was sealed in before it could gain the decisive results hoped for, the Battalion took its full share in holding on to this strategic position which had been won. The retention of the Anzio bridgehead against the fiercest of enemy assaults was to prove a battle-winning factor in my plan for the taking of Rome. A few months later the Anzio force broke out to join hands with the advancing armies in the capture of the first capital city in Europe to fall to the Allies. Rome fell on June 4th.

After the 1st Battalion left the Mediterranean, it returned to England to re-form with new recruits. I was sorry to see them go. They had fought with me in North Africa and in Italy where they had displayed the dash and gallantry I knew so well of old, but I was glad to know that they had partaken in full measure of our victories.

The story now passes to our sister Battalions which fought in North-West Europe from Normandy to the Baltic and who, during those eleven months' fighting, won fresh battle honours to be added to that proud number already carried on the colours of the Irish Guards.

In recording the deeds of the Regiment on the battlefields of Europe, we must not forget that individual Irish Guardsmen served with distinction in nearly all theatres of operations where the Forces of the Crown were in action against the enemy. Although their deeds are not recorded in this book, they have made their contribution to the records of the Regiment and played their part as good Irish Guardsmen.

I hope that this book will be widely read. It is the record of a great fighting Regiment, which has not only upheld the tradition of the Irish Guards in battle, but which has added fresh lustre to the long history of the Brigade.

When it comes to this business of fighting, the proudest claim a man can make is that he is a front line soldier. I am glad that in my earlier days my front line service was with the Irish Guards.

May 20th
1949.

Alexander of Tunis.
Colonel
and Field Marshal.

PREFACE

THE writing of this History has stretched over the commands of two Lieutenant-Colonels, Colonel C. A. Montagu-Douglas-Scott, D.S.O., and Colonel J. O. E. Vandeleur, D.S.O. In Colonel Andrew and Colonel Joe I had always at my call the two best sources for the campaigns in Norway, the Mediterranean and North-West Europe. I am most grateful to them for their confidence and patience.

The basis of this History has been the admirable War Diaries kept by a series of Battalion Intelligence Officers. I was an Intelligence Officer myself, and I know how tempting it is to let the days slip by and then, weeks later, to fill up the blank spaces with "Nothing unusual. Some shelling." I succumbed to temptation and I have paid for it. To this basis I have added a mass of individual records and reminiscences. Officers and men lent me their diaries, letters and papers for months on end, without complaint, and went over battles with me again and again. I hope that I thanked them properly at the time, especially those (Lieutenant-Colonel D. M. Gordon Watson, M.C., and Captain D. Drummond, to name only two of many) who wrote long accounts of isolated actions. And in particular I must thank R.S.M. Coppen, M.B.E., and his clerks who cheerfully turned the Orderly Room upside down to unearth small details and did all the typing and indexing, and my brother, Eamon Fitzgerald, M.C., who prepared most of Part V, the Campaign in North-West Europe.

I have tried above all things to be accurate, not only because this is an official record, but as a tribute to the many old friends and comrades who may read what I have written, and still more to those who will never read it and to whom I have dedicated this book.

DESMOND FITZGERALD.

CONTENTS

PART V

THE 2ND AND 3RD BATTALIONS IN NORTH-WEST EUROPE

ILLUSTRATIONS

MAPS

PART I

•

THE 1st BATTALION IN NORWAY

CHAPTER I

The North-Western Europe Force

ON 8th April the Royal Navy laid mines at certain places in Norwegian waters. The Allied Governments stated that they had been forced to do this because German naval and merchant shipping had been constantly using these territorial waters in order to evade the British blockade. The Germans had done the same thing in the 1914-1918 war, but the Norwegians had laid minefields themselves in order to stop it. This time the Norwegian Government did not see its way to taking similar action. When they were told that the Allies had done it for them, they met to draft a protest against "the violation of the Norwegian neutrality."

On the morning of 9th April the Germans announced to the world that they had taken such steps as were necessary to "eliminate the North of Europe definitely from the British plans for extending the war." This meant, in fact, that German troops had marched into Denmark and had landed in Norway by sea and by air. They described this as an impressive way of showing that aim which Germany was pursuing in all her military actions—"to safeguard peace and protect the weak." The Swiss Press could not conceal their alarm at such a statement, for though no one could lay mines off their coast, they were peaceful and very weak.

Denmark was occupied during the morning. "No incidents occurred anywhere," said the Germans. "On the Norwegian coast notable resistance was offered only near Oslo. It was broken during the afternoon. Oslo itself is now occupied."

Early that morning—at 5 a.m.—the German Minister in Oslo had called on the Norwegian Government, told them that German troops were landing and asked that no resistance be offered. Dr. Koht, the Prime Minister, replied that Norway would resist as long as possible and ordered total mobilization.

The Norwegian Army consisted only of a permanent cadre of 1,900 officers and N.C.Os., with a yearly call-up of 12,500 men for 84 days' training. With the exception of the Polar Division, which was in the far north watching the Finnish frontier, it was not mobilized, and what arms and ammunition it possessed were scattered in depots all over the country. The Navy consisted of a couple of elderly warships and a few submarines, trawlers and armed whaling ships. The Air Force was negligible—and anyway, German parachutists and airborne troops had landed on every aerodrome in the country.

For the Norwegians the invasion was the "Ragnarokk," the "last day" prophesied in the Edda, the ancient Norse poems still taught in their schools. It is the time when man will forget the laws even of brotherhood—"axe-time, sword time, wind-time, wolf-time," when "flames will leap down from heaven itself," as indeed they did.

The Allied Supreme War Council immediately announced that they would extend the fullest possible aid to the Norwegians. Mr. Churchill, however, added a proviso: "It is not the slightest use," he said, "blaming the Allies for not being able to give substantial help or protection to neutral countries if they are held at arm's length until these countries are attacked on a scientifically prepared plan by Germany."

Germany would probably have preferred to control the Scandinavian states economically and absorb all their products—iron ore, timber, foodstuffs and manufactured goods—without having to invade and then garrison them. But she was well prepared to fight if the Allies attempted to interfere. As far back as 1937 the German General Staff had drawn up routine plans for the invasion of Denmark and Norway and had since then been checking and perfecting them. During the months of February and March, 1940, transports had been collected in the German Baltic ports, as the British Government knew, and Austrian mountain troops had been withdrawn from the Western front to practise embarking and disembarking.

The German Rear-Admiral Lutsow claimed, in an official statement, to have known on 28th March that the British Government had decided to lay mines off the Norwegian coast in order to stop the import of Swedish iron ore via Norway to Germany and to divert it into their own ports. If this statement is true, the Germans had nearly a fortnight in which to launch their invasion. The German troops, on their own showing, embarked and set sail at least two days before the minefields were laid. Also, a German battle fleet, consisting of the *Scharnhorst* and *Hipper* with cruisers and destroyers, put to sea and led the British North Sea Fleet out of Scapa Flow on a wild chase into the Arctic Sea.

The Allies, on the other hand, though they knew that Germany was preparing to strike, could not guess where the blow would fall. The Navy certainly had no hint. After having laid their mines, the Navy withdrew, and so could not intercept the German transports which were already on their way. Nor did they prevent the Germans screening their communications by mining the Skagerrak. These lost hours, during which a large part of the German invasion fleet might have been sunk, were the most vital in the whole campaign.

The Germans landed at Bergen, Stavanger, Trondheim, Egersund and Narvik. Their plan was to gain complete control of Southern Norway and establish a general defensive line from Trondheim to the Swedish frontier before the Allies had moved at all. The Foreign Minister, Ribbentrop, boasted that no Englishman or Frenchman would be able to set foot in Norway till the war was over.

Every detail of the German campaign was meticulously planned. Their commanders-designate had been sent on holidays to Norway and seemed to know every bit of the country. They were equipped with excellent maps, based on the Norwegian Staff maps, but handier and designed to fit in with the operations. The Allies, and frequently the Norwegians themselves, had often to rely on the sketchy relief maps published by the Norwegian State Railways for genuine tourists. Every German soldier had a neat Norwegian phrase book and a bundle of proclamations to stick on walls. The Germans had also carefully organized their Norwegian supporters through the Nordische Gesellschaft, a society for the "propagation of Nordic culture and ideals." This society had contacts in nearly every Norwegian village and town. One of the members was Vidkun Quisling ; another was the commander of the garrison of Narvik. The Norwegian warships in Narvik fjord went down fighting ; the garrison did not fire a shot.

The Allies' plan was much the same as that of the Germans, only the other way round. The Norwegians were trying to hold the two valleys, Gutbrand and Osterdal, up which ran the railway from Oslo to Trondheim, and the only roads to the north. British and, later, French troops were to land at Namsos and Andalsnes, a hundred miles either side of Trondheim, recapture the port, and establish a defensive line from the sea to the Swedish frontier which would confine the Germans to the comparatively level country of the south until the Allies were ready to descend from the hills. Simultaneously, Allied troops would land near Narvik and eliminate the isolated enemy forces in that area. Command of the sea and local air superiority were essential to the success of this plan.

Norway is a long, narrow mountain plateau, broadening and sloping towards the south. It stretches over thirteen degrees of latitude ; this means that the distance from Lindesnes in the south to the North Cape is about the same as from Lindesnes to the Pyrenees. The length of the coast, measured in a straight line, is nearly 1,700 miles ; if the fjords and greater islands are included, it is more than 12,000 miles.

The population of this enormous country is only about two million. Even more than the English, the Norwegians are an essentially maritime people. Their whole history, life, economy and country are inextricably bound up with the sea. One man in five is a seaman, manning the Norwegian merchant fleet, the third largest in the world, exceeded only by England and Germany. During the 1914-1918 war Norway, though neutral, lost half her total tonnage and 2,000 seamen, but in the interval between the wars she built up her fleet again. Of the whole population, one man in twenty-five is a fisherman, coastal, deep sea or whaling. In the north, and particularly the Lofoten Islands, the vast majority are fishermen, landing about 800,000 tons of cod and herring alone each year. The north prospers on and reeks of fish.

Those Norwegians who are not seafarers are farmers, although only 2½ per cent. of the country is arable land and only a quarter of it will support even forests. "Our country has a sufficiency of stones," wrote Ibsen sadly to Edward Grieg. Into this rocky, mountainous country run a series of fissures, from west to east, dividing it into separate compartments between which communications are very difficult except by sea. Patient and skilful engineering has succeeded in driving one tortuous road through the country from south to north. The formation of the undersea coastline allows only the warm Gulf Stream into the fjords, keeping out the icy Arctic waters. This gives Norway ice-free ports in winter, a comparatively mild spring and a warm summer.

It is, however, a country of violent seasons. The Gulf Stream does not prevent a temporary "ice age" appearing inland every winter. In the north the sun does not appear at all for eight months of the year, and work has to be done by artificial light even at midday. During the four months of summer perfectly clear photographs can be taken at midnight. From the middle of April to the middle of August there is no real darkness in the whole of Norway.

This was the country which the German Generals chose for the first trial of strength. Norway had known nothing of war for over a hundred years. She was now experiencing the full effect of modern warfare as perfected by the Germans.

On 1st April, 1940, the Commanding Officer, Lieut.-Colonel Faulkner, M.C., received a warning that the Battalion would very soon leave London to complete its mobilization in a Division. The Brigade Commander, Brigadier W. Fraser, gave the 10th as the probable date of the move. The 24th Guards Brigade had existed as a formation since December—on paper. There was no Brigade Staff until one was now hastily assembled. Of the three Battalions, the 1st Bn. Irish Guards and the 1st Bn. Scots Guards knew each other of old. The 2nd Bn. South Wales Borderers, however, had just returned from a long tour of duty in India. Nowadays all three battalions in a brigade always work and live together before going into action. The Commanding Officers call each other by their christian names ; the Adjutants should be close friends, denouncing in harmony the iniquities of Brigade H.Q. ; the Quartermasters should be linked together by loans and secret agreements, and all the officers should visit each other's messes. But in 1940 nobody in the Irish or Scots Guards knew anything about the South Wales Borderers or even where they were.

Until more definite orders came, there was little that could be done except hand over all commitments to the 2nd Battalion, issue battle-dress and draw from Ordnance the full scale of equipment as laid down for Home Service by that best known of all Army Forms, G1098. The companies drew extra Bren guns, to give one to each section, and an anti-tank rifle for each platoon. The Mortar Platoon handed in their training dummy and got in exchange two 3-inch mortars. The normal training went on. The King visited the Battalion during training on the 4th, which proved to the Guardsmen that the Battalion was really going to move. The day after the King's visit, packing up began in earnest. Stores were checked, accounts closed, leave stopped, and a small advance party sent over to Hyde Park Barracks to join the Scots Guards, who were to move off first.

Everything had to be packed in small boxes, and the heavier equipment broken up into man loads. This gave the Battalion their only guide to the future. It ruled out France, and meant that they would be going to some desolate place where all stores would have to be man-handled ashore.

On the 7th the Movement and Administrative Instructions arrived from the Director of Mobilization—a pile of technical documents, which were soon covered by notes by the Commanding Officer:

> " What does 1st Reinforcement consist of ?"
>
> " The 2nd Bn. have still to send us 25 men and the Training Bn. 50 or 60. Adjutant to get a Bn. Move Order out immediately."

Captain B. O'Neill produced the order the following morning. The Company Commanders, the Transport Officer, the Quartermaster, the Regimental Sergeant-Major, the Drill Sergeants, the Pioneer Sergeant, the President of the Officers' Mess and the Sergeants' Mess Caterer called their little conferences and started the machinery that would put the Battalion on a train at Euston at eight o'clock on the evening of the 10th, taking everything they could possibly need, and leaving behind a spotless barracks. The Transport Officer, Captain P. Whitefoord, M.C., saw that he need be in no hurry. It would be a good week before he would have to take the transport and the carriers up to Catterick. This would give him time to fit the new tracks and overhaul the engines. Information seeped down through the Battalion.

"Is it right that you are going up to Catterick to join the 49th Division ?" asked the 2nd Battalion men. "That is what they say."

The next day's papers changed the questions :

"Have you heard the news ? The Germans have invaded Norway." "Will it take the Battalion ?" "I wonder where the Jocks are."

The 1st Bn. Scots Guards had disappeared into Euston station a few days before. There had been no word from them or from the Battalion's advance party, under Captain D. H. Fitzgerald. Through his office window the Transport Sergeant, P.S.M. McCleary, watched his drivers cleaning their trucks with the comfort of a man who has plenty of time. A ring on the telephone brought him the Adjutant's voice: "The transport will move tomorrow. The carriers must be loaded on to flats at King's Cross by eight o'clock in the morning." "Tomorrow morning, sir ? The new tracks are not on yet and we're still deficient of spare parts. We will have to work all night, sir." "So you will. Also the Battalion is confined to barracks."

The Quartermaster (Lieutenant McCarthy) and the Pioneer Sergeant went round rooms looking for barrack damages. "Are your men all busy ?" "Yes, sir, they are out with paint pots stencilling the serial number 2595 on all the boxes and baggage they can find." " Don't forget the bicycles. The Armourer is checking them now.

Put bands of white, grey and white and a big red B on them. Don't spare the paint; there is plenty of it."

Under the archway the Armourer watched the orderlies stacking the bicycles. "This one has got a broken pedal, sir; they said you'd mend it." "Not only have I got to mend your bicycle for you, but I've also got to take it down to the station and load it carefully into a special van. What for? So that you can break it again—if you ever see it again. Do you realize that I've got some thirty Brens and fifteen A/T rifles to inspect? Where's the W.T. Sergeant? Does he know that he's got to take the ammunition from the magazine direct to the station and distribute it on the train?" "I do," said P.S.M. Bingham. "The Companies drew what they have got to carry this morning. They didn't want a hundred rounds for each A/T rifle, but that is what is laid down. [Do you know the old story about the Staff Officer in Egypt? 'Tell me, my man,' says he to a Guardsman, 'who carries the Boys rifle?' 'Ah sure, sir,' says the Mick, 'de boys carry deir own rifles.'] I gave the Pipe Major eight thousand rounds mixed ball and tracer for his A/A Brens to shoot the Luftwaffe out of the sky."

In the offices and the Mess, the Company Commanders went through the orders. "We wear full 'Christmas Tree Order'—'Change of Quarters' with additions. British warms, with a haversack slung on either side, and respirator at the alert. We all know that the neat square of webbing in the middle of the chest is a perfect aiming mark for snipers, but there it is. You've seen the list of officers, so the suspense is over."

2/Lieutenant D. M. Kennedy was beaming. "Where's my servant? Hackett! Hackett! Give back that Guardsman's greatcoat, webbing and big pack, and tell the Platoon I won't be in the rear rank after all. Pack my Colt and Mauser, and the Remington with the telescopic sights, and put the small pistol and the knuckle-duster somewhere handy."

The newspapers were full of news from Norway. There was one report, "Narvik captured in snowstorm," but Mr. Chamberlain said: "Our information is that the Germans have landed at Bergen. There have been some reports of a similar landing at Narvik, but it is very doubtful if these are correct. I am informed that there is another place of a similar name in the south of Norway, and it is very possible that there has been some confusion." Mr. Chamberlain meant Larvik.

On the evening of the 10th the Battalion paraded on the square. Round the sides gathered the 2nd Battalion and the families from the married quarters. Along Birdcage Walk was a row of Green Line buses waiting for the Battalion, with their signs still showing Brighton, Horsham or Lingfield, and in crude chalk lettering "To Norway"—"See the midnight sun"—"North Pole Express."

It was the first time that the whole Battalion had appeared in battle-dress and certainly the first time that the officers had worn it. There was only one man wearing service dress—Colonel Faulkner. The Adjutant took over the parade.

" Battalion, stand at—ease. Call the roll." The officers inspected their platoons: "Check that man's kit, Sergeant-Major." "One mess tin, ground sheet, two pair socks, one cap comforter, holdall complete, two towels, soap, two pair laces, housewife, canvas jacket and trousers, one pair canvas shoes, one shirt, one vest, small kit, clasp knife and lanyard, A.B. 64 and identity discs, field dressing, gas cape, gloves, wallet, anti-gas eyeshields and ointment, ration bag. Kit present and correct, sir " ; and so on down the ranks.

"Got your knife, fork and spoon ?" "Yes, sir." "Wearing your long drawers ?" " Yes, sir." "This man's water-bottle is empty. Take his name, Sergeant-Major." "Guardsman Murphy, empty water-bottle, sir."

The Adjutant reported to the Commanding Officer: "Battalion present and ready to march off, sir." "Good ; tell those men to fall out, and then march off to the buses."

The eight Guardsmen-in-waiting, standing under the archway, turned to their right, saluted and walked away, easing off their big packs as they went. The companies filed into the buses. The families crowded round the open windows. "Goodbye, goodbye. Take care of yourself." "Don't worry." "Keep your head down, Mick," shouted the 2nd Battalion.

"Go back to the Naafi, you," replied the 1st. "They need real soldiers now."

The Major-General and the Regimental Lieutenant-Colonel, Colonel T. E. Vesey, were at Euston to say goodbye. They launched it by putting a case of champagne into the Commanding Officer's carriage. The train moved off. A Guardsman put his head out of the window.

"Goodnight to you all now."

PARADE AT WELLINGTON BARRACKS PRIOR TO EMBARKING FOR NORWAY.
Capt. B. O'Neill, Lt.-Col. W. D. Faulkner, M.C., Major C. L. J. Bowen and Capt. T. H. M. Grayson

HARSTAD

OFFICERS OF THE 1st BATTALION

Battalion Headquarters.

Lieut.-Colonel W. D. Faulkner, M.C.
Major C. L. J. Bowen.
Captain and Adjutant Hon. B. A. O'Neill.
Captain and Quartermaster T. D. McCarthy, M.B.E.
Lieutenant A. D. P. O'Neill (Medical Officer).
Father Kavanagh (R.C. Chaplain).

H.Q. Company.

Major J. A. Hacket-Pain.
Captain D. M. L. Gordon-Watson, M.C.
Lieutenant H. L. S. Young.
Lieutenant J. Gilliat.

No. 1 Company.

Major V. V. Gilbert-Denham.
Captain B. O. P. Eugster, M.C.
Lieutenant E. C. FitzClarence.
2/Lieutenant D. R. S. FitzGerald.

No. 2 Company.

Captain J. R. Durham-Mathews.
Captain D. H. FitzGerald.
Lieutenant F. R. A. Lewin.
2/Lieutenant G. P. M. FitzGerald.
2/Lieutenant J. E. Vesey.

No. 3 Company.

Captain L. W. Armstrong-MacDonnell.
Lieutenant D. Mills-Roberts.
Lieutenant I. H. Powell-Edwards.
2/Lieutenant D. M. Kennedy.

No. 4 Company.

Captain H. C. McGildowny.
Lieutenant C. A. Montagu-Douglas-Scott.
2/Lieutenant D. L. Cole.
2/Lieutenant J. S. O. Haslewood.

CHAPTER II

The "Monarch of Bermuda"

ON the morning of the 11th April, the troop train steamed slowly into Glasgow. Up and down the carriages the Company Sergeant-Majors shouted, "Get your equipment on." The train went straight on to the King George V Dock, pulling up alongside the *Monarch of Bermuda*. As the companies were filing up the gangway a man turned to his neighbour. "When I was on the reserve," he said, "I was saving up for a cruise. I reckoned I'd have enough for a fortnight's 'Tour of the Northern Capitals' by the summer of 1940."

The guides and stewards were there to take the Battalion to their cabins and berths. "Four of you in there—there was only one the last time, but he was a New York stockbroker. Two sergeants in here ; an actress once complained about this cabin, but you'll find it all right."

Big packs were slung in the luggage racks, rifles dumped where there used to be golf clubs. R.S.M. Stack reported to Colonel Faulkner in the largest of the three staterooms that had been allotted to the Commanding Officer, "The Battalion flag has been hoisted, sir. Some sailors made a fuss, but the Police Sergeant settled it. The companies have been detailed to find an A/A post and submarine sentries. There is to be a boat-drill practice this afternoon, after which the Company Quartermaster-Sergeants will issue those extra containers for the gas masks. Someone thinks that the Germans will use arsine gas."

The morning papers came aboard. *The Times* carried a headline "Recapture of Bergen and Trondheim." The Swedes reported that the British had recaptured Bergen and the Norwegians Trondheim. The Speaker of the Norwegian House of Commons, according to Reuter, had had a message from the Commander of Bergen to say the British were in possession of the town. None of these reports were true, but they were good examples of the confusion and wild rumours which existed after the German landing.

The ship sailed at three o'clock in the afternoon. The men crowded to the rails, watching the banks of the Clyde. "A sailor told me that we would pick up the rest of the convoy tomorrow off Scapa Flow." "One told me that there was piles of Arctic clothing on board. We can't be going that far." "Will we have an escort?" "I am sure the Germans will try to sink us. They say that the shores of Norway are clogged with drowned Germans." "Are you in a boat?" "No, I've been detailed for a raft." "I'm taking no chances; I'm going to Mass on Sunday."

The four days at sea were calm and peaceful. Every morning long queues trailed round the decks, filing past heaps of heavy clothing. Storemen handed out quilted sleeping bags, kapok greatcoats, sheepskin jackets, thick sweaters of every colour, white fur caps, mittens and long woollen stockings. Each man got a pair of special snow boots, one size larger than normal, so that he could wear at least two pairs of stockings. The scale of issue was as for winter in Tientsin, the coldest of the peace-time army stations, supplemented by the comforts accumulated for a possible Finnish campaign. F. S. Smythe of the Everest expedition, and E. Shackleton, son of the Arctic explorer, had advised the Minister of Supply. The Battalion was equipped for a trip to the North Pole. The German radio mocked at these Polar outfits and said that the British intended to fight only in uninhabited regions, but the fact remained that the Battalion was never cold in Norway. The Germans also showed articles of this equipment to neutrals as evidence that the British had long been planning the invasion of Norway.

With the Battalion now at sea, there could be no breach of security, so Colonel Faulkner called the officers to his stateroom to hear the orders he had received in London. The Brigade was to land at Narvik and occupy the peninsula; secondly, maps were to be issued so that the battalion and company areas could be allotted and studied.

"Gentlemen, I have just heard that neither of these is possible. The maps are in another ship and the Germans are in Narvik. H.Qs. are now trying to choose another base."

The news of the German occupation of Narvik came over the ship's wireless. The German radio described the scene in Narvik port. German soldiers—Austrian mountain troops—had landed on the afternoon of 9th April. They were now busily unloading "huge quantities of war material" and tinned food and distributing it by sleigh to their outposts. The German soldiers were said to be enjoying excellent meals of soup and frankfurter sausages, and to be particularly pleased—not unnaturally—that there had been no resistance. An agreement had been reached with the local Norwegian commander and he had submitted to the German instructions. The Norwegians, according to the commentator, had "placed their horses at the disposal" of the Germans, and were giving them "a restrained but friendly welcome." The commentator ended by saying that more mountain troops were being landed and that everything was going smoothly "in truly German fashion."

Meanwhile the convoy sailed steadily northwards. The Battalion could see their companions and escort—four other liners, the *Empress of Australia*, two Polish ships, the *Batory* and the *Chobry*, plus the *Reino del Pacifico*, the battleship *Valiant*, two cruisers, an anti-aircraft cruiser, *Cairo*, a net-laying ship, and, scattered round the horizon, twelve destroyers. A large flying boat circled monotonously overhead. Later the convoy split in half. Three of the liners with an escort dropped behind and set a course towards Namsos.

On Sunday evening, the 14th, the convoy was off the Lofoten islands, entering submarine zone. From the coast came a breath of intense cold. They were very far north indeed, some two hundred miles inside the Arctic Circle. The Battalion woke up next morning to find rock closing in on each side of them like the jaws of a trap. This was their first experience of a fjord.

The convoy had rounded the north of the Lofotens during the night and was now steaming in line ahead southward down the Vaags Fjord, between the islands and the mainland. The clear, smooth snow ran down to the water. Occasionally the Battalion could distinguish "an object a little less white than the others—the lightly coloured stem of a leafless birch." At intervals along the mountain sides rose a wooden house or a painted wooden steeple. Great clouds of eider duck rose from the water.

The transports circled twice while the destroyers took soundings. About midday a noise they had heard twice already on the voyage brought everyone on deck. It was depth charges. The seamen sat in the sun with supreme indifference, and the Guardsmen asked them why the destroyers had hoisted a black flag.

"U-boats."

The men went on talking. The subject under discussion was seagulls. One of the Guardsmen had shot a seagull on the way out and had been astounded at the amount of blood that had welled up to the surface of the water out of that little body.

Suddenly a destroyer rushed past them up the fjord, rocking the narrow sea. The crew shouted triumphantly, "We got one." They had sunk a U-boat and picked up six survivors. They had also picked up the U-boat's log, from which they learnt the rendezvous of the German submarine flotilla. The U-boats reported at the right time and place ; so did the Navy, and got every one of them.

A cruiser steamed slowly past. "That's *Aurora*." It was the Battalion's first glimpse of the cruiser, soon to become a familiar friend. They were to meet again in later years in Algiers, Bône, Bizerta, Brindisi and Naples. Now, flying the flag of Admiral Lord Cork and Orrery, she led the convoy towards Harstad. The little fishing villages on either side of the fjord at first took little notice of the long line of ships. Occasional groups gathered on the waterside and waved. The Battalion watched them and waved back.

"It looks like Switzerland." " Yes, just like Switzerland."

" Reminds me of Switzerland." "Yes, but there is more water."

"Have you ever been to Switzerland ?" "No. Have you ?" "No."

"Look at the snow. Even the sky is white." " It's very bare and quiet."

"Too much winter." "What I don't like is that there is no night."

Others reminded each other that, according to Mr. Churchill, they had come to purge the sacred soil of the Vikings of Nazi tyranny.

"Here come some Vikings in 'puffers.' " Fishing boats, flying the Norwegian flag, had put out from the shore, their engines spluttering and puffing. They hung round the convoy, like small boys running beside and behind a column of marching troops. These broad wooden boats had two tall masts, a high engineer's cabin in the stern, and amidships a wide space of decking. They lurched heavily in the swell, and the crew slid from side to side on the layer of snow, fish scales and frozen sea-water that covered the planks.

By one o'clock the convoy was off Harstad—"a cluster of wooden houses in a bay among the mountains." A whaler with a landing party cautiously approached the quay. A couple of officers landed, spoke to Norwegians, and then fired a Very light—"No enemy here." Harstad had become the northern base of the North-West Expeditionary Force. The destroyer *Electra* drew up alongside to disembark the Battalion. The men were ready, wearing their Arctic coats, pullovers and snow gloves and carrying two kit-bags stuffed with winter comforts. The Norwegian boats puffed up importantly and took off the remainder.

It was on 15th April that the 1st Battalion landed at Harstad. In 1914 the Battalion had gone abroad with the first flight of the B.E.F. and had fought through the retreat from Mons. In 1940 the Battalion landed for action five days after the real war began. At home the British public waited for news of this tiny force—but nobody guessed how few they were—who had disappeared into the darkness of the northern spring.

The British Army, we are told, should be a projectile fired by the Navy to strike the enemy at his weakest point. The Navy had carried the 24th Guards Brigade safely across the North Sea and launched it against the Germans in Northern Norway. Other projectiles had been fired at central Norway, at Namsos and Andalsnes. If these forces could hold on till the Irish Guards and their companions had cleared the Narvik area, their combined force would move down and chase the Germans out of Norway.

These hopes and plans ended in failure and depression. The campaign was a tragedy, made more grievous by endurance of the few troops who did the fighting with inadequate material. From the beginning of May a sense of ineluctable fate hung over Norway. There remained only an unshakable confidence in the magnificent spirit and companionship of the Battalion and in the skill and gallantry of the Royal Navy. The discipline, tradition and steadfast courage of the Battalion saved it from annihilation on the *Chobry* and disintegration at Bodo, and brought it proudly through the collapse with dearly bought experience and credit. But all the battles in Africa, Italy, France, Holland and Germany, longer and bloodier though they were, could not efface the memory of the Norwegian campaign as the worst of all experiences.

What happened in Norway ? Briefly, it was this. The Battalion sat round the shores of the Ofoten Fjord, slowly edging closer in to Narvik, waiting for Force H.Q. to make up their minds. The question was, would it be possible to lay on a naval bombardment effective enough to cover an assault landing ? This question was never decided. After three weeks the Allied troops in central Norway were evacuated to save them from complete destruction. There is only one way through Norway to the north. Now it lay wide open. The Staff ordered the 24th Guards Brigade to move nearly two hundred miles south, to Mö, the narrowest part of Norway. They thought, apparently, that there was no reason why the Brigade should not hold up the entire German Army at Mö for ever, but out of the whole Brigade only the 1st Bn. Scots Guards ever arrived at Mö. The *Chobry*, carrying the Battalion, was bombed and sunk, and H.M.S. *Effingham*, carrying the 2nd Bn. South Wales Borderers, struck an uncharted rock. The Scots Guards could not hold on and began a hundred-mile retreat on foot. The Battalion refitted as best they could and went south again, this time to Bodo to hold the road a hundred miles behind the Scots. After the Scots had passed through, the Battalion held on for a week and was then evacuated to Harstad. Meanwhile the French and Poles had captured Narvik, fighting with great gallantry and suffering heavy casualties, but every ship and man was now needed at home. On 4th June the Battalion went back to England.

CHAPTER III

Harstad and the Narvik Fjord

AS the Irish Guards jumped ashore on the slippery pier of Harstad, all they knew was that they were the men who would do the first fighting of the war, who would engage the German Army on the ground that the German generals had chosen. Except for their families and friends, no one knew that they were there. The only British troops ever named as fighting in Northern Norway were "two companies of Scots Guards." The German wireless announced that the landing had been made by "hired volunteers and unemployed."

A warm sun was shining. The thick snow dripped from the roofs on to the solid piles heaped up by the side of the streets. Ankle deep in slush, the Battalion marched up through the town in single file, past the Grand Hotel. The hotel was the most comfortable building in the town and had already been chosen as the H.Q. of Major-General P. J. Mackesy, C.B., D.S.O., M.C., G.O.C. the Narvik sector of N.W.E.F. A Norwegian interpreter came out and joined the Commanding Officer. Like everybody else in Harstad, he was astonished at the sight of the Brigade. "The people have never seen so many soldiers." And in fact peaceful Norway, with its bare two million inhabitants, had known nothing of war for over a hundred years.

Battalion H.Q., H.Q. Company and No. 1 Company halted outside a large school near the quay. A billeting officer was on the porch.

"Your Brigade H.Q. and the Scots Guards are also coming in here, so you can only have the Infants' Wing."

The school books were still lying on the desks. Arne Aornelinsen had left his "Norsk" copy-book behind—a yellow book with a design of square churches, seagulls and Viking longships with dragon-head prows. Drummer Hughes picked it up and later used it for his observation reports. It was saved from the general destruction of documents and now lies in Regimental H.Q.

No. 2 Company was half a mile out of the town. Nos. 3 and 4 Companies trudged another four miles south along the Vaags Fjord to find the villages of Kannebogen, Mekile and Breivik. Their feet were soft after four days of gymnasium shoes aboard ship. The road —there was only one—was deep in snow. Straggling houses made it difficult to tell where a village began and where it ended. It was even more difficult to tell one village from another, for there were no signposts and no notices and the Norwegians did not recognize a strange pronunciation of names. Lieutenant I. H. Powell-Edwards was already murmuring, "Oh, for a hot bath, a week's leave, and a mention in despatches !" Lieutenant Gilliat and the Signal Platoon, staggering through the snow with drums of cable, laid telephone lines behind the companies. It took two days and all one night to unload and distribute the baggage. The Staff did not know when the transport would arrive, and suggested that a Norwegian might be willing to lend his lorry. He did so, but at very irregular intervals.

The Battalion settled into billets for the next four days. The large wooden-frame houses, raised on posts above the snow level, were warm and comfortable. The walls and floors were bare and scrubbed or painted white, with a black iron stove in the centre of each. The Norwegians wandered in and out. These were the descendants of the Norsemen who harried Ireland centuries ago, and of that old Norse King, Magnus Barefoot, who was killed near Dublin fighting desperately, according to a Norwegian history book, "to obtain a footing in a boggy place he longed to possess." They were silent people ; in fact, the other Norwegians say that the Lofoten Islanders speak so slowly that they say one word today and another tomorrow. At Kannebogen Major R. McGildowny challenged the young ladies of the village to a snowball fight. "This is to establish friendly relations," he explained to the Commanding Officer. A small Officers' Mess was established behind the school in Harstad. " I am glad we brought N.A.A.F.I. stores for the Mess," wrote Colonel Faulkner, " as we can get nothing here." A captured German trawler, however, supplied some very good fish for everybody.

The next day Colonel Faulkner wrote to R.H.Q. : "Harstad is too full of troops and I am most anxious to get the rest of the Battalion out of the town." More ships put into the harbour. The town filled up with troops, clerks, signallers, bakers and Pay Corps men, but no more fighting troops and no transport. That afternoon the German bombers came. The first raid was during a conference in the Battalion Orderly Room (Classroom IIB). " Look at your maps." The officers spread out the large sheets.

"These look more like charts than maps—all contours and white spaces, scale 1 in 50,000, no grid, and made in 1909."

"You see where we are—on the island of Hinno."

The tangled mass of the Lofoten Islands lies off the Norwegian coast, like a seahorse with its head reared to the north and its tail trailing out south-west into the sea. Its body is formed by the largest island of the group, Hinno, separated from the mainland by the Vaags Fjord, which runs north and south. Harstad is on its north-east corner. The great West Fjord runs up from the south-west between the tail of the seahorse and the mainland, along the south of Hinno, and joins the Vaags Fjord at the island's south-east corner. At their junction the West Fjord bends to the east and becomes the Ofot Fjord and runs nearly forty miles into the mainland to Narvik. Half-way up it bulges to the north to form Bogen Bay. At Narvik it splits into four subsidiary fjords. The sea had thrust an arm into Norway with fingers pointing to Sweden. The squat thumb is Bogen Bay ; the forefinger is Herjangs Fjord, with the town of Bjervik at the tip ; the middle finger Rombaken Fjord, ending only five miles from Sweden ; the third finger is Beis Fjord and the little finger Trangskjomen. Between Herjangs Fjord and Rombaken is the Oijord peninsula, with the town and harbour in the crook at the tip ; between Beis Fjord and Trangskjomen is the broad Ankenes peninsula, with the little town and harbour of Ankenes on its north side across the fjord from Narvik.

There was singularly little information about the Germans. They held Narvik, the peninsula and railway to Sweden in strength. They also held the Ojord Peninsula and Bjervik and had dug themselves in on the Norwegian Army camp and training ground at Elvegaarden, on the high ground overlooking Bjervik and the coast road. For the rest, there was nothing definite except that they had patrols out in the mountains.

"The South Wales Borderers have already landed at Skaanland, a village on the mainland some fifteen miles down the Vaags Fjord. The Brigadier now wants us to secure Bogen Bay. The Navy also want it as an anchorage." Colonel Faulkner looked over at Captain J. Durham-Mathews. "Tomorrow No. 2 Company will cross to Skaanland. From there you will march the ten miles overland to the village of Evenes on the Ofoten Fjord and the west end of Bogen Bay. Drop off a platoon there and carry on round the coast road to Lenvik on the east side of the bay. The Battalion will join you in a few days' time."

The first bomb fell fifty yards from the Orderly Room. The officers bent their heads over the maps. Through the silence came the crackle of flames and then long bursts from a Bren. The second bomb threw the officers into a heap on the floor. Colonel Faulkner appeared lost in meditation. "Have we too many eggs in one basket ?" he murmured.

"Get out of here !"

Wooden houses were crumpled in ruins. Across the road a large shop, the Carrier Platoon's billet, was in flames. "What shall I do with this ?" A Guardsman was rocking the till in his arms. Lieutenant H. L. S. Young padded through the broken glass towards his platoon. "That Bren gunner is only annoying the Germans. The Mess is going to be very draughty without any windows."

All afternoon and night two bombers flew in low, bombed, went home, loaded up and came back again, and again and again. They concentrated on the water front. The military policeman on point duty was killed ; P.S.M. Higgins had his Pioneer Platoon sheltering beneath the pier.

"They can do exactly as they please. Thank God there is only two of them !"

"No. 2 Company's baggage on top should stop splinters."

"Somebody said they had shot one down and the officers have all rushed up the hill behind to look for the wreckage."

Before the bombers came next morning, No. 2 Company embarked on three fishing boats. The Harbour Master fussed round, asking innumerable questions in broken English. Captain Durham-Mathews reported him as a Fifth Columnist.

The Company sailed away into the blue, taking with them the best available wireless. The signallers at Battalion H.Q. sat by their sets and waited. The Signal Officer, Lieutenant Gilliat, claimed that he could hear faint call-signs ; no one else could. The rest of the Battalion sat round their stoves, brewing tea and frying fish, telling and retelling the story of the naval actions at Narvik. On 10th April Captain Warburton-Lee, R.N., led his destroyers into Narvik Fjord and engaged a superior German Force. At the cost of his own life and the destroyers *Hunter* and *Hardy* he sank one German destroyer and seven supply ships and left three destroyers ablaze. Three days later our destroyers returned with the battleship *Warspite* and sank seven German destroyers. This for all practical purposes eliminated the Germans' brand-new destroyer fleet.

There were no cigarettes, no news, no definite orders.

"Our plans seem rather uncertain," wrote Colonel Faulkner.

"We get plenty of orders, usually cancelled later. In fact, the arrangements seem rather peculiar all round."

After thirty-six hours' silence from No. 2 Company, Major Bowen, with two Norwegian interpreters, set out after them in a small fishing boat.

On the morning of the 18th H.M.S. *Vindictive*, a converted repair ship, put into Harstad Bay and flashed a message, "Have orders to take you to Bogen immediately."

The Quartermaster requisitioned the one civilian lorry to transport the 25 tons of baggage and hired two buses to bring in the outlying companies. For five hours the Battalion waited for a chance to embark. German bombers flew up and down the quay, methodically demolishing it. When at last the sky was clear, the minelayer *Protector* ferried the Battalion out to *Vindictive*.

German air superiority would not allow *Vindictive* to take a direct route through the narrow Vaags Fjord. A ship of her size could only have used such confined waters under cover of darkness, and there never was any darkness. *Vindictive* sailed right out into the ocean round the Lofoten Islands and up the West Fjord eastwards towards Narvik. It was a pleasant voyage. The sea was calm, the Battalion was comfortable, and the ship's canteen was well stocked with cigarettes and tobacco at Navy prices. German aeroplanes followed *Vindictive* out of Harstad and picked her up again on entering the West Fjord, but made no attacks.

"I had a very comfortable night in the Captain's cabin," wrote Colonel Faulkner. "No incidents, except that we hit something very hard in the middle of the night. No one knew what it was, but it made a tremendous noise, and all the sailors thought we had been mined and went for their lifebelts. As we had none we were able to keep calm."

Early the next afternoon *Vindictive* dropped anchor off the village of Liland in Bogen Bay. Lieutenant I. H. Powell-Edwards leant over the rails, his gooseberry eyes fixed on the shore. He meditatively swung his gas-mask over the side and then dropped it. He passed his hand over his head with a gesture of Russian fatalism. "I won't need that any more."

A fleet of fishing boats, flying the White Ensign, put out from the shore. The Flag Officer Narvik had " pressed" fourteen of them into the Royal Navy and had appointed a Flotilla Commander. The first boat came alongside and a naval officer shouted up that he wanted to take the Commanding Officer ashore first. This was the Flotilla Commander ; he was now under the orders of Colonel Faulkner.

Major Bowen and Captain D. H. FitzGerald were waiting on Liland Pier ; No. 2 Company occupied the village, having left one platoon under 2/Lieutenant G. P. M. FitzGerald at Evenes. The local civilians had reported that German ski patrols were operating ten miles east of Liland, but there was no definite information. The Battalion, with one eye on the sky, landed quickly and disappeared into the houses scattered round Liland. The baggage, as always, took longer and was not unloaded until early the following morning.

The Norwegian Government had announced the recapture of Narvik ; the B.B.C., relying on this and on an American journalist who claimed to have been there himself, also stated that Narvik had been in Allied hands for some days. The one definite fact known to the Battalion was that the German 3rd Mountain Division, commanded by General Dietl, held Narvik. The Germans knew it too ; their wireless described how the "simple Alpine songs" of the Austrians mingled with those of the Norwegians.

"We Germans have eyes to see and hearts to feel. It is a great experience to stand as a German soldier on neutral soil to protect a wonderful and unique country. One visitor [*sic*] prefers the lonely heights of the Norwegian mountains ; another the lovable population with its interesting folk-lore ; one will be attracted by the great memories of Viking days ; but all these features together make up the great fairy tale that is Norway."

Colonel Faulkner suspected that the simple Austrians and Bavarians were doing rather more than brooding over the scenery in a dream of Teutonic sentimentality. They had certainly occupied Bjervik and Elvesgaarden at the head of the Herjangs Fjord. From Bjervik the road cuts across the base of the promontory that divides Herjangs Ford from Bogen Bay and runs straight due west for seventeen miles to Lenvik on the east coast of the bay. The road then turns north and follows the coast-line. At the northern point of the bay it crosses a narrow isthmus formed by the bay on one side and the large lake of Strand on the other. This lake and the mountains behind and beyond it stretch out to the north-east and form a barrier to any troops other than skilled mountaineers. On the isthmus the little town of Bogen commands the road. So far the road was guarded only by a Norwegian outpost at Lenvikmark, half-way between Lenvik and Bjervik, which could be, and was, easily by-passed by German patrols. The original plan had been to occupy Lenvik, but Colonel Faulkner decided first to establish a firm base at Bogen.

At nine o'clock the following morning two platoons of No. 2

Company, followed later by the third, marched out of Liland for Bogen. They pointed out, as a matter of principle, that they had done all the work so far, but were really quite pleased to be setting off on their own. Three saloon cars and a procession of horse-drawn sledges crawled along behind them carrying their stores and ammunition. They took over Bogen that afternoon. Captain D. Mathews was "practically king of it, quite unmoved, and in close liaison with the locals, to whom he talks in what he thinks is their language." He appointed Lieutenant Lewin deputy-governor of Bogen, and taught the inhabitants one phrase of English. Every morning and afternoon Lieutenant Lewin drove round the town in a horse sleigh, with six children on board, all singing "Run, Rabbit, Run." Smiling Norwegians waved and bowed politely as they passed, courteously repeating their English phrase, "We hate Freddy Lewin."

Lieutenant J. Gilliat was in general a keen officer and in particular an enthusiastic Signal Officer. While he kept the Battalion War Diary he filled it with references to signal procedure and information about communication. A hasty evacuation by the Battalion is described by the entry " Three telephones lost " ; an obstinate stand by No. 4 Company at Pothus Wood draws the comment, "Without their telephone to Battalion H.Q. they could never have held on." Lieutenant Gilliat's professional trust in the power of communications meant that telephone lines were always laid out to companies as soon as possible. It also meant that the lines were always being tested. Major R. McGildowny disliked being disturbed, for he was essentially a tranquil soldier and a great believer in the doctrine of economy of effort. To save himself a long trudge through the snow to answer the telephone, he hit on the idea of sticking pins in the receiver. After this there were many sad entries in the War Diary, "No. 4's telephone again out of order."

On the 20th Lieutenant Gilliat writes that by 6 p.m. visual communication was established by heliograph from Liland to Bogen. The first message was passed from No. 2 Company to No. 4, who had taken over their area in Liland. After twenty-five minutes' hard work No. 4 Company signallers deciphered it. "Captain D. Mathews says, will you return his towel immediately. You will know it by the name *Monarch of Bermuda*." "Later," writes Lieutenant Gilliat seriously, "F procedure was adopted in case our signals might be read by enemy observers."

Encouraged by their success, the Signal Platoon became more ambitious and began flashing lamps at the ships lying in the bay. The naval signallers sent back a stream of dots and dashes. After the chastened signallers had asked them not to go quite so fast, Lieutenant Gilliat was able to report that by using a trawler as a relay station he was able to talk to the cruiser *Aurora*. The first message to the Navy set the standard of future co-operation. "Are there wounded sailors at Ballangen. Please confirm if report correct. Medical supplies lying on quay at Harstad." Back flashed the answer from *Aurora* : "Information correct. Thank you for taking so much trouble."

A later message was not so successful. A Norwegian naval commander telephoned to say that five enemy submarines had been sighted. He rang again to say that they were now submerged and moving at full speed towards Narvik. A flurry of flashes passed between the Battalion, the trawler, *Melbourne* and *Aurora*. Two minutes later another telephone message caused more signal activity, this time apologetic. "For submarines, please read whales."

The countryside was snowbound. It was difficult and exhausting, when not actually impossible, to move on foot anywhere except along the one road. To locate the enemy long-range patrols were essential, and these could only be done on skis. "We could do with Jimmy Coates and his lot here," wrote Colonel Faulkner, "but failing that, I do not see much chance of anything serious for a bit."

"Jimmy Coates' lot" was the volunteer ski battalion formed for service in Finland, called the 5th Bn. Scots Guards, and sent to Chamonix for training. The Chasseurs Alpins, who really could ski, were on their way out, but would not arrive for some time. Meanwhile the obvious alternative was to make use of the local Norwegian troops, who had been born on skis and knew the mountains from infancy. That morning a telegram arrived from Norwegian Divisional H.Q., the only official communication from them Colonel Faulkner ever received : "Norwegian volunteers at Bogen are not to be used by British troops as their task is only to defend their homes." The following morning these Norwegian troops evacuated, without notice, their advanced post at Lenvikmark and dispersed to their homes, which were now being defended for them by No. 2 Company.

The only thing to do now was to adopt a long-term policy and start teaching the Guardsmen to ski so that the more skilful ones could be sent out on patrols next winter. It was disheartening to hear very small children speaking perfect Norwegian, but it was even more disheartening and, in the circumstances, irritating to see them ski-ing down to school. The foothills of the mountains rising gently up behind the village of Liland made a perfect "nursery slope." Those men who showed any signs of ever being able to ski were collected into classes. The chief instructors were Captain D. Mathews,

Lieutenant P. Whitefoord, and a Guardsman who had been junior ski champion at Montreal. Every evening for the next three weeks the classes gathered on the hillside. The rest of the Battalion turned out to watch and offer sympathy and advice.

"No snow casualties yet," wrote Colonel Faulkner, "but I fear the worst." By sheer good luck there were no broken limbs. Nobody was allowed on skis until he had learnt to toboggan. The majority of the Battalion never "passed off" tobogganing and so spent the evenings sliding down the road into the village.

On the evening of the 22nd Lieutenant P. Whitefoord, the Transport Officer, arrived with forty drivers but no trucks. He had sailed from England the day before the Battalion, but had had to leave the transport and carriers behind with fifteen of the drivers to look after them. He left another twelve men at Harstad to wait for the arrival of the Transport ship. The Battalion never got its transport. In this country of vast distances, with companies scattered miles apart, it could never count on a truck of its own to move rations or stores, and could never make use of the Carrier Platoon except as a reserve infantry platoon. When the transport eventually arrived, it remained at Harstad, being cleaned, oiled and polished until it was driven for the first time in Norway—into the sea.

From Bogen, No. 2 Company sent in all the information that could be gathered from the inhabitants. Bjervik was the main enemy base after Narvik. The Germans were apparently using the big school there as a barracks and had established posts in the hills overlooking Bogen bay and town. An enterprising Norwegian produced a photograph of German machine-gun posts on the road to Lenvik, three miles west of Bjervik.

On the 22nd the Brigadier set up his H.Q. at Skaanland and immediately sent for the Commanding Officer. Lieutenant D. Mills-Roberts had, by walking up and down waving his stick and shouting loudly, persuaded a Norwegian to lend him a small car. He filled the back of it with bundles of letters for the Army Post Office, helped Colonel Faulkner to squeeze into the front seat and drove noisily and slowly off to Skaanland. It was late at night when they got back. The Company Commanders were waiting at Battalion H.Q. "It is a curious fact," Colonel Faulkner told them, "that the 24th is the anniversary of Gallipoli. On that date, the day after tomorrow, the Battalion is going to make an assault landing and capture Narvik. There is only one assault landing craft available, so the first platoon to land will have to maintain itself for half an hour before another platoon can reach it."

The officers waited in anxious silence. "The Carrier Platoon will land first." Lieutenant H. L. S. Young twirled his long fair moustache and did his best to look unconcerned and, if anything, pleased to have the interesting experience of being the first man to step ashore. "The destroyer *Bedouin* will take us out on a reconnaissance tomorrow morning."

Captain M. Gordon-Watson, the Intelligence Officer, was immensely proud of his naval knowledge. "That's a Tribal class—like *Zulu* and *Ashanti*. Chap called McCoy commands her."

The plan, in outline, was to take the town from the north. Narvik stands on the western end of a rocky promontory between the two fjords, Rombaken and Beis Fjord. The main harbour is in the south side, opening on to the Beis Fjord. There is a subsidiary harbour, Vasvik, on the north side, with a pier and a small knoll just behind it. Preceded by a heavy naval bombardment, the Battalion was to land at Vasvik in the order 3, 4, 1 Companies, advance Battalion H.Q., 2 Company, H.Q. Company. The beaches were known to be mined and covered by machine-gun posts in the rocks. The Carrier Platoon, therefore, was to land on the pier itself and make a dash for the knoll, from which it was to cover the landing of the first platoon of No. 3 Company half an hour later. Nos. 3 and 4 Companies were to secure a bridgehead from which No. 1 Company would advance inland and take up a position astride the railway, which skirted the Rombaken Fjord, and cover the approaches from the east. No. 2 Company, which would begin to land approximately five hours after the initial landing, would then fight its way into the town of Narvik. The whole plan depended on the effect of the naval bombardment, which could not be judged till the last minute. The Flag Officer, Narvik, was directing the operation and he would make the decision whether or not the Battalion was to land.

The Company Officers moved over to Battalion H.Q. in the hope of being offered a drink. Lieutenant Young found the strange new politeness of his brother officers particularly ominous. Major T. Hacket-Pain, who was to stay behind and hold Liland and Bogen with the officers and men left out of battle, was both relieved and disappointed. All the Company Seconds-in-Command were staying out of battle. Their hearty "Wish I was coming with you" had the genuine ring of insincerity.

The next morning the Orders Group—that is the Commanding Officer and Second-in-Command, the Adjutant, the Company Commanders, Captain M. Gordon-Watson and Lieutenant H. L. S.

Young—went out to the ***Bedouin.*** As they came aboard a rating handed each of them a naval officer's cap, which they solemnly wore while on the bridge, as a ruse to deceive any German observers. A row of well-set-up khaki caps would presumably have alarmed the Germans. At first the weather was misty and visibility poor, but as the destroyer approached Narvik, the clouds lifted and the sun poured through, throwing into sharp outline every feature of the shore. A low range of hills ran round Narvik promontory; behind the range was a broad depression before the mountains rose up steeply. In this depression lay the town, invisible from the front and out of reach of the flat-trajectory naval guns. *Bedouin* came round into the mouth of the Rombaken Fjord, close in to the northern shore of the promontory. The "O" Group got a perfect view of the future company areas and lines of approach. They could see the railway and, through a broad gap, the town and the harbour opening on to the Beis Fjord; there was no sign of life anywhere. It was snowing hard when the destroyer returned to Liland and the Company Commanders had to fight their way back to their companies through a blizzard.

In the early hours of the 24th the naval bombardment of Narvik began. It was a bitterly cold morning with a howling gale flinging the snow into the faces of the Battalion and lashing the fjord into tempestuous waves. The companies lined up on Liland pier, muffled up to the eyes, waiting to be ferried out to the *Vindictive.* The fishing boats were awash with water and pitched alarmingly in the waves. One of them was badly crushed against the bows of the *Vindictive,* but all the men were hauled on board before she sank. One by one the Guardsmen were heaved up the rope ladders. One diminutive sailor had a long struggle with No. 1 Company, the biggest men in the Battalion. Lieutenant B. O. P. Eugster was bad enough—"God! King Kong himself!"—but at the sight of the enormous Lance-Corporal O'Donovan words failed the rating.

At 8.30, as the last man came over the side, *Aurora* flashed the message "Negative embarkation." The Naval Staff postponed the operation. The result of the bombardment had not been satisfactory, but the main reason was that in such weather they could not guarantee that the landing craft would ever reach the shore. By midday the Battalion was back in Liland, except No. 2 Company, who returned direct to Bogen. The speed of this disembarkation shows how seaworthy the Battalion had become. It is hard enough to clamber aboard ship in heavy equipment and studded army boots; it needs real skill to swing down a ship's side to the heaving deck of a small boat.

That evening a Norwegian came in with information about Narvik. Vasvik pier was mined. It was later calculated that the amount of explosive found under the pier was enough to blow Lieutenant Young ninety feet into the air. According to this Norwegian there were some 3,000 German troops in Narvik. Some were sailors and marines off the sunk destroyers, but the majority were Austrians. Two hundred ski troops had crossed over the Oijord peninsula before the ferry was sunk, but he assured Colonel Faulkner that there was no need to worry about this as they could only approach Liland through Bogen. Anyway, judged by Norwegian standards, the Germans were poor skiers. When entering this information in the War Diary, Lieutenant Gilliat remarked that it would seem better to have poor skiers by the Norwegian standard than good skiers under the Norwegian command. The Norwegians had seen no field guns, but plenty of mortars. The local defences consisted of machine-gun posts, protected by a mine belt, and a line of slit trenches dug in the snow about a hundred yards from the shore. The Germans evidently expected to be attacked on the northern side, for their defences were strongest on that side and they had moved their H.Q. to the south. They seemed to have plenty of food and stores, which were replenished every day by parachute from transport planes. Of the normal 10,000 inhabitants there were only 4,000 left in the town, but they were in good spirits and "patiently awaiting the coming of the British."

Both the snow and the naval bombardment continued all next day. In the afternoon the Brigadier came to Battalion H.Q. with a new plan for capturing Narvik. The method now suggested was to clear the Oijord peninsula and from there to launch an attack on Narvik across and around the Rombaken Fjord. The 12th Bn. Chasseurs Alpins had just arrived and had been put under the command of the Brigade. The Brigadier had ordered the Chasseurs to land at Bogen in two days' time and prepare to advance eastward across the hills to Bjervik. As the other half of the plan, he proposed that the Battalion should land somewhere on the Oijord peninsula at a point to be chosen by the Commanding Officer. Finally, to protect the landing of the Chasseurs, the Battalion was to move down the coast road and secure the eastern side of Bogen Bay.

The next day, the 26th, No. 2 Company took to their boats again, sailed down the coast and landed at Lenvik without incident. A small party was left behind at Bogen to welcome the Chasseurs. During the afternoon the look-outs reported the approach of a strange craft. A large Seine barge, very low in the water, came slowly in to the shore. A short, fat man, wearing a huge beret, jumped ashore.

He explained that he was the Quartermaster of the Chasseurs, and had brought the advanced party and essential stores. The Frenchmen then began to roll ashore many barrels of wine.

Aurora was lying off Bogen ready to take the Commanding Officer on a reconnaissance cruise. Colonel Faulkner, Captain Gordon-Watson and Lieutenant H. L. S. Young came over from Liland and were picked up by a naval cutter.

Captain Gordon-Watson and Lieutenant Young, determined to miss nothing, were up on the bridge very early the following morning. Although their object was to reconnoitre the Oijord peninsula, their main interest was in the naval gunnery task, which was to bombard Bjervik and shoot down the German aeroplane which dropped supplies there every morning. Captain Gordon-Watson wrote an account of the day.

"*Aurora* sailed at three o'clock in the morning, the Chief Engineer having reported to the Commanding Officer, who was sleeping in the Captain's bed, 'Engines present and ready to march off,' or words to that effect. We sailed towards Narvik and before turning north-east into Herjangs Fjord exchanged a few signals with the Polish destroyer they called *Whiskers*. *Zulu* could be seen farther over towards Narvik.

"As we passed Troldviken we saw the remains of a German destroyer which had been chased ashore off that point. *Aurora* sailed up the western edge of the Oijord peninsula to Bjervik. The town seemed deserted at about 5.30 a.m. However, on the road to Gratangen we could see a column of stationary M.T. We opened fire on these at 2,400 yards with 6-inch guns. As the first shot fell a little short, we both let out a subconscious 'Short.' However, the third shot set one lorry on fire and before long at least three of the vehicles were in flames. A charabanc which still remained was demolished later in the morning. Right down by the beach were about fifteen vehicles and two petrol pumps. Unfortunately they were surrounded by houses and we could not shoot. We then tried to demolish a bridge, but the target was too difficult for flat trajectory and we gave it up.

"The cold was intense, with a 55 m.p.h. east wind, and we all decided it was time for a hot bath and breakfast.

"At 10.00 a message came to the ward-room, 'Parachute plane sighted, action stations.' We rushed up to the bridge, only to find it was a false alarm. In the meantime we saw about thirty Germans moving in extreme open order across Bjervik. They all went into two red houses and eventually moved up the road and disappeared near the shattered cars. They presented a very poor target and must have realized it as they did not seem to worry much about the bombardment.

"After this we turned to the major gunnery task of the day—the large school house. Three shots and then a salvo of four sent the whole building up in flames 300 feet high. *Zulu*, who had by now joined us, demolished a telephone exchange and the lines with 4.7's and pom-poms."

There was no sign of the German supply plane, so *Aurora* and the two destroyers moved south and turned into the Rombaken Fjord. Along the side of the Narvik peninsula they saw many tracks, trenches and emplacements, but little sign of life. The destroyers moved close inshore and shot up some cables running into the sea. At midday they saw in the distance the German supply plane heading for Bjervik, well out of range. *Aurora* then turned for home and passed very close to Narvik. The harbour was full of sunk shipping. From the water protruded the stern of H.M.S. *Hunter*, sunk a fortnight before in Captain W. Warburton-Lee's brilliant destroyer action. There were a number of machine-gun posts on the shore, and a hut which had obviously been turned into a strong point. The 4-inch guns opened up on it. After three shots the signal came down, "Hut destroyed."

To return to Captain Gordon-Watson's account: "That was the end of the morning's shooting. About forty shots were fired. The 6-inches made a terrific crash and cotton-wool was very necessary. We then went down for lunch, which was an excellent one. I was especially pleased as I was given a tin of ship's tobacco without even having to 'angle' for it. I promised the Navigation Officer a white fur cap in exchange."

From this short extract, Captain M. Gordon-Watson's three main interests in life clearly appear—destruction, food and his pipe.

From what he saw, Colonel Faulkner decided against a landing in the Oijord area. "As far as the reconnaissance was concerned," wrote Captain Gordon-Watson briefly, "it was decided that the Oijord area had no merits." "The chief things that impressed me," wrote Lieutenant H. L. S. Young, "were the lack of movement, the fact although we were close inshore the whole time we were only fired on once (a few rounds during the early part of the night), and the uselessness of a landing at anywhere else but Narvik, owing to the immobility through lack of roads."

In Bogen Bay, Colonel Faulkner transferred to his own "flagship," the largest of the fishing boats. Hoisting the Battalion flag, they chugged round the cruiser, exchanging compliments. This courtly ceremony was interrupted by the crash of the 4-inch guns. Three German bombers were overhead. The cruiser's guns kept the aircraft up at a great height, but some of the bombs fell unpleasantly close. In the fishing boat they could clearly see the bombs glittering in the sun directly overhead and called for more speed from the engines. Thousands of stunned fish floated up to the surface. When the bombers had gone the Norwegians scrambled into rowing boats and had the easiest day's fishing in their lives. The "puffer" reached Liland pier just as a seaplane flew in low over the village. It was an old Walrus from H.M.S. *Southampton*, carrying the Admiral to *Aurora*. The anti-aircraft post by the pier greeted it with a sharp burst of Bren gun fire. The seaplane climbed steeply and then came down again and circled round for recognition. The Bren gun opened up again. "Who is in charge of that post?" asked Colonel Faulkner. "Lance-Corporal Ludlow, sir." Lance-Corporal Ludlow (generally known as "Twenty to Four" from the angle of his feet) was marched into the Commanding Officer's Orders the next morning as "idle in the recognition of aircraft." Sympathetic friends were waiting for him outside Battalion H.Q. "What did you get ?" "Reprimand." "What for ?" "Missing a low-flying admiral."

Honest regimental soldiers always like to be as far away as possible from Brigade H.Q. The ideal distance is one which is too far for the Brigade Commander to walk over and look at the Battalion when he has nothing else to do, but not so far as to make the regimental officers' necessary visits a series of wearisome journeys. The distance between Liland and Bogen was just about right, so that at least the Commanding Officer, Adjutant and Quartermaster were glad to hear that Brigade H.Q. proposed to move from Skaanland to Bogen.

Brigade H.Q. and the Chasseurs Alpins both landed at Bogen the following day, the 28th. The Chasseurs took over Lenvik from No. 2 Company. Earlier in the morning a German ski patrol had approached the village. The sentries opened fire and a brisk exchange of shots followed, with no casualties on either side. The French, when they had taken over, sent a patrol out after these Germans, but it was too late.

No. 2 Company returned to Liland that evening. The story of the skirmish lost nothing in the telling. It was the first encounter with the Germans and well No. 2 Company knew it. The other companies had to listen in patience. When they got a chance they described the German magnetic torpedo that had been washed up on the beach, and how a naval officer, dressed in "degaussing" kit, had disarmed and dismantled it.

The Allies were now beginning to close in round Narvik. The Chasseurs were in the hills behind Bogen ready to move across the mountains to Bjervik and the Oijord peninsula, north of Narvik. The South Wales Borderers were standing by to land on the Ankenes peninsula, south of Narvik. When these two operations were completed, Narvik would be invested on three sides. This was the plan that the Brigadier told Colonel Faulkner. That evening the Brigadier set out on a personal reconnaissance of the Ankenes peninsula, leaving Colonel Faulkner in command of the Brigade.

The following morning, the 30th, the South Wales Borderers landed on the south side of the Ankenes peninsula. The only casualty was the Brigadier himself. He had landed from a destroyer ahead of the Borderers and began walking overland towards the town of Ankenes on the Beis Fjord opposite Narvik. The Germans held Ankenes and the hills above it. They could not stop the South Wales Borderers landing on the southern coast, but they were not going to allow a red tabbed and capped figure to walk into the town. From the destroyer the Brigade Staff could follow the progress of their commander and his escort. A sudden burst of machine-gun fire drove him into a convenient church. The Brigadier reappeared on the church tower; the Germans opened fire again. The Brigadier came out of the church door; the Germans put down three mortar bombs. The Brigadier retired back into the church. This happened several times with the mechanical regularity of a cuckoo clock. Finally, the Brigadier decided to make a dash for the beach. Half-way there he was slightly wounded by a mortar fragment, but he made it. From the beach he was evacuated to Harstad. The command of the Brigade automatically devolved on Lieutenant-Colonel Trappes-Lomax, of the 1st Bn. Scots Guards, the senior Commanding Officer.

For the first fortnight of May the Battalion remained on the northern shore of the West Fjord, guarding the roads leading from Narvik. "I would not be surprised," Colonel Faulkner wrote to R.H.Q., "if you have heard rumours in London this week of the goings on here and some of our troubles." Rumours were all there was in London. The communiqué of 27th April said "Nothing to report from the Narvik area." *The Times*' comment was that it was difficult to get reliable news from Norway except that "cleaning up operations were continuing from Harstad."

"It is an anxious time," Colonel Faulkner continued, "especially for Trappes and me, and I shall be glad when plans are settled and settled in the right direction. I am not, as you know, subject to alarms and worries, but it seems to me that we are invited to take on responsibilities which Battalion Commanders are not often invited to take. I am not in the least depressed, but slightly angry and my nose going round just a little bit. The men are longing to fight. When they have to, I hope it will be with a reasonable prospect of success."

There was another reshuffle of the Battalion positions. No. 3 Company moved to Lenvik to take over No. 2 Company's old positions from the Chasseurs Alpins. The Chasseurs moved eastwards into the mountains towards Bjervik. The Battalion never saw them again. A French account says: "The Chasseurs were dispatched somewhat hastily in a direction where information had led them to believe the enemy had no large forces and found themselves caught by machine-gun fire, surrounded by mines, and trapped in the snow without adequate provisions. They could neither advance nor retire, and at that altitude were almost frozen."

The news from Southern Norway was bad and getting worse. On the 4th it was officially announced that the Allied forces in the south had been evacuated "in accordance with the general plan of withdrawal from the immediate neighbourhood of Trondheim." In the first days of the invasion the Germans had seized all the principal ports and airfields. They had, therefore, complete supremacy in the air, and were also able to land tanks and artillery on a scale that the Allies could not equal. To save the Allied forces in the south from complete destruction, they were evacuated from Namsos and Andalsnes on the night of 2nd/3rd May.

The German Air Force was now free to turn its whole attention to the Narvik area. There were few profitable targets on land, for all the troops were widely dispersed and well concealed. The Germans, with obvious good sense, concentrated on the ships in the fjord, so as to deprive the Allies of their naval supremacy by exploiting their own air supremacy. The German high-level bombing was unpleasantly accurate. "I do not mind the bombs on land," wrote Colonel Faulkner. "I do not much like being aimed at when I am aboard ship—they are rather good shots."

There was a particularly heavy series of raids—nine in all—on the 4th, during which the Polish destroyer *Grom* was sunk, going down in two minutes with heavy casualties. A surprise attack by Heinkel 111's caught *Aurora* in a narrow neck of the fjord where she had no room to manœuvre. One of their bombs "ripped open a turret like a sardine tin." *Aurora* steamed slowly out to sea to bury her dead.

From their positions along the edge of the fjord the Battalion watched this continuous bombing in complete safety and comparative comfort. They had a ring-side view of the battle between the ships and the bombers. The air sentries posted along the coast could always tell when a destroyer was coming up the fjord. "See that bomber up there ? Bet you a ship is coming." The Germans would spot a ship entering the Ofoten Fjord, fly ahead to the narrowest part of the fjord and there hover in wait for it. There was nothing the Battalion could do except watch. One night a battery of Bofors anti-aircraft guns drove over from Skaanland and set themselves up along the road. In the morning the Adjutant, Captain B. O'Neill, found one just outside the mess door. It was soon removed. Major T. Hacket-Pain was particularly hostile to the Bofors. They could do no good, he said, and would only let the Germans know that the Battalion was living in the village. The guns never fired a shot, and moved away in the night as silently as they had come.

Only close fighter support could protect the Navy, the ports and bases from constant bombing attacks. Unfortunately, the Allies did not possess one aerodrome. There was a flat area at Skaanland, and a small civil aerodrome at Bodo, a hundred miles to the south, which might in time have been made into fighter bases. But no work could be done till after the thaw. A company of the Scots Guards was sent down to Bodo to protect the aerodrome till engineers and pioneers could be assembled to develop it. Meanwhile the weight of German bombing increased. Harstad was being remorselessly battered into ruins.

"We are well scattered now," wrote Colonel Faulkner, "so I hope the bombers won't bother us any more. All the men are longing for a fight, especially after the air raids, which they looked on as a deliberate insult. We are in the country and in a wonderful place. H.Q. is in a little white house five hundred yards from the sea, and the Battalion is in good billets. Sun and blue sky and snow-covered mountains all round. I have a private fleet of fourteen large fishing boats, each holding fifty men and a naval officer, under my command. They lie off my house and fly the national flag and look very fine. Would you mind if I wore a naval cap and asked 'Chief Petty Officer' Stack to pipe me on board? Talking of clothes, Eddie FitzClarence wears a large fur collar, but that is nothing to the appearance of many of the others. We have issue sweaters, white, brown, grey, dark blue and sky blue, which look very fetching indeed especially when worn with a leather jerkin, white cap and goggles."

The Battalion settled down to a routine of fatigues and training, chiefly recreational, which came as "a complete anti-climax to all the alarms and excursions." The mornings were occupied with fatigues. There were always supply boats to be unloaded on to the pier, under the direction of the Quartermaster, now also the Harbour-master, Lieutenant McCarthy. The snow was just beginning to melt, breaking up the poorly laid road. Fatigue parties were out every morning working on the road to keep it fit to bear even the very limited volume of traffic.

The warm sun turned everybody into "big bronzed brutes." Officers and men spent pleasant, lazy afternoons fishing and boating. Some men even bathed, including the doctor, Captain A. D. P. O'Neill, "who cannot, therefore, be normal." "I have ordered Fr. Kavanagh and the Doctor to catch some fish as all the Guardsmen are doing," wrote Colonel Faulkner, "and have promised Fr. Kavanagh a Cardinal's hat if he wins the contest." The most assiduous fisher-man was R.Q.M.S. Butler. All day long he sat on the edge of the pier, his glasses on the end of his nose and a line drooping listlessly in the water. At night, when he settled down to sleep on a pile of ammunition boxes, the line was still tied to his wrist. "Does the R.Q.M.S. ever catch anything?" Lieutenant M.-D.-Scott once asked the Quartermaster. "No, not Sammy Butler," was the reply, "he's too slow to catch a cold."

Each platoon was a self-contained unit. They were billeted in the Norwegians' houses and did their own cooking. The R.A.S.C. could only send boatloads of bully beef and biscuits from Harstad. Later they sent a small party of cooks with flour and coal, to set up a field bakery. The bread was poor, and by then the men had acquired a taste for the local rye bread, but the coal was most useful and rapidly disappeared. The Norwegians were only too willing to take English money, as well as the kronen issued at pay parades, in exchange for meat, vegetables and dried fish.

The countryside was transformed as the snow melted. Crops that had been hidden by the snow came up so quickly "that you could almost see them growing." Every house now seemed to have a large cache of food. Lieutenant John Kennedy was delighted to find "bags of lovely spuds"; these were, in fact, the Norwegians' seed potatoes, but that did not save them. The Germans also supplied extra food, wood, and pioneers' equipment. A few miles down the fjord a 5,000-ton German store ship had been driven ashore by the Navy. It was loaded with guns, tracked vehicles, motor-cycles, hundred of sets of horse-shoes, crates of cigars and tinned food. Official and unofficial salvage parties went through the holds like a swarm of locusts.

The Company Officers established their own messes, where the food was usually better than at Battalion H.Q. Lieutenant Andrew M.-D.-Scott arranged large luncheon parties at No. 4 Company, to which invitations were always eagerly accepted. Lieutenant E. Fitz-Clarence, at No. 1 Company, was a keen rival host.

There was only one man who could draw on the local supply of alcohol: that was the Doctor, who had installed the R.A.P. in the local apothecary's shop and drew on the medicinal brandy. Otherwise the situation was acute. Sergeant Ritchie, the Mess Sergeant, was " tearing his hair." "We have gone on rations in the hope that the drink will last a fortnight," says a sad letter. "The N.A.A.F.I. has not yet arrived, so it is a good thing we brought out some drink and cigarettes, for this is a dry country, not even beer or wine. The ration is one whisky and water, one port, one sherry, one gin a day; you can swop these with another officer by arrangement. This would not suit many of the Whites' Club boys very well. Perhaps you will give us a thought after lunch at Wellington."

There were two main inconveniences—no baths and no mail. "Bathing is a difficulty, as there are no baths at all here and the locals seem to keep perfectly clean without washing. I thought this was the place where young ladies gave you a bath, but no one has offered to give me one yet." Each company improvised bath-houses. H.Q. Company took over a large dairy. Eight men were put into the big boiler for scalding milk churns, allowed to simmer to a delicate shade of pink, and then were tipped out for another batch. "Still no post here, but one is reported on the way at last. Getting none for a month must be a record unbroken since the Crimea." The first mail arrived on the 9th—bundles of letters and newspapers. The first man to get his mail was, of course, the Quartermaster. He eagerly opened his bundle of *Daily Mirrors* to get up to date with the comic strips, and saw the headline, "Narvik in Allied Hands." "What the —— hell do they think we are!" He has never trusted the Press since. The mail included a local delivery; there were many postcards from girls in Harstad.

The Regimental Colonel wrote that a draft of reinforcements was standing by in readiness to sail. "We do not want them this minute," wrote Colonel Faulkner in reply, "but one never knows. Actually the military and political situation in this area has shown signs of temporary improvement, but it is the kind of place where changes of plan take place from time to time. After thinking that we were in rather a bad area we now think that we are probably best off and are all hoping that the 2nd Battalion are all right and wondering where they are.

I do not expect they were left long in their training area."

Colonel Faulkner wrote this on the afternoon of 11th May. At that time the 2nd Battalion was on the march to Tunbridge Wells; they were met in the bivouac area by orders to move to Dover immediately to embark for the Hook of Holland.

"It is hard to see," says one military critic, "why when the evacuation of the main body in the south had been decided on and carried out, the isolated operation in the north was continued; it could have no ultimate effect on the German campaign and involved a dispersal of valuable warships which led to serious losses." This, however, is criticism after events in France which Force H.Q. could not foresee. The capture of Narvik was still the main object of the Allied forces, and the Battalion was still the chosen instrument. There were certainly many "changes of plan." On the 7th May Colonel Faulkner made another reconnaissance of Narvik. The Naval Staff had already chosen a beach on which the Battalion was to land; Colonel Faulkner and Colonel Trappes-Lomax rejected it as quite unsuitable. They chose another beach, but the Navy said they could not provide craft to land there, so the whole operation was again postponed.

On the 10th the Battalion was turned out again. Force H.Q. at Harstad intercepted and decoded a German message that Bjervik had been evacuated. The Brigade Major telephoned orders for the Battalion to land at Bjervik as soon as possible. Colonel Faulkner was doubtful; a brief reconnaissance in the destroyer *Bedouin* made him even more doubtful, and, anxious to have more information before he committed the Battalion, he ordered Lieutenant E. FitzClarence, with an interpreter and the four largest men of No. 1 Company, to land under cover of the destroyer's pom-poms, seize the first civilian they met and ask whether there were any Germans in the town. If there were no Germans, No. 1 Company would land from *Bedouin*, and the rest of the Battalion would follow in *Aurora*. If the Germans were still in the town, Lieutenant FitzClarence and his party would have to run for it.

That evening *Bedouin* came in to Liland pier, took on Battalion H.Q. and No. 1 Company, and put out again into the mouth of the Herjangs Fjord. In an hour everything was ready. The landing party was in the assault landing craft. Lieutenant FitzClarence could not prevent Captain M. Gordon-Watson from taking command of the pom-poms and was, for the last time, urging him to be careful. "Hold hard, signals from the shore." The destroyer put about and went closer inshore. "Cancel operation."

On Liland pier Major Bowen sighed with relief when he saw

Bedouin acknowledge the signal. For nearly an hour signallers had been flashing lamps and torches without being able to catch the destroyer's attention. Lieutenant Andrew Scott rubbed his burnt fingers ; he had been striking matches as long and short flares. They had received another telephone message, this one from the Brigadier himself, who had returned from Force H.Q. There had been a mistake in the decoding of the German signal ; it really referred to a place forty miles away. The French Foreign Legion were already in transports on their way to storm the beaches of Bjervik and fight their way into the strongly held town.

It was after midnight when No. 1 Company disembarked from the *Bedouin.* The next afternoon they embarked again, crossed the fjord and landed undisturbed in the ruins of Skjomnes. This little town on the western end of the Ankenes peninsula had been heavily bombed during the preliminary reconnaissance by Major Gilbert-Denham and the Company Officers. It was not bombed again, as there was nothing left to bomb. The French and the South Wales Borderers held the southern half of the Ankenes peninsula and were preparing to clear the whole peninsula. No. 1 Company were not expected to take part in this operation, but were there just to strengthen the position of the South Wales Borderers. The Battalion was now scattered round the shores of the Ofoten Fjord—reading clockwise, a platoon at Evenes, No. 2 Company and No. 4 Company and Battalion H.Q. at Liland, No. 3 Company at Lenvik, and No. 1 Company now at Skjomnes.

The following evening the fleet, led by H.M.S. *Resolution*, sailed up the fjord towards Bjervik. "There goes *Vindictive*, carrying the Foreign Legion."

"The Battalion," says the War Diary, "were almost disappointed that they were not chosen for this task."

"Almost" is the operative word. At midnight the sentries reported, "There's a lot of firing going on." There was hardly any need for them to report this, for the thunder of the naval bombardment filled the fjord, each broadside mingling with the echoes of its predecessors to make one continuous roll. The watchers on the northern shore could only see the glow of the burning town, but No. 1 Company could see the battleships, the flash and smoke of the guns, and the small dots that were landing craft and launches filled with troops. After an hour there was a sudden silence, and then the faint sound of machine guns, as the Foreign Legion landed on the beaches. The Legion captured Bjervik after sharp fighting and went on to storm the strong German position at Elvergaarden. A Polish brigade landed at Bogen and marched twenty miles across the hills and descended on Bjervik just after the French had captured it. Together they cleared the rest of the Oijord peninsula.

The whole area north of Rombaken Fjord was now in Allied hands. The Germans now held only the Narvik peninsula, with the narrow strip running from Narvik along the railway to the Swedish frontier, and the northern half of the Ankenes peninsula, including the town of Ankenes. After a month of slowly building up and deploying the Allied forces, there was now a reasonable prospect of capturing Narvik. But there was now also the possibility that the Germans from the south might get there first.

The collapse and evacuation of the Allied troops in the south had freed the main German forces. The only Allied troops now opposing the Germans in their advance northwards were some Independent Companies and a few ill-equipped Norwegians. It was essential to hold, or at least to slow up, the German advance until Narvik could be captured and more Allied troops be released. The best point at which to hold the Germans was Mö, the narrowest part of Norway, where a fjord ran inland to "almost within hailing distance of the Swedish frontier." Force H.Q. therefore decided to leave the capture of Narvik to the French and Poles, and to move down to Mö all the available British fighting troops—that is, the 24th Guards Brigade.

LILAND

EMBARKING INTO
PUFFERS, NORWAY

CHAPTER IV

The "Chobry"

ON the morning of the 13th, the Polish Carpathian Brigade took over the Ankenes peninsula. From all round the fjord the scattered units of the 24th Guards Brigade converged on Skaanland. The orders were for the battalions to sail at four-hour intervals, the Scots Guards first in the two destroyers, then Irish Guards in the *Chobry*, and finally the South Wales Borderers in H.M.S. *Effingham*. Three old river boats and one flat-bottomed barge put in to Liland to transport the Battalion and three times the normal reserve of ammunition. The barge was dangerously overloaded. The steamers were unseaworthy and so top-heavy that men and kitbags had to be packed as ballast into the water-logged holds. Bodies are less perishable than bullets and bombs. All three steamers and the barge left Liland together and arrived together alongside the *Chobry* at five o'clock in the afternoon. Part of Brigade H.Q., a battery of field gunners and some Fleet Air Arm officers were already on board, but no preparations had been made to load the Battalion. It was three o'clock in the morning before the last man and last box of ammunition were loaded.

The Scots Guards sailed that morning. "We should be under way in four hours' time." Captain Brian O'Neill sat smoking "like a piquet officer"—one Balkan Sobranie after another—waiting for the operational and sailing orders. He waited all day. "The *Chobry* now remained at anchor within 400 yards of the *Resolution*, *Cairo*, and other warships, until 1830 hrs., 14th May, thus endangering the troops to an unnecessary risk from air attack." At six o'clock a Liaison Officer arrived from Harstad. "*Chobry* will sail immediately." He brought no other orders—nothing except a vague apology for keeping the Battalion waiting. Captain O'Neill dispatched him with the cold professional rudeness of an Adjutant. "Five hours you've kept us waiting. During that time we've been bombed three times and it was pure good fortune that the ship was not hit."

"It is a hard thing to say," wrote Captain Gordon-Watson later, "but it is possible that this delay contributed to the loss of much valuable life when the ship was again bombed and hit."

At half-past six the *Chobry* steamed slowly down the fjord, followed by a German observation plane. When she reached the open sea, the *Chobry* was sailing alone through the peaceful evening sunshine. The German aeroplane had disappeared; the naval escort, the destroyer *Wolverine* and the sloop *Stork* were out of sight over the horizon. As the evening grew chilly, the Battalion went below to eat and sleep. The *Chobry* was a new Polish motor ship, comfortable and well provisioned. "This is the way to go to war," said one officer. "It's all very well," said Colonel Faulkner, "but it only needs one bomb. It would go through this ship like a hot knife through butter. Also, I have no information at all. I do not know whether our landing will be opposed or not, but I think it will be pretty sticky, particularly if the German aircraft spot us. We will land about four o'clock, so I will advise you all to go to bed early and get some sleep while you can. Nobody ever gets enough sleep in this country."

At midnight three Heinkels bombed the ship. The entries in the War Diary are laconic: "0015 15th May, H.M.T. *Chobry* bombed and set on fire. Ship abandoned. 0930, Arrival of *Stork* and *Wolverine* at Harstad."

Naval reports are notoriously brief and unemotional. The Commodore, Rear-Admiral Burke, R.N., wrote to the Admiralty:

"The calm courage shown by the troops can hardly—if ever—have been surpassed and is best illustrated by the following:—

"Embarked 2 a.m.; under frequent bombing attack all day cooped up at anchor—300 or more were collected on the forecastle—whole midship part of the ship a raging furnace—enemy planes overhead—50 tons of ammunition in the hold—rescuing destroyer alongside. Not a man moved until I gave the order, which was not until I judged that men from the rest of the ship had got off. When they did move, they did so at a deliberate walk, some even refusing to part with their rifles. It was naturally not possible to single out anyone particularly, but I did notice the very admirable conduct of the Roman Catholic Chaplain."

"I turned in about 2330," said one of the Fleet Air Arm officers, Lieutenant Compston, R.N., "and went to sleep almost immediately. The next thing I remember was the crack of machine-guns and the roar of aircraft engines overhead. Familiarity truly breeds contempt, and my cabin companion and I decided it was no good getting up and hoped that the enemy would miss us as he had done for the past few days. Unfortunately this was not the case, and no sooner had we turned over to go to sleep again than there was the most deafening roar I have ever heard or want to hear. The ship had been struck abaft by large calibre bombs—one at least incendiary. My cabin collapsed immediately, and the lights went out. I left the cabin and ran through the adjoining dining saloon—the floor of which was covered with glass and debris—cutting my feet rather badly, and on reaching the port side of the ship saw that she was already ablaze."

Lieutenant J. Gilliat shared a cabin with Lieutenant C. A. M.-D.-Scott. "He had the bottom bunk, because I am more agile than he. At about 1130 I was awakened by a bang, not a big one, as I thought it might be stores being moved. As my feet touched the floor, the lamp burst and glass flew around the room. I grabbed my watch and life-belt, put my feet into boots (unlaced) and went out into the passage, followed by Andrew Scott in similar undress. I must have looked like a slightly obscene pantomime dame. The passage was dark and a thick acrid smoke gripped one's throat. I thought we were done for." The boots belonged to Lieutenant C. A. Scott.

"It was the unluckiest thing in the world that the bombs all landed near by the senior officers' cabins," wrote Captain M. Gordon-Watson. "I'm afraid the first one must have killed Jack D.-Mathews and Freddie Lewin and the second or third the Commanding Officer, John Bowen, Tommy H. Pain and Brian O'Neill."

"The cabins collapsed like a pack of cards," said one of the Brigade Staff Officers, "lights went out, the whole of the top decks amidships were immediately ablaze and very soon the main staircase seemed to have disappeared."

Guardsman Draper, the sentry at the head of the stairs, was killed at his post. Of the servants and orderlies sleeping in the corridor outside the cabins, Guardsman O'Connell had his arm broken and Armer was pinned to the ground and badly burnt. Guardsman Armer, the C.O.'s orderly, extricated himself from the wreckage and struggled through the smoke to his cabin. There was no trace of Colonel Faulkner. Guardsman Allen dragged Major Gilbert-Denham out of his cabin and carried him up to a life-boat. Captain D. H. FitzGerald was having a shower when the first bomb exploded. He and his servant, Guardsman O'Shea, were trapped in the bathroom and had to get out into the sea through a port-hole. Lieutenant F. Lewin, who shared his cabin, was killed in his sleep.

The fire spread rapidly, for the explosion had wrecked the sprinkler system. P.S.M. Morrow, and Guardsman Sullivan, the Battalion Fire Orderly, struggled to get the hoses working, but there was no water in the hydrants. "Theirs was a very creditable performance," said Lieutenant I. H. Powell-Edwards, "since this task appeared almost hopeless from the start." The flames reached the ammunition stacked on the deck. "We formed lines and began chucking the mortar bombs and ammunition cases overboard." The crackle of .303 and the red and green flares of exploding Very lights mingled with the steady firing of the A/A Brens under L./Sergeant O'Halloran to look and sound like an A/A barrage. The Heinkels circled overhead at a respectable height, "waiting to machine-gun the boats," thought Lieutenant J. Gilliat gloomily. So, too, thought Lieutenant Compston, R.N., "but to our surprise they were gentlemanly enough not to machine-gun us in the water as we expected. Their main interest seemed to be to take photographs."

After the first explosions the Battalion was ordered up on deck. The fire divided the ship into two halves, with the result that most of the men had to go forward and most of the officers aft. The companies filed up from their mess decks, in full kit, carrying their rifles and Brens. "Get on parade—face that way." At the sound of R.S.M. Stack's familiar voice the companies formed up in mass, D./Sergeant Hoey in front, D./Sergeant Peilow in rear. The sentries already on deck acted as markers. Only one man jumped overboard; he broke his neck on his lifebelt.

The lifeboats forward could not be lowered, for "the power was cut off and the electric winches were unworkable; the herculean efforts of the Guardsmen on the hand winches proved of no avail." There was nothing to do but wait till the escorting destroyer came alongside. Father Cavanagh began to recite the Rosary. On a burning ship in the Arctic Circle men said the prayers that they had learnt in the quiet churches and farmhouses of Ireland. Rescue parties searched the burning wreckage and brought the wounded up on deck. Sergeant Johnson, the Medical Sergeant, cleared an area on the promenade deck for an R.A.P. and there collected and tended the casualties. His first two casualties were the doctor, Captain A. D. F. O'Neill, and Captain R. McGildowny, both of whom were unconscious. Only four men were now reported missing—Guardsmen J. O'Donnell, Widdison, P. Killian and R. Tweed. Guardsman Callahan—"Mushy" Callahan of No. 3 Company—knew that they must be trapped by fire down below in the hold. He threw a rope over the ship's side and swung from porthole to porthole till he discovered them, and then hauled them out one by one up on to the deck.

The winches aft were still working, so the Polish crew lowered the first flight of lifeboats. These were already full with mixed loads of soldiers, sailors and wounded. Lieutenant Compston, R.N., with his boat load, "cast off and drifted away from the *Chobry* to see the escorting destroyer, H.M.S. *Wolverine*, approaching fast to come along the starboard side. We headed for the other ship—the sloop *Stork*. At this moment I must praise the courage and devotion to duty of the men of your Regiment who, in spite of finding themselves in an element which is certainly not their own, showed the greatest calm—many of them carrying their kitbags and rifles to the lifeboats and waiting patiently to embark—without the slightest sign of panic. We had great difficulty in parting them from their weapons." No mere naval disaster could shake the effect of the Depot, reinforced by a Sergeant shouting at them, "Take care of those rifles; they are government property."

"In the lifeboat," continues Lieutenant Compston, "they were magnificent, and once they had been told to obey orders of one officer, they never faltered. I shall always be grateful to one Guardsman who gave me his battle-dress tunic to put over my cold and wet silk pyjamas, which was all I stood up in. Another Guardsman gave me his scarf and they all did their best to keep the most scantily clad of us from freezing in the incredible cold. We had rather difficulty in getting the Polish crew to row and do as they were told—possibly this was because I was a British officer and they had their own ideas—but on the whole they were calm. Eventually in the crowded lifeboat we managed to get Guardsmen to man the oars. They did as we asked them and after about thirty minutes in the water we managed to row alongside the sloop *Stork*. They still behaved with the greatest reserve, obeying every calmly given order of the N.C.Os. because as the boat was crowded there was a great possibility that if they disembarked too quickly she might have overturned."

The crew lowered the second flight of boats aft while they could, and then slid down the rope after them. Some men, led by the Quartermaster, who ruptured himself, followed them, and swam to the half-empty boats.

Lieutenant B. O. P. Eugster, M.C., also started to go down a rope, very slowly in the orthodox P.T. style, hand over hand. A solid block of six Polish sailors slid down on top of him and swept him into the sea. He was wearing bright pyjamas when he went into the water; he came up stark naked. Lieutenant H. L. S. Young could not swim; Lieutenant P. M. FitzGerald did not like the look of the water; Lieutenant C. A. Scott, questioned the Polish Captain and learnt that it would take the ship twenty-four hours to burn herself out and sink, though she might blow up at any moment. The three of them decided to stay on board and stop anyone else from sliding down into the water. If the ship blew up, everyone would go into the water anyway; if it did not, they might as well keep warm and dry.

By the time the escort came up there were some twenty heads bobbing about in the sea, for the fire amidships was spreading and forcing isolated men overboard. The *Stork* launched the whaler to pick them up. She herself stood off astern, engaging the bombers with her guns, and taking on board the lifeboats. H.M.S. *Wolverine* came alongside starboard.

"We closed on their burning and sinking ship," said Commander Craske, R.N. "I never before realized what the discipline of the Guards was. We got a gangway shipped forward and the men were ordered to file off on to us. There was no confusion, no hurry, and no sign of haste or flurry. I knew that there might be only a matter of minutes in which to get them off. I had four ropes fixed so as to hurry up the transfer. They continued to file steadily off in one line. I cursed and swore at them, but they had orders to file, and they filed. I saw someone who seemed to me to be a young officer and in no measured terms I told him to get them off by all four ropes. In a second they conformed to this order by one of their own officers, still steadily and without fuss or confusion. Their conduct in the most trying circumstances, in the absence of senior officers, on a burning and sinking ship, open at any moment to a new attack, was as fine as, or finer than, the conduct in the old days of the soldiers on the *Birkenhead*. It may interest you to know that 694 were got on board in sixteen minutes."

Two years later Admiral Craske wrote to the Regimental Lieutenant-Colonel: "You will not know me. My son, Commander R. H. Craske, R.N., was in command of H.M.S. *Wolverine* in May, 1940. He lost his life in H.M.S. *Barham* in November, 1941, and amongst the papers he had treasured is your letter to him referring to the rescue of the Battalion from the *Chobry*. He never mentioned the affair till the following December, when he was awarded the D.S.C., and then told us very little, except that any rescue would have been impossible but for the superb discipline of the men of the Battalion."

The "letter" was a message from Officer Commanding, 1st Irish Guards dated 16th May, 1940: "I wish to convey to you the deepest gratitude and admiration of all ranks for the bravery and skill displayed by officers and crews of H.M.S. *Wolverine* and *Stork*. It was entirely due to your gallant action that so many lives were saved."

"The sailors were wonderful," wrote an officer, "and made coffee and cocoa and gave us clothes. We had a seven-hour journey back to Harstad and were bombed all the way. Not a good ending."

The destroyer *Wolverine* arrived at Harstad first and discharged its load of survivors on the quay. "What a funny feeling it is to have nothing except what you stand up in." They came ashore wrapped in blankets and naval greatcoats over pyjamas and dungarees. Stretcher-bearers carried the wounded off first, and laid them in a little tin shed. From there, the worst cases, Major Gilbert-Denham, Guardsman Corbett and Guardsman Sliney, were taken straight to the Base Hospital. D./Sergeant Peilow jumped ashore and doubled away to look for a square. He found one and put out company markers, while R.S.M. Stack ordered the men straight on parade. They fell in—"a proper Battalion parade"—and waited for the other boat to arrive. The Scots Guards R.Q.M.S., still at Harstad with their Base Details, with real charity, sent down containers of tea and mounds of "wads." The Officers and the Company Sergeant-Majors waited on the quay for the *Stork* to come in. Everybody was desperately hoping that Lieut.-Colonel Faulkner would be on board. As the *Stork* came in, they saw Captain M. Gordon-Watson in pyjamas standing on the bridge and shouted enquiries. "Where's Colonel Faulks ?" "No Sign." "Jack." "Never Seen." And so on, I almost cried.

The Company Sergeant-Majors collected their men off the sloop and called the roll on the square. "We were surprised to find so few men missing." The Battalion marched out of the town to the village of Ervik.

"As senior able-bodied officer, though only temporarily," Captain M. Gordon-Watson, M.C., took command, and made H. L. S. Young his Adjutant. He wrote a long letter to R.H.Q.: it was naturally rather disjointed, for which he apologized, "as there are so many things to think of."

"We have suffered a terrible tragedy—one thing I feel sure of, the Hun knew we were in that ship from the first. I cannot tell you what it is to us to lose the best Commanding Officer anyone ever had. Of the wounded, 'Clubs' Gilbert-Denham is very bad with a broken ankle and shoulder, wounds on his leg and shock. He had an operation last night which has straightened out his leg and shoulder. He had two blood transfusions and is doing very well and they said yesterday that if he pulled through the forty-eight hours he would be all right—he seems *most* likely to do so.

"Armstrong MacDonnell has a badish injury over his eye but will be all right though he will go back to England they tell me. Ronnie

McGildowny is shocked and with a few superficial injuries to his face. He will be all right in a few days. Denis FitzGerald is rather badly shocked and very deaf in one ear but it should get all right soon. Basil Eugster is in hospital for a couple of days as he fell into the water. I'm afraid poor Guardsman Sliney died of injuries, but Father Cavanagh saw him, and he died, I think, content. Guardsman Corbett also died. John Vesey is all right though he was rather shocked. The Doctor, by the way, is concussed and will probably have to go back. I have just heard that A. McDonnell has been put on a boat for England with Guardsman O'Connell and Armer—the doctor may be on it too. I have not had time to see yet.

"George Brodrick is now back with the Battalion. Derek Mills-Roberts was sick, and was not with us, neither was Patrick Whitefoord and the M.T. which is intact. A lot of mail went down with the ship, so families will miss a lot of letters. We have lost *all* our equipment except what we stand up in, except for odds and ends. The drums, fifes and bugles were not in the ship and we have saved five pipes. Could you arrange with Edward Smith & Co., to send out S.D. caps and stars for all officers here except Powell-Edwards, Mills-Roberts and Whitefoord? I am trying to arrange compensation for personal effects—Officers and Other Ranks. In the Navy they get it, and as we were under orders of Flag Officer Narvik at the time I don't see why we should not get it. I believe there is no 'Financial Adviser' here so it may be difficult. Perhaps you could help. I, for instance, must have lost about £100 worth of kit—telescope binoculars, service dress, glasses, riding breeches, etc. I've lost four pairs of spectacles. People are asking about Arctic and Field Allowance which are in King's Regulations which we do not get. Father Cavanagh lost all his Mass equipment and asks me to ask you to get Father 'Dolly' Brookes to give you his set to send out here.

"Could you send us out a nominal roll of the Battalion?

"General Auchinleck, the new G.O.C., came round and saw all troops yesterday and told them how impressed he had been with the way they had 'taken it.'

"At the moment the situation is as follows :—

Hospital : Gilbert-Denham (will not be fit).
Armstrong MacDonnell (home).
Denis FitzGerald (fit in about a fortnight).
McGildowny (fit in week).
Eugster (out tomorrow).
Mills-Roberts (sick; out in about a week).

H.Q. :	Gordon-Watson (Acting C.O.). Young (acting Adjutant). Gilliat (O.C. H.Q. Company). Whitefoord (M.T.).
1 Company :	FitzClarence. Desmond FitzGerald.
2 Company :	George FitzGerald. John Haslewood (transferred from 4 Company).
3 Company :	Powell-Edwards. Kennedy.
4 Company :	Scott. Brodrick. Cole.
Base Details:	John Vesey.

"Denis FitzGerald will presumably go to 2 Company and Basil Eugster to 1 Company or we could put him to H.Q. and let John Gilliat go back to Signals. I will sort it out and let you know. Ronnie McGildowny will be back as Commanding Officer in a few days. I cannot tell you how upset we all are about the loss of so many officers that we all loved so much."

The Battalion began to refit as best it could. The Ordnance Depot had a very small reserve, so that there were not enough Bren guns, only one Tommy-gun "to be treated with great reverence," and no mortars. Rifles, steel-helmets and webbing were provided by a Pioneer company and the H.Q. staff. The Quartermaster—his rupture strapped up with string and sticking plaster—scoured Harstad with a posse of storemen who stripped every man they met. By this means every Guardsman was at least armed, but that was about all, for there could be no replacement for the personal equipment—the hundred-and-one-odd articles a soldier is supposed to possess. After a few days the minor casualties reappeared from hospital. Captain Armstrong MacDonnell was "determined to get at the reins," but the doctors shanghaied him on board a ship sailing for England, and Captain R. McGildowny was released to take over command. An officers' "soviet," or council of war, made out the final order of battle:

Commanding Officer ...	Captain H. C. McGildowny.
Adjutant	Captain D. M. L. Gordon-Watson, M.C.

H.Q. Company.

Signallers: Lieutenant J. Gilliat.
Carriers: Lieutenant H. L. S. Young.
Mechanical Transport: P. S. M. D. McCleery.
Intelligence: Drum-Major Stone.

No. 1 Company.

Captain B. O. P. Eugster, M.C.
Lieutenant E. C. FitzClarence.
2/Lieutenant D. R. S. FitzGerald.

No. 2 Company.

Lieutenant G. S. Brodrick.
Lieutenant D. Mills-Roberts.
2/Lieutenant G. P. M. FitzGerald.

No. 3 Company.

Lieutenant N. S. P. Whitefoord, M.C.
Lieutenant I. H. Powell-Edwards.
2/Lieutenant D. M. Kennedy.

No. 4 Company.

Lieutenant C. A. Montagu-Douglas-Scott.
2/Lieutenant D. L. Cole.
2/Lieutenant J. S. O. Haslewood.

Base Details.

Captain D. H. FitzGerald.
2/Lieutenant J. E. Vesey.

CHAPTER V

Pothus Wood

THERE were too few troops and too much to be done in Norway for the Battalion even to hope to be left in peace for long. From the day after they landed, Force H.Q. poured in demands for men for fatigues, guards and special duties. The "week's rest" was a period of steady hard work, under constant bombing.

The Navy required a small party for special duty on the armed trawler *Raven*. Sergeant Smith took six men of No. 4 Company and disappeared for the rest of the campaign. When he rejoined the Battalion in England he wrote an account of their privateering.

"Commander Sir Geoffrey Congreve, R.N., was in command of the *Raven*, a Norwegian steamer of about 500 tons. He advised us to write to our relatives as we would probably be away from port about five weeks, and promised us plenty of fun with the Boche. We sailed about midnight on the 19th, flying a Norwegian flag, with our own white ensign unbroken at its halliards on the main mast. Next we were told to dress up as Merchant seamen in overalls and caps and were detailed off in three watches. At first we cruised along down south into Nazi Norway on reconnaissance. During this tour several German planes swooped down to look at us. One plane was so inquisitive that he came right down and circled round us. After satisfying himself that we were one of his craft, he waved to us and flew away. When this reconnaissance was finished, we called at the deserted town of Sandressjeon, where we helped ourselves to a lot of timber, and converted the S.S. *Raven* into a 'Q' boat, covering our guns in wooden cases with collapsible sides. The ship's armament consisted of one Bofors anti-aircraft gun, one Oerlikon gun, five Bren guns, two Lewis L.M.Gs., two French machine-guns and two German machine-guns, for which there were unlimited supplies of ammunition. Every man of the crew had one revolver or rifle, or both, with hand grenades. We were now in a position to take on any target, and we went searching for trouble well and proper. A message from a Norwegian telling us of Germans on an island close by gave us our first experience of a landing party. We searched the island thoroughly, but all we got for our labours was a deserter from the Norwegian Army, who would have been shot but for the timely intervention of a captain in the Norwegian Army, who was attached to us as an interpreter. A rumour that the enemy were transporting troops in Norwegian fishing boats had us sailing south again at full speed. We made contact with the enemy, who proved to be Germans dressed in Norwegian clothes, and their mission was cable cutting in British-occupied territory. We took possession of their boat which we ordered to steam to our base. Our Commander had decided to explore every part of the Norwegian coast-line in German hands, entering every fjord and taking stock of the enemy's strength from Narvik to Trondheim. This feat demanded great daring and superb navigation by our Commander, who succeeded in taking his ship into such perilous waters with narrow fjords and shallow water.

"On 30th May we went on to Bodo which was about to be evacuated. Our job was to assist the destroyers which were taking off the British troops from the town. Here we met our own Battalion, who were returning after their noble stand against the Germans in Pothus Wood. We were last to leave after searching the town for stragglers. We left Bodo, with its burning oil and petrol tanks, in absolute ruins to the advancing Germans, and we went back to our base to await further orders from the Admiralty. After taking on more coal and water we set sail again to stem the advance of the enemy who had reached Rosvik. We learnt that they were using motor-boats to carry their troops across the fjords. Our first encounter with the enemy was when we met their empty boats coming back for more troops. This party consisted of one high-powered motor-boat towing three barges. They ran their boats aground and tried to hold us off by firing from the shore, but we silenced them with Bren gun-fire and destroyed their boats with heavy gun-fire. We continued along the fjord and we were fired on by 4-inch mortars and heavy guns at a range of about 1,400 yards. Considerable damage was done to our ship with one casualty. It was late in the evening, and our Commander decided not to venture in until the following day, as the ship was badly in need of attention. We took refuge for the night in a quiet place some distance from the enemy who left us in peace. Early next morning we sailed down the fjord and saw the enemy constructing rafts, all of which we destroyed. By this time the enemy had brought his machine-guns forward and they made life very unpleasant for us for about two hours. During this action two warehouses and a church were set on fire. When we were well clear of the enemy, the Commander said, 'Well done you Irish Guards! It's your Bren gun-fire they don't like.' The same night we sailed back to Harstad, and the next day our Commander flew back with six planes of the Fleet Air Arm and bombed the enemy. Next we were instructed to proceed to Eff Fjord, about twenty-four hours' steaming from Harstad, and our job there was to cut the telephone cables. The water in the fjord was too shallow to take our ship, so we had to lower our motor-launch to travel the last ten miles. The men selected for this job were the 1/Lieutenant, three seamen, two Irish Guardsmen and myself. Our job was to guard the sailors whilst they cut the cables. We were informed that the enemy were about 15 kilometres away. This operation lasted a considerable time. During the night we were disturbed by a patrol. After considerable manœuvring on our part into a good position, we were successful in surrounding them. We discovered that it was a Polish patrol investigating the wire cutting. Our officer, having a knowledge of French, relieved a nasty situation.

"Our next encounter with the enemy was on our way home, in the West Fjord. We had just finished setting fire to a big oil container, when we were chased by an armed German trawler which troubled us considerably, but was finally scared away by the automatic firing of our Bofors gun. At this point, we were joined by one of our own trawlers which we had to escort home as it had run short of ammunition. We were again attacked by another trawler, which soon got tired of facing our guns and steamed rapidly away, out-distancing us, as our ship had less speed. The coast-line of Norway was rapidly disappearing behind us, when suddenly two enemy bombers swooped down and bombed us until their load of bombs was exhausted. One stayed circling round us, whilst the other went away to give information of our position to his base. Later we were again attacked by eight of the same type of aircraft, who bombed us for two hours, dropping ninety-eight bombs, but causing little damage to our ship. Then they tried machine-gunning us from close range, but we scared them off by our anti-aircraft fire. After this we were left severely alone, and we steamed into Aberdeen in good time."

The 17th May is Norwegian Independence Day. "You must not lose heart," King Haakon told his people, "You may be certain that for the future generations to have to rebuild our country after all this destruction it will be of vital importance that we did everything to keep Norway a free and independent country. If we can see it from this point of view, then perhaps the ordeal will become easier for us."

The Battalion, of course, saw it from this point of view and certainly did not lose heart when, on the 19th, General Auchinleck ordered them south for further "ordeals." There was no alternative. The South Wales Borderers had also failed to reach Mö. They too had been delayed and had not sailed till the 15th. To avoid the fate of the *Chobry*, their ship, H.M.S. *Effingham*, was diverted to the inner route down through the fjords and islands. She struck an uncharted rock and went aground. The Scots Guards were thus left entirely unsupported, and could no longer hold Mö single-handed. They had already started a long weary retreat and were now "in a bad way." Nearly a hundred miles north of Mö, the Saltdal Fjord runs thirty miles into the mainland, more than half-way to the Swedish frontier. This was the most southerly position the Allies could now hope to hold. There was already in this area a force of independent companies and Norwegians. The G.O.C. therefore ordered the Battalion and a troop of the 166 Field Battery, R.A.—the only available men and guns—to join this force and with it to establish a defensive line, through which the Scots Guards could withdraw and at which the Germans' advance would be halted.

In the afternoon of the 20th, the Battalion embarked on destroyers and "puffers." The Germans were, as usual, bombing Harstad. The town was burning and in the harbour a tanker full of petrol for the Fleet Air Arm was in flames, giving "not a bad impression of purgatory quite adequately staged." H.M.S. *Walker* and *Firedrake*, carrying Nos. 1, 2 and 3 Companies, went well out to sea to round the British minefields. H.Q. and No 4 Company's old "puffers" would not face the open sea and so preferred to hug the coast and chance the minefield. Even in the calm coastal water, one of the "puffers" nearly sank. Another, with part of No. 4 on board, piled itself up on a reef. As the young naval officer in charge had been violently sea-sick the whole of the way, and was quite helpless, Lieutenant J. Haslewood launched a skiff and dragged the "puffer" clear. Bodo seemed deserted at midnight, there was nobody who could give any information about anything. The Battalion settled down to sleep on the quay amid the piles of equipment salvaged from H.M.S. *Effingham*. The Company Quartermaster-Sergeant and Specialist Platoon Sergeants made up a few deficiencies. P.S.M. Byrne, the Mortar Sergeant, found a 3-inch mortar barrel. "The Borderers would surely be pleased to lend us this." "Now we want a base plate." He found one in a shed. "Now we have a mortar."

The next morning a stray staff officer suggested that the local H.Q. might be at Hopen, a small fishing village some ten miles up the fjord. The Battalion moved to Hopen in "puffers," disembarked and marched inland to the village of Godones. There they waited while Captain McGildowny had found the local Commander, Colonel Gubbins. All British troops in the area were amalgamated into a force called Stockforce, commanded in the field by Lieut.-Colonel Stockwell, but directed by Colonel Gubbins. It was not till the 23rd that a decision was made to hold up the Germans in the Saltdalen valley. That afternoon Lieut.-Colonel Stockwell, Captain McGildowny and Lieutenant H. L. S. Young crossed the fjord to reconnoitre the valley.

The Saltdals Fjord runs inland due east for thirty miles to the village of Fauske. At Fauske it turns sharply and runs seven miles due south of the town of Saltdal-Rognan. The Saltdalen valley is the geographical continuation of the fjord and cuts down south through the tangled mass of mountains and lakes. It is the only practical route from Mö northwards. The North Road and the Saltern river both enter the valley near the Swedish frontier level with Mö and run side by side down to Rognan. The road stops at Rognan and begins again at Langset on the north-eastern side of the fjord. The normal connection between these two towns is the ferry, but there is a track through the foothills of the mountains round the edge of the fjord. The river, swollen by the melting snow, rapidly gathers speed and volume and is very soon unfordable. The road enters the valley east of the river, and runs along the eastern bank till it reaches the area of Pothus ten miles from Rognan. Opposite Pothus a thickly wooded razor-backed ridge juts out from the mountains ; behind it a turbulent tributary river runs down to the Saltern. Before reaching this ridge, the main road crosses the river by an iron girder bridge and runs through the fir woods on the western bank down to Rognan. A rough track climbs over the ridge and crosses the tributary by a light suspension bridge, and continues along the eastern bank till it too crosses the Saltern by a footbridge three miles farther down.

When Lieut.-Colonel H. Stockwell and Captain R. McGildowny saw this area—the spur, the rivers, Pothus bridge and the woods and terraced hill on the west bank—they decided that here was a bottleneck at which to halt the German advance up the valley. The Germans could outflank the position either by working through the rough wooded ground on the west bank till they reached the road and open country two miles behind the bridge or by taking to the mountains to the east of the valley. A strong force covering the woods could stop the first manœuvre ; posts in the mountains could indefinitely delay the other. The position was undoubtedly a strong one, if held by enough troops to cover the ground. A brigade supported by a Field Regiment, R.A., would probably have been adequate. Stockforce H.Q. could only provide one battalion, the Irish Guards, a troop of 25-pounders and a section of Norwegian mortars and machine-guns. Stockforce also nominally controlled three Independent Companies, and hopefully detailed them to "picquet the heights" in the mountains on either side of the valley.

Captain R. McGildowny decided to put a company forward on the left flank on the high ridge east of the river ; a company on the right flank on a slight plateau overlooking the bridge and the woods ; a company in the rear between the road and the river to cover the centre of the position and the river behind the ridge, and to hold the fourth company in reserve in Pothus Wood. One company would thus be far forward of the rest of the Battalion and well out of any small-arms support.

The companies landed at Rognan at intervals on the 24th and moved straight up the road through the flat, cultivated land and the thick woods of the valley. This was a prosperous agricultural district, very different from the bleak foothills round Narvik. Instead of an occasional thin silver birch stuck in the bare expanse of hillside, there were close plantations of firs with long clearings on which the open fields stretched away to the hills. Along the road were dotted small wooden houses and farm buildings. "Look at the walls of the houses —they are riddled with bullets." The Saltdalen valley was within easy flying distance of the advanced German fighter aerodromes. For days German fighters had been flying up and down the road ; when they could not find any transport or troops, they "smartened up" the houses which offered the only cover between the woods. Even a solitary man on the road was liable to be machine-gunned. Captain Gordon-Watson was attacked by a large Dornier while he was chugging peacefully down the road on the pillion of the Master Cook's motor-cycle. Sergeant Cox accelerated wildly, and Captain Gordon-Watson equally wildly returned the fire with his pistol. A running and inconclusive fight followed, with six rounds of .38 ammunition on one side and on the other "what seemed to be small cannon shells, for they exploded in the road." No. 2 Company was machine-gunned at Rognan and No. 3 Company was machine-gunned just as it was entering its area, but the Battalion moved into position without any casualties. With the German Air Force so active, Captain McGildowny could not know how much of the Battalion would eventually reach him, so he put the companies out in position piecemeal as they arrived. He explained the plan to the last arrival, No. 2 Company :

"No. 1 Company are on the ridge on the far side of the river. From there they can cover the bridge and prevent the Germans getting observation down the valley. When the Scots Guards have passed through, the main girder bridge will be blown. No 1 Company will hold their position as long as they can, and will then withdraw back into reserve. There is a platoon of No. 3 Company guarding the suspension bridge. When they and No. 1 are across, the suspension bridge will be blown behind them. No. 4 Company on their plateau can command a long stretch of river and the road and No. 3 can cover the tributary behind the ridge, so that once the bridges are blown, the Germans will have great difficulty in crossing the rivers, particularly as they will have no darkness to cover them. There are Norwegian machine-gunners on No. 4's flank who can shoot across on to the road in front of No. 1 Company."

It was a perfect summer's day. The hot sun thawed the ground and beat down on the Battalion as they dug into the soft soil. The Guardsmen sat on the edge of their slit trenches, smoking and chatting, beating off swarms of ants and midges, and quietly watching the German fighters overhead. Once dug in the Companies could remain still and hope to be unobserved ; Battalion H.Q. was not so lucky. The German pilots would inevitably see the stream of runners, cyclists and visitors—often unnecessary—turning off the road into Pothus Wood.

Force H.Q. promised a wireless set for No. 1 Company. They sent the set and the operators to different places, neither of which was Battalion H.Q. When they were joined up, the operators admitted that they had not the faintest idea how to work the set. The Signallers set out to lay a telephone line across the bridge, but ran out of cable half-way. The only communication with No. 1 Company was by runner.

The evening drew in, with no sign of activity anywhere. The night was as cold as the day had been hot. The Battalion wrapped themselves up in their sweaters and greatcoats and went on smoking in the clear light. An old Norwegian truck brought up the rations from Rognan and dumped them round the Companies. It was nearly midnight, but few men could sleep ; they propped themselves up in their trenches, chewing biscuits and reading old newspapers. At midnight the Scots Guards passed through the Battalion position. The Battalion heard the slow, shuffling tramp of tired men. They came down to the roadside and in silence watched the lines of tattered men hobbling past. The two battalions had often passed each other on the march, but this time there were no jeers, no greetings. No Irish Guardsman shouted "Get up off your knees" ; no Scots Guardsman replied "Having a good rest, Mick?" Lieutenant Powell-Edwards stood in deepening gloom, "Tottering columns, crumbling ruins, defeat of an empire," he muttered as he turned back to go round his platoon positions once again. "I've read of this sort of thing, but now it is happening to me."

The sappers blew up Pothus Bridge. No. 1 Company were left holding their hill unsupported, and connected to the rest of the Battalion only by a long, roundabout track, the footbridge and the suspension bridge.

The Germans were only a few hours march behind the Scots Guards. Early that morning their leading scouts appeared on bicycles round the corner of the road in front of No. 1 Company. They were riding hard and fast, like professionals, with their heads well down over the handlebars. The Norwegian machine-gunners shot them into a tangled heap of bicycles and bodies. For several hours there was silence, while the Germans brought up their infantry and support weapons. While the mortars and machine guns were being set up and ranged, the infantry worked their way forward down the river. About eight o'clock as the Companies were stretching their cramped, cold bodies in the sun and breakfasting on water and biscuits, small parties of Germans began crawling up the hill. "Come to us," they shouted, "we are your friends." These invitations irritated P.S.M. Thompson. "I went forward and kicked the bushes," he reported to Captain Eugster, "but I could not find anyone." The Germans came closer and threw stick-grenades ; the Company replied with bursts of Bren fire. The steep, rocky, scrub-covered ground gave excellent cover from small-arms fire. Bullets ricocheted off rocks, humming up into the air well above the heads of the men crouching in the hollows and trenches. No. 1 Company flung Mills grenades and 2-inch mortar bombs. Such a use of 2-inch mortar bombs is contrary to Small Arms School regulations, as being highly dangerous. The "grenadier" must unscrew the cap, bang the nose hard on a rock to arm the bomb and then throw it high in the air so that it lands on its nose and explodes. It needs nice judgment to strike a blow hard enough to arm the mechanism without exploding the bomb prematurely. Temporarily discouraged, the Germans withdrew down the hillside. The troop of 25-pounders and the Norwegian mortars came into action. They put down defensive fire along the base of the hill whenever they heard an outburst of small-arms fire. Such fire might inconvenience the Germans, but it could not prevent them attacking again.

The Germans now had their mortar and machine-gun batteries well established and thickened up their concentrations on both forward companies. The men deepened their slit trenches and sat tight. They learnt the inestimable value of a hole in the ground, when they went to North Africa two years later the collective memory of the Battalion saved them unnecessary casualties for they were well below the ground before—instead of after—the arrival of the first mortar bombs. Battalion H.Q. rang up to report the situation, but Stockforce H.Q. did not answer the telephone. A runner was sent and came pack with the news that the house headquarters had occupied had been burnt to the ground ; he brought with him three charred whisky bottles as evidence.

"The German pilots saw the yellow signal cable," said Lieutenant Gilliat.

"In that case," replied Captain McGildowny sleepily, "we can expect them here soon."

At two o'clock, five Heinkels made a trial run over Pothus Wood. They formed up in a line ahead and flew along the western edge of the wood machine-gunning steadily. Up and down they went, raking the wood with the methodical accuracy of ploughmen. Battalion H.Q. by the road on the eastern edge of the wood watched this fascinating performance. They lay on the ground in a long line. "When I blow the whistle," shouted R.S.M. Stack, "jump up and double across to the far side of the wood." While the Heinkels were climbing to turn, the long line of men raced through the wood and dropped panting behind the bullet-scarred trees. One Guardsman was slightly wounded.

During this air activity, the German infantry attacked No. 1 Company again. They rushed over the ridge hurling grenades. The Brens got some, but the rest had to be driven back by the riflemen. During the close fighting, Guardsmen Tierney was killed and Captain B. O. P. Eugster was wounded in the shoulder. When the attack was beaten off, he sat down to consider the situation. It could only be a question of time before the Germans overwhelmed the isolated and unsupported Company. The left-hand platoon had already reported that the Germans were moving round the flank. Nothing he could do could prevent the Germans from working wide round the left flank higher up the mountain side, so the next attack would come from the flank and rear as well as from the front. This lull which followed the failure of the Germans' second attack would certainly be the Company's last chance to withdraw.

In the late afternoon, Captain Eugster ordered Lieutenant E. FitzClarence to lead two platoons down to the suspension bridge. Half an hour later, he himself withdrew the remaining platoon. They wrapped a wounded Guardsman in a blanket and carried him down the hill, but he died on the way. When they got to the river they found no one there and the bridge already blown. They walked along the bank but everywhere the river, swollen by the melting snow, was too fast and deep to ford. It did not take the Germans long to discover that the position had been abandoned. They came up over the ridge and opened fire on the platoon down below. The men whipped the slings off their rifles and knotted them into a chain. Guardsman (Red) Murphy stripped "to the buff," tied one end of this chain round him, and plunged into the river. The current, racing like a herd of wild horses, swept him a hundred yards down stream before he struck a small island near the far bank. Captain Eugster anchored himself in the middle of the current to help each man across. P.S.M. Thompson remained on the bank and threw into the water any man who hesitated. All the time the Germans were getting closer and their fire more accurate. When the whole platoon was across and away, P.S.M. Thompson joined Captain Eugster on the island. The two of them lay there, shivering miserably, for three hours before the fire slackened. On the way back to Rognan, they found a boat, which should not still have been there, and crossed the Saltern river. Captain Eugster, swinging a revolver in his left hand, stalked into Battalion H.Q. to report, and was promptly evacuated to the hospital at Bodo.

The withdrawal of No. 1 did not greatly alter the situation. It had been part of the original plan and in fact the Germans could get no observation from the ridge. What was unforeseen, however, was the speed with which the German Alpine troops took to the mountains and began to outflank the whole position even while their ordinary infantry was attacking No. 1 Company's positions. It was a perfect example of the old mountain-warfare maxim. "Go high and wide" and could only be stopped by sending a defensive force higher and wider. The highest point in the hills on the east flank was a peak 2,500 feet high. Lieut.-Colonel Stockwell ordered No. 2 Company to move across from Pothus Wood and climb to the top of that peak. "Your objective is spot height 800 metres. If you can get there before the Germans, I think we can hold them here a good while yet." He also sent one of the independent companies to hold a position half-way up the mountain side below No. 2 Company. Stockforce had now given up hope of permanently holding the Germans, and was frankly fighting for time—time for the Scots Guards to rest and re-form; time for the South Wales Borderers to arrive; time for the French and Poles to capture Narvik; time for reinforcements to arrive from England and France. In England, the 2nd Battalion had just landed at Dover which they had left forty-eight hours before in a desperate last-minute effort to hold Boulogne; in France the Germans were closing in on the last of the Channel ports, Dunkirk.

Earlier in the afternoon, Drummer Hughes of the Intelligence Section 2 and a Norwegian officer had set up an observation post opposite Pothus Bridge. "About 1500 hrs." wrote Hughes in his report, "we saw movements on the other side of the river about 800 yards south of the bridge. Shots were being exchanged between the enemy and some of No. 4 Company. Whilst the enemy were thus engaged, I got two ground sheets and tied our rifles and ammunition in them. We then crossed the river by the girders underneath the shattered bridge. I had just managed half the bridge when I nearly slipped in and lost our rifles, but we got across all right. We lay low for an hour and then made our way up the opposite hill. This was easy owing to plenty of cover. We found a good observation post and from there saw a group of enemy lying around a machine gun. We returned across the river and reported the position of the machine gun. Very soon afterwards our artillery blew up the machine gun post beyond hope of it going into action again. We then reconnoitred the country forward of No. 4 Company on the right flank and spent the rest of the day sniping the billets where the enemy were, which proved successful for me. I used a Norwegian rifle which I had found far more accurate than my own and easier to sight."

No. 4 Company were now in direct contact with enemy. Their main positions along the top of a slight hill were protected by advance section posts dug in farther down the forward slope. These posts held up the first German attempts at infiltration, and were then ordered to fall back on the main company positions. The gunner of No. 17 Platoon's forward section left his Bren behind. The Platoon Commander, Lieutenant D. Cole, ordered him to go back and get it. The man returned in a few minutes. He could not get back to his old position, he said; the German fire was too heavy. Guardsman J. Wylie came up and saluted, "I'll go, Sir." He loved weapons for their own sake, and could never bear such beautiful pieces of mechanism damaged or lost. He got the Bren gun, returned for the tripod and then went back a third time to collect some picks and shovels. There was no more talk about German fire being too heavy to cross. Guardsman Wylie was awarded the D.C.M. for this action ; if he had not won it then, he would have been awarded it later on many occasions in North Africa and Italy. He enjoyed fighting—"It's a great life if you don't weaken"—and preached a simple fatalistic philosophy—"You are all right if your name is not on the detail ; if your name is on the detail, you're for it, and if you're for it, you're for it ; so go to sleep now." He was killed commanding a platoon on the Anzio beach-head in February, 1944, the last casualty before the Battalion was withdrawn.

The Germans dug in opposite No. 4 Company to keep it occupied while they sent patrols round the flank. Parties of two or three got behind the Battalion and sniped the road. Strange figures in Norwegian peasant dress appeared in the woods and farmyards. Guardsman Tracey had a long conversation with two strapping blonde women. "They were great girls" he said as he pointed them out to Lieutenant Powell-Edwards. That unlucky officer strolled towards them ; the "girls" resented his curiosity and opened fire on him with sub-machine guns.

No. 2 Company crossed the footbridge at 7 p.m.; at 4.30 a.m. on the 26th the leading platoon under P.S.M. Ferguson occupied Pt. 800, the highest peak in the mountain range. They had climbed the last 1,500 feet up almost perpendicular cliff, and had crawled up to the skyline on their hands and knees through the snow.

During the night, German engineers built a pontoon bridge half a mile south of Pothus bridge, Drummer Hughes and the Norwegian officer watched them at work. "We had about eight shots but they found us out and gave us a hot burst of machine-gun fire, which was badly aimed as we got away unscathed. We decided to await developments ; our idea was to see which way the troops would advance when they had finished the bridge. At six o'clock in the morning the 26th, we saw the enemy bring up two boats. Two hours later, they began loading the boats with a machine-gun and long boxes which we surmised was ammunition. We sniped them and accounted for three, but they machine-gunned us and we had to crawl away." They were able to report that the Germans had evidently decided to concentrate on the right flank. A steady stream of troops was crossing the pontoon bridge and disappearing into the woods on the western bank.

Lieut.-Colonel Stockwell gave out orders to the various unit commanders personally, but the only officers who could be found to attend his conference were Captain R. McGildowny and the Commanders of Nos. 3 and 4 Companies. These officers met Lieut.-Colonel Stockwell in a corner of Pothus Wood at four o'clock. They were there for two hours while Lieut.-Colonel Stockwell struggled to make himself heard above the roar of German aircraft. "Battalion H.Q. Irish Guards will withdraw at the discretion of the Commanding Officer ; the forward Company will withdraw at 1900 hrs." This left Lieutenant C. A. M.-D.-Scott exactly an hour to get back and to withdraw No. 4 Company from close contact with the enemy. Battalion H.Q. began to pack up. "Better clean up the area first" said Captain McGildowny, "there are lots of old papers and tins lying about."

Lieutenant C. A. M.-D.-Scott wondered how he was to extricate his forward platoons in full view of the enemy, and how and when the Companies would really be evacuated from Rognan. Lieutenant J. Haslewood took the orderly's bicycle and pedalled back at top speed to find, seize and hold some boats. On the way he met a lorry and directed it up to No. 4 Company H.Q. Into it were loaded the stores and the Company Sergeant-Major, "Nanny" Nairn, who had hurt his foot. The problem of extricating the platoons was solved by a *deus ex machina*. A British aeroplane appeared. One old Gladiator wobbled out of the sky and shot down three Heinkels in quick succession. It then started machine-gunning the astonished and horrified Germans in their trenches. The platoons promptly withdrew under the cover of this remarkable and completely fortuitous air support. C.Q.M.S. Byrne—who closely resembles Hitler—collected the Company and kept them going at a good pace. They passed through Battalion H.Q., who should have been already away, and through No. 3 Company, which had left a platoon under Lieutenant Powell-Edwards to cover their withdrawal. It was No. 4 Company's proud boast that they did not lose a man or a weapon ; they left Norway with one Bren gun more than when they landed. The Signallers and Clerks of Battalion H.Q. attached themselves to No. 4 Company as it passed through. The Pioneer Platoon moved off independently a little later, leaving the A/A Section, that is the Drums and Pipes, and a few odd men behind with Captain Gordon-Watson. This party stayed behind to load the reserve ammunition on to the charabanc. The Regimental Sergeant-Major was reluctant to abandon the dump he had so laboriously collected, and quoted the Force H.Q. order that ammunition was to have priority over personnel in the use of transport. Captain Gordon-Watson and a couple of men drove the charabanc away just after eight o'clock ;

the remainder set off in single file to march down the road to Rognan ; there were twenty-three of them, led by Drum-Major Stone followed by Sergeant Ward and Guardsman Sullivan. The Regimental Sergeant-Major brought up the rear. They had not gone very far when a machine-gun suddenly opened fire on them from a farm-house 200 yards off the road. "We never knew how it got there." Drum-Major Stone ran to the woods on the left of the road. The others dropped into the ditch on the right of the road. The German machine-gun continued firing, but the pipers with Brens could not locate it. "Make a dash for it," shouted R.S.M. Stack and ran across a field to a gully behind the house. He was followed by one Guardsman ; the remainder stayed in the ditch. The Sergeant-Major and the Guardsman crawled down to the village of Nesby, two miles from Rognan. Here they expected to find No. 3 Independent Company, but heard instead the familiar challenge of Irish Guards. A platoon of No. 3 Company and one from No. 4 Company under Captain P. Whitefoord, M.C., and Lieutenant D. Cole, had taken their place and held the position till midnight.

The Intelligence Section, manning the forward O.Ps. had to make their own way back. "I reached Battalion H.Q. about 2100 hrs.," said Drummer Hughes, "and found it deserted, so I lay low in the Orderly Room trench and had something to eat. I had just finished my meal when I heard noises and movements on the side of the hill opposite my trench. It was the enemy advancing along the ridge. By keeping in the wood I advanced parallel with them for about 300 yards, then lay low again. They passed me about 900 yards to my left-hand; as they did not make their way towards the wood where we had been camped, I knew I was comparatively safe. I scouted the woods looking for a bike but I only found two boxes containing signallers' kit, which I destroyed by tearing the plugs and wires out and smashing the plug boards with my rifle. I also found two boxes of mortar ammunition which I buried. I then made my way down the road towards the town, where I met a section of No. 3 Company. Knowing the hills on the right of the road, I led them over the hill on to the river edge. There we lay low until I scouted the ground thoroughly ahead. I asked the men to get rid of their packs and all web in case they had to swim. We then started to crawl on our stomachs, each man 15 yards apart. We successfully made our way until we were forced to run for it across an open stretch about 200 yards along the river bank. I went first with the N.C.O. about 10 yards behind. As he could not swim it was the only possible way of advancing. I ran about 30 yards when a machine-gun opened out on me.

I fell flat and gave the signal for all the section to jump in the river. We then made our way by letting the current sweep us along and holding to boulders on the side. We all got round safely and we then doubled through thick undergrowth, where we were halted by a swiftly flowing river. There we were joined by P.S.M. Higgins and a party of about forty men. As the majority could not swim we were confronted with a rather big problem. P.S. Higgins' idea was to tie all our rifle slings together. We did that and it was tied round my waist and I swam across. I tied it on to a branch of a tree which overhung the river and flung the other end to the men. It was made fast and all came over by clinging to the line. We then were picked up by a bus." The Regimental Quartermaster-Sergeant was making his last journey in a requisitioned charabanc to collect the ammunition dumps along the road. With one man sitting on the roof, to provide anti-aircraft fire, the charabanc rattled into Rognan in time to catch the last boat.

"At midnight," says the War Diary, "the Battalion, less those unaccounted for, left Rognan by 'puffer' for Finneid." "Those unaccounted for," included the whole of No. 2 Company, half of Battalion H.Q. and a few men of No. 3 Company. The Battalion landed at Finneid early the next morning, the 27th May, and marched to Fauske. Each little Norwegian town possessed a municipal charabanc. The one here had already been commandeered by a Major Kermit Roosevelt. That afternoon he delivered to the Battalion part of No. 2 Company and went back for the rest who had already reached Langset on the coast road.

High up on the mountain peak, No. 2 Company had had no idea of what was going on. Down in the valley they could see small dots moving along the road and round the woods. It certainly looked as if the Battalion was withdrawing, but their orders were to hold their position and they stayed there. Late in the evening—26th—they saw a solitary figure climbing towards them. "From the speed he is making it must be a Norwegian." It was one of Lieut.-Colonel Stockwell's interpreters, who wanted to make sure that there was no one left behind. He produced a copy of a message that he had given hours previously to the Independent Company to pass on to No. 2 Company. "Withdraw immediately to Rognan by quickest possible route." "Why haven't you gone?" he asked. "There hasn't been another man on these mountains for the last three hours. You had better hurry if you want to get back, as the Germans have occupied Pothus Wood and are moving fast on Rognan." They looked down into the valley and saw the footbridge disintegrate in a cloud of smoke.

"Never mind," said the Norwegian, "somehow we will get back." "We must reach the fjord and after that we will follow the coast-line."

Throughout the day the men "unaccounted for" at Rognan arrived in twos and threes. Guardsman P. O'Shea marched in with a small party of Guardsmen and men of the Independent Companies. Captain Gordon-Watson was convinced that O'Shea must have saved this party; by persistent questioning he learnt that O'Shea had, in fact, taken charge of the other men, and had shepherded them through the rivers and over the hills.

By the evening the only men still missing were the twenty men of Battalion H.Q. under Sergeant Ward. Drum-Major Stone left them in their ditch, when he saw that they could not cross the road to join him in the woods. When he eventually reached Rognan the boats had gone and the Germans were marching in threes down the street. He walked into Fauske alone, and promptly wrote a report for the Chief Cipher Officer, Harstad—"Sir, I have the honour to report that Battalion H.Q. was cut off and came under heavy machine-gun fire. I escaped with my cipher into the woods, but there finding that the chances of escape were small I destroyed the cipher by fire."

At Fauske the Companies were spread out on a desolate promontory overlooking the village and covering the road along the north shore of the fjord. It was a temporary position, little more than a place for the Battalion to eat and sleep, while Lieut.-Colonel Stockwell and Captain McGildowny chose the next position. It was a dreary day. The Quartermaster suddenly arrived from Bodo in a taxi with the depressing news that Major Gilbert-Denham had died of his wounds. The continual air raids on the hospital near Harstad gave him no chance to recover. Every officer felt the death of "Clubs" Gilbert-Denham as a personal loss. He was an unusually kind man; he actually spoke to ensigns during their first six months at Wellington.

At midnight 27th-28th May, the Battalion marched out of Fauske. The whole of Stockforce was concentrated in the Valnes peninsula, four miles to the west, where it could block the roads and approaches to Bodo. Two independent companies remained as outposts at Finneid. Two Norwegian Battalions came up to guard the passes through the hills to the north. The main position in the woods and hills round Aasen in the centre of the peninsula was held by the Battalion, three independent companies, a detachment of Royal Engineers and a troop of the 166 Field Battery, R.A. The 2nd Bn. South Wales Borderers joined the Force and came in to reserve at Valnes on the north-west side of the peninsula. The companies reached Aasen in the early hours of the 28th. Outposts covered the approaches and the main coast road to Bodo, while the companies dug positions on the edge of a wood overlooking a valley to the east of the village. The men settled into the barns of deserted farms, and relieved the suffering cows of their surplus milk. There was no wire and few tools. Force H.Q. sent over all it could spare—half a dozen Tommy-guns and one machine-gun. After much discussion at Battalion H.Q., Guardsman Donaghty was installed behind the machine-gun covering the main coast road.

Fifty German cyclists were reported to have entered Langset, the ferry village on the east of the fjord opposite Rognan, but there was no definite information. The companies heard firing in the distance, but saw nothing except a stray Norwegian patrol. The bombers, however, were active all day. They drove Battalion H.Q. out of its farm-house to join Force H.Q. at Valnes. The Quartermaster, Lieutenant McCarthy, again arrived from Bodo by taxi. "The Germans have reached Boulogne and Calais. God knows what is happening to the B.E.F." After this, the news of the capture of Narvik fell rather flat. The French, Poles and Norwegians had taken the town after twelve hours' heavy fighting, and had driven the Germans eastwards along the railway towards the Swedish frontier.

For the Battalion in its remote fjord the news raised the inevitable question "What is going to happen to us ?" The next day Lieut.-Colonel Stockwell ordered the withdrawal and evacuation of the whole of Stockforce. At midnight, the Battalion marched westward again, passed through the Scots Guards and reached Hopen, twenty-seven miles away, early on the 30th. The "puffers" were waiting, and carried the Battalion to Bodo through a driving rain-storm.

Bodo had been bombed into ruins. The Battalion tramped through the flames and ashes of the town to the woods and villas on the outskirts. There they got their first wash for many days, and cooked a meal in the deserted houses. No. 4 Company occupied the Spanish Vice-Consul's house. Guardsman McEvoy made a brief survey of the wardrobes and collected an armful of silk underclothes. The Company officers gladly changed their tattered vests and pants.

At midnight—everything in Norway seemed to happen at midnight—the message came up from the harbour, "Destroyers *Firedrake* and *Fame* at Quay. Five minutes to get on board." Sailors standing at the head of the gangway ruthlessly threw overboard anything they considered superfluous. They seized the large tea chest full of the Battalion documents, giving the Orderly Room Clerks just time to snatch out a nominal roll and a casualty list before throwing it into the sea. One stretcher case was tenderly brought up the gangway.

The ship's surgeon insisted on seeing the "casualty" and the truth came out. In a ruined house a Guardsman had found a bottle of gin. "I thought it was one of them light Norwegian wines," he said afterwards. To save the reputation of the Battalion, his Company Sergeant-Major had knocked him unconscious with an oar and covered him with a blanket. The Battalion's reputation suffered another temporary setback. Lieutenant C. A. M.-D.-Scott rushed down to have a shower, but forgot to warn the ship's officers and explain why he was wearing a highly coloured silk petticoat.

CHAPTER VI

The Evacuation

THE Battalion landed near Harstad the following morning, the 31st May, and moved into their old billets at Ervik. They spent three days there once again re-equipping with what little equipment there was left in Harstad and ploughing through their arrears of mail. From the bundles of letters and newspapers they got their first idea of the campaign in France. The first news of the 2nd Battalion came in a letter from the Regimental Adjutant:

"We had had a very bad week here, starting with the 2nd Battalion being sent off to Holland at very short notice last Sunday, 11th. They landed in the Hook during the night and were severely bombed on two occasions before they withdrew in daylight on the Tuesday. They were very lucky to get away. Their total casualties were eleven other ranks killed, seventeen wounded in hospital and a certain number of others with small wounds at duty. We started to get rumours about the 1st Battalion on Wednesday, 15th, but got no official news until Friday about midday when we got the names of the Officer casualties. They were a terrible shock to everybody and we feel very much for those of you who have got to carry on and take their place. We have heard no details of how seriously wounded any of the officers are on the wounded list and have got only a rough idea as to what happened. We have done our best to make it as easy as possible for all their next of kin and they have been very brave over it all. We are anxious to get further details. We are informed that the other rank casualties were four killed and twelve wounded, but so far have got no names."

The news from France was getting steadily worse. Everybody could see that there was no prospect of reinforcements for Norway; on the contrary, it looked as if every man and ship would be needed in England. On the 2nd, General Auchinleck, the G.O.C., came over to Ervik to present decorations. In addition to those awards already announced "for gallantry on H.M.T. *Chobry*," he made immediate awards of the D.C.M. to Guardsman, now L./Corporal, J. Wylie and Guardsman P. O'Shea, of the M.M. to Drummer Hughes, and of a bar to the M.C. to Captain B. O. P. Eugster, M.C. It was a sad day for P.S.M. McCleary, the Transport Sergeant. With tears in his eyes, he watched his spotless trucks being driven one after another off the quay into the sea.

The following day the Battalion moved to Borkones ; at midnight the destroyer *Echo* took them out to sea and transferred them to the liner *Lancastria*. The *Lancastria* lay off the coast for three days, while the convoy assembled round her—two other transports, H.M.S. *Vindictive*, two destroyers and H.M.S. *Valiant*. They sailed for England on the 8th; 300 miles off Trondheim in a calm sea and under a clear sky two German bombers picked up the convoy. They circled overhead dropping incendiary bombs and then streaked back towards their base. In the *Lancastria* the Battalion waited anxiously for the inevitable attack by a series of bombers. Over the clear horizon rolled a thick bank of mist ; the convoy plunged thankfully into this heaven-sent cover. An hour later the Battalion heard the engines of the German bombers as they patrolled over the fog bank, but the fog held good till the convoy was well out of aircraft range. "We would have been even so relieved if we had known that H.M.S. *Glorious* had been sunk by the *Scharnhorst* not so very far behind us."

On the 10th June—two months after they left Wellington Barracks—the Battalion landed at Greenock. Lieut.-Colonel E. Mahoney was waiting there with a draft of reinforcements. They had embarked a week before but had been taken off the ship just as they thought that they were at last sailing for Norway. Lieut.-Colonel E. Mahoney took over command and moved the Battalion to Coatbridge. After four days of reorganization and entertainment by the local citizens, the Battalion moved south to Northwood, an outer suburb of London. The Battalion was to spend the next two and a half years in the suburbs of London. Their first task on arrival at Northwood lasted, with variations, for all that time, digging trenches on the golf course to repel German parachutists.

Each campaign usually adds a few foreign words to a soldier's vocabulary. The whole Norwegian campaign is contained in the two phrases brought back by the Battalion—"Shnay" for snow and "Tyske flee" for German aeroplane.

The Irish Guards were not forgotten in Norway. In Tunisia in May, 1943, the Adjutant found a Red Cross postcard in the pocket of a dead Guardsman. The signature was Christina; the postmark Harstad.

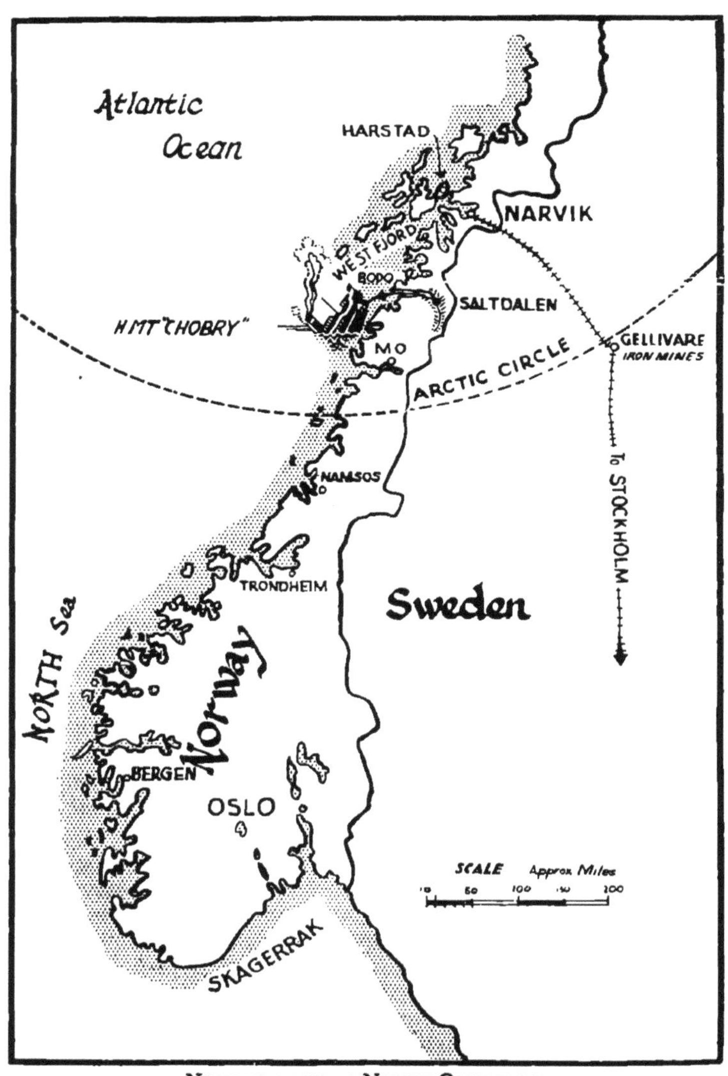

NORWAY, SHOWING NARVIK OPERATIONS

PART II

•

THE 2nd BATTALION IN HOLLAND AND BOULOGNE

CHAPTER I

The Hook of Holland

ON 10th May, 1940, the German Armies invaded Holland across the eastern frontiers. Simultaneously, they struck directly at the central administration of the country by landing troops on the beaches north of The Hague and dropping parachutists all round it. The Netherlands Government, in imminent danger of being isolated and captured, appealed to the British Government for help. There were very few trained troops in England ; the most the War Office could promise was a force of Marines and a battalion of the Brigade of Guards.

At the time the 2nd Battalion Irish Guards was on the move to Tunbridge Wells. The departure of the 1st Battalion for Norway a month previously had not greatly disturbed the steady routine of Wellington Barracks. The 2nd Battalion remained there for another fortnight—a long fortnight on public duties or confined to barracks as companies-in-waiting. They took it for granted that some time sooner or later they would join the 1st Battalion. Meanwhile, they taught Canadians how to mount King's Guard, went for route marches through London or trained self-consciously in St. James's or Hyde Park. They did, in fact, receive orders to move to Norway, but two days later the order was amended, and Camberley was substituted for Norway. On the 22nd April, the 2nd Battalion marched out of Wellington Barracks. At Old Dean Camp, Camberley, it joined the 2nd Bn. Welsh Guards and the 5th Bn. The Loyal Regiment to form the 20th Guards Brigade. There was little now to look forward to except the Whitsun leave.

The Whitsun leave parties got away as early as they could on 10th May. They were well out of reach before a War Office telegram arrived cancelling all leave. The Germans had invaded the Low Countries at dawn. This was no reason, however, for cancelling the Brigade's first night exercise. Early the following morning the Battalion returned to camp, tired and dirty. Little groups of officers and Guardsmen were still standing among the tents talking and eating when they heard shouts, starting at the Orderly Room and spreading throughout the camp, "Pack up, Pack up. Prepare to move." England, it seemed, and Kent in particular, was in immediate danger of being invaded by German parachutists. The 20th Guards Brigade, as one of the few bodies of troops available, was moved hastily down to the area of Tunbridge Wells.

It was nearly midnight on the 11th May before the Battalion had settled down among the oast-houses and sheds of Beltring Hop Farm, near Paddocks Wood. No sooner had he arrived than the Commanding Officer, Lieut.-Colonel J. C. Haydon, O.B.E., was summoned to Brigade H.Q. He found the Brigade Commander, Brigadier W. L. Fox-Pitt, M.C., in the Wellington Hotel, Tunbridge Wells. The orders were brief: "You will command a composite battalion of the Brigade; this battalion will embark at Dover for Holland tomorrow afternoon, or rather this afternoon. Report to the War Office in the morning at ten o'clock for further orders." Colonel Haydon did what he could that night, but he had to leave all the organization of the Battalion to the Adjutant, Captain H. S. Phillpotts. About a quarter of the Battalion had gone on leave, away beyond the reach of telegrams, so a company had to be hastily borrowed from the 2nd Bn. Welsh Guards. The early morning was disturbed by messages from Brigade H.Q. that parachutists had landed in large numbers in four places in Kent. Parachutists or, as it happened, no parachutists, Colonel Haydon left to keep his appointment in London, leaving the Battalion to assemble, collect stores and move down to Dover. Some of the men going on leave to Ireland had been stopped in time at Holyhead and sent back to the Battalion. Since no one in uniform was allowed into neutral Eire, they were in civilian clothes, and their kit had been left behind in Old Dean Camp. They made themselves look as much like soldiers as possible, but most of them, including C.S.M. O'Connor, could not get boots and marched to battle in highly polished pointed shoes. By a tremendous effort, the Quartermaster, Lieutenant Keating, got back from leave in Ireland. The first thing he thought of was pay for the men; he extracted £2,000 from the local bank and wrapped the notes carefully in a belt under his shirt.

Colonel Haydon got his orders from General J. G. Dill, Vice-Chief of the Imperial General Staff.

"A force of 200 Marines landed at the Hook of Holland during the night (11th/12th May) with orders to secure a landing place. The

Battalion under your command will proceed to Holland, disembarking at the Hook. On arrival, you should get in touch with the local Dutch Commander, and the Commander of the Marines from whom you will ascertain the latest information."

This was very necessary, for singularly little information was reaching England. As far as the War Office was concerned, the situation in Holland was "necessarily obscure," which meant that nobody really knew what was happening there.

"Your object," continued the orders, "will then be to move your battalion towards The Hague and to co-operate with the local Commander in his operations to safeguard the Government and to restore the situation in The Hague. In assisting in these operations, you will carry out any task allotted your battalion, if you consider the task a reasonable operation of war. You will not, however, come under his orders and will not hesitate to refuse requests for assistance which would, in your opinion, entail useless sacrifice of your men. In the event of the Netherlands Government evacuating The Hague, you will endeavour to withdraw to the Hook for re-embarkation in His Majesty's ships. You should endeavour to keep the War Office informed of your situation and movements."

The Battalion reached Dover on Sunday evening. There was no time to sort and stow the baggage in the correct order for unloading. The two Channel steamers, S.S. *Canterbury* and S.S. *Maid of Orleans*, were standing by with steam up ; their captains were clamouring to sail immediately so as to reach the Hook before full daylight the following morning. The Battalion was bundled straight from the train into the ships. Because of the rush, many of the men still did not know where they were going—the popular theory being that the Battalion was going to garrison the Maginot Line to replace some battalion of the B.E.F. that had moved forward into Belgium. As soon as it was really dark, the ships put out to sea with an escort of destroyers. At the last moment a large packing case of maps, a special wireless for direct communication with the War Office, and a Dutch interpreter in British battledress were flung on board the *Canterbury*. The Battalion, now dignified with the code-name Harpoon Force, spent a miserable night in a rolling sea.

The convoy reached the Hook as dawn was breaking on Whit Monday, 13th May. Nobody really knew whether or not the Germans had yet occupied the port ; it was with relief that they saw a British destroyer in the harbour and Marines standing on the quay. One stray German aircraft came over, circled round, dropped a bomb and flew away. Otherwise, the landing was without incident. There were no signs of war in the Hook, except for a few Dutch soldiers, and nothing to be seen towards The Hague. But in the east the sky was reddened by the flames of burning Rotterdam. Colonel Haydon scribbled a note for the ship's captain to take back to the Regimental Lieutenant-Colonel. "When you see Sinclair, ask whether we can be allotted air-support. I am certain we shall need it, and there are no arrangements for it."

As each ship tied up, the companies filed off and moved into positions within the perimeter held by the Marines. There they remained while the Commanding Officer made a brief reconnaissance. The Hook of Holland is only a small village looking straight out on to open country. The village and the quay together form admirable and well-defined air-targets. The village is rectangular, with streets running straight through it at right-angles to each other. The surrounding countryside was bare, except for the single line of trees along verges of the main roads, with no cover anywhere for troops and vehicles. Fortunately, there was still a ground mist, but this natural protection could not last for more than a few hours.

As yet, there were no vehicles to conceal, for the Marines had not been able to collect any in the neighbourhood. Some transport was essential ; without it, the Battalion could not move on The Hague. The local Dutch Commander, who had been found eating bacon and eggs in the Hotel Amerika, did all he could to help and after a long conversation with someone in The Hague decided that a column of vehicles would arrive at noon for the use of the Battalion.

Colonel Haydon had now seen enough to realize that to make the Hook really secure it would require at least one infantry brigade supported by artillery and anti-aircraft guns. He wirelessed his opinion back to the War Office, adding that even so he intended to march on The Hague as soon as the promised transport arrived and could be loaded. The War Office replied that a second battalion might disembark at the Hook the following night. To this Colonel Haydon could only say that the arrival of only one more battalion without any supporting arms could not make any difference to the situation. In his opinion, the decision should be taken immediately either to reinforce the Hook strongly or to evacuate the place altogether.

The Companies now moved into new positions on the outskirts of the village, thus expanding the perimeter and placing the general one a little farther away from the quay. There was still little room for manœuvre but to hold even this area all the rifle companies had to be employed in the line. This left no reserves other than the few men who had been brought over as reinforcements for the Welsh Guards Company. Battalion H.Q. moved out of its first home—an air-raid shelter—into the Hotel Amerika, a restaurant in the main street. The Dutch Commandant was still there ; he sat in silence at a small table all day unmoved by bombing, receiving an occasional report from a junior officer. He could give little information, but he had a direct military telephone line to The Hague. Conversation with him was difficult as the interpreter had disappeared. Shortly after Battalion H.Q. was installed, the Military Attache at The Hague rang up to pass on an urgent request from the Dutch High Command. "Could the Battalion please stay in the Hook, guard the port and keep open the road to The Hague?" The reason for this request soon became clear.

About midday, Colonel Haydon and his Adjutant, Captain H. S. Phillpotts, were walking up and down the quay, watching a crane slowly unloading the Battalion's stores, and sailors loading crates of diamonds from Amsterdam on to the destroyer *Windsor*. A fleet of long black cars, with motor-cyclist outriders, suddenly swept down the road and drew up sharply by the quay. Almost before they had stopped, the doors opened and a man jumped from each car. The largest man—a burly giant in plain clothes who had appeared from the largest car—marched smartly towards the two officers. Captain Phillpotts tentatively drew his revolver. " They are so smart," he said, "they must be Germans." The civilian clicked his heels and bowed ; Captain Phillpotts cocked his pistol ; "Her Majesty the Queen of the Netherlands has arrived." The two officers looked from the Dutchman back to the cars, and there saw a middle-aged lady, Queen Wilhelmina. While Colonel Haydon took charge of the Queen, Captain H. S. Phillpotts went on board the destroyer H.M.S. *Malcolm*. There he told the senior Naval Officer, Captain T. E. Hasley, that the Queen had arrived and would no doubt require his help. "Nonsense," said the Captain, "she left yesterday." He was persuaded that he must be thinking of the Princess Juliana, that the Queen was certainly on the quay and no doubt required a passage in one of His Majesty's ships, and so came ashore to put a destroyer at the disposal of the Queen. The royal party went aboard and set sail for Flushing. The Queen had told Colonel Haydon that she intended to transfer her household to the Island of Walcheren, but apparently she was later prevailed upon to go straight to England.

The departure of the Queen, which her party expected to be followed shortly by that of the Dutch Government, removed one of the two objects for which the Battalion had been landed. Colonel Haydon asked the War Office by wireless whether his original orders still held good, and was he still to move to The Hague in an attempt to restore the situation with one battalion? Meanwhile, the promised transport had arrived—fifty-five brand new Dutch Army lorries, under the command of a young lieutenant who openly fretted at every minute he spent away from The Hague. Colonel Haydon was not going to leave the Hook till he got an answer from the War Office; he had already refused two requests from the Dutch Commander-in-Chief, the first to take the whole force to Rotterdam and the second to take it to Amsterdam. The Dutch Lieutenant was equally determined to return to The Hague immediately. They compromised by the Battalion keeping six lorries, and the Dutchman driving away with the rest. The Companies spent the afternoon watching the roads and the sky, loading their stores on the lorries and preparing to march to The Hague if need be.

About six o'clock in the evening the sentries halted a convoy of cars on the outskirts of the village. It was the Dutch Government. Their departure removed any lingering doubts there may have been in Colonel Haydon's mind that the whole position in the country was rapidly disintegrating and that there was no longer any confidence at The Hague to be restored. Hard behind the Government came the Diplomatic Corps. With them was the lost interpreter, now resplendent in full-dress uniform and field boots. It was hardly necessary for the head of the British Military Mission to say that the situation had deteriorated during the day. One look at the diplomats crowding on the destroyers was enough to make that quite obvious. There was very little other information. The forces available for the defence of Rotterdam, as far as was known, were six battalions. These were supposed to be holding the western exits of the city, but it was not known whether there were any Dutch troops between it and the Hook.

The Germans caught the tail of the Diplomatic Corps. It was the first heavy air-raid on the battalion area. Flights of bombers roared over the village, bombing and machine-gunning. The Battalion had been expecting this all day, but they could offer no effective opposition. The anti-aircraft gun posts came into action at once. They were necessarily in very exposed positions, but they fired continuously throughout the raid. L./Sergeant J. O'Donnell's A/A post was particularly exposed, but he stood to his gun, pumping a steady stream of tracer, till he collapsed badly wounded by machine-gun bullets. L./Corporal J. Flynn on another post had a personal feud with one aeroplane which singled him out for special attention. His tripod was hit six times, but he kept on firing till the gun itself was hit twice and destroyed. This air-raid killed seven Guardsmen and wounded twenty-three. Three of the casualties were wounded some distance from the R.A.P. A local doctor treated them and then, with the best intentions, drove them to a hospital in The Hague, where, unfortunately, the Germans collected them. The rest of the wounded were taken on board the destroyer and evacuated to England. Captain H. S. Phillpotts was slightly wounded in the arm but concealed his wound till the following morning.

The rest of the evening and the night were quiet. A message at last came through from the War Office. "In view of the departure of the Queen and the Dutch Government," it said, "steps were being taken to arrange for the evacuation of the Force." The Battalion spent the night wondering what these steps might be.

The German bombers came again the following morning. The first air-raid, at 9.30, was heavier than the previous one, but fortunately the casualties were less. Four Guardsmen lost their lives and four were wounded. At first the bombers singled out Battalion H.Q. for special attention. The Bren-gunners in the area, L./Sergeant McGrath, L./Sergeant J. Armstrong, and L./Corporal Reardon, stood their ground and did their best to discourage the Germans with a steady stream of fire. When the raid began, most of the officers were attending a conference in the Hotel Amerika. The first flight of bombers scored a direct hit on the roof of the hotel and another on the house next door. As soon as the noise of falling glass and masonry had subsided, the officers hastily decamped into an air-raid shelter just outside the door. Only Captain P. Pole-Carew remained where he was, safely under a billiard table. There were two shelters, one originally occupied by Battalion H.Q. Clerks, the other by the R.A.P., both now crowded with unhappy civilians. Work was impossible and thought difficult in the crowd of women and children and distraught fathers looking for members of their families. The bombers returned for another run over their target. This time they scored a direct hit on the R.A.P. shelter. The bomb did not penetrate, but one end of the shelter caved in under the explosion. A Medical Orderly, Guardsman Kiely, was sitting directly underneath the bomb burst, but his nonchalant treatment of the whole incident kept the wounded calm and the civilians quiet. The Medical Officer, Lieutenant M. R. Grace, R.A.M.C., the Medical Sergeant, L./Sergeant F. Cross, and the rest of the Orderlies were all out in the streets hard at work. The wounded Guardsmen were but a fraction of the casualties. The streets and roads were littered with dead and dying civilians. Refugees had started to trek out of the Hook down the road towards The Hague. On the other side of the village, an endless stream of refugees were pouring in from Rotterdam. Father Stoner, O.S.B., the chaplain, described the morning as a confused kaleidoscope of horrors. Some of the refugees were pushing dead children on handcarts and perambulators. Every now and then a German plane would swoop down and machine-gun them again. There were no signs of panic ; in fact, no one even bothered to take cover in the ditches beside the road. All the morning the Germans bombed and machine-gunned the refugees. A naval officer writes : "It was deliberate and calculated murder. By no stretch of imagination could the pitiful crowd have been mistaken for armed troops." Father Stoner and Pipe-Major Cosgrove organized the stretcher bearers to pick up as many civilians as possible. While Father Stonor worked amongst the dying, the stretcher-bearers carried the living to the doctor. But there were far too many victims, scattered for miles, and great numbers of them had to be left unattended.

It was now only too clear that the Germans could have little difficulty in breaking through the slender Dutch opposition at Rotterdam and pressing on to the Hook. They had already reached The Hague, for during the night, German snipers had infiltrated into the streets. Although there had so far been no contact, except from the air, a German mechanized attack could very easily, logically and rapidly develop. To such an attack the Irish Guards had no adequate response. It was indeed probable that the Germans were already moving up from Rotterdam, and were using their air superiority to bomb the Irish Guards into a static and quiescent state until they themselves were ready to mount an attack.

Just after the first air-raid, the destroyer flotilla leader, H.M.S. *Malcolm*, put into the harbour. The Senior Naval Officer came ashore to say that he could now provide ships for evacuation. Knowing that the War Office had already made preliminary arrangements for evacuation, Colonel Haydon had no hesitation in ordering the Battalion to embark. There was no need to worry about loading stores ; the bombing had destroyed them all. The reserve ammunition, neatly stacked in sand-pits, was burning and exploding, the wireless instruments and trucks had been smashed and the Dutch lorries were in flames. The Companies began to move down the quay at 11 o'clock. "As each half-platoon of the Irish Guards was detailed," wrote an officer of the destroyer H.M.S. *Whitshed*, "they marched down the jetty and on board as if they were parading in the forecourt of Buckingham Palace. It was grand to watch them."

At midday, the destroyers *Malcolm* and *Whitshed* steamed out with Headquarters Company on board. An hour later, the rest of the Battalion and the naval demolition party sailed on H.M.S. *Vesper*. At ten o'clock that night, forty-eight hours after they had left, the Battalion landed at Dover. After a night in the rest camp and the Lord Warden Hotel (bed and breakfast, 15/- a head) the Battalion returned to Old Dean. They drove into the camp through the lines of Welsh Guardsmen, whose cheers were deeply embarrassing to all but Lieutenant du Boulay, who was ready to tell the first of many stories about "the Hook." Sitting in the sun outside their old tents, they found it hard to believe that it had not all been a dream. Six days later the nightmare recurred.

COMPOSITION OF HARPOON FORCE

Battalion Headquarters

Lieut.-Colonel J. C. Haydon, O.B.E., Commanding Officer, 2nd Irish Guards.

Major G. St. V. J. Vigor, Second-in-Command, 2nd Welsh Guards.

Captain H. S. Phillpotts, Adjutant, 2nd Irish Guards.

Lieutenant D. Hornung, Intelligence Officer, 2nd Irish Guards.

Attached

Lieutenant M. R. Grace, Medical Officer, R.A.M.C.

Captain Phillips, Interpreter, Dutch Army.

Captain J. J. Stoner, Chaplain.

Headquarter Company

Major T. G. Lindsay, Officer Commanding 2nd Irish Guards.

Lieutenant J. F. Marnan, Signal Officer, 2nd Irish Guards.

2/Lieutenant P. O. Davison, Transport Officer, 2nd Irish Guards.

2/Lieutenant P. D. Lindsay, Mortar Officer, 2nd Irish Guards.

No. 1 Company (2nd Welsh Guards)

Captain C. H. R. Heber-Percy.

Captain A. H. S. Coombe Tennant.

Lieutenant C. A. St. S. P. Harmsworth.

2/Lieutenant J. E. L. FitzWilliams.

No. 2 Company (2nd Irish Guards)

Captain J. W. R. Madden.
Captain P. W. B. Pole-Carew.
Lieutenant J. B. FitzGerald.
2/Lieutenant M. V. Dudley.

No. 3 Company (2nd Irish Guards)

Captain C. K. Finlay.
Lieutenant E. A. S. Alexander.
2/Lieutenant N. A. R. O'Neill.
2/Lieutenant P. P. Jeffreys.

No. 4 Company (2nd Irish Guards)

Captain L. D. Murphy, M.C.
Captain P. F. I. Reid.
Lieutenant D. W. S. P. Reynolds.
2/Lieutenant N. H. Du Boulay.

First Reinforcements

Captain C. R. McCausland, 2nd Irish Guards.
2/Lieutenant G. G. Romer, 2nd Irish Guards.
2/Lieutenant N. T. C. Fisher, 2nd Welsh Guards.

Strength of Companies

Headquarter Company, 174 2nd Bn. Irish Guards.
No. 1 Company, 201 2nd Bn. Welsh Guards.
No. 2 Company, 91 2nd Bn. Irish Guards.
No. 3 Company, 90 2nd Bn. Irish Guards.
No. 4 Company, 95 2nd Bn. Irish Guards.
Total (including attached)—651.

CHAPTER II

Boulogne

LATE on Tuesday morning, the 22nd May, the 2nd Battalion once again marched into camp from yet another night exercise. They were dirty, tired and hungry, so they wolfed the breakfasts that were waiting for them and scattered to their tents to sleep. They did not want to hear another sound till the Duty Drummer blew "Cook-house" and the Quartermaster-Sergeants shouted "Come and get it." At 11 o'clock a despatch rider drove up to Battalion H.Q. and a few minutes later the camp was torn by shouts of "Pack up." "Prepare to move." At first the Battalion thought it must be a joke, but the Commanding Officer, Lieut.-Colonel Charles Haydon, knew it was no such thing. "The order to move that afternoon," he said, "could not have arrived at a more inconvenient or tiresome moment." The War Office, however, could hardly be expected to know that the two battalions of the 20th Guards Brigade had had no sleep that night ; all it knew, or cared, was that the German armies were sweeping through France and that the Channel ports were undefended. The War Office had already ordered the Rifle Brigade into Calais ; it now ordered the 20th Guards Brigade to embark at Dover for Boulogne.

At half-past three that afternoon the Battalion drove out of Old Dean Common Camp at the head of the Brigade column. The weather was hot enough to be called a heat-wave and the Battalion drove all afternoon in perfect sunshine. The roads were lined with people, the women and children in bright summer dresses and the old men wearing straw hats. For the first time in their lives the soldiers heard civilians shouting "Up the Army," and it made them think that there must be something very wrong somewhere. The column halted on the heights above Dover and waited for darkness to fall before driving down to the harbour. They found two channel steamers at the quay, the *Biarritz* for the Welsh and the *Queen of the Channel* for the Irish Guards. After a quick meal of stew, bread and tea, the Battalion set to work to load their equipment and stores into their ship. As the equipment was checked and loaded it became painfully noticeable what equipment was there to load. They did not know what they would find on the other side, but they hoped that there would at least be some mortars, grenades, anti-tank mines and wire, for the Battalion had none of these elementary weapons of war. There was no signalling kit. For anybody who fought only in the later stages of the war, it is a shock to read in Colonel Haydon's official report "In an operation of the kind undertaken, wireless sets should be issued to each battalion and Brigade H.Q." In spite of Colonel Haydon's repeated statements that a Battalion without its own transport loses at least 50 per cent. of its efficiency, the ship's captain could not be induced to take any vehicles on board except motor-cycles and the carriers. There was no room for them, he said, and the Battalion had to be content with the hope that they might be able to borrow a few lorries in Boulogne. The port authorities had already received a signal from a trawler lying off Boulogne: "Enemy tanks reported two miles south of Boulogne." The only thing the Brigade had to deal with an armoured division was one platoon of four 2-pounder anti-tank guns, commanded by 2/Lieutenant A. Eardley-Wilmot. These guns, Brigade H.Q. and a box of umpires' white arm-bands were loaded into the destroyer H.M.S. *Whitshed.*

A brief air-raid alarm cleared the quay of dockers and sight-seeing officials which for the first time gave the Battalion a chance to study the capacity of the *Queen of the Channel.* It was quite obvious that she was much too small to take the Battalion and such equipment as it had. Colonel Haydon persuaded the War Office to allot him another small ship, the *Mona's Star.*

No. 1 Company, under Captain C. R. McCausland, the men of the Mortar Platoon, the dismounted truck drivers, the Pioneer Platoon and some of the heavier equipment were left on the quay to wait for the *Mona's Star.*

The main body of the force sailed just before dawn. The destroyer *Whitshed* led the way followed by the *Queen of the Channel* and the *Biarritz*, with the destroyer *Vimiera* on their beam as an additional escort. It was a cramped and uncomfortable crossing. All the officers with their baggage were crammed into a single cabin while the Guardsmen lay out all over the decks. The *Mona's Star* did not sail till some hours later. In this way the Battalion got separated and No. 1 Company occupied their position only half an hour before the Germans attacked it.

At half-past six on the morning of the 22nd of May, the *Queen of the Channel* berthed at Boulogne. It may still have been fine in England, but in France it was raining heavily. The Battalion unrolled their long oil-skin gas-capes (originally issued as a protection against showers of mustard gas) and lined the deck. The quay was a scene of squalid confusion. It looked as if thousands of suit-cases had been emptied on the ground by maniac customs officers, and trampling over this sodden mass of clothes, bedding and filthy refuse was a horde of panic-stricken refugees and stray soldiers waiting to rush the ships. The Battalion could not even disembark till sailors and Guardsmen with fixed bayonets had cleared a lane through the sorry mob. The tide was low, none of the cranes was working and refugees, with the ingenuity of despair, found endless ways to board the ship—everything conspired to delay the unloading. Fretting with impatience, the Battalion waited in the Customs shed. The shed was already occupied by some Belgian troops and the Commander-in-Chief's chargers ; the horses at least seemed pleased to see them. The Battalion was still there at eleven o'clock when the ships backed out of the harbour crammed with two train-loads of wounded from the B.E.F. and refugees from every army and nation in Western Europe except the German.

Meanwhile the Brigade Commander, Colonel Haydon and the Commanding Officer of the 2nd Bn. Welsh Guards were walking round the outskirts of Boulogne choosing a perimeter for the defence of the town. The force only consisted of two battalions so it was simply a question of which battalion should hold which half of the perimeter. The Brigadier ordered the Irish Guards to hold the right half, the one covering the southern and western entrances to Boulogne. As soon as he heard this, Colonel Haydon sent back word to the Battalion to move up to Outreau, a suburban village on the main road from the south. Loaded with all the ammunition they could carry the platoons marched in single file up through the town. They had to force their way through the crowds that jammed every street, pressing down the hill in a wild effort to reach the ships. When they reached Outreau they sat down on the pavements to rest and smoke and think about food while Colonel Haydon showed the officers the positions he had chosen for the Companies. There was a bakery in the main square of the village and the delicious scent of new bread filled the air. Father Julian Stoner, the chaplain, suffered acutely. "Never have I felt so hungry," he said, "as when I watched a French woman handing out long loaves of bread to a crowd of Belgian soldiers ; but, although famished, none of the Irish Guards joined in and I could hardly be the first. All the shops were, of course, empty."

To cover Boulogne, Colonel Haydon had to stretch out the Companies in a wide semi-circle of over two miles from Outreau down to the sea on the west of the town. No. 1 Company and No. 4 held the main position at Outreau, No. 2 Company covered the area between Outreau and the coast road and No. 3 Company was on the extreme right. The three Companies, Nos. 2, 3 and 4, were in position by one o'clock and having learnt a hard lesson at the Hook of Holland, dug like beavers. Even so, it was difficult to shake off the effects of years of restricted training; one Guardsman asked his platoon-commander "Are we allowed in these gardens, sir, or are they out of bounds?" 2/Lieutenant Antony Eardley-Wilmot brought up his little French 37-mm. anti-tank guns and put one in Outreau to cover the main road and the other to cover the coast road. As yet, there was no sign of No. 1 Company. There was no sign either of the Germans or French, though there were said to be some French troops between Nesles and Samer, two small towns to the south-west. Since nobody in Boulogne could tell him anything, the Brigadier told the Battalion to try and find the French. Lieutenant Peter Reynolds "borrowed" a car and offered to drive to Nesles. With two motor-cyclists alongside and three Guardsmen in the back he drove cheerfully and furiously down the road. In about an hour he reappeared, with bullet-holes in the back of the car. He had seen neither French nor Germans but someone had fired at him from the woods round Nesles.

No. 1 Company and the first Germans both arrived at Outreau at three o'clock in the afternoon. Captain Conolly McCausland got his company into their positions on the left of the Battalion's line outside the village. Small parties of Germans, with single tanks, appeared on the ridge which overlooks the village from the south. The first shells fell on No. 1 Company almost before the Guardsmen had broken the ground for their trenches. So far the Germans had only a few light infantry guns which did little damage. By half-past five, however, they had brought up field guns and then put down a heavy concentration, again on No. 1 Company. Behind the line of shells came tanks and infantry. The leading tank advanced up the main road. Lieutenant Eardley-Wilmot and his anti-tank gun were waiting for it, and they stopped it dead in the middle of the road with seven direct hits.

The German infantry came on. After confused fighting they were halted but only after they had got in between the forward left-hand platoon and the rest of No. 1 Company. Half an hour later, German aeroplanes bombed and machine-gunned Outreau, and under cover of this, their infantry attacked No. 1 Company a second time. This attack was also beaten off and the Germans withdrew to think again. They brought up more artillery and fresh troops. Two hours later they shelled the whole Battalion front heavily ; then, when it was quite dark, launched a third attack on No. 1 Company. They got round in behind the left-hand forward platoon. Captain McCausland ordered it to withdraw, but two sections had already been overrun. L./Corporal Mawhinney, an enormous man with a soft, gentle voice, commanded the third section. There was a German tank within thirty yards of him, but L./Corporal Mawhinney managed to extricate his section without loss. So far No. 1 Company had had all the fighting. Their casualties were very heavy, but they had halted the Germans all evening and still held their main position.

A German motor-cycle platoon commander published an account of this action, from his point of view, in the Army magazine *Die Militarwoche*. "After Abbeville had fallen," he wrote, "the German armoured formations pushed on towards Boulogne. Late in the afternoon we were just outside Boulogne, in Outreau. The tanks were leading ; behind came the motor-cyclists. Suddenly the advance halted. From ahead came a lively sound of fighting, the sharp bark of our 20-mm. guns (those mounted on the German tanks Pz. Kw. II) and furious machine-gun fire from our tanks. In between there were dull, heavy thuds. An enemy anti-tank gun? Then a dispatch rider dashed up. 'Motor-cyclists forward.' In a flash we had dismounted and were worming our way forward on both sides of the houses. Fifteen yards ahead the road bent sharply to the left. There stood two of our own tanks, hit by the enemy anti-tank gun. A tank lieutenant explained the situation. Round the bend were two anti-tank guns which covered the whole road and were in positions covered from direct fire. Our job is to capture these guns, so that the advance may go on. And we must do it, for every minute will save us casualties.

"The Company Commander decides to put in one platoon on the left of the road and one on the right, and take the enemy position from both sides at once. Brief instructions are enough, and the men prepare for action.

"No. 3 Platoon vanished into the houses to the right, and for us the job begins with getting through a thick hedge. In two minutes we have got through, one by one ; and we deploy for an attack. We creep unseen almost to the ridge—just in time to see the flash of a shot from the enemy position. Did that one catch No. 3 Platoon which had a shorter journey than we ? Section No. 1 gets its machine-gun into position and fires a burst. At that instant hell is let loose. The houses ahead of us and the little wood are occupied by the enemy. Burst after burst of machine-gun fire comes whipping into the long green grass. We crouch in the thorns and nettles while the bullets whistle over us. Where are the bastards ? We can't find where the shots are coming from. There must be regular fortifications, as if there wasn't enough to deal with already. Meanwhile we have found that a direct attack on the enemy anti-tank guns is impossible.

"Now it has grown dark. Every attempt to get within grenade-throwing distance of the enemy fails because of his defensive fire. Corporal B. is killed in trying to reach the enemy machine-gun. Shot in the head. The enemy is shooting too damned well. We managed twice more to get in a series of shots at the anti-tank position, when suddenly we hear several sharp explosions and shouting. Then all is quiet. I shout across to find out if No. 3 Platoon has reached the objective. Sergeant H. replies that it has been taken. The enemy's left flank was weakly protected, but in one sector he had dug strong defences. No. 3 Platoon had managed to get unseen within grenade-throwing distance and to capture the two anti-tank guns. In doing so, 2/Lieutenant B. was severely wounded."

The destruction of No. 1 Company's forward platoon and the two anti-tank guns left nothing to prevent the Germans moving down the road under cover of darkness. Since the Germans knew that the remainder of No. 1 Company could sweep the road with fire when there was enough light to see, it seemed inevitable that they would attack down the road again that night. The Carrier Platoon, the Battalion's only mobile reserve, moved up into Outreau to block the road behind No. 1 Company. But the Germans did nothing more that night, except shell and wait for their tanks to come up at dawn. It was an uncomfortable night ; Colonel Haydon spent it wondering how he was going to recapture No. 1 Company's lost position. It was impossible to launch a counter-attack until he and the troops could see what and where to attack. That made the earliest possible time dawn, and the Germans were notoriously fond of attacking at dawn. Moreover, the front was so wide that all four rifle companies had to be up in the line. Had there been mortars, guns or air support ready to hand, the Battalion could have recaptured the lost position, but there were none of these things, and not one of the seven despatch riders sent out to report the situation and ask for supporting arms could find Brigade H.Q.

The Battalion stood-to from half-past two in the morning, expecting a dawn attack. The Germans did not attack till half-past seven.

They started on No. 1 Company's front as before, but spread their attack to No. 4 Company, concentrating on Lieutenant Reynolds's platoon. This platoon held a hump of high ground near a reservoir; it was the forward platoon of the Company and the destruction of No. 1 Company's forward platoon the previous night left its position exposed and precarious. First the Germans shelled the position and then switched their guns and mortars on to the rest of the Battalion while their tanks moved forward on to Peter Reynolds's platoon. For an hour the Guardsmen held up tanks by rifle-fire alone, but they could not continue doing so indefinitely, for sooner or later the German tank commanders were bound to decide to chance it and drive straight on to the position they had already isolated. Lieutenant H. S. Leveson tried to get his carrier platoon up to help Lieutenant Reynolds, but only himself and his leading section were able to reach him. By now No. 4 Company Commander, Captain L. D. Murphy, M.C., thought that Lieutenant Reynolds should be withdrawn if he was to be saved at all. But it was already too late; the Platoon was completely surrounded, and every time Captain Murphy tried to reach them he was beaten back by machine-gun fire. In this attack, Lieutenant Peter Reynolds was killed, and Lieutenants Jack Leslie and Pat Butler (wounded) were captured.

Colonel Haydon now determined to reorganize the whole position. Captain McCausland collected all his remaining men and at nine o'clock withdrew No. 1 Company to the centre of Outreau village, where they defended the road down into Boulogne. At the same time, Captain Murphy withdrew his remaining platoons to cover the area between No. 1 and No. 2 Companies. No. 3 Company, under Captain Finlay, remained where it was, as yet untouched. Thus the line now ran from the centre of Outreau through some fields, which gave a field of fire of some 150 yards, on to the northern exits of Outreau, and thence to the sea. Though shorter than the original line, it was still too long and too thinly held to withstand a concentrated attack on any one point. Colonel Haydon sent Major Ross, his second-in-command, back to find some inner line of defence that could be held with only three companies, leaving one in reserve. "At this stage," he said, "I did not yet realize that No. 1 and 4 Companies had already been reduced to almost microscopic numbers." Of the 107 men of No. 4 Company who landed in Boulogne, only nineteen returned and only forty of No. 1 Company. Most of these casualties they had lost already, so the Battalion now had only two and a half rifle companies left.

A light railway runs through the middle of Boulogne, curving round behind the Battalion's present position. At half-past ten the Companies began withdrawing to the line of this railway, from which they could defend the west of the town and the main road from the south. The remnants of No. 1 Company held the village till the rest of the Battalion was established in the houses and gardens along the railway. They and the Germans were within fifty yards of each other. For two hours the Company beat off every attempt to outflank or rush them. "The holding of this post by No. 1 Company," said Colonel Haydon, "in spite of the very heavy losses it had suffered, reflects the very highest credit on Captain C. R. McCausland, 2/Lieutenant G. G. Romer and the other ranks who held the post."

The Battalion held the line of the railway for another two hours against constant attacks and under perpetual shell-fire. The R.A.P. had from the first been in a garage just behind the railway; inside it the doctor, Lieutenant Grace, and Father Julian Stoner were hard at work on the steady stream of wounded. Father Julian came out to see what was happening. In the open daylight the situation did not seem so bad as it had done in the dark garage with the sound of incessant firing and the shelling growing nearer and nearer. "I think I had expected to see corpses everywhere, but the only person in sight was Lieutenant Patrick Davison standing behind a wall with a revolver in his hand. The noise of rifles and machine-guns soon showed that there were really hundreds of men all around me, but our own men and the Germans were all hidden." The Bren-gunners were using up magazines as fast as their comrades could fill them. It needed a constant stream of fire to stop the Germans slipping across the railway and down between the houses into the town. Some of the barrels got so hot that they warped and jammed, leaving the section with only their rifles.

In his official report, Colonel Haydon afterwards wrote, "It has been hard to avoid the impression in the Battalion that the weapons with which they are issued are not equal to the tasks which they are called on to perform. In order to counteract any such impression, it has been pointed out to all ranks that at the Hook of Holland and Boulogne they have been attempting to play a tune when only half the orchestra was present, and that had artillery support, mortar support, air support, grenades, tanks, mines, wire and good communication been available the result in both cases would have been very different. Even as things were, it took a fully equipped, fully supported and highly mobile force a full day to drive the Battalion back a distance of one and a half miles."

About one o'clock the Battalion fell back farther towards the centre of the town. They marched away down the streets in a long column. Sergeant Gilchrist, L./Sergeant Carragher and L./Corporal Burke stayed behind with Bren guns and anti-tank rifles to guard the vulnerable tail. The Germans immediately began shelling the streets. The Companies scattered into the houses, while the Bren gunners collected the little ammunition there was left and set up their guns to cover the side streets. The shelling continued for an hour and then suddenly stopped. The officers and sergeants, sheltering in the doorways, heard the rattle of tank-tracks on the cobbles and then saw five German medium tanks coming slowly down the street. In front of them walked a man dressed in civilian clothes, waving his hands and shouting that the tanks were French. The man and the three leading tanks went on down the hill ; the two rear ones remained in the street. One halted outside a house in which a section were sheltering ; the other was immediately in front of Battalion H.Q. The sergeant was wondering what he could do, when a civilian walked in the back door. The stranger quickly unbuttoned his mackintosh to show a French uniform, pointed to the front door and said "Français." The sergeant opened the door cautiously to have a look at the tank which was noisily turning round. The "French officer" fled out of the back door, and "taking time from him" the section flung themselves on their faces just as the tank's shots rocketed down the passage. Next door in Battalion H.Q. they were all lying on the floor peering anxiously at the tank. Lieutenant J. Marnon, the Signals Officer, was the most uncomfortable, as he remembered only too clearly that he had left a motor-cycle parked outside the door. Every now and then the tanks fired a burst of machine-gun fire into a door or window. The only hope for the Battalion was that the Germans would not search the buildings or stay for very long. They did neither. Within half an hour the tanks that had gone down the hill came back and all five of them withdrew. The Battalion in the houses had felt trapped, but the Germans, who had expected to find the street full of troops and found it deserted, must have suspected an ambush. Their training taught them to expect mines and concealed guns ; how could they know that there was not a mine in Boulogne nor a gun left that could penetrate their armour ? As the companies were coming out of the houses, two small German tanks swept up the street. A Guardsman with an anti-tank rifle managed to get in a quick shot. They were very small tanks indeed, but even so a direct hit on the back of one of them made no impression whatsoever.

It was now about three o'clock in the afternoon. A despatch rider brought Colonel Haydon orders from Brigade H.Q. to evacuate, but no other information of any kind. A patrol went down to the harbour to see what was happening. On the quayside they met Lieutenant Sir John Reynolds, and returned to say that the dock area was clear. The Battalion marched down to the quays, headed by an advance guard, ready to drop Bren guns at any side roads which might be held, and covered by a rearguard. German snipers were already installed on the roofs and it took the Battalion a full hour of detours and small skirmishes to reach the harbour area. They barricaded the streets with cars, trucks and barrels, set up posts to cover these road-blocks and hid the rest of the Battalion in the sheds and warehouses. There was a cafe on the quayside which many Guardsmen thought would afford excellent cover. But Drill-Sergeant Kelly had seen it first ; he was already there, standing guard over the rows of coloured bottles. "They are poisoned," he said, and everyone believed him. They were only there a few minutes. The first orders were cancelled and the Battalion came out of the houses to defend the harbour area till everyone else was evacuated.

About 4.30, the destroyer H.M.S. *Whitshed*, came alongside the quay. A naval officer wrote an account in *Blackwood's Magazine*. "The machine-gun fire sounded very close and as the destroyer, going into action, cleared a long shed on the quay, the Captain suddenly saw what was going on. A section of Irish Guards were engaging with rifle-fire an enemy machine-gun post established in a warehouse, as coolly and methodically as if they had been on the practice ranges. 'Tell the foremost guns to open fire' the Captain yelled. The guns swung round and with a crash two 4.7 H.E. shells tore into the building and blew it to the skies. Meanwhile as the German infantry now passed ahead of their tanks and infiltrated closer and closer to the quays, the fine discipline of the Guards earned the awed open-mouthed respect of all. Watching them in perfect order, moving exactly together, engaging target after target as though on parade ground drill, it was difficult to realize that this was the grim reality of battle. They were truly magnificent, and no sailor who saw them could ever forget the feeling of pride he experienced." Naval landing-parties joined the Battalion. Seamen and Guardsmen fought side by side till the destroyers received the signal that Boulogne was to be evacuated entirely. Guardsman Griffiths joined the naval platoon commanded by a Lieutenant James, R.N. The report reads : "He told the naval officer that he had found an abandoned Bren gun and would like to use it as he was sure he could work it. The naval officer accepted his offer, but before it could be put into force, the naval platoons were ordered to retire. It was then that Griffiths asked the naval officer if he might remain and give what cover he could to the retiring platoons. The last seen of Griffiths was his very gallant and efficient volume of fire pouring into large numbers of approaching German infantry. It was undoubtedly due to Griffiths that the naval platoons were able to withdraw without loss, although one or two casualties were suffered by wounding."

Only two destroyers could be berthed in the harbour at a time. When each pair had loaded as many troops and refugees as possible, they put out to sea for Dover, and two more destroyers took their place. The 20th Guards Brigade held off the Germans while the wounded and thousands of stray soldiers were embarked. All the time German aircraft were bombing the harbour. Their main attack came at seven o'clock when the destroyers *Keith* and *Vimy* were alongside. "Aircraft from the north," shouted the naval look-out. Twenty bombers were flying steadily over the town. Suddenly nine British fighters swept out of the sky and tore into the German formation. Sailors and Guardsmen cheered hoarsely as one bomber after another crashed in flames. Then, "Look! Overhead." A cloud of sixty "Stuka" dive-bombers had shot past the heavily engaged fighters and were "peeling off" to dive. This was the moment for which the Germans had been waiting to make the final assault on Boulogne. As the first bombs dropped, German infantry poured down the streets of the town. "The din was appalling. To the deafening roar of guns was added the scream of falling bombs, the snarl of crashing planes and the angry hornet noise of dive-bombers. Huge fountains of mud and water rose alongside the destroyers drenching everybody at the guns." *Vimy* backed out of the harbour; she had a slight list and was on fire aft. *Keith* followed, keeping up an incessant bombardment of the heights north of the town. The destroyer flotilla Commander sent a signal to the Admiral at Dover "I do not consider we are justified in going on with the evacuation without fighter protection." He had not long to wait; in a few minutes nine British fighters appeared, and he signalled "In we go, boys." *Whitshed* (for the second time) and *Vimiera* entered the harbour. They loaded troops as quickly as they could, units from the B.E.F., mostly Durham Light Infantry and Gunners. All was now strangely quiet, except for occasional bursts of machine-gun fire. The destroyers cast off, each carrying more than 500 troops. "Not many of the passengers were Guardsmen," wrote a naval officer, "as the majority of that Brigade had to wait till the end." Amongst those who did embark, however, were the ten survivors of the anti-tank platoon which *Whitshed* had landed the previous day. A burly Guardsman climbed on to the bridge and deposited a bottle of champagne on the chart-table. "Thanks for the double ride," he said and hurriedly disappeared. H.M.S. *Whitshed* afterwards presented her bridge-emblem to the 2nd Battalion as a memento of this day.

At eight o'clock the Navy and the Army received the order from Dover that Boulogne was to be evacuated immediately. As soon as *Whitshed* and *Vimiera* were clear of the harbour, *Wild Swan* and *Venomous* entered. The Battalion moved down to quayside in sections and platoons, and the bulk of it sheltered on the lower level of the quay on the inner (southern) side. As soon as the first two destroyers had berthed, a third, H.M.S. *Verity*, followed, to speed up the evacuation. "From seaward *Verity* watched the two leading destroyers pass safely into the inner harbour. All was still quiet when she, herself, went ahead towards the breakwaters. When she was within a few yards of the entrance, there was a sudden sheet of flame from the low hills to the north as a hidden battery opened fire. This was followed by another, and a general bombardment broke out. The intention was obvious." If the Germans could sink a destroyer between the breakwaters, she would effectively block the harbour. The only part of Boulogne the British still held was now the quay on which the Guards Brigade was waiting and which small Bren-gun squads were defending. German tanks drove down the opposite quay parallel to them. They concentrated their fire on *Verity*, hit her amidships, and set her on fire. H.M.S. *Verity* promptly went full speed astern, firing every gun she could bring to bear. The faster she went the quicker the flames spread, but she reached the open sea and saved the troops on the quay from certain destruction. Meanwhile, the two other destroyers were steadily embarking the wounded.

Having failed to sink the *Verity*, the German tanks and guns turned their attention to the quay, and for the next forty-five minutes poured fire into it. The range was so close that every shot was a direct hit. The quay was built of huge blocks of granite ; it stood up to the fire, but the air was full of flying chips. The noise of the explosions above them and of the ships' guns below them deafened the Guardsmen. Straight in front of them, they could see the tanks on the opposite quay ; behind them they could hear the brief bursts of Bren-guns as the rearguards beat the Germans off their quay. "It says a great deal for the discipline of the troops," wrote Colonel Haydon, "that no move of any sort or kind was made toward the destroyers until I gave the order, and then the move was carried out slowly and efficiently." A naval officer afterwards broadcast a description. "The courage and bearing of the Guardsmen were magnificent, even under

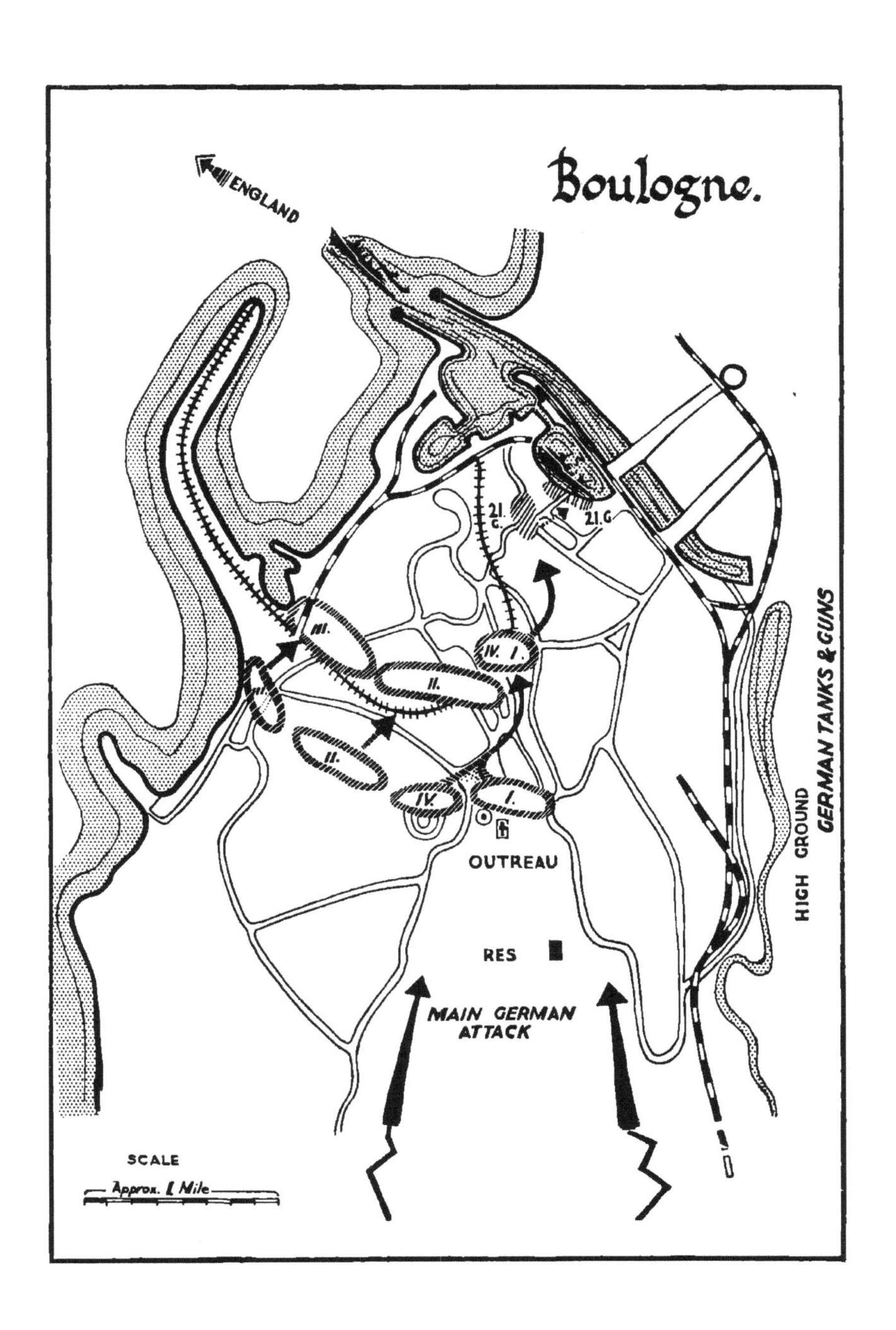
Boulogne.
ENGLAND
III.
III.
II.
II.
IV. I.
IV.
I.
21. C.
21. G
OUTREAU
RES
MAIN GERMAN
ATTACK
HIGH GROUND
GERMAN TANKS & GUNS
SCALE
Approx. 1 Mile

a tornado of fire with casualties occurring every second. They were as steady as though on parade and stood there like rocks, without giving a damn for anything." The Battalion, in turn, was filled with a boundless admiration for the sailors manning their guns on the open decks. Their gunnery was splendidly effective. The *Wild Swan* sent a large German tank on the opposite quay spinning like a cart-wheel, and blasted the top floor off a hotel opposite when she spotted a machine-gun firing on the Battalion from an upper window.

The wounded were slowly lowered from the quay and taken below and then the Battalion leapt on board. It was low water and a long jump from the quay down to the deck ; a number of men missed and fell into the water, but they were all fished out by the sailors. The wounded were taken down to the boiler room. The heat below decks was like a furnace and the congestion stifling. Half-naked sailors cracked jokes with the Guardsmen as they forced their way through the crowd with shells and cordite for the guns.

At half-past nine the last Bren gun squads came running down the quay and leapt on board *Wild Swan*. The destroyers cast off ; *Wild Swan* was aground and her Captain only extricated her by magnificent seamanship. "It was dark when I came up on deck from the inferno below," writes an officer. "I found a seat on a torpedo tube with some Guardsmen and we talked about the sea and our admiration for these sailors, until the flickering light that was the signal lamp of the wounded *Verity* was joined by another which proved to be the *Dover Castle*." The Battalion landed at Dover at midnight, entrained for Fleet and reached Tweseldown Camp at 6.30 on the morning of 24th May. For the second time within ten days the Battalion owed its existence to the seamanship and courage of the Dover Destroyers.

APPENDIX

A. Officers of the 2nd Battalion Irish Guards

Lieut.-Colonel J. C. Haydon, O.B.E.
Major J. F. Ross.
Major T. G. Lindsay.
Captain H. S. Phillpotts.
Captain C. E. McCausland.
Captain L. D. Murphy, M.C.
Captain C. K. Findlay.
Captain J. W. R. Madden.
Captain P. W. B. Pole-Carew.
Captain P. F. I. Reid.

Lieutenant J. D. Hornung.
Lieutenant E. A. S. Alexander.
Lieutenant J. F. Marnan.
Lieutenant D. W. S. P. Reynolds.
Lieutenant J. B. FitzGerald.
Lieutenant H. S. L. Leveson.
Lieutenant H. R. Grace (R.A.M.C.).
2/Lieutenant P. O. A. Davison.
2/Lieutenant P. D. Lindsay.
2/Lieutenant G. G. Romer.
2/Lieutenant D. A. Reid.
2/Lieutenant M. V. Dudley.
2/Lieutenant R. McN. Cooper-Key.
2/Lieutenant N. A. R. O'Neill.
2/Lieutenant P. P. Jeffreys.
2/Lieutenant J. N. I. Leslie.
2/Lieutenant R. C. Hubbard.
Captain J. J. Stoner (Chaplain).
Lieutenant and Quartermaster J. Keating.
2/Lieutenant G. R. Fisher-Rowe.
2/Lieutenant Hon. P. T. Butler.
Lieutenant Sir John Reynolds and 2/Lieutenant A. R. Eardley-Wilmot, Attached H.Q. 20th Guards Brigade.

B. Strength of Battalion when Embarking at Dover.

H.Q. Company	257	Other	Ranks.
No. 1 Company	100	,,	,,
No. 2 Company	111	,,	,,
No. 3 Company	104	,,	,,
No. 4 Company	107	,,	,,

C. Casualties (as known on the return to England).

Known killed in action	2
Died of wounds	1
Known wounded	13
Believed to be in Hospital	11
Missing	174
Total ...	5 Officers and 196 Other Ranks

INTERLUDE

•

THE YEARS OF TRAINING

INTERLUDE

The Years of Training

IN June, 1940, the Regiment consisted of three battalions—the 1st Battalion at Northwood, in the 24th Guards Brigade, the 2nd Battalion at Woking, in the 22nd Guards Brigade, and the Training Battalion at Hobbs Barracks, Lingfield. The 24th and 22nd Guards Brigades were both held in reserve as counter-invasion forces to defend London by halting the German columns in the outer suburbs and killing the German parachutists on the golf-courses where they were expected to land. The coastal defences of the country were sadly under-manned as the inevitable result of the losses of men and equipment in France, and had, at first, to be entrusted to half-trained troops. By comparative standards, the Training Battalion was a trained force and was by any standard disciplined ; it was therefore despatched to Britain's front line to meet the Germans when they stepped ashore. On 14th July, under the command of Lieut.-Colonel The Viscount Gough, it moved to Dover, leaving behind in Lingfield only the recruits who had joined in the previous fortnight and a small maintenance force. For three and a half months the Training Battalion occupied the Western Heights as part of the garrison of Dover.

The Western Heights had been fortified against the last threatened invasion. During the Napoleonic Wars British soldiers and French prisoners had built a complicated fortress—a conglomeration of redoubts, redans, caponiers and bastions, detached and undetached, all surrounded by the cliffs and a deep wide moat crossed by three draw-bridges, each with a real portcullis. Subsequent generations of soldiers built the Grand Shaft and the North Front Barracks, nailed down the draw-bridges and allowed the portcullises to rust in their grooves. The Training Battalion took over the barracks, manned the caponiers, cleared and mined the moat, got the draw-bridges to work and, instead of portcullises, hung up submarine nets weighted with blocks of concrete. While part of the Battalion manned the old stone loopholes and anti-aircraft posts, the rest dug light machine-gun emplacements and mortar pits and festooned the approaches with wire. Then they sat and waited for the German invasion barges to put out from Calais and watched the Battle of

Britain as it was fought out in the air above them and the sea below them. Sometimes the air battle descended to their level and the Bren gunners took a hand. The anti-aircraft posts on the roof of South Front Barracks were above the barrage balloons that protected Dover Harbour. There were twenty posts in all, and when a German aeroplane dived to machine-gun the balloons they all opened fire. The War Diary proudly records their two successes : "Major Gordon-Watson shot down a Messerschmitt 109 on 31st August, and the guns of No. 3 Company a Dornier 17 bomber on 29th September." "On how few occasions," it continues, "can young soldiers have been provided day after day with such targets as low-flying aeroplanes manned by real Germans intent on the conquest of Britain. The roar of the barrage was a fine novelty for the young Irish Guardsmen preparing to join a service battalion."

The entry in the Diary for 15th October, 1940, is typical : "A morning of intense air activity. Dog fights over the cliffs and Channel are almost continuous. Bursts of machine-gun fire, punctuated by A.A. fire from the coastal batteries, the whine of diving aircraft and the crack of Bren and Lewis guns form a long, rampageous symphony."

The Training Battalion was, in fact, the point of what the Press and newsreels called "Hell Fire Corner," for on a balcony outside No. 1 Company's Mess the photographers mounted their cameras. Officers and men went to the cinema in Dover and listened, with quiet satisfaction, to the commentators describing the constant danger of their lives. They did not need to be told of the courage and persistence of the sailors and merchant seamen in the Channel, for they saw it with their own eyes every day. "The outstanding event of the day," says the War Diary on 22nd August, "was the passage of a convoy sailing very close inshore, going up the Straits towards the Port of London. Instead of provoking the usual cloud of dive-bombers, the coming of the convoy was heralded from far down the coast by a series of terrific bangs which were at first thought to be the explosion of depth-charges dropped by our own destroyers against lurking submarines. Soon, however, a series of vivid flashes could be seen through the sea mist from the direction of Boulogne, and as the convoy came abreast of us, it was obvious that it was being shelled by a battery of four long-range guns from the French coast. Three big shells fell with a heavy concussion right into the harbour. Battalion H.Q. was promptly transferred to the Tunnel. The convoy passed unscathed, but some desperately near misses brought vividly home the gallantry of the officers and men of the Merchant Navy who incur such risks almost daily, without a chance of hitting back. It is of interest to record that the time-lag between the flash of discharge over in France and the explosion of the shells among the convoy was 55 seconds." The Germans had hauled the big guns from the Maginot Line and turned them against the Channel convoys and Dover. From then on the guns fired regularly, concentrating on the harbour, but throwing occasional shots on to the Western Heights. On 11th September two shells hit a barrack block and wounded two officers (Captain Mathew and Lieutenant Boulton) slightly and three men, one of whom, Guardsman Haller, died of his wounds. These were the Battalion's only casualties. "Luckily the Grand Shaft Barracks had been evacuated a few days previously. At this time the companies were living in ancient caponiers in the Drop Redoubt and the Detached Bastion, dark and damp maybe, but covered with upwards of twelve feet of earth."

In September, when the German Air Force concentrated on London and the invasion shipping concentrated in the Channel ports, the Battalion lived in a perpetual state of "alarm." The War Diary for the 21st September reads : "The sea is very calm today with a mist and a light rain across the Straits. The day for the invasion, perhaps. The sentries gaze endlessly across the water through binoculars. Occasionally the mist lifts and the French coast is dimly seen. Some ships are stealing past Cap Gris Nez. Then the mist falls again like a curtain across the stage. In the evening it clears, the clouds disperse and the French coast seems but a few miles distant. Enemy aeroplanes pass overhead at a great height and fly inland. The night is brilliant with a full moon. Once again the R.A.F. bomb the French channel ports. Gun and bomb flashes, searchlights and tracer-shells illuminate the sky from Calais to Boulogne."

The next day was unforgettable ; the Regiment dined out on the story for years. At midday Garrison H.Q. sent an urgent message "President Roosevelt has just heard from a source in Berlin, which he considers most reliable, that invasion of England is timed to start at 3 p.m. today." Battalion H.Q. passed it on to the companies with the addition, "No men will proceed out of barracks. The Battalion will stand to at 1330 hrs. Posts will be warned to expect dive-bombing attack." By half-past one every round of the small reserve of ammunition was dumped in the posts and by the loop-holes and every man was waiting for the Germans, finger on trigger. The minutes dragged, and with each new minute the watchers expected to see the barges appear out of the sea mist. After all, a despatch rider had sped direct from London and the news could not be just another "bar." Three o'clock came, but no Germans. At a quarter past, the magazines were taken off the guns ; at twenty past a second message came from Garrison H.Q. : "*Re* previous message. Correction. For ' England ' read 'Indo-China.' Revert to normal." The rest of the Battalion's time in Dover continued to be normal as is shown by the entry in the War Diary for 2nd October : "Intermittent shelling began at breakfast. It sounded as if a new gun is ranging. Air-raid warning sounded off and on throughout the day. One enemy plane dropped several bombs in the harbour. In the afternoon there was a Rugby football match between the Battalion and the Navy. The Navy were handicapped by being four men short—substitutes being found by the Royal Artillery—consequently the Battalion won comfortably."

Meanwhile, the recruits had been piling up in Hobbs Barracks, Lingfield, and the small detachment that had been left there in June had by October increased to over 1,200 men. From this increase was born the 3rd Battalion by the most rudimentary form of reproduction. When the "invasion weather" broke in November the Training Battalion in Dover was ordered to move to Northwood to relieve the 1st Battalion. The command and administration were, therefore, split. The Dover companies moved to Northwood with the new title of "The Holding Companies," under the command of Major J. O. E. Vandeleur. Lieut.-Colonel The Viscount Gough returned to Lingfield and the companies there became the Training Battalion proper. As the recruits were trained in Hobbs Barracks they were passed on to the Holding Companies, swelling their numbers till, in February, 1941, they were large enough to be constituted into a battalion. The same thing was happening in the whole Brigade of Guards.

According to the popular military theory at this time the infantry was already an obsolete arm. The Germans had won the Battle of France with unsupported armoured divisions, and the only answer to them was more armoured divisions. The 1st Battalion did not hold with this theory ; they trained, under the Second-in-Command, Major C. A. Montagu-Douglas-Scott, to perfect a system of infantry anti-tank action which was first taught to the Brigade and then to the whole Army. They knew then, what was so clearly proved once again afterwards, that when all is said and done, when all the bombs have been dropped and all the shells fired, when all the tanks have "milled about" or "driven wedges," victory depends on men who will sit tight in a hole in the ground and are prepared to get up and walk steadily forward till they meet men like themselves, on their own two feet.

Of course, "armour" is also essential, and as soon as Britain began producing tanks in quantity the Army began forming new armoured divisions. In June, 1941, after conferences and decisions "at the very highest level," it was announced that a Guards Armoured Division would be formed consisting of two brigades, one of tanks and one of lorried infantry. The 20th Guards Brigade was broken up and reassembled as the 5th Guards Armoured Brigade ; the 32nd Guards Brigade became the infantry. The 2nd Battalion left Woking, and on the 16th September, 1941, they arrived at Fonthill Gifford Camp on the edge of Salisbury Plain and began to train with their new tanks. After two weary years on Salisbury Plain—an eternity, it seemed, of "stunts," "maintenance" and courses—they moved to the Yorkshire wolds for months' more training before the invasion of France.

The 1st Battalion was the first to see action again. In November, 1942, the 24th Guards Brigade mobilized for active service as an ordinary infantry brigade. It shed its surplus men and equipment and moved to Ayrshire to join the 1st Division on an urgent and secret operation. The operation was cancelled, without the Battalion ever knowing what it was, and the Battalion lodged in the grandstands and offices of Ayr racecourse till it sailed for North Africa at the end of February, 1943, under the command of Lieut.-Colonel C. A. Montagu-Douglas-Scott. From then on the existence of the 3rd Battalion was imperilled by the casualties of the 1st. The first-line reinforcements that the 1st Battalion took out with it were drawn from the 3rd Battalion, and in the succeeding six months the 3rd Battalion had to send out 26 officers and 600 men to make good the 1st Battalion's losses in its Tunisian "blood bath." The 3rd Battalion was ordered to work on the basis that it would always be required to provide drafts for the 1st. It disintegrated into draft companies, training companies and a demonstration company permanently at the School of Infantry. The other regiments, too, "were feeling the draught," particularly the Scots Guards, who had two of their four battalions fighting abroad. In July, 1943, the 3rd Battalion was ordered to send its best-trained company to the 4th Bn. Scots Guards in the Guards Armoured Division.

"This appeared to be the end of the 3rd Battalion," wrote Colonel J. O. E. Vandeleur, "who were now left with a skeleton Headquarters, about half their Support Company and nothing much else." The Battalion, however, was saved by more Scots Guards casualties abroad. "In October, 1943, much to their astonishment, the remnants were ordered to Malton in Yorkshire to link forces with the 4th Bn. Scots Guards, who were to be disbanded," wrote Colonel Vandeleur again. The composite battalion at first consisted of "X" Company and Right Flank Company of the Scots Guards, the Irish Guards company already there, and the remainder of the 3rd Battalion. The Right Flank Company was later withdrawn ; but by then the 1st Battalion had suffered such crippling losses in Italy that it was due to be sent back to England, and the 3rd Battalion, free from competition, was able to form a third Irish Guards rifle company. By June, 1944, the 3rd Battalion, predominantly Irish Guards, was ready to take the field.

PART III

•

THE 1st BATTALION IN NORTH AFRICA

CHAPTER I

North Africa

ON 8th November, 1942, the Allies landed in French North Africa. A few days later the 24th Guards Independent Brigade Group mobilized for active service. This was the first stage in a move overseas. Theoretically, of course, the Brigade had always been "on active service," but during two years in billets it had accumulated around itself a thick padding of stores and "attached men." Also, it was an Independent Brigade Group, with a fourth battalion, its own gunners and ancillary troops and enough transport of its own to carry every man. All this had to go—the extra battalion, the coaches, the comforts and the old soldiers whom the battalions had kept in spite of their flat feet and rheumatism because "the battalion wouldn't be the same without Murphy 99." 24th Guards Brigade lost its independence, and was absorbed into the 1st British Infantry Division to replace the 1st Guards Brigade, which had been shipped separately to North Africa.

The Battalion's roots were deep in Sanderstead and the extraction was painful. Many men had married local girls and even more had set up their homes in the neighbourhood. In the following years the shopping streets of Croydon buzzed with the anxious gossip of wives, trailing little Mickie or Bridget behind them, and the *Croydon Times* might well have been a regimental gazette. On a grey evening in late November the Battalion marched down Sanderstead Hill for the last time, and instead of swinging into the Muncipal Car Park as it had so often done, took a train for Scotland. The 1st Division was scattered along the Ayrshire coast, training in "Combined Operations." It was at that time part of an assault force called 125 or alternatively Morganforce. The object of the force, under either name, was never disclosed ; the battalions were merely told to prac-tise landings from the sea and "encounter battles" in "a rough hill country where the local population can be expected to be impartially hostile to all comers." And that is what the Battalion did in countless exercises on the coast and over the moors. In the intervals it worked ceaselessly to turn the stands and offices of Ayr racecourse into a barracks fit for Guardsmen. "The next unit," said the War Diary smugly, "will not find this place in the revolting condition in which we found it." The racecourse had been a Transit Camp, and looked it. Major Sam Bucknill and Captain Simon Combe had gone up to Ayr before the Battalion to meet some officers of the 19th Field Regiment, R.A., the gunners allotted to the Brigade, and together to take over the racecourse. Hercules entering the Augean Stables had less cause for dismay than they. By the time the Battalion arrived they had scraped over the top layer of dirt. Guardsmen and Gunners removed the rest, and so began in fatigues a friendship that was invaluable in battle.

Two months of schemes and swabbing culminated in a peculiarly uncomfortable expedition to the Combined Operations School at Inveraray. Half-way through the course the senior officers were suddenly recalled ; 125 Force was scrapped and the 1st Division "reverted to War Office control preparatory to an immediate move overseas on full divisional scale." The Battalion had done too much splashing round Inveraray Loch to be anything but pleased. "We learn with some relief that for the time being we are to be spared a landing from Assault Craft and that we will sail in a large convoy with our full equipment and transport instead of the exiguous assault scale—one blanket, 100 rounds, 48 hours' rations per man—and we will land in comparative comfort at a proper port."

The Battalion gathered from the Divisional Commander, Major-General W. Clutterbuck, that the change was in some way connected with the Casablanca Conference. That made it North Africa, for, according to the strategists of the Mess and the barrack-room, Churchill and Roosevelt must have decided that it was time to get a move on in North Africa. The First Army was stuck in Tunisia, and would remain stuck until it got reinforcements. It was all very well for critics, both professional and amateur, to say "Algiers was supposed to be a spring-board ; the First Army are using it as a sofa," but even the Battalion knew that the grandiose title "First Army" concealed little more than a couple of divisions of fighting troops. "It's North Africa for us, boys." The officers and drivers who took the transport to Cardiff and Liverpool a few days later could have confirmed this opinion. They watched the trucks and carriers being hoisted into the ships of a slow convoy, all boldly marked "Algiers" ;

the sailors told them they were going to Algiers ; the dockers pointed out and named the ships bound for Algiers ; and then a Port Security Officer swore them to silence and secrecy. Other Security Officers ordered the Battalion to remove its designations and Brigade signs ; they carefully explained that this was not to hoodwink the citizens of Ayr but to defeat spies at the other end of the voyage. The Guardsmen unpicked the green strips embroidered with "Irish Guards" from their battledress shoulders and put them in their paybooks. The Dragon's Wings of the old 24th Guards Independent Brigade Group were collected for burning. "The Dragon's Wings have gone for good," says the War Diary, "and we will later be given the white triangle of the First Division."

The command of the Battalion was changed as suddenly as its object. Lieut.-Colonel C. A. Montagu-Douglas-Scott replaced Lieut.-Colonel H. S. Phillpotts, M.C., and Major D. M. L. Gordon-Watson, M.C., became Second-in Command in place of Major C. R. McCausland, M.C. Colonel Andrew slipped into what seemed his natural place. No doubt an ancestry stretching back into the murderous wars of the Borders had something to do with it, but whatever the reason, he was a born commander. To a natural gift was added practical experience. His father, Lord Herbert Scott, had commanded the first troops of the Regiment to go into action, the Irish Guards Mounted Infantry in the South African War, and naturally put his son into the Regiment. Andrew Scott served for three years as a slim young ensign, and then retired to the Stock Exchange, where he sharpened his wits and increased his bulk. In 1939 he returned as a subaltern, and began the steady rise that ended in the command of 1st Guards Brigade and the acting command of 6th Armoured Division. In Norway he commanded a platoon and then a company, in Sanderstead he trained No. 4 Company till he became Second-in-Command and trained the whole Battalion; then he was moved to the Royal Military College as Chief Instructor, and had become Commandant of the Infantry O.C.T.U. when the Regimental Lieutenant-Colonel recalled him to the Battalion. Andrew Scott was a man who liked comfort and insisted on it when it could be obtained. Unnecessary discomfort, he said, was the sure sign of a poor soldier ; the Irish Guards were good soldiers and as a result the Battalion under his command was the best fed, the best housed and the best entertained in North Africa and Italy. He was also a man of remarkable stamina and determination. The Battalion never saw any change in him ; he was the same on the Anzio Beach-head as he was in Sanderstead—confident, authoritative and chatty. He was as good a conversationist in some muddy trench as he was in White's Club and days of continuous fighting made him look more like a Regency buck. He was a great Commanding Officer.

There was another important domestic gap to fill. The Quartermaster, Lieutenant J. Stack, M.C., was transferred to the 33rd Guards Brigade Support Group. His successor as Regimental Sergeant-Major, R.S.M. H. F. McKinney, succeeded him as Quartermaster. This too was a popular and most successful appointment. The Officers' Mess welcomed Hugh McKinney with open arms ; the Guardsmen hung about the Stores with broad grins waiting for a chance to salute the new Quartermaster. McKinney was a man of dynamic energy who would stick at nothing to get the Battalion what it needed. He established a network of friends and agents in every office and dump round the Mediterranean ; somehow they were all under some obligation to him and found it difficult to refuse him anything. The system of trade agreements he established among the Quartermasters of the Division would have done credit to the Foreign Office. No man so deserved, and got, the gratitude of the Battalion.

"Send up O.R.Q.M.S. Phipps." This was a private code message to Regimental Headquarters as well as a request for the expert form-filler. It meant that the Battalion had been given a date for embarkation and that the clerks were up to their eyes in paper. The Barrack Guard could see the lights in the Orderly Room burning all night, as Sergeant McCashin, Lance-Sergeant Kelly and the others worked in shifts, checking, entering and re-checking every individual man and piece of equipment on innumerable forms. It seemed that every authority in the British Isles wanted to know something about the Battalion. How many cobblers were there ? how many Presbyterians? how many men had been on a sanitary course ? Sickness and accidents meant emendations, and more work for the bleary-eyed Guardsman Cross, the typist. One final exercise—a night attack on a hill, said to be the most common operation in a certain campaign—caused havoc in the Battalion. First the new Sergeant-Major, R.S.M. McLoughlin, broke his ankle, and then on the way home a stray truck from another unit ploughed its way through a platoon of No. 1 Company. More promotions, more replacements, new nominal rolls and a bitter disappointment for the Sergeant-Major. On 27th February everything was ready, the names on the lists fitted the bodies on the ground, and to keep them like this the racecourse gates were shut and the telephones disconnected.

Breakfast was at four o'clock on the morning of the 28th. The Battalion needed a good two hours in which to load itself with the staggering amount of equipment called "Embarkation Order." At half-past six, while it was still dark, the Battalion paraded by the light of bonfires of burning straw palliasses. Then the dark mass of the companies lumbered slowly and silently out of the main gate. It was very like a funeral.

A convoy of eight liners was mustered in the Clyde to carry the Division and a contingent of service troops and R.A.F. ground staff. After a sleep and tea in the train, the Battalion was in the high spirits of an excursion party by the time it reached Greenock. Even the sight of the Clydeside in a drizzle did not depress them. They jumped with a heavy clatter into the waiting tenders and after a short, wet passage, poured into the side of the P. & O. liner *Strathmore.* O.R.Q.M.S. Phipps was left standing alone on the quay, a bundle of spare forms under his arm and the tears running down his cheeks. "Have a pint for us at the Windsor, Charlie" shouted the last boat-load. "Oh, I will," he replied, "indeed I will."

ORDER OF BATTLE *28th February,* 1943

Battalion H.Q.

Lieut.-Colonel C. A. Montagu-Douglas-Scott	Commanding
Major D. M. L. Gordon-Watson, M.C. ...	Second-in-Command
Captain J. M. Park	Adjutant
R.S.M. Peilow (Acting)	
R.Q.M.S. Grey (Acting)	
Drill-Sergeant Rooney	
Drill-Sergeant Kenny	

H.Q. Coy.

Captain J. B. S. Fitzgerald	Coy. Commander
Lieutenant B. T. Synge	Signal Officer
Lieutenant D. G. Madden	M.T.O.
Lieutenant D. J. L. Fitzgerald	Intelligence Officer
Lieutenant J. J. Nunn	Pioneer Platoon
R.S.M. McKinney (Acting)	Quartermaster
Captain G. F. Barnes	M.O.
Rev. Fr. J. F. Brookes, C.F.	Chaplain
Captain P. A. G. Rawlinson	Carrier Pl. Cmdr.
Lieut. J. St. G. Gunston	Second-in-Command, Carrier Platoon
Lieutenant O. F. McInerney	Mortar Officer

Lieutenant R. N. D. Young	Anti-Tank Platoon Commander
Lieutenant M. McN. Boyd	Second-in-Command, Anti-Tank Platoon
C.S.M. Stone	C.S.M.
C.Q.M.S. Barratt	C.Q.M.S.

No. 1 Coy.

Major H. L. S. Young	Coy. Commander
Captain O. S. Chesterton	Second-in-Command
Lieutenant F. A. Mahaffy	Platoon Commander
Lieutenant M. J. Eugster	Platoon Commander
C.S.M. Malone	C.S.M.
C.Q.M.S. Mercer	C.Q.M.S.

No. 2 Coy.

Major S. J. R. Bucknill	Coy. Commander
Captain J. T. Egan	Second-in-Command
Lieutenant C. D. Lesslie	Platoon Commander
Lieutenant A. W. Rochford	Platoon Commander
Lieutenant A. M. C. Askin	Platoon Commander
C.S.M. Ferguson	C.S.M.
C.Q.M.S. Stuart	C.Q.M.S.

No. 3 Coy.

Captain D. M. Kennedy	Coy. Commander
Captain R. Prendegast	Second-in-Command
Lieutenant M. F. Rawlence	Platoon Commander
Lieutenant C. D. Kennard	Platoon Commander
Lieutenant T. C. Keigwin	Platoon Commander
C.S.M. Moran	C.S.M.
C.Q.M.S. Pestell	C.Q.M.S.

No. 4 Coy.

Captain I. H. Powell-Edwards	Coy. Commander
Captain G. B. Ismay	Second-in-Command
Lieutenant A. H. T. Smith	Platoon Commander
Lieutenant D. C. Attlee	Platoon Commander
Lieutenant J. G. A. Pym	Platoon Commander
C.S.M. Kiely	C.S.M.
C.Q.M.S. Babington	C.Q.M.S.

1st Reinforcements

Captain D. Drummond
Lieutenant J. F. Sandberg
Lieutenant A. P. Thorn
Lieutenant J. C. Dodds
Lieutenant D. C. W. Lloyd-Thomas
C S.M. Kinane
C.Q.M.S. Smythe
Lieutenant C. F. Larkin Liaison Officer

The *Strathmore* was a large ship—some 11,000 tons—of the P. & O. Line, transformed into a trooper apparently by the simple method of clearing every available yard of space below decks and screwing hooks into the beams for hammocks. The Guardsmen were packed like sardines or, as they said themselves, like negroes in a slave ship. "The people who arrange these things," wrote Colonel Scott, "never realize that two Guardsmen take up the room of three ordinary soldiers." The heat at night with every porthole and door shut was stifling and the men lay in their hammocks gasping like winded cods, the sweat running off their faces. But a good soldier can sleep anywhere, and by ten o'clock each night rows of snoring bodies swung gently to and fro.

The officers and warrant officers—all except the most exalted—were crammed into small dormitories made by fitting extra bunks in the cabins. The cabins soon looked like frowsty jackdaws' nests, festooned with equipment and the shiny products of the barber's shop. The Indian stewards did their best to sort out the tangle every morning, but from the first they concentrated on getting their officers into sea-water baths and keeping them there. "No matter what we ask for," wrote one officer, "our steward, one Abdul, nods brightly and rushes away ; a sound follows as if the whole sea was pouring into the hold and Abdul returns beaming 'Bath now please.' These stewards and the lascars are the only part of the crew we ever really see. The Ship's officers are too busy to appear, though all the rumours are supposed to emanate from them. The tiny lascars run around under the Guardsmen's feet. George Ismay, who was a director of the Cunard White Star before he became Second-in-Command of No. 4 Coy., protected them with all his authority. 'Don't tread on the lascars. They are the saviours of the British Empire.' Impressed by this, the Guardsmen have tried to talk to them, but the only ones who know any English are the old wizened white-haired ones, but who are also very gloomy; only the mention of Gandhi raises any sign of interest from these patriarchs. Questions about the war drew the same sad reply. 'No letters, no money, no Calcutta'; we feel much the same."

Compared to other troopers in which the Battalion later travelled, the *Strathmore* was a comfortable ship. There was enough deck space for everybody by day, there was a well-stocked canteen and above all the meals were regular and good. Two eggs for the first breakfast was a good start which defeated even the most hardened grumblers. "The food was quite excellent," wrote Major Gordon-Watson in an account which showed that neither his interests nor his style had changed since the Norwegian campaign. "All lost no time in filling up those little corners that rationing at home had left neglected. Five-course dinners with Sole Colbert, Chicken a la King, grape-fruit and oranges were no exception. Captain D. M. Kennedy on no occasion failed to have less than two helpings of each."

At half past ten on the night of 1st March, 1943, the ship slipped anchor and moved slowly down the Clyde, so slowly that at first it was hardly noticeable. The men who went up on deck when they heard the beat of the propellers saw nothing but mast-head lights in a thin blanket of rain. When daylight came the ship was in the middle of the convoy, sailing three abreast with an escort of a destroyer and corvettes. The Battalion felt cheated by the size of the escort; they had expected a battleship, an aircraft carrier and a flock of destroyers. Through the low clouds and mist came an occasional glimpse of the coast of Northern Ireland—each headland identified firmly by a man who said he knew it well. "It's your last chance to swim for it. Over you go, the Battalion won't miss you." The Englishmen in the Battalion affected to be unimpressed by the soft outline of the blue hills of Ireland. But for even the most unimaginative Irishman—and there are many such—this was the real moment of parting. They were, after all, getting the same last glimpse of Ireland that their forefathers had seen as they sailed away to join the Irish Brigade in France. The Regiment always claimed to be descended from the Irish Brigade.

"We're not so old in the Army List,
But we're not so young in the ring,
We carried our packs with Marshal Saxe,
When great Louis was our king."

The soldiers of the Irish Brigade also had hoped to come back one day.

The ship heaved rhythmically in the heavy swell, making half the Battalion queasy and a quarter really ill. The swell and the suffering increased after dark and the groans rose and fell with the movement of the ship. Good sailors are always callous, and the strong-stomached men who attended breakfast the next morning tortured their companions with descriptions of the plates of fat bacon waiting for them in the galleys. The convoy had rounded Ireland during the night and by midday was well out in the Atlantic off the Bay of Biscay. The sun came out and the sea was as calm as a bucket of milk. Pale convalescents tottered up on deck to sit in the pleasant warmth, and began to think of food. From then on, the voyage was calm and uneventful. "There were I believe some U-boats about," wrote Captain I. H. Powell-Edwards vaguely, "but except for some gun-fire one night, never really explained, we slept pretty comfortably."

The days passed in a steady routine, as the convoy zigzagged round the Atlantic. On the horizon the escort stood like dots; occasionally a flying-boat circled overhead, and nothing ever happened. The only alarm came just before the convoy turned into the Mediterranean. There was a flurry of activity four miles to starboard, one of the destroyers bore down on the convoy flying a black flag, the ships' sirens hooted at each other and the convoy turned itself inside out. To the half disappointment of the Battalion none of the other ships were torpedoed, but it was a wonderful opening for reminiscences of the *Chobry*. One fine afternoon a school of porpoises broke through the convoy. They were at first identified as a submarine and then as a sea-serpent. Lieutenant P. A. G. Rawlinson said they were dolphins and called for tennis balls. He knew his Shakespeare because he had once played Henry V in a school play in which his handsome appearance and fair wavy hair made him a great success with the female audience, but he ought to have known his brother officers better. "Why tennis balls? Golf balls would be much better—easier to throw." Some of course, wanted to shoot the porpoises, and Major H. L. S. Young wondered if they could be caught on a salmon rod.

The busiest officer in the Battalion was the chaplain, Father Brookes. He said Mass every morning for a remarkably large congregation and heard confessions in his cabin from a constantly reinforced string of penitents. Next to him came the officers in charge of the two main troop-decks, Captains George Ismay and Jim Egan. "They were worth their weight in gold," wrote Colonel Scott, "which in the case of big Jim is no inconsiderable item." The officers, after the morning inspections, spent their days on the

Swimming Pool Deck—a raised platform in the middle of which was a large hole. They had all carefully packed a collection of pocket-size classics, but none of them managed to get down to them; instead they read in a desultory way novels from the ship's library, such as "Lefty Rides the Range" and "The Corpse in the Coffin." In the evenings they all crowded into an "ante-room," formerly the Smoke Room, to play bridge and write letters. Every evening Lieutenant Jackie Pym (whose chubby face made him look even younger than he was, which was very young) was shown the notice still over the door, "Children and Nurses strictly forbidden to enter."

The Guardsmen's days passed as peacefully. The mornings began with fatigues and a little gentlemanly P.T., ending at 11 o'clock in time for the opening of the Canteen where they bought bottles of fizzy lemonade, chocolate, and sweet biscuits, cigarettes at 1/8 for 50 and 3 lb. bags of sugar which they ate raw in handfuls. Smoking steadily, they then began to write the day's bundle of letters; all over the ship day after day, broad-nibbed pens drove remorselessly across pads of paper. The "Romeos" sacrificed length to safety by writing only on letter-cards, in case the censoring officers should muddle the letters and the envelopes. In the afternoons everybody attended the ship's Tombola or Housie-Housie school. Half the price of the cards for this went to some ill-defined charity, the other half to the winner. A sailor perched like a muezzin in a lifeboat chanted the numbers in the language of Housie-Housie players—Kelly's Eye, Piccadilly Ladies, Two Jews, Clickety Click. The Guardsmen sat round marking their cards in silence till a shout showed that someone had filled a line on his card. This claim was verified and his friends escorted the winner to the canteen where they spent his prize money for him, and then back again to the Tombola, which had not stopped. Tea ended the day, and there was nothing to do except go to sleep.

The Battalion saw land again in the 8th March, when the convoy sailed through the Straits of Gibraltar into the Mediterranean. It was a warm and sunny day with a sea like glass. The ships did no more zigzagging but steamed straight along the coast of Africa as fast as they could go. The Battalion instinctively kept an eye on the bright blue sky, but still nothing happened. It was most encouraging.

The O.C. Troops now thought it safe to announce that the convoy was bound for Algiers. He issued an Army pamphlet "Notes for Troops proceeding to North Africa." From this a Guardsman learned that if he was asked to dine with an Arab he should wash his hands and always leave some scraps on the plate for the women of the household to eat in the kitchen. Almost as useful were the bundles of maps and intelligence reports produced from a strongroom. With the help of these Lieutenant D. Fitzgerald lectured all companies on the situation in Tunisia.

Three Allied Task Forces landed in French North Africa on 8th November, 1942. The two which landed at Casablanca and Oran were purely American ; the third which landed at Algiers was mainly British. This British force was at first a Brigade Group till in the course of the next few days it became the First Army, under the command of Lieut.-General Anderson. The instructions given to General Eisenhower, the Allied C-in-C, were first to secure his bases and then to launch the First Army eastwards from Algiers into Tunisia to seize the ports of Tunis and Bizerta. After two days of sporadic fighting the local French forces, under Admiral Darlan, decided to join the Allies. "The Armistice came in for some criticism on the political side," wrote General Alexander afterwards, "but it seems to me very likely that it may have considerably reduced the duration of the war, for if the Germans had first been given sufficient time they could probably have built up sufficient strength in their Tunisian bridgehead to hold out all the summer of 1943. As it was, General Eisenhower was able to turn all his attention to the task of pushing the First Army at full speed towards Tunisia." The First Army, in spite of its name, consisted of only one infantry division, reinforced later by an armoured regimental group, two Commando and two parachute battalions. Algiers and Tunis are separated by 560 miles of mountainous country and are connected by two roads and an indifferent railway. The Germans had certainly been surprised by the Allied landing, but within 48 hours they were flying troops into Tunisia at the rate of 1,000 a day to form a new Army under General Von Arnim. The chance still remained, however, of snatching Tunis by a quick grasp, and General Eisenhower took it. The First Army made a dash for Tunis by land and sea and air. It occupied Bougie on 11th November and Bone on the 12th. A week later it had covered 500 of the 560 miles and had reached Beja, 60 miles from Tunis. There, in the mountains that protect Tunisia on the west, it met the Germans.

Tunisia is an oblong of mountains with a narrow coastal plain on its eastern seaboard. One steep desolate range succeeds another in heartbreaking succession whichever way you turn, till you reach the plain of Carthage, the semi-circle of flat ground that stretches round the city of Tunis for some ten to fifteen miles. Bizerta, the naval base in the north, is more closely hemmed in, and south of Tunis, by Cape Bon, the mountains sweep right down to the sea.

Six routes only cross this long mountain barrier and all six of them can be easily blocked. The two northern ones converge on Bizerta—the coast road from Bône through Tabarka and Mateur and a road and railway from Souk Aras through Souk el Arba and Beja to Mateur. South of these runs the main entrance to Tunisia, the road running straight from west to east from Souk Aras through Le Kef to Medjez el Bab, where it enters the valley of the Medjerda river. Another road strikes up to Tunis from the south, through Tebessa and Pont du Fahs. Farther south still are two parallel roads leading to the ports of Sousse and Sfax. The only important connection between these different routes is a road from Beja through Oued Zarga to Medjez el Bab.

The central route is the best, the easiest and the traditional approach to Tunis and its ancient predecessor, Carthage. The Medjerda Valley opens as a funnel through the hills into the coastal plain, but it is a funnel in which there are, or can be, three stoppers. The first stopper, while the funnel is still narrow, is the town of Medjez el Bab, "The Gate of the Pass." Medjez is the key to Tunis, "Who holds the pass holds Carthage," said Hannibal; that, at any rate, is the tradition, and the exact words as well as the principle may well be accurate, for once Hannibal lost the pass he was defeated by Scipio Africanus on Zama, the plain, and Carthage fell. General Alexander held the same opinion. "I was determined," he wrote later, "to hold our gateway into the Tunis plain and ordered the town to be held at all costs." East of Medjez the hills veer away to north and south but they leave behind them two ugly heaps of rock to command the valley, first the Djebel Ahmera, "Longstop Hill," and then the Djebel Bou Aoukaz, "The Bou." Medjez, Longstop and the Bou—every yard of these was soaked in blood before Tunis fell.

On 17th November the First Army advanced from Beja, still making its dash for Tunis. A small armoured force—"Blade Force"—raced ahead of the main columns down the Medjerda Valley. It passed through Medjez, which it found held by French Gunners who had declared for the Allies, and pushed on towards Tebourba and Djedeida. It got no farther. The Germans fell on it in the hills, cut it to pieces and forced it back on to Medjez. The First Army meanwhile had been advancing steadily in two columns, one on Medjez and the other on Mateur. In Christmas week it made its second attempt to capture Tunis. The 1st Guards Brigade stormed Longstop Hill, but on Christmas Day the Germans recaptured it, and the attack petered out in torrential rain. "This ended the attempt to take Tunis in a rush and it was clear that we should have to build up forces for a deliberate operation. It was also clear that the enemy would be able to build up faster than we could for his lines of communication through Italy and Sicily were more reliable and shorter than ours from the United Kingdom and the United States, and from his ports of entry to the front they were very short and over good roads in flat country. It was necessary therefore to go on the defensive in the northern sector."

The Germans took the offensive for the next three months. Having accumulated enough troops to outnumber the First Army they pressed continual attacks to drive it back into Algeria. It was a period of bitter local actions, fought in appalling weather. The First Army clung to its positions until more troops, guns and tanks could be shipped from England or come up from the desert to launch a grand offensive from those very positions. One by one the hills round Medjez were abandoned, but the town itself was held as the tip of a narrow salient. The first trickles of reinforcements were all flung into action as soon as they arrived, for the constant German pressure gave the First Army no time to build up a reserve.

The First Army grew slowly. The 78th Division was completed on 1st December, the 6th Armoured Division on 15th December, the 46th Division in February, 1st Division in March, 4th Division in April. It was in February that the balance of forces began to swing slowly in favour of the Allies. The Eighth Army drove the German Desert Army out of Tripolitania and followed it into the deep south of Tunisia. The Combined Chiefs of Staff, at the Casablanca Conference, had already decided to set up one fighting command for Tunisia and to give General Alexander responsibility for the entire conduct of operations. General Eisenhower, in Algiers at Allied Expeditionary Force Headquarters, remained the Commander-in-Chief. On 17th February he officially appointed General Alexander Deputy Commander-in-Chief and Commander of the 18th Army Group. The Army Group consisted of the First Army under General Anderson, the Eighth Army under General Montgomery, the American II Corps and the gallant but ill-equipped French 19th Corps, making in all nine Allied Divisions in contact with the enemy with two more on their way from Tripoli. Paragraph 3 of the Directive to the Deputy C.-in-C. read, "Your mission is the early destruction of all Axis forces in Tunisia." The Axis forces then amounted to the equivalent of fourteen divisions, of which about half were Italian, and included one Italian and three German armoured divisions. "I expected," wrote General Alexander, "to be able to build up to a strength of about twenty divisions by May, if all went well, but at the moment

Rommel was being reinforced faster than I was and his normal intake was about a thousand men a day." On the day he assumed command General Alexander laid down the principles of victory. Separate British, French and American Sectors were to be organized under their own commanders. The "bits and pieces" were to be collected and reassembled into their proper formations. The front was to be held by static troops while the armoured and mobile forces were withdrawn and grouped to form a reserve striking force. All troops were to be extensively trained and re-equipped. Finally, immediate plans were to be prepared to regain the initiative, starting with carefully planned minor operations. A new spirit came into Tunisia.

As Rommel's Army fell back into Tunisia the Germans too created an Army Group H.Q. to control their forces. Tunisia was all they had left in Africa as a battlefield and a bridgehead, and they expected to hold it for a long time. "Army Group Africa" under Field-Marshal Rommel controlled both the forces which had been hurried into the country to oppose the First Army and those which had been driven back into the country by the Eighth Army. General Von Arnim remained in command of the north with his forces now called the 5th Panzer Army. The desert Army in the south, still containing the old Afrika Korps, became the First (Italian) Army under the command of a General Messe. Von Arnim's troops were first class. The first arrivals were naturally airborne troops, the Koch Storm Regiment and the Barenthin Regiment, both composed of officer-cadets and instructors from the training schools. These Regiments, with various independent battalions, mountain troops and Grenadiers withdrawn from Russia, held the front from the sea to the Medjerda. The 334 Infantry Division, a new formation, covered Medjez. On its left, covering the Goubellat plain, was the 10th Panzer Division, a division which had fought in France. They were reinforced by more Grenadier Regiments and by a heavy battalion of the new Mark VI "Tiger" tanks. South of them came the Italian divisions reinforced by Germans, and then, facing the Eighth Army, the old desert army with the 21st Panzer Division in central reserve. Rommel's long-term policy was defensive, but his first necessity was to drive back the Allied forces ranged along the length of Tunisia so as to give his armies room to join, breathe and fight. Having abandoned Tripolitania and fallen back on the Mareth Line he dealt a swift blow at the Americans in the plain west of Faid. His object was to make sure that they would not come in on his rear when he was heavily engaged with the Eighth Army, and in this he succeeded. He also very nearly succeeded in disrupting the whole front in Tunisia and causing a withdrawal, if not a disaster. General Alexander hastily took command. "It was clear to me that although Rommel's original intention had been merely to give such a blow to the U.S. II Corps as would leave his right rear free while he prepared to meet the Eighth Army, he now had much bigger ideas." British troops, including the 1st Guards Brigade, rushed down from the north to meet and help the Americans. They halted the Germans west of Kasserine, and on 22nd February, Rommel called off the attack. "His withdrawal was, as always, well conducted with a most liberal use of mines and explosive devices to discourage pursuit."

Then Von Arnim took a hand in the north. He launched his Fifth Army in a series of attacks all along the front from the sea to Medjez. He kept the Allies at full strain at a time when the Kasserine crisis had forced them to weaken the northern sector and had caused some disorganization. His intention must have been to drive the First Army back into the mountains and to recapture Medjez. As the 1st Division convoy approached Algiers the Germans advanced steadily towards Beja, till they overlooked the Beja–Medjez road from the north and Medjez represented the extreme point of a dangerous-looking salient. First Army H.Q. was inclined to evacuate Medjez on the ground that its fall was almost inevitable and that a withdrawal into the mountains to the west would produce a stronger defensive position and an economy in troops, but General Alexander would not hear of it. "The most important feature in our favour," he said, "is that we retain our essential gateway at Medjez el Bab."

CHAPTER II

Medjez el Bab

DURING the afternoon of 9th March the convoy turned into Algiers Bay. From the sea Algiers looked like a stage back-drop : the startling blue sea, the glaring white town embracing the quays and cranes and climbing steeply into the green hills, till only an occasional red roof showed through the trees. The Battalion recognized it from the pictures. They could pick out the Kasbah, the old Arab quarter, and passed on the story that a soldier a night was murdered there. "Not that it is any chance you have of getting murdered," said the old soldiers. "It is only the Germans will be interested in boys with no money."

The *Strathmore* docked at six o'clock while it was still light. The men hung over the rails shouting to American dock operators and throwing cigarettes to Arab loungers. They soon stopped giving cigarettes to Arabs, but they did not yet know that cigarettes were currency, worth at least an egg each. Night fell before the Battalion disembarked, and with darkness came the rain. Algiers was less attractive now. It looked dirty and squalid in the glimmer of lamps ; the comic Arabs became damp and surly and the port officials became more irritable with every new order they shouted to the ship. The Battalion relapsed into the state of resigned patience which is the soldier's protection. There was no transport for anything ; everybody would have to march to a staging camp outside Algiers. "*Outside* Algiers, what did I tell you ?" "Oh, well, let's get on with it," said the Battalion. The first platoon was filing down the gangway when a sudden blast of sirens made them jump out of their skins. The ship rocked as the anti-aircraft gunners let off the barrage they had been holding back all the voyage. Searchlights meandered across the sky, throwing a convenient light on the quay. Shrapnel pattered on the tin sheds and there was not a sign of an Arab or a docker.

"It's an air raid," shouted the Sergeant-Major, perhaps unnecessarily. "Pay no attention. Stack your kit-bags neatly by companies and fall in on the markers." The Battalion threaded its way through miles of warehouses and railway lines to a "check point" at the Quai l'Orient. Here they found a seething mass of soaking troops through which every unit in the Division was trying to fight a way. A harassed man in a kiosk told the Battalion to go to Sidi Moussa. "How far is it ?" "Another twelve miles." "How do we get to it ?" "Five miles straight up the road to Maison Carrée, turn right, seven miles down on the left." "Is it a camp ?" "Not yet."

At two o'clock in the morning the Battalion, with clouds of steam rising from it, passed through the sordid town of Maison Carrée and, two hours later, halted by an open field. A row of marquees flapped dismally in the rain and another row lay sodden on the ground. Till the transport arrived two days later, the Battalion was isolated in this glutinous wilderness. The only break in the steady rain was an occasional cloud-burst, under which the tents collapsed in a deluge of disaster. Captain Powell-Edwards almost revelled in the discomfort. "For the three days we were there," he wrote, "it was rain, rain, rain, mud, mud, mud, mud always ankle deep, in places knee deep, of the texture of paint, evil-smelling, fabulous, frightful, awful." It was as much as the cooks could do to boil water on smoking, spluttering stoves, and the Battalion lived mainly on tea and biscuits—like City typists, only not so well paid—with a lump of bully beef or cheese. The French colonial in the nearest farmhouse did a famous trade in oranges. When the men had spent their few francs he charged a silver piece for an orange ; it did not matter whether it was a half-crown or a threepenny bit, you only got one orange for it, and he would not accept holy medals as Irish coinage. Seedy Arabs, dressed in sacks, hung about the camp in the vain hope of being allowed to shine shoes or steal something. Drill-Sergeant Rooney and other veterans of Cairo and Palestine drove them off with roars of "Imshi ! " It was like shouting at sparrows ; the Arabs scattered and returned, flapping and chattering. For most of the Battalion there was nothing to do but go on route marches and hope for letters. The men wandered around the camp and looked at the nearby farms trying to distinguish what had been a field from what was plough, and sheep from goats. The only man who had a good word for the place was Pipe-Major Phair. Algerian reeds are the best in the world, and he had the luck to find a hut built of magnificent specimens. He happily dismantled it to cut into chanters for the pipes.

On 13th March the Battalion left Sidi Moussa. "The Brigade will proceed to Bone," said the orders, "marching personnel by sea, wheels and tracks by road." Seven hundred and seventy-two men of the Battalion marched the fifteen miles back to Algiers harbour and the transport and carriers started a 300-mile drive in the opposite direction. The Navy was running a shuttle service between Algiers and Bone with two mail-boats from the Glasgow–Belfast service, the *Royal Ulsterman* and the *Royal Scotsman*. The Battalion squeezed into the *Ulsterman*. There were men who knew the boat well, and they pointed out that she had only been built to carry 400 at most. The *Ulsterman* sailed at dusk, followed by the *Scotsman*, appropriately carrying the 1st Scots Guards, and two destroyers carrying the 5th Grenadier Guards. It was like spending a night in an old tram. The men had to sit bolt upright on wooden benches as the ship belted along through a sharp chop. At dawn the wind dropped, the sun came out and the ship settled down to a steady race through the smooth water. A steady gush of muddy water spouted out of her side as the Battalion washed themselves and their clothes. The engine-room was festooned with drying vests. Then, after breakfast, up on deck to watch the coast slide by. Four Bren teams mounted their guns on the after deck beside a 12-pounder gun. The sailors were glad to have someone to talk to because, they said, they never had anything to do. The Battalion and the sailors passed the time of day till four o'clock when the *Ulsterman* rounded the cape into Bone Bay and the Battalion went below to get dressed.

"Action stations! Aircraft." The Battalion poured back on deck and were driven down below again. There were three dots on the horizon, enlarging into Italian torpedo planes. The officers raced to the after deck, all determined to see and, if possible, to fire something. The guns of the *Ulsterman* and the destroyers opened fire, but the aircraft came on. "Come nearer, oh, do come nearer," begged the Bren gunners. Guardsman Merriman fired the first shot in the Battalion's Mediterranean campaigns. It was followed by a fusillade of Bren fire and a confused babel of fire orders and encouragement. Captain Mungo Park was hopping with excitement, his borrowed Bren bouncing on the rail, and R.S.M. Peilow shouting "Another magazine for the Adjutant!" The aeroplanes dropped their torpedoes and veered off. In the silence which followed Captain George Ismay, who had been leaning over the rail apparently unimpressed, announced clearly, "There is a torpedo going to hit us. It is just like the films." And so it was. There was the long white wave streaking towards the ship, and soon we could see the torpedo itself, a small one. "It will hit us just beneath where we're standing," continued

Captain Ismay. Nobody moved. "It's missed!" Still nobody moved; then slowly they began to collect magazines and get ready to disembark.

This is the entry in the ship's log: "At 1625 hrs. H.M. ship in Bone channel observed three twin-engined aircraft, distance five miles, flying in formation about three degrees above horizon. Shortly after sighting, aircraft turned and were seen heading towards H.M. ship. Officer of the watch immediately gave orders for action stations. *Oakely* [a destroyer] opened fire and splashes were seen falling below aircraft. Two aircraft approached H.M. ship from abeam and one torpedo from each fell into water at an estimated inclination of 162 degrees right from about 2,000 yards. Heavy and accurate fire was opened at short range by all, including Bren gunners from 1st Bn. Irish Guards. Helm was put hard aport. Aircraft turned away to port and were last seen heading in an easterly direction. H.M. ship swung about 50 degrees to port helm and then reversed, and ship was swinging to starboard when two tracks were seen approaching, one abaft the beam and clear, the other before the beam at about 190 degrees. Helm was again put hard aport, but had little effect, and it seemed inevitable that torpedo would hit port quarters. It actually passed four yards astern, as estimated by the officer i/c 12-pounder gun."

The town of Bône is built beside the ruins of the ancient Hippo, and the huge Basilica of St. Augustine towers over it. The harbour had been heavily bombed and its squalid wreckage merged into the remains of Roman villas. The nearer you get to the front the better things are organized. Here the Brigade staff had already arrived, there were trucks to carry the baggage and the Battalion had only four miles to march. The tents of "Cardiff Camp" were pitched on a long high dune beside the sea, flanked by a salt marsh. The close turf felt like a carpet after the mud of Sidi Moussa. When their tents were suddenly blown down in the middle of the night, the Battalion consoled itself with the official announcement that the bad weather ended punctually on 15th March. It still rained heavily in bursts, like exaggerated April showers, but in the intervals the sun shone and the water drained away to give the Battalion a dry, sandy bottom. Captain Powell-Edwards produced the old-fashioned folding chair and table he carried everywhere and sat outside his tent. "Bone is quite fun," he wrote, "with wine, oranges, baths in a cruiser and the most luscious rumours." As far as the Battalion could make out, the fighting seemed to be mainly in the hills north-west of Medjez el Bab, that is above and behind it. The Germans were still pressing attacks against Beja and the road to Medjez el Bab. Their progress varied with each rumour, but all rumours agreed that they had made some progress. "I expect we will move up soon after the transport joins us," said Colonel Scott. "Till then, take it easy." The Battalion took his advice and stuffed itself with tangerines.

The Battalion did not mind much when it went into the line, but it did want to know where it was going to be on the 17th of March. "Probably still here," was all Brigadier Colvin could say, but that was good enough. Shamrock had been flown out to General Alexander in Algiers and was brought to Bône by his A.D.C., Captain Sir Rupert Clarke. Colonel Scott asked the Brigadier to present the shamrock, and invited to lunch the officers of the cruiser *Aurora*, then lying in the bay. The Adjutant and Sergeant-Major chose a flat stretch of ground and put the Battalion through a few rehearsals. The Quartermaster descended on the Naafi in Bône and extracted from it extraordinary supplies of beer, chocolate and cigarettes. His method was simple. He walked into the dump and demanded them. The head clerk looked as if he was going to ask a question, but the Quartermaster said firmly, "It's St. Patrick's Day tomorrow, you hadn't forgotten, had you ?" Captain John and Lieutenant Desmond FitzGerald were sent out to buy local produce. They inspected and rejected pigs which resembled greyhounds, very active and bad-tempered beasts, and loathsome old goats, but bought two huge casks—Bordelaises—of sweet red wine. The wine was recommended by some Zouaves, who fixed a fair price for it, and also gave the Battalion two sheep, the property, so they said, of the French Republic. In return they accepted an invitation to the Sergeants' Mess party. To be on the safe side the Sergeants held their party on the evening of the 16th. It was in the true style—beer, whiskey, smoke and singing. There was wine for those who wanted it, but the Sergeants urged their guests not to touch such dangerous stuff. The Zouaves did not need urging ; they happily drank much more dangerous mixtures and smiled in bewilderment at the rebel songs and the repeated references to General Hoche and '98, the Irish Brigade, Kevin Barry and Terence MacSweeney. They insisted on singing a song they had specially practised in honour of the glorious Irish Guards, "Ce n'est qu'un au revoir, mon vieux." It was "Auld Lang Syne" in French, but even the Scots Guards present said nothing about it and joined the applause. The singing died down about midnight, and the bullfrogs in the marshes took over from the Sergeants.

The Battalion paraded on St. Patrick's Day in the morning. "It makes one proud to see them," wrote Brigadier Colvin. "An American liaison officer with us was so moved when the Battalion marched past that he blubbed freely." With the shamrock General Alexander sent a message from himself: "Welcome to the Micks. Now we'll get cracking."

Early the next day the Battalion piled into troop-carrying lorries and drove out of Bône. It was just as well. Too many men had been deceived by the sweet taste of the wine at their dinner and drank it like lemonade. Those whose stomachs stood the strain "proceeded" to Bône and took the town apart. "I am still getting reports from Bône," wrote Colonel Scott a week later. "The terrible ruffians, even when they were being conveyed under escort managed to pelt the Military Police with bully tins. However, we are miles away now, thank God."

Hour after hour the troop-carriers trundled along the switchback road, up and down, right-handed corner, left-handed corner, down and up. As long as they followed the coast road to Tabarka there was at least something to look at, but when they turned south and plunged into the thick cork-oak forests the Battalion fell into a cramped doze. The hum of heavy tyres was such a familiar sound. The Brigade had been ordered to a concentration area near Chardimaou, between Souk Arras and Souk el Arba. Chardimaou was said to be a convenient place to hold a reserve brigade which might be needed anywhere in the line at short notice, say twenty-four hours. The transport on its way up from Algiers had been diverted and had been driving all through the night so as to get there about the same time as the troops. Colonel Scott sent the Intelligence Officer and the Quartermaster on ahead of the Battalion, to drive as fast as they could. This small advance party reached Chardimaou in the pouring rain and found the map square allotted to the Battalion to be a dismal olive-grove. Shaking off despair and digging their truck out of the mud, they divided the grove into company areas, posted a Guardsman to order all vehicles to stay on the road, persuaded the nearest farmer to supply pure water, and sat over a smoking fire to await the Battalion. The Battalion never came to Chardimaou. An agitated staff officer from H.Q., First Army, stopped the convoy at Ain Dram. The Germans were attacking again; Tamara in the north was falling, or had fallen; the line had been stripped to reinforce the north, and now Beja was in danger. Hurry, hurry, hurry to Beja.

The Brigade was rushed into the line with just what the men were carrying—rifles, Brens and a hundred rounds. The 46th Division was "pushed" as the Battalion said, and wanted the Brigade deployed in double quick time to cover the town and, incidentally, Divisional H.Q. "Beja was bloody," wrote an officer. "Ruined and typhus-ridden, a dreadful place to reach at one o'clock in the morning. And, besides, Beja was in the line ; we could see the gun-flashes in the mountains less than two miles away." The R.A.S.C. lorries dumped the Battalion in a cemetery. It was pitch dark and pouring with rain. While the companies huddled under tombstones, the officers studied their maps by torch-light in the mortuary. Major H. L. S. Young showed a gloomy satisfaction in his surroundings and could be heard muttering something like "Told 'em they'd all be stiff as kippers." As soon as it was light the Grenadiers marched out of the town "under cover of heavy rain." The Scots Guards and the Battalion waited for their transport so that when they moved up into the hills beyond the Grenadiers they should be fully armed and at least partially fed. The transport did not arrive till mid-morning. It was the best they could do, explained Lieutenant Dennis Madden ; they had covered 380 miles in a day and two nights. The last night's drive from Chardimaou was a nightmare. After two trucks had run off the road into ravines the column halted every half-hour for five minutes while the drivers got out and ran round in the biting rain to wake themselves up. The dawn was lurid, but it came too soon. It was clear daylight as the convoy started to run down a long, straight valley headed by the sign-board, "Look out and up. This is ' Messerschmitt Alley." With our own forward airfields sunk in mud, there was nothing to stop the German fighters taking a quick run over from the Tunis aerodromes for half an hour's machine-gunning. The wreckage along the sides showed how regularly they chose this stretch of road. The drivers put their boots down on the accelerator and kept them down till they saw the notice boards of Beja—"Keep out. Typhus."

The "situation map" in the 46th Division H.Q. was an alarming affair. Blue arrows pointed at Beja from all directions, and there were far too many of the conventional signs for enemy tanks. Still more alarming was the "Mine Museum." Laid out on the floor of a stable was every kind of German and Italian mine, big ones and little ones, mines to disintegrate a tank, and mines just big enough to drive a bullet through a man's foot ; Teller mines, Schu mines, Bar mines, Box mines, anti-personnel mines, mines which jumped up into the air and sprayed steel balls at chest height, booby-trap mines, concrete mines, timed mines which needed three pressures before they exploded, and finally Italian egg grenades and German rifle grenades, which could be left in the grass for someone to kick. The curator, an enthusiastic Sapper, said that Tunisia was sown with mines, and he was not far wrong.

The Scots Guards moved up into the hills during the afternoon, and Colonel Scott went with them to see the lie of the land. He was talking to the Brigadier when the Divisional Commander drove up in an armoured car. The Germans were pressing down on Djebel Abiod and the whole line had to be reorganized once again to free more troops for the defence of Beja. "Leave the Grenadiers where they are and motor your Scots and Irish to Medjez to relieve the 38th Brigade." The Beja–Medjez road was cut, so they would have to go round sixty-five miles by way of Teboursouk and Thibar. The 78th Division, who owned the Medjez salient, wanted the relief completed before dawn. "This makes our third division in twenty-four hours," said Colonel Scott. "Watson can bring up the Battalion ; it is the sort of job he likes. I'll take the company commanders straight off to find the 38th Brigade."

The "dangerous looking Medjez salient" was the hinge of the Allied line. From the south the line came up almost dead due north from Bou Arada and across the Goubellat plain to Grenadier Hill, where the 1st Guards Brigade were holding the short southern flank of the salient. At Medjez the line turned sharply back due west twenty-five miles to Beja, where it turned north again. The 38th Brigade were holding the eastern three miles of the northern flank covering the Beja road. Colonel Scott in the big Humber car, and the four rifle company commanders in their jeeps, like a hen with her chicks, passed through the vineyards of Thibar, where the monastery of the White Fathers housed the casualty clearing station, and the prize olive groves of Teboursouk, and drove straight up the main road to Medjez el Bab. Three miles short of Medjez, where a poplar avenue began, they saw the battle-axe sign of the 78th Division and the code number of a brigade headquarters pointing up a track. Half a mile up the track they found the Brigade H.Q. in the White House, a rambling farmhouse surrounded by cactus hedges and liquid mud. The Beja road lay another mile and a half north, but between it and the White House ran a parallel chain of low ridges which just covered the main road from the Germans in the real hills to the north. The Battalion was told to take over these ridges from the Buffs. "Carry on up the track and you will find them in the small farm, Diar el Hammar." Beyond the White House the track got steadily worse. The owner of Diar el Hammar had built a better and much shorter approach to his house from the Beja road and had so far abandoned this one as to plough in long stretches of it. The farm buildings were tucked beneath a low hill set slightly in front of the rest of the chain. The track, with aimless perversity, came up over a low hill well to the left and trailed along its northern face in full view of the Germans before it eventually turned back down to the farm. It was no wonder that the farmer had abandoned it even before the Germans came. The positions held by the Buffs were simple, because they were the only ones possible on so wide a front—three companies strung out along the top of the ridges, and one in reserve. Once the company commanders knew which was theirs—"Saville, you'll be in reserve, John on the left, Sam in the centre and Pol on the right"—they took one look at them, noted the names of the Buffs' platoon commanders, and walked straight back across country to the main road. It was already dusk, so with them went about half the Buffs. They had not much to say. "It's not too bad, but very wet. The worst part is the patrols."

A Northamptonshire battalion on the left flank covered the relief with standing patrols on the Beja road. Well before midnight Colonel Scott was able to tell the Northamptons, with thanks, that they could go home. The companies were in position. There had been nothing to it, they had just squelched through two miles of mud and stepped into the empty trenches. The Bren gunners set up their guns and stacked the magazines in neat piles ; the riflemen took the grenades out of their pouches and put them on the parapet, eased off their equipment, pulled their greatcoats round them and squatted down to wait for the dawn and breakfast. This was "the line," but it might well have been "a scheme," except that there was less fuss. The company commanders walked along to the farmyard to collect their trucks. They found nobody there except the doctor, Captain Barnes, and Sergeant Thorogood, the Medical Sergeant, busily turning a cowshed into an R.A.P. by lighting a fire in one corner and balancing a stretcher on two old boxes. Everybody else was out on the track manhandling the transport. The heavy lorries sank to the axles and beyond in the glutinous mud. The Guardsmen pushed and lifted them forward yard by yard and watched them slither forward on the firmer patches, their wheels spinning, but they sank again. The carriers burnt their clutches and slipped their tracks struggling to haul the lorries through the morass. Lieutenant Madden, a mud-caked giant, hoarse with shouting, flogged the last ounce of energy out of every man. "We'll get them through if we have to carry them. Take them one at a time." It was a cold wet night, with a thin drizzle of rain, but the men were working in their shirt sleeves, the sweat running off them. Swearing and almost weeping they flung themselves on the lorries. "Big Jim" Egan came to give a hand. "This is like the main road to Cavan," he grunted from beneath a three-tonner, "the nearer to Cavan, the mainer it gets." The last lorry lurched down the dip into the farmyard as the first rays of dawn came up over the hills. "The transport's in, sir," reported Lieutenant Madden, and started to scrape the mud off his enormous boots. Colonel Scott looked at him, "You'd better join Joshua Nunn," and pointed to the Pioneer Officer lying spreadeagled on the floor, snoring. "The Adjutant will get it unloaded." The companies needed no telling; they had stripped their trucks as they came in, and already the roar of petrol burners told the platoons in the trenches that tea was on the brew.

The new day, 20th March, brought the first casualties. A flight of infantry-gun shells buzzed through a gap in the slopes on to No. 2 Company's headquarters. They wounded Guardsman Brown, the mess waiter, and two other men, damaged Major Bucknill's jeep and punctured a teapot. "We hope," says the War Diary, "that this is not going to be a frequent occurrence."

At first light on 20th March most of the platoons came back over the crest of the ridges, leaving only the Bren gunners on the forward slope. This was the system on which all hills were held in Tunisia by both sides. By night "bodies on the ground" were needed to hold the long, exposed slopes, but during the day the Bren gunners could cover the ground with fire while the riflemen lay on the reverse slope. Medium machine guns such as the Germans used would have been better than Brens, but there were none on the establishment of an infantry battalion. The Battalion got hold of four old Vickers guns just before it left Medjez and formed its own Machine-gun Platoon, but during this period it had to rely on Brens fixed on tripod mountings. The companies found, or dug, themselves trenches, which as the days went by they elaborated into rough shelters to keep out the rain and splinters. They could never equal the magnificent vaults of the Germans, carved out of the living rock or burrowed deep into the earth, lined with armour plate and carpeted with straw, but they did their best with sand-bags, ammunition boxes and ground sheets.

The ridges held by the Battalion were little more than undulations in the rolling floor of the Medjerda valley. The corn was sprouting lush and bright green in the sticky black earth. It was no higher than lawn grass at first, but in the following weeks, when the sun came out, it grew so fast that you could almost watch it till it smothered the trenches and had to be scythed at night to open a field of fire. When Captain O. Chesterton, or somebody in No. 1 Company, broke the only scythe and hid the remains, the Guardsmen had to use their clasp-knives. "My company—No. 4—was on the right flank," wrote Captain Powell-Edwards, "which consisted of an extensive gravel pit on the reverse slope from the Hun and, forward, a farmhouse and, some 200 yards to the left, another gravel pit. The two platoons in the forward positions could not move at all by day, a state of affairs that could become very trying after a time. Each platoon would do three or four days in the left-hand forward position, getting up their food by night, then move to the farm, then back for a rest to the gravel pit on the reverse slope." No. 2 Company, in the centre, had nothing but a bare slope where the ridges flattened out, and they suffered the most from the sweeping rain. Diar el Hammar farm lay behind the left-hand shoulder of the ridges. It was a pronounced shoulder which effectively shielded the farm from the front before it dropped down to leave a flat defile between itself and an ugly excrescence on the left called Mortar Hill. No. 3 Company held this shoulder and covered the defile. It kept two platoons on the forward slope and its third on the reverse slope, peering round the edge. By night it visited a group of Arab huts and a long stone barn in the mouth of the defile ; there was usually a stray German, alive or dead, to be found there and if there was not, the men could pass the time by painting insulting messages in dog-German on the wall of the barn. The shoulder was crowned by a wrecked Hurricane aircraft, conveniently placed to shelter observation posts. Gunner and Mortar Platoon observers sat on all day in the shade of its wings, patiently watching the valley and the hills. Very rarely did they see anything move ; when they did they shelled it. No. 1 Company, in reserve, held a hill behind and overlooking the defile. They shared a secluded hollow called Happy Valley with the carriers and mortar trucks. It looked like a gipsy encampment, with the camouflaged trucks standing round like caravans and dozens of small fires burning under blackened tins of tea or stew. A battery of field guns led an independent life beside the farm. They had been there when the Battalion arrived and stayed there till replaced by Major Streatfield's battery of the 19th Field Regiment.

Battalion H.Q. was installed in the farm. The farmer had built himself a neat little white villa on the hillside above the farmyard, and there he lived by himself. To anyone approaching from the rear it looked like a doll's house, stuck on the top of the ridge, waiting to be knocked down. But it never was knocked down ; it was never even touched. It stood on a false crest so neatly placed beneath the true crest that the German gunners could not get at it. The shells fell around it, on the track leading to it, and skimmed over the roof to land in the farmyard below, but not a tile was shifted nor a window broken, except by the Battalion. Colonel Scott had an eye for houses, and it did not take him long to see the peculiar qualities of the Doll's House. Also there could not be much wrong with a house in which the lugubrious farmer continued to live. "Monsieur Joli Bonbon" was as pessimistic as a man could be, and enjoyed wondering, out aloud, which side had done him the most harm, but he had never bothered to move into his fine cellar. Battalion H.Q. took over half the house and transformed it into a Mess and Command Post. "Kew Gardens must get their most unpleasant and obscene specimens of cactus from here," wrote an officer. "The gloomy proprietor is a great cactus lover and has hundreds of horrid little pots about, like aspidistras. As we were always pricking our fingers on them, I have had them removed by the pioneers, who wore wiring gloves for the job." Monsieur accepted everything with resignation until the Signal Platoon began to dig an underground telephone exchange and wireless station in the middle of his shrubbery. Then he struck ; he stood on the porch and denounced the signallers in rolling periods. "It is the mark of civilized man to plant trees. When the Romans left the barbarians cut down all the timber for firewood, and look at our valley now, parched in summer, sodden in winter, ridden with malaria. In this country a tree has a Frenchman under it. For years I have nursed these plants, protected them from the sun and my Arabs. They were my gift to posterity ; they were to make this place fit for my son to live in, and now you are going to destroy them. I cannot stand it. Occupy my house, gut my barn, ruin my machinery, trample the wheat, drive away my Arabs, but leave me the trees. C'est la guerre, mais soyons civilisés, quand meme." Lieutenant Brian Synge, who had been civilized at Winchester, replied with dignity that the Irish Guards abhorred vandalism and moved the site of the telephone exchange. "He need not have been so upset," said Sergeant Sullivan. "I told the boys to go easy with the bushes. Still, I see what he means ; it is a terribly bare country."

From its positions the Battalion looked across 3,000 yards of corn-land to the steep hills that enclosed the Medjerda valley on the north. In the evening, when the light was fading, a blue and mauve haze covered these hills, smoothing the jagged edges and softening them into friendly tranquillity. They looked so peaceful, lying like leviathans stranded on the shore. It was a cruel delusion. They were rough and stony, with outcrops of sheer rock and a bald, boulder-strewn top; their sides were pocked with a horrible kind of gorse and thorn bushes, while on the lower slopes an occasional miserable olive shrub struggled for existence against goats and Arabs. Two main features faced the Battalion. On the left was a long, steep razor-backed hill called Recce Ridge; on the right was a similar, but larger, hill with a cliff face on which was perched the white fortress village of Chaouach. The break between these two was filled by a sugar loaf. The main German strength, as far as the Battalion knew, was concentrated on Recce Ridge and the Sugar Loaf, but they had seeped down from their commanding positions to establish outposts in the valley. Their patrols controlled the "no man's land" up to the Beja road. This road, with the railway behind it, ran at the foot of the Battalion's position. Its white surface glittered in the sun and gleamed in the moonlight; both sides had sown its verges with mines. Sometimes a solitary Arab picked his way down the centre of it, nervously looking to the left and right, and twice a stray truck from Beja careered down it and went up on mines under the Battalion's nose. Across the valley to the north-east Longstop Hill made itself only too obvious. The Battalion saw the puffs of smoke in its horrid bulk when the Allied air forces bombed it, as they did every day, but the smoke cleared, the noise rolled away and Longstop and the Germans remained.

By day the scene stretched before the Battalion as still and as familiar as a painted landscape target. The shift of colours in the changing light was the only variation, and sometimes before dawn a thick mist filled the valley like milk. The surface was serene. Below the surface was the 756 (Edelweiss) Mountain Regiment.

CHAPTER III

Recce Ridge

"WE are now trying to reorganize ourselves," wrote the Brigadier on 22nd March, "and at the same time be offensive to the Hun who is getting rather above himself at the moment." During its first week in Medjez the 24th Guards Brigade consisted of the Scots and Irish Guards and a line battalion—("I am making frantic efforts to recover the Grenadiers," continued the Brigadier, himself a Grenadier)—with artillery, sappers, tanks and a reconnaissance regiment belonging to the 78th Division. It was the same in every other brigade ; the continual German pressure had forced apart the neat groupings of battalions and services. During this week the Germans reached the high tide of their success in Tunisia. "On 22nd March," says an official report, "the position was that although the key positions of Beja, Medjez el Bab and Bou Arada remained firmly in British hands, the enemy had pressed uncomfortably close, especially to the Medjez–Beja road. In view of the fact that the final attack on Tunis would have to be mounted and launched from the area of Medjez el Bab, it was essential that the enemy be driven out of the commanding positions he had acquired north-west of the town."

The Battalion did not yet know anything of a final attack on Tunis, but it did know that before anything could be done it must sweep the Germans out of the valley back into the hills. The two main enemy outposts in the valley were M'Dakrene and Sidi Naceur. Sidi Naceur was a deserted "woggery on a wadi" (an Arab village set on the edge of an old water-course) half-way between the town of Medjez and the hills. It covered both the entrance to the valley from the east and the approach out of the valley towards Longstop. It was also a useful base for patrols against the defences of Medjez.

M'Dakrene lay at the foot of Recce Ridge opposite No. 3 Company. It was the home of a prosperous landowner—and looked it—a large white house with a red roof, now rather battered by shells, flanked by rambling farm buildings and surrounded by trees. No. 3 Company could catch a glimpse of a wide veranda and ornamental gardens and could clearly see the dormer windows above the trees.

There was not a sign of life in it, but the Arabs swore there were men with telephones in the attic and more men with guns in the cellars. The Battalion started work on the night after it arrived, the 20th. By patient observation the gunners had located a German section post on the outskirts of M'Dakrene farm. "We've been saving it up," they said. To which Colonel Scott replied, "We'll soon have them out of it and see who they are," and sent for Lieutenant M. Rawlence. Michael Rawlence made a brave show of pleasure at being chosen to lead the Battalion's first patrol. It deceived nobody in Battalion H.Q., least of all Colonel Scott, but it made things much easier for them, and they were grateful. Night patrols are part of the duty of a subaltern, but that does not lighten the responsibility on the officers who have to order him out. Of all the things an infantryman has to do to earn his keep, patrolling is the nastiest. There are men who enjoy a set-piece battle ; many men are quite happy in the line, but everybody hates patrolling. No amount of experience can reduce the nervous strain of walking or crawling through the dark, waiting for the sudden shots. But in time you do at least get an idea of what is likely to happen in a particular area—if that is any comfort. Lieutenant Rawlence and his patrol had nothing to go on ; they would have to find it all out for themselves.

The plan for this patrol was simple. They were to go out as soon as it was dark, wait for three artillery concentrations to fall and, after the third one, to rush the German post and haul out the occupants. Lieutenant Rawlence picked six men from his platoon of No. 3 Company and they spent the rest of the day resting in the farm, feeding like fighting cocks. As night fell they went through the ritual of emptying their pockets, checking their weapons for the ninety-ninth time, blacking their faces and smoking one last cigarette.

The patrol started soon after dusk. "I looked at the man next to me," wrote Lieutenant Rawlence. "His face, beneath the burnt cork and mud, was set in concentration and expectancy. Down the slope we went, past a wrecked Stuka as far as a wadi where we paused for a moment while I crawled forward to see that everything was clear. The landscape was flooded with moonlight. There was a gentle sound of trickling from a stream below me but apart from that, silence. Although one bush looked very like a man, I decided that it really was only my imagination and that the wadi was clear. We crossed it carefully, for in a place like this a tuft might hide a mine and between any two bushes might be stretched a booby trap wire. The first nervousness wore off and, like a boxer once the fight has started, we were so immersed in the present that we had no time to imagine the future. Suddenly there was a small bang, and a Very light—a German Very light—hung in the air about 300 yards on our left. We stopped still, waiting like statues till the light died, and then moved on. After another ten minutes of careful progress there was a noise just ahead of us as if all hell had broken loose. Every man dropped on his stomach with his gun to his shoulder. Twenty seconds of apprehension dragged slowly by . . . it had only been a brace of partridges. Now there was a small Arab village to circumvent and two more fields and then we should reach the outskirts of the farm, where we were going to wait for our artillery concentration to fall. A dog barked, and then another, and finally every dog in the village was howling its head off. 'Down, and crawl.' Having gone on all-fours through two fields of standing corn, still wet from the morning's rain, we arrived at our forming-up place soaked to the skin and very muddy. Five minutes to go and I found myself praying that the artillery would get a direct hit with every shell. Three minutes to go, I was wondering how many Germans there were in the post. One minute to go. 'Stop moving about there.' Then a fusillade of reports came from our own lines and we heard the comforting whirl of shells through the air as the first concentration landed beautifully, on and around the enemy post. There was a scream and a shout, which was lost as another concentration crashed down on the post. 'Get ready.' And as the third and last concentration came down, away we went into a slight dip. As we came up the other side there was one wild and rather inaccurate burst of fire and two of our men were hit. We covered the last fifty yards yelling with excitement and firing as we went. 'Kamerad! Kamerad!' and two Germans climbed hurriedly out of their trench. We looked quickly round. There was one German killed and three wounded. We searched them for documents, collected our own wounded and started back with our prisoners. The other Germans in the area were obviously not sure what was going to happen next, as Very lights kept on going up and machine guns fired bursts on their fixed lines, none of them near us. We remembered hearing that the Germans had often ambushed patrols on their return journey just before they regained our lines. The prisoners recovered somewhat from their fright and seemed to be resigned to their fate. Far from being truculent, they wished as fervently as we did that there would be no more trouble that night. The tension increased as we crept across country till we reached the foot of the final slope. Fifty yards up it we were halted by the comforting sound of a voice saying quietly, 'Halt, who goes there?'"

The following night Lieutenant Rawlence and a larger patrol went out again to clear the farm-house itself. The plan was much the same ; they hung round the outskirts while the guns poured in concentrations. There was no response. They rushed the buildings and, after searching every corner, unearthed an aged Arab. He said he was the caretaker and that the Germans had left, taking everything with them, but had promised to be back soon. At that moment the Germans unleashed their guns and mortars on the farm. Guardsman Calahane was wounded in the legs and Lieutenant Rawlence in the chest and head. The Arab whisked away like a rabbit. The patrol dragged Calahane into a shed and prepared to "repel boarders," while Lieutenant Rawlence walked about the farm-yard like Banquo's ghost, till it was time to go home. Calahane had to be carried carefully and slowly, but Lieutenant Rawlence stayed on his feet till he reached the R.A.P., and there he collapsed. A fragment of metal had passed right through him, piercing one lung and tearing an ugly hole in his back on its way out. Everyone who could came to see Calahane and Lieutenant Rawlence before they were lifted into the ambulance. They were drawn by curiosity as well as sympathy. The atmosphere of the R.A.P., the sweet smell of new blood and the sickly smell of old blood, the heap of dirty stained battledress, the mixed tobacco and candle smoke, the white faces emerging from the rolls of blankets, familiar and yet very altered, the buzz of voices centring round the doctor, soon became as ordinary and dull as company orders, but this time it was new and horribly fascinating. Men walked away meditatively. "Poor old Calahane." "Rawlence must be as strong as a horse."

Every night the patrols went out. "Sometimes at midnight pandemonium would start in the valley and we would go up to the Gunner O.P. and watch the flares and the tracer and listen to the Tommy guns and Brens yapping and spluttering. Every morning the patrol reports went in to Brigade H.Q. "Patrol from 1st I.G. Lieutenant Rochford and three men. Patrol searched Sidi Naceur. Just before leaving the village one M.G. fired on patrol at 15 yards range. The patrol returned fire with four Tommy guns and four grenades. The result was a scuffle and the M.G. ceased firing. In the interval the patrol returned to the huts. The M.G. started firing again and a small mortar opened up. All shots went wide and there were no casualties in the patrol. There is a strong probability that the No. 1 on the German M.G. was killed."

A series of such patrols persuaded the Germans to abandon Sidi Naceur, and then the Battalion concentrated on Recce Ridge. It had already sent a strong patrol to "probe" the enemy's defences on the Sugar Loaf (Point 305) and found them to be good. On the night of the 24th, Lieutenant Keigwin, Sergeant Roberts, Lance-Sergeant Pearson and thirteen men of No. 3 reached the foot of the Sugar Loaf and started to climb it. Lance-Sergeant Pearson took a Bren gun round one side to cover the patrol as it clambered up the rocks. "Half-way up the hillside the patrol was challenged and fired on by M.G. 38's, belt-fed guns on swivel mountings. The Germans (or Austrians) fired continuously for an hour wasting an enormous amount of precious ammunition, and lobbed small grenades over the side of the hill." Most of the fire was directed on Lance-Sergeant Pearson. In fact, he drew it on to himself by firing tracer at each gun in turn. Underneath the machine-gun fire the riflemen fought a brisk skirmish in twos and threes, while Lieutenant Keigwin made careful, almost pedantic, notes. He added two pieces of general information : "(1) At least two Germans here speak good English. One of them shouted 'Felix, Felix—they're English. Louie's been wounded.' (2) The German grenades are similar in type to our Bakelite No. 69. The fuse gives off a green light while burning ; the explosion is sharper than the 69, but the blast effect is less." The patrol, its work done, fought its way back. Eight of them got straight home. Lance-Sergeant Roberts was caught in the dark and marched off up the hill. Guardsman Harris, just behind him, pretended to be dead and was left alone. Lance-Corporal Cartlidge slept out in a gully and returned the next morning, damp but undamaged. Guardsman Walsh and another Harris (Harris 66) lay up for the whole of the following day and tried to come in through the Scots Guards lines the next day. Harris 66 trod on an anti-personnel mine and died of wounds ; Walsh escaped more lightly, winged by a sentry. The remaining men of the patrol, Guardsmen Beasley, Flannery and May, did not return.

Every night for the next week men went out to chart the top of Recce Ridge. Lance-Sergeant Landers and Guardsman Maquire found two machine-gun posts. Lance-Sergeant Henderson and Lance-Corporal Duckworth climbed the ridge at its western end and walked along the side of it about 200 yards below the crest. "The Germans never saw us till we reached the end of the Recce Ridge and started down into the gully," said Sergeant Henderson. "There we were fired on by rifles from a platoon position on the Sugar Loaf. We took cover. The Germans came in search of us, firing in our direction. They came on top of Corporal Duckworth, who emptied his Tommy-gun magazine into the leading man. I rolled away down a ravine, calling to Corporal Duckworth to follow, but he did not come. I was then fired on from the slope of Recce Ridge itself and dived under cover of a bush, to find myself within two yards of an enemy post. I lay there, hardly breathing, till six in the morning, when the Germans ' stood down ' and went back over the ridge, and I crawled away."

Scrap by scrap the Battalion pieced together a picture of the Recce Ridge. The Germans had their main positions just behind the crest and in the little re-entrant valleys beyond it. The foot of the forward slope clearly did not interest or worry them ; it was loosely mined and irregularly patrolled. The bare upper part of the forward slope was covered by fire from the flanks and guarded during the nights by a series of section posts, most of which were on the western half and only a few yards down from the crest. Every patrol agreed that they had no trouble till they were well up the slope. Deserters and their usual method of escape confirmed this general picture. They used to slip away from their posts just before dawn and take refuge in the bushes at the foot of the ridge ; there they lay till the following nightfall when they set out across the valley to surrender themselves about breakfast-time. Each morning usually brought an Austrian or a Pole who had had enough of the war. They complained about everything, the shelling, the food and their officers. The Poles felt no need to justify their action, but the Austrians poured out self-pity and explanations. Like all deserters, they said that every single one of their former comrades was anxious to desert and would surrender immediately if attacked. After spending an hour or two under the stairs of the Doll's House, with a cup of tea and a lump of bully, they were taken up to the O.P. and invited to point out their old positions. Only one man refused to do so ; he was a Pole who said he was not going to betray anyone, even a German. He was the only deserter the Battalion felt any sympathy for.

Both sides shelled each other as best they could. The Division's own artillery was deployed behind the Battalion, and whenever the Gunner officers thought that their teams needed practice, which was frequently, they shelled Recce Ridge. They made neat lists of the enemy posts found by patrols or given away by the deserters and pasted them regularly. It was alarming for an infantryman to see the pains the Gunners took to work out the time at which the troops opposite should be having their breakfast. The German gunners, for their part, favoured tea-time. There was usually a scattered morning delivery, but every afternoon about four o'clock

No. 3 Company, Battalion H.Q. and the area behind it received a steady shelling for a half an hour or so. It was so regular that appointments were made for "after the tea-time stonk." Most of the shells landed on No. 3 Company's forward platoon and on the track between the farm and the Doll's House. The platoon was always in its slit trenches, and nobody lingered on the track so that there were remarkably few casualties, only one of them fatal. Guardsman Hurley, of No. 3 Company, was badly wounded in the stomach. The doctor's report said of him : "This Guardsman, due to excellent treatment given him by Guardsman Harrison, was in good condition considering the length of time he lay in the open until he could be treated by the M.O. and evacuated to dressing station for a blood transfusion," but Hurley died a week later. Sergeant Maquire and Lance-Corporal Brough, the Regimental Policemen, and Lance-Corporal Piggott, a piper, were slightly wounded ; Guardsman Bowen, a young pioneer, was badly wounded in the leg.

The greatest misfortune of this period was self-inflicted. On the night of the 26th the Commanding Officer, the Adjutant and Lieutenant R. D. N. Young of the Anti-Tank Platoon, with Guardsmen Doyle and Dowding, were blown up on our own mines. It was a pitch-black night, raining slightly, and they were coming back from a round tour of inspection, riding in one of the anti-tank gun portees. Their last call was on a new anti-tank gun position in front of No. 2 Company, and they turned for Battalion H.Q. down a track leading past the company. This track could not be used by day for it was in full view of the Germans, but the company kept a patrol on it by night. They knew this, and drove very slowly, with Lieutenant Young standing on the running board beside Colonel Scott and the driver. The portee went up on a "necklace" of Hawkins grenades. The only one left conscious was Colonel Scott ; he stopped the shooting which followed the explosion and ran to the R.A.P. for the ambulance. The driver found Lieutenant D. Young in the ditch covered with small wounds. The other three were in the back of the portee, their legs broken and mangled. They never said a word, even when their legs had to be straightened to get them out of the wreckage. Lieutenant Young eventually returned to the Battalion, his back like a nutmeg grater, to be killed in Italy ; the other three were out of action for good. Doyle and Dowding could be consoled by the thought of going home, but not Captain Mungo Park. He had worked and hoped to be a regular soldier and this wretched accident wiped out his past and destroyed his future. He left Dublin in 1939 to enlist as a Guardsman, falsifying his age to do so. At the Depot he was called "the Boy," and "Boy Park"—not eligible for man's privileges—he remained even after he became Adjutant. He was really happy in Medjez, bursting with energy, and keenly looking forward to going into action with the Battalion. The Adjutant is supposed to be the best-hated man in a battalion, but it was not possible to hate, or even formally dislike, Mungo Park. His high spirits were infectious, for nobody could resist his peculiar combination of a "dead regimental" officer and a schoolboy out on a treat. "I am miserable about poor Mungo," wrote Colonel Scott, and so was the whole Battalion. His was one of the uncounted tragedies of the war. For years he swung himself round on sticks, in and out of hospitals, but nothing could mend his foot and at last he resigned himself to becoming a miller. Lieutenant Desmond Fitzgerald became Adjutant in his place, and Lieutenant Dennis Madden Intelligence Officer.

During its first week at Medjez the Battalion had not much time for the outside world. It got the news from the B.B.C. that the Eighth Army had attacked the Mareth Line and learnt from Brigade that the 1st Division had taken over the whole Medjez area—the 78th Division and the 1st Guards Brigade being withdrawn to prepare for some attack in the north—but it remained untouched till the 26th. That morning Lieutenant Synge, after washing and shaving like a cat in a mess tin of water, telephoned the usual message to Brigade: "Situation unchanged. Patrol reports on their way by D.R." Instead of a grunt of acknowledgment he got the reply, "Stand by for a galaxy of Sunrays," which he interpreted to Colonel Scott, "There are some generals coming to see us." About midday a string of beflagged jeeps tore down the track and decanted the hierarchy of V Corps into the Doll's House—the G.O.C., Lieut.-General Allfrey, the Divisional Commander, the Brigadier, and the C.R.A., the Chief Gunner of the Division. It began as a social call, with introductions and polite enquiries about the health and the comfort of the Battalion, but the officers eyed the C.R.A. with suspicion, for such men do not normally visit infantry battalions. Colonel Scott called for wine, and Sergeant Bates lugged in a jerrican which Father Brookes had just got from Thibar monastery. The wine tasted slightly of petrol, for the jerricans were not water tins as Father Brookes had thought—only Father Brookes did not know this as he never drank it himself, and nobody had the heart to tell him. After the wine, which was quite good, petrol and all, the Corps Commander described the general situation. The Eighth Army, in the south, was nearly through the Mareth Line, but the

Germans were still fighting stubbornly there while they prepared a new position north of Gabes. The First Army was set to attack a sector in the north which the Germans had stripped of troops to reinforce the south. If the Germans wished to send any more reinforcements to the south or to re-stock the north at short notice, they must turn to Medjez, "and that," said the Corps Commander, "is where you come in."

"The Corps Commander has ordered us to attack Recce Ridge with the idea of destroying as many Germans as possible, making them think it is part of a big attack and making certain that troops from here cannot go to Rommel's help in the south. The whole attack is laid on by Division, supervised by the Divisional Commander himself and in detail by our own Brigadier, with the C.R.A. in charge of the artillery. As you will see, this is a big set-up when the only troops involved are a company and a few carriers and mortars. The job is a hazardous one, but the Brigadier wishes us to succeed in the first thing we are told to do. The enemy are strong in fire power—machine guns and mortars—but we will be supported by two field regiments, two batteries of mediums and two batteries of heavy guns, no mean force and the heaviest support, I suppose, a company has ever had." Those were the orders Colonel Scott passed to the company commanders. In short, one company was to make a raid disguised as a full-scale attack, to impress the Germans. Captain John Kennedy was enthusiastic, but the other three, who were older, did not like it. "It was a nasty sort of job," wrote Captain Powell-Edwards afterwards, "which entailed an advance across the valley in the dark, a climb up the slope, a battle on the ridge and then a withdrawal in daylight across the valley again. Well, there it was—but who was going to take it ?" It took No. 2 Company. The Intelligence Officer brought the decision to Major Bucknill that evening. It was raining hard, and he crawled into the low bivouac where Major Bucknill and Captain Egan lay steaming like two great bears in hibernation. "Jim," said Major Bucknill, "our whisky ration is in one of my boots. Fish it out and we'll drink to the Company. Back for breakfast and no bones broken."

Breakfast in Battalion H.Q. the next morning, the 27th, was a gloomy meal. Captain Mungo Park was gone, Colonel Scott was quite silent, and Lieutenant Desmond Fitzgerald, the new Adjutant, and Dennis Madden, the new Intelligence Officer, sat brooding over maps and a large watercolour panorama of Recce Ridge made by Guardsman Fox. The Adjutant had already written the "Intention" paragraph of the operation order : "No. 2 Company will kill or capture all enemy in area 'Three Re-entrants'." Then Major Bucknill came in. "What are the Three Re-entrants?" he asked. The Adjutant drew a crude sketch. "It is where the Germans live."

"What about the Sugar Loaf?" "We'll have to neutralize that somehow." In the course of the day each of the higher commanders returned to see, amend and approve the plan of attack. The objective, and the approach to it, were already fixed—one by the Corps Commander and the other by nature—so that part of the plan was

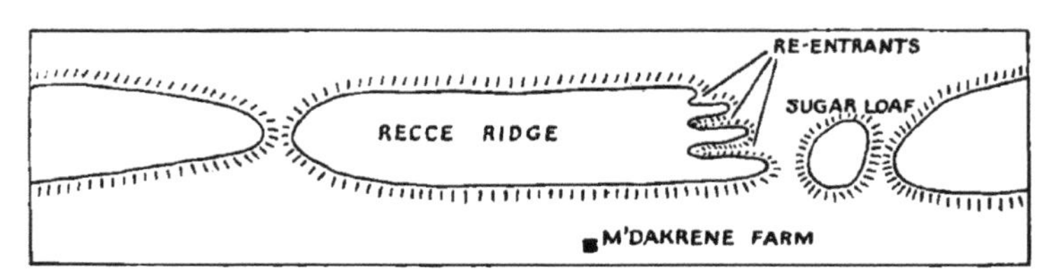

simple. The success of the operation depended on three other elements—surprise, accurate timing and the isolation by gunfire of the Germans to be attacked. The C.R.A. and his staff produced a "Divisional Artillery Task Table" as intricate and precise as a Bradshaw, and detailed two Gunner officers with wireless and signal lamps to go out with Major Bucknill in case anything should go wrong. The Company was timed to reach the base of the ridge at about three o'clock in the morning. It was to climb half-way up the slope and lie there till 5.30 a.m. From 4.30 onwards the field guns were to shoot general harassing fire on to the top of the ridge—nothing alarming, but enough to discourage any German from leaving his trench to walk about the forward slope. At 5.30 a.m. the Company was to start climbing again, slowly and quietly, one platoon, called the Fire Platoon, going slightly ahead of the others. The platoons should time their climb to arrive just below the crest of the ridge by 6 a.m. Dawn was due punctually and suddenly at six o'clock. Equally punctually at six o'clock all the guns were to fire an intense concentration on the top of the ridge for ten minutes. Under that concentration the fire platoon was to reach the top and install itself. At 6.10 a.m., by which time it would be light enough to see, the concentration would lift by stages and scatter on to the re-entrants in the rear, the Sugar Loaf, and the flanks, and the two assault platoons, covered by the fire platoon, were to sweep over the top of the ridge. The quicker the job was done the better. When they had finished, a series of white flares would bring down smoke from the guns to cover their withdrawal. The carriers and mortars would move out to M'Dakrene farm at dawn to see the Company home. The ambulance would be waiting on the Beja road.

On the 29th No. 2 Company changed places with No. 1 and retired into the Happy Valley for the day. They checked the guns and filled the magazines with new, clean ammunition, drew a bandolier of fifty rounds and primed two grenades each, discarded their battle-dress jackets and put on cardigans instead, tied their personal belongings in sandbags with a label, padded their steel helmets so that they would not clatter, blackened the brass of their equipment and their faces. The two gunners, Captain D. Bethell of the 19th Field Regiment, and Captain Whitehead of the 138th Field Regiment, joined them with their wirelesses and signallers and went through the plan once again with Major Bucknill. Captain Egan, Lieutenant Askin, the three sergeants and the ten men who were "left out of battle," did the housekeeping while the others sat around in their greatcoats. At eleven o'clock the Quartermaster brought them an enormous meal to keep them warm, as he said, in the early hours. Major Bucknill had dinner in the Doll's House. He said he was quite happy, and indeed no sign of misgivings appeared on his kind, cheerful face or in his one good eye.

At midnight Lieutenant Nunn and five pioneers, armed to the teeth, went out with a mine detector and swept a stretch of the Beja road and the track leading to M'Dakrene. They found three Teller mines on the track, recently laid and hurriedly covered with fresh soil of a colour different to the surface. The mines were not booby-trapped, and the pioneers extracted them easily enough. Corporal Freeman returned to Battalion H.Q. with the mines, which he put on the table, and a message that the carriers would be all right so long as they stuck to the track. The rest stayed out all night to keep the track open and to watch M'Dakrene.

At 1 a.m. on 30th March No. 2 Company filed down the track past the Doll's House and through No. 3 Company. It had not rained all day, and it was a clear, cold night lit only by the stars. A sharp wind blew across the valley from the ridge. No. 11 Platoon went by led by Lieutenant Colin Lesslie; then came Major Bucknill with C.S.M. Ferguson ("the Skipper"), Lance-Corporal Fildes, carrying the Company's wireless, and Captain Bethell, R.A., with his signallers; after them came No. 10 and No. 12 Platoons. Lieutenant Tony Rochford, commanding No. 12 Platoon, brought up the rear; he waved cheerfully as he disappeared into the dark. Half an hour later Captain Kennedy reported that No. 2 Company was all across the Beja road and that there was not a sound to be heard.

About five o'clock Colonel Scott, with field-glasses the size of hock bottles, and the Brigadier went up to the observation post under the Hurricane. The Adjutant and the Signal Officer were there already with the control set. They could say that the Company was all right so far, because Corporal Fildes had been sending a regular tuning call—a faint whisper—"Paddy two, Paddy two." At half-past five Corporal Fildes spoke at last, "Sunray for Sunray," and Colonel Scott snatched the spare headphones from Lieutenant Synge. Sam Bucknill's voice was conversational. "No trouble so far. We dodged two patrols on the way over. We are more than half-way up the slope and have been for some time. It is much steeper from now on. Colin will start climbing again in a few minutes. Have the guns got one up the spout ? So long. Over." "All set here. Good luck, Sam. Off." Fifteen minutes ticked slowly by on the watch propped up in front of the O.P. The irregular harassing fire continued monotonously like maroons as it had done for the past hour—bang bang ! pause, bang ! pause, bang, bang, bang ! pause. A thin crackle drifted across the valley. "Listen." It came again, louder and longer. "My God ! M.Gs." "And grenades. Listen." "And mortars. Look." Short flashes burst on the hillside and faint white pillars of smoke appeared against the dark background. Suddenly Major Bucknill came up on the air. "I want support on the eastern edge, now." The F.O.O. must also have been calling to his guns at the same time, for a troop behind the farm immediately shot a short concentration. The noise of the shell bursts rolled away, but the crackle of small arms continued. It was just beginning to get light, and then with a violent crash the barrage came down on Recce Ridge.

After ten minutes there was a break in the gunfire while the barrage lifted to the rear of the ridge. Through their glasses the observers could see dots moving on the crest of the ridge ; there were very few of them, and they soon disappeared. The wirelesses were quite dead, and nobody could see the flicker of a lamp or a Very light. For an hour the guns fired their set tasks. The unnatural silence which followed was cut by the short tapping of Brens and the long, hysterical whir-r of Spandaus. There was still no call for artillery support, no signal for smoke. In the O.P. the Brigadier was tugging his moustache while Colonel Scott never took his eyes from his glasses. "What can be happening, Andrew ?" As if in answer Colonel Scott shouted "Here they come. Oh, thank God ! Well done !" Small groups of men came over the top, joined each other and split apart again as mortar bursts puffed up between them. They trickled down the slope, halted and turned back. The firing increased, and now the Spandaus drowned the Brens. More groups came round the side of the hill and disappeared into the dark undergrowth. There was firing on the top and bottom of the ridge, but the middle was dead. Colonel Scott called for smoke and the guns started again, raining canisters on the ridge. The fall of smoke brought a wild outburst of firing, but it died away as the wind dispersed the cloud into wisps. All along the line of its position the Battalion watched and listened. The firing on the ridge became irregular. There was no sound of Brens now, only isolated rifle shots answered by the faint rattle of Schmeisser machine-pistols. "It's all over now, one way or the other," said Colonel Scott. "Keep up the smoke as long as possible." He ordered Captain Rawlinson's little force back from M'Dakrene and sent Lieutenant McInerney and two detachments of mortars out on the left to help the men of No. 2 Company on their return journey. "They will be coming back by sections, if at all." It was half-past eight.

Five wounded men came back on the left—Sergeant Deazley, Sergeant Mears, Guardsman McCafferty and two gunners, and were picked up by Lieutenant McInerney. Two unwounded men came in later on that night, Guardsmen Mills and Cox. That was all out of 103 officers and men.

The German gunners had put down defensive fire as soon as they heard what was happening on Recce Ridge. Apart from the base of the ridge, their main targets were the area of M'Dakrene, the Beja road and No. 3 Company. Captain Kennedy, Major Gordon-Watson, M.C., and Guardsman O'Shea, D.C.M., his servant, were caught in the barn to which Major Gordon-Watson had brought them to get a closer view of the battle. Kennedy and O'Shea were wounded; Major Gordon-Watson, who was lying between them, was untouched. M'Dakrene got a severe battering. The Bren carriers and the two mortar carriers joined Lieutenant Nunn near the farm at about 6 a.m. Captain Rawlinson, in the leading carrier, turned into a gully and dismounted the Bren gun, after which Lance-Corporal Lumley drove the carrier farther up the gully. Sergeant Hughes, in the second carrier, dismounted his gun and crew and had gone scarcely ten yards from the carrier when it got a direct hit from a shell which killed the driver, Guardsman Ditchfield. The mortar carriers then moved up to put down a smoke screen in front of the farm. The first one was blown up on two mines; the explosion killed Sergeant McCarthy, wounded Guardsman Lang and Guardsman Curran, a Bren gunner, who was lying on the ground near by, and overturned the carrier so that Guardsman Rice, the driver, was pinned underneath by his legs. Simultaneously a machine-gun from the farm buildings opened fire on them. Lieutenant Nunn and Sergeant Hughes tried to lift the carrier off Guardsman Rice while Captain Rawlinson covered them with a Bren, but they could not do it. Sergeant Englishby got his mortar into action and, under cover of its smoke, Lance-Corporal Lumley brought his carrier back to help. As this carrier was passing the wreck of Sergeant McCarthy's carrier it, too, was blown up and Lance-Corporal Lumley was killed. Captain Rawlinson collected the wounded and ordered the three remaining carriers back to the line of the railway. Then he and Lieutenant Nunn extricated the surviving men on foot out of the little valley of desolation. Guardsman Rice had to stay there, but they surrounded him with water-bottles and cigarettes, and he said cheerfully that he would be all right. A few hours later Captain Barnes, Drill-Sergeant Kenny and Sergeant Thorogood drove out in the ambulance to rescue Rice. They parked the ambulance at the gates of M'Dakrene and took out a large jack and the surgical kit. Six Germans jumped through the hedge and ran round them, saying "Prisoner." Captain Barnes and Sergeant Thorogood paid no attention, but went on sorting their knives and needles ; Drill-Sergeant Kenny glared at them and told them to "fall out." A German officer and more men appeared. Captain Barnes explained what he wanted in a mixture of German, French and English, while Drill-Sergeant Kenny hurriedly shut the doors of the ambulance because he had just remembered that there was a Bren gun inside. The German officer marched his men over to the gully where Rice lay smoking and singing to himself. The Germans heaved up the carrier and Rice was freed. Captain Barnes then said good-bye firmly and drove home. "The Germans were young, 17 to 20, pale, not sunburnt like our Guardsmen," says the War Diary. "Their appearance confirms the reports of deserters that they lie up all day in deep dugouts in farms and villages. Identification of our Regiment was almost certainly secured."

The Battalion sat up all night in the hope that more men of No. 2 Company would come home. But only two came—Guardsman Ayres, who was wounded, and Guardsman Potts, unwounded. No more than seven ever returned from Recce Ridge till after the war. Of the ninety-six men reported as missing nineteen were killed, including Major Bucknill and Lieutenant Rochford, and more than half were wounded, including Lieutenant Lesslie, C.S.M. Ferguson and every N.C.O. The accounts of the six survivors were naturally confined to the events immediately around them. A German C.S.M. gave himself up that evening, but he could only describe a confused mêlée on the top of the hill, which he did not like, and so left. For the full story the Battalion had to wait.

"Unfortunately the Germans were expecting us," wrote Lieutenant Colin Lesslie after he had escaped from a prisoner-of-war camp. German prisoners, taken later, said that they had been expecting an attack on Recce Ridge for the past ten days. Their posts were changed every night, and they had a reserve company standing by for an immediate counter-attack round the side of the ridge. On this night they had two platoons entrenched on the forward slope. Captain Bethell, R.A., also escaped from prison camp. "The fact that did stand out," he wrote, "was that the Company fought in a manner beyond praise. The leading platoon bumped a section post near the top of the hill. It opened fire at once and a number of others joined in. Lieutenant Lesslie rushed this post, but was himself wounded and his platoon held up. He sent a message to Major Bucknill that either a left flank or a right flank movement would probably deal with the situation. Major Bucknill ordered Lieutenant Rochford's platoon, No. 12, to the right flank and called for gun fire to help him. All three platoons succeeded in reaching the top and waited for zero hour. The enemy caused heavy casualties with stick grenades, but No. 12 Platoon eliminated two section posts with hand grenades and bayonets." As No. 11 Platoon was coming up on the left of No. 10, Major Bucknill shouted to Guardsman Potts to get Lieutenant Rochford up from No. 12 Platoon to take command of No. 10, as Lieutenant Lesslie had been wounded. "At zero hour the concentration arrived," continued Captain Bethell, "also a concentration on the Company from eight enemy mortars. This caused casualties to the Company H.Q. and the Gunner parties and destroyed all our wirelesses. When the concentration lifted the platoons on the left and right went in to the attack and tried to reach the enemy posts dug in on the reverse slope. They were picked off as they became silhouetted against the sky. One Guardsman in particular carried out the assault in a very gallant manner, advancing on the enemy with a Bren gun on the hip. The attack went on in spite of the fact that the Company Commander and one platoon commander were killed and the other officer, Lieutenant Lesslie, was already wounded. The remainder of the Company engaged the enemy continuously though under heavy mortar fire and machine-gun fire from both flanks and rear." Major Bucknill led the attack on the right, Lieutenant Rochford the attack on the left, leaving the wounded Lieutenant Lesslie in charge of the fire platoon. They were both killed. Lance-Sergeant Mears and Guardsman Ayres of No. 11 Platoon were behind Major Bucknill as he led the rush down into the first re-entrant gully. The two of them were wounded, and the last they, or anybody, saw of Major Bucknill was a glimpse of him charging on, firing a Tommy gun.

"The Company found themselves completely surrounded," wrote Lieutenant Lesslie. "Heavy small-arms, mortar and artillery fire was put down on the Company, and casualties were heavy. The only hope was to hold on until our own artillery put down smoke to enable us to get out." The remnants of No. 11 and No. 12 Platoons came back out of the gully to join No. 10 on the top of the hill. For an hour they held the top while Lance-Corporal Fildes and the other signallers flashed their lamps. But nothing could be seen at Battalion H.Q. The wounded crawled down the slope to a little hollow in the hillside where C.S.M. Ferguson and the stretcher-bearers did what they could. An hour's steady firing all but exhausted the ammunition. Lieutenant Lesslie ordered what was left of the Company to get away down the hill as best they could while the Bren gunners, and himself, stayed at the top to cover them. "The Platoon Sergeant and the N.C.Os. of No. 11 Platoon," he said, "were all either killed or wounded. Guardsman Horan was the only Bren gunner of this platoon left. In order to get a better field of fire he stood up and fired magazine after magazine from the hip, in spite of my shouts at him to get down. He continued to stand on the top of the ridge while the Company was thinning out behind him, and by some miracle he was not hit. After the action was over and I had been taken prisoner a German officer asked me whether 'the soldier who had been standing up all the time was still all right.' I was glad to be able to say he was. Guardsman Horan was taken prisoner with the remainder of the Company who survived. The Germans were already at the bottom of the hill, and as smoke could not be brought down, there was no way of escape."

The German Corps commander, Major-General Weber, issued a special Order of the Day: "Encouraged by his successes achieved against the Manteuffel Division, the enemy believed on 30th March, 1943, that he could attack elements of this Corps Group with impunity. His attacks on the positions of the 756 Mountain Regiment were not only severely repulsed but, in the counter-thrust carried out by III Battalion, 756 Mountain Regiment, eighty prisoners were taken. I heartily congratulate the Mountain Battalion and expect that all elements of the Corps Group will come up to the standard of this Battalion when the time comes. For the rest we are only waiting for the moment which brings the order to attack to show the enemy the stuff we German soldiers are made of. Heil Hitler." While the Germans were preening themselves the Battalion replaced the lost company. There were about ninety Irish Guards first-line reinforcements in a camp near Algiers. "It takes such a hell of a time to get them up," wrote Colonel Scott, and until they arrived a company of Grenadiers filled the gap. On the 5th of April Captain John Fitzgerald marched over the hill with sixty men ; they were battered and travel-stained, but very relieved to find any of the Battalion left at all after the rumours they had gathered on their journey. Lieutenant Dodds brought the rest of the men two days later, and by the evening of the 7th the Battalion had a brand new No. 2 Company in position, but no reinforcements left in Africa.

The new No. 2 Company was just in time to see Recce Ridge captured by the 11th Brigade of the 78th Division. The Battalion had a grandstand view of the battle, and Lieutenant D. Madden reported its progress in the ***Sanderstead Echo***, the daily news-sheet issued by the Intelligence Section. "In the early hours of this morning, the 7th, the 78th Division crossed the Medjez–Beja road well to our left in a drive to capture Toukabeur and Chaouach. The first objective for the 11th Brigade is Point 512, the cone-shaped hill to the left (west) of Recce Ridge. At 0350 hrs. 150 guns opened fire and kept up a bombardment for well over an hour on Point 343, the hill lying against Point 512. From then on machine-gun fire has been gradually approaching the hill. This operation naturally had its repercussions on us. No. 3 Company submitted manfully to spasmodic mortaring. A number of patrols went out to give warning of any counter-attack and to capture a prisoner, if possible, as there have been rumours of fresh troops arriving on Recce Ridge." The *Echo* of the 8th reported that the attack was going well. "The Northamptons, the battalion on our immediate left, had difficulty in capturing Point 343 and suffered considerable casualties. Last night was quiet. Occasionally mortar bombs fell on us. Apart from this, a few Very lights, odd sounds of rifle fire or bursts of M.G. fire were all that disturbed the stillness of the night. At 0600 the bombardment of Point 512 began. Between 0600 and 0700 hrs. the 19th Field Regiment alone fired 2,500 shells. Shortly after the shelling ceased infantry could be seen on the near side of Point 512 making their way to the top. They disappeared from view near the summit. A few of our tanks could be seen lower down. It is reported that about 0800 hrs. the Germans hoisted a white flag and surrendered Point 512. From about 1000 hrs. onwards our troops were seen advancing towards the west end of Recce Ridge. The position at midday seems to be that the left battalion of the 11th Brigade is attacking Toukabeur, while the troops on the right are clearing Recce Ridge." The Northamptons, supported by Churchill tanks, finally took Recce Ridge from the flank and rear at midday on the 9th. The Germans withdrew their mortars and anti-tank guns early in the morning and left their infantry to fight it out. The 756 Mountain Regiment was quite prepared to face men, but threw up their hands as soon as the Churchill tanks appeared. "Farther north the operation has gone equally successfully," reported the *Sanderstead Echo*. "The result of the battle has been the elimination of the salient which protruded westwards into our front. The Germans have withdrawn to the line of Longstop Hill, Chassert and Grich el Oued, in front of Medjez."

The Battalion received what was in effect the drill order, "Change direction right. Right form." The line now ran northward from Medjez instead of westward, but there was nothing between the Scots Guards in the outskirts of the town and the 11th Brigade in the hills round Chaouach. The Battalion therefore swung right on the pivot of No. 4 Company's position and put half its strength into Sidi Naceur. No. 1 and No. 4 Company, with sections of mortars, anti-tank guns and sappers, some Bofors anti-aircraft guns and a private medical unit under Captain A. D. F. O'Neill—all commanded by Major H. L. S. Young—moved quietly out on the night of 9th April. Their orders contained one piece of advice: "There will no doubt be anti-personnel mines. The Germans have a careless habit of leaving the covers lying by the roadside. Anyone who sees these covers will realize that he is near a minefield and step warily." The only casualty was No. 4 Company's three-tonner which, loaded to the springs with petrol, ammunition, blankets and cooks, went up on an ordinary mine in the middle of the plain. It made the best single fire ever seen, proved the agility of the cooks, who all jumped clear, provided an irrefutable explanation of any missing equipment for months, and gave every man in the company a fresh start, as all the conduct sheets were destroyed. "Young Force," as it was called, lived peacefully in Sidi Naceur for ten days, troubled only by occasional shells from Longstop and voracious fleas from the Arab huts.

CHAPTER IV

The Final Offensive

THE best description of General Alexander's plan for the final assault is, naturally enough, in his own despatch. "My object was to complete the destruction of the forces still opposing me as quickly as possible in order to obtain the use of the ports of Tunis and Bizerta for the invasion of Sicily. The enemy positions presented to us two fronts at right-angles facing west and south. I decided, for topographical reasons, to make my main attack on the western face of this perimeter. My intention was to break through to Tunis and thereby split the enemy forces in two. I would then leave the smaller body of enemy to the north to be mopped up by the Allied troops on the spot and, turning south with the greater part of my forces, drive the larger body of enemy on the right flank of the penetration against the line firmly held by the Eighth Army. It was particularly important in carrying out this manœuvre to prevent the enemy establishing himself in the peninsula terminating in Cape Bon, where he might have been able to hold out for some time. I ordered General Anderson to prepare a large-scale offensive to capture Tunis. I informed him that I was placing IX Corps under his command and that II Corps (U.S.) would simultaneously be attacking Bizerta. I indicated that the area for the main attack by V and IX Corps, with four infantry and two armoured divisions, would be on the front from Medjez el Bab to north of Bou Arada, with V Corps attacking north-east on the axis Medjez–Massicault and IX Corps on a parallel axis." The Medjez–Massicault road, the main road to Tunis from the west, "was the most direct route and gave the best opportunities for the use of tanks ; we had fought all winter for our foothold at its gate. For these very reasons, however, the enemy defences were here at their strongest. The final plan was worked out in the following form : The Eighth Army was to start its (holding) attack on the night of 19th-20th April. The First Army was to attack on the 22nd April. IX Corps would begin in the early morning with the 46th Division and the 1st and 6th Armoured Divisions. V Corps would attack in the evening with the 1st and 4th Divisions south of the river, directed on Massicault and the 78th Division in the mountains north of the river with 'Longstop' as their first objective. II Corps' (U.S.) attack was timed for the next day, 23rd April."

The enemy commander, General von Arnim, still had over 200,000 troops to hold a front of 120 miles. General Messe's Army, mixed German and Italian, held the southern front. The German Afrika Korps held the angle between the two fronts. The order of battle of Von Værst's 5th Panzer Army on the west was relatively unchanged. The Manteuffel Division was in the northernmost sector, then 334 Division in the mountains north of the Medjerda and 999 Africa Division, now almost complete, astride the river. In the area of V and IX Corps was the Hermann Goering Division, reinforced with additional infantry and tanks, including part of a very recently arrived heavy tank battalion. As soon as Messe was back on his Enfidaville line, von Arnim removed the 10th Panzer Division, still his strongest armoured formation, and transferred it to the area between Sebkret and the Medjerda. "This was clearly the most threatened point, and it was vital to have an armoured reserve to cover the plain of Tunis," writes General Alexander. "It was, however, the only reserve that Army Group Africa had, and it is a little surprising that von Arnim made no effort to create a larger one by shortening his line at less important points. Nor did he attempt to construct any defensive systems in rear of his present line, except for some not very impressive perimeter defences round Tunis." The enemy had no intention of evacuating Tunisia, but was, on the contrary, using every possible means to rush in reinforcements. On the 18th April, for instance, Allied fighters intercepted off Cape Bon a large flight of German transport aircraft carrying troops and shot down fifty of them.

Before the armoured divisions could break through to Tunis the infantry had to punch a hole through the German defences in front of Medjez. The brief "Information—Own Troops" paragraph of the Battalion's operation order sets out the arrangements for this opening phase of the offensive: "V Corps is attacking with 1st Division in the centre; 1st Division is attacking with 2nd Infantry Brigade on the right, 24th Guards Brigade on the left and 3rd Infantry Brigade in reserve. 24th Guards Brigade is attacking with 1st Scots Guards on right, 5th Grenadier Guards on the left and 1st Irish

Guards in reserve." This meant in effect that the 24th Guards Brigade was to clear the right bank of the River Medjerda and the "Bou," which rose out of it to dominate the road to Massicault. The Brigade was to start from a system of gullies called Tella Sefra, marked on the map in front of Medjez and Grenadier Hill, and the Brigadier ordered the Battalion to secure these gullies beforehand. On the 18th April No. 3 Company, under Captain R. H. Prendegast, joined the 5th Grenadiers on their hill and from there went out to find Tella Sefra. The 1st Bn. The Duke of Wellington's Regiment was deployed on Banana Ridge, which covered the area between Grenadier Hill and Medjez. Behind these two battalions—Grenadiers and Dukes—the infantry and guns of the 1st Division rolled into assembly positions.

On the night of the 19th April the Battalion handed over Diar el Hammar to K.S.L.I. and marched away down the track past the White House. The mud of a month ago was now as hard as brick and powdering into dust. It passed Baharine Farm with its dressing station and graveyard, crossed the Medjerda by the "Forth Bridge"—the first long Bailey erected by the Sappers in Tunisia, and a favourite target of the Germans—and marched towards the base of Grenadier Hill. Support group and the transport stopped at a little farm off the main road. The companies tramped on to a long, dry wadi, where they were to kick their heels and pass the time as best they could for forty-eight hours. No. 3 Company, meanwhile, had found a route to Tella Sefra. That night Sergeant Maher took out a special patrol of Grenadiers, under a Lieutenant Frederick, to choose "forming-up" places for their battalion. With them and in Sergeant Maher's special care went a Tank officer, the forerunner of a brigade of Churchill tanks which was being unloaded at Bône. Part of this brigade was to go straight into action in support of the Grenadiers, and the officer had posted ahead to find "tank runs" through the gullies out into the open plain. He was a man of peculiar importance and of a high "security" value, for the Churchills were to be a complete surprise to the Germans. The patrol reached Tella Sefra safely, found a way out of the gullies and went on into the plain. The tank officer declared himself satisfied and the patrol turned for home. Lieutenant Frederick was leading, Sergeant Maher, the tank officer and a corporal brought up the rear. A German fighting patrol cut straight into them. Lieutenant Frederick was killed, the centre of the patrol scattered into the gullies, and the tail was left out in the plain, on the wrong side of the Germans. The tank officer, fresh from England, thought the game was up, and said so. Sergeant

Maher, now in his second war and third campaign, took control. "My orders, sir, are not to let the Germans get you." They crawled away through the tall hay, lay up all day, and the next night Sergeant Maher returned with his charge, rather tired and very thirsty, but unidentified.

A jumbled line of low hills stretched across the front from Grich el Oued on the banks of the Medjerda nine miles eastward to the Massicault road. They were the outworks of the massive "Bou" which lay four miles behind them, and it was from them that an attack on the "Bou" itself would have to be launched. The Brigade plan, therefore, was to secure this line of hills by "a night attack supported by artillery followed by daylight exploitation supported by tanks and artillery." The Battalion was in reserve for the night attack, and its role depended entirely on the course of events. If all went well, it was to pass through the Grenadier and Scots Guards and capture some isolated hills nearer the "Bou." The only thing the Battalion had to do on the 20th was to lay a telephone wire to Brigade H.Q. and carry the rations and water across half a mile of rough ground. The platoon commanders read out the orders for the attack, repeating the notes which Colonel Scott had added: "(1) The usual German practice is to allow their forward troops to be overrun and then to counter-attack violently before we have consolidated. (2) When the Battalion is co-operating with tanks, wounded men lying in such places as cornfields are liable to be run over; a wounded man, or his nearest comrade, must stick his rifle by the bayonet into the ground beside him; hang a helmet on it if you can. (3) All enemy anti-tank guns fire H.E. (4) Water supply will be difficult. It may not be possible for every man to have his water-bottle filled every day."

The dark came down to end a dull day. Sergeant Bates was very late with Battalion H.Q. dinner—"the road was blocked with tanks and guns"—and it was half-past ten before they got their tin plate of stew and mug of lukewarm tea. Into the middle of this unappetizing meal slid Major McBarnet of the Scots Guards. "There is a big flap on. Brigade could not get you on the telephone. The Hermann Goering boys have attacked us first." It was the last and best-timed demonstration of the tactics that had become traditional in Tunisia, the spoiling attack.

The Battalion repaired its telephone line and waited for more news. "At about two o'clock in the morning," wrote Colonel Scott, "the reports became pretty serious. The infantry of the Hermann Goering Division had come across Banana Ridge, cutting through the

Duke of Wellingtons and had captured most of the 19th Field Regiment's guns which were right forward behind the ridge. The Grenadiers were engaging the enemy from their localities. Our own No. 3 Company was isolated, but Captain Prendegast reported that there was no immediate threat of attack on him, only a certain amount of shelling and mortaring which, although unpleasant, had not yet caused any casualties. Shortly afterwards tanks were reported to be mustering on the Goubellat plain to the south, and I was ordered to move the Battalion as quickly as possible on to the hill Djebel Touila, covering Medjez." Touila lay to the right of Grenadier Hill and slightly behind it in the middle of a wide gap through which a main road led in from the Goubellat plain. The Battalion was in position between four and five o'clock, with Nos. 1 and 4 Companies on the hill and No. 2 Company at its foot on the Goubellat road "with the task of destroying any enemy infantry that venture into the open," which Captain J. B. Fitzgerald passed on to the company as "If you see a German, shoot him." The Adjutant went back to wake up the transport and to bring the anti-tank guns and machine guns up to Touila. When he returned Lieutenant Madden hugged and pounded him. "I am glad to see you. We thought you were gone. A Guardsman said he left you in the farmyard firing into a crowd of Germans until they jumped on you." "Those were not Germans," said the Adjutant when he had recovered. "They were some Bofors gunners who thought they were urgently needed in Teboursouk. I was a bit abusive, but I did not actually fire. Tell Colonel Andrew that Drill-Sergeant Rooney has them down below and that they are now very keen to try out their Bofors against tanks."

As dawn broke on the 21st the Battalion heard the clank and clatter of tanks—a noise like chains dragged across asphalt. The Brigade Commander had gone back to meet the Churchills on their transporters and had rushed them across country into a "hull down" position in front of Touila. "A masterly stroke," wrote Colonel Scott. "We then watched what could be called a school solution battle." The Germans attacked with a regiment of infantry supported by tanks. "The Grenadiers and No. 3 Company held their localities, pounding the enemy with fire. Our heavy armour was waiting for the German tanks and created havoc among them." The Churchills were posted like a line of sentries behind a slight slope, and the Battalion could see the flash and hear the heavy thump of their guns. Solid shot from the German tanks streamed over the slope and slapped into the hillside. "Very exciting it was," admitted Captain Powell-Edwards, "to see them belting away at each other not much farther off than you could kick the garden roller." The Battalion's anti-tank guns and the Bofors joined in, claiming hit after hit. The messages from No. 3 Company were jubilant. The Battalion saw and heard the Grenadiers' machine guns firing steadily as they cut the German infantry to ribbons. The surviving battery of the 19th Field Regiment meanwhile had been shelling its own guns to stop the Germans taking them away. At about nine o'clock the Germans called off the attack. They retreated across Banana Ridge, urged on their way by the Dukes. The gunners recaptured all their guns, some rather battered, and everything was the same as it had been twenty-four hours before. The Battalion later saw the German orders for this attack—Operation "Lilacblossom." "They committed five battalions of infantry and seventy tanks to smash their way into Medjez. The minefield which protected the main position had been lifted the previous night to let our own tanks through, otherwise the German tanks would have run straight into it. At the time we thought that the Germans must have known that this minefield had been removed, but since reading their orders I see that it was a lucky stroke just hitting the day the mines were lifted. If they had got through to Medjez there was nothing to stop them rolling down the main road to Teboursouk ; they would have created havoc in our lines of communication and put back our attack for an unknown period. The factor which saved the day was the brilliant timing of Brigadier Colvin in getting the Churchill tanks into position at first light across unknown country."

The Battalion spent the night and the next day on the hill Touila. By their attack the Germans succeeded in postponing the Division's attack for twenty-four hours, that was all. Instead of advancing from Tella Sefra about midnight on the 21st/22nd, the Brigade waited till midnight 22nd/23rd April. No. 3 Company moved into Tella Sefra and saw the Scots and Grenadiers go through unmolested. The Battalion's advance to Tella Sefra was like a well-rehearsed night exercise. The platoons crossed Banana Ridge in "artillery formation" with shell bursts exploding in the spaces between them to give realism. No. 3 Company led the Battalion into a maze of gullies cut out of sandstone and gravel by the erratic winter floods. The narrow crevasses gave good cover, but each shell burst showered chips and pebbles on to the dozing Guardsmen.

By the morning the Grenadiers and Scots were across the mile of plain that stretched eastwards from Tella Sefra, but had met determined opposition on the far side. The Grenadiers were fighting for the village of Crichet el Oued, and the Scots Guards were stuck in the open at the foot of the line of hills. Colonel Scott went to see Colonel Barne of the Scots Guards. "I found him and his H.Q. in an extremely hot position, being shelled and mortared from all sides. He had already committed two companies to battle, and the situation in the hills was extremely obscure. I was then ordered to put a company under his command to give him a reserve, as it was not likely in the circumstances that the Battalion would be able to pass through the Scots that day, as originally planned, to attack the next set of hills. I chose No. 1 Company under Captain C. Chesterton, and it was sent up on a hill to help one of the Scots Guards companies. It was during this engagement that Lieutenant Eugster was so badly wounded that he subsequently died." Lieutenant Michael Eugster heard that enemy tanks had been sighted, as indeed they had been, making towards the company. There were no anti-tank guns near by, but there was a wrecked Churchill abandoned by its crew. He climbed on to it to use its six-pounder gun ; as he was swinging the gun round an H.E. shell struck the turret.

In the meantime the Battalion moved out of the gullies on to the edge of the plain. It was very hot, and they lay in a shallow depression, panting. It was the first day of the real Tunisian summer, and as the sun mounted the heat became scorching. The men discarded their jackets and from then on fought in their shirt-sleeves. From then on, too, everybody was always thirsty. Every now and then a wounded man from the Scots Guards, or No. 1 Company, was carried past them. The Germans were clearly bringing up their guns, for the shelling steadily increased. They also turned out their air force for its last big effort. While the Allied bombers flew over to Tunis miles up in the sky, the German fighters bombed and machine-gunned the infantry. No. 3 Company got a direct hit in their gully, which decapitated them. Captain Prendegast, Lieutenants Lloyd-Thomas and Askin, and C.S.M. Moran were wounded and two Guardsmen killed. The Machine-Gun Platoon was caught on the road by a Messerschmitt, which pumped cannon shells into its trucks, killing Guardsman Barry and mortally wounding Guardsman Ridge. Ridge was a fine heavy-weight boxer and as handsome a man as ever stepped out of County Galway. When the Adjutant went to say goodbye to him there was not much left of him except his courage. "I am afraid, sir, this is a bit of trouble you can't get me out of." This day, the 23rd of April, was Good Friday.

The Battalion remained in its assembly area for the night and following day. "It was extremely hot, and there was very little shade, and every few hours some violent alarm took place, such as reports of heavy tank attacks, so that the rifle companies and the support company were deployed in battle positions all day." Colonel Scott spent most of the morning at the Scots Guards H.Q. where "the position was still rather confused in front, owing to a breakdown in the wireless communications, but we eventually discovered that their main objective, Hill 145, had been taken by a company under Lord Lyell." He took this news to Brigade H.Q. that evening. "I was told that it was too late to put in a further attack that night, but was ordered to make a reconnaissance early the next morning for an attack on Points 151 and 187, two hills beyond the Scots, which could not be seen from our present positions. I returned to the Battalion about eight o'clock." The big Humber car had been manœuvred into the depression. The blinds were drawn and Colonel Scott settled down to study the map. Major H. L. S. Young lay on the ground outside, racked with a kind of dysentery. "At half-past eleven Lieutenant Sandberg, my liaison officer, arrived from Brigade with orders that I was to attack Hills 151 and 187 that very night with zero hour at 0200 hrs. . . . This was obviously an extremely difficult proposition. We had only two hours, no reconnaissance had been made, and there was no possible way to identify the objectives in the darkness. I managed to get the commanders of Nos. 1 and 4 Companies, Captains Chesterton and Powell-Edwards, together at about a quarter-past twelve. They had no time to give any orders to their companies, even if they had been in a position to know what orders to give, and they eventually arranged to meet on the start line, which was to be the positions of the Scots Guards. They got there about a quarter to two. In the meantime I had discovered that the Scots Guards company on Point 145, in the immediate path of our attack, was again out of contact with its battalion and consequently could not be given any warning of our attack. Even if we should ever, by fluke or fortune, find our objectives, we should certainly have to fight our way through the Scots Guards to get there. Captain Powell-Edwards was waiting for me on the start-line. He told me that he had no idea where the objective was, nor could he find anybody who did know. He had taken a compass bearing off the map, but in his opinion it was practically impossible to get the companies to the right hill with our own troops somewhere in the darkness. His appreciation was correct. I spoke to the Brigade Commander on the wireless and said that, much as I regretted having to question an order, I could not commit the Battalion to this task. He agreed when he heard my reasons and called off the attack. I was extremely relieved that he backed me up in my decision." Brigadier Colvin had had his orders from Division, and he now had the invidious task of explaining why he had postponed the attack to a Divisional Commander who had already taken to bed with some internal disorder. The Battalion never forgot it to him. The two companies—relieved, but slightly puzzled—marched back to their positions.

Next morning—the 25th—the company commanders went across to the Grenadiers in front of Crichel el Oued, which was the only place from which it was possible to get a glimpse of the two Hills 151 and 187. The Battalion spent the day quietly under spasmodic shell fire. It was Easter Sunday, and Father Brookes managed to say one Mass in a sheltered gully, and then went round the companies hearing confessions. In the afternoon the 2nd Infantry Brigade on the right flank made a full-scale attack supported by tanks which, as far as the Battalion could see, was moderately successful. On the left, across the River Medjerda, the 78th Division was fighting hard for Longstop Hill. The company commanders returned after dark to get their orders. From the low line of hills that bounded the Medjez plain a string of long, steep hills led north-east parallel to the Medjerda into the main bulk of the Bou Aoukaz. They had a generic name, Djebel Rhaouass, but they were known by their "spot heights," Point 145, Point 151 and Point 187. After Point 187 there was a break of a mile—the Gabgab Gap—before the first feature of the Bou Aoukaz rose sharply out of the plain. This was a long, bare ridge marked Asoud on the map, with a pimple at either end, Point 212 on the south, Point 214 on the north. Points 145, 151 and 187 were stepping stones to the "Bou"; the Hills 212 and 214 buttressed the "Bou" and were its dominant feature. That night the Battalion marched through the main body of the Scots Guards, skirted Point 145, where the company was now expecting them, and at five o'clock on the morning of the 26th attacked Points 151 and 187. It was a straightforward night attack, carefully prepared and entirely successful. Nobody was hurt, except a few Germans, and two complete German sections were scooped up before they could get away. By daylight the Battalion had consolidated its position, with Nos. 1 and 4 Companies on Point 187, No. 2 on Point 151 with No. 3 behind them, and Battalion H.Q. in the ravine between Point 151 and Point 145. The Battalion was now stuck straight out in front of the rest of the Division. The Grenadiers were on two hills, Points 119 and 133, to the left rear; on the right flank there was nobody. As soon as dawn broke the Germans began shelling the

Battalion. From their positions on either flank they could see both sides of the Djebel Rhaouass and fire straight into them. It was a most uncomfortable day. The men crouched in shallow holes or squeezed behind rocks, lying as still as they could. The Germans were using their 88-mm. guns as snipers' rifles, and fired at any sign of life. One casualty inevitably led to others, for when men left their shelters to pick up a wounded comrade, they were chased over the hill by a solid shot and H.E. In all, thirty men were killed or wounded on this sweltering, passive day. The carriers ran a continual service back to the field ambulance from the old German dugout which served as the Battalion's R.A.P.

"I reported to Brigade H.Q. about six o'clock," wrote Colonel Scott. "Our Brigadier was in conference at the time with the Brigade Commander of the 2nd Infantry Brigade, who was acting for the Divisional Commander, who was sick. The acting Divisional Commander was afraid we had lost contact with the enemy, and said that the Brigade must put in an attack that night on Djebel Ben Aoukaz. Our Brigadier explained that it would be extremely difficult to lay on a brigade attack at that time of the evening (it got dark at seven), as he would have to prepare an artillery plan and get his commanding officers together. He did not see how he could do it, and would prefer to send out strong patrols to discover the enemy's positions. The acting Divisional Commander then stated that if he was not prepared to attack that night he would have to attack next day by daylight. Brigadier Colvin was very loath to do this, but he knew that he could not possibly do an attack that evening, so he replied that if it had to be done by day, he would like to do it at last light, that is about half-past six."

The Battalion knew very well that it had not lost contact with the Germans. It could see an observation post on Point 212, and the fire that was being poured into its positions could only come from an array of mortars and guns spread along the front, some of them at point-blank range. For its own comfort, and to reassure the acting Divisional Commander, the Battalion sent out a patrol that night to Point 212. It was a full platoon of No. 4 Company commanded by Lieutenant Attlee, a ruthless young man. They climbed Point 212 and, after a brief struggle, destroyed the German observation post and brought back an artillery officer and two sergeant-majors. Sergeant Lynch marched the prizes into Battalion H.Q. The officer was quite ready to talk; he had got as far as saying that they had strict orders to hold the "Bou" to the last, when he changed the subject to his home town in Germany. To jolly him along, the Adjutant said that he himself had been there, and asked if it was still standing. This was a tactical error ; the German laid his head against a carrier and wept copiously. Sergeant Lynch urged him to be a man, but since it was Sergeant Lynch who had killed his late companions, the German took no comfort. Everybody was very embarrassed, particularly the German sergeant-majors, and he had to be sent away still sobbing.

"A night attack on this particular feature was comparatively easy," wrote Colonel Scott, and he said so the next morning to the acting Divisional Commander. "It was eventually agreed that this was what we should do. The Brigadier gave out his plan, and Lieutenant-Colonel Mackay, commanding the 19th Field Regiment, made the artillery plan. Zero hour was 1830 hrs. The Battalion's objectives were Hills 212, 214 and 181 on the left and a small hill, Point 128, in the plain to the right. The Scots Guards were to capture Point 226, the farthest point on the 'Bou,' and the Grenadiers to take Hills 171 and 154 on our left. I ordered No. 3 Company, supported by No. 2 Company, to capture Point 128, No. 4 to capture Point 214 and No. 1 to pass on to Point 181." The destruction of the German observation post on 212 made it less dangerous to move about on Rhaouass. By squirming backwards and forwards over the crest the company commanders could get a general view of the "Bou," and an ugly sight it was. The only approach to it was across open ground ; that was its strength. After its peak Hill 187 flattened down northwards for 500 yards to the broad defile of the Gabgab Gap. A mile to the north-east Asoud, with its pimples on either end, rose sharply out of the plain. The country to the left, between Asoud and the river, was like a basket of eggs, a series of bumps boxed in by higher hills. To the right of it stretched mile after mile of gently undulating corn. A track ran out of the Gabgab Gap to cross the plain ; on either side of it lay a square olive grove and a few Arab huts. The olive groves offered the only cover in the whole area. Colonel Scott decided, therefore, to launch the attack from the forward edge of the nearest grove, the one east of Point 187, hoping—and it could be no more than a hope—that the fading light would shield the Battalion as they came down off the hills and crossed the open ground. "At midday Brigade told us that zero hour had been put forward by Division to 1600 hrs. This meant that the attack would be in broad daylight in the heat of the afternoon."

CHAPTER V

The "Bou"

THE Battalion assembled behind Hill 151 at three o'clock. It was a blazing hot afternoon; the sun flashed off the rocks, and every footstep raised a little cloud of dust. A short spur from Point 151 protected the companies while they formed up—No. 3 under Captain Kennard, No. 2 under Captain J. B. Fitzgerald, No. 4 under Captain Powell-Edwards, and No. 1 under Captain O. Chesterton. A few shells crashed into the spur. In single file No. 3 Company swung round the edge of the spur and out into the open plain. The Battalion followed them, stepping a long steady pace. There was the olive grove, a low line of dark green across a wide expanse of yellow-green corn, shimmering in the heat. It was under a mile away, but it seemed the other side of the world. From the spur to the corn was only a couple of hundred yards, but before the first man reached it the German guns opened fire. "They threw everything but their cap-badges at us." Guns, mortars, and those abominable machines the six-barrel mortars, everything within miles, let drive. The platoons spread out into open order and plunged into the waist-high corn. The fire intensified and the whole cornfield was ripped and torn. Part of it was burning smokily. Amid the tall poppies that stood out over the corn there sprang up a new crop—rifle butts. They appeared suddenly, and so thickly, that it was almost a surprise to look beyond them and see the thin line of men plodding steadily on towards the olive grove. "We could not believe it," said a German prisoner afterwards. "We thought nobody could cross that plain." "Thank God for drill," said one Guardsman, "it keeps you going." They fixed their eyes on the olive grove—it looked so peaceful and safe—and made the well-tried jokes. "Ah, well, I've seen it before on the pictures" and "I would not care to take my girl out in this." Captain John Fitzgerald, Lieutenant J. Pym and C.S.M. Malone were

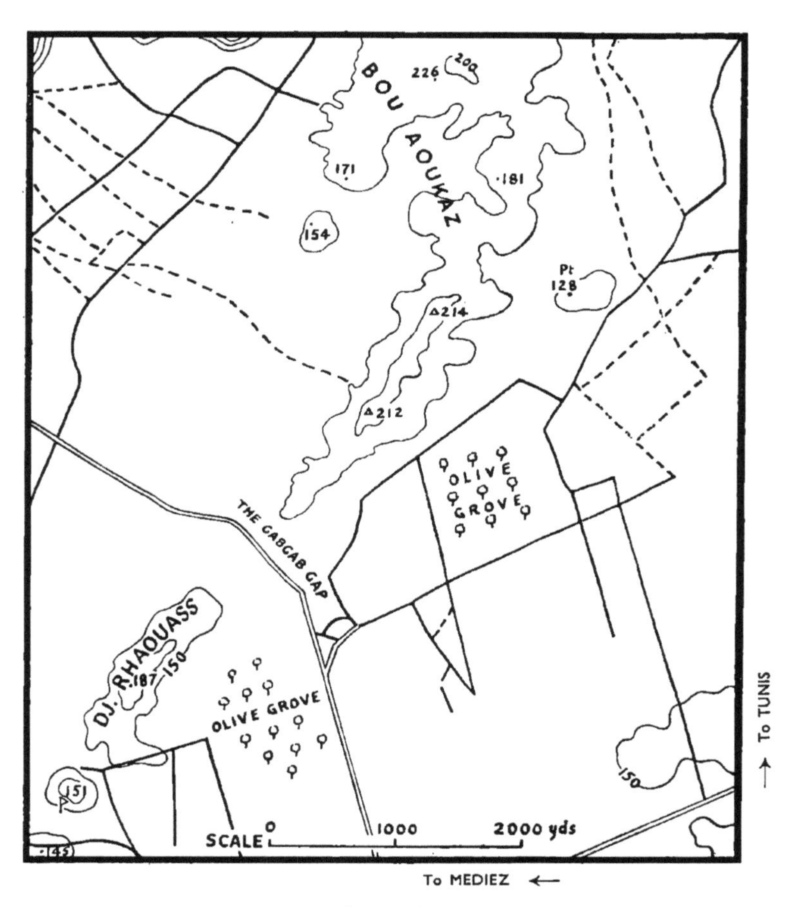

THE "BOU" AND APPROACHES

but three of the many killed. Captain I. H. Powell-Edwards and Lieutenants C. A. Larking and D. Lloyd-Thomas were wounded.

The olive grove was a registered German target. They pounded it systematically, working up and down the straight lines of stumpy trees. "Bash on, boys !" The companies tramped through the grove, Nos. 2 and 3 veering to the right and Nos. 4 and 1 to the left. Nos. 2, 3 and 4 Companies each now had only one officer left, Lieutenant Keigwin, Lieutenant Kennard and Lieutenant Attlee. Battalion H.Q. halted on the forward edge of the olive grove. The ground had been ploughed by some industrious French colonist, but the furrows ran the wrong way, so that while they could press their heads and legs down below ground level, their middles protruded. No cover was any good against the heavy shells. R.S.M. Peilow was killed and the tree he was sheltering under disappeared in the explosion. About six o'clock the position was that the troops on the left were pinned some three or four hundred yards in front of the olive grove, and that the troops on the right were fighting in the second olive grove. As soon as No. 4 Company emerged into the open again Lieutenant Attlee, the only surviving officer, and C.S.M. Kiely were wounded. Sergeant Lynch laid Lieutenant Attlee in a hole, stood to attention, saluted, and asked "Leave to carry on, sir." The Company struggled on another few yards through the fire. Then Captain Chesterton brought up his company and absorbed the remnants of No. 4. No. 1 Company got its 2-inch mortars into action and advanced again behind a thin film of smoke. A burst of machine-gun fire from a small stone farmyard caught them in the flank. Lieutenant Mahaffy swung his platoon round to rush this post ; he himself was killed, but the platoon finished the post. In the outburst of mortar fire which followed Captain Chesterton was wounded. The Company crawled on through the corn. They could see the Germans on the hill, and Sergeant Gundel was trying to keep their heads down with a Bren gun. Captain Chesterton, wounded a second time, got on his wireless to Colonel Scott. "We will be able to take the hill as soon as it is dark. Can we wait till then—about half an hour ?"

Colonel Scott had already decided to concentrate the Battalion on Points 212 and 214. Nos. 2 and 3 Companies were fighting a brisk hand-to-hand action with infantry and armoured cars in the second olive grove. They cleared the infantry, but had more difficulty with the armoured cars, which bounced up and down the rides between the trees blazing away with their machine guns. One Guardsman was run over, but recovered in time to throw a grenade

BATTLE OF THE "BOU"

Face page 170

at the back of the armoured car. Point 128 lay beyond this second grove and, according to the map, should have been a well-defined spur running out from 214. When Captain Kennard and Lieutenant Keigwin emerged with their battered companies they saw only a smooth bump in the open plain. Lieutenant Kennard reported back. "We can get this Point 128, but I don't think it is much good to us." "Stay where you are," replied Colonel Scott, "and close on 212 after dark." "I asked leave from Brigade," he wrote afterwards, "to establish all my riflemen on Point 212 and abandon this exposed place 128. The communication with Brigade was done via the No. 18 set to rear Battalion H.Q., where our link passed it on. At the same time, and in the same way, artillery concentrations were brought down on various enemy positions which Captain Chesterton and Lieutenant Kennard indicated to me over the wireless."

As soon as it was dark No. 1 Company renewed the attack. It plodded silently up the hill, bayonets at the ready, while the shells were still falling on the top. The Germans did not wait for it ; a bevy of fifty or sixty of them scurried along the ridge and away down the far edge. Battalion H.Q. collected the remnants of No. 4 Company and joined No. 1. By messenger and wireless every effective man was gathered on to the hill. Captain Kennard brought up the thirty survivors of No. 3 Company, and Lieutenant Keigwin arrived a little later with twenty-five men. One hundred and seventy-three men out of four rifle companies and Battalion H.Q. reached Hill 212 that night. The rest lay down in the corn or in the olive groves calling to the stretcher bearers, or silent, and marked only by a rifle butt silhouetted in the glow of burning Arab huts.

The top of the ridge was bare rock, with only a few pockets of earth. The men worked all night digging, hacking and shifting boulders to get the slit trenches built before dawn. The hill and the plain were an ant's nest of activity. The carriers ran loads of ammunition, rations and water from the Battalion's old position as near as they could to the foot of the ridge and gave lifts back to the walking wounded. Father Brookes, with a team of "beaters," walked backwards and forwards over the plain and along the course taken by the companies. He still had with him three young Germans who had surrendered to him some time in the afternoon as he was walking along swinging his blackthorn ; they were an embarrassment till he turned them into stretcher-bearers. The ambulance came up through the Gabgab Gap and collected the wounded off the track. Doctor Barnes temporarily patched them up by the light of the headlamps and gave them morphia to ease the jolting journey to the rear.

Father Brookes and Doctor Barnes between them cleared the wounded from the plain before dawn. The dead could afford to wait. The Germans, too, were busy. The Battalion could hear the clank and clatter of their half-tracks ferrying up fresh troops and the faint throb of tank engines. Every now and then there was a confused brush in the dark, the flare of a Very light and a burst of wild firing. But both sides were absorbed in their own affairs and preferred to leave each other alone for the time being. The Battalion sent a patrol to investigate Point 181. It found a Scots Guards company on Point 181 and returned with two "Jocks," who thought that their other companies had reached their main objective, Point 226. "This was comforting news, and we prepared for the counter-attack we expected at dawn."

No counter-attack came at dawn. Everything was perfectly still till a fatigue party ventured down the hillside to pick up more of the stores. Machine guns promptly opened fire from the olive groves and a couple of tanks, hull down behind the rise of 128, drove them back up the hill with well-placed H.E. That was that. The Battalion looked in the other direction towards the River Medjerda. It could just see the Grenadiers on the hill away to the left, but there was no sign of the Scots Guards or anything else. Captain Egan lumbered off towards Points 181 and 226 with the two Scots Guardsmen. He returned, puffing, to say that the Germans were on both these hills, and that the Scots Guards were now somewhere in the area of Point 117. The problem before Colonel Scott was how to get the supporting weapons on to the hill. "After some time I realized that it was an impossibility, as no carriers could get up so steep a hill. There was no chance of getting the anti-tank guns, mortars and machine guns up there except on foot, which in the case of the guns, anyway, was out of the question. This also applied to the big No. 19 wireless set which was the only link with Brigade H.Q., and it was essential to be in touch with them if one was to command the battle. There was a very big gap between 212 and the rest of the Battalion still at 151, and no prospect of getting any more help. This presented, to my mind, a most serious situation as there were no troops on the right flank and no anti-tank guns to cover the gap. The Germans only needed to make a flanking movement to cut off the troops on the hill. There was nothing to stop them taking up a position on Hill 132 immediately behind 212 on the Medjerda side of the Gabgab Gap. I went to see the Brigadier." Colonel Scott and Lieutenant Synge left the hill at 8.30, only just in time. At nine o'clock the Germans made their flanking movement and cut off the hill.

The 173 men on Hill 212 realized that they were isolated till nightfall at least, and took stock of their position. There were five officers left for what had once been four companies and advance Battalion H.Q.—Captain Egan, Captain D. Fitzgerald, Lieutenant D. Madden, Lieutenant C. Kennard and Lieutenant T. Keigwin. The only senior N.C.O. was Sergeant Lynch of No. 4 Company. They had with them just what they had been able to carry up during the night—some twenty boxes of .303, three or four sacks of bread and bully, and a dozen jerricans of water and tea. That was enough small-arms ammunition to be going on with. As long as the one wireless set, a No. 18, worked it could call for artillery support, but so far no mortars or machine guns had reached the hill. The length of the ridge was 1,000 yards and the men were spread out along the top in company groups. No. 1 held Point 212, Nos 2 and 3 held Point 214, and No. 4 and H.Q. held the saddle between the two points. "Force H.Q." as the Adjutant, Lieutenant Madden, Sergeant Kelly and the two signallers, Guardsmen Vare and Hayman, called themselves, found a pocket of earth behind No. 4 Company and dug a trench there. An overhanging rock near by was reserved for the wounded. The position they held was vital to the whole attack on Tunis. General Alexander said so in his despatches. "The capture of this mountain (Bou Aoukaz) was essential to the whole conduct of operations in order to clear the left flank of the attack. The fighting on the mountain was severe, and the enemy counter-attacked many times ; major credit for the success must go to the 1st Irish Guards." The Germans said so by the price they were prepared to pay for the recapture of the hill. On that morning, Wednesday, 28th April, 1943, 173 Irish Guardsmen, armed with Brens, rifles and two grenades each, held the hill. On Friday night, the 30th April, after five large attacks, eighty Irish Guardsmen, armed with Brens and rifles, still held it.

At Brigade H.Q. a squadron of the 1st Reconnaissance Regiment and three companies of the North Staffordshire Regiment were put under Colonel Scott's command. "It was decided," he wrote, "to form a bastion on Points 151 and 187," and he has described the action from "this sort of stronghold." Major Gordon-Watson, Captains Ismay and Drummond, and Lieutenant Dodds came up from "B" Echelon. "We set about putting the place in as strong a state of defence as possible. About two o'clock the Germans counter-attacked with about twenty tanks and supporting infantry. They came from the south and got through the Gabgab Gap, cutting off the force at Point 212. They attacked Point 212 and then, round about four o'clock turned their attention to Point 187 and tried to take that ridge, which was exactly what I was afraid of. However, we loosed off everything we had got, anti-tank guns, M.Gs. and mortars. I can only imagine that they must have thought that we were a much stronger force than we were, for from that time the enemy put all their forces against Point 212, whereas if they had made a persistent attack against Point 187, it would have been very strong betting against holding them up. As it was, Point 212 was cut off from us, and the only way to get supplies up there was by carriers running the gauntlet of German tanks from all directions, and even then everything that was got up had to be carried about half a mile up the hill. The German tanks that had come through the Gap were between us and the Grenadiers. Our Churchill tanks were behind a rise in the rear, and I hoped that they would come forward, but unfortunately they could not get farther than the bottom of Point 187, as the Gap was guarded by Tiger tanks. Consequently, the Churchills could give no support to the troops on 212 who were again being attacked. The Germans now held Point 132, and their tanks were machine-gunning 151. There was considerable shell and mortar fire. We had no artillery officer with us, but Major Gordon-Watson, on 151, passed information on the Mortar Platoon's power telephone to Battalion H.Q., where the 19 set passed it on to Colonel Mackay, the Field Regiment commander. At about six o'clock a concentration was brought down on the German infantry and tanks and the Churchills moved forward. They were able to drive the Germans back through the Gap, but the Tigers still held the gap itself. During the night the carriers dumped some supplies at the foot of 212 and evacuated those wounded who had made their way down to the bottom of the hill.

"On the 29th Major Young, who had returned from hospital, and Lieutenant Synge got a machine gun up to Point 212. The method of inter-communication now was that information from 212 was sent by the Adjutant by 18 set to Hill 151, where the 18 and 19 sets were, and either I or Major Gordon-Watson contacted Brigade for any support that was asked for. Points 187 and 132 were taken over by the North Staffordshire Regiment, and the 1st Bn. The Loyals were in the area of Point 117. The Germans attacked in strength at mid-morning with some forty tanks. They broke through Point 132 and established themselves on Point 117, eliminating the Loyals. Their infantry took Point 132, menaced 187 and made a half-hearted attack on the Grenadiers. Our artillery was very active and knocked out fifteen enemy tanks, but the penetration right into our positions made the targets difficult. At nightfall the enemy infantry and fifteen tanks or so still lay across the only supply route to Point 212. Three attempts were made to supply Point 212 but none got through.

"I went to Brigade and asked for reinforcements, and was told that two companies of Gordon Highlanders would be available. I arranged for the officer in charge of the Gordons to report to me at 10 p.m. and had guides to take his companies up to Point 212. We also planned to send up Captains Ismay and Drummond and a carrier convoy of supplies under their escort. The Gordon officers were delayed and did not appear till three in the morning, and then lost their way back to their own companies ; it was daylight before they found them and too late to get up to the hill. Captains Ismay and Drummond took the supplies forward unescorted. They got up on the hill themselves, but they had to leave the supplies at the bottom.

"While I was at Brigade H.Q. the Brigadier had got under way an admirable scheme for a tank sweep of the olive groves, which would have broken up the German force which was assembling there for yet another attack on the Hill 212. This attack was to have gone in at 0400 hrs., and I am sure it would have had a spectacular success. Undoubtedly it would have prevented the Germans from making their last grand attack. However, this plan was cancelled by Division in the early hours of the 30th. I have never heard why, but there must have been some very good reason as, otherwise, the plan seemed excellent.

"On the morning of the 30th the Adjutant told me by wireless that the men were getting tired. They were short of water and fairly short of ammunition owing to the difficulties of getting it up the hill, but were in a very high state of morale, having had the satisfaction of whipping the Germans on each occasion they had appeared. Major Young, he said, was on his way back to give a full report. He rang off, saying that another attack was being made on the hill. I went to Brigade to try and raise some reinforcements for the troops on the hill, as it was impossible that the eighty men—all that was left—could continue to hold on against such heavy odds. The Brigadier ordered a company of Grenadiers to cross the valley and reinforce 212. At this time the fighting which was being reported through the wireless was desperate and hand to hand. Major Young arrived at Brigade H.Q. and explained the position on the hill when he held it before the present attack. Even then there were too few troops to man the position properly. At that moment the great news came through that the enemy had again been put off the hill.

"The afternoon was quieter. Enemy tanks and guns were still shelling us. By now we had a telephone line to our own guns and Lance-Corporal Barrow and Signaller Irons amused themselves directing the fire of batteries and chasing tanks around the country-side. Doctor Barnes was up to his eyes in work in the Battalion's R.A.P., so the Field Ambulance lent Doctor O'Neill, who had been with the Battalion for years. O'Neill set out straight away for 212. The Divisional Commander told me I could withdraw the troops that night and that the Gordon Highlanders would be able to hold the hill. I gave the Adjutant this news, which was very gratefully received. However, at about 7 p.m. I had a message from Brigade H.Q. saying that the Divisional Commander now said that in no circumstances was I to withdraw my men. This was most regret-table, as the men were whacked to a standstill and had not unnaturally been looking forward to coming out as soon as it was dark. Lieutenant-Colonel W. S. Stewart-Brown had now taken over our Brigade in place of Brigadier Colvin. I told him my opinion, and he agreed to me putting up sixty fresh men from support company and anywhere I could find them. Lieutenant J. C. Gunston took these troops up to the hill that night, and about three o'clock in the morning of the 1st May the men from 212 rejoined Battalion H.Q.

"The Germans by now appeared to be fed up with taking such heavy knocks, as they had been doing, and things were comparatively peaceful. On 2nd May the Battalion, less Lieutenant Gunston's force, which was now reinforcing the Scots Guards on Point 117, withdrew about a mile to the banks of the Medjerda where they were held in reserve."

The Adjutant wrote a report of the defence of the hill. It began formally: "Sir, I have the honour to submit the following account of the events which took place on Points 212 and 214 and the ridge connecting them after you left to report to Brigade H.Q. on the morning of Wednesday, 28th April:

"*Wednesday, 28th April.* After a quiet morning the enemy began to mortar the ridge heavily about midday. The only result of this was that any slit-trenches that were not finished were rapidly deepened. The top of the ridge, however, was bare rock and it was very difficult to find good cover or digging ground. At about 1400 hrs. 88-mm. guns and tanks, firing H.E., opened up on the crest from close range in the olive grounds. This fire was heavy, most accurate and most unpleasant. The Germans had clearly set to work to 'soften' the defences. The men were withdrawn to the top of the reverse slope, leaving on the eastern side only look-outs dug in as well as possible. Both then and throughout the following days casualties were heavy among the look-out men, but there was never any lack of volunteers for the task. At 1500 hrs. the fire intensified. Salvos from six-barrel mortars screamed through the air like Green Line buses and crashed in quick succession along the ridge. The look-outs shouted ' Here they come ! ' German infantry were climbing the slope up the end of the ridge nearest to Point 214. This was the first opportunity the Guardsmen had of engaging the enemy personally, and they took it eagerly. Nos. 3 and 4 Companies—we still called the small groups companies—moved up to the crest, and as soon as the shelling slackened halted the Germans half-way up the hill with rifle and Bren fire. When the Germans were already wavering a section of No. 1 Company came over from the right flank, which was not engaged. The increase in the volume of fire had a splendid effect. The Germans turned and ran back down the hill. We were astonished at the sight, but soon recovered. The Guardsmen went forward and shot down the fugitives till they disappeared into the corn below. Two German officers who tried to rally their troops were picked off by rifles. The whole force was elated by this success, and from then on morale was at the highest possible level. The Guardsmen never for one moment doubted their ability to thrash and to go on thrashing the Germans as long as our ammunition and water held out.

"After this attack the mortar and shell fire began again and continued steadily till Friday night. I cannot remember any time during that period when we were not being shelled and mortared, and later machine-gunned and sniped as well. But, worst of all, was the thirst. The days were blazing hot, and the shelling churned the ridge into a naze of dust ; but we had only some half-dozen jerricans of water and two tins of cold tea. Half a water-bottle for twenty-four hours was the ration, and by the end we were all croaking harshly. The tea we kept for the wounded. There was a brief shower of rain on Thursday night and we caught a little muddy, but very welcome, water in groundsheets. The only other source of supply was from the Germans. After dark men used to crawl forward and unhook the water-bottles from the dead bodies on the slope. One man got down to a wrecked carrier at the foot of the hill and brought back three tins of canned peaches. He gave them to me for the wounded, and for the next three days I doled out the juice spoonful by spoonful. It was the only physical comfort we had to offer to the dying.

"At six o'clock that evening the Germans began to work round the left of the ridge and got into a Gully below Point 214. They had already got round the right through the Gabgab Gap, and their tanks were firing along the ' reverse ' slope of the ridge. Preparations were made to meet another attack, which duly came at about seven, when it was nearly dark. This time the Germans tried to scale Point 214 from the north-east. No. 2 Company went round the western side of the hill and caught the enemy in the flank. In spite of this the enemy succeeded in reaching the top of 214. Since life would have been intolerable if the enemy had held this point, Lieutenant Kennard led a bayonet and Tommy-gun charge and the enemy was swept off it and grenaded down the hill. The Germans continued to press their attacks on the northern half of the ridge and were nearly on to the flat top. It was getting dark and the situation looked serious. At the moment of greatest need Sergeant Musgrove and his 3-inch mortar team came running along the reverse slope, carrying their mortar. The mortar had had to be abandoned that morning at the southern foot of 212. Sergeant Musgrove had quietly rescued it in the half-light. It was assembled in record time—they threw it together—and all twenty bombs were shot over the ridge at minimum range, with alternative switches to left and right. The effect on the enemy could be judged by the screams which followed each burst. No. 4 and No. 1 Company men then ran forward and destroyed the leading enemy troops, who had been cut off from the main body by the mortar fire. If we had had more grenades we could have done even more damage. As it was, the Guardsmen finished by throwing rocks after the Germans. Captain Egan was wounded at this stage. A bullet, which would have missed an ordinary sized man, hit him in the arm and spun him round like a huge top. ' It was the angry r-r-roars of the k-k-kerry bull that d-d-decided the Germans,' said Guardsman Kane. Kane always stammered, but the excitement made him worse. He was an excellent Bren gunner and had been having the time of his life perched on a boulder methodically firing regulation bursts of three or four rounds.

"During the attack a troop of the Reconnaissance Regiment, No. 11, I think, made a dash across the Gabgab Gap. They had to ditch their carriers at the foot of 212 and scrambled up the slope pursued by Germans and cheered by No. 1 Company. Only a handful of them, commanded by a Sergeant Salt, got home. They fought alongside No. 1 on 212 and were invaluable. The whole troop has our unqualified gratitude and admiration.

"The Germans retired and throughout the night we could hear them digging half-way up the hill and collecting their dead and wounded here and on the plain below. The roll of one German company was called by what sounded 'a very bad type of C.S.M.' as Sergeant Kelly described it, and we were glad to note that he was deficient of a good half of the names called. The deficiencies in our own roll did not bear thinking on. There was no rest for anyone that night. We expected the Germans to make a sudden rush at any moment : it seemed the obvious thing to do, and if it came it would succeed or fail in the first minute. Lieutenant Madden stalked up and down the ridge all night, like a sentry on patrol. It was a great comfort to see big black Madden pass and repass and to hear him say, 'They're still digging.' The wounded who could walk were sent down the western slope to get back as best they could. It was at least a chance of getting their wounds treated before they went gangrenous and, as Guardsman Hickey, the senior stretcher-bearer, said, 'I have no time for the gangrene.' The wounded who could be moved were carried down to the western foot. By great good luck Lieutenant Nunn got two carriers through from 151 and was able to send these wounded back to the R.A.P. He himself replaced Captain Egan on the hill. No. 2 Company produced a prisoner from somewhere. He belonged to the 2nd Bn. 47th Regiment, and said that his battalion had left Enfidaville the previous afternoon and was rushed out to the attack by lorry.

"*Thursday*, 29*th April*. We fully expected a dawn attack, as our prisoner was very anxious to be evacuated before dawn, but none came. C.Q.M.S. Mercer appeared, to our surprise and pleasure, leading a small pack train of men so bowed beneath the weight of ammunition boxes that they could hardly climb the hill, much less bother about the enemy fire. He had brought two carriers across the plain in the early light, but the rest of their cargo had to stay at the bottom. He had the good sense to bring with him a large sack of cigarettes—enough to give every man a tin of fifty. Guardsman Hollingsworth smashed the boxes, festooned himself with bandoliers, and ran along the positions dishing them out. Hollingsworth was an old man as Guardsmen go, and I put him in charge of the ammunition thinking that it would be a sedentary occupation. In fact, it was an arduous and dangerous task, but no man could have done it better. He was continually passing up and down the firing line, dragging heavy boxes through shell fire and answering the shouts, 'Hollingsworth! Ammo!' At one stage, when he had only twenty rounds in his reserve, he made three separate journeys down the hill to C.Q.M.S. Mercer's dump without saying a word. On the third journey he was wounded in the leg, but brought in the box, and the first indication that he had been hit was when the stiffness made him limp—even then he passed it off as rheumatism.

"It was not till nine o'clock that the Germans came on again, this time in even greater strength, and all along the line of the ridge from 212 to 214, including both points. The first warning came from the Reconnaissance Regiment, who had taken over the expensive duty of finding the look-out man on Point 212. A German company was forming up for the attack just below Point 212. By leaning over the top it was possible to see them. This is what Lance-Corporal Kenneally did, and he decided that this was the right moment to attack them himself. He charged down the bare forward slope straight into the Germans, firing his Bren gun from the hip as he went. The Germans were thrown off their balance by this extraordinary assault. Having cut right through them, Kenneally turned and began shooting men who were still goggling up the slope. It was too much for the Germans. They all started firing in all directions at once, trying to follow Lance-Corporal Kenneally as he leapt about the hillside. They were still firing at each other when No. 1 Company came forward and finished them. Lance-Corporal Kenneally walked slowly back to the top of the hill. No. 4 Company dealt with the attack in the centre in a more conventional way with the help of most of No. 1 Company which, thanks to Lance-Corporal Kenneally, was now free to move over. The attack on the left was put in with more persistence and had the support of the reserves originally intended for the right and centre. For some time it looked as if the Germans might succeed in reaching the top of 214. Two tanks and an armoured car crawled uncomfortably far up the hillside and fired steadily to cover their infantry. Nos. 2 and 3 Companies had to lie low till the Germans were at close quarters and then rise up and beat them back. Between the jigs and the reels there was not much time for thinking, as one man put it. The tanks then withdrew, but the armoured car swung round and climbed the southern face of 181 till it was level with the defenders of 214. Lieutenant Keigwin dealt with this tiresome machine. He had a large American rifle, of which he was very proud, and four armour-piercing bullets. He crawled forward, took careful aim and put two of the bullets into the engine. The crew then foolishly tried to dismount their machine gun, but were caught with it half-way out by Sergeant Ashton and a section of No. 3 Company. That was all for the time being.

"After a few hours' respite another attack was made by fresh German troops. By this time we were getting quite used to them, and as usual drove them off. We watched and waited eagerly for the

SERGEANT P. KENNEALLY, V.C.

Face page 180

Germans to waver under the fire ; at the first sign of it the Guardsmen jumped out of their holes and rushed at them. It was a highly successful policy, and made a nice change, as Guardsman Foran said. C.Q.M.S. Mercer led No. 4 Company into a very neat charge, with himself on one flank and Sergeant Lynch on the other to keep the dressing. On the left, Lieutenant Kennard launched a counter-attack which swept away the Germans and carried on across a gully up the slopes of 181, where there were two new German machine-gun posts, which he particularly wanted to get at. He fired the only revolver shot known to the Battalion in Tunisia ; it dispatched the No. 1 on the nearest machine gun. He and his companions captured the two guns and turned them on to the retreating Germans. We had not enough men to hold this position as well as our own, so No. 3 Company came back bringing one machine gun with them and draped with belts of ammunition.

"The rest of the afternoon would have been quiet if we had not been shelled by our own guns. An abortive tank attack was apparently being made in the plain between us and the river, and this shell fire moved in one-hundred-yard lifts along the ridge and finally concentrated on and beyond 214. Lieutenant Keigwin was deafened and concussed. Then smoke canisters were showered on the ridge, which must have puzzled and alarmed the Germans, for they dispersed the smoke with ten minutes of concentrated blasting by their six-barrel mortars. Guardsman Hayman sent our protests over the wireless. He was the only operator left now as his assistant and friend, Guardsman Vare, had been killed in the previous attack. The aerial waving above the crest made him a natural target, and he had an inconceivable number of near misses, but he preserved an admirable calm when any mistake or distraction would have meant the loss of contact with the Commanding Officer and the artillery. Shortly after this shelling Major Young and Lieutenant Synge arrived with a Vickers machine gun and team. The team set up their gun just in time to get a good shoot on German infantry who were following a tank attack below us towards 187. We could see them arriving in lorries at 128, debussing and spreading out across the plain. Unfortunately a direct hit from a tank gun disabled the Vickers and killed or wounded all but two of the crew, which included Major Young. As a result of this attack two German tanks got round to our rear between us and Point 132, and began climbing the approach to Point 212. The gradient and the rocks halted them, as we hoped it would, for we could not rely on the Hawkins anti-tank grenades to do more than frighten them. They opened fire on us from behind, an example which was followed by other tanks which had reached Point 117. At nightfall the Germans mounted a mortar and a machine gun on the slopes of 132 and 212 respectively, and we could not drive them off because they were protected by a Tiger tank, the first we had seen.

"About midnight Guardsman J. Nicholson suddenly walked up to Major Young to say that he had found 'some infantrymen' in the plain and could bring them up if we wanted them. Guardsman Nicholson had been wounded in the attack on 212 and had been sent back to the R.A.P. on the Wednesday morning. On Thursday evening he walked out of the Field Ambulance hospital 'to be with the boys again.' It was a remarkable achievement. Officers with maps in daylight and little danger lost their way trying to reach 212, while Nicholson with only a general idea of the positions, and in the pitch dark, not only found his way through the enemy lines, but went back and brought up a body of troops lying within 200 yards of the enemy tanks. He had come across the survivors of a Loyal company, which had been overrun, imposed his command on them and told them not to move till he came back. They followed him on to the hill and were superimposed on the existing sections to thicken them. We expected more reinforcements from another unit, but these never appeared. Otherwise it was a quiet night. The men 'off duty' sat on the rocks and took their boots off to air their feet. It was an opportunity also to clear some of the corpses from the top of the ridge. The Germans killed there on Wednesday morning had already putrefied in the sun, and the flies were beginning to bother us.

"*Friday, 30th April.* Just after dawn Captains Ismay and Drummond arrived, smartly dressed in full fighting order. They had brought two carriers of rations and very necessary ammunition to the bottom of the hill. Major Young and some wounded returned to Battalion H.Q. in the carriers. German activity started almost immediately afterwards and we were able only to get up a very small proportion of the supplies. The machine gun on the slope of 212 was raking the back of the hill from that flank and the tanks on 117 were firing straight into it. First Lieutenant B. Synge was badly wounded, and then Lieutenant J. J. Nunn was killed in attempting most gallantly to reach and recover the ammunition we needed so badly. On the other flank, by 214, the Germans were edging forward again, dragging heavy machine guns behind them. Lieutenant Kennard was wounded in a skirmish; the only surprising thing about this was that it had not happened before. I ordered him to hand over his command to Sergeant Ashton, but even so he continued to visit ' the company ' after intervals of rest and limped about on a broken rifle, cursing the Germans.

"At eleven o'clock the Germans made their last and biggest attack of all. It opened with a violent bombardment. The 88 mm's. and tank guns tried to knock the top off the ridge with H.E. and solid shot, while the field guns and six-barrel mortars pounded what used to be the reverse slope. ' There is no doubt about it,' shouted Lieutenant Madden, ' they are very keen to get this hill.' Captain George Ismay must have been killed some time in the preliminary bombardment. He had taken charge of No. 4 Company, and was last seen on his way through the shell bursts to a forward trench. No trace of him was ever found. Captain Drummond did not last much longer. Hickey and I had to stuff field dressing after field dressing into a hole the size of a teapot in his back, after he had been shot through the shoulder in the early stages of the attack.

"The German infantry came up in exactly the same way as before, but in greater numbers and with greater persistence. We noticed a higher percentage of officers than we had ever seen with any troops—half were in front leading (these were easily picked off) and half were behind, driving on their troops (these were harder to get at). The assault on 212 was broken up by Lance-Corporal Kenneally and Sergeant Salt before it got under way. In the words of the citation awarding him the Victoria Cross : ' Lance-Corporal John Patrick Kenneally repeated his remarkable exploit on the morning of the 30th April, 1943, when, accompanied by a sergeant of the Reconnaissance Corps, he again charged the enemy forming up for an assault. This time he so harassed the enemy, inflicting many casualties, that this projected attack was frustrated. The enemy's strength was again about one company. It was only when he was noticed hopping from one position to another further to the left in order to support another company (No. 4), carrying his gun in one hand and leaning on a Guardsman (Cafferty) with the other, that it was discovered that he had been wounded. He refused to give up his Bren gun, claiming that he was the only one who understood that gun, and continued to fight all day with great courage, devotion to duty and disregard for his own safety. . . . His extraordinary gallantry in attacking single-handed a massed body of the enemy and breaking up an attack on two occasions was an achievement that can seldom have been equalled.' On the left the Germans actually got over to our side of 214 and flooded along the top of the ridge.

Shepherded forward by tanks, the Germans fell on No. 2 Company. The Guardsmen rose to meet them and they fought it out on the edge of their trenches. ' What with tanks sliding around on the rocks and the Germans shouting their heads off, it was a real fracas,' said Lance-Sergeant Fitzpatrick. Two sections were overrun and led away, but one of them, under Lance-Corporal Ferguson, took an opportunity to brain their captors and rejoined the Battalion after twenty minutes' absence, for which Lance-Corporal Ferguson asked to be excused. (The others escaped from a prison ship when it was bombed in La Goulette harbour and reported for duty in Tunis.)

"In the confusion the rest of the force had a moment to organize a counter-attack. Sergeant Ashton led No. 3 Company against Point 214, where Lieutenant Kennard came careering through them. Lieutenant Madden gathered No. 4 Company and hurled himself and them along the ridge. These charges shattered the Germans, and the whole line swept forward cheering and shouting ' Up the Micks ! ' We chased the enemy halfway down the slope, firing ' into the brown,' and bayoneting the less fleet footed. I have never seen anything like it, and it was with great difficulty that the men were restrained from going down into the cornfield. I should mention here that Lance-Corporal Lockley, whose conduct throughout was exemplary, spotted a senior German officer trying to rally his men. Lance-Corporal Lockley pursued this officer almost down into the plain and eventually shot him ; immediately afterwards he himself was caught by a machine gun and killed. The Germans proved the value of this officer by sending up two tanks which placed themselves on either side of him to protect him and remained there till nightfall, regardless of the shell fire I had directed on to them. Lieutenant Madden was hit by a shell fragment as he came over the top of the ridge ; he lived long enough to hear that the Germans had been ' seen off.' It was very lonely on the hill without him. It is literally true to describe him as a tower of strength, for wherever the fighting was the closest, wherever the shelling was the heaviest, there was Dennis Madden, head and shoulders above the rest.

"This complete failure of their strongest attack evidently broke the Germans' hearts, for they never made a proper full-scale attack again, though throughout the day small parties continued to try and work their way up and continued to be shot down. The shelling also continued. Guardsman Hickey, that prince of stretcher-bearers, was so badly wounded that his leg had subsequently to be amputated. He was, as usual after an attack, working on the forward slope, and was actually bandaging a man when he was hit. We then saw a company of Grenadiers starting to cross the wide valley below us from their hill to ours. It was a heartening sight, and we were glad to have them when they came for, though everything was practically over, their presence gave us a chance to relax a little. Some time in the afternoon the plain behind us was cleared and we were able to evacuate the wounded. Dr. O'Neill, whom we had last seen in Ayr, somehow insinuated himself on the hill. He had already been wounded by the time he reached the top of the hill, and was hobbling on a pick-handle, but was just the same as he used to be on the sick parades.

"About 1800 hrs. one company of Gordons appeared and the Grenadiers withdrew. The other company of Gordons took the wrong turning and walked into the Germans. When it eventually came up I took our men into reserve on a ledge halfway down the reverse slope. At 0300 hrs. Saturday, 1st May, we were relieved. One hundred and seventy-three men reached Points 212 and 214 on Tuesday night ; 80 left it on Saturday morning, which included those men such as the M.G. section, who managed to get up during the siege. The conduct of the Battalion throughout these days was beyond all praise. They were short of food, short of sleep, short of ammunition, very short of water, continually shelled, mortared and machine-gunned, sniped and often surrounded ; but never did I see anything but a fixed determination to hold our positions—for ever if need be—a complete contempt for the German infantry, and a stolid and cheerful endurance of the German fire. After the repulse of the first attack morale was at the highest, and I have never seen the Guardsmen more cheerful. There was no suggestion of complaint of any kind, and the most dangerous and uncomfortable tasks were carried out almost before the order was given. Very few orders were given by me or anybody else—there was hardly any necessity, for the whole force acted as one cohesive and intelligent body. Every man, including those with the longest ' sheets,' did his duty, and more than his duty. I always knew the Battalion was good, but I never guessed it was so good, and personally I shall never forget their courage and uncomplaining endurance, their unfailing cheerfulness, the silence and patience of the wounded and the kindness and gentleness of the men to their wounded comrades and the spirit of co-operation among themselves. As they said themselves, ' We are all Micks together, and the Micks muck in.' It was an honour to be with such men."

A great white cross now stands on Hill 212. "To the memory of the Officers, Warrant Officers, Non-Commissioned Officers and

Guardsmen of the 1st Bn. Irish Guards who died on and around this hill April 27th–30th, 1943. *Quis separabit?*" Who indeed?

Such was the part the Battalion played in the capture of Tunis. It now sat back to watch the massed divisions of the First and Eighth Armies deliver the final blow. There were 440 men left, counting everybody from the cooks and drivers in "B" Echelon to the wounded with the Battalion such as Captain Powell-Edwards and Lieutenant Kennard, who had extricated themselves from the machinery of evacuation, and the sixty men under Lieutenant Gunston and Lieutenant McInerney still on the hill, but only 110 of them were riflemen. On 3rd May the Battalion moved across to the banks of the Medjerda, where the 110 riflemen were formed into one company under Captain Kennedy, who had just returned from hospital, and everybody changed into khaki drill so as to finish the campaign in the correct summer dress. The casualty roll, however, was not yet closed. Lance-Sergeant Somers and Lance-Corporal Reddington were mortally wounded and Lance-Corporal Kerr was seriously wounded when their anti-tank gun portee went up on a mine in the middle of the "rest area." A long-range gun, somewhere in the north, fired an occasional shell; one of them fell by a group of men gathered round the water truck, wounding Sergeant Wallace and three Guardsmen and killing Sergeant Maguire, the Provost Sergeant, who was marshalling the queue. Doctor Barnes was killed by a chance shell as he was handing over the old R.A.P. behind Point 151. Meanwhile, the 4th British Division, the 4th Indian Division, the 6th Armoured Division and the 7th Armoured Division were assembling on the plain in front of Medjez and behind the Battalion. It was an overwhelming display of armed force. The whole of this stretch of two and a half miles was packed, wheel to wheel, with four hundred guns, myriads of trucks and droves of tanks. Overhead, flocks of fighters patrolled the sky. Officers from the 4th Indian Division besieged the Battalion for information. "On 6th May, at 0330 hrs., they advanced to the attack side by side on a very narrow front. The massed artillery of the First Army, backed by dumps of ammunition which we had been nourishing so long for this event, fired concentrations on known enemy locations. At dawn the air forces went in. It was their greatest effect in the war up to date, over two thousand sorties of all sorts. The weight of the attack was too much for the defenders, already weakened physically and morally by the heavy fighting since the 22nd April. By 1030 the first infantry objectives were captured. The two armoured divisions, which were close on the heels of the attacking infantry, at once

MEMORIAL CROSS ON THE "BOU"

FATHER BROOKES, ADJUTANT, COLONEL MONTAGU-DOUGLAS-SCOTT AND SERGEANT DOONAN ON THE "BOU"

passed into the lead. The impetus of the offensive was so strong that it carried them by nightfall as far as Massicault, half-way to Tunis. At first light on the 7th May the 6th and 7th Armoured Divisions moved forward once more from Massicault. Despite his best efforts the enemy had been unable to organize a defence in the area of the breakthrough. There was a sharp skirmish at the junction of the Medjez and Bizerta roads, a little sniping from isolated houses on the outskirts, but at 1145 hrs. the 11th Hussars and the Derbyshire Yeomanry entered Tunis."

Although defeated, divided and disorganized the enemy was not yet destroyed. They planned to fall back on Cape Bon and there to "do a Dunkirk." The 6th Armoured Division put a stop to that by cutting across the base of the Cape from Hammam Lif to Hammamet, while the infantry divisions spread a net across the plain to catch the Germans streaming down from the hills to the north. On the 8th May the Battalion marched fourteen miles to El Bathan, a village set in the wide olive groves which fringe the Tunisian plain. They wound along the dusty tracks, through the old battlefields, by the foot of the "Bou," past a cemetery where the Germans had buried some of our dead, and camped round an empty Italian farmhouse. The following day, Sunday, 9th May, after Father Brookes had said Mass for a most fervent congregation, and Captain Kennedy had taken a photograph of the whole Battalion, Colonel Scott read out two messages. The first was from the Divisional Commander: "Now that this particular phase of the operations is over, may I express my very great admiration for the gallant conduct of the 24th Guards Brigade. The 1st Division was selected to bear the brunt of forcing an entry through the crust of the enemy to enable the armour to break through. All three brigades had very strong enemy positions to attack which they did most gallantly, but the relentless courage, the cheerful sacrifices and the great tenacity of the 24th Guards Brigade was outstanding, and indeed without it the victory of the First Army could never had been achieved. While it is impossible to differentiate between the conduct of all three battalions, I think the story of the Irish Guards on Hill 212 will always stand in red letters on the pages of that glorious Regiment's history. Your losses were great and terrible, but my heart goes out to you in thankfulness that such courage should produce a reward, the true value of which, at this time, no man can assess." The second message was from General Alexander: "Heartiest congratulations to you and all ranks of the Battalion for your magnificent fight, which had not only added fresh laurels to the illustrious name of the Regiment, but has been of the utmost importance to our whole battle. I am immensely proud of you all ; I am very sorry about your losses."

On the 10th the 1st Division moved on towards Cape Bon, but the Brigade changed places with the 128th Infantry Brigade, as it was now too weak for anything but guard duties. The Battalion took over control of the pontoon bridge across the Medjerda at Djedeida. It watched a ceaseless stream of traffic flowing in both directions. Much of the traffic consisted purely of sightseers, enthusiastic Americans who had driven up from Algiers, and who were prepared to pay a good price, in money or cigarettes, for souvenirs, German helmets (with holes carefully punched by the Guardsmen), bayonets, waterbottles and all the junk that litters a battlefield. The Arabs, driving their flocks and herds out to pasture, paid a small toll in kind—unofficial, but very nourishing. On the 13th the Battalion entered Tunis. It occupied a large Italian farm, formerly a German headquarters, at Manouba on the outskirts of the city. As it settled down for the night under an ostentatious moon it heard the song of "Lili Marlene" for the first time. It was being sung, very well, by five thousand Germans who were waiting to be officially captured. That same day General Alexander sent a signal to the Prime Minister : "Sir, it is my duty to report that the Tunisian campaign is over. All enemy resistance has ceased. We are masters of the North African shores."

INSPECTION OF SUPPORT COMPANY, 1ST BATTALION, BY FIELD-MARSHAL THE VISCOUNT ALEXANDER

1ST BATTALION MARCHING TO THE VICTORY SERVICE AT CARTHAGE CATHEDRAL, MAY, 1943

Face page 188

GUARD OF HONOUR TO H.M. THE KING

Face page 189

CHAPTER VI

Tunis

THE Victory Parade in Tunis on 20th May involved as much preparation and more staff work than a major battle. The Battalion crowded down to the Avenue Jules Ferry and climbed on the tanks of the North Irish Horse to get a view of its own contingent marching past the saluting base. Colonel Scott commanded the 1st Division contingent, and Major Young commanded the sixty picked Irish Guardsmen who took part. The highly polished, neatly dressed Guardsmen were followed in the parade by a horde of Moroccan Goums, wearing dressing gowns and slippers, and then by a regiment of the French Foreign Legion, which had fought alongside the Battalion in Norway. On the first free Sunday Father Brookes sang a High Mass of thanksgiving in Carthage Cathedral for the Battalion and the 78th Division. When the sound of the pipes leading the troops drifted into the great, still Basilica, one of the white-robed priests sprang from his stall and rushed down the aisle, crying "I must see the boys, I must!" His name in religion was Pere Angelicus, but he had been born Flynn in Westmeath. The Archbishop, Primate of Africa, a prelate of immense dignity, was taken round the company lines at Manouba in a jeep. He wrote afterwards to "Le Regiment de St. Patrick, Guardes Irlandais," to say how touched he had been by his reception and to promise his prayers for his "chers soldats et aimables sous-officers." In June the Battalion found a guard of honour for His Majesty the King. It was the smartest guard ever seen—even the Grenadiers admitted as much. The immediate awards for gallantry had been made by General Anderson, but the four surviving medallists of the campaign—Sergeant Lynch, D.C.M., Lance-Sergeant Ashton, D.C.M., Lance-Sergeant Pearson, M.M., and Guardsman Nicholson, D.C.M.—were presented to His Majesty.

Three months of "public duties" in Tunis gave the Battalion time to absorb a flood of reinforcements from the 3rd Battalion and the disbanded 33rd Guards Brigade Support Group. These duties were tiresome rather than onerous. There was always something to be guarded or regulated in Tunis—the Kasbah, road-blocks, prison camps, stores and ammunition dumps, and until more men arrived the Guardsmen were doing "twenty-four hours on and twenty-four hours off." As the drafts came in the one rifle company divided into two, then three, and finally, by the middle of August, the Battalion was up to strength with four rifle companies. The new men were disappointed to find that there were drill parades in Africa just the same as in England, and were horrified to hear, on arrival, that the first parade was at 5 a.m. The day had to start early, as the heat in the afternoon was crippling and the best place to be was either in the water or asleep on the sand at Sidi Bou Said, the favourite bathing place of the Bey of Tunis and his wives. Having got there first, the Battalion secured the best bathing chalet and stretch of beach, and maintained it against the envious civil administrators by producing a fictitious grant from the Bey himself whose furniture and harem the Battalion had somehow saved from ruin. In the cool of the evening the Battalion either entertained its friends at Manouba or descended on Tunis with the hope of finding something more than the usual tomatoes and sweet red wine. The invasion of Sicily in July gave the Battalion a new occupation—"housekeeping." It supplied and fed troops waiting for embarkation and conducted them, like slave-traders, into the landing-ships.

At the end of August, after many false alarms, counter-orders and changes of division on paper, the 24th Guards Brigade rejoined the 1st Division for training on the south coast of Cap Bon. The Battalion marched some forty miles in two days to a small farm just outside Hammamet. "I sweated out so much salt that my cap looked like Lot's wife. The men marched very well, and the poor first-line reinforcements, who had only arrived the night before, made the grade all right except for ten men, who developed malaria." The companies pitched their bivouacs and tents in the olive and fig groves and began to build elaborate cook-houses. Battalion H.Q., always known as "Whites," occupied half the farmhouse, canopied by hanging vines and surrounded by caper-bushes. Before the Battalion left Manouba it learned that Lance-Corporal Kenneally had been awarded the Victoria Cross. Letters and telegrams of congratulation poured in ; everyone who ever had anything to do with the Battalion wrote or called, and the stream followed the

Battalion down to Hammamet. On 27th August General Alexander made the presentation. "A tremendous day," wrote Colonel Scott. "General Alexander arrived accompanied by the Corps Commander, the Divisional Commander, Lieut.-General Bradley of the U.S. Army and Major-General Lemnitzer, the American Deputy Chief of Staff. The Battalion was formed up on three sides of a square in a rather dusty field and very hot sun. The place was stiff with reporters and photographers. We had no idea what sort of a parade General Alexander wanted, but he said on arrival that he wanted to go round the whole Battalion. He did this, and then Kenneally was marched up to him through the Battalion by R.S.M. McLoughlin. After he had pinned the cross on Sergeant Kenneally he made a speech to the Battalion, congratulating them personally on having played a vital part in his victory, and probably total victory. Then he ordered the Battalion to march past while he stood at the saluting base with Sergeant Kenneally on his right. General Alexander and his party came on to Battalion H.Q. Mess where they had an excellent luncheon, arranged by Simon Combe, under a mulberry tree. The Americans were highly pleased to get ice-cream, and I mixed General Bradley a rum-and-lemon cocktail which he said was the best he had had since he was in the Country Club, Richmond West, adding 'And boy, could that nigger shake them.' "

Sooner or later the 1st Division was bound to be sent to Italy, but as the weeks and months went by the Battalion assumed that it would always be "later." Every rumour turned out to be false, and every warning order was cancelled. A new commander, Major-General R. Penney, C.B.E., D.S.O., M.C., took over the Division and launched a series of exercises. It was difficult to enter wholeheartedly into these "stunts," but the Battalion did its best and drove for hours along the Tunisian roads and marched for miles over the hills of Cap Bon. When at last, in the middle of November, the Divisional Commander announced that the Division would be moving at the end of the month the Battalion felt that, this time, it must be so; they could not decently be left any longer in North Africa. The Battalion left Hammamet just after midnight on the 29th November. It was a bad period for a move, for the area and district commands had by then had time to lay their hands heavily on all transport and movements. With the usual acquisitiveness of Base H.Q. they had demanded the surrender of all vehicles "surplus to Battalion establishment," and by a stubborn mathematical error did not provide enough R.A.S.C. lorries to carry the Battalion, much less the various stores it had accumulated. But Captain J. Egan was an ingenious transport officer, and that evening a curious assortment of vehicles drove out of cactus plantations and olive groves to form a convoy. First came the conventional jeeps, trucks and troop-carrying lorries, then the Battalion's private vehicles—old Italian rattletraps, huge German diesel lorries, a couple of strange French machines that looked like horse-boxes, and several quiet, retiring trucks that had officially been destroyed by enemy action over six months ago—and finally came six bright yellow desert lorries belonging to the Foreign Legion. But for the Foreign Legion, the Battalion would have had to do what other units did—leave half their personal stores behind and come back the next day for what few remnants the local Arabs had not fancied. After years on British rations the Foreign Legion had just changed over to French Army rations, and they sadly missed their whisky, tea and bully beef. Major Gordon-Watson and the Adjutant went to say "au revoir" to their friends of the 1st Regiment,—Barbe bleu, Beaujolais,and le Petit Chevre. Major-Gordon-Watson talked of the old days in Norway; the Adjutant presented a farewell gift from the Battalion, and they returned leading the six lorries, each flying a huge tricolour and driven by Legionaires. Colonel Andrew Scott eyed the convoy anxiously. The springs of every vehicle were flat under the weight of "stores" heaped on board it, for the Battalion was leaving nothing behind that could conceivably be of any use. "Do you think they can all reach Bizerta?" he asked.

The Battalion drove slowly through the night, skirting Tunis and passing the huge American supply dumps, where the only sign of life was the gleaming teeth of the Negro sentries. At seven o'clock in the morning they reached "Texas Staging Area," a collection of tents scattered on a hill overlooking Bizerta Lake. When they saw the signboards the Battalion looked forward to stuffing themselves with American rations, but the nauseating smell of old sump-oil soon told them that the cooks of the camp were British and were using the A.C.C. crude open oil-stoves. It had been raining in Bizerta, and the camp was muddy, cold and windswept. The lorries struggled up the hillside, dumped the Battalion, slithered back down to the harbour to be loaded immediately on board a Liberty ship. Somebody in a remote headquarters had, as always, issued a precise Vehicle Loading Table, but no battalion regarded this document as anything but a statement of the minimum. After a few words with the naval officers, Colonel Scott had no difficulty in loading every vehicle he wanted. The ship was bound for Naples, and the one thing the Battalion knew about its own destination was that it was not Naples. The ship cast off, and Captain Egan shouted goodbye. "God knows when we will see you again."

Most of the Battalion had expected to sail straight away, and they did not fancy the prospect of kicking their heels in "Texas." "Take it easy," said the older Guardsmen. "It's like the crossing to Ireland. You've got your sailing ticket all right, and now you must wait for a boat." This was quite an accurate statement. "Movement Control" had brought the Division up to Bizerta and were now looking for ships to carry it to Italy. The following morning it produced two Landing Ships Tank, and with the note of frantic urgency that marked all its messages demanded Support Company and a rifle company down in the docks within an hour. This was easy enough for Support Company, who just jumped into their carriers, but for No. 1 Company it meant a wild scramble and a long sweating march in greatcoats and big packs. Their destination was announced to be Taranto, and reasonable efforts would be made, it was said, to send the rest of the Battalion to the same port. After four days, and some very unpleasant suggestions that the Battalion should cross the stormy Mediterranean by half-companies in small landing craft, three liners, the *Llangibby Castle*, the *Lutetia* and *Cuba*, put into Bizerta for stores and were seized by the Divisional Commander. The Battalion marched down to the Transatlantique Dock on the morning of 4th December and filed up one gangway into the *Llangibby Castle*. An American embarkation officer insisted on checking each man against his name on each of six nominal rolls. "I don't doubt your word," he told the Adjutant, "but it is the routine." The Adjutant spoke to the C.S.Ms., the C.S.Ms. spoke to the companies and the "routine" was followed. As the American called the names in alphabetical order the Battalion filed up the gangway by platoons, answering to any name. Embarkations did not normally, in the American's experience, go as smoothly as this, but whenever he called a Guardsman back to confirm the name, he was always satisfied. "What's your name ?" "What name did you call, sir ?" "The five O'Donnell boys." "I'm one of them, sir." The ship was overcrowded and short-handed, but the sailors, as always, did their best to make the soldiers comfortable. The previous passengers had been Moroccans, admirable fighting men, but peculiar in their habits, so the rest of the day was spent in swabbing the mess decks. The convoy sailed the following morning. The Battalion crowded on deck to see the last of Africa. Sergeant Harrigan began to sing his own version of "Galway Bay," and the Battalion took it up, repeating fervently the verse that begins—

> "Oh the wind that blows across the sea from Tunis,"

and ends

> "And the Arabs gathering cactus in the hedges,
> Speak a language we have no desire to know."

PART IV

THE 1st BATTALION IN ITALY

CHAPTER I

The Approach March

THE *Llangibby Castle* docked—at the wrong quay—in Taranto on Tuesday, 7th December, 1943. It was a clear, fresh morning and the sun gleamed on the fortifications of the Old Harbour and on the marble crozier of an enormous statue of a bishop. "St. Patrick ! " cried the enthusiasts, and pointed out something in the statue's hand that might have been a shamrock. The doubters appealed to Father Brookes. "What would the Eyeties be doing with St. Patrick ?" He, speaking *ex cathedra*, said it was the next best thing to St. Patrick, a later Irish saint who had delayed in Taranto on his way to Rome long enough to become the town's patron saint. "Adsit omen." The Battalion disembarked in high good humour. It was an immense relief to be back in Europe, to step ashore on the right side of the Mediterranean. The companies laughed and boasted as they assembled on the quayside. "All we have to do now is just lead on. By the right, quick march, and you'll be home, boy." These, and other jokes, may have been simple and hackneyed, but they were the best expression of everybody's feelings. The happiest man was probably Major Gordon-Watson, M.C., for on top of the joy of being out of Africa, he had seen H.M.S. *Aurora*, the cruiser the Battalion knew so well in Norway, and was already planning to force an invitation to its wardroom.

The Company Sergeant-Majors called for silence in the ranks, the Pipers, after an opening wail, started "St. Patrick's Day" and the Battalion marched through the side streets of Taranto out into Italy.

The Battalion eyed the countryside with critical interest. There were the same familiar rows of olive trees, but the trees were bigger and somehow seemed European. The houses looked like houses, and not overgrown tombs. Some of the passing Italians looked like Arabs, and the Battalion shouted "Yoo-hoo Mahomet !" and "Saida

Wog," but all the same it cheered them because they were not Arabs. It passed derelict road-blocks and heaps of rusty barbed wire, which recalled the Home Guard defences in England. Three miles up the main road they found an open field and a shed full of tents. This was the Staging Camp, but it was a fine day and they were in Italy, so nobody minded. They flung off the big packs, pitched the tents and then went to buy fruit, postcards, Italian phrase-books and holy medals from the touts who already besieged the area. The first thing was to trace Support and No. 1 Company. Under heavy pressure from Colonel Scott, the British stationmaster disclosed that Major Young had taken a ticket to Canosa, small town north of Bari. Later that evening Major The Lord Kilmarnock, the D.A.Q.M.G., arrived with an empty lorry. "Recreational transport," he explained. "Who'd like to come in to Taranto ? You will all be moving to Canosa tomorrow." Apart from this there was no information except a general idea that the Division would join the Eighth Army in the hills beyond Foggia. "Taranto looked quite an attractive place," wrote one of the officers who accepted Kilmarnock's invitation, "but dinner in the Bella Rosa was mediocre and the cognac in the Officers' Club was real rot-gut." The Guardsmen who made the journey found that a box of matches would buy most things and a bar of chocolate would procure everything.

The following evening—the 8th of December—the Battalion boarded an Italian train. There were a few ordinary carriages, third-class dining cars, but it consisted mostly of large goods wagons. It was the first time the Battalion was faced with the traditional "8 horses or 40 men" wagons, and at first it did not like the look of them, but there were enough of them to give two wagons to each platoon and sufficient floor space for each man. With blankets, candles, cards and rations the Battalion made itself comfortable for the night. At intervals they looked out to see the Italian countryside moving slowly, very slowly, past in the bright moonlight. The train reached Barletta soon after dawn. It halted outside the town for rather longer than was intended as someone, who preferred to remain anonymous, drew off all the water in the boiler to make tea and shave. This halt enabled Father Brookes to offer a lift to what appeared to be an entire seminary; it was eagerly accepted and Italians of every age and clerical rank swarmed on board. The train eventually moved on, shedding priests all along the line, and reached Canosa about midday.

The demesne of Monte Garrafa lies along a bare hillside six miles outside Canosa. In the scramble for battalion areas, Major H. L. S. Young had grabbed the manor-house and the granaries. Monte

Carrafa was a square, medieval building, half farm-house, half fortress. It looked uncomfortable and cold, but it was infinitely better than a tent in the frozen fields. The rooms all opened off the central courtyard, storerooms and workshops on the ground, long, high living rooms on the upper floor. The outlying granaries were full of ashes and charred tins, ration stores fired by the Germans in their retreat ; the Brigade Major threw them in with the house, as neither of the other battalions fancied them. In two days, by using the back-log of "punishment men," the granaries were clear, white-washed and warm with stoves.

The Battalion settled down to spend Christmas in most seasonable weather. It was bitterly cold, with a few hours' bright sunshine every day and a light snowfall every night. As soon as the transport arrived from Naples, the Quartermaster and his henchmen disappeared into the hills, armed to the teeth in case, they said, they met bandits at lonely farms. They returned with a load of pigs and turkeys, which led a precarious existence till Christmas Eve. Christmas Day began with Midnight Mass in the chapel attached to the house. As the men poured out of the chapel afterwards it was like a country church in Ireland. They stood around in the moonlight, joining together into groups and breaking up, wishing "Happy Christmas" and discussing the presents they had been able to send home. In the morning there was the traditional football match, Officers *v.* Sergeants, with the traditional smoke canisters. Colonel Scott got much advice from the side lines, D./Sergeant Rooney made most unfair use of his weight, and Captain S. H. Combe cheated shamelessly. Sergeant Kennedy and his cooks had been working since dawn, and at midday produced a gargantuan meal, the like of which was never seen in England. Lance-Corporal O'Donnell, his moustache specially waxed, made a long speech, of which no one heard a word, for it was lost in the cheers. It was a good and a long day. On Boxing Day the orders and counter-orders began. At first the 1st Division were warned to relieve the 8th Indian Division on the Eighth Army front, and indeed an advance party had already gone up there. All previous orders were cancelled on New Year's Eve, and another advance party, under Captain O. F. McInerney, set out in all the trappings of secrecy. They themselves did not know where they were going to ; they were to meet a guide at a rendezvous near Foggia. Speculation was drowned in the Sergeants' Mess New Year party. A seedy Italian band played alternately "Tipperary" and "Lili Marlene" in one corner of the low, dimly-lit barn. "It only needed a few women and it might have been a night-club." A big clock ticked out the minutes to midnight. The first toast of the New Year was to Fallen Comrades, and then the cheerful cries of "Happy New Year" and "May the next one be at home." R.S.M. McLoughlin announced the next attraction: "Sergeant Wylie, D.C.M., will oblige with a song—'On the road to Castlebar'—a fine song and a fine singer."

"January 1st, 1944. Very wet and cold," wrote Lieutenant J. Quinn in the War Diary. "This would have been a cheerless beginning to the New Year but for the opportune issue by the Quartermaster of the long-awaited Africa Star ribbon. Intense sewing activity lasted till tea time. After this there was an excellent concert given by the Regimental Band in the large barn which is Support Company Mess." The Regimental Band had come out to the Mediterranean for a tour of duty a month previously, but it was only now—and that only by using the greatest influence—that the Battalion had secured them. Lieutenant Willcocks and his thirty musicians had been shuttled round Italy in 3-ton lorries; the pleasure they gave, however, more than made up for any discomfort they may have suffered. They arrived just in time to move with the Battalion and stayed with it, entertaining the whole Brigade, till it embarked for Anzio.

On 2nd January the Battalion drove across Italy to Gragnano, a small town on the south side of the Bay of Naples. It started at the favourite Army time, in the small hours of the morning. "Breakfast was at midnight, and soon afterwards the first elements of the Brigade began to move. The Battalion, which was last in the convoy, passed the starting point at 0335 hrs. Just before we reached Foggia it became light—the dawn of a clear, sunny day. By about seven o'clock we could clearly see everything to the mountains on the promontory of Manfredonia. We had a memorable journey through green valleys and snow-topped mountains by Ariano and Avellino. From Avellino the road down into the valley was precipitous, giving us an impressive aerial view of miles of country. The snow was thawing on the streets of the villages; the lorries skated down, occasionally crashing into the ditch or the wall of a house, to the laments of the Italians. Just as it was beginning to get dark we came up over the last hills and a strong pungent smell hit us in the face. It was Naples. We caught our first glimpse of Vesuvius, with a thin wisp of cloud-like smoke trailing from the summit." Here Lieutenant McInerney, "the Dentist," his teeth and glasses glistening, met the Battalion to lead it through San Severino, Pompeii and Castellamare.

Gragnano is a spaghetti town; miles of "pasta" are, or were, turned out of the huge factories which lined the main street. There was no spaghetti being made now, and the factories, with their large drying-rooms, stood empty as ready-made barracks. The Battalion spent a fortnight at Gragnano, living from day to day. "It seems inadvisable to make any detailed arrangements for very far ahead," says the War Diary soberly. "There is a strong feeling that important events are impending and are perhaps very imminent." It was obvious to the simplest Guardsman, but not, we hoped, to the Italians, that a force was being collected for a landing somewhere. The Battalion was ordered to practise "Combined Operations"; it had spent years in England jumping in and out of boats, so it contented itself with one simple exercise. Even that one exercise had to be done from the wrong kind of ship, but that worried neither Colonel Scott nor the Battalion. Their interest lay in where they were going to land and, even more, in what was going to meet them. "We will get ashore all right. People over-rate the difficulties of landing from the sea. After all, it is only a kind of approach-march. You get into boats instead of buses, the difference being that sailors are more reliable than Army drivers." Conference succeeded conference at Fifth Army H.Q. in the Royal Palace of Caserta. At first only the Commanding Officer knew the landing point; everyone else was left to speculation—the South of France, Corsica, Yugoslavia, North of Rome; a few said "South of Rome," and one man persisted in "England." On the 13th January Colonel Scott gave the officers the orders for Operation "Shingle." "We land south of Rome, at Anzio.

"Personnel, other than those officers already 'briefed' under Brigade arrangements will on *no* account be briefed until they are on board ship." The "security" of Brigade H.Q. was strict. The officers studied maps and photographs in a secluded room—no notes, no maps to be taken away. The rest of the Battalion knew only that they were to be part of the 6th U.S. Corps, and they looked forward with interest to seeing their Corps Commander. Major-General Lucas, of the U.S. Army, visited the Battalion on the morning of the 7th. By a carefully timed coincidence, he saw No. 1 Company returning from a route march, very fresh and smart—as well they might be, for they had come from just round the corner. They saw a pleasant, mild elderly gentleman being helped out of layers of overcoats. The Corps Commander remarked that they were big men, expressed the opinion that the main guard, under the command of Sergeant Bird, was "mighty fine," drank a cup of tea and drove away, leaving the Battalion slightly puzzled. On Friday, the 14th, the Battalion learnt its allocation of shipping space and craft. The

Adjutant, Sergeant Kelly and his staff retired into the Orderly Room for twenty-four hours to draw up the "loading-tables." It was like a nightmare jig-saw puzzle, in which the pieces were alive and kept changing, and the makers frequently altered the pictures they wanted made up. Support Company and the Transport, on reduced scale, were to be loaded separately on two tank landing ships. Three times they were ordered down to Castellamare harbour; three times they were sent back to the Battalion, who got tired of saying goodbye. On the 19th January the tank landing ships opened their bows and the carriers, anti-tank guns, mortars and trucks were allowed on board. The four infantry landing craft allotted to the rest of the Battalion had a capacity of 120 men each. H.Q. Company had to be severely pruned and the four rifle companies somewhat clipped to reduce the total figure to 480 officers and men. It was done by leaving behind in Gragnano, to be shipped in the "follow-up" convoy, the seconds-in-command and other men who would in any event have been left out of the first battle.

The Battalion was ready to march off at midday on the 20th. Nobody had very much to do except dress themselves, for everything that had to go had already been loaded and if anything had not been loaded by now, it was too late. The rear party fussed around like mothers trying to get their children off to school in time. The companies paraded in full fighting order in the broad main street of Gragnano. The Italians had never before seen the Battalion massed and dressed for war. They were used to groups of Guardsmen walking amiably down the streets buying cakes, fruit and wine; they had even seen a little company drill, but they were not prepared for this sort of thing. They stood nervously in the doorways, and only the very small boys ventured out along the walls behind the rear ranks to try and finger somebody's Tommy gun, or beg for cigarettes or biscuits. There is in the Army a military Travel Agency called Movement Control. Its name implies its duties, but every soldier was convinced that the object of this organization was to cause as much trouble and discomfort as possible to innocent fighting battalions. This time Movement Control suggested that the Battalion should march inland two miles, wait in an open field for an indefinite time and then march down to Castellamare Harbour through Gragnano. The Adjutant refused point blank. Reluctantly a little man, wearing a large armlet marked "M.C.," admitted that perhaps it would not make any difference if the Battalion waited in Gragnano until the time when they would have passed through it for the second time. It made a difference of four miles to the Battalion. Colonel

Andrew had no intention of wasting the Regimental Band and every intention of embarking with full military pomp. The Band played the Grenadiers down to the harbour and then drove back to Gragnano. They formed a circle in the street, with Captain Willcocks (D.M.) in the middle, and gave a short concert of light music.

The Battalion marched out of Gragnano headed by the Band playing the Regimental March, "St. Patrick's Day." They swung down the hill into Castellamare. The brave sound of "The Minstrel Boy" and "The Wearing of the Green" and the steady tread of Guardsmen rang through the shabby streets. Italians lined the pavements and crowded the main square, clapping and cheering "Viva, Viva !" as if the whole thing was for their benefit—as indeed to a certain extent it was. Colonel Andrew Scott, standing on the pedestal of a statue, took the salute. It was the way that men should go to war.

Support Company and the transport was already loaded in the tank landing craft. The companies filed up the ramps on to their infantry landing craft—long, narrow shallow-draft ships like miniature corvettes. These landing craft are troop-carrying egg-shells ; apart from the engines there is nothing inside them but three large cabins, fitted with old wooden tram-seats, into which it is possible to cram 120 men. Loaded with equipment, carrying rifles, Bren guns, Tommy guns, Piats and bombs, mortars and bombs, wireless sets, camp kettles, water-cans and rations, the Guardsmen stumbled down the narrow iron ladders into the "cabins." The officers were further burdened by long rolls of maps which they were not to distribute till the convoy had set sail. It was terribly crowded below decks. Somehow or other the men sorted themselves out and found a place for their equipment and their bodies. "Can we smoke ?" was, as always, the first question. There was nothing now to do but wait and smoke, smoke and wait, till the Navy put them on shore again. The officers urged their men to get some sleep, as it might be the last chance for a long time, but only physical exhaustion could bring sleep in such quarters. The convoy assembled in Naples Bay. There were ships as far as the eye could see—L.C.Is., L.C.Ts., small craft, landing ships, M.T.Bs., mine-sweepers, destroyers, an aircraft-carrier and a couple of cruisers. About seven o'clock the convoy sailed. It headed out to sea through the channel between Cape Sorrento and the Island of Capri, and then steamed south—a simple ruse to deceive any German reconnaissance planes. A destroyer, with General Alexander on the bridge, cut through the long line of ships flying the signal "Good luck to you all." At dusk the convoy turned on its tracks and steamed north up the coast. It was a dark, still winter night. There was no moon, but the stars gave enough light to see the dark outlines of the ships and the faint phosphorescent glow of their wakes. It was eerily quiet. Standing on deck it was just possible to hear a low murmur from the cabins, otherwise there was no sound but the soft wash of the water. It was stifling in the cabins and thick with smoke; the men, in their socks, slipped up on deck to watch the dark Italian coast. As they passed the mouth of the River Garigliano they could hear the thuds and see the pin-point flashes of gun-fire. "That's to help us, and when we land there won't be any more need for it."

Meanwhile, down below decks, the Company Commanders on each of the four landing craft were preparing their "briefings." The men crowded into the largest cabin. The officer shone a light on the large-scale map of Italy and began. "We are landing at a place called Anzio tomorrow morning. Anzio—here it is, thirty miles south of Rome. This is the idea. . . ."

ORDER OF BATTLE FOR OPERATION "SHINGLE."

Commanding Officer ... Lieut.-Colonel C. A. Montagu-Douglas-Scott, D.S.O.
Second-in-Command ... Major D. M. L. Gordon-Watson, M.C.
Adjutant ... ... Captain D. J. L. FitzGerald, M.C.
R.S.M. McLoughlin.
R.Q.M.S. Grey.
Drill-Sergeant Rooney.
Drill-Sergeant Kenny.

H.Q. Company.

Coy. Commander ... Captain S. H. Combe.
Intelligence Officer ... Lieutenant J. C. Quinn.
Signals ... ... Lieutenant F. Collin.
Pioneer ... ... Lieutenant G. Bland.
M.T. ... ... Sergeant Quinn.
Quartermaster ... Lieutenant H. F. McKinney, M.B.E.
Medical Officer ... Captain D. O'Neill.
Chaplain ... ... Father Rudesind Brookes, O.S.B.

Support Company.

Coy. Commander ... Major H. L. S. Young.
Anti-Tank ... ... Captain R. D. N. Young.
Lieutenant M. Boyd.

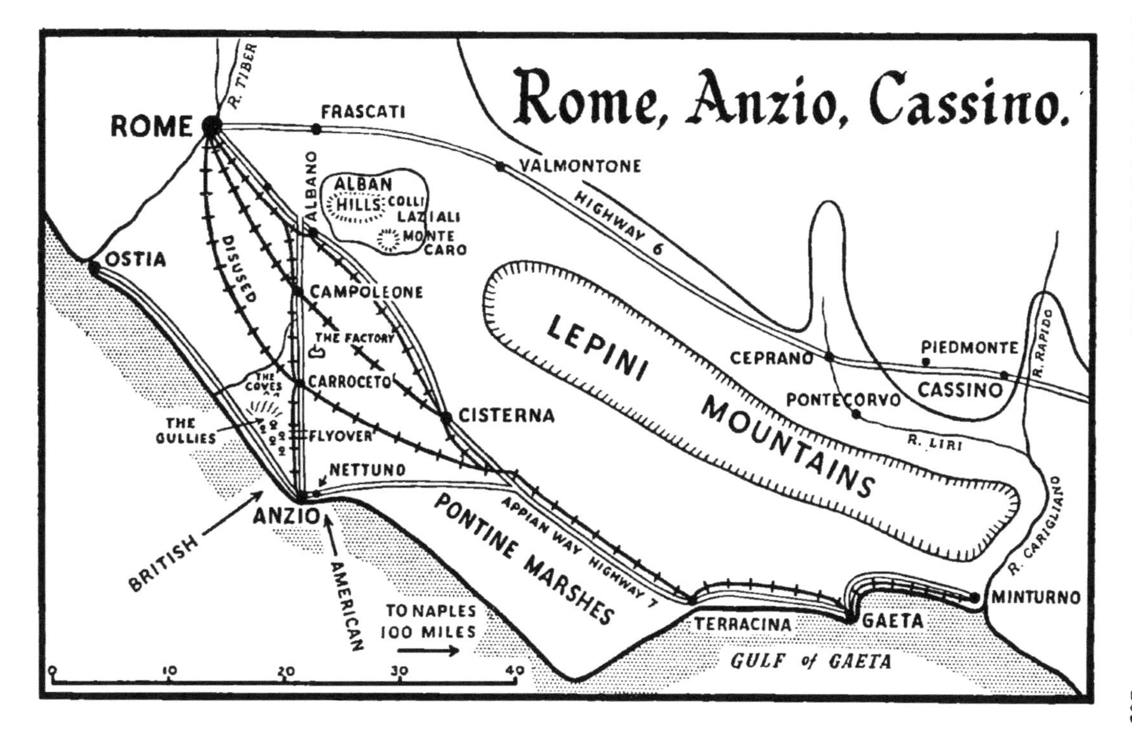
Rome, Anzio, Cassino.
R. TIBER
ROME
FRASCATI
VALMONTONE
HIGHWAY 6
ALBANO
ALBAN HILLS
COLLI LAZIALI
MONTE CARO
OSTIA
DISUSED
CAMPOLEONE
THE FACTORY
CARROCETO
THE COVES
THE GULLIES
FLYOVER
NETTUNO
CISTERNA
LEPINI MOUNTAINS
CEPRANO
PIEDMONTE
R. RAPIDO
CASSINO
PONTECORVO
R. LIRI
R. CARIGLIANO
MINTURNO
ANZIO
BRITISH
AMERICAN
PONTINE MARSHES
APPIAN WAY HIGHWAY 7
TERRACINA
GAETA
GULF of GAETA
TO NAPLES 100 MILES
0 10 20 30 40

Carriers	Lieutenant T. Bell
Mortars	Lieutenant A. Bell.
Machine Guns ...	Lieutenant D. Lambert.
	C.S.M. Stone.

No. 1 Company.

Coy. Commander ...	Major Sir R. Stewart-Richardson.
Second-in-Command ...	Captain D. O'Cock.
	Lieutenant P. Da Costa.
	Lieutenant C. Bartlett.
	Lieutenant P. Grace.
	C.S.M. Gilmore.

No. 2 Company.

Coy. Commander ...	Major G. P. M. FitzGerald.
Second-in-Command ...	Captain P. R. B. Keogh.
	Lieutenant A. M. Burton.
	Lieutenant Hon. C. Brand.
	Lieutenant H. Gillow.
	C.S.M. Pestell.

No. 3 Company.

Coy. Commander ...	Captain D. M. Kennedy.
Second-in-Command ...	Captain O. F. McInerney.
	Lieutenant Earls-Davies.
	Lieutenant Hon. S. E. Preston.
	Lieutenant C. Musgrave.
	C.S.M. Moran.
	C.Q.M.S. Smythe.

No. 4 Company.

Coy. Commander ...	Major I. H. Powell-Edwards.
Second-in-Command ...	Captain D. Drummond.
	Lieutenant T. Keigwin.
	Lieutenant P. Harcourt.
	Lieutenant J. C. Dodds.
	C.S.M. Mercer.

Reinforcements : 17 officers, 294 other ranks.

Note : As long as there were three platoons in a company, one subaltern was left out of battle, his platoon being commanded by the platoon sergeant.

CHAPTER II

The Anzio Plan

THE campaign in Italy became in the first three months what it was to remain till the end—a slow, painful advance through difficult mountainous country against a determined and resourceful enemy who made the best use of the unending natural obstacles. The Germans clearly intended to force the Allies to fight a slow and costly frontal battle up the backbone of Italy. The only way to frustrate this intention was to turn their flanks. The Eighth Army had considerably quickened their advance by small amphibious attacks, and the landing at Salerno had hastened the capture of Naples and the joining of the Fifth and Eighth Armies. At the beginning of November, General Alexander ordered a concentrated frontal attack aided by an amphibious assault in the rear. The Eighth Army was to capture Pescara and strike westwards to cut the German lines of communication ; simultaneously the Fifth Army would attack up the Liri and Sacco valleys. When the two attacks were going well, the Fifth Army was to land a third force somewhere on the coast south of Rome. The Fifth Army planning staff chose the beaches and small port of Anzio, some thirty miles south of Rome. A good road runs out of Anzio to join Highway 7, one of two main roads south, at the foot of the Alban Hills. A direct thrust up this road would threaten the German communications and put the assault force in a good position to meet the main army advancing from the south. To the south the area was bounded by the Pontine Marshes. The flat country inland is overlooked by the encircling Alban and Lepini hills, from which guns could shell the assaulting force, but it was necessary to accept this "disadvantage." The main political and military objective was Rome. Mr. Winston Churchill, the Prime Minister, had already declared that, "whoever holds Rome holds the title-deeds of Italy." Its capture would enable the Italian Government to hold up its head and would give the Allies an important group of airfields.

This first plan came to nothing. The Eighth Army attacked across the River Sangro on the 26th November in appalling weather. The roads were impassable, the rivers were in flood and the Germans were in strength. The soldiers of the Eighth Army were already exhausted by crippling exposure and remorseless hardship. They did manage to break through part of the German defences, but were halted twenty-five miles from Pescara. The Fifth Army attack was no more successful. The strength of the enemy's defences, the heavy rain and the flooding of the River Garigliano all combined to stall the attack. The capture of Monte Comino was in itself a remarkable feat, but it did not lead to a general advance. The Fifth Army still needed to break through the Mignano Defile before the way was clear to Cassino. Air reconnaissance revealed that the Germans had built yet another defensive system in front of Rome—the Gustav Line. Hitler had given up delaying tactics and was now determined to fight for Rome.

Almost as soon as the original plan was abandoned a second and similar one was undertaken. Every day of fighting in the hills and river valleys proved that some plan on the same principle would have to be devised if the Allies were to gain a quick military decision leading to the capture of Rome. With the Fifth Army on the west coast stuck in the Liri valley, and the Eighth Army halted in front of Pescara on the east coast, it seemed that the only way to get to Rome was by sea. "Anzio" was officially revived in Tunis on Christmas Day at a Grand Conference between the Prime Minister and all the Mediterranean Commanders-in-Chief. It would be folly, said Mr. Churchill, to allow the campaign in Italy to drag on and to face the invasion of France in the spring with the task in Italy half finished. The object now was not merely to capture Rome, important politically as that might be, but to annihilate the German Army south of the city, and so quicken the whole Italian campaign and prepare the ground for an attack against Southern France. The Combined Chiefs of Staff agreed to an amphibious operation in Italy, provided that it did not in any way interfere with the plans for the great invasion of France in the summer of 1944. The Naval representative said that they would somehow provide enough landing craft. The Air Force representative said that they could prevent the Germans bringing reinforcements down from the north. The conference therefore ordered General Alexander to launch an amphibious assault behind the enemy's right flank to form a beach-head, to advance and secure the Colli Laziali, the highest of the Alban Hills. The plan, as agreed, called for an assault force of two divisions with airborne troops and armour, to be combined with an attack by the main forces between the Abruzzi mountains and the mouth of the Garigliano river.

The greatest problem was the shortage of landing craft. Most of the craft in the Mediterranean were already due to sail for England, but by some complicated juggling the Royal Navy managed to keep enough ships and landing craft to carry the assault divisions to Anzio and maintain them there for a fortnight. The Royal Navy, as always, overcame all physical difficulties, but even it could not hold the ships and craft in the Mediterranean later than the 5th February. Under the existing plan therefore, the success of the operation would depend on the amount of stores that could be accumulated on the beach-head during that fortnight.

The Fifth Army planning staff reassembled at Caserta with a Naval planning staff under an American Rear-Admiral, Lowry, and with an American air commander, Major-General Cannon. The assault was to be launched on, or as soon as possible after, the 20th January. Its object was to cut the enemy lines of communication and threaten the rear of the German 14th Corps. The chosen instrument was a mixed corps made up of the American 3rd Infantry Division, an American armoured force, a parachute regimental combat team, a battalion of Rangers, the British 1st Infantry Division, a British armoured regiment and two Commandos. It was given a name, the 6th U.S. Corps, and a commander, the American Major-General Lucas. The 1st Infantry Division had just landed in Italy to join the Eighth Army. The Eighth Army was also to lend the Fifth Army the 5th Division to replace the 3rd American Division withdrawn from the front. It was of the utmost importance to conceal these transfers from the enemy, so the Eighth Army was ordered to keep up a constant pressure on the Germans in front of them. Before the landing, the Fifth Army was to launch a full-scale attack so as to draw into battle all the enemy reserves south of Rome. It was then to break through and join 6th Corps at Albano.

General Eisenhower, at that time still Supreme Allied Commander in the Mediterranean, would have preferred the assault force to be composed of troops of only one nation. He felt that the administrative difficulties of a "mixed corps" had been overlooked in favour of high policy. He was, however, told that any such problems could easily be overcome. His native good sense was borne out by the experience of the troops in the beach-head. Most British and American soldiers admired each other and were anxious to help each other, but they rarely knew what the other was doing. Time and again the British units made attacks with the assurance of Corps H.Q. that

American troops would support and "conform," only to find that the Americans concerned had heard nothing, and so did nothing, about it. The same must have happened equally frequently the other way round. When the British and American battalion commanders could talk to each other personally there were no difficulties, administrative or tactical. That amorphous body, Corps H.Q., on the other hand, always put a complete block in the normal channels of communication. The brigades soon discovered that it was fruitless to ask Division H.Q. to ask Corps H.Q. what the Americans were doing. The only way to extract the information was to send an officer to ask the American subordinate commanders themselves. The answer always began, "Oh. Didn't you know. We told Corps yesterday to tell you." The reason given for using a "mixed corps" was that there was not time to assemble either an exclusively British or exclusively American corps. Anyway, the reshuffle that would be needed to assemble a "one nation corps" would be so great that the Germans could hardly fail to discover it. General Alexander felt that he had achieved the strongest possible combination by securing two first-class formations—the 1st British and 3rd U.S. Divisions—and that, in Major-General Lucas, he had secured a capable force commander. Furthermore, the only competent parachute force was the 504th Regiment of the 82nd U.S. Airborne Division. The British Airborne Brigade was actually in the line where it would be difficult to replace ; and anyway, it had had no experience in air landing.

The Anzio landing was now a major operation in its own right. The planners conceived that it would be necessary to supply the assault by sea for at least fifteen days, as it was highly improbable that the main Fifth Army could join the beach-head in any shorter time. The Navy, however, said that with their existing number of ships and programme, they could only maintain the force in the beachhead for eight days, and indeed, after the 3rd February there would only be six landing ships left in the Mediterranean which they could use. Under these conditions the operation was extremely hazardous. The Germans were certainly building and reinforcing new defensive positions across the peninsula, but should the Fifth Army attack fail to draw in all the enemy reserves, the Germans would be able immediately to muster against the landing at least three divisions and two battle groups. The assault force was to be landed with eight days' supplies to face these German troops. If it was not joined by the main Fifth Army within the eight days, either more supplies would have to be shipped or the force would have to be evacuated. An evacuation, even if successful, would involve a total loss of equipment, a heavy loss of life and a serious loss of landing and assault craft badly needed for the invasion of both Northern and Southern France. The political repercussions of an evacuation—an Italian Dunkirk—would be a godsend to the Germans. The immense propaganda value of crushing a continental landing was not lost on Hitler. He later bombarded the German troops round the beach-head with orders, encouragements and pleas to drive "the invaders" into the sea at all costs. All this the new Supreme Allied Commander, General Maitland Wilson, had to consider, but he judged the military prize to be well worth the risk. So, also, did General Alexander. "The operation appeared justified, even at considerable cost." The Prime Minister had already stated his views. "We cannot leave the Rome situation to stagnate and fester for the three months without crippling amalgamation of 'Anvil' (the landing in Southern France) and thus hampering 'Overlord' (the great invasion plan). We cannot go on to other tasks and leave this unfinished job behind us." It was essential, however, to get more landing ships and craft. On 8th January General Alexander saw Mr. Churchill at Marrakech. As a result of what he said means were found to provide twenty-four additional landing craft, which meant that the beach-head force could be maintained to the end of February, if necessary, without affecting future operations.

The plans were now well under way and the operation had been given a code name, "Shingle." Two naval task forces, one American and one British, had been assembled to embark and land the troops.

British Task Force, commanded by Rear-Admiral T. H. Troubridge, R.N.:

- 1 H.Q. ship.
- 4 Cruisers.
- 8 Fleet destroyers.
- 6 Hunt destroyers.
- 2 A.A. ships.
- 2 Dutch gun-boats.
- 11 Fleet minesweepers.
- 6 Minelayers.
- 4 Landing craft guns.
- 4 Landing craft flak.
- 4 Landing craft tanks (fitted with rocket projectors).

U.S. Task Force, commanded by Admiral Lowry, U.S.N. :

1 H.Q. ship.
1 Cruiser.
8 Destroyers.
2 Destroyer escorts.
6 Auxiliary minesweepers
12 Patrol craft.
20 Submarine chasers.
18 Yacht minesweepers.
6 Air rescue boats.

The Tactical Air Force allotted most of its strength to cover the landing. The 12th Air Support Command and two American wings from the Desert Air Force were to provide direct air support, while the tactical bombers were put on heavier missions. The close day-to-day air support of the beach-head forces, however, would have to come from the aerodromes round Naples, because there was not enough shipping space to land more than one Spitfire squadron, granting that it was possible to maintain an "air-strip" on the beach-head itself. The Coastal Air Force prepared to protect the assault convoy in Naples Bay and half-way up to the landing beaches. The threat from the German Air Force was not very serious. Part of their bombing fleet had already been withdrawn from Italy, and the R.A.F. planned to deal with the remainder of it by blasting the airfields.

The beaches were poor and could only be used in good weather. If the port was wrecked the only alternative, a most unsatisfactory one, was a floating pontoon causeway over the beach. The supply of the force, therefore, very largely depended on the capture intact of Anzio Harbour. Even the harbour, however, was unusable in bad weather. The weather experts could only give a firm forecast for forty-eight hours at a time, so all stores had to be loaded in such a way that they could be discharged in that period.

The Germans clearly had no intention of withdrawing from any position until they were forced to do so. Their heavy losses and the constant strain, however, would in the normal course of events force them to regroup and relieve their troops in the line some time in January. With any luck, the landing and the general offensive would catch them in the middle of this movement. The main Fifth Army attack, it was hoped, would force them to commit their reserves to hold the Liri valley, then they would have to withdraw some of these same reserves in order to crush or contain the Anzio threat to their rear. By the 16th January the Fifth Army Intelligence thought that the Germans in front of them were weakening. This, if true, meant that the Germans must put all their reserves into the fight. "Once weakened on the main front, and with his forces split, he would have little chance of containing our thrust up the Liri valley." That was the considered opinion of the planners. There would be at the most only one division and four parachute battalions in the Rome area immediately available to throw against the landing on the first day. After that, they could probably raise another infantry division and S.S. regiment and a few battle groups, and possibly the Hermann Goering Panzer Regiment. When they saw what the Allied plan was they might later be able to bring the 26th Panzer Division from the Adriatic coast. They also had two divisions up round Florence which they could bring down, but the R.A.F. proposed to delay these by bombing the roads and railways.

The final plan ordered 6th Corps to secure a beach-head in the vicinity of Anzio and then advance on Colli Laziali. The assault would take place at 0200 hrs. on the 22nd January. The Navy's original plan was to make a feint at the mouth of the River Tiber the day before the landing. This was cancelled, since the most probable result would be to draw south, and so near the real landing, the German forces north of the river. Instead, the Navy proposed to bombard Civitavecchia just as the assault convoy arrived off the beaches. There would be no preliminary naval bombardment of the Anzio beaches, but the rocket ships would fire a barrage five minutes before the first troops stepped ashore. The American Naval Task Force was to land three regiments on the beaches east of Anzio. The British Task Force was to land a brigade group and two Commandos on the west beaches. The American Rangers would land in the port of Anzio from the old Irish cross-channel steamer, H.M.S. *Royal Ulsterman*—the same ship which, a year before, had carried the 1st Bn. Irish Guards from Algiers to Bone. These three forces would then form a bridgehead seven miles in depth around Anzio. After the establishment of the beach-head, the objective of the whole force was to cut the two main roads about twelve miles south-east of Rome. The operative words for this section of the plan were: "After the establishment of the beach-head." The report does not say how long this was intended to take. The planners calculated that the Germans could throw a division against the beach-head on the first day. This worried them. They ordered the bulk of the 1st British Division with a regiment of tanks and two regiments of artillery to be held in reserve to deal with this possible counter-attack. "504th Regimental Combat Team," continued the plan, "will land behind the 3rd U.S. Division and also pass to 6th Corps reserve." These few words cancelled the parachute drop which was at first considered vital to the success of the operation. Now, however, in the words of the official report, "the hazardous mission appeared to offer too few advantages to offset the risks." Instead of jumping out of aeroplanes to cut the Anzio–Albano road before the landing, the parachutists were now going to walk ashore like everybody else and later than most. The official reasons for the change are unconvincing. It was said that a parachute drop would give the Germans early warning of the landing, but there was no need to drop the parachutists until the leading assault troops had actually landed. It was also said that the advancing troops of the 1st British Division would not be able to distinguish American parachutists from German soldiers. Parties of fully equipped paratroopers had already visited each battalion in the Division. The British greatly admired their equipment, but it never occurred to them that there would be any difficulty in distinguishing them from Germans. There are two things in particular that a Guardsman can tell at a glance—an enemy and a good commander.

The orders given to Brigadier Murray, the commander of the 24th Guards Brigade, put a different emphasis on the objects of the landing. In his own account of "Shingle" he lists them in this order: (1) To draw German reserves away from the Fifth Army; (2) to *threaten* the German lines of communication between Rome and the Fifth Army front, and (3), in co-operation with the main Fifth Army, to capture Rome and destroy the German forces south of Rome. "The impression I had before we landed was that we were in for hard fighting on D Day and D+1 and that any early advance to cut the German lines of communications was not likely, though we all realized the importance of this and hoped it would come off." When the plan eventually got down to the level of battalion commanders, Lieut.-Colonel Andrew Scott, D.S.O., and Lieut.-Colonel G. Gordon-Lennox quickly made up their minds. The Scots Guards were landing as a fourth battalion in the assault brigade. That left only the Grenadiers and the Irish in the 24th Guards Brigade to be landed at dawn as reserves for the assault. They urged, with every conceivable argument, that their battalions should be organized as two mobile striking columns, each with tanks and self-propelled guns under command. If the landing was opposed, or immediately sealed off, they would fight as normal reinforcement reserves. But if the landing achieved surprise, as it well might, then the advantage must be pressed home. They repeated this again and again. It would be known by dawn whether or not the landing was a success ; if it was, then the two battalion columns should—in fact, must—be launched straight up the main road to Albano. Just before the main road reaches Highway 7—the Appian Way—it forks to form a rough triangle. One battalion would go up one fork, the other up the other, to establish road-blocks on the Highway. If parachutists were dropped round the Colli Laziali, they could join the battalions to form a stronghold in the triangle ; if they were not, the battalions could manage well without them. The sudden appearance of a determined force on one of the Germans' two main routes south would create chaos in the supply columns and might easily stampede the German commander into ordering a general withdrawal. If the main landing force could not reach the Highway then the battalions, their work of disorganization done, could withdraw in good order into the secure beach-head. The news of the landing did, in fact, throw into a flurry the Germans in Rome and all down the line to the southern front. Highways 6 and 7 were a stream of staff cars beating it back to Rome bearing officers and men who considered that their presence so far south was no longer necessary. The Grenadiers and Irish could have picked up most of these military refugees and harried the others. The Germans at the front would have been looking over their shoulders instead of straight ahead. The words "What might have been" are the saddest in life ; they are the keynote of the Anzio landing.

CHAPTER III

The Landing at Anzio

THE convoy dropped anchor off Anzio a few minutes after midnight on Saturday, 22nd January. The submarines *Ultor* and *Uproar* were waiting as "markers" on either side of the port. Naval scout parties were sent ashore to signpost the beaches. The assault craft were lowered and marshalled, and at one o'clock the first waves headed for the shore. The moon had not yet risen and from the beaches came no sound or sign of life. At ten minutes to two the rocket ships broke the silence with salvoes behind and on either side of the beaches. Still no response came from the shore. Ten minutes later the two "first wave" battalions of the 2nd Brigade—the 2nd Bn. The North Staffordshire Regiment and the 6th Bn. Gordon Highlanders—stepped into the sea some four miles north-west of Anzio. Their assault craft hit and stuck on a hidden sand-bar a hundred yards out, and they had to wade ashore. They found a few scattered mines, but no enemy and moved slowly forward through the bushes and trees above the strand to the coast road. It took over an hour for the craft to turn round, collect and land the other two assault battalions, the 1st Bn. The Loyal Regiment and the 1st Bn. Scots Guards. Wireless silence was broken at half-past two, but the Battalion in its landing craft only heard that surprise was complete and that all was going well. The moon rose about the same time, and from the decks three miles out at sea the Battalion could see the outline of coast and even pick up some of the landmarks they had seen on the air photographs. They had to wait till the assault brigade had secured the initial bridgehead. The 1st Loyals advanced north-west along the coast road to the stream Caffarella, seven miles from Anzio. On the right flank the Scots Guards advanced down the road towards Anzio. They flushed a few convalescent German soldiers, in pyjamas, out of a beach-hut. In the centre the North Staffordshires and the Gordons advanced north towards the Campo di Carne and plunged into the tangled wilderness of the wood called Selva di Nettuno. The Commandos and American Rangers landed at Anzio itself, captured the small dock area and proceeded to mop up the weak defences of the town and the neighbouring seaside resort of Nettuno. On the beaches east of Anzio—X-Ray Beach—the two assault brigades of the 3rd U.S. Division met no opposition or obstacles and advanced slowly inland.

When dawn broke the Battalion could see the sea around them full of craft and ships and the air above full of aeroplanes. It promised to be a clear, sunny day. There was an atmosphere of jubilation, mixed with a sense of "this is too good to be true." The operation was running far more to plan than any exercise had ever done. Nobody had had a clear idea of what the landing was going to be like, beyond a hazy picture of wading up to their necks through water churned to foam by bullets and stained scarlet by blood, to cling to a few yards of sand in the teeth of two German divisions. Certainly nobody expected to see the vast armada spread out on the calm sea, as peaceful as a painted ship upon a painted sea, but not as idle. Launches and landing craft wove patterns through the larger ships, landing troops, guns and H.Q. staffs. At seven o'clock the L.C.Is., carrying the Irish and the Grenadier Guards, moved slowly in to the shore. The Battalion could now see the beaches, the flags, the signposts, the unemployed anti-aircraft guns, and the tractors winching guns up the sandy dunes to the hard ground beneath the trees. Fifteen miles behind the beach they could see the solid mass of the Alban Hills and, farther to the east, the long high range of the Lepini Hills, enclosing the flat plain to make a huge amphitheatre. On either side of these hills ran the two main roads to the southern front; on the south side, Highway 7—the old Appian Way—from Rome through Albano, Velletri, Cisterna, Terracina and Gaeta, and on the north side through Frascati and Frosinone to Cassino.

The Battalion landed dry-shod. "Ducks," large amphibious jeeps, met the L.C.Is. at the sand-bar and ferried the companies into a floating pontoon pier. It was all very gentlemanly, calm and dignified. Major Young, with a large black umbrella hung on his arm, stepped ashore with the air of a missionary visiting a South Sea island and surprised to see no cannibals. It was quite clear that the landing had achieved complete surprise. "I only hope we are taking advantage of it" was everyone's unspoken and spoken thought. The Battalion, anxiously counted by the Adjutant, filed up the sandy track to the coast road and then along between the trees on the coast side towards Anzio. They passed Italian farm labourers on their way to work and greeted them politely. The Italians showed singularly little interest. "Dove Tedeschi ?" asked the Guardsmen. "Niente Tedeschi," replied the Italians, and jerked a thumb vaguely north-westward. "Roma." "Rome," translated the scholars. "We will give the Holy Father a holiday," said one enthusiastic man, "and make Father Brookes acting unpaid Pope." The Battalion halted in the roadside woods, with the Grenadiers between them and the main Anzio–Albano road. This old Roman road runs due north from Anzio to join the Appian Way—Highway 7—four miles north-west of Albano. It was a wide, well-made road, but open and straight as an arrow ; an observer on the hills could see the entire length of it. It was the only main road leading north and the only short cut to Rome. All the other roads, if they were not mere tracks, branched off sharply outside Anzio east and west and only reached the Appian Way by devious circuitous routes. The beach-head centred on this road ; all the fighting in the following weeks was basically only fierce efforts to extend the Allied hold on it or to defeat the German attempts to cut it.

The Battalion stretched itself out under the bushes to wait, chat and smoke, while Colonel Andrew, Lieut.-Colonel Gordon-Lennox of the Grenadiers and the Brigade Commander, Brigadier Murray, drove down the road in a jeep to find the Scots Guards and Lieut.-Colonel D. Wedderburn. "It was a great relief," said Brigadier Murray, "to feel that it had all been so easy. We realized that we had gained complete surprise and felt that this was the moment to go forward. But it was not to be, and we had to obey orders and remain in our concentration area." The Brigadier could not appeal against these orders as there was no one to appeal to. "I expected to find the Divisional command post," he said, "but they were not to be found as they did not land until the following day." By a private arrangement the Brigade Commander of the 2nd Brigade transferred the Scots Guards back to Brigadier Murray, and the 24th Guards Brigade undertook to keep in contact with the American Rangers on the right (west) of the main road. For the Battalion the main event of the morning was the sight of General Alexander and Rear-Admiral Troubridge driving up and down the coast road. General Alexander was optimistic ; "I am very satisfied," he told Colonel Andrew. The sun was now well up, and the Germans were just beginning to shell the beach-head. "I don't feel safe except at sea," said Admiral Troubridge. "This is most unfair, as really I am a non-combatant on land." The cruisers and destroyers at sea replied to the German guns, and at last the Battalion felt the local war had started.

So the Battalion waited all morning and afternoon in the woods by the sea, walking restlessly up and down, collecting wood for fires, making tea and eating the stale haversack rations that had been packed in Gragnano. At what should have been tea-time, by which time everyone had smoked too many cigarettes, the Battalion crossed the road and moved into the southern outskirts of the Selva di Nettuno three miles inland. By the evening the whole Brigade group—the three battalions, the 19th Field Regiment, R.A., and Self-Propelled Battery, R.A., a Medium Battery, R.A., the Brigade Support Group and the 137th Field Ambulance—were ashore and concentrated between the Selva di Nettuno and the sea. "It had been an extraordinary day, and though all had gone well, we could not but feel we were losing a golden opportunity." Only the Scots Guards, on the main road two miles to the east of the Battalion, saw any sign of the Germans. One of their patrols shot a stray German and took a couple of prisoners. Down in Anzio the tank landing ships and craft were discharging vehicles and stores. "So successful were the unloading arrangements," says the official report, "that by midnight 90 per cent. of the personnel and equipment of the assault convoy, amounting to 36,034 men, 3,069 vehicles and large quantities of stores, had been put ashore." A few feeble German air raids and some desultory shelling did not interfere with the work in the port and on the beaches. "Because of careful preparation by an experienced planning staff," continues the report complacently, "complete co-operation between all Services and faith in a successful conclusion to the task, the landings had proved a model of amphibious operations. The pre-assault air plan had been successful in cutting the enemy lines of communications in three places between the Pisa–Rimini line and Rome, had rendered the Rome airfields unserviceable and had made impotent the enemy reconnaissance units in the Perugia area, so that our final preparations and initial landings went unnoticed by the enemy reconnaissance. Our feint against Civitavecchia by naval bombardment on the night 21st/22nd January occupied the enemy's attention until well after dawn." Admittedly there is bound to be a difference in the point of view of a soldier who fought on the beach-head and anyone who sat in Naples, Bari or Algiers. An Irish Guardsman certainly would not give "an experienced planning staff" the pride of place among the reasons for the success of the landing. The planners may blow their own trumpet, but the soldier remains deaf and ascribes the "model" success to the important fact that there were no Germans there, that the Royal Navy, as always, did its job and that the troops walked ashore. The absence of Germans was due to the initial choice of Anzio, the work of the air forces and the misjudgment of the Germans. The Battalion's opinion of the planners that night was coldly bitter.

As soon as the sun went down, before six o'clock, it turned bitterly cold. The Battalion's transport was not yet unloaded—not being part of the 50 per cent. quoted in the report—so the Battalion had nothing but what they stood up in. A chilling mist rose from the dank wood ; water dripped from the trees on to the shivering men, and seeped out of the ground to form puddles, which froze at midnight "The night," says the War Diary, "was memorable chiefly for the extreme cold." The doctor, Captain D. O'Neill, an ingenious man, found three dirty old German greatcoats, which he kept at his Aid Post—a ditch under a tree—in case anyone got wounded by a shell. The coldest, weariest man in the Battalion was the Commanding Officer, Lieut.-Colonel Andrew Montagu-Douglas-Scott, D.S.O. His hand and forearm were swollen and red from a septic cut; the doctor had fed him on M & B tablets all the previous night and day, and now the depressive reaction of the drug set in. He lay in silent misery on a bank until the doctor spread one of his German greatcoats over him. The rest of them paced ceaselessly up and down the rides and paths in the wood, sitting down when they thought they were tired enough to sleep, and walking again as they found it too cold to sit. Only the carrier drivers got any rest; they switched on their engines and slept fitfully in the driving seats. It was a very long night.

When at last the sun rose on Sunday, the 23rd January, it brought no warmth, but it did bring the transport up from the harbour. The platoon trucks were stripped in an instant and each man got his greatcoat and blankets. The Battalion was not supposed to have any tents, and the staff of Divisional H.Q. had accounted for every inch and pound of equipment on the lorries, but the Irish Guards were old soldiers, and they had been to war before. Within half an hour every man had had his breakfast and the lucky ones, who had drawn the first "shift," were in one of their platoon's four bivouac tents, rather squashed, certainly, but under canvas. With shelter over them and tea and tinned bacon inside them, the Battalion came to life and went to sleep. The men slept till the rain woke them at midday ; the officers and non-commissioned officers waited for the order to advance.

The delay and inaction caused unconcealed disquiet amongst the

Battalion. Officers and men discussed it endlessly amongst themselves. It was about the only thing to do in the sodden, freezing woods. There was a sickening feeling of anti-climax. Every man had been keyed up for a bold, impressive stroke, an enterprise which would probably be bloody, but would certainly be spectacular. The unexpected ease of the landing had raised hopes even higher. There were no Germans, what was stopping the Division ? The men could not understand it, and the officers found it difficult to explain. The orthodox answers—the necessity of securing a firm base before advancing, the need for landing and accumulating supplies, the inadvisability of doing anything rash—all sounded very unconvincing. The 23rd was a completely wasted day, spent unloading the lorries and reconnoitring possible or impossible counter-attacks in every direction and in all parts of the beach-head. It was still bitterly cold, and now it was raining, but at least the Battalion had its blankets and greatcoats and a few tents, and could huddle in miserable groups under the dripping trees. At midday Brigadier Murray saw the Divisional Commander. "There are no orders for us," he told his battalion commanders afterwards, "but we have been given some rather vague counter-attack roles." There was a report that the German 3rd Panzer Grenadier Division, supported by a regiment of the 90th Light Division, had been withdrawn from the Fifth Army front to meet the threat of the 3rd U.S. Division north-east of Anzio. This was the first news that the landing had achieved anything. "Our own future movements depend to a large extent on developments in that sector," ended the Brigadier. "Meanwhile, we are to stay where we are." Meanwhile, also, the German garrison in Rome were recovering from the panic into which the news of the landing had thrown them. The Romans hastily put back the Swastika flags hoping that no one had noticed the Union Jacks and Stars and Stripes. Captain Colin Lesslie and the other escaped prisoners of war, sheltering in the Vatican, sadly unpacked their bags.

The first German reaction had in fact been a hasty concentration of the Hermann Goering Panzer Division. Air observers had seen an increase in the road traffic on Highway 6 westward from Frosinone to the Colli Laziali area, and heavy traffic on both main roads leading north-west from the southern front as well as west from the Eighth Army front. The Intelligence had estimated that, by the evening of 23rd January, the Germans could mass two divisions against the beach-head. Two Panzer Grenadier regiments, the 29th, from Pescara, and the 104th from the Liri valley, were already around the beach-head, and behind this screen the Germans were concentrating more troops round Velletri. It looked as if they had already committed their Tenth Army reserves to meet the attacks along the whole Fifth Army front. On the very day that 6th Corps landed the Germans launched a series of heavy counter-attacks on the main Fifth Army, and did nothing round Anzio. The following day, the 23rd, their counter-attacks in the Liri valley increased in intensity, but they still did not touch the beach-head. It was clear proof of their weakness in the Rome area. The Battalion could not understand why Corps Commander did not take any advantage of this local and purely temporary weakness. The first order came that evening. The Divisional Commander ordered the Brigade to send an "armoured reconnaissance" to the village of Carroceto, and beyond, if possible. As there were no tanks available the Brigadier found it "difficult to see how the armoured part of the task was to be done," but he ordered the Grenadiers to send out a patrol at dawn, with carriers to act as "armour."

At dusk, German aircraft bombed the harbour and beaches. They sank H.M.S. *Janus* with glider-bombs and so damaged H.M.S. *Jervis* that she had to move to Naples. Every anti-aircraft gun and most of the Bren guns in the beach-head pumped shells and bullets into the sky. Streams of tracer wove intricate patterns through which the German aeroplanes streaked back home.

IRISH GUARDSMEN ON THE MAIN ROAD TO ROME, EIGHT MILES NORTH OF ANZIO. 25.1.44

A SHERMAN TANK OF THE 46 ROYAL TANK REGIMENT COVERING IRISH GUARDSMEN AS THEY ADVANCE ALONG THE ROAD NORTH OF ANZIO. 25.1.44

Face page 222

View of the main road to Rome taken from road bridge, Campo di Carne, about eight miles north of Anzio. 25.1.44

Corporal Doak, 1st Battalion, with Two German Prisoners. January/February, 1944

Face page 223

CHAPTER IV

Carroceto

THE beach-head now consisted of a semi-circle round Anzio of roughly seven miles diameter. It was bounded on the north by a convenient road which ran from west to east, just where the woods of the Selva di Nettuno ended and the flat plain called Campo di Carne began. This flat plain, broken by innumerable gullies, stretched northwards for three miles to the Buonriposo Ridge and the village of Carroceto. Beyond Carroceto the ground sloped up gently northwards to Campoleone and Albano at the foot of the towering Alban Hills. The Campo di Carne road crossed the main Anzio–Albano road by an embankment and fly-over bridge. This was the present outpost position held by a battalion of the 2nd Infantry Brigade. Nearly three miles beyond the fly-over bridge, just south of Carroceto, was another and longer embankment and a bridge on which a disused railway line crossed the main road. Standing on a swell in the ground about a quarter of a mile to the right of the village was a cluster of large new buildings. This was Aprilia, the pride of Mussolini, and the municipal centre of the reclaimed marsh-lands. The whole area had been for centuries a malarial bog, shunned by all sensible men, and inhabited only by a few web-toed fever-ridden cork-cutters. The little port of Anzio stagnated to the constant hum of mosquitoes ; its only claim to fame was that it was the birthplace of the Roman Emperor Nero, and Nero is the only man who is known to have loved Anzio. Behind the town stretched the notorious Pontine Marshes and festering bog-land, overgrown with scrub and cork-oak. Two of the things the Italians are really good at are digging canals and building roads, but even they, land-hungry as they were, could do nothing with this desolate area till Mussolini poured in men and money to win prestige for the Fascist party. It was a remarkable achievement.

They dug a spider's-web of canals and irrigation channels to drain every bit of land that was not beyond redemption and turned it into pasture and plough, but even now when it rains the ground becomes a spongy, sodden mass. They built a series of farm-houses, all neatly numbered and in three patterns, and installed ex-service men as colonists. On the northern edge of the former marsh land they built a model "community centre," and on the slight ridge north of it a model co-operative farm. Aprilia, the "community centre," had everything recommended by town-planners—shops, health clinics, a church, offices, municipal wine stores and, largest of all, a town hall and Fascist headquarters surmounted by a tall square tower like a chimney stack. From a distance it looked like a factory, and "The Factory" the Allies always called it. The tower was a landmark from the sea to the Alban Hills.

The Grenadier patrol drove under the fly-over bridge at dawn and up the road. They returned in the afternoon to say that there were some Germans, probably about a company, and one or two tanks, in the village and the Factory, but nothing very formidable. The Brigadier and every man in the Brigade had been waiting all day hoping for orders to advance. Nothing came until the evening. At eight o'clock the orders at last arrived. The Brigade, supported by two troops of British Sherman tanks and some self-propelled guns, was to capture Carroceto and the Factory as a "spring-board" for an attack by the American Armoured Division the following day. The left flank would be left wide open, but the right would be protected by a parallel advance by the American Rangers. The Rangers, unfortunately, did not hear of this arrangement till late the following evening when everything was over. The Brigadier pointed out that the Germans had been given two days' grace—plenty of time to prepare trouble for the Brigade. He was told that he would not meet any trouble. "Delighted with the idea that at last we were to advance, I accepted this, but not without some misgivings. I ordered an advance guard, consisting of two companies of Grenadiers in R.A.S.C. lorries and a squadron of tanks, commanded by Colonel Gordon-Lennox, to pass under the fly-over bridge at 7.30 in the morning. After them would come the remainder of the Grenadiers, then the Irish and the Scots, all on foot."

At half-past seven precisely, the Grenadier carriers and lorries and the tanks shot under the fly-over bridge and careered up the road. It was a cold, crisp morning with bright sun. The whole atmosphere was somehow unreal. It was too like the opening phase of an exercise. Both sides of the road were lined by marching

Grenadiers ; trucks drove slowly along the centre. Standing at the entrance to the rides in the woods, the Irish and Scots Guards waited their turn. The Commanding Officer and Adjutant drove ahead of the Battalion up to the fly-over bridge. A line of little farms, later to become hideously familiar as they were slowly knocked to pieces by German shells, fringed the road and the Italian farmers and their families stood at the doors waving handkerchiefs and clapping. From the top of the bridge they could see a marching line of Grenadiers advancing steadily towards Carroceto. Not a shot had yet been fired.

Behind the embankment of the Fly-over was a row of beflagged jeeps ; on the bridge itself was every red hat in the Division—the Divisional Commander, the C.R.A. and the three Brigadiers. They saw the Grenadiers reach the embankment and bridge in front of Carroceto, and saw them halt there. The advance guard could not get through the village. "Things are getting sticky," said Brigadier Murray gloomily. Looking down the long straight main road they could see the white plumes of air-bursts over the trees. The long lines of Guardsmen were still marching steadily down each side, but from Carroceto came the rattle of small-arms fire. Against the dark hulk of the Alban Hills, the backcloth to the whole scene, they could see the flashes of the 88-mm. guns firing those air bursts. It was maddening to see the exact position of the guns and yet be impotent. The fly-over bridge was the best observation post in that sector of the beach-head, and it seemed unnatural that the Germans did not shell it. It soon seemed so to the Germans, too, for a shell burst on the road and killed a military policeman beneath the bridge. The next shells climbed up the embankment, scattering the exalted spectators, making this the first and only time that a group of men stood on the fly-over without being killed. The first attempt of the Grenadiers to rush the Factory failed. Colonel Gordon-Lennox was wounded but continued, in Elizabethan fashion, to command his battalion from a mattress. At eleven o'clock their leading company cleared the houses of Carroceto and the Grenadiers prepared to launch a full battalion attack on the Factory. The Factory was the key to the whole situation ; whoever held it controlled the road between Campo di Carne and Carroceto itself, and the country to the north of it. Meanwhile, the Battalion tramped up the road to and past the Fly-over. After this they had nothing to do. Apart from the sound of firing, it was still like a training scheme, with a long halt while the umpires disentangled some "bog." The transport was strung out along the road, each truck automatically drawn up under a small, leafless tree. Officers and men lay in the ditches shouting for information to the passing despatch riders and wandering over to the Italian farm-houses. Tuesday was baking day in the Pontine Marshes. The housewives and their daughters were all busy round their outside ovens. The Guardsmen exchanged biscuits and chewing gun from the American "K" rations for hard hot bread and assured the farmers in their new Italian that there was "niente pericolo."

The Grenadiers attacked the Factory at half-past two, preceded by a barrage of medium and field guns. As soon as they had captured it the Battalion moved up to hold the left flank and Carroceto station. The Company Commanders and Battalion H.Q. drove straight to the railway bridge, the companies plodded across country up towards the embankment. No. 1 Company passed under the railway and went on some five hundred yards up the main road. No. 4 came up behind to the embankment on the right of the bridge, to cover the right flank and the gap between No. 1 Company and the Grenadiers in the Factory. On the left flank, No. 3 Company was forward, holding the railway station and stretching back round to the embankment a thousand yards north-west of the bridge. No. 2 Company came in between No. 3 and the electric railway line to strengthen the left flank. The Battalion was thus in a rough semi-circle round Carroceto, with the Grenadiers on the right in the Factory and the Scots Guards in reserve back down the Anzio road. On the right the U.S. Division was echeloned back, making slow progress towards Cisterna ; on the left the 2nd Brigade was holding the line of the Molletta river over two miles in the rear. The 24th Guards Brigade had, in effect, pushed a thin salient up the road into the enemy's outpost line. Both flanks were exposed, and all their positions and the only road leading to them were in full view. The Germans' main positions lay a mile farther on. The Factory had been held by a company of the 2nd Bn. 29th Panzer Grenadier Regiment of the 3rd Panzer Grenadier Division. The rest of this battalion held the main road in front of No. 1 Company, with another battalion on its right opposite No. 3 Company and a third battalion in reserve. Farther over on their right—that is the Battalion's left flank—were infantry of the 90th Panzer Grenadier Regiment supported by tanks. In front of these Germans was a screen of semi-independent machine-gun squads and snipers. Some of them surrendered with alacrity, and the companies picked twenty of them out of the houses and culverts, but others remained intact and active, busily machine-gunning anyone they could see. Major Gordon-Watson gave them an excellent

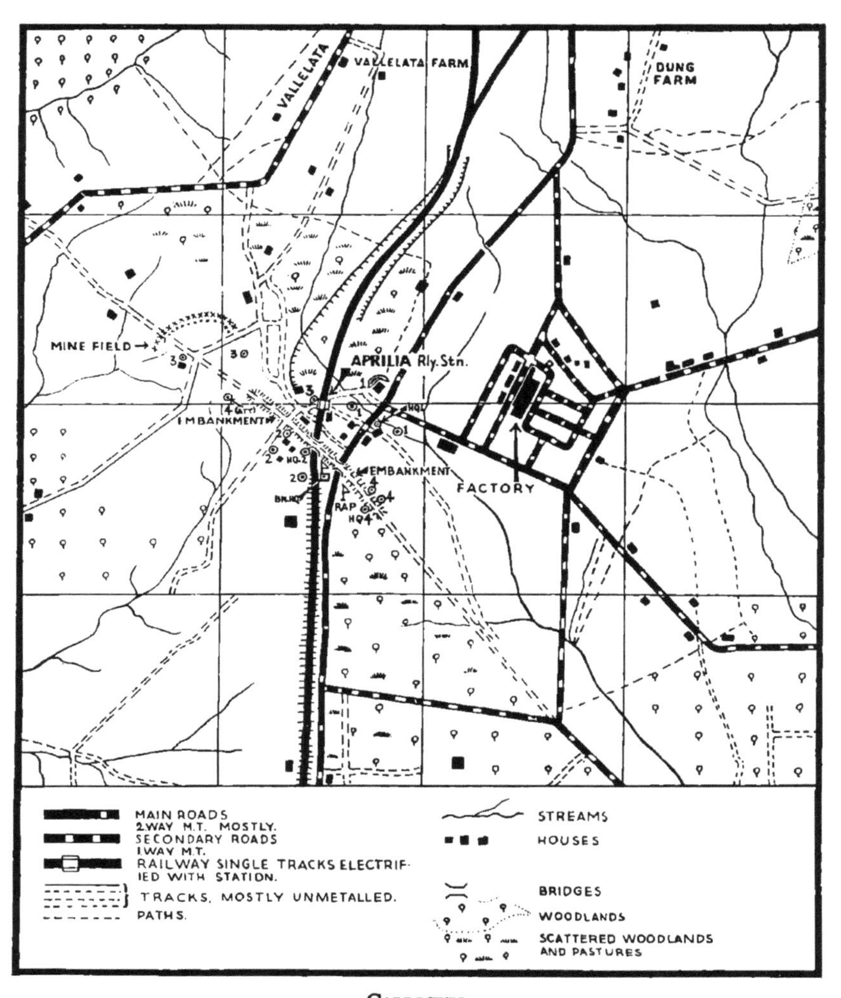

CARROCETO
(1) Carroceto "Factory." (2) The "Embankment." (3) Aprilia Railway Station. (4) Positions occupied by the Battalion, 25th-29th January.

target. He offered to lead Colonel Andrew Scott up to the station, assuring him that it was perfectly all right. North of the embankment, the permanent way of the Anzio electric railway is raised about a foot above the ground. Major Gordon-Watson's quiet stroll to the station ended with both of them lying under the ballast while machine-gun bullets clattered into the stones above them. They crawled slowly towards the station. Corporal McNally, who had a section of mortars already there, watched their approach with kindly interest. "You want to be careful, sir!" he shouted. "There are machine gunners about." "What on earth do you think we are doing now?" replied Colonel Andrew. "Get on your wireless to No. 2 Company." Major George FitzGerald sent out Sergeant Wylie and a small patrol; they soon found the post and despatched the two young Germans behind the Spandau. As soon as he was released, Colonel Andrew was called to Brigade H.Q. Major Gordon-Watson returned to move Battalion H.Q. into a large farm-house behind No. 2 Company. The trucks drove into the courtyard, the men piled into the house and sheds. They set up Signal and Intelligence offices, a guard-room and a cookhouse, dug trenches and latrines, posted sentries and allotted alarm posts. In the companies the platoons were carrying ammunition, tools and blankets out to their section positions. Back in "B" Echelon, in the woods, the Battalion's dinners were ready, and the Quartermaster, Lieutenant H. F. McKinney, and the Company Quartermaster-Sergeants were sitting in the "cookers" ready to drive up to the Battalion as soon as it was dark.

The Company Commanders walked round their areas. Captain John Kennedy strode restlessly backwards and forwards between the platoons of No. 3 Company. He has described his position in detail. "The one feature which stood out was a farm-house on the highest piece of ground in the vicinity. Not only did it dominate the disused railway bed leading down to the bridge over the road, but it also covered the valley to the west. This I called Baron Preston's Castle, because No. 14 Platoon were in it. North of it, on the far side of the old railway bed, was another farm-house, facing up the wide, shallow valley running north. Beside this farm-house, just on the brink of a small slope, were some magnificent bomb-craters; as the ground was not planted with any crops they would not be noticed from any distance. That is where I had my H.Q. and No. 13 Platoon commanded by Sergeant Dunne. One hundred and fifty yards to the right again (the north-east) lay Carroceto railway station. I had already told Lieutenant Musgrave to get 'steaming' there.

By now it was just dark and beginning to drizzle. Telling Lieutenant Preston and Sergeant Dunne to lose no time in digging in, as there was no knowing what the morning might bring, I made my way up to the station to see how No. 15 Platoon were getting on. I found Lieutenant Musgrave in the middle of reorganizing, as he had just been having an argument with a German machine-gun post. The sole survivors of the post were a paratrooper and a very badly wounded warrant officer; we gave him some morphia and got him an ambulance. No. 15 Platoon's position was fairly straightforward. The station was defiladed from the front, the north, but gave a beautiful shoot to the north-west, covering the craters with cross-fire. Inside the station the platoon had the protection of deep cellars, whilst outside they had the soft plough running alongside the tracks in which they were already digging their Bren-gun slits. At the south end of the station two 17-pounder anti-tank guns had already pulled into position. Back at Company H.Q. I found Sergeant Dunne laying trip-wires round the position. The more I looked at those bomb-craters the more I thanked the pilot who had dropped the bombs, as even from a distance of thirty yards it was impossible to pick them out; and for slit trenches dug round the circumference it was perfect."

Between Company H.Q. and Lieutenant Preston's farm the old railway bed ran in a cutting. A hundred yards behind them it emerged from the cutting, ran for a few yards on level ground, and was then gradually built up into the embankment which carried it over the electric railway to Anzio and the main road. A small, narrow lane crossed the bed at this one level point, and along this lane Sergeant Cawood installed two 3-inch mortars to support No. 3 Company. No. 3 Company was also given four of the Battalion's 6-pounder anti-tank guns and a section of the Battalion's private medium machine-gun platoon. Lieutenant M. Boyd brought up the anti-tank guns and Sergeant McDermot the two Vickers medium machine guns. Captain Kennedy, Lieutenant Boyd and Sergeant Wyles, the detachment commander, investigated "Baron Preston's Castle." "Round it were small gardens suffering from the usual effects of winter in war time. On the east end of the house—like all other farm-houses in the district—was a small cow-byre, round which stood large white oxen, the cows amongst them easily noticeable by the pained expression on their faces from lack of milking. It was very reminiscent of Norway. Grunting amongst the chickens was a long thin, black and pink sow, who looked as if she had been on hunger strike since the day she was born." Captain Kennedy never explained what happened to that sow, thin as she was. Sergeant Wyles moved his anti-tank gun in beside a little shed behind a row of small cedars. Corporal Hennessy's gun was about twenty yards away, defiladed by the garden hedge. The machine gun section set up their guns with Corporal Nicholson's section to cover the broad valley running due north. This little force was covered in turn by the rest of the platoon and by Sergeant Ashton's section of No. 13 Platoon in the bomb craters. Sergeant Bowers and Corporal Donovan took their guns to the other sections of No. 14 Platoon. Guardsmen McManus and Carruthers, the Company signallers, had already installed themselves in the farm-house by the bomb-craters. "The house was a pathetic sight. Once it had been in good order and kept neatly, but the hasty withdrawal by the inhabitants had left it an untidy mess. They had even gone so far," continued John Kennedy indignantly, "as to take nearly all the food, leaving only a bowl of milk, a bit of black bread and some half-made cheese. As Lieutenant Boyd and I had had no dinners, we made quick work of this. 'O' Group was 'sounded for' over the air. Finding my way to Battalion H.Q. was no easy matter, and I crashed heavily three times on my way there, which did not do anything to improve my outlook on life."

Colonel Andrew was waiting for the Company Commanders in the big red farm-house that Major Gordon-Watson had chosen as Battalion H.Q. He did not like it, and he said so. This house was the biggest in the neighbourhood. It stood two hundred yards west of the railway line, beyond the cover of the embankment, and separated from the road by five hundred yards of mud criss-crossed by innumerable narrow but deep drainage ditches, as well as the railway line. To get to it the trucks had to drive round the far side of the embankment along the very track on which Colonel Andrew had been trapped by the machine-gun and come in from the north through No. 2 Company's positions. The crestfallen Major Gordon-Watson explained away these disadvantages; it was raining, it was dark and the Germans could not see anything, anyway; they would be away at dawn. "I tell you," said Colonel Andrew firmly, "I am not staying in this house tonight. You will find me in my car under the railway bridge." and that is where the Commanding Officer and the Adjutant spent the next three nights. The big square Humber car was tucked into the stone wall under the bridge; it looked perilously exposed, but it was a difficult shot for the German gunners. Guardsman Higgins, the driver, who had mysteriously been born in Dakar, watched it anxiously during the heavy bombardments, but in the three days the car suffered only a cracked windscreen and a perforated radiator.

The Company Commanders threw off their gas capes and asked if they could have a glass of whisky. It is the firm belief of all company officers that there is an unlimited supply of whisky at Battalion H.Q. Major George FitzGerald, of No. 2 Company, arrived first as he was nearest. His small black figure exuded misery as he sat fingering his moustache. Major I. H. Powell-Edwards came across from No. 4 and asked in a resigned voice, "Just what is going on ?" Then came Major Rory Stewart-Richardson. He was almost too cheerful. His large face, with sandy hair all over it, glowed, and he began to fill in the time by telling a familiar story of one of his macabre adventures in New Guinea. He had once, it seems, found a gold mine in some desolate jungle. "Unfortunately, my two companions died of fever on the way back," it always ended, and he could never understand why everybody always laughed. Major H. L. S. Young, the Support Commander, came in, carefully folding the large black umbrella which was now an essential part of his battle equipment. The rain dripped off his nose and his fair moustache. "You look very brushed up, Inky," he said to Major G. P. M. FitzGerald. "What has Watson done to you ?" The last arrival was Captain Kennedy, who burst through the door, startling everybody in the room, and shouting, "Will we be in Rome soon ?"

Colonel Andrew sat placidly with his elbows on the table till they had all got their maps out, and then began, "I've just come back from Brigade H.Q. They want us to do what they call a reconnaissance in force up the road towards Campoleone tomorrow morning. We have got two troops of Shermans of the 46th Royal Tank Regiment in support and a call on our own 19th Field Regiment, the mediums of the Scottish Horse and the self-propelled guns of the 24th Regiment. At the same time the Divisional Commander does not want us to get involved in a major battle. Now, we know the Germans are on the main road . . ." "Jerry's up the road ; it's more than flesh and blood can stand," murmured Major Young in exaggerated accents of fear. "Shut up, Savill.. I want a patrol to try the parallel side roads on the right flank leading past the Factory. Jimmy . . ." Lieutenant J. C. Quinn leant forward earnestly. "Send your Intelligence Section out to test them. The Battalion will be down on the road by the bridge at eight o'clock. The Adjutant will give you the order of march." Captain D. J. L. Fitzgerald was scribbling busily in his notebook and tossing little lists around the table. "I'm going to put the main force up the side roads on the right and only a weak token force up the main road to keep them occupied. You will all 'stand to' before dawn, of course, as it's my opinion that the Germans must attack soon, and we've already given them plenty of time to prepare. And now I'm going back to my car."

"I don't envy that patrol," said Captain Kennedy as he watched Lieutenant Quinn brief Sergeant Bennett, "It's the dirtiest night we've yet come across."

The rain poured down all night. The German shells squeaked rather than whistled in their flight and slapped heavily into the mud. A thin gleam of light shone regularly from Battalion H.Q. farm-house as runners in shining ground-sheets squelched in and out with reports, questions and complaints from the companies. Occasionally came the faint, indignant cry, "Put that light out!" Just before dawn on the 26th a violent hailstorm stung the Guardsmen from damp misery to fretful wakefulness. They heaved themselves to their feet to a thin tattoo of hailstones hopping off steel helmets, and leant forward over the slit trenches, ready for a dawn attack. The shelling increased, but there was no sign of an attack. For an hour they waited till it was fully light, and then stood down, leaving only the sentries in the positions. The gun crews started hauling their guns out of position; the sections boiled water for tea on their Tommy-cookers; the platoon sergeants started loading tools and spare ammunition on to the trucks.

Everybody was busy preparing for the next advance, but not for long. Brigade postponed the "reconnaissance in force" till half-past ten, and now said one company would be enough. "Put them all back." Guns were pushed back through the mud, machine guns reassembled and the trucks unloaded. With a collective shrug the Battalion sat down to eat a sodden breakfast. Advance Battalion H.Q. dug new trenches in the embankment beside the railway bridge; only rear Battalion H.Q.—the spare signallers, the pioneer platoon, the R.S.M. with the ammunition trucks—remained in the farm-house. Captain Kennedy reported enemy tanks, nine silhouettes, sitting in the mist not a mile away. The words tumbled out over each other, as they always did when he was excited, and the Irish accent got stronger. "At first I thought they were some Shermans which had come up on our flank, but the picture portrayed by my glasses drove all doubts from my mind that they were American tanks for, standing on the turrets and hulls in their field-grey coats, also looking through Zeiss glasses, were the crews of at least two troops of a tank squadron. A ray of sunshine piercing the mist showed the tanks to be Mark IV specials and Mark VI and, from a side view, the long

88-mm. guns. As they turned to disappear their long-barrelled guns looked like the snouts of crocodiles."

The anti-tank guns were still out of position and most of the Company was still having breakfast in the railway cutting. Ten seconds after the shout "Stand to," the cutting was empty. The Company rose from the ground like a cloud of duck and disappeared into their platoon positions. Sergeant Wyles and Corporal Hennessy's guns were behind their positions, and it was only a question of unhooking them from the tractors and wheeling them forward. Sergeant Bowers's and Corporal Donovan's guns had already been towed out of No. 14 Platoon's area ; the crews manhandled them back, "showing the most remarkable calm." The mist lifted now, revealing the clear valley in front of them. It was not a deep valley, but wide and long, and straight north between the main road and the Vallelata ridge to the west. Their rear on the west side was well protected by the gullies and streams of the Buonriposo Ridge, the only approach being up the railway bed. "How I wished that we had mined these gullies where the railway crossed them."

The rattle of tracks on tarmac distracted Battalion H.Q. A troop of Shermans pulled in under the embankment ; the troop leader climbed out to report to Colonel Andrew that he was ready for the "reconnaissance in force." He was warmly welcomed. "You have come in nice time to deal with a counter-attack we are expecting." This was certainly not what the troop leader was expecting and he showed no enthusiasm. While they were talking there had been a lull in the shelling. Then the heavens opened. At eight o'clock precisely a concentration slammed down on the embankment. During the last three days the Germans had been massing every gun they could lay their hands on, guns of every age, kind, calibre and nationality—German guns, Italian guns, Czech guns, French, Russian and Yugoslav guns—modern 105-mm. and 220-mm., strange old field pieces and monster railway guns. The air was full of iron dug from every mine in Europe ; the fragments were marked in every known language west of the Urals. Into the middle of this drove Major Streatfield, a battery commander of the 19th Field Regiment, and the forward observation officers of the Scottish Horse and the 24th Self-Propelled Regiment. "Where's it coming from ?"

"There's nothing you can do about it," said Colonel Andrew. "Tell your counter-battery people to deal with it, and you wait for the attack that is due any minute. What's the news from Kennedy ?" Kennedy replied, "There's not yet a target fit for Major Streatfield. But there will be soon," he added hastily. The Germans were doing things in style ; they had kept guns in reserve for close support, and these they now turned on Lieutenant Preston's farm-house. Amongst the first shells was an armour-piercing solid shot, which cut a haystack neatly in two and set fire to it. Two tanks rolled forward out of the valley, shooting as they came. Sergeant Wyles and Corporal Hennessy, in the garden of the farm-house, held their fire till the tanks were within four hundred yards, and then fired their guns for the first and last time. Both tanks burst into flames and billowed clouds of black oily smoke into the air, "filling the Company with delight." There were other tanks to replace those destroyed, and they concentrated their fire on the anti-tank guns. Shell after shell tore through the garden hedge, crashed into the house or landed in the garden, ripping up clouds of mud and smoke. Out of the wreckage, through the explosions and above the crackling of the ammunition in the burning tanks, came the faint cry of "Stretcher-bearer." Captain Kennedy's admiration for his Company medical orderly confused his speech. "Amidst the shelling, to answer the call, went Corporal Morley, quite unperturbed, to treat what people were left alive."

The Germans launched their infantry. Through his glasses Captain Kennedy saw a herd of them advancing down the Anzio railway, two companies up and one in reserve. Their determined attitude reminded him of the riders in the Prince of Wales's Chase riding into the stone wall at Punchestown. It was a target fit for Major Streatfield's guns. Sergeant Cawood, the 3-inch mortar detachment commander, lay beside him watching the Germans as a cat watches a mouse, till they came between 1,000 and 1,500 yards away. "Fire target. Sergeant Cawood, do your stuff !" The Germans came on through the few ranging rounds, but disappeared into a welter of explosions. It was a savage barrage. The German attack was completely broken, and within a few minutes there was neither sight nor sound of any of them. "Did that suit you ?" asked Major Streatfield, R.A., over the wireless. "Highly delighted," replied John Kennedy. "So far we are in the win."

But Lieutenant Preston's platoon were not sharing in the win. Captain Kennedy looked up to see two sections disappearing over the rise, some of the men carrying wounded comrades. The reason was only too obvious, for round the corner of the house poked the muzzle of an 88-mm. gun. There were two 17-pounder guns of the Royal Artillery anti-tank battery that should have been able to get this German tank and its companions as they came up from the left rear of the Battalion. Early that morning the unhappy little gunners had hooked their guns to the tractors and driven them into the shelter of the Battalion H.Q. farm-house. There they sat till the tank shells crashing into the farm-yard drove them out. A shell took the corner off the roof ; a second crashed into the bottom of the house, exploded inside and wounded Guardsman Higginson. The gun crews made frantic but belated efforts to get their guns into action. Lieutenant Burton, Lance-Sergeant Milner, Guardsmen Gibson and Hitchen ran across from No. 2 Company to help them. A direct hit from a tank killed three of one gun crew and wounded Lieutenant Burton, Lance-Sergeant Milner and the two Guardsmen, both of whom died. The other 17-pounder fired one round and then jammed. The German tanks and guns turned on the farm-house and pounded it to pieces. Rear Battalion H.Q., under Lieutenant G. Bland, the Pioneer Officer, and the Regimental Sergeant Major, had spent an uneasy morning there. The first salvo killed Guardsman Ayres and wounded R.S.M. McLoughlin, Sergeant Mitchell of the M.T. and Guardsman Milne, the doctor's servant. The survivors hastily decamped, bringing the wounded with them. It took eight men and a door to carry the seventeen stones of Lieutenant Burton across the rough ground. R.S.M. McLoughlin reported to the Adjutant by the bridge. He had cut away the sleeve of his battle-dress jacket and was firmly grasping his massive forearm. The blood trickled through his fingers. "It's nothing, sir, really it isn't," he said. "Why did I have to be hit so soon ? Don't let them evacuate me." His square red face, with its fierce black moustache, was as disappointed as that of a child cheated of a pantomime. Three days before the Battalion left Scotland for North Africa, R.S.M. McLoughlin had broken his ankle on a night exercise. He rejoined after the Tunisian campaign. His ambition in life was to fight with his Battalion, and now he was wounded. The Adjutant watched him trudge wearily to the R.A.P. "If such a thing were possible, I'd say that the Sergeant-Major is crying."

Captain D. J. L. Fitzgerald turned to his small slit trench by the bridge and found crammed in it Guardsmen Graham and McEvoy, his own and the Commanding Officer's servant. "We thought we would come and join you, sir," they said in unison. "Ayres is dead," added Graham gloomily. "You can keep this hole," the Adjutant told them, "but now go and dig a long and very deep trench for the Commanding Officer and myself, with room for two visitors—very deep." Five yards from the bridge just off the road, Sergeant Little, the senior despatch rider, was digging a shelter in the embankment for himself and his motor-cycle. A high-velocity shell whipped over the embankment and exploded on the road with a sharp crack. The splinters hummed through the air, but no one paid any attention to them. Sergeant Little dropped his spade and sat down slowly; the colour drained from his face, leaving his fair moustache bright golden. "I've been hit." "Poor chap," said McEvoy. "Help him away, Graham. His trench will do us nicely."

Meanwhile, the Sherman tanks were sitting under the lee of the embankment, taking cover like everyone else. Colonel Andrew ordered a troop to go over and help No. 3 Company on the left flank. The troop started their engines; the first tank could not move, for it had bogged itself already, the second got stuck on the railway line; only the third ploughed on towards No. 3 Company. Captain Kennedy sent Corporal Cruttenden out of his slit trench to fetch the tank commander over to the O.P. to show him the ground. "I was horrified to see Corporal Cruttenden return a few minutes later saying that the tank commander was not able to leave his tank." The tank moved on till it was almost level with Company H.Q. Knowing that if it went on much farther, they would lose a good tank, Captain Kennedy went over himself, climbed on the turret and tried to point out the ground. "The tank commander appeared to know all he wanted about it, and seemed unwilling to take advice. He also disliked the idea of getting out of his machine. I did not blame him as the shelling at that time was very heavy. I crawled back into the O.P. and stood horrified to watch the tank turn about, traverse its gun 180 degrees so that it was facing over the engine, and then reverse slowly in the direction of the farm-house. For us it was a hair-raising performance as there could only be one outcome. Yard by yard the tank moved, inch by inch more of it showed over the top of the crest until at last, there was a crash followed by a whine. We did not see what had been damaged, but we knew the tank had been hit, for it shot forward a hundred yards, passing over the tracks it had just made. Everybody felt disappointed, but it was not the moment to worry about the loss of one tank. We had to make other plans."

It was now after ten o'clock. The shelling continued unabated, but the German tanks and infantry had been beaten into temporary quiescence. The Germans were reorganizing; an armoured car, with a large red cross, was working up and down the side road through Vallelata Farm, stopping every now and then to pick up wounded. The Commanding Officer took the opportunity to reinforce No. 3 Company. He sent over a platoon of No. 4 Company, under Sergeant Guilfoyle, to cover the former "Baron Preston's Castle," and ordered Lieutenant John Bell to send them more mortar ammunition.

Sergeant Ashton, D.C.M., reported that there were some very live Germans in Lieutenant Preston's farm with one and possibly two machine-guns. Lieutenant Boyd confirmed this; he knew it for certain, because he had just ridden up to it on a motor-cycle. Captain Kennedy and Sergeant Dunne, with a Piat ("both were a great encouragement"), crawled out from Sergeant Dunne's platoon position to take a good look at Preston Farm from a perforated haystack. "It was easy enough to see who occupied the farm, for we were greeted by the familiar ' Brrrrr ! ' of a German M.G.42."

On the right of the road there was a culvert through the embankment. It was low, narrow, dark and evil smelling—but it was safe. Major Young and the doctor, Captain O'Neill, had ousted from it a couple of young Germans, confiscating their rifles, and had installed in it the R.A.P. and Support Company H.Q. All Support Company, except the two wireless operators, were gradually squeezed out by the wounded. The ambulance was running a non-stop shuttle service up and down the road direct to the Casualty Clearing Station just outside Anzio; but it could not cope with the pressure. The casualties poured in and overflowed out of the culvert into an "annexe" in the drainage ditch at the foot of the embankment. Between bandaging wounds, the medical orderlies worked to deepen the ditch and roof it with old iron fencing and earth. The patience and gratitude shown by wounded men is one of the few things which it is worth being in battle to see. Not only on this occasion, but at all times, the silent courage of maimed, battered, bleeding Irish Guardsmen lying in the open or, if they were lucky, in some muddy ditch, was a living monument to the strength of the human will in the depths of human misery. A man drained of blood gets very cold; there is not much a man with a shattered thigh can do for himself; a man whose chest has been torn to ribbons by shell-splinters would like to be moved out of the barrage. But they did not say anything, they didn't ask for anything; they smiled painfully when the orderlies put a blanket over them or gave them a drink of water and a cigarette, and just shut their eyes for a moment when a shell exploded particularly close. The very men who complained most loudly about the few potatoes in the stew were the ones who assured the doctor most firmly that they had "no complaints."

The scene along the embankment was "like a Bank Holiday crowd lining the stands for Surrey *v.* Middlesex at the Oval," said Major Gordon-Watson. It was more like a colony of dispossessed moles going to earth. The keenest diggers were the men of Rear Battalion H.Q. With a hoarse shout of "Follow me, pioneers !" Lieutenant

Bland had led them from their temporary refuge in the ditches round the farm-house across the road to the embankment. They brought with them a strange collection of Italian agricultural implements, antique spades and long-handled shovels, and dug for their lives. The Pipe-Major, Pipe-Sergeant Phair, Sergeant Kelly, the Orderly-Room Sergeant and Lance-Corporal Cross, a clerk, crawled along a drain through the shell-fire. As they reached the road a paving stone from the sky fell with a thud on the Pipe-Major's back. "I'm dying," he gasped. "You old fool," said Lance-Corporal Cross unfeelingly. "Show us some blood, and we'll believe you." Over with No. 3 Company Lieutenant Boyd had already started constructing a dugout "which looked as if it were going to be stronger and harder to get into than St. Kevin's bed at Glendalough."

Meanwhile, the German tanks were still sitting in Preston's Farm and along the ridge on the left flank, shooting and machine-gunning across the Battalion. The Battalion soon saw what they were there for. More tanks, with armoured cars and lorry-borne infantry appeared round Vallelata Farm. The field guns broke up this new concentration of infantry. After this the Germans gave up trying to capture the Battalion's position with infantry and turned their attention to the Grenadiers in the Factory. The field guns followed them round; their task was to smash the German infantry, and most effectively they did it this day. The tanks, however, remained where they were. Colonel Andrew at last got the use of the medium guns. "Little Robin Redbreast," whose real name was Major Campbell-Preston, the battery commander of the Scottish Horse, had been trying for the last hour to get permission to shoot. His urgent pleas had to go through all the usual channels—through Brigade and Division to Corps H.Q., to be checked with his original orders to support the "reconnaissance in force"—now forgotten by the Battalion, but keenly remembered in the caves by Nettuno—delayed while somebody went out to see how many shells there were, and finally granted. "They've told me to be very economical," he told Colonel Andrew, "but if you want it, I'll shoot every shell in the beach-head." Now, at last, there was a chance of shifting those tanks that covered every movement in the Battalion's area. "Robin Redbreast" controlled the guns, Captain Kennedy observed the fall of the shells, and the Commanding Officer, through the Adjutant, controlled Captain Kennedy.

"I'll turn them inside out with a few well-directed salvoes," Kennedy promised, and he was as good as his word. "Hello, Able 3. Shot—Over," the Adjutant passed on the gunners' message that they had fired. The first salvo crashed heavily in the ploughed field five hundred yards over the target. "The sensation was terrific, as all morning the Germans had been landing similar stuff on to us, and now it was our turn." "Able 3. Correction—500 South-East—Over." "Able 3. Wait. Able 3. Shot—Over." The messages passed up and down the human and wireless chain, while Captain Kennedy, as he says himself, vividly pictured the great guns plunging on their pneumatic tyres as their recoil dug them deeper and deeper into the ground. "Dead on!" he shouted excitedly. In Battalion H.Q. trench, "Robin Redbreast" was pink with pleasure. "We'll try them with three rounds from each gun first." Back to Kennedy went the news. "Able 3. Shot. Three rounds gunfire—Coming up now." One German tank got a direct hit and blew up, the rest moved off hastily. If there had not been Germans still watching him, Captain Kennedy would have got out of his trench and danced a jig—or so he said.

"Good God! It's not yet twelve o'clock." It was only now that anyone bothered about the time, except for a vague idea and hope that it would soon be dark. As the sun rose higher in the sky the shelling increased. The clear midday sun gave the German observers in the Alban Hills, on Monte Caro and the Colli Laziali, a perfect view. They could sit in comfort on the terrace of an old monastery—founded by Henry Stewart, Cardinal Duke of York—on Monte Caro above the Rocca di Papa with a cup of coffee in one hand and a telephone in the other, and direct their guns as if they were playing on a sand-model. The Battalion knew they were under direct observation, but thought that there were at least a few corners in which they were concealed. Officers who climbed Monte Caro afterwards realized that there was, in fact, no single place in which a man could move without being seen. The Germans knew where the Battalion was to a square foot; it was only a question of landing a shell on that square foot. The Germans now produced their show-piece, a monstrous railway gun, which flung a shell the size of a bus—fortunately it seemed to travel at about the speed of a bus, so that the Battalion had warning of its approach. "You'll have to get the bombers on to that gun; we don't like it," Colonel Andrew told the Brigadier. "I have tried to," replied the Brigadier, "but they say it disappears into a tunnel after every shot." "Well, tell them to bomb the railway line, then, and get the heavies on to it." "I'll try to, Andrew, but it's all so difficult. I've asked for more tanks, but was refused. The only tanks I've got left, besides the few with you, are a troop with the Scots Guards, and I've just sent two of them to the

Grenadiers. It leaves us very weak on the flanks." No. 1 Company, in Carroceto village, gave a running commentary on the Grenadiers' defence of the Factory—"they seem to be doing very well. . . . The Germans are withdrawing. . . . They are sending back about fifty prisoners."

There was now nothing to do but sit tight till the Germans ran out of ammunition and reorganize during the lulls—if there were any. Father Brookes took the chance to read his office—he paced delicately up and down the track behind the embankment, a steel helmet perched on top of his cap, and his nose buried in his breviary. It was a very comforting sight. Nine Sherman tanks had been destroyed by tank or shell-fire in the Battalion area, the three survivors huddled under the embankment practically on top of Battalion H.Q. They could do no good there and were only drawing fire. The Adjutant, shouting above the noise, at last convinced the squadron leader that their best place, from every point of view, was on the left flank behind No. 3 Company. "I'll even show you where to go," he said and took the squadron leader's arm. "Oh, God, don't tear my arm off !" screamed the squadron leader, and sank to his knees gurgling. The Adjutant stood for a second wondering what he had done as a thick torrent of blood ran out from under the body down the pattern of a tyre-track. "Don't let me bleed to death." The squadron leader's irritated voice woke him up ; he knelt down and put his hands up to the wrists into the squadron leader's side. The doctor ran up and whipped out a shining pair of scissors. "Don't cut my new leather jerkin whatever you do," said the squadron leader and fainted.

Drill-Sergeant Kenny took over from R.S.M. McLoughlin the duty of marshalling the transport and distributing fresh ammunition. He had the trucks spread out under the embankment, drawn in as near as they could go. "I'll let no more in or out till after dark," he said, "It's not worth it. We've lost enough already." As he spoke a heavily laden Grenadier 3-ton lorry careered up the main road, took one look through the bridge, did not like what it saw, and swung in among the Battalion's transport. The German guns had been following the Grenadier lorry up the road and they were on to it in a flash. The third shell hit one of the Battalion's ammunition 15-cwt. trucks, which blew up with a resounding explosion. The fourth hit the Grenadier lorry slap in the middle of its load of mortar bombs. The men, crouching in their holes along the embankment only a few yards from it, held their breath for an even greater explosion. But it did not happen like that—it was worse. The lorry went on fire, and for half an hour mortar bombs exploded in twos and threes.

Lance-Corporal Cross, an orderly-room clerk, a sedate man who normally lived in a world of Army forms and typewriters, was nearest to this inferno. He peered cautiously over the top of his slit trench and saw the Grenadier, Drill-Sergeant Armstrong, still in the cab of the lorry, struggling to open the door. With admirable courage and promptitude he leapt out, wrenched open the door, and dragged the wounded Armstrong into his own trench. He kept him alive till the lorry was burnt out and then carried him to the R.A.P. On the other side of the road the farm, where Battalion H.Q. had been, was burning fiercely. "My kit, my kit!" stammered Major Gordon-Watson, and darted off to salvage what was left of it. He spent the next three months making out a complicated claim for compensation.

The haystacks round Lieutenant Preston's farm had burnt themselves to ashes, but where the tanks had been hit there were still oily clouds of smoke hanging in the air. From the railway cutting beyond the farm came a faint sound of clanking; it stopped, somebody shouted, and then it started again. No. 3 Company knew what those sounds were—it was one tank towing away another. From the map there was only one place where the tanks could cross the railway cutting. With his tongue stuck out in concentration, Captain Kennedy worked it out with a protractor—bearing 290 degrees grid, range 1,500 yards. Sergeant Cawood fired one ranging smoke bomb from his mortars, the tank engines stopped abruptly and a column of white smoke rose from the cutting. The mortar crews stacked bombs ready for use and waited for the engines to start again. At the next sound "the mortars coughed their bombs into the air. As the last ones were beginning to leave our end we heard the slow roll of them beginning to land on the target. We must have been doing some good, and even if we were doing no good, both Michael Boyd and myself liked firing mortar bombs, and so did Sergeant Cawood and Sergeant Ashton." Sergeant Cawood ordered more bombs to be set and primed. After ten minutes they heard again the familiar hum of engines; this time Captain Kennedy decided to give them a minute before firing. "That minute seemed to take an age, but when I gave the word those mortars turned themselves into machine guns, for they spat out bombs quicker than I had ever known a mortar crew were capable of doing. Michael Boyd's expression can only have been equalled by mine for amazement when, above the noise of falling bombs, came a most resounding crash. A jet of orange flame giving way to black smoke rose into the air. Sergeant Cawood shouted for more fire. 'We've hit one.' Corporal Borland, the detachment commander, got more bombs per minute down his two mortars than have ever been put down any other two mortars in the world. Another similar explosion rent the air, leaving behind it the minor noises of bullets crackling just as does the hide of a joint of pork over a big fire."

Having thus disposed of the two German tanks, Captain Kennedy and Lieutenant Boyd cautiously approached Preston's Farm. "Outside the cowshed I heard a movement and started to stalk it only to discover that it was a wounded ox. Moving round and keeping in the shadows, our attention was attracted by a pig sniffling in the ground." It would be. "I stalked up on the pig, coming across a body. The pig darted away with a startled grunt, and at that moment I saw a camouflaged steel helmet. It was one of ours. I was highly delighted that there were at least some of our fellows left in the farm. How they had done it was a miracle, because for the best part of the day they had been subjected to a terrific bombardment and had had a tank, from the marks of its tracks, not more than fifteen yards from them." In the first trench were Lieutenant Preston, Sergeant Parke and Guardsman Carey, all intact. Lying on the ground beside them was the body of Guardsman Angell, wearing Sergeant Bowers's jacket. Behind them was the twisted frame of an anti-tank gun. They had been trying to manhandle it round to replace Sergeant Wyles's and Corporal Hennessy's destroyed guns when it had been smashed under their hands. Twelve German tanks, said Lieutenant Preston, in a hull-down position had covered a party of armoured cars and one Tiger tank into the farm-yard where they had taken prisoner seventeen of the platoon. He thought, even then, that there were still two tanks on the road about seventy yards away. Captain Kennedy assured him that there had been, but that they were now burnt out down the valley. "As we came round the side of the house we saw the full savagery of war, for there, with its straight barrel cocked into the air, its shield bent, and its trailer and carriage twisted, was Sergeant Wyles's gun, the crew dead and stiff as they had been reloading it. The small building beside it was a smashed heap. Farther up the garden was Corporal Hennessy's gun, two of the crew dead. But to the front, as I went to see the damage, the slit trenches came to life. From two twisted heaps of metal which showed where an M.G. section had been, heads appeared, twice as defiant as before." No. 16 Platoon, under Sergeant Guilfoyle, moved up to relieve Lieutenant Preston and the survivors. Captain Kennedy's tour of the destruction was not yet complete. "Passing down the road to Battalion H.Q. was a sad sight. The first thing I saw was the burnt-out wreck of my jeep, which like all other things in the cutting, had been hit by the tanks in the early part of the day."

As the evening slowly drew in the shelling decreased. The Battalion began to think about food, and got out of their trenches to stretch their cramped legs. The battlefield, as far as the eye could see, was studded with fires—burning houses, burning vehicles and burning tanks. A chill thin mist rose from the ground, and small groups of men gathered round the still burning wreckage of trucks to eat their evening stew. An odd shell still fell round the embankment, but now nobody could be bothered with them. The best bonfire was just behind Battalion H.Q. A railwayman's small wooden hut had somehow escaped the shelling, but it could not escape the Battalion's cooks. Guardsman O'Keefe chose it as a kitchen for Support Company and in a few minutes had it in flames. Clutching his blankets, camp kettle and food, he came pelting out of the blaze. "I had an old bird," he said, "but I was near roast like a plump partridge myself." The Adjutant and Sergeant Kelly sat by the glowing beams checking the casualties. From shelling alone, although every man was dug in below ground level, the Battalion suffered ninety casualties, of whom twenty were dead. In addition, there were the twenty-seven casualties of No. 3 Company and the anti-tank guns. No. 4 Company, on the right flank, suffered as much as anybody. They were the only company to lose their Company Commander. Major I. H. Powell-Edwards was carried to the R.A.P. with a cruel wound in the stomach. "It is useless my ever doing any training," he said resignedly. "I always get wounded on the first day." With the dark came silence, and so ended the day which Father Brookes described as the worst day he had spent in this war or the last. It was in fact the first time that British troops sat through a bombardment equal in concentration, duration and intensity to the barrages of Flanders.

It was a quiet night, but the shelling started again promptly at dawn. One of the first of the day's victims was C.S.M. Mercer, so No. 4 Company was now under new management, Captain David Drummond and C.S.M. Lynch, D.C.M. The Brigade's orders for the day were to hold on to what they had got. The air hummed with excited messages from Corps H.Q. that an armoured division—the 1st U.S. Armoured Division—was going to sweep through to Rome that afternoon.

Neither the Battalion nor the Grenadiers saw any German infantry in front of them, but the U.S. Rangers, who had joined the Grenadiers on the right, reported that they had met strong opposition. The armoured division were not going to do anything rash. They wanted to be sure the road was clear before they started. Division ordered the Battalion to send a patrol at once to Campoleone. The Brigadier protested that the men were much too tired and that it was essential that the patrol commander be given time to be properly briefed. The "planners" in their caves would not hear of such things. Lieutenant J. C. Dodds took his platoon of No. 4 Company and a section of carriers and set off up the road to see how far he could get. They got two miles. The Commanding Officer waited anxiously till a motor-cyclist roared back with a message. "Having taken two prisoners, we took up a defensive position round a linesman's house, Number M.23. We saw a dozen Germans coming down the road and opened fire on them. Another section noticed thirty or forty had worked round to the left. The Bren guns engaged them while the platoon got into the carriers and moved back to high ground where we could observe them. We are now at the cutting in the bend of the road where the road from the Factory joins the main road."

"Tell Mr. Dodds to come back immediately," said Colonel Andrew. "They have found out quite enough." For the next hour he was pestered by a series of flamboyant American officers in gaudy jeeps, all claiming to be the General's aide. "What General ?" "Why, the Commanding General of the 1st Armoured Division. The General wants to know if there are any roads on which he can deploy his armour." "I'll show you on the map, and if you'll wait a bit, there is an officer due in from patrol who can tell you more." "Oh, no, we're in a hurry for Rome," they all said and let in the clutch. The Battalion watched the long column of tanks as they went by nose to tail that afternoon and responded politely to the cheers of the crews. The column halted. The ones south of the railway bridge turned round and drove away without any explanation. A few minutes later the leading tanks, who had passed through the bridge, came pelting back down the road. There was no time to cheer. After this "foray," as it was now described, the Brigade's orders were changed to "Advance as best you can." Brigadier Murray called Colonel Andrew and Colonel David Wedderburn of the Scots Guards to his headquarters, and confided his troubles. "It is not a happy day. The situation is so vague, and the enemy is obviously in some strength. I do not like the situation a bit." The Brigade Commander was already beginning to show the physical effects of too little sleep and too much worry. North of the Factory the ground sloped down to a little stream valley and then rose slightly to form a long narrow ridge which ran parallel to the main road half-way to Campoleone. It was a very slight rise, hardly noticeable in ordinary country, but in the flat plain of Anzio it was a prominent tactical feature. Half-way along this ridge, opposite the railway halt, M.24, was a large group of farm buildings. This farm had an Italian name—Mandria—but it was never known by it; it was called first "Scots Farm," then "—— Farm" by the Battalion, bowdlerized to "Dung Farm" by Brigade. But these titles were all to come; that evening it was just "the large farm," and it was decided that the 1st Bn. Scots Guards should occupy it during the night. This they did without difficulty or casualties, except the tragic loss of Major T. Tyldesley-Jones, an old friend of the Battalion, who was blown up in his carrier by a mine.

By dawn the following morning, the 28th, the Scots were firmly entrenched on the ridge. They were now in a subsidiary salient. The Germans were in the woods on their right—the Macchia de Casale—in front of the U.S. Rangers, on the main road and flat plain on their left in front of Carroceto, and were digging a main line of defence straight across the front, where the left parallel road turns right to cross the main road. The Brigadier planned to bring the Grenadiers up on the left of the Scots to the area of the railway halt, M.24. This was not enough for the Divisional Commander, Major-General Penney. He wanted the line of the road in front of the Scots Guards captured, so that the 3rd Brigade could pass through immediately to capture Campoleone, and he wanted it done at once. This sudden urgency was merely irritating. The Brigade had sat doing nothing for three days, when there were no Germans in front of them and there was a certainty of success. Now, when the Germans had arrived in force, it was to be flung into an attack at an hour's notice. The Germans attacked the Scots Guards, which confirmed the Brigadier's fears that the enemy were in strength. He determined to give the Divisional Commander first-hand evidence to pass on to Corps H.Q. by bringing him up to the embankment. They arrived in the middle of a sharp bombardment and piled panting into Battalion H.Q. trench; their satellites piled in after them, squeezing the wireless operator, Corporal Hayman, M.M., and the Adjutant out into the open. Nos. 1 and 3 Companies reported that there were at least three new infantry companies in front of them—paratroopers, they thought. Lieutenant Quinn produced for inspection and interrogation two fresh prisoners, just taken by No. 1—a trembling obsequious youth, and a tough, bitter warrant officer. The German warrant officer was obviously a regular soldier; he stood stiffly to attention, would not open his rat-trap mouth, and refused to explain his parachutist's flash, a printed recommendation for outstanding service in Crete, or the campaign ribbons on his jacket. The youth babbled obsequiously from the ground. He belonged to a pioneer work battalion, he told the Adjutant; they had been brought across from the other side of Italy specially to dig trenches and emplacements for parachutists and Panzer Grenadiers. "They are real soldiers," he explained. His company were engaged in digging machine-pits along the main road for the warrant officer's company. They had got captured when the warrant officer led him too far in the search for good positions. He was glad to be captured, he grinned, "nichts mehr Krieg, boom, boom," but the warrant officer was furious. The Divisional Commander's face set in disbelief. "That warrant officer is not a parachutist; he may have been once, but now he is just one of a scratch lot of troops that the Germans scraped up wherever they could." His audience sighed.

The Brigadier made his plan. The Irish were to stay in Carroceto for the time being, to hold the left flank. The Grenadiers were to hand over the Factory to the Sherwood Foresters battalion of the 3rd Brigade and move up level with the Scots Guards during the night; then the two battalions would attack the German positions some time during the following day. The Scots Guards' H.Q., a hay barn on top of their ridge, gave the best observation over the plain. The Brigadier and Colonel Andrew drove off to meet Colonel Wedderburn of the Scots and Major Miller, acting Commanding Officer of the Grenadiers. Two hours later Colonel Andrew returned. "A terrible thing has happened. After we'd had a good look at the ground and discussed the plan, the Brigadier went home. David Wedderburn and I stayed there talking with Dusty Miller while we waited for his company commanders to come up for orders. We waited some time, and then a Grenadier officer ran into the farm, badly shaken and incoherent. As far as we could make out, all the Grenadier Order Group, in two jeeps, had driven straight up the road into the German lines. They missed the turning up to the farm, easy enough to do if you are driving fast. It has finished the Grenadiers for the time being. Christopher Ford, Hugh Luttrell and Harding are missing, presumably killed, which leaves them with only subalterns to command the companies. They cannot really launch an attack till they get more officers. Fortunately John Stanley, their Adjutant, did not go with the 'O' Group, and he is now with the Brigadier explaining the situation to him."

Colonel Andrew's solution was for the Grenadiers to move up level with the Scots during the night; there was no great difficulty about this and it would give them something to do to stop them endlessly discussing their disaster. The main attack should be postponed when the Battalion would do the rest of the Grenadiers' part. The Grenadiers rejected this vehemently; they could not do anything, they said, except get out of the Factory. The Brigadier was convinced of this and took Captain Lord Stanley back with him to convince the Divisional Commander. The final arrangement was that the Grenadiers should be withdrawn for rest and reorganization, the whole operation postponed twenty-four hours, and that the Irish Guards would attack with the Scots Guards. The Grenadiers were to move out as soon as it was dark.

Colonel Andrew, as a good neighbour, went up to the Factory and offered the Grenadiers a few officers to help them move from this singularly unpleasant place. The agricultural settlement, which was called the Factory, was grouped round a main square. All the buildings in the square had been shattered by British and German gunfire and a few German bombs. There were, however, a few houses and offices still standing in the lanes of the square. The "removal party"—the Adjutant, Lieutenants Bell and Boyd, Drill-Sergeant Kenny and Sergeant Bennett—drove into the square, but could see nobody in the dark ruins. They drove round till they heard a hum of conversation. They pushed through a door covered by blankets and found themselves in a long room lit by a score of guttering candles—the Grenadier Battalion H.Q. Lieutenants Bell and Boyd helped to move the Grenadier anti-tank guns and carriers, but there was nothing for the Adjutant, Drill-Sergeant and Sergeant Bennett to do except to free some Grenadier officers by going out to meet the Sherwood Foresters battalion, who were already on their way up. The Grenadiers marched off down the road to the area of the fly-over bridge, where they rapidly reorganized and were soon back fighting ferociously.

The German stocks of ammunition showed no signs of running out, and the shells continued steadily all day with the inevitable casualties but, as before, it slackened off after dark. Lieutenant Preston and a patrol had been out all day exploring the left flank and the road, little better than a track, which ran through Vallelata Farm parallel to the main road. They had made a wide sweep through the low hills of the extreme left flank, which took them over eight hours. On their way back they had walked into a German tank harbour area. The tanks were out for the day, but they lay up till they saw them coming back and counted thirty of them. "You should be able to get them at breakfast time," suggested Lieutenant Preston. He marked the area as exactly as he could on his map, and the Commanding Officer sent the reference to the medium gunners. The gunners replied they would be glad to oblige and could spare eight hundred shells. At dawn the following morning, just as the Battalion lit its Tommy-cookers for the first cup of tea, a steady stream of shells whistled overhead on their way to the Germans. "That should at least make things a little easier tonight" said Colonel Andrew as he set out for a final conference at Brigade H.Q.

The 6th Corps had now been on the beach-head a week. The original landing force, the 1st British Division and 1st U.S. Division, had been reinforced by the 45th U.S. Division and the 1st Armoured; but the Germans had been reinforcing their troops at the same time, and much more effectively. The Allied Air Force, in spite of all they had said before the landing, had not been able to prevent the Germans moving troops down from the north of Italy. This troop movement may have helped the partisans in Yugoslavia and the Maquis in the South of France, but it certainly did not help the Fifth Army sitting in front of Cassino.

The Corps Commander decided that if he was ever to achieve the second object of the Allied landing—the capture of the Colli Laziali and a subsequent advance on Rome—he must launch an offensive. He followed the old plan that was marked on the maps in Caserta. This described a two-pronged attack—the 1st British and the 1st U.S. Armoured Divisions in the centre to drive up the main road to Albano and seize the hills above it, simultaneously the 3rd U.S. Division, on the right, to capture Cisterna, cut Highway 7 and push on to Veletri. Meanwhile, the original beach-head positions would be held by the 45th U.S. Division. The main thing wrong with this plan was that it was at least five days too late. It all depended on the 1st British Division being able to break a hole in the German defences; after that the 1st U.S. Armoured Division would, in theory, sweep all before them. All that was needed, they said, was for the infantry to reach the line of Campoleone. The 3rd Brigade had not yet been committed to battle, and was therefore allotted the task. The 24th Guards Brigade was told that all they had to do was to clear the area two miles beyond Carroceto so that the 3rd Brigade could have a flying start. Brigadier Murray gave his orders to the Scots and Irish Guards. They were to capture the line of the little road that ran across the front, a mile south of Campoleone and about three-quarters of a mile in front of the Scots Guards' present position. As soon as it was dark the Irish Guards were to walk forward on the left flank until they came on a level with the Scots Guards H.Q. There they were to sit until eleven o'clock when both the Scots and the Irish would start walking forward again. Just in case there might be an odd German tank, the Irish Guards could have the loan of two platoons of American tank destroyers (M.10's). The details the Brigadier left to Colonel Scott and Colonel Wedderburn.

Colonel Andrew returned to the embankment, collected the company commanders and they all went up to the Scots Guards H.Q. "It was a most beautiful farm that had obviously been well stocked ; there were the usual cattle, some dead from shell-fire, in the well-fenced paddocks round a big hay-shed at the end of a fine modern cow byre. The whole place, minute by minute, was beginning to age with the strain of war as shell after shell crashed into buildings, vehicles or the road." The officers tried to see the ground over which they had to attack. The area was in shape a blunt wedge, its long straight bottom the main Albano road just below them, its base the Carroceto embankment, its sloping top the Vallelata road and its blunt point was their objective, the half-mile of sunken road where the Vallelata road turned east at right-angles to cross the main road. The electric railway from Albano crossed the sunken road on a bridge four hundred yards from the main road and ran south roughly parallel to it. Between the two was another disused bed on which the line had run before the Italians decided to straighten it, and a long narrow gully and stream. The whole plain was a network of intersecting drainage ditches, invisible till you were on the brink, or at the bottom, of them. A line drawn across from east to west, from the Scots Guards' farm through the road police and maintenance station, M.24, on the right-hand side to Vallelata Farm on the left-hand, cuts the rectangle roughly in two. This line had to be secured first to give the attacking companies a clear start. Colonel Andrew therefore ordered No. 3 Company, with a platoon of American tank destroyers, to start before the rest of the Battalion and clear the left road up to Vallelata Farm. He arranged with Colonel Wedderburn for the Scots to send a patrol down to M.24. The assaulting companies were No. 1 on the left and No. 2 on the right. When they reached the half-way line No. 1 was to make contact with No. 3 and No. 2 with the Scots Guards patrol. Then Nos. 3, 1 and 2 Companies and the Scots Guards battalion would complete the attack. No. 4 Company, in reserve, would advance only some five hundred yards to a railway halt to secure a firm base and Battalion H.Q. Again, when the objective had been captured, No. 1 was to connect with No. 3 and No. 2 with the left-hand Scots Guards company.

"Zero hour" had been laid down as 11 p.m. ; all should be over by midnight. The whole object of attacking early in the night was to give the companies time to dig trenches and get the anti-tank guns and the supporting arms into position before dawn. It was vital to get up the supporting arms, as Colonel Andrew said again and again. Even if the Germans were much stronger than Division alleged, the Battalion could capture the objective in the dark ; whether they remain there depended solely on the arrival of the guns and tank-busters in good time to deal with the German tanks at first light. The Battalion knew from sad experience that it was fatal to be content with promises that the tanks or anti-tank guns would be sent up "at dawn." They would be too late if they did not start till dawn ; they must move up during the night and be there ready to fire as the first glimmer of light appeared in the sky. Forty minutes before the attack started—that is, from twenty-past ten—the field and medium guns would fire a barrage, starting just beyond the railway halt and creeping up to the objective. The H.Q. staff persisted in their belief that the ground was only lightly held and that there would be no serious opposition after this barrage had rolled over the Germans. At half-past ten the following morning, according to the Corps plan, the 3rd Brigade would capture Campoleone and then the armour would "pass through" to cut Routes 6 and 7 and end a crowded day by going to the top of the Colli Laziali.

The Company Commanders clambered up the bales of hay to the roof of the barn and peered out over the scrubby olive trees on to the plain. Only Captain Drummond could see his company's objective; the rest could just catch a glimpse of roof-tops, marking the line of the transverse side road and patches of the ground they had to cross. They could not see any Germans ; "but it was soon obvious that there were many there," said Major George FitzGerald, "for we were strafed by machine guns on our way back." While they were away yet another of the "General's aides"— a new one, a bull-necked man smoking a cigar—drove up to Battalion H.Q. demanding information about the roads to Rome. Captain D. J. L. FitzGerald directed him up to the Scots Guards H.Q., but he added, "You want to be very careful ; it's easy to go too far and be killed." "I would not like that to happen," said the American as he drove away. The Adjutant saw him again the following day. He was sitting in his jeep beyond the farm gates, his hands lolling on the wheel, the cigar clamped in his teeth. He was as dead as a door-nail.

CHAPTER V

The Battalion's Night Attack

BY nightfall everything was ready and the Battalion was waiting for the Duke of Wellington's Regiment, to whom they were to hand over their positions. As soon as it was dark, the Quartermaster-Sergeants brought up the dinners and a large batch of mail. Many of those letters were never read, for the men stuffed them in their pockets, impatient for the dawn. There was as yet no sign of the "Dukes." At a quarter to eight, three-quarters of an hour before zero, Colonel Webb-Carter arrived alone ; his battalion had been so harried by orders and counter-orders and impeded by the thick mass of 3rd Brigade transport on the road that it would be at least another hour before they reached the embankment. Even though the "Dukes" would only be in these positions for the night, they must be firmly established there before the Battalion attacked. It is an elementary principle, none the less true for being frequently forgotten, that in any battle you must have "one foot on the ground." If all the troops are on the move at the same time, any minor reverse causes infinite confusion. Colonel Andrew postponed the attack for three-quarters of an hour. There would now be no time, or need, for a halt on the "start line"; the companies would attack straight through, pausing only to shake themselves out. This change did not affect the Scots Guards, but it did affect the gunners, and the air hummed with calculations and sums. The American tank-busters, two platoons of "C" Company, 894th Tank Destroyer Battalion, drove up and parked in the shrubbery round the largest house in Carroceto. Major Stewart-Richardson met them politely. When he referred casually to the attack, their two officers, Lieutenants Smith and Siercks, had no idea what he was talking about ; nobody had yet told them anything except to join the Irish Guards. Colonel Andrew hastily gave them their orders—Lieutenant Smith's platoon to advance with No. 3 Company up the Vallelata side road; Lieutenant Siercks's platoon to join the support column of anti-tank guns and machine-guns which Major Young was going to lead up the main road to Nos. 1 and 2 Companies as soon as the objective was captured. Captain Kennedy was as pleased as a child with a new toy. He led off the willing but puzzled Lieutenant Smith and put him in command of a column consisting of the tank-busters, a platoon of Middlesex Regiment machine-gunners, Sergeant Cawood's 3-inch mortars and the companies' trucks. "Sergeant-Major Moran will be your second-in-command, and Sergeant Parkes and a few men your escort. Will that do you ?" Lieutenant Smith thought it would do fine. Major Young approached Lieutenant Siercks more delicately. Later on, when the first part of this tiresome business was over, he was going to drive up the road, and would Lieutenant Siercks mind following him when he gave the word? Lieutenant Siercks said he would not mind at all. Allied co-operation had begun.

The "Dukes" arrived before nine o'clock. The companies hoisted themselves out of their trenches ; the officers and sergeants put the "Dukes" into place, and then all moved down to the road. No. 3 started up the side road. "The take-off was perfect," said Captain Kennedy, "and we little thought we should see this battle area again, for we were sure that we were now on our way to the Colli Laziali." No. 2 walked up the railway in single file past the station, No. 1 joined on behind them and then came No. 4 and Battalion H.Q. The Adjutant stood under the bridge peering at No. 4 Company and Battalion H.Q. as they tramped by to catch Corporal O'Donnell, the Police Corporal, the oldest man in the Battalion and the father of the largest family, and keep him out of the attack on some excuse. Corporal O'Donnell slipped by in the dark ; he died of wounds that night.

The moon had not yet risen, and only the flash of a distant gun and the croaking of frogs disturbed the dark, quiet night. The companies filed up the railway, the dark shuffling figures trailing like the caravan from old Samarkand. In the night air voices carry far, so the few orders were given in whispers. The electric cables, drooping from the shattered standards, knocked off steel helmets and wound round ankles. Every time a cable was touched it twanged and reverberated away into the dark. It sounded like a choir of gigantic harps. The sudden crash of the barrage drowned every other noise. "On reaching the start line," wrote Major G. P. M. FitzGerald, "the companies got into their deployed positions. This was somewhat difficult at first, the noise was excessive and many of the shells were falling very short." The forward companies wirelessed back that they had seen nothing of the Scots Guards or No. 3 Company, but that otherwise all was well. Colonel Andrew replied that the Scots had begun their attack, but that No. 3 Company was out of wireless touch. He himself, with the Adjutant and both wireless sets, was going up to the Scots Guards' farm, the best place from which to control the battle. At eleven o'clock Nos. 1 and 2 Companies stepped forward on either side of the railway line, each with two platoons up. No. 4 Company and Battalion H.Q. were still some way behind, trudging up the railway.

Silently the companies tramped forward, following the barrage. They passed the railway halt and pressed on, sliding down into the drainage ditches and climbing up the other side, jumping the smaller ones. Each man guided himself by the man on his left or right, and the two inside men of each company guided themselves by the railway line. They reached half-way to the objective without a shot. No. 4 Company, still in single file, could not see the forward companies, nor could they see the railway halt, but Captain Drummond, a precise man, calculated that they must have "all but reached our allotted position." That moment a Very light shot up into the sky, flooding the plain with brief light. In the simple words of Lieutenant Bland, "Up goes a Very light and down comes the dirt." A machine-gun on the left opened fire on No. 1, another on the right fired on No. 2. A succession of Very lights and flares shot up on all sides ; shells poured into the railway halt. Five more machine guns joined the one on the right. There were six machine guns in a line on the narrow stretch between the railway and the road. They shot a solid curtain of bullets into No. 2 Company. Lieutenant Gillow, the commander of the right-hand platoon, fell severely wounded in the first burst. Both platoons ran forward into the fire and dived into a small gully. Sergeant Murphy took over his platoon. The nearest fire came from a small house on the railway bed. Shouting to the other platoons to watch out and to his own "Follow me," he made a dash for the house. It was too late for the Germans to surrender. There was a machine-gun post and two rifle posts in front of the house. Each section commander, Lance-Sergeant Dempsey, Corporal Day and Lance-Sergeant Cartledge, automatically swung his section on to a post and destroyed it. The left-hand section plunged round the house on to another post, the remainder of the platoon, led by Sergeant Murphy, pressed forward. Yet another machine-gun, fifty yards behind the house, opened fire at point-blank range. Mixed amongst the bullets were rifle grenades. Meanwhile, the left-hand platoon under Lieutenant C. Brand had pushed slowly forward on the left. It was quite clear from the number of machine-guns and the number of Germans that they were in amongst the main defensive positions. The reserve platoon under Sergeant Gundel, coming forward to help them, was caught in the right flank by a blast of machine-gun fire from the other side of the road, the objective of the Scots Guards.

Major G. FitzGerald was walking with Lieutenant Brand's platoon. The flash of tracer bullets showed a solid line of machine guns in front of them all pumping out bullets as fast as they could. As he said himself, he took "the only course available, which was to pass round the left and get up to No. 1 Company." This course was made available by Lance-Corporal M. T. O'Brien, the platoon's 2-inch mortar man. The platoon was pinned down by a series of machine-guns and was being hammered out of existence by mortar bombs. Corporal O'Brien carried his own small mortar forward towards the nearest stream of tracer till he could see the muzzle flashes, set it up, and shot bombs in that direction till the gun stopped firing. The platoon then filed through the gap in the row of machine guns. Sergeant Gundel, in command of the reserve platoon, had already crossed the railway line. On the right he could neither see or hear anything but fire from all sides and the grunts of wounded men. The fire seemed thinner on the left of the railway, and there was no sound of Brens, which meant either that No. 1 Company was entirely and instantaneously destroyed, or that it was advancing steadily under some kind of cover. Though always prepared for and expecting the worst, Sergeant Gundel considered that he had already met the worst and switched his platoon. No. 1 Company had indeed found cover in the drainage ditches. On the left of the railway line there were fewer machine guns and the ditches conveniently ran north and south. It reached the line of the side road with only one casualty. They were met by fire from two houses on the embankment near a railway bridge. Lieutenant Bartlet led his platoon forward and cleared the Germans from one house. Guardsman H. Taylor, a Bren gunner, captured the other one by walking in the front door and killing all the occupants. Major G. FitzGerald collected the remnants of Lieutenant Gillow's platoon, joined Lieutenant Brand, and together they crossed the railway line. They had had a clear passage up a gully, except for a brief tussle with invisible German grenade-throwers in which Sergeant Wylie was wounded in the cheek. Sergeant Gundel brought up his depleted platoon. The two companies amalgamated and established four strong platoon positions on the line of the sunken road, which was the left half of the Battalion's objective. Their position was bounded on the right by the railway bridge over the sunken road and on the left by the bend where the side road comes up on the level again and turns south. Both were held by German infantry and tanks. The companies were alone with the enemy all round them. No. 3 Company, on the left, had not been able to clear the side road; the Scots Guards on the right had not been able to clear the main road and road junction, though they had also reached the outside flank of their objective. It was just after midnight. The general position was that the Germans held a small salient in the tip of the Brigade's not much larger salient. Majors G. FitzGerald and R. Stewart-Richardson set up one joint H.Q., not only for the sake of company and conversation, but because No. 2 Company's wireless had broken down. Lance-Corporal Holwell, No. 2 Company's signaller, took his set to pieces by the light of a shaded torch; he worked by himself some distance from everyone else, as every gleam drew a heavy burst of fire.

For the past hour Colonel Andrew Scott, Captain Desmond Fitzgerald and their signallers, Lance-Corporal Barrow and Lance-Corporal Hayman, M.M., had been kneeling in two trenches at the side of a barn in "Dung Farm." Corporal Barrow dragged out bales of hay to build a parapet, "The finest sainfoin and clover you could wish to see," he said. The Scots Guards were fighting beside, in front, behind and, it seemed, on top of them. The Germans pumped shells into the farm buildings, reducing the neat cow-byres, barns and houses into a blazing shambles. With painful monotony the high-velocity shells skimmed the ground and crashed into the farm-yard. Four lorries, towing the Scots Guards' anti-tank guns and carrying their ammunition, exploded one after the other in a sheet of purple flame. A charred mummy in each seat was all that was left of the drivers. The hay barn was on the forward edge of the Scots Guards' positions. In front of it were an open paddock, some woodpiles and then a line of hedges and olive trees. Behind these hedges sat the German machine gunners. There is something peculiarly fascinating about the flight of tracer bullets. They curve in a slow, graceful arc, glowing with a soft, almost friendly light. The eye is irresistibly drawn to them and then down the line of flight to the muzzle. There is a strong pull of attraction, something like vertigo, for it is hard to realize that anything so decorative can be so deadly. For the Commanding Officer and the Adjutant, the dark world was hung with a web of tracer. They could see the faint streaks down by the railway. Bright streams poured over them and over their heads to clatter into the walls and trees. The left-hand company of the Scots Guards went forward to attack the machine guns that they could see firing from the hedge in front. On the other side of the barn the right-hand company had already crashed into the olive groves. The left-hand Scots reached the woodpile and there stopped. The company commander decided to withdraw his company round behind the barn and put them on the right. To withdraw troops from close contact with the enemy is always a difficult and dangerous operation. To do it in the dark invariably leads to chaos and often to rout. The men do not know what is happening; all they see is that their comrades are withdrawing, and they do not know why or whither.

The Scots Guards tramped back over the Irish Guards command post. Colonel Wedderburn stormed out of the dark and met the company half-way down the barn. His language was remarkable. Colonel Andrew and Captain D. FitzGerald listened with amazement and admiration. The gist of his remarks were: "What were they doing? Why were they coming back? Where was the Company Commander? About turn; this is the way, follow me." That was all the Scots Guards needed. They had got confused in the dark, but now they recognized their Commanding Officer's voice and it was quite clear what he wanted. They were only too glad to do it and, headed by Colonel Wedderburn, they lumbered forward again into the woods and machine guns. Colonel Wedderburn came back panting. "That was a close thing," he said. "They are in the wood now, but they have got stuck. The right-hand company have got to the line of the side road, but that is not a great deal of help to us, as they cannot clear the wood." "We must clear that wood," said Colonel Andrew, "otherwise I will not be able to get up my anti-tank guns to my forward companies. My two forward companies have reached the line of the side road, too, and, like yours, on the outside flank. It is quite clear that the Germans have built a strong position around the cross-roads and will fight to hold it. The companies are more or less all right while it is dark, but if I don't get guns or tanks up to them they will be cut to pieces by the German tanks as soon as it is light." No. 4 Company and Battalion H.Q. reported that they were in position. When the first Very lights went up the German defensive fire crashed down on them and machine guns opened fire on fixed lines. They ran forward to a cutting and crawled towards the railway halt. The halt, being marked on the map, was the centre of the Germans' "defensive fire tasks," and the shells rained into it.

The Guardsmen dug furiously in the soft banks round the house and in the cutting. The officers of Support Company, Major H. L. S. Young, Lieutenants A. Bell, Lambert and M. Boyd, had walked up the railway with No. 4 Company with the original intention of going straight up to No. 1 and No. 2 Companies to choose positions for the anti-tank guns and mortars. They were caught here in this fire.

As soon as the wireless was working to the command post in "Dung Farm," Major Young asked for news about the two roads north. Both of them were still held by the Germans. Neither the Scots Guards, nor No. 2 Company, had been able to oust the Germans from the cross-roads on the main road, and there was no word from No. 3 Company. It appeared that the Vallelata road had not yet been cleared, but might be soon as across the plain came the sound of firing and the glow of something burning. This was, however, the noise of C.S.M. Moran's private battle in the rear of the company. In their advance across country to the Vallelata road the platoons had by-passed the forward German posts, some in the ditches and one in a farm-house on the road itself. The noise of the engines and the clatter of the tank-destroyers gave these posts their first target, and they poured heavy machine-gun fire and mortar bombs into the column. C.S.M. Moran jumped out of his truck, collected the escort and rushed the farm-house. They killed the Germans in the house and plunged into the ditches after the others. On the road a carrier exploded ostentatiously, lighting up the whole column with its flames. C.S.M. Moran went back and found that Corporal Borland, the carrier commander, was dead, Lieutenant Smith badly wounded by his tank-buster, and the column being devastated by mortar bombs. He took command, ordered the tank-destroyers to engage the German posts, while he turned the trucks and carriers round and took them back to safety. He then walked up the road to tell Captain Kennedy what had happened. Captain Kennedy got his wireless working for the first time that night and reported to Battalion H.Q. Colonel Andrew then told Major Young that as both roads were impassable, he must find some way of bringing the supporting arms up the centre to the forward companies. Major Young and Lieutenant Bell went back down the railway line to bring the carriers and anti-tank guns up to No. 4 Company. The area between the railway halt and Carroceto station was now alive with Germans. These Germans had lain silent and motionless while the shells fell round them and the companies tramped over them. Some of them had even slept through the whole thing, but now there was enough noise to waken the dead and they were all busy firing their Spandaus and sub-machine guns more or less at random and chiefly to encourage themselves. This, however, did not make Major Young's and Lieutenant Bell's journey any less unpleasant.

To get back to Carroceto village, where the supporting arms were still waiting, they had to crawl down ditches and eliminate those snipers that were in their way. Lieutenant Boyd stayed with No. 4 Company and, together with Lieutenant Quinn, took charge of Battalion H.Q. Lieutenant Lambert and Sergeant Bennett set out to find No. 2 Company and discover what was the position there. The constant shelling and machine-gun fire had wounded a dozen men, some of whom were serious cases. Lieutenant J. Quinn and Guardsman Miles of the Intelligence Section followed Major Young and Lieutenant Bell down the railway line, carrying the most serious casualty on a stretcher. They could not get through the German posts and had to come back, but set out again without the stretcher and in time reached the R.A.P. They met Lieutenant Bell as he was bringing up his carriers to clear the area behind No. 4 Company. One of the carriers was fitted with stretchers and came up to the halt with the supporting arms convoy. Major Young and his officers installed four 3-inch mortars and two anti-tank guns in the cutting beside the halt. This made the area a secure little fortress ; there was nothing more for No. 4 Company to do but to beat off any attacks and to hope that the other companies were as firmly established.

No. 1 and 2 Companies, meanwhile, were digging positions along the sunken road by the railway bridge. The ground here was hard and stony. The picks and shovels clanged and sparked in the darkness. "It did not make things any easier," said Major FitzGerald, "when the noise of approaching tanks became obvious. It is interesting to note," he added professionally, "the effective use the Germans make of three or four tanks in the moonlight." These tanks moved slowly up the side road and sprayed the digging Guardsmen with their machine guns. It was an irritating distraction. It meant that the Guardsmen had to lie flat on the ground till a cloud passed over the moon, then dig furiously while the cloud lasted and lie flat again before the moon reappeared. Guardsman Montgomery and Guardsman Taylor took their Bren gun to the extreme right of the companies and there settled down to engage the German tanks. .303 bullets cannot, of course, be very effective against armour plate, but it did at least force the German tank crews to close their visors and so limited their vision. It also had the effect, which Guardsmen Taylor and Montgomery ignored, of so infuriating the tank commanders that they devoted most of their time to trying to kill these two Guardsmen.

After an hour the German tanks gave up this profitless occupation and moved slowly up the road to pass under the railway bridge. Lieutenant Bartlet was waiting for them under the arches. He slid "75" grenades under the tracks of the leading Tiger as if he was dealing cards. A "75" is a small flat anti-tank grenade, a sort of portable if ineffective mine. These grenades exploded with a sharp crack as the tank ground over them. It can have done no damage to the tracks, but it did frighten the commander. The tank backed out from under the bridge and sat by the side of it with its gun poking round the corner. The others stayed with it ; here they could not be deadly, but only very unpleasant. The Guardsmen of the two companies were now all below ground ; here they were secure till dawn, but if dawn came before the British tanks or anti-tank guns, then they would have to face the German tanks in the open with small arms, grenades and, of course, their bare hands. All this Major G. FitzGerald had to report to Colonel Andrew through No. 4 Company. No. 1 Company's wireless could only reach No. 4 Company ; No. 2's own wireless set was still out of action. There was no sign of No. 3 Company until Lieutenant Preston and two Guardsmen walked out of the dark. No. 3 Company was not on the left flank, it was somewhere behind them, near the railway line. "They can't get forward and I can't get back." This was the last news Nos. 1 and 2 Companies had from the outside world, and the last they gave, till dawn, for their remaining wireless set then went off the air.

No. 3 Company had not, in fact, got as far as Vallelata Farm. After their "perfect take-off" they had advanced across the open country, following a track from the embankment till they reached the Vallelata road—"a fairly good guide from the point of view of the map," said Captain Kennedy, "but in relation to the ground there was not much resemblance." So far, all they had seen of the Germans was a patrol which ran away before they could catch it, but here they got caught in the German defensive fire. The company was well scattered, so only three men were slightly wounded, but what was more serious was that the wireless set was shaken and thrown off net. Leaving Lieutenant Musgrave and Sergeant Dunne to press on up the road, Captain Kennedy led the rest of the company and advanced northwards along the Vallelata ridge to outflank the German defenders. "We continued on so for about half an hour and realized that we were in an area very strongly held, as every farm-house was occupied and the sentries were awake. In the course of these adventures we took some prisoners, who very rashly left their farm-house to take cover from a salvo of shells passing near by. These prisoners were very useful and gave us some idea where the Germans were."

The whole ridge was strongly held, and there was no prospect of outflanking the defences. Everywhere they went they woke up dozing machine-gunners, and the fire of one post alarmed and brought into action a group of others. The prisoners pointed in all directions and flicked their ten fingers open and shut; there was certainly something in what they said or signified. From the Vallelata road behind and below them came the sound of firing and confused shouts, so they struck back towards it. They came on Lieutenant Musgrave and Sergeant J. Dunne storming a farm-house, a little operation which Sergeant J. Dunne completed by charging through the backyard to kill the last two Germans. Captain Kennedy re-formed his company and took his bearings. "Over to the east the whole plain was a mass of green and yellow lines of flame stabbing the darkness. Here and there patches became lit up as a concentration of shells burst in ditches and hollows." The moon had now risen, and the next farm-house up the road stood out quite clearly, silent and apparently unoccupied. Captain Kennedy and Lieutenant Musgrave stood looking at it, wondering whether or not it was Vallelata Farm, for neither they nor anyone else had realized that there were so many farm-houses dotted along the road. C.S.M. Moran interrupted them with the news that the houses behind them, which they had by-passed, were so strongly held that the column of trucks and anti-tank guns could not get up the road. Captain Kennedy decided that, as they were already overdue on the objective, they would first of all clear the road up to No. 1 Company and then dispose of the German posts behind them. Lieutenant Musgrave led his platoon quietly up the road. His leading section heard voices and the sound of digging from the farm. They thought they must have hit No. 1 Company, and that the loudest voice of all was the Company Commander, Major Stewart-Richardson. Captain Kennedy crawled forward to make sure, hoping they were right. "It was a commander of sorts, all right," he said, "admonishing some soldiers in a very thorough fashion—the unfortunate part was that he was doing it in German and the smell of the place left no doubt that they were Germans. Slipping back, I told Lieutenant Musgrave and we prepared to attack. I had hardly done this when the Germans started to walk down the road. I gave Lieutenant Musgrave a machine-pistol we had taken off one of the prisoners and told him to keep these Germans covered whilst I brought the rest of the Company into the assault. I had just got back to the Company when I heard the Germans opening fire. The Company got into the field on the right of the road, and we shot up the house until no further movement or fire came from it. Lieutenant Musgrave did not return." He was shot down in the middle of the road as he came out to challenge the Germans.

All along the road behind this farm, and from the ridge on the left, machine-guns opened fire, shooting on fixed lines across the front and down the road. Captain Kennedy revised his plan—rather than try again to force a way up the road or across country on the left of it, he would strike to the right (east) towards the railway and try to get up to the objective that way. This, he knew, was the route No. 1 Company had taken, and he hoped to find some trace of it. The Company tramped slowly across the plain till they were challenged from a ditch by a Guardsman of No. 1 Company. This man had been left behind as a guide ; he pointed out the direction his company had taken, but it was now a maze of tracer. Lieutenant Preston and two men branched off to slip between the German posts. The Company moved on, but all the time they were going south-east—that is, slightly backwards—so that when they hit the railway line they were behind No. 4 Company and not very far in front of Carroceto station. Here they found an outpost of the Foresters, of the 3rd Brigade, waiting to attack the next morning—a depressing meeting, as it meant that, after a night of wandering and skirmishing, they were back at the start-line. There was nothing for it but to begin again. They handed over their prisoners and began to walk up the railway line towards No. 4 Company. Half-way there they came on Lieutenant Lambert sitting in one of the machine-gun platoon's carriers with the headphones of his wireless over his cap. Drumming in Lieutenant Lambert's ears was Colonel Andrew's insistent broadcast : "If anyone sees Kennedy, tell him I want him here, in ' Dung Farm,' now." Everything but time goes slowly in a night battle. It was now nearly four o'clock.

As "Dung Farm" was the only commanding feature in the area, so also it was the only defined artillery target for the Germans. Their guns were still pounding it into a shambles, mangling and mixing the remains of men and cattle. Their infantry were still holding the wood in front of it down to the cross-roads. Up till three o'clock, however, everybody in "Dung Farm," even the wounded, was cheerful. In night attacks delays and unexpected checks are usual ; they are disappointing, but not disheartening.

While there were still some hours of darkness to look forward to, there was still time for either No. 3 Company or the Scots Guards to clear one of the roads. The Guardsmen of Nos. 1 and 2 Companies rested in their rough slit trenches, shivering with the cold and keeping an eye on the German tanks. At intervals, Major G. FitzGerald made tentative enquiries on the wireless. His voice sounded apologetic; he did not want to nag, but when would the support weapons arrive? No. 4 Company, firmly entrenched around the railway halt, kept up a steady exchange of fire with the German machine-gun posts. In "Dung Farm" the shelling slackened and the flames burnt low. But as the minutes passed the cold soaked into everybody, and with it the realization that the two Battalions by themselves could not get the support weapons up to the forward companies. At half-past three Colonel Andrew wirelessed to Major G. FitzGerald, "Sit tight. We'll get some tanks for you." He then turned to the operator of the large No. 19 set. "Get me the Brigade Commander himself." It was time for a clear decision. Only tanks could shift the Germans; if there were no tanks available the forward companies must be withdrawn on to No. 4 Company while it was still dark. "It won't be dark much longer. It's nearly four o'clock," said Colonel Andrew. "Wait," was the reply, "I will come up to you myself." It was a long wait.

Meanwhile, Captain Kennedy ran all the way from the railway to "Dung Farm." He ran back again with orders to collect No. 3 Company, the carrier platoon and the American tank-busters into one force and to try again to force a way up the side road on the left flank. "As we left the farm," he said, "the grey light of dawn was slowly appearing in the east, which meant that we had about an hour, perhaps less, to get forward to Nos. 1 and 2 Companies."

With the dawn arrived the Brigadier, grey with exhaustion. To him the situation "to say the least of it, did not appear good." The squadron of tanks in support of the Brigade had now only five "runners" left, and even these could not be used without the permission of Divisional H.Q. "We must have those tanks, and more," said both Colonel Scott and Colonel Wedderburn. It is hard for anyone who is not at the crisis of a battle to realize how vital time can be, and the agony of waiting. It may have been only minutes, but it seemed like hours before Divisional H.Q. replied to the Brigadier's appeal. The squadron could be used; but there were no more tanks available. "That's —— it." All over the plain, stiff, cold red-eyed men blinked and moved uneasily. They could see each other, and they all knew what that meant. The Brigadier made the only possible decision. "I decided to support the Scots Guards with tanks and to withdraw the most advanced companies of the Irish Guards."

The five Sherman tanks rattled through the farm-yard to join the Scots Guards. Behind them came the commanders of the Field Regiment, R.A., restive after six hours' inactivity and worried by the low stock of smoke-shells. At a quarter-past six—on the 30th January—Lance-Corporal Hayman, M.M., reported "No. 2 Company is back on the air. It's Corporal Holwell talking." There was no time then to congratulate Corporal Holwell, and there never was another chance for he was killed a few minutes later. If ever one man saved his comrades, it was Corporal Holwell. But for his unshakable courage and skill the companies could have got no orders to withdraw and would have remained where they were till they were destroyed. Colonel Scott ordered Major G. FitzGerald to extricate the two companies, fight a way back to No. 4 Company and re-form in "Dung Farm." "When the companies got the order to withdraw," wrote Major FitzGerald afterwards, "the situation was not very bright. We decided to take the obvious route back down the railway line. As we were quietly leaving our positions a German officer came running towards us flourishing a revolver. He was duly killed, but the shots attracted the attention of a nest of machine-gunners." Whole belts of bullets swept across the open stretch of ground that lay between the sunken road and the nearest cutting on the railway line. Only a man who could run had any chance of surviving. The wounded were collected in the safest place, under the bridge over the sunken road. Lance-Corporal Moriarty, a medical orderly, had spent the night finding casualties and bringing them in. He now chose to stay with them, and remained there the whole of the day, while the battle eddied round them, easing and comforting them, till they were rescued and evacuated, and then, "at about 2359 hrs. on the 30th," as his Company Commander wrote afterwards, "he reported back as if he had been on a Battalion scheme." The Bren gunners and Major George FitzGerald remained in position to cover the withdrawal. The remainder, under Major Rory Stewart-Richardson, made a dash for the embankment. "The Bren gun covering fire was not very effective, because of the long range and the number of German machine guns, and the companies received rather heavy casualties getting into the embankment. C.S.M. Gilmore, who had been invaluable throughout, was mortally wounded along with Lance-Corporal Holwell, to whom too much praise cannot be given." The covering party followed.

The Companies paused in the embankment while they prepared

to fight their way back down the railway line. The only help they could get was smoke. Directed by Colonel Andrew Scott and the artillery commander, the field guns showered smoke canisters around the railway line. But it was impossible to concentrate an effective screen. What was needed was a thick fog; all that could be provided was a thin intermittent mist, through which the keen morning breeze whipped large gaps. Major George FitzGerald decided to cover the immediate rear and to divide the companies into its platoons, each of which was to batter its own way through the Germans. Two Bren gunners of No. 1 Company, Guardsmen H. Taylor and W. Montgomery, set up their guns on the top of the cutting and engaged the nearest Germans. The top of the cutting was dead flat, and these Guardsmen's heads and shoulders made perfect silhouette targets. Taylor and Montgomery, however, were as steady and accurate as if they themselves were firing at Figure 4 silhouette targets. On their return, both Company Commanders repeated over and over again that, but for the courage and devotion of these two Guardsmen—"old steely-chests of No. 1"—the companies would have suffered far heavier casualties.

Lieutenant Patrick Da Costa led off the first platoon. He was killed almost immediately and his platoon broken into small parties by a German attack. Lance-Corporal O'Brien took command of the largest fragment and brought them back to No. 4 Company by bounds. He himself, with a Bren gun, provided the covering for each bound, running the gauntlet every time to catch up with his party and cover them over the next stretch of open ground. The other platoons followed by slightly different routes. Lieutenant Stephen Preston was killed by machine-gun fire from the flank as he came out of the first railway cutting with the second platoon. Major Stewart Richardson, following behind, was wounded over the eye by a mortar fragment, but could still see enough to gather the platoon and return the Germans' fire, while Lieutenant Bartlet, behind him, led his platoon slightly left down a gully. Lieutenant Brand, with the last platoon and Company H.Q., joined Major Stewart Richardson and together they launched an attack down the railway line. It was a bloody little battle. Squads of Germans dotted along the railway, who had lain low during the night, now resisted savagely. The German mortars fired indiscriminately along the railway line. They did not seem to care whether or not they hit their own troops, but they must have done, and they certainly killed and wounded numbers of Guardsmen. The German 88-mm. guns by the cross-roads joined in firing air bursts. Through this turmoil of mixed fire, over the bodies of their friends who had been killed the night before, the Guardsmen attacked post after post, driving the Germans back before them into the waiting arms and muzzles of No. 4 Company. Slightly less than half of the two companies who had set out the previous night reached No. 4 Company that morning. The two last men to come in were Major G. FitzGerald and Guardsman Montgomery. Guardsman Taylor had been wounded in the leg, but he hobbled back with his gun, covered by the untouched and unmoved Montgomery. Twice on the way back Montgomery halted in open ground to return the fire of German machine-guns ; once he planted himself firmly in the standing position to engage, and silence, a concealed Spandau only 150 yards away from him.

Nos. 1 and 2 Companies re-formed as one company behind "Dung Farm." They were tired and dirty, but there could be no rest, as the Scots Guards in front of them were still being attacked. One complete Scots Guards company was destroyed by a heavy tank and infantry assault. The new composite company moved up into the farm. The forward platoon held a flower garden on the right flank. The Scots Guards had meant to use it as a cemetery and had already dug a dozen graves ; some of them were still empty and the Guardsmen sank gratefully into them. It was now light enough for the Gunner observation officers to see and call artillery concentrations down on any German movement. This prompt and heavy shelling discouraged the Germans and gave the Brigade a pause. "I again appealed for more tanks," wrote the Brigadier, "and at about nine o'clock they arrived. As we had no reserves available I got a loan of a company from the K.S.L.I. of the 3rd Brigade, who were close at hand, and with the new squadron of tanks they went forward to clear the cross-roads. As soon as the tanks got busy the Germans put up their hands. If only we could have had them sooner how different things might have been."

Meanwhile, No. 3 Company and the 2nd Platoon, "C" Company, of the 894th American Tank-Destroyer Battalion had set out to sweep the left flank. The company, now organized into two platoons, piled on the M.10 tank-destroyers, with Captain Kennedy and the American Lieutenant Siercks in the leading one. Captain Kennedy has left a full account : "As we hit the side road we were well spread out, our guns facing east and west alternately down the column. Behind us came the carriers looking very small in comparison to the M.10's. The sun was now up, shining like a big red ball of fire, bringing to us a new day and new spirits. I signalled to the Guardsmen on the tanks to man the .55 Browning machine guns, and to open fire when they saw us do so from the leading tank. They had not long to wait, for the first target was the house where we had lost Lieutenant Musgrave the night before. We all opened fire on it like a line of old men-of-war engaging the enemy at sea. No fire was returned, but all of a sudden some men ran out waving a Red Cross flag. Some Guardsmen ran over to them to discover what was up and the M.10's pulled into some dead ground. Almost immediately the Germans started to shell us in earnest. The Company dismounted and took cover. I gave them an impromptu lecture on 'Infantry Tank Tactics,' and we prepared to clean up every single house in the district. This task turned out to be easier than we expected, because one sniper in a house only a hundred yards away gave himself up, as he could not bear the suspense of having tanks so close to him. He was a Frenchman and gladly gave us the location of every German position he knew. No. 13 Platoon, under Sergeant Dunne and two tanks, advanced to attack the first house covered by fire from the two other tanks. The attack went very smoothly and far faster than we expected, as Sergeant Dunne went through the house like a dose of salts, driving 'Krauts' out in all directions. The two covering tanks then moved up to the next farm-house where more Germans surrendered, again from all directions. From this farm-house No. 15 Platoon, under Sergeant McKeown, and a section of No. 13, under Corporal Kane, launched a successful attack on a strong German force entrenched in an embankment. They returned plus prisoners and spoil, and the whole Company and the tanks concentrated round the farm-house."

Just after midday Captain Kennedy reappeared in "Dung Farm" with the fifty-five prisoners No. 3 Company had collected during the morning to say that the left flank was now clear. By this time the Germans had given up the attempt to recapture the ground they had lost during the night and had fallen back on the right flank as well, leaving the cross-roads undefended. This was what the Divisional Commander, Major-General R. Penney, had been waiting for all morning. He had come up to "Dung Farm" just in time to hear, in fascinated silence, Captain Kennedy's account of his adventures. He sent Captain Kennedy back to continue his privateering and ordered the 3rd Brigade to move up and press home the second stage of the attack on Campoleone at three o'clock.

The 3rd Brigade's advance began quietly, but as soon as their leading troops crossed the sunken road that had been Nos. 1 and 2 Companies' objectives, they met strong opposition. Salvos of 150-mm. shells crashed into "Dung Farm." Enormous clouds of black smoke erupted as the heavy shells exploded, and the noise was deafening. Through the confusion of noise the distinctive sound of Bren guns and the thud of the tanks' guns told the Battalion that the 3rd Brigade were pushing slowly forward. But the attack had started late, and the winter days were short. When dusk fell the Duke of Wellington's and the K.S.L.I. were established just short of the Campoleone railway, which was to be the objective next day. All hopes of the armour "going through" that day had been abandoned before the attack started, and in fact where the "Dukes" now stood was as far as the beach-head forces were to reach until the final break-out in May.

As soon as the 3rd Brigade had crossed the sunken road, No. 3 Company sallied out of their farm-house. They were met by a shot from a house so close to their farm that it was almost part of the same building. Sergeant Dunne led his platoon into an immediate attack and found, in the parlour, four German youths with two Spandau machine guns. These Germans had been there all day, but for some reason—probably self-preservation—they had not made a move until they thought they were being directly attacked. The survivor spoke English well and claimed to have been educated in Vienna. "In spite of his education," said Sergeant Dunne, "he did not have the intelligence to realize the situation. A few minutes after we started to attack him he left his rear completely unguarded, and so he succeeded in doing nobody any damage, as from the time he started firing he could not have had time to fire more than one belt before our party slipped round to his rear." They then noticed Lance-Corporal Moriarty, the medical orderly of No. 2 Company, leaning on a gate watching this little episode. He reported to Captain Kennedy, "I have about forty-five men, mostly wounded, and a few prisoners under the railway bridge up there. Can you get them back ?" Captain Kennedy and No. 13 Platoon carried the wounded back to their farm-house, put them on the M.10's and sent them, with the unwounded, to Battalion H.Q. in "Dung Farm."

As the night closed in, No. 3 Company withdrew to Carroceto to refuel the tanks and feed the men. The Company Quartermaster-Sergeant and cooks already had dinners ready in the cellars of the station. "There was plenty for all, and both Irish Guards and Americans ate like only soldiers can. After dinners, in spite of their tiredness and without a word being given, they started gun-cleaning on an unprecedented scale. It might as well have been for St. Patrick's Day parade." The Battalion was now in semi-reserve and in part responsible for the right flank. The defence was centred round Battalion H.Q. and the company in "Dung Farm," with No. 3 resting in Carroceto village and No. 4—a firm rock in a sea of battle—firmly entrenched round the railway halt. It was a quiet night, but it passed all too quickly in the reorganization of the Battalion. The reinforcement company, which had landed the day before, marched up from the "B" Echelon area in the woods by the sea. Nos. 1 and 2 Companies were re-formed and No. 3 Company strengthened by new officers and men. Even so, the Battalion was under strength, but another batch of reinforcements was said to be on the sea from Naples.

At dawn on the 31st January, No. 3 Company handed over Carroceto to the Grenadiers and returned to their old farm-house. Lieutenant Hall, who had joined the Company during the night, led the way with No. 15 Platoon. They found that the Germans had moved in during the night, but quickly ousted these interlopers and No. 13 Platoon chased them across country into the scrub beyond Vallelata Farm, where the last of them was killed as he made for cover. One odd sniper remained, causing annoyance all day till the evening, when Sergeant Dunne found time to deal with him personally, routed him out of his lair in a culvert and despatched him. No. 13 Platoon pressed on to occupy a spur in rising ground covering the side road and plain. This was as far forward as they could go ; beyond it the Germans were strongly entrenched in a network of deep gullies. The Company spent the rest of the day in small forays, hunting German artillery observers off the crest of the rising ground.

At half-past ten the 3rd Brigade resumed their attack on Campoleone. They made a series of costly efforts to cross the railway line there, but every time they were beaten back. The Germans had turned every house into a fortress, by blowing out the back wall and driving tanks through the house into a front room and shooting through the windows. At five o'clock the Divisional Commander called a halt, and the 3rd Brigade dug themselves in on the south side of the railway line. Since the Battalion's next move depended entirely on the outcome of the 3rd Brigade's attack, it had been standing by all day, waiting for news. The Guardsmen saw the tanks of the 1st U.S. Armoured Division drive up the main road and, without surprise, they saw them drive back again. There was to be no "armoured break-out" that day either. Just as it was getting dark, Nos. 1 and 2 Companies moved up to the sunken road and reoccupied the positions they had left the previous morning. "It will be seen," wrote Brigadier Murray afterwards, "that the position held by the Division was most unsatisfactory. From Carroceto northwards the position was held by two brigades, pushed out some five miles on a mile and a half front, with both flanks exposed to an attack from a numerous enemy. We did not at all like it, but gathered that the armour would soon be moving through. There was heavy shelling on the whole front from time to time, and fairly heavy air attacks both by day and by night on Anzio and the echelon areas."

The Battalion spent the whole night choosing positions and digging trenches. The area it had to hold, covering the front and the whole left flank, was so great that long open stretches gaped between the companies. These gaps could be adequately covered by small-arms and gun fire during the day, but during the night whole armies could march through undetected. The only possible defence was to range the guns on to these areas as "defensive fire" tasks, and to send out as many patrols as possible. The huge rectangle of ground between Nos. 1 and 2 Companies forward on the sunken road, No. 3 Company in its farm-houses half-way down the left flank, and No. 4 Company securely lodged round the railway halt, remained an unoccupied and confusing wilderness. Battalion H.Q. settled into a ditch and culvert just behind No. 2 Company. It was the best position that could be found in the dark, but it was offensively evident from the shell-holes and the bodies of the previous occupants, both British and German, that the gunners of both sides knew its range. The wireless operators dug little caverns for the sets into the stiff walls of the ditch, and the others lay down to sleep in the oozing mud under the culvert.

With the light on the 1st February began a day of steady shelling. As soon as they could see, the Guardsmen lifted the many corpses they had been sleeping on, buried them decently, and then continued deepening their trenches. The mortars and machine guns had been brought up during the night and were now disposed so as to cover the gaps between the companies. A platoon of No. 4 Company, under Lieutenant Paul Harcourt, moved across to the right rear of No. 3 Company to act as "long stop" and give some little depth to the defence. Lieutenant Mark White and a section of No. 4 Company were called up to man an observation post on Point 115, a small hill rising between the Battalion and the Duke of Wellington's Regiment at Campoleone. Apart from the shelling, the day was quiet. As far as the Battalion knew, the next day or two was to be a period of reorganization and pause for the Brigade and Division as a whole, while the American forces on the right drew level and captured Cisterna. Then, it was said, both British and Americans would drive on towards the Colli Laziali and, of course, the "armour would pass through." Inside the 24th Guards Brigade the Grenadiers extended themselves along the Carroceto railway embankment and the Scots Guards came over to the left flank in between No. 3 Company and the Grenadiers. These moves greatly strengthened the base of the salient, but left the apex as weak as before. By now all the commanders in the Battalion, from section leaders up, were exhausted by ten sleepless days and nights of fighting, reorganizing, planning and patrolling. Colonel Scott decided that it was high time to give them twenty-four hours' rest, and furthermore, that such an opportunity as this would hardly occur again. He ordered up the "second eleven." Major Gordon-Watson, the seconds-in-command of the companies and all the officers and non-commissioned officers who had been "left out of battle" came up and relieved their superiors. Each company sent back to "B" Echelon the twenty men who had been the most hard pressed and worked and replaced them with men out of the new draft of companies. Back in the woods by the sea these weary men bathed in petrol drums, ate a huge meal of American rations—largely cherry jam—and subsided into a sleep that ignored the air-raids and the "bouncing bombs."

The night was comparatively peaceful, but the day which followed, 2nd February, was noisy and dangerous. The German heavy guns pounded the whole area and during the intervals, presumably while the gunners rested, single Messerschmitts skimmed over the houses machine-gunning the line of the ditches. The only casualty, however, from air-strafing was in Battalion H.Q., where Guardsman Grey, the elderly and dignified servant of Captain S. Combe, the relief Adjutant, was wounded in the arm as they both stood shaving in front of one broken mirror. Lieutenant Mark White, in the observation post on Point 115, reported that parties of infantry, large and small, were moving up under cover of the shelling. About a platoon of them, he said, had accumulated in a large two-storey house in front of him; there did not seem to be a back door as they all went upstairs by a front staircase. The machine guns of the Middlesex (Support) Regiment were trained on the staircase; the medium guns fired a sudden salvo on to the house, the Germans bolted down the stairs. There was something distressingly automatic about their death. After this the Battalion sent back to the medium guns a list of all known or suspected German positions, and the medium gunners opened retaliatory fire. This had the effect of cooling off the Germans and gradually the shelling subsided. In all, the Battalion suffered eight casualties.

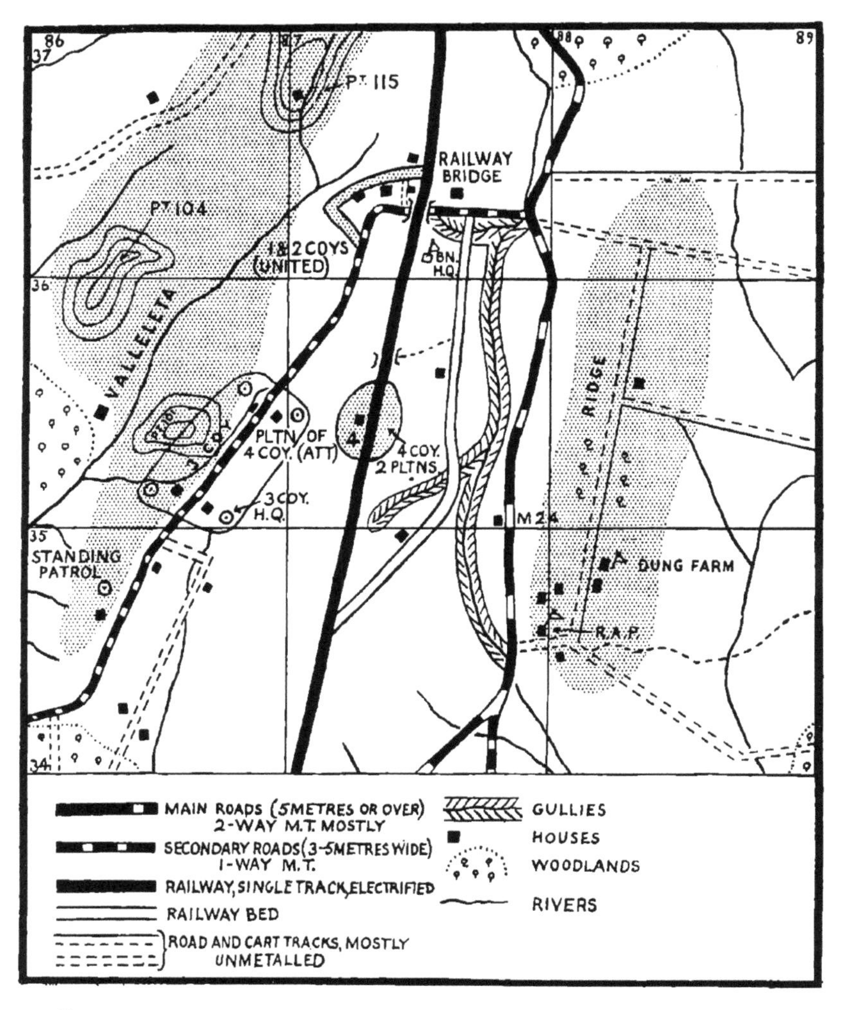

Positions finally occupied by the Battalion after Night Attack of 29th/30th January.

The night was disturbed by a powerful German patrol, which made its way undetected right up to Battalion H.Q. Sergeant McConnell, sitting by a Bren gun on top of the culvert, held it back till the rest of Battalion H.Q. scrambled out of their trenches and "saw it off" ; the patrol disappeared without a trace into the darkness. This incident was alarming, not because of the patrol itself, but because of the obvious ease with which it had slipped between the companies. And yet, what more could the Battalion do ? To scatter sections along the line of the salient was to invite piecemeal destruction by night. As the Brigadier wrote afterwards : "The Division was not in good position to stand a heavy attack, as the narrow salient with open flanks courted attack. The battalions were on a wide front and had no wire or mines, but it was decided that our present positions were to be held and we had to accept it."

CHAPTER VI

The German Night Attack

EARLY the next morning Divisional H.Q. issued a general warning order, "Strong counter-attacks to be expected." The only reinforcement they could raise, however, was a battalion of American parachutists, who were held back in reserve. The Germans had by now assembled a counter-attack force of four new divisions, one of them armoured—the 65th, the 715th the 4th Parachute Division and the 26th Panzer Division—all good, tough divisions, well equipped and up to strength. The endless ridges and gullies running parallel to the salient on the left flank, opposite No. 3 Company, gave them splendid assembly areas and covered approaches so deep and convenient as to be practically natural communication trenches all the way to Rome. The Battalion also heard, first from its prisoners and then from Divisional H.Q., that the S.S. Division, "Reichsführer," was on its way into the line. "Those will be the boys," said the Battalion and went on with breakfast. The day was peaceful for the Battalion, though they heard the sound of the 3rd Brigade receiving and defeating some small attacks. The stillness of the afternoon was broken by the bleating of a thousand sheep. Like a dirty, ragged wave a huge flock surged over the crest of the Vallelata ridges and scampered crazily through No. 3 Company. Those wise after the event later said that it was a typical German trick to use poor dumb animals as mine-detectors, but at the time no one felt anything but gratitude.

At half-past nine the Battalion settled down for the night. Dinners were dished out and the ration trucks sent back ; the artillery and mortar defensive fire tasks were checked and the Company Commanders set out on their rounds. At eleven o'clock—2300 hours dead—the heavens seemed to open and a violent barrage fell on the Battalion. It lasted precisely five minutes, a neat military time, as

Major Gordon-Watson pointed out to Brigade H.Q. There were three minutes of nasty silence and then the barrage began again, even more violent this time, and concentrated on the left flank and rear. Captain O. F. McInerney, who had relieved Captain Kennedy in the command of No. 3 Company, called for defensive fire on to the ridge and gullies opposite him. But already some Germans had slipped through the gaps under cover of the bombardment, for burst after burst of machine-gun fire came whipping through No. 4 Company's positions. No. 3 Company's area was held by its own platoons, the medium machine-gun platoon, a detachment of 3-inch mortars, and three of the Battalion's anti-tank guns. The Germans now concentrated on overwhelming No. 3 Company's area by weight of numbers. They first showered mortar-bombs on the farm; this was a mistake, for the phosphorous charges fired the haystacks, which burnt with a bright, steady flame, throwing "a pretty pink light" out into the night. The Guardsmen could now see their enemies.

"They came on in a mass, very hard, thick and fast after the barrage," said Lance-Corporal Fahy; "the machine-gunners mowed them down, but they came on just the same." Guardsmen Flanagan, Nicholson and Maloney, who manned one of the forward Vickers M.M.Gs., fired all their ammunition, 8,000 rounds, straight into the wavering line of silhouettes, "but nothing seemed to stop them, they came on shouting and gesticulating wildly as if doped." Lieutenant Harcourt could hear them shouting, "Seig Heil! Gott mit Uns!" but he was just too far away to see clearly what was happening, so the running commentary he sent back over his telephone line to No. 4 Company H.Q. was a "sound picture" rather than an eye-witness account. As soon as the M.M.G. had fired its last round three Germans jumped into the trench, shouting "Hands up, Englishmen!" The three "Micks" were not going to stand for any insults; they flattened the Germans with their fists and made off to No. 4 Company. Meanwhile, the Germans surged in waves against the farm-house. Captain McInerney reported their strength to be "at least one battalion"; the Operation Order for this attack, found later in Rome, showed that two battalions and two special companies had been turned on to No. 3 Company alone. Their casualties must have been staggering, for the platoons cut them down in swaths as they came out of the dark into the glow of the burning haystacks, but the German commanders had their reserves and they were determined to beat down the resistance. They shovelled in fresh troops, passing them round the left flank of the Company between it and the Scots Guards, and driving in on Lieutenant Hall's platoon and Company H.Q. from the flank and rear. They obliterated Lieutenant Hall's platoon and swarmed into the farm-yard. "I never saw so many people killed round me before in all my life," said Lance-Corporal Donnan, who was captured, escaped, re-captured and escaped again. Captain McInerney reported that his headquarters was "in a critical position, for the Germans are at the door," and that was the last that was heard of him until a Red Cross prisoner-of-war postcard arrived at his home some months later. With Company H.Q. the Germans took the only wireless, so that the Battalion did not know what had happened to the platoons of the Company.

Of the three platoon commanders, Lieutenant Patrick Alcock, of No. 14 Platoon, was captured, Sergeant M. Dunne, of No. 13 Platoon, was captured but escaped, and Lieutenant Hall, of No. 15 Platoon, did not survive to give an account. Sergeant Dunne told his story the next afternoon. "While I was standing in my platoon area on the night of 3rd February I heard the prearranged signal from the forward observation post and, knowing that an attack was imminent, immediately ordered the platoon to 'Stand to.' I ran round to the officer in charge of the support 4.2 mortars, who was in the house at the rear of my platoon, informed him that the enemy were attacking in strength and told him that the defensive fire plan must be laid on immediately. On my return I ran into the heavy enemy barrage and had to take shelter in a nearby cowshed until I could cross the open ground to my platoon. On reaching my platoon I found Guardsman Burke badly wounded lying in his trench. I lifted him from the trench and sent another Guardsman for the stretcher-bearers. Then Captain McInerney joined me and I explained to him that I had already told the 4.2 mortar officer to bring down the defensive fire. He left me to return to Company H.Q., and I did not see him again. Whatever happened I do not know, but the defensive fire was never brought down, and I saw the enemy at the far edge of the gully in front of us. My platoon at once engaged the enemy, as did No. 15 Platoon on my left, joined by the attached machine guns. The hay-ricks in front of Nos. 14 and 15 Platoons were set alight and the Vickers machine-guns brought heavy fire to bear in front of our positions. Then, on my platoon front, the enemy seemed to move over to both flanks, and only a number of enemy snipers remained. Next I observed the enemy attacking Company H.Q. from the rear, and after approximately thirty minutes the firing quietened down. I then decided to withdraw my platoon to Battalion H.Q. to support them in defence of their positions, knowing that Nos. 14 and 15 Platoons had been overrun.

"After giving orders to my section commanders we moved forward, then swung to the right. We made good progress until we reached the railway, then we came under heavy fire, which I thought came from our own troops. I shouted to them and then found that the embankment was strongly held by the enemy, thus making our objective almost an impossibility. I left two sections of my platoon in the gully, which runs from the road to the railway, whilst Lance-Sergeant Ashton, Lance-Corporal Wilson, five Guardsmen and myself went forward to the high ground. On reaching this we were pinned down by fire from both flanks and the rear, and Lance-Corporal Wilson (who was the link-man) reported to me that the two sections in the gully had been cut off. I remained with this section on the high ground overnight and at eight o'clock the following morning Lance-Sergeant Ashton and Guardsman Swift were badly wounded by enemy machine-gun fire. The enemy by this time had encircled the section and, having exhausted our ammunition, we were taken prisoner and put in the gully. We were later moved to a house, leaving Lance-Sergeant Ashton, as we were refused permission to carry him with us. Guardsman Swift was able to accompany us, with help. We had been in the house for about an hour when one of our tanks opened up on it, causing the enemy to seek safety in the trenches outside. We were left under a guard of two Germans, whom we overpowered, and made our escape, taking them with us. We made our way back by the gully, taking two more prisoners, then passed through the mortar platoon, who were in the gully under the railway line. On reaching the road we handed over the prisoners, and Guardsman Swift and myself were conveyed by carrier to the dressing station." In this account Sergeant Dunne forgot to mention that he himself was wounded early in the night.

Lieutenant Alcock gave his account after his release from a prison camp. "At nightfall on the 3rd February my platoon took up its night-time positions around a farm-house on the forward slope of the ridge held by the Company. The platoon then settled down for the night. About eleven o'clock a heavy concentration fell on the Company area. It lasted for about thirty minutes and a large number of haystacks were set on fire. One of my sections was forced out of its trenches near the haystacks, and I ordered its commander, Corporal Murray, to take it to an alternative position. I then went round the remainder of the platoon, which I had ordered to 'stand to' at the beginning of the concentration. Unfortunately the Germans turned their machine-guns on us at this moment and their fire bursts caught Corporal Murray's section as it was getting into its new position. As I returned to my Platoon H.Q. I heard Lieutenant Hall, who had evidently gone out in front of his positions, shouting for fire from his Bren guns, and saw a Very light signal go up from him for the medium machine guns to open fire. Then my platoon was attacked from three sides, and I could hear fighting all round Company H.Q. We continued firing until our ammunition was nearly exhausted—not without effect, judging by the shouts and screams we heard. The Germans gave up trying to rush us, but from about midnight to four o'clock in the morning kept us pinned in our slit trenches by persistent accurate Spandau fire. During the fighting I was cut off together with my platoon Sergeant, Sergeant McKeown, a few men from another section and the crew of an anti-tank gun. About four o'clock, since the enemy were clearly in possession of the Company area, I considered the possibilities of getting through, either to the Scots Guards on the left or to Nos. 1 and 2 Companies on the right. I split the men into parties of three and explained to them the lie of the land. I set out with Sergeant McKeown and a Guardsman. We were captured at first light while trying to cross the new German front line."

Immediately after No. 3 Company went off the air Lieutenant Harcourt, in No. 4 Company's "long-stop" platoon, saw Germans moving across a dip towards the railway line. He engaged them with H.E. bombs from his 2-inch mortar, which produced shouts of alarm and despondency, and passed the word to his Company H.Q. Captain Keigwin, in temporary command of the Company, ordered the other two platoons to put up parachute flares from time to time and to await an attack on the halt. But the Germans made no attempt to assault this position and contented themselves with shelling and continuous sniping from all sides. With No. 3 Company now gone, the gap between the companies in the sunken road and the Scots Guards was nearly a mile wide. There was nothing to prevent the Germans walking through this gap and nothing but No. 4 Company to prevent them reaching the main road and so cutting off the apex of the salient which contained most of the Battalion and the whole of the 3rd Brigade. Major Gordon-Watson explained this danger to Brigade H.Q. and asked that tanks and infantry be moved up to Carroceto ready to go into action at dawn. "A couple of sweeps with infantry and a troop of tanks would clear the whole situation," he said. At the same time he could hear the Scots Guards passing the same request over their wireless. The reply from Brigade was encouraging. "Yes. Heavy friends are coming; they should be with you at first light." "How many?" "A whole squadron, and you can have six busters now." Two tank-busters, commanded by a Lieutenant Jarvie and a Lieutenant Sertz, made their own way up to Battalion H.Q. and parked under the railway bridge to deal with any German tank that tried to cross the road. The other four, however, remained in Carroceto and demanded guides. Captain R. D. N. Young and Lance-Corporal Donnan went back through the snipers to meet them and bring them up, but they might have saved themselves the trouble, for these tank-busters refused to budge.

The Germans, meanwhile, were moving more and more troops through the gap into the central plain. Some of them set up machine-guns between No. 4 Company and the forward companies and kept up a steady fire, but most of them seemed to spend the night tramping around firing Very lights. A succession of red and white lights shot up, varied by an occasional pillar of green smoke or a flare. These were, presumably, signals of some sort. They had no immediate results, but the general effect was eerie; it was like being in a jungle and seeing the bright eyes of animals shining from the darkness, hoping they were deer, but suspecting they were tigers. The Battalion did its best to confuse the signals by firing a Very light of its own after each German one on the chance that the addition of a red light to the Germans' green and white would change the signal from "I am here; be careful," to "Put heavy concentration here immediately." "And so the situation continued till dawn," wrote Major Gordon-Watson, "with brisk exchanges of fire between Corporal Carr in a nearby house, Sergeant McConnell on a Bren behind a knocked out 88-mm. gun, and the tank-busters versus four or five enemy machine guns."

At dawn the firing died down and the Germans went to earth. It was a cold, grey morning with a thin drizzle. The long-promised Sherman tanks came into sight, but only into sight, on the main road behind "Dung Farm." There they halted, but as it seemed that it would only be a matter of minutes before they came on to Battalion H.Q., Major Gordon-Watson prepared his plans for sweeping away the Germans. What he did not know—and what the Battalion did not know till afterwards—was that the tanks could not get up the road and had been diverted to the support of the infantry battalion on the hill forward of "Dung Farm." The Battalion waited and waited. Meanwhile, German Tiger and Mark IV tanks began to appear among the houses forward of Nos. 1 and 2 Companies. They knocked out one of the tank-busters and poured in fire from yet another direction.

The remaining tank-buster, however, tucked in under the railway bridge, did "great work with the magnificent 3-inch naval gun and as far as we could see accounted for three tanks."

Back at No. 4 Company, Captain Keigwin had established an observation post in the top room of the halt, manned by Guardsman Donaldson. "Either Lieutenant Dodds, Lieutenant Boyd (whose 6-pounder gun was in our area) or myself," he wrote, "were up there most of the morning. We could see the enemy crawling about in groups and firing on No. 1 and No. 2 Companies' area. I tried to get the gunners on to this target, shouting the corrections from the upstairs window down to the wireless set, but with limited success, as I suppose they had to go carefully with their ammunition. At about ten o'clock I spoke to Captain Combe, the Acting Adjutant, on the wireless, and he told me that the Battalion had been promised tank support immediately and that they would so sweep the ground between us clear of the enemy. ' No,' he said, ' Our heavy friends, the beetle-crushers, have not actually arrived, but they are on their way.' Then the wireless, so carefully nursed all night by Guardsman Buckley, broke down. At last, an hour later, we got it going again and on getting through to Captain Combe he told me that the situation had greatly deteriorated. I was ordered to concentrate the Company and fight my way forward to help Battalion H.Q."

During this period of silence for No. 4 Company the Germans attacked and captured the forward half of "Dung Farm" hill at the very same time as the Sherman tanks were moving forward to help the defenders. Battalion H.Q. could see it happening. "Whilst the Sherman tanks were taking about a hundred prisoners in the rear of the unit on our right, a large body of men in the forward positions laid down their arms and surrendered to the enemy, some of them taking their blankets with them. There appeared to be no earthly reason why this should have happened, and even the Germans seemed to be totally unprepared for such a turn of events. Guardsman Montgomery, the right-hand Bren gunner of Nos. 1 and 2 Companies' right-hand platoon was the first to react. He swung his gun round and opened fire on the Germans, without worrying too much about the blanket-carriers. Major Gordon-Watson joined in, firing two magazines from Sergeant McConnell's gun, and then remembered to tell Brigade H.Q. "The alteration that this action makes to the situation must be too apparent to need explaining, completing as it does the enemy's bid to isolate Battalion H.Q. and the forward companies." Brigade H.Q. replied with a suggestion that the Battalion recapture the hill itself. By the time Major Gordon-Watson had explained that the only men in the Battalion not already closely engaged with the enemy were the twenty-odd men of Battalion H.Q. the Germans had already reinforced the hill and set up machine guns to fire down on the Battalion. "Spandaus began to rake the railway bridge with fire and made life most unhealthy in the ditches." Major Gordon-Watson concentrated what remained of the Battalion in Nos. 1 and 2 Companies' position where the railway bridge would give some protection from this plunging fire, and ordered No. 4 Company to join them. Sergeant McConnell, with his Bren gun, remained on the right flank tucked in under a derelict 88-mm. gun.

No. 1 Company called in its outlying platoon. Lieutenant Robert Aikenhead, its commander, only arrived the morning before, and most of his men were from the new draft. He had spent a quiet morning lobbing 2-inch mortar bombs at the Germans round his position. "I noticed a lot of vehicles on fire on the hill to our right. Then I saw a lot of prisoners being taken there, and thought they were Germans, as little firing seemed to come from that sector. Some time after this I got a message by runner telling me to withdraw my platoon to the sunken road on three blasts of the whistle. By this time we had come under heavy machine-gun fire from what I presumed to be tanks in a 'hull-down' position. I never managed to spot where they were. Also the house to our rear was being shelled by 88's and all the 'shorts' fell on to the platoon—and there were a good many of them. I then got another message by runner saying 'Come at once, before it is too late.' We had a 150-yard dash across the open under heavy machine-gun fire. How no one was hit I can't imagine. A lot of small shells met us as we entered the sunken road. I sent my platoon to the top end of the cutting out of view of the enemy, and told them to wait for me there while I found out what was happening from Major Stewart-Richardson, the Company Commander."

Major Gordon-Watson and Major Stewart-Richardson met under the railway bridge for a consultation. Battalion H.Q. found "the new position not much of an improvement on their old ditch." Indeed, the whole force—the two companies and Battalion H.Q.—was now surrounded and overlooked. Tank shells from the hill were whistling right under the bridge and exploding on both sides of it, and the whole road was swept by direct machine-gun fire. Heavy 105-mm. shells fell monotonously into the sunken road, blowing in the slit trenches in the banks. One shell alone killed and buried a complete section. The remaining tank-buster decided, with good reason, that it could do nothing more of any use, backed out of the bridge and made off down the road. To Major Gordon-Watson "it seemed no time for dilly-dallying, and the only way out of a rather impossible situation was for Battalion H.Q. and the companies to withdraw independently." He told Brigade H.Q. what he thought and got the Brigadier's permission for No. 1 and No. 2 Companies and Battalion H.Q. to withdraw and separately to fight their way back to No. 4 Company. It was, however, too late to stop No. 4 Company, who had already set out on their relief attack, and were temporarily "off the air"; they could only hope to meet them half-way.

The fighting in the Battalion area now broke up into three separate actions—Nos. 1/2 Companies' withdrawal, Battalion H.Q. withdrawal, and No. 4 Company's attack. Each one was a distinct and yet essential part of the Battalion's task—to disrupt the German attack, to hold the Germans off the main road and to deny them possession of the central plain until the 3rd Brigade could be brought back from the Campoleone railway line, and finally, to extricate as many men as possible from the German encirclement. The Brigade Commander described the day briefly afterwards: "The situation was very serious, and something had to be done at once. The enemy were showing signs of activity on the Grenadiers' front, and I told the Divisional Commander that I expected an attack on Carroceto might develop which, if successful, would involve the encirclement of the best part of the Division. Luckily a brigade of the 56th Division had landed that morning, and they were moved straight into battle. Of these welcome reinforcements, one battalion was allotted to the Grenadiers in reserve, one to counter-attack the lost positions of the Gordons on the hill, and the third battalion to the 3rd Brigade. Fighting was very confused on the Irish Guards' front, mainly in platoon and company groups, which in spite of a very difficult position, held on. Later in the afternoon much of the lost ground was recovered, including German prisoners, and the battalion of the 56th Division retook the Gordons' lost position. This allowed the 3rd Brigade to be withdrawn into reserve, but most of their transport had to be abandoned. After the 3rd Brigade had passed through, the Irish Guards were withdrawn into reserve for reorganization about a mile in the rear of the Grenadiers. The line that night was held from left to right by the North Staffs, the Grenadiers, the Scots Guards and an American parachutist battalion, with the London Irish Rifles (of 56th Division) in the Factory. It had been a most difficult and confusing day, and we were indeed very lucky to get at least the best part of the 3rd Brigade back. This was largely due to the Irish Guards who stood their ground and kept fighting in spite of the general confusion all round them. . . . The cost, however, had been heavy." The cost is best shown in figures. On the morning of the 4th, the total number of Battalion H.Q., No. 4 Company and the combined Nos. 1 and 2 Companies was 260 men. Of these, 140 answered the roll in "Dung Farm" that evening.

Major Stewart-Richardson intended to lead No. 1/2 Company back to No. 4 on the west side of the railway line, the way it had come in the first night attack. He met Lieutenant Aikenhead and, with him, climbed to the top of the cutting. "There," wrote Lieutenant Aikenhead, "we were bowled over by a shell. Stewart-Richardson was badly hit in the left arm, under the arm-pit. He could not pick himself up. I put him on his back, and he started to fight, and then stopped. I thought he was dead, but it proved to be otherwise. I dressed his wound, gave him morphia, placed him on a stretcher and covered him with blankets. While this was going on, John Vesey came up." Lieutenant Vesey was the only other officer in the Company, and he now took command. His platoon and the other one were entrenched just forward of the sunken road. For the past hour they had been attacked at regular intervals by small groups of Germans whom they regularly repulsed, collecting three or four prisoners from each attack. They had about fifteen in all, a dispirited bunch, who did not like the sunken road and had had enough fighting, but did not want to accompany the Irish Guards. "However, we persuaded them to come with us, thinking it a waste to leave them behind. We set off, skirting the Germans on our left. We could not 'feel our right' too much, as there were more Germans there. We reached the area where No. 3 Company had been the night before, but found them gone. We now had to contend with our own artillery fire, which was most unpleasant." They put their prisoners and a few men as guards in a barn while they advanced on the farmhouse. "It was full of Germans; they were in fact all round us. We saw them rush the barn, and the way we had come was closed. We went down in a ditch and were fired on from all sides. We thought of many schemes to get out of the mess we were in, but none seemed to make any sense." And so began the second fight at Vallelata Farm. Each man settled down in the best bit of ditch he could find, counted his ammunition, kept twenty rounds for himself, and passed what was left up to the Bren gunners. Here they would stay till dark, for ever, or till the Germans hauled them out. And that is what happened. Some were killed, others were swamped by repeated assaults, and a few lay hidden in the labyrinthine ditches till nightfall, when they made their way back through the Germans to Carroceto.

On the other side of the rectangular plain Battalion H.Q. and No. 4 Company were, all unknown to each other, fighting towards each other. While Major Gordon-Watson was talking to Major Stewart-Richardson under the railway bridge, Captain Combe had collected Battalion H.Q. and Lieutenant Grace's platoon of No. 1/2 Company in their old ditch. Major Gordon-Watson chose his servant Guardsman O'Shea, D.C.M., Lance-Corporal Cross, an orderly-room clerk, and Lance-Corporal Dodds of the Intelligence Section as a combined escort and point section, and at their head plunged into the network of ditches and gullies. The rest of Battalion H.Q., under Captain Combe and Captain R. D. N. Young, threaded their way behind in single file. The gully was narrow, overgrown and extremely muddy. The "point section," lightly armed and laden, travelled fast, leaving an ever-increasing gap between themselves and the main body, stumbling along. As they rounded a corner they came face to face with four Germans sitting in a culvert. One of them levelled his Schmeiser sub-machine gun, but dropped it hastily at the sight of the muddy Major Gordon-Watson waving a muddy revolver. The gully seemed to be paved with Germans. Fifteen yards farther on there was another culvert, which contained five Germans. This time a blast from the Tommy guns of Lance-Corporal Cross and Guardsman O'Shea cleared the way, and they stepped over the Germans on a cattle track. Two German officers, chatting unconcernedly, walked straight into them. Major Gordon-Watson shot one dead ; the other made a dash for a bush and slid behind it. Major Gordon-Watson fired and missed ; the German fired and missed. Major Gordon-Watson dived across the track into the mouth of the next gully. Corporal Dodd walked slowly towards the bush and, when he thought he had got near enough, emptied his magazine into it. The whole party, shepherding their prisoners, ran down this new gully, jumped over a bank and landed on top of ten Germans in two slit trenches. "It was a real mix-up," said O'Shea. "I didn't know which way my hat was on." The first to recover was Lance-Corporal Cross ; though his hands were more accustomed to typewriters than fire-arms, the execution he dealt was fearful. The surviving Germans surrendered. It was only now, when there was a moment to pause, that Major Gordon-Watson realized that he and his little party were alone. There was no sign of the rest of Battalion H.Q., and no possibility of turning back, so they went on to the main road. Lance-Corporal Dodd "borrowed" a motor-cycle from a despatch rider who was taking cover in a ditch. As always with these temperamental machines, it would not start when it was needed, and Lance-Corporal Dodd had to push it up and down the road, at first kicking and cursing it, and then pleading with it as some Germans started to shoot at him. He bumped down the road on two flat tyres till he saw some of No. 4 Company and found Captain Keigwin. Major Gordon-Watson, still waving a revolver, headed straight for "Dung Farm," while Corporal Cross lined up the twelve prisoners and marched them down the road in step and in order of height.

The rest of Battalion H.Q. were now temporarily in German hands. As they plodded through the winding gullies, the Germans closed in on them, attracted by the firing. Rows of grinning German faces, and rows of Spandaus, appeared over either side. The gist of their remarks was apparent even to non-German-speakers, and the column halted with ill-grace and a lot of muttering. The Germans slid down the banks, removed the arms and reversed the order of march. With a guard on each man, the column marched back the way they had come. Captain Combe, at the head of the column, spoke to his particular guard in a polite voice, "I am going to do you in when I get a chance." He did not have to wait very long for the chance. They emerged from the gully into the sunken road, climbed the bank and continued northwards. As they came into the open a flight of bullets halted and disconcerted the Germans, but not Captain Combe. He walked on, picked up a rifle from the bank and shot his guard. The other Germans did not seem to notice this interlude so, much encouraged, Captain Combe changed the rifle for a Tommy gun and emptied the magazine into the nearest clump of Germans. Lieutenant John Bell followed his example by clubbing down his attendant German, and Sergeant McConnell and Guardsman Montgomery snatched the machine pistols from their guards. This was a signal for a general slaughter of the escort. Every Irish Guardsman picked up something—a rifle, a spade, or even petrol tins—and laid about him. Of the thirty Germans who formed the escort, twenty were killed, nine taken prisoner and one was "missing." They dusted themselves down, re-equipped themselves from the litter of arms and turned back once more to the railway bridge. Here they found the carriers where they had left them, and still intact. Standing between the carriers and the bank was Lance-Corporal Moriarty, the stretcher bearer, mounting guard over a dozen wounded men he had collected. The wounded were lifted into the carriers, the unwounded piled on board. Lieutenant John Bell and Captain Young started the engines and the overloaded carriers drove "flat out" down the track past No. 3 Company's old positions to reach the Scots Guards or Grenadiers by Carroceto. Just after they started, Captain Simon Combe noticed a large form lying by the roadside covered by a tarpaulin, heaving like a stranded whale. There could be only one such form on the beach-head. He jumped off the carrier. It was as he thought—Major I. Stewart-Richardson. The huge bulk was bundled on to the carrier and they started off again, rocking from side to side. The Germans made no special effort to stop the convoy; they may have fired at it, but there was already so much metal in the air that nobody would have noticed a little more.

No. 4 Company's action was remarkably successful. When Captain Keigwin got the order to attack he went upstairs to look out of the window. He could see the enemy machine-gun posts dotted all over the fields on both sides of the railway line, and that it would be quite impossible to go straight up to the bridge. The Sherman tanks had by now established themselves on a firing line just off the main road opposite the halt, so Captain Keigwin decided to work round to the right by the main road and then bear left up a gully to the sunken road and railway bridge. No. 17 Platoon withdrew from its "long-stop" position without casualties, though each man in it was fired on. Within a quarter of an hour the Company was under way with Lieutenant Dodds's platoon, No. 16, in front, followed by No. 18 Platoon, with No. 17 Platoon in the rear. They just skirted the tanks, which were firing hard at the Germans on the skyline near No. 3 Company's late position, and then moved along the left-hand side of the main road. Some two hundred yards beyond the tanks they branched off left up the gully. Like all gullies, it was very overgrown, a tangle of bushes and brambles. "We ran straight into a large body of Germans and, after a few bursts of Bren and Tommy gun fire, about forty ran out with their hands up. Elated by this, we proceeded to winkle them out at a great pace. Wheeling round the next corner, Lance-Sergeant Weir led his section in a charge against another group of Germans. These Germans were ready for them and met them with long bursts of fire. Lance-Sergeant Weir was shot through the shoulder, but the bullet only stopped him for a moment, while he recovered his balance. He led his men full tilt into the Germans and they killed those who delayed their surrender with the traditional comment, 'Too late, chum.' While lying on the ground waiting for the stretcher-bearers he directed his section to the assault of an adjacent machine-gun, and saw it captured and his section re-formed before he was carried away. 'After this the opposition became thicker and stiffer. The enemy had a tremendous number of M.G.34's—about one to every three men—and we began to have casualties,' said Captain Keigwin. There was little chance of getting any farther frontally, so he sent No. 17 Platoon, the only one not committed, across the main road to get forward on to the rising ground and to shift the enemy with fire from the right flank. Lieutenant Harcourt led the platoon round with great dash, opened fire, and the Germans in the gully in front of us proceeded to pull out, several more giving themselves up." While the main body gathered the prisoners, Lieutenant Harcourt's platoon pressed on into an olive grove, and there they ran into an enemy company entrenched. "Germans began to appear from their holes all over the place. Lance-Corporal Foran, a big, black ' Mick ' from County Clare, and a fine fighting Guardsman, who had been promoted for gallantry in Tunisia, dodged in and out between the trees and did great execution before he himself was killed."

It was at this stage that Lance-Corporal Dodds found Captain Keigwin and told him what had happened to Battalion H.Q. "Major Gordon-Watson says you are to close on ' Dung Farm.' " Captain Keigwin thereupon concentrated the Company, bloated like a boa-constrictor with prisoners, in the ditches near the main road and sent a runner to recall No. 17 Platoon. The Guardsman returned, saying that he had been forward and come under heavy fire, but the fire was all directed at him and there was no sign of No. 17 Platoon. It was surprising how easy it was for a large body of men to disappear in a comparatively flat plain. The deep gullies swallowed up a platoon without a trace. When the last man turned round one of the innumerable bends, and the rustle of undergrowth or squelching of mud died away, they were gone beyond recall except by wireless. No. 17 Platoon fought its way out of the olive grove and the Germans who had captured the rising ground, recrossed the road, and headed for where Lieutenant Harcourt knew Battalion H.Q. should be. They reached the culvert and climbed over it to find Germans in possession. Neither side were prepared for this encounter. Some Germans tentatively laid hands on Lieutenant Harcourt and the leading men, but not for long. They shook themselves free and the men in the rear opened fire, while they backed out through the culvert. The return journey was slow and hazardous, but by nightfall Lieutenant Harcourt had brought his platoon back to "Dung Farm."

Captain Keigwin had taken the rest of No. 4 Company back to "Dung Farm" and there they remained, dug in behind the road embankment till dusk. "We suffered one or two casualties by the farm through heavy enemy shelling, but apart from these, and some of No. 17 Platoon who were still missing, the Company was fairly intact, and the wireless set still with us. It is difficult to estimate the number of prisoners taken, but we sent back well over a hundred under escort, apart from the very many others who went back on their own."

News of the German attack did not reach "B" Echelon, where Colonel Scott and the "first eleven" were resting, until after dawn that morning, 4th February. Up till then Brigade H.Q. had regarded it as a routine, though somewhat large, attack with which the men on the spot could deal. When the news did reach Colonel Scott it came down like a hammer stroke. "1st Bn. Irish Guards surrounded. One company destroyed, remainder holding on, but isolated." The Commanding Officer and Adjutant drove to "Dung Farm" immediately, passing the halted Shermans on the way. "What is wrong with them ?" There was little more to be learnt at "Dung Farm," except that the forward part of the hill had been captured, which meant that the Germans now overlooked the Battalion. He ordered Major George FitzGerald to collect every available man in "B" Echelon, form them into a company of sorts, and hold them ready to move up to the farm. The first real news came from Major Gordon-Watson, who arrived panting and alone. The remnants of the Battalion joined No. 4 Company behind "Dung Farm" and covered the approach of a battalion of the London Scottish. In mid-afternoon the London Scottish attacked to clear a way forward to the 3rd Brigade. When the 3rd Brigade had successfully withdrawn down this alley, the Battalion was ordered to take up a reserve position behind the Grenadiers and North Staffords. The Adjutant drove back in the pouring rain to find the safest and most comfortable place. Attracted by the noise of firing, he turned off the main road down a muddy lane and found a squadron of self-propelled guns in a wide valley south of a low hill. "There are some handy caves over there," said the gunners, "You can have them." A series of wide galleries had been cut into the side of the hill to excavate gravel, and gave the hill its name, Cave di Pozzocana. The Battalion occupied these caves just after nightfall. One of the roomy single caves was already occupied by refugees from Anzio, but the Battalion left them undisturbed in their desirable semi-attached residence. There was room for all ; better still, the caves were dry and it was possible to build large fires out of the empty shell cartons. On the way to the valley the Battalion had filed past a barn ; as they passed each man tore out a bundle of straw. They bedded down around roaring fires and slept, while the newly-formed company from "B" Echelon stood guard.

Single men and small groups continued to rejoin the Battalion during the night. By dawn on the following day—the 5th—the Battalion was 270 strong. Another eighty men were sent up as reinforcements during the day, so that now it was possible to have three rifle companies—Nos. 1, 2 and 4, each about seventy strong—leaving No. 3 Company in suspended animation, to be revived as soon as more reinforcements arrived. The Battalion's only duty now was to guard its own left flank, and this it did quite peacefully that night.

CHAPTER VII

The Caves

AFTER a night's sound, warm sleep the Battalion emerged from the caves blackened by smoke and grimy with gravel dust, but ready to go on with the war. The Quartermaster had brought up the cooks' lorries before dawn and the flare of the petrol cookers lit up the mouths of the caves. Breakfast was an enormous meal, composed of the whole of the previous day's rations—bread, jam, porridge, bacon, stew, potatoes, "duff" and custard, if anyone wanted it, all washed down by floods of tea—real "Sergeant-Major's brew"—boiled to a bitter blackness and then sweetened with condensed milk. Even the heaviest eaters were bloated into silence. Water was put on the burners and the Battalion washed and shaved. The smooth red skin, the hall-mark of a Guardsman, appeared once more. Having cleaned themselves, the Guardsmen cleaned their weapons. The Quartermaster brought up every Bren and Tommy gun he could lay his hands on—and he had a remarkably long reach—but there were no replacements in the beach-head for the lost mortars and anti-tank guns. A few more men and officers arrived, the last of the reserves. The only orders from Brigade H.Q. were "to dump three days' rations and ammunition forward and work on improving defences." The nearest the trucks could get to the caves was a farm—called "Ration Farm"—half-way between them and the main road and some three hundred yards north. It was an exposed spot to use as an *entrepot*, but there was nothing better, and the high stone farm-house sheltered the courtyard where the fatigue parties unloaded the truck. "Ration Farm" dominated the flat, open country forward of it right up the Carroceto railway embankment. It was already occupied by a reserve company of American parachutists. Lieutenant Anthony Bell and his dismounted carrier platoon joined them and held the farm for a week. It was a singularly unpleasant position, for the house was an obvious target, but it was the best—indeed, the only—vantage point in the area and had to be secured. Lieutenant Bell installed himself in an upper room with a wireless set, and directed the guns. He was regularly joined by two American observation officers, which relieved the monotony and increased the fire power. At the end of the week the Germans, after many attempts, at last got the right window and put an 88-mm. shell into the room. The explosion lifted the roof, killed the two American officers and badly wounded Lieutenant Bell.

But on this first day in the caves—the 5th—things were quiet; it was exhausting rather than dangerous. All day long men trudged from one side of the valley to the other, humping ammunition and rations from "Ration Farm" to its twin on the south side of the valley, perversely called "Carrier Farm," with a stop at the caves to check and change loads. The sticky black mud clung to the boots like a ball and chain. At the same time the Battalion was being reshuffled once again into four rifle companies, each of roughly seventy men. The Company Commanders and Company Sergeant-Majors got a nominal roll of their new companies, the result of the night's work by Sergeant Kelly, Sergeant Sweeney and Lance-Corporal Cross, the orderly-room staff, who had checked every single man. Sergeant Kelly had come from "B" Echelon with a nominal roll of the Battalion as it was on the morning of the 3rd. Sitting round a leaping fire of cardboard shell cartons, they crossed off the "known killed" and "known wounded" and then toured the caves and later stood at the head of the breakfast queues by the tea containers, ticking off the names. It was a heart-breaking job. From these lists the Company Sergeant-Majors collected their Guardsmen, while Colonel Scott showed the officers the new positions.

The defence was based on the caves and the low plateau above them, which were held by Nos. 2 and 4 Companies. No. 1 Company, under Captain David O'Cock, crossed the valley to "Carrier Farm." Captain O'Cock had been second-in-command of No. 1 Company for six months in Africa and Italy, but "when I took over No. 1 Company on 5th February," he wrote, "there were very few faces among them familiar to me. Major Rory Stewart-Richardson, the Company Commander, had been wounded. Of the platoon commanders, Da Costa was dead, shot through the head, and Grace had his legs broken. Replacements for these two had been John Vesey and Robert Aikenhead, but they were now both missing. The officers I now had were Lieutenants Charles Bartlet and Gallwey. C.S.M. Gilmore—that splendid man—had been killed, so that C.Q.M.S. Smilie was made my Sergeant-Major, and Sergeant Moore imported as C.Q.M.S. There had been such heavy losses that there were only twenty-three left of the original 120 who went to make up the Company, but my numbers were made up to eighty by a draft from the reinforcement camp. In the rear of the caves there was a small hill with a farm building on top which overlooked a wooded gully running down in the direction of the enemy. I was given the task of occupying this hill by night and keeping the gully under observation by day. I was also ordered to wire and mine the gully. During the day I passed these orders on to my platoon commanders in the normal manner, and as soon as it began to get dark the necessary digging was started. Company H.Q. was set up in a disused garage attached to the farm buildings."

At nightfall the Battalion moved out into the newly-dug slit trenches and stayed there till dawn, when, like some nocturnal animal, it retired back to the warm gloom of the caves, leaving only the Bren gunners in position. With breakfasts came the first salvos of the German six-barrel mortars. So far, these abominable instruments of war had been absent from the beach-head. The previous evening, however, a German mortar officer, absorbed in his duties, had driven into the Scots Guards' lines. He took pleasure in telling his captors that he had found excellent positions for batteries of "six-barrels," and advised them "to do a Dunkirk while there was still time." Despite the loss of their commander, the German mortar crews dutifully clocked in to work at first light and were still hard at work when the Battalion finally left the beach-head.

The Brigadier called in the middle of gun cleaning, after breakfast; he looked exhausted, and sank gratefully into an old deck chair, which had been transported from the beach by the Quartermaster. An orderly was sent through the passages to No. 2 Company to fetch a "Kennedy Special"—a mug of hot rum and dried lemon. As he drank it, the Brigadier gave the latest news and orders, and as he spoke the Guardsmen moved quietly out of the shadows to hear what he had to say. The Battalion's role was now to sit tight and beat off all attacks—this, in fact, applied to the whole beach-head force, for the next move was to come from the main Fifth Army to the south. The Brigadier had decided to concentrate the Brigade as much as possible, for the Scots Guards forward of the station were "very much out in the blue," and the North Staffordshire Regiment, temporarily transferred from the 2nd Brigade to the 24th Guards Brigade, had a very wide area to hold on the left flank. He therefore ordered the Battalion to send one company to reinforce the Scots

Guards and with the remainder of its force to support the North Staffords and, if necessary, counter-attack their positions. To tighten the defences and close the gaps he proposed to withdraw the American parachute battalion into reserve round "Ration Farm," beside the Battalion, to move the Grenadiers back slightly so that they could take over part of the North Staffords' area, and finally to withdraw the Scots Guards to Carroceto embankment. Colonel Scott now had to choose a company for the Scots Guards, and he choose No. 4 as being the strongest and the one with the greatest number of its original men left intact. Captain David Drummond, the Company Commander, met Colonel Wedderburn at Carroceto station and told him that he would bring up his company as soon as it was dark. During the afternoon officers of the other companies walked across country through a tangle of bushes to see the positions of the North Staffords, who were in contact with the Germans to the immediate north. The Germans did not interfere with this combined professional, social and constitutional stroll, and the party returned with a rough idea of how to get to the North Staffords should they be called on to help. The North Staffords definitely expected that they would need help for, according to them, another big attack was brewing. Colonel Scott realized and accepted that, as things were, the Battalion was bound to be used to bolster the line, but, as he said himself, "I don't like being a little Dutch boy, running up and down plugging holes in the dykes."

Dinners came up early, to let No. 4 Company get away in good time. Their departure was hastened by an "alarm" from Divisional H.Q. : "Indications that enemy may attack with tanks about 0400 hrs. 7th Feb. Area unspecified. All troops to be warned verbally, *not* by telephone or wireless. All reliefs and readjustments to be completed by 0001 hrs. 7th Feb." The "troops" received this message just as, in the old days, they would have received the news—if news it could be called—that there would be a Battalion parade on Saturday morning. Anyone looking at the men spooning potatoes out of their mess-tins, or at No. 4 Company rolling the gas capes, would have said that they were unimpressed and even uninterested. C.S.M. Lynch, D.C.M., with no apparent preparation or change of expression, suddenly let out a shrill shout, "No. 4. Get on parade !" The scattered figures squatting on the grass and in the cave mouths coalesced into three platoons ; the sergeants called the roll. Captain Drummond, dressed with scrupulous neatness down to the last gaiter strap, saluted the Commanding Officer. "Permission to march off, please, sir." "Yes, please. I hope you won't be away very

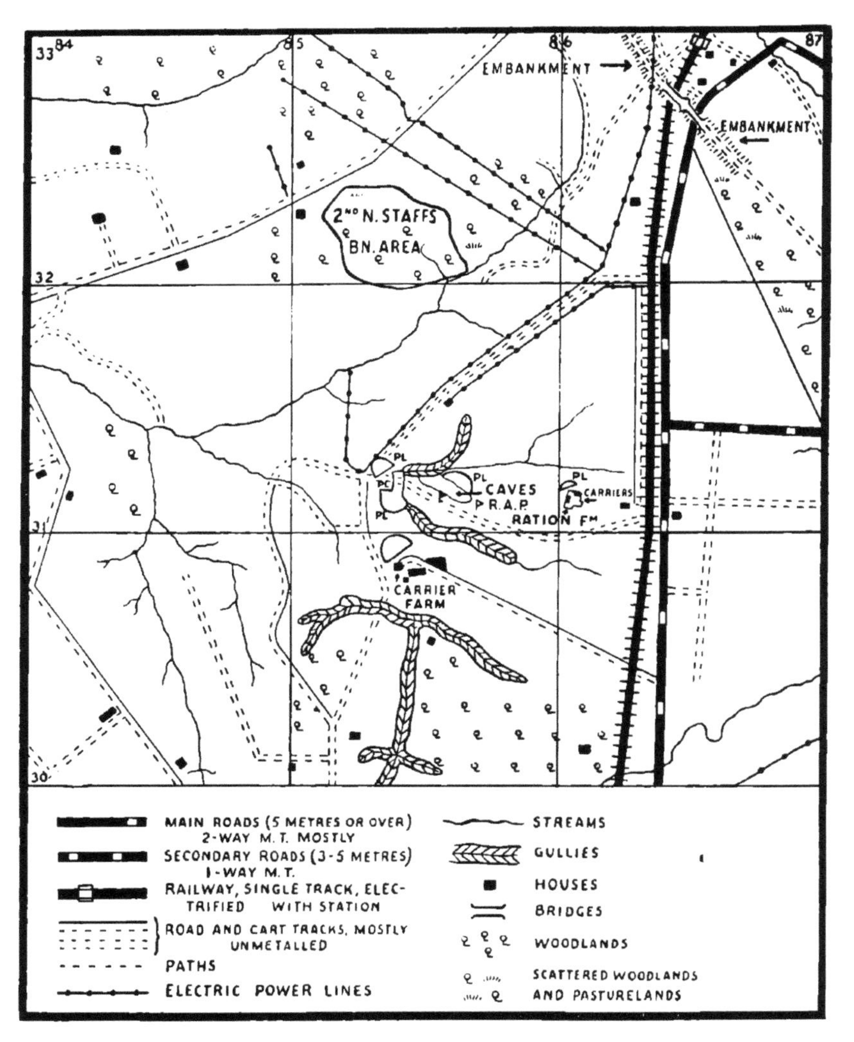

POSITIONS OCCUPIED BY THE BATTALION IN THE CAVES FROM 4TH TO 12TH FEBRUARY

long. I'll come and see you to-morrow morning." No. 4 Company disappeared up the narrow muddy track that led to the main road, and the Battalion never saw them again.

The night was cold, but undisturbed. There was no sound from the left flank, and not even a wind to rattle the wire and tin cans that had been strung across the stream-beds and gullies. But to the north, round Carroceto, the gun-fire was incessant, and the horizon was lit constantly by a flickering light. "No. 4's getting it." Just before dawn, when the Germans should have attacked, it began to rain, which was worse. It rained all day, a steady miserable stream, but otherwise there was an ominous calm. The North Staffords passed back some prisoners they had captured during the night—four tired, dirty, tattered men from the 71st Infantry Regiment. These Germans, after the usual complaints that they were over-worked and underfed, which might be made by any infantryman in the world, explained that their regiment was only holding the line with skeleton companies while something big was being prepared. This was obviously true, but the most intelligent-looking prisoner, who might have known something more definite, was so distressed by the loss of his comb that he could talk of nothing else. He finally plucked up courage to ask Drill-Sergeant Kenny for the loan of one—the reply was so discouraging that he subsided into sobbing silence.

The rain stopped at dusk and the sky cleared of clouds to reveal a full moon. Captain D. O'Cock came down from "Carrier Farm" at dinner time to complain about an errant gunner officer. "I was sitting in my new headquarters," he said, "when I saw a jeep driving up the hill straight through the Company's night positions. We had taken a good deal of trouble to stop any movement in the area during the day-time, so I stamped out to interview the driver. It was a Gunner major, so I slightly modified my language. When I explained that he was in the middle of my Company's position, he replied that this was not the front line, so what did it matter? I told him that, as a Gunner, I should have expected him to realize that we were well within enemy artillery observation, being on the top of a hill, and within range of the type of cannon used at Waterloo. I was even more incensed when I discovered that he was in no way connected with our Brigade, and was merely looking for somewhere to put his anti-tank guns. He said he wanted to put two 17-pounders in among my farm buildings, so I begged him at least to send them up after dark, and to try not to run over any of my men, who would then be in their slit trenches." Colonel Scott soothed him, saying, "The anti-tank defence has been put on a divisional basis," and gave him a drink. He was half-way down the mug when they heard and saw shell bursts on "Carrier Farm." "The fruit of the Gunner's visit," he cried, finished his drink in a gulp and ran off shouting "Thank you!"

About nine o'clock Lieutenant James Quinn, taking a turn on the wireless, heard the North Staffords announcing an attack in strength on their left flank. This was followed by a warning to all that "a party of some fifty Germans have broken through and are moving in direction of the fly-over bridge." Then the little Corps of Signals operator, Corporal Hislop, sang out cheerfully, "They say that all their companies but one are off the air, and that Battalion H.Q. is surrounded. The corporal on their set sounds worried." "I don't blame him," said Colonel Scott and ordered a general "stand-to." The signallers and orderlies of Battalion H.Q., who had been on duty all day, were kicked awake and put to man the mouths of the caves. "Here we are and here we stay. They will have to smoke us out like bees." The babel on the air continued. The Adjutant was on the set, trying to keep track of the battle. The Scots Guards, and with them No. 4 Company, seemed to be all right, but the Grenadiers were in a bad way and were also asking for help. He heard the Brigadier promise the Grenadiers a company of American parachutists, heard the North Staffords appealing again and yet more urgently for help, and then heard what he had been expecting, the Brigadier asking to speak to "Andrew." Theoretically, the Brigadier should have called "King Roger Queen"—or whatever was the Battalion's code sign for the day—and said, slowly, clearly and avoiding all individual mannerisms of speech, "Put Sunray on set," but he was tired, hard-driven and human; besides, everyone knew who "Andrew" was. Colonel Scott could not, and did not, conceal his reluctance to send a company—nearly half the precious men left to him—out into the night, first to find and then to extricate the remnants of the North Staffords. "We have not the men to spare for gestures. It is throwing good men away. This is now the position to hold, and we can do it if you will cut your losses. Some of the North Staffords are trickling back. Unfortunately we have shot one or two in the dark and the others are veering south towards the Fly-over. By the morning you will have enough survivors to put in a proper counter-attack." The Brigadier accepted all these, and more and stronger arguments, saying, "I know, but we must help." The Brigadier had his own worries. "I spoke myself to Divisional H.Q. more than once that night, and told them I considered the situation so serious that the 3rd Brigade should be brought up from reserve to the

Fly-over. I was told that there was nothing to worry about and that they were certain we could clear up the situation ourselves in the morning. It was not considered to be a major attack, so I sat on the wireless with the reports becoming more and more gloomy as the night went on. I sent Geoffrey Hood (the Irish Guards liaison officer) down to the Fly-over, where he did a great job of work in collecting a quantity of North Staffords, who were walking back to Anzio and sent them up to the Irish Guards."

Colonel Scott remained by the wireless for a few minutes after his conversation with the Brigadier. He sat in silence, slowly tearing up an old letter, before saying to the Adjutant, "Tell David to take out No. 1 Company," and then went back to the fire and emptied his pockets into it. The Adjutant tried to make his voice sound non-committal, almost nonchalant, but the effort only made him croak. "We will be ready in about twenty minutes," replied Captain O'Cock. "Try and keep in touch with me." They talked at intervals after No. 1 Company had set out, Captain O'Cock giving a commentary on his progress and what he could see, the Adjutant guiding him by the map and explaining the various sounds of battle. "I think this must be them. Yes, it's their left-hand company." After an interval, Captain O'Cock's voice came up again. "Their Battalion H.Q. are clamouring for us to join them. Do we go?" The Adjutant had to reply, "Yes. You must get through to them." Another crackling silence and then Captain O'Cock "came up" for the last time. "We've hit the Germans." Nothing more was heard from or of No. 1 Company until Rome Radio gave the names of a few prisoners. At dawn twenty bedraggled men of the third platoon filed down the gully into the valley of the caves, but they knew nothing of the rest of the company. They had got held up at a stream crossing soon after setting out, and when they got across the Company had disappeared. They had tried to catch up, but at each gully junction had to guess which way to turn and so, as was natural, had got lost. They marched towards the sound of firing till they came on an American battalion. "An officer said he could use us, and after we had held some trenches for some hours showed us the way home."

About the same time that No. 1 Company disappeared the parachutists of the 3rd Bn. 504th Airborne Regiment, now under command of the 24th Guards Brigade, withdrew to "Ration Farm." Their commanding officer, Colonel Freeman, came down to the caves. His first words endeared him to the Battalion. "Those Krauts, I sure hate their guts." From him, and his troops, the

Battalion learnt the word "Kraut," and never afterwards called the Germans anything else. Colonel Freeman was a tall, melancholy gentleman from Virginia, with a slow drawl and a captivating manner. Every morning during these days he strolled into Battalion H.Q. to discuss the previous night and the forthcoming day. Every morning Colonel Scott greeted him, "Hiya, Colonel, what d'ya know," and invariably Colonel Freeman replied " 'Morning, Colonel. Not a goddam thing." These American parachutists were "real soldiers"—higher praise than that the Battalion could not give. Colonel Freeman later wrote his opinion : "I wish to convey to you the admiration of both my troops and myself for the British soldiers and officers under your command. Their attitude and conduct under the most trying conditions was superb. Their cheerful and immediate obedience to orders, difficult both to give and to execute, inspired me. I congratulate you and those under you for what you did. One thing I frankly envy—that is the unfailing courtesy and kindness with which we were treated. I fear I may have appeared rude in comparison, because we sometimes employ an approach direct at the expense of the finer qualities."

While the two Colonels were chatting amiably, about Krauts and mint-juleps, the Brigadier appeared in the mouth of the H.Q. cave with news as gloomy as his appearance. The Germans had attacked from the flank between the Carroceto embankment and "Ration Farm" behind the Grenadiers. They had not yet reached the main road, but, without being too pessimistic, it looked as if the Grenadiers, as well as the North Staffords, might be "written off." The Brigadier ordered the parachutists "to sweep the battle area," supported by the Battalion and a squadron of tanks. No. 2 Company moved to "Ration Farm" to join the Americans and remained there to form a continuous line from the main road to the left flank of the caves. The Americans attacked in the red light of a lurid dawn supported by the small-arms fire of No. 2 Company. They were all morning fighting their way across the open water-logged ground, but by midday they had reached the Grenadiers. The ground and the main road itself were swept by machine-gun fire from the Buonriposo Ridge on the left flank, the North Staffords' former position. The Germans on the ridge showed every sign of pressing home their success. "Prisoners and captured documents," announced Divisional H.Q., "show that this attack is planned by the 1st Parachute Corps with headquarters at Grottaferratta, behind the Alban Hills, with the objective of establishing a firm base from Buonriposo Ridge to Carroceto and Aprilia." Early in the afternoon two battalions of the 3rd Infantry Brigade, the Sherwood Foresters and the K.S.L.I., tried to recapture Buonriposo. The results of this counter-attack were not very clear or very encouraging; there were too many Germans, and they refused to be ejected from the Ridge.

At nightfall it began to rain again. "Rain stopped play" is one of the oldest jokes in the Army, but there were still people to make it once again that evening. The lull gave the Division the chance to form a rough defensive line south of the embankment composed of the Foresters and the K.S.L.I., the Battalion and the American parachutists. Forward of this line were the parachutists at Carroceto bridge, the Grenadiers strung out along the embankment, and the Scots Guards and No. 4 Company in Carroceto station. There was no detailed news of No. 4 Company. It was impossible to visit them, and the Battalion had to be content with the statement that "they were doing all right." As soon as it was dark the Grenadiers fell back on Carroceto bridge, and the Battalion kept touch with them by a non-stop carrier patrol, under Lieutenant Boyd, up and down the main road. At half-past two in the morning there was a sudden outburst of shelling—the usual prelude to an infantry night attack. The Battalion "stood to," but the attack fell on the Grenadiers. After an hour the Germans abandoned this attack, but when the Battalion heard the continued noise of fighting from their right front they realized the real object of the shelling and the attacks. The Germans were after the Factory, and they left everything else in peace, except for shelling, until they had captured it from the 168th Brigade. The 9th was, therefore, a passive day for the Battalion. They waited for the fall of the Factory with a dull feeling of inevitability. The beach-head forces were going back to where they had started, and they had started without the Factory. After the capture of the Factory the Brigadier ordered the Scots Guards to fall back and join the Grenadiers, "to hold the embankment and as many houses as they thought fit." The death of Sergeant O'Connell of the carrier platoon was a private loss which weighed far more in the mind of the Battalion. He was killed by one of the routine "air-bursts."

All night the Battalion waited for news of No. 4 Company, slightly encouraged by the promise that the whole of the Mediterranean Air Force was going to be turned on to the Germans at first light. Dawn came; a few aircraft flew over and dropped a handful of bombs—"the markers," said the Battalion—and then the heavens opened with a cloudburst. There would be no bombing that day and, worse still, there was no news of No. 4 Company. Colonel

Scott and the Adjutant drove in a carrier to Brigade H.Q. In Tunisia, during the peaceful days after the campaign, nothing could induce Brigade H.Q. to live anywhere but in a remote and desolate wadi, but in the beach-head it was drawn irresistibly into a series of farm-houses. As each farm was shelled into ruins on their heads Brigade H.Q. moved patiently to another one, where the process was inevitably repeated. They did not seem to suffer more casualties than anybody else, but it was difficult for the battalions to keep track of their moon-light flits. Lieutenant G. Hood, the liaison officer, met Colonel Scott and led him through the mud and driving rain into the dark candle-lit room where the Brigadier was sitting talking to the commanding officer of the Duke of Wellington's. Nobody seemed to know much about the situation on the embankment, but everybody agreed that it was desperate. The Grenadier and Scots Guards were hanging on precariously, and Divisional H.Q. had at last agreed to relieve them with the "Dukes." A counter-attack was to be put in at first light the following morning by the U.S. 1st Armoured Division and the U.S. 45th Division, to recapture the Factory; all the "Dukes" had to do, they were told, was to hold on at all costs till dawn when "the armour would go through." The phrase was familiar, but no comment was made. Colonel Scott wanted to see Colonel Wedderburn and find out more about No. 4 Company. The carrier drove back down the Campo di Carne road in the steady rain, turned right under the Fly-over bridge and rattled down the main road as fast as the driver could flog it, for it was in full view of the Factory and the bullets from the machine-guns on Buonriposo Ridge were whistling around it. The embankment was a scene of peculiar desolation. The rain beat down on a litter of smashed equipment and burnt vehicles, shattered ammunition and derelict tanks. Lying on his back was a Gunner officer, shot through the head, and then run over by a tank. It was not a pretty sight. Up on the embank-ment the sodden, exhausted remnants of the two battalions crouched in their slit trenches. Battalion H.Q. was in the culvert under the embankment, where the Battalion R.A.P. had been, knee-deep in water and crowded to capacity. Looking tired, but unmoved in the babel, was Colonel Wedderburn, surrounded by Americans, Sappers, Gunners—all that could be scraped together to reinforce the Scots Guards and Grenadiers. Outside, snuggled close up to the embank-ment, were four American tank-destroyers, the only comforting sight to be seen.

About No. 4 Company Colonel Wedderburn could only say what he afterwards wrote: "For four days No. 4 Company, 1st Bn. Irish

Guards, was under my command. I wish to put it on record how proud I, and indeed the whole of the 1st Bn. Scots Guards, was to have them fighting with us and to say how much we all admired them for the magnificent and self-sacrificing way in which they fought. For the whole of these critical days they held their ground in the area of Carroceto station in the face of intense shell, and mortar and M.G. fire. On two occasions fighting patrols were found from them. Both patrols had to be carried out under observed small-arms fire from the enemy, but on both occasions the patrol did great and valuable work. The first captured between twenty and thirty prisoners, and the second not only killed numerous Germans, but also found out much needed information regarding enemy positions. It is impossible to say, during the great defence that they put up, how many casualties they inflicted on the enemy, but it was abundantly clear to all who were there that the number must indeed be high. It is sad that this great Company should, in the end, have been overwhelmed by a greatly superior enemy force of tanks and infantry, but no body of men could have stood up to the final weight of the attack that the enemy put in ; an attack with tanks covering all the windows and doors of the station building where what remained of the company of Irish Guards were holding out, and with a strong force of enemy infantry assaulting covered by the tanks. Their casualties were not in vain, the ground which the Scots Guards were ordered to hold until relieved was held, and No. 4 Company, 1st Bn. Irish Guards, played a great part in the magnificent defence put up by the whole Battalion."

Colonel Scott and the Adjutant drove slowly back to the caves. They were both old "No. 4" officers, and every man in the Company was a friend of years. It did not seem possible that the Company—"our Company, No. 4"—should be annihilated. What would the Battalion be like without it ?

At eight o'clock the "Dukes" took over the embankment. The Scots and Grenadiers marched away into reserve, and the Battalion was transferred to the command of the 3rd Brigade. Lieutenant James Quinn, the Intelligence Officer, went up to meet them. "An alert-looking Irish Guardsman presented himself," wrote their C.O. "He said he was their Intelligence Officer, and brought a message from Andrew Scott to say that he strongly disapproved of my present headquarters and advised me to join him in his large cave some five hundred yards back. Apart from the personal comfort of being with Andrew, there were the additional benefits of being in close touch with the only firm body of troops between us and the

Campo. I therefore set out to talk things over with Andrew. That remarkable officer was as cheerful and helpful as ever, but the glutinous mud made his headquarters inaccessible for my purposes, and we therefore pulled the carriers out of the mud and struggled back to our headquarters."

The rain stopped at dawn. In the greyish light, No. 2 Company saw a long column of tanks advancing slowly up the road towards Carroceto—about seventy of them, in single file. "The armour was going through at dawn." The column paused and the three leading tanks rolled under the bridge and out the other side. The Germans knew what to do—they brought their guns down on the road and turned mortars on the embankment. From the far side of the embankment came the clatter of Browning machine-guns and the thud of anti-tank guns. One more tank went through the bridge and then shot back again. The whole clanking column turned and slowly rumbled back towards the sea. "What good they did," said the Brigadier, "I never heard," and neither did anybody else. The American infantry doggedly continued their attack alone, but they could make no progress. The German guns shifted from the main road to the farm-houses. "Ration" and "Carrier Farms" were heavily and accurately shelled.

The Italians living in their separate cave had, so far, taken no part in the war, but one of them, called Vittorio, was the owner of "Ration Farm," and he was depressed by this turn of events. He came forward with the story that it was all due to some Fascist spies, and that he could show the Battalion where these spies were and so contribute to the Allied victory. He was put in charge of Guardsmen Montgomery and Adamson, two of the most forbidding-looking and resourceful men in the Battalion. They returned in about an hour with a small Italian Army captain, a smaller and even more terrified civilian, and a huge Alsatian dog. From the conversation which followed the Italians got the impression—as well they might—that they were going to be shot out of hand and fell on their knees weeping bitterly. Vittorio, the informer, repeated many times that, since the dog was an Alsatian, it must have been supplied by the Germans for the special purpose of carrying messages. The Italian captain swore that it had been his since it was a puppy, so the Sergeant-Major suggested a simple test. The dog was led away round a corner, and the Italian was told to call it. The Italian began confidently, but when no dog appeared, his voice rose in tones of shrill despair, particularly when he noticed Guardsmen Adamson and Montgomery significantly shifting Tommy guns from hand to hand. The Adjutant decided to look at the dog before doing anything hasty, went round the corner and found it, struggling desperately and half-strangled by a rope tied to its collar. Hanging on the rope was Major Kennedy. "A grand little dog," he said. "It took to me at once." The Italians were reprieved and sent to Brigade H.Q., who had no use for them and sent them to some Corps "cage," where they were lost.

The Germans attacked again that night and forced two companies and the Battalion H.Q. of the "Dukes" to withdraw to "Ration Farm." The "Dukes" counter-attacked, however, the following morning (12th) and recaptured the embankment. The sun came out once again and the weather cleared for flying, which meant that the Battalion had a quiet day while the bombers kept the Germans underground. Later that evening the Battalion was relieved by the Gordons and marched back to the wood where they had spent their first night on shore.

CHAPTER VIII

The Last Actions of No. 4 and No. 1 Companies

I. No. 4 COMPANY

No. 4 COMPANY reached Carroceto after dusk on the evening of the 6th February. They found that the American parachutists had had no orders and proposed to remain where they were, curled up in their "fox holes" until they heard from their own Battalion Commander. Captain Drummond, by urgent entreaties and with the help of the Scots Guards, persuaded the reluctant Americans that it would be "according to schedule" for them to leave. An hour later, when it was quite dark, the Americans "pulled out," leaving behind them, as they always did, cartons of cigarettes and packets of candy. The Guardsmen felt uncomfortable and unsafe in the "fox holes," wide and shallow, more like a saucer than a grave, and one by one began to dig themselves regulation-pattern slit trenches.

Before the new trenches were ready, salvos of shells landed on top of and just in front of the Company's positions. The Gunner at the Scots Guards H.Q. was bombarded with abuse. "Your shells are falling on us. Get the guns to pitch them up a bit." "We're not shooting," replied the F.O.O. "That is a German stonk. They have guns behind us, down by the sea on the left flank of the beach-head." The ground was littered with bags of cordite and unused shells, dumped by a battery of self-propelled guns which had previously occupied the area. Company H.Q. hastily removed as many of these unwelcome objects as they could find in the dark and threw them into the water-logged gullies. The continuous shelling inevitably caused casualties. Two sergeants were wounded and C.S.M. Lynch, D.C.M., was knocked unconscious and concussed, which left the Company with only one senior non-commissioned officer, Sergeant Guilfoyle. Later in the night the shelling was followed by heavy machine-gun fire to the west. The Germans were apparently attacking the Grenadier positions on the high ground to the west. At about eight o'clock in the morning—the 7th—when the digging had almost been completed, Colonel Wedderburn ordered the Company to withdraw to the railway station and there to form a strong-point. To Lieutenant Dodds the station "seemed too easy a target, and the open fields vastly preferable, especially when we saw the shattered transport and the large portions of the station which littered the yard." The Company moved back at once, and Captain Drummond "dovetailed" (as he called it) his defensive positions in with those already occupied by the Scots Guards. This was not as easy as it sounds, for the area of the station included gravelled yards and stretches of asphalt. No. 16 Platoon, under Lieutenant M. White, eventually dug in around a goods shed, about fifty yards north of the station itself; No. 17 Platoon (Lance-Sergeant Havers) on some banks to the east of the station yard, while No. 18 Platoon (Lieutenant Dodds) and Company H.Q. occupied the actual station building. Two sections of No. 18 Platoon went upstairs and covered the approaches to the east and west from the windows. The platoons outside spent the remainder of the night breaking the crust of concrete and gravel to dig a second lot of trenches, while the men inside the station fortified their rooms with furniture, mattresses, sacks of corn, bales of straw and boxes of earth. The night was made still less pleasant by heavy rain which filled the trenches with a foot of freezing water. By dawn the men of Nos. 16 and 17 Platoons were sodden, stiff and tired, but they were below ground.

Spasmodic shelling during the morning caused a number of casualties to No. 17 Platoon. A sharp concentration killed Guardsman Moran and buried him and his companions by blowing the bank down on their trenches. Lance-Sergeant Duffy, crouching in a nearby trench, heard "fearful shouts" and, looking up, saw Guardsman Lyons's head sticking up out of the earth. Lance-Sergeant Wright and Lance-Sergeant Duffy dug out Lyons and two other men alive, but poor Moran was already dead. Lieutenant White supervised the excavation. "Very placid he was in the barrage," said Lance-Sergeant Duffy, "and whenever I was feeling a bit upset I looked across to Mr. White and felt O.K. again." "On the whole," said Lieutenant Dodds afterwards, "it was a chancy business to remain out of a trench or the houses for any length of time. The shelling continued at intervals throughout the day, and at times the shells seemed to fall like rain, so that one could hardly distinguish one explosion from another. The noise was magnified by the buildings and became most tiring."

It was not till about midday that there was any sign of the German infantry. A small group of them, carrying a large white flag, appeared on the rising ground about a mile to the north of the station. The sentries in the upstairs windows said it looked like a burial party or

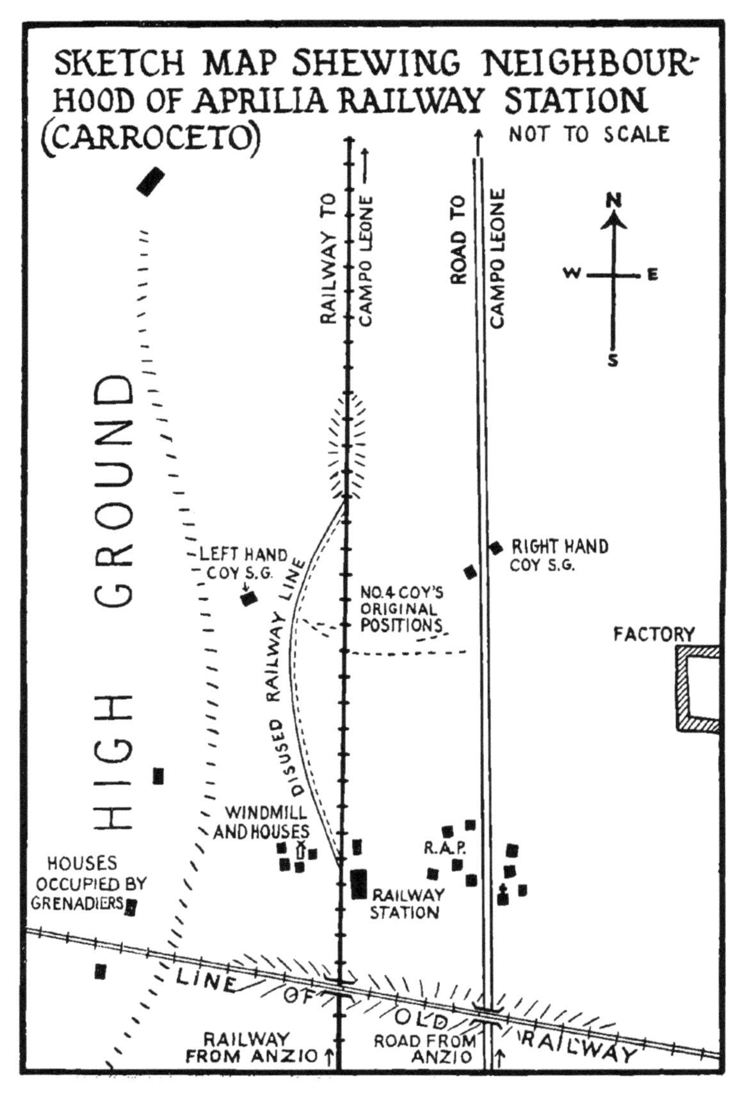
SKETCH MAP SHEWING NEIGHBOURHOOD OF APRILIA RAILWAY STATION (CARROCETO)
NOT TO SCALE
RAILWAY TO CAMPO LEONE
ROAD TO CAMPO LEONE
N
W
E
S
HIGH GROUND
LEFT HAND COY S.G.
RIGHT HAND COY S.G.
DISUSED RAILWAY LINE
NO.4 COY'S ORIGINAL POSITIONS
FACTORY
WINDMILL AND HOUSES
R.A.P.
HOUSES OCCUPIED BY GRENADIERS
RAILWAY STATION
LINE OF OLD RAILWAY
RAILWAY FROM ANZIO
ROAD FROM ANZIO

stretcher-bearers searching for wounded, but reported that there was a much larger body of men, some sixty or seventy, advancing down an irrigation ditch parallel to the small party. The white flag party then wheeled away into dead ground and did not reappear, but the large body came out into the open and marched steadily ahead. The Scots Guards carried two machine-guns upstairs and opened fire out of the windows. The Germans halted abruptly, and the survivors promptly retired. "We don't want to stop them surrendering," said Colonel Wedderburn, "but we can't take any chances." An hour later more, or possibly the same, Germans reappeared and began advancing down the line of the railway, under cover of the embankment. The Scots Guards 3-inch mortars and the artillery halted them with a sharp concentration and held them down while a company of the Scots Guards made a sortie which dispersed them. In the late afternoon the sentries in the top storey again reported a white flag on the high ground to the north, and also that, just as on the first occasion, a large party, this time of 100 or so, was advancing down one of the irrigation canals. Colonel Wedderburn ordered Captain Drummond to go and meet these Germans and to bring them back if they wished to surrender, but to take an armed party with him in case the Germans tried any "funny business." Captain Drummond borrowed a large Red Cross flag from the R.A.P. and walked up the railway with two Guardsmen, feeling like "part of a misplaced May Day procession." Lieutenant White and his platoon followed two hundred yards behind.

The ground to the west of the railway line was a network of irrigation ditches, along which the party threaded their way. After about 1,000 yards they found two bunches of Germans sheltering in the ditches behind the embankment and under the "cattle creeps" which ran under the railway line. There were about fifteen Germans in all—a miserable-looking crowd, filthy dirty, soaking wet and surrounded by a number of their own dead, who must have been killed that morning. Captain Drummond in loud, if ungrammatical, German offered them safety and honourable imprisonment. After some discussion amongst themselves they threw down their arms and agreed to come. During these negotiations there was a certain amount of unpleasantness. Other Germans, whose heads could just be seen in dripping grass, kept interrupting the conversation by sniping. These Germans were either only trying to scare Captain Drummond away, or else were the worst shots in the German Army, for although the range was only a bare one hundred yards, they did not score a single hit—not even an "outer" on their own side.

Their presence, however, made the new prisoners very uneasy; it was clear that they did not want their captors hurt or angered in any way, and vehemently disclaimed any connection with the snipers. They also professed to know nothing of the large party which had been seen from the station, but it is also possible that they did not understand Captain Drummond's questions. Urged on by their prisoners, the expedition returned unmolested.

"For the rest of the day nothing startling happened in the immediate neighbourhood of the station, though the German artillery did not forget us," wrote Lieutenant Dodds. "The two remaining Scots Guards companies, however, had a more eventful time and were in contact with the enemy on and off till dark. The continued racket and shelling naturally made refreshing sleep an impossibility. The Company was always alert, and though they never really knew what was happening and were continually rather hungry, uncertain of even one good meal a day, and on duty for long periods because of the shortage of men, there were no complaints."

In the evening, when it was comparatively quiet, Captain Drummond re-formed the Company. With the casualties it had suffered, it was now capable of mustering only two platoons, each of about twenty-five men. There seemed "no point in having a platoon outside the buildings," so No. 16 Platoon was scrapped and its men joined Nos. 17 and 18 Platoons who were respectively manning the upstairs and downstairs windows of the station and the doors and windows of the goods shed. "Maybe they will give us a rest tonight," said the Guardsmen, "and let us take a drop of kip." They lay down on concrete floors and most of them managed to get half an hour's sleep before the shelling and the alarms started again. There was the sound of heavy fighting to the west and, as the Company "stood to," it wondered how the Grenadiers were getting on, and whether or when the Germans would shift their attack. As soon as it was light the following morning—the 8th—the Company looked toward the houses on the rising ground to the west, and saw German helmets. This was the first intimation that the Grenadiers were no longer in their old positions. The machine-gunners upstairs opened fire and conducted a long-range duel all morning. "There were rumours that the Factory had been taken, but nobody seemed to know anything," wrote Lieutenant Dodds. "An American battalion appeared on the scene, with only a hazy idea of where anything was, but filled with the quiet determination to do something. Colonel David Wedderburn told me to persuade the Americans to clear the ridge, but their commander had other ideas and disappeared with his battalion in single file over the hill to the left, thereby nearly completing a circle."

At midday, just as the idea of a lunch was occupying all thoughts, Colonel Wedderburn decided it was "uncomfortable" to have the Germans sitting on the ridge overlooking the station, and therefore ordered Captain Drummond to clear the houses and drive the Germans off the high ground. It was a task for a strong company at least, but Captain Drummond had only one weak platoon, for the other must be left to hold the station. As a form of compensation, Colonel Wedderburn promised the support of a troop of tanks and the usual call on the guns. When the Shermans arrived the troop commander insisted that he could give adequate support from the station and would only agree to one of the three tanks accompanying the platoon as close support. The platoon just had to make the best of this. They watched the guns and the tanks almost flatten the houses and "set off feeling quite confident that there would not be much spirited resistance after that." The platoon walked up the line of the old railway with the one tank following them. They breasted a small rise and came into view of the first house. The tank fired a few rounds and the Germans inside bolted. "Money for old rope," said the platoon, and pushed on towards the house. Half-way there, they noticed that the tank was not following them. The commander refused to come any farther on account of some ill-defined danger from an 88-mm., which he thought might shoot at him from the rear. There was nothing to do but leave the tank where it was and go on alone. To make things more awkward the wireless set "packed up." From now on the only communication with the station was to send a runner to the tank with a message to be relayed by the tank's wireless. About one hundred yards from the house the platoon came under fire from one Spandau shooting down the railway line and another from the second house. Guardsman Burke was killed and three others wounded. Running, twisting and side-stepping through the fire, the leading men burst into the second house. Germans in the farm-yard and outbuildings kept a stream of fire and threw grenades in through the windows. Guardsman English, a Bren gunner, and Guardsman Kerr, like terriers after rats, shot and bayoneted their way through every stable and up into every loft. "There's another in that straw. Keep his head down while I fork him out."

The Spandau to the north was still firing across three hundred yards of open ground and had hit some of the men moving into the garden. Lieutenant Dodds and six men slipped through the gate and tried to rush the post. Half-way across, another gun opened fire, killing Guardsman Moores and wounding another man. Flat on their faces, they heard the dull crack of the platoon's 2-inch mortar, and then the thud of the Scots Guards 3-inch mortars. The smoke bombs burst in front of them, but the fresh wind, blowing across the high ground, swept the screen away. Edging themselves forward to a shell-hole, they scraped at the soft earth with the heads of their entrenching tools. The houses had been cleared, but the Germans were still firmly entrenched on the high ground, and could not be shifted from their positions by an odd twenty men. All the Germans had to do was to wait till their tanks came up or till nightfall, and then recapture the houses with fresh troops. The German machine-guns on the flanks were firing long bursts covering the only line of withdrawal and trying to keep the Guardsmen boxed up in the farm. Their fire was wild, only the first few shots of each burst being properly aimed, and they hit only one of the returning men, Lance-Sergeant Haver. "Fourteen casualties left behind, as well as Lieutenant Dodds and six men presumed killed or wounded. The Germans are dug in all over the high ground, and are now working round behind it to our left rear," was Captain Drummond's report. The Scots Guards sent out a carrier ; the Germans allowed the crew to pick up the wounded and then took the whole lot prisoners.

The Company sank back into the slit trenches, cautiously lit cigarettes, and waited for darkness to bring up the evening meal. C.S.M. Lynch brought up the containers of stew and took charge of the Company again, dishing out mess-tins of stew. Into the middle of the meal walked Lieutenant Dodds. He and his party had lain in their shallow holes till dark and then walked back through the German positions. After the meal the Company was reorganized again into two platoons of seventeen and eighteen men each. The men huddled up in their blankets, dozing in corners, while the sentries leant forward, peering into the dark. In the station, H.Q. men and stretcher-bearers were brewing tea on the Tommy-cookers, attending the wounded and trying to get some sleep themselves. "The first sign that life was not going to be a bed of roses that night was the sound of tanks rumbling down the main road," said Lieutenant Dodds. "They stopped about one hundred and fifty yards away from the embankment at the end of our front drive. The anti-tank gunners in the area had apparently decided that the opposition was too great and preferred to remain inconspicuous. Our tanks, which were waiting behind the embankment for just such an occasion, seemed to think this was none of their business." Soon afterwards a Guardsman came downstairs to report, "There is a German tank just outside the door." One of them had left its fellows and driven up the station drive. This report was confirmed by a harassed Gunner officer who came back from a reconnaissance; he had assumed that the tank was on his side, and it was not till he had laid his hand on it that he saw the black and white cross. The tank itself cannot have realized that the station was occupied, but it seemed just as well to get rid of it before it learnt any better. "Frantic messages to the Brigadier and the tank commander were of no avail. Then the tank woke up and began to make itself more unpleasant by firing its machine guns at the windows of the station. Two Scots Guardsmen went out into the dark with a Piat and the two remaining bombs; they did their stuff, but the bombs did not explode. The tank, which was a Mark IV, appeared to be angered by this and started using its heavier armament, but luckily it only had solid shot for its gun." The shells blasted holes in the building, through which bursts of machine-gun fire were sprayed. Inside the station everyone lay flat on the floor, covered with broken glass. The few remaining windows and doors were smashed down by rifle butts to reduce the danger of flying splinters. There were no anti-tank guns and Brigade H.Q. could not provide a tank or a tank-buster, so the German tank could do what it liked. Back in the caves the Battalion's signallers heard the Scots Guards Adjutant saying to Brigade H.Q.: "The position here is tantalizing. There is a —— great German tank sitting outside my door demolishing my house brick by brick."

By midnight the station was a scene of complete desolation. The staircase had been knocked down, and the only way to get upstairs was by a rickety ladder. The one cellar was crowded with wounded men who could not be evacuated; they were safe enough, although one shell which had bounced off several walls did penetrate to the bottom of the stone steps. Anyway, there was nowhere else to put them, for the Scots Guards R.A.P. had been captured, the doctor and chaplain marched off as prisoners, and two tanks were sitting on the ruins. And so the night wore on. The station had to be held as long as possible, for it commanded the main road and the railway line, but it was clearly no longer any use as a headquarters. Colonel Wedderburn made a reluctant decision to move his headquarters back behind Carroceto embankment. By four o'clock in the morning all the Scots Guards had managed to get away from the opposite side of the buildings to the tank. No. 4 Company, two signallers with a No. 11 wireless set, about forty wounded and the dead remained in the station buildings. The two parts of the Company itself were divided. "Since the arrival of the tank," wrote Captain Drummond, "we had been unable to get in touch with Lieutenant White's platoon in the shed, for it almost always noticed any movement and dealt with it." In spite of this, Captain Drummond and three Guardsmen slipped out to the food dump in the yard and strolled back with cases of compo ration under their arms. "The morning looked like being the beginning of further difficulties, so when the look-out situation had been reorganized, I told the Company to feed before daylight."

The section upstairs, under the command of Lance-Corporal Milne, had been battered by shell-fire, but were in good spirits and fired at the tank whenever they could see it. The dawn broke slowly and, in the half-light, their view of the tank improved. So did the view for the Germans, and their fire became more accurate. Guardsman Boland, going up with a message for Lance-Corporal Milne, was knocked off the ladder down on to the men below. "He's dead," said the stretcher-bearer. "Put him over there." Captain Drummond looked sadly at Boland, his servant for many years, and then sent his last message over the wireless. "We must have a tank-destroyer up to settle this tank." "The Germans were only a hundred yards away," said Lance-Sergeant Duffy afterwards, "and we could hear them calling to each other. They started to fire H.E. Guardsman Duffy was killed and Guardsman Murphy—'Old Jock'—had is thigh broken. I went over to Murphy and another 88-mm. shell hit me in the back. I was taken down to the cellar, which was full of dead and wounded, and lost consciousness. When I came round, the cellar was full of Germans."

The storm of high explosive gave way to a long continuous burst of machine-gun fire and, without other warning, German infantry burst into the station. "Our own breakfast was late," said Lieutenant Dodds, "and C.S.M. Lynch was just cooking some very appetizing sausages, when an automatic weapon was fired through the door and the signallers fell over the wireless. The door opened and Germans walked in." The "dead" Guardsman Boland sat up and asked angrily, "What is coming off here ?" As an old Signals officer, Captain Drummond thought first of the frequency and jumped to the set to spin the dials round. He might have saved himself the trouble and danger ; one of the Germans smashed the set without even looking at it. The Germans were parachutists, good soldiers, and what they themselves called "very korrect."

Captain Drummond, Lieutenant Dodds and their companions were marched out into the yard. They then saw three other tanks and two self-propelled guns sitting on the railway line covering the station and the shed. There was no sign of Lieutenant White's platoon and no sound from Lance-Corporal Milne's section in the upper storey. Lieutenant White's platoon had been swamped at dawn. As soon as it was light the German tanks had closed on the shed and poured fire in through the doors and windows until the parachutists were on top of the Guardsmen. The section in the upper storey had seen some of this attack and had fired on the parachutists, but were silenced by the fire from the tanks. This section, however, continued fighting all morning and, with the Scots Guards' machine-gun crew who were with them, held out till three o'clock in the afternoon. A brief counter-attack by a troop of Sherman tanks gave them a welcome opportunity to shoot a number of Germans, but the counter-attack was driven off and the German tanks then methodically demolished the top storey and collected the few survivors out of the ruins.

The prisoners were marched off at once, but the wounded had to stay in the cellar for another twenty-four hours. Early the following morning the Germans brought up an ambulance and began to move the wounded. Lance-Sergeant Duffy and Guardsman Callaghan were the first to be carried out ; Callaghan was almost immediately killed by a shell burst "very convenient" to the ambulance. The German driver was, according to Lance-Sergeant Duffy, either drunk or very stupid, for he had no sense of direction, and at first drove into the British lines. They passed a private of the Duke of Wellington's Regiment, who had cut his hand opening a bully-beef tin, and was walking back to his R.A.P. The "Duke" thumbed a lift, the Germans leapt out and bundled him into the back of the ambulance. To this day that "Duke" does not know what happened to him. All the way to Rome he repeated plaintively, "The platoon sergeant will have my life for being away so long."

II. No. 1 COMPANY

When No. 1 Company disappeared into the dark on the night of the 7th February nobody knew what had happened to them. The Battalion watched and sent out patrols, but not one man of Captain David O'Cock's two platoons returned. It was not till Captain O'Cock returned to England after the defeat of Germany that the story was told, and he told it himself.

"The afternoon of the 7th passed quietly, but after dark we were subjected to a hail of ' air-bursts '—shells whose fuse is set to burst when they are thirty to one hundred feet from the ground. Fragments of metal fly in all directions. There were casualties from these shell-bursts, chiefly in a wiring party that was out at the time. While I was arranging for the evacuation of the wounded, I was called to the wireless set. The Adjutant said that the North Staffords had been heavily attacked and that their Battalion H.Q. were hard pressed. My orders were to take the Company and, as arranged, to put myself under their command. At this time there came a steady sound of small-arms fire from the direction of the North Staffords, and tracer bullets were cutting criss-cross patterns all over the sky. It seemed that we should have a better chance of reaching them unmolested if we approached from the left, instead of taking the direct route I had been shown the previous evening. Having asked, and been granted, permission to do this, I recalled the wiring party and gave out orders for this nebulous operation. The Company had only three Bren guns, none of which was at all reliable, and no mortar. There was enough ammunition for the riflemen, which was something, but we could well have done with a little extra automatic fire power. I decided not to take a Piat, owing to its weight and the difficulty of carrying the bombs, and also because the likelihood of our getting a shot at a tank was remote. I thought it unlikely that the Germans would be using tanks in a night attack of this sort, but it turned out that I was wrong, although we never came up against them.

"We set off down a gully, with Company H.Q. in rear of the leading platoon. As we threaded our way along the gully it became apparent that what I had taken to be one large engagement around the North Staffords' H.Q. was in reality two quite separate battles. From the position we were now in, it was impossible to decide which of these battles concerned us. I wirelessed back to Battalion H.Q. and was informed that the Grenadiers were also being attacked away to the right, and that we must therefore keep to the left. The gully took us too far left, so we struck to the right across country and, shortly afterwards, passed to the right of the American battalion I knew to be on the left of the North Staffords. Fortunately it was not a dark night and, helped by the light of bursting shells, tracer bullets and two burning houses, it was easy enough to see as we made our way along.

"Very soon after this we came upon 'C' Company of the North Staffords' battalion. They had been forced to withdraw several hundred yards from their position and were expecting a tank attack with infantry at any minute. The company commander got through to their Battalion H.Q. and got permission for my company to stay with him and help to resist the threatened attack. I set about getting the Company into position. It was only now that I was informed that the platoon which had been in rear had got lost, thereby reducing my force to approximately fifty all told before even being in contact with the enemy. The expected attack failed to materialize, so I got the second-in-command of the North Staffords on the set and explained that everything was quiet where we were, for the time being at least. He said that they were very hard pressed at Battalion H.Q. and asked us to come along at once. I gathered from 'C' Company that parties of Germans had already passed behind us, all the other rifle companies having been overrun. To avoid getting caught, therefore, we moved off in two waves, each of one platoon with Company H.Q. in the centre. As soon as we got close to the burning houses we were fired on by a machine-gun from the left. My wireless set had unfortunately gone 'dis' by this time, but the last orders I had received over it had been that I was to reach my objective at all costs and give what help I could. The issue, therefore, seemed clear enough. We were now within some one hundred and fifty yards of the North Staffords' H.Q., where it was possible to see and hear the exchange of shots. We were well in the open, but being so spread out, our numbers appeared quite formidable in the dim light. There was no hope of hiding and trying to send a reconnaissance party forward to contact the headquarters, as we were already under fire. Accordingly I decided to go straight on and break through the Germans into the perimeter held by the North Staffords. I shouted a few warlike cries, such as 'Keep going,' and 'Come on the Micks!' as much to let the North Staffords know we were British, as for any other reason. We got in easily enough, and as there was quite a considerable amount of firing going on, the Company got down immediately into battle positions with platoons facing outwards. Almost at once the second-in-command of the North Staffords came up to me, and we introduced outselves to each other without much formality. He asked me to come along with him to see his Commanding Officer. At the time bullets were whizzing all round us. and as we turned to go a shot struck him and he fell in his tracks. I do not know whether he was dead or merely unconscious; he made no sound at all, but simply crumbled up. He had no runner with him, so I called out loudly, 'Are there any North Staffords here?' I cannot say I could hear anyone shout back 'Yes,' but the noise of rifle and machine-gun fire was so intense that my voice may easily have been drowned. In any case, anyone hearing me was doubtless far too occupied with his own battle to shout back. What I did hear, however, was my own name being urgently and persistently called. I ran in the direction of the sound and found that it was coming from Lieutenant Charles Bartlet, my second-in-command, who told me that the Germans were withdrawing from in front of him, and wanted to know if we could follow.

"I had to make up my mind pretty quickly. So far we had failed to contact the North Staffords, and the only link with them, their second-in-command, had gone. In front of us I could see a small valley, and on the other side of it ground which was rather higher than that on which we ourselves were. If the Germans could once reach that higher ground and establish themselves on it, they would be able to sweep us with machine-gun fire, for we had no cover beyond a few scrub bushes. On the other hand, their withdrawal was by no means organized, and if we followed them up at once, we would have a good chance of driving them back altogether and occupying the high ground ourselves. We would then be able to make contact again with the North Staffords in our time. This seemed the better plan, and we decided to give chase. It is, however, impossible in the middle of a confused battle like this, at night, to apply 'battle drill' or any other accepted set of fighting rules. None of us knew the ground we were fighting over, and we could see little more than the dim outlines of the hills and of men moving. Moreover, we had casualties and were few in number, and last, but not least, our blood was up. I gave the order to advance; we were more like an excited pack of hounds than anything else. The platoon commanders were shouting to their men; the platoon sergeants were assisting them. The Germans fell back rapidly and our first drive took us to a deep irrigation trench which ran the length of the valley. Here I reorganized the Company, which appeared to be about thirty strong. To our right the trench was filled with a large number of German wounded, and their groans became shouts and screams of fear when we arrived. It was obvious that they expected us to finish them off; it was equally obvious that the North Staffords had taken a heavy toll of them during the defence of their headquarters.

"I explained to the men that it was essential to occupy the high ground in front, and that we would breast the slope well spread out in two irregular lines. When I gave the order, the men moved forward readily and we reached the crest without more than two or three casualties. However, as soon as we moved over the crest, we got a very unpleasant surprise. It was a false crest; the ground sloped gently upwards for another two hundred yards, and the Germans had established at least two machine-gun posts on the horizon. About eight of us had crossed the crest and the remainder got down behind it. At this moment Charles Bartlet received a whole burst of machine gun bullets, which tore a wide hole right through his leg. Sergeant Haydon attempted to block the bleeding with his field dressing, but this was too small, so I collected two or three handkerchiefs and we managed to make a tourniquet. His wound was so bad that we hardly dared move him, but we managed to get him into a fold in the ground where he very soon fainted from loss of blood. Our own machine guns were all three out of action, but not far away was an abandoned German machine gun, which I crawled over and collected. It had an unused belt of ammunition in it, but appeared to be jammed, so I handed it over to Lieutenant Gallwey to see if he could get it to work. Scouts went out on either flank to see if we could get round or if we were likely to be attacked from these quarters. In the meantime, we were returning rifle fire in the direction from which the enemy fire was coming.

"It was tempting at this stage to try to withdraw to our original position, but on checking the wounded, I decided it was quite impossible to move Bartlet, and we had lost more than I had thought in scaling the hill, so that there were barely twenty unwounded left, and I was reluctant to abandon those who had been hit. Guardsman French, who was the only stretcher-bearer left, was doing the best he could fixing up those who had been hit and, until this job was completed, I decided to hold on. It was not very long before the scouts reported that large bodies of Germans were moving round on us from both flanks. I was soon able to see a certain number for myself, moving across the skyline to our left. We seemed to be on the spot. There was no sound from behind us, and the North Staffords' H.Q., if there was now anything left of them, may have had a chance of getting away. We could not get the German machine gun to work, but we were still under fire and must have been silhouetted when we showed ourselves on the crest, for we invariably drew a burst of fire if we did. Suddenly, from quite close to us on our right flank, we heard shouts of 'Surrender!' This was a bit of a poser; for want of anything better to do some of us shouted 'Surrender!' back as loudly and as arrogantly as we could. A machine-gun opened up from behind us somewhere. and the men on the reverse slope were well under fire. We could see nothing to attack. We had no cover where we were, and it was not really necessary for the Germans to come and get us. However, they did, and so we were mopped up, and in this unsatisfactory manner our night action came to an abrupt conclusion." That was the end of No. 1 Company.

"The sequel to this battle," continues Captain D. O'Cock, "which, for all the faults of management on my part, had been thoroughly exciting while it lasted, was depressing. Peremptorily we were ordered forward and lined up under cover of a machine gun. I sincerely hoped that we were not going to be mown down in a row. We were not. The German officer spoke French, and I was able to explain to him that I had had heavy casualties and that I had left a sergeant with the wounded. This was, in point of fact, Sergeant Haydon, who had displayed the utmost gallantry throughout. In the circumstances the German officer was comparatively courteous, and said that he would do his best for our men. He would not, however, let us leave anyone else behind to look after them. I passed the order round among the men that they were now to act on their own initiative, without orders, and to escape if they could.

"We were herded together by our guards, and started to move off in the direction of the German lines. Just then, however, a fairly heavy 'stonk' opened up, which may have been mortars, but was probably our own artillery. This somewhat disorganized our procession, so when the next shell fell close at hand I made a break for it and dashed straight at the burst. I hoped in this way to be hidden by the smoke and have a reasonable chance of getting away. The idea was all right, but it was down hill, and I was running as fast as I could, with the almost inevitable result that, before I had gone more than fifty yards, I took the most imperial toss. However, I was not hit, and I succeeded in getting away. I plodded along in what I believed was the direction of our own lines, but the ground in that area was studded with little hills and copses and bushy undergrowth and soon I was hopelessly lost. Shell-fire was pretty heavy and too close to be comfortable; quite a lot of fighting seemed to be going on around and about. Several times a group of Germans passed close to me, but being alone I found it easy to conceal myself from them.

"Eventually I found my way into a fair-sized wood just as the first light of dawn was beginning to show in the sky. I had a look out of the far end of the wood and saw what I took to be British soldiers on the far side of a narrow road, facing away from me. I wasn't going to take any chances of getting picked up again, so from the ditch at the side of the wood I shouted 'Are you English?' The answer was quite obviously 'No,' so I popped back into the wood again. The wood now came under heavy shell-fire and as I was the only person in it, a large number of shells must have been expended by one side or the other in trying to get me out. I managed to find some sort of a shelter in a leafy ditch under the roots of an old tree. Shells were exploding uncomfortably close, and I worked extremely hard with my hands to try and hollow out some sort of a dugout. I was still engaged in this occupation when a shell landed in the ditch right alongside me and caught me the most almighty clip in the left leg. For some time I just lay back feeling sick, until I noticed the blood staining my trouser leg, so I fixed myself up with a field dressing. I had thought at first that my leg was broken, but I saw that this could not be the case, as the shrapnel had entered the fleshy part of my thigh. However, it was extremely painful and grew more so as the day wore on. I still had my wrist watch and at about one o'clock I decided to take a look around. My leg by now was stiff and rather numb, so moving was less painful than it had been, though awkward. The battle had moved on and everything was very quiet. I retraced my steps over some of the ground I had covered the night before, but there was no one about. I reached some high ground under cover of the scrub and, with the help of the hills to my left and the sea in front, I was able to form a fair opinion of where I was and of the best route back to our own lines. The silence proved too good to last. Suddenly I found myself the centre of a mass of bursting mortar bombs, both H.E. and smoke. There was nothing I could do but just lie down and hope for the best. For the next twenty minutes or so I had a thoroughly unpleasant time. I had no idea whether the barrage was our own or the enemy's, and I didn't much care. Bombs were raining down in hundreds ; fortunately, just where I happened to be, they were nearly all smoke and, as none of them scored a direct hit, I survived. Nevertheless, I was nearly choked by the fumes.

"Late in the afternoon, to add to my discomforts, it began to rain. I was cold and wet, hungry and thirsty, in pain and tired out, and, in fact, I was thoroughly miserable. As soon as it got dark I set off again, though it was a slow process by now. Eventually I reached a long irrigation ditch and followed it, as it seemed to be running in the right direction. General firing had begun again and bullets were passing uncomfortably close, so I presumed that I must have found my way on to the scene of another battle, though to whose lines I was closest I hadn't the faintest idea. I had no option but to keep dragging myself along until I found out. Soon I began to make out the lines of a mud parapet across the ditch some twenty yards in front of me, and almost at the same time I was called upon to halt, unmistakably in German to my utter disgust. I called out 'Wounded,' which was apparently understood, as I was summoned forward. It was not yet quite dark and bullets were pinging round me regularly, as the trench along which I was crawling was very shallow, and from time to time I must have exposed myself. I realized the bullets must be coming from our own rifles and that, with a bit of luck, I should have been crawling into our own trenches. On my way to the parapet there was a dead German blocking my path. His face was bright green in the half-light, and he must have been there some time. It was an unpleasant business crossing over him, keeping as close to him as possible for safety's sake. When I reached the parapet, a German soldier hoisted me over and I found myself in a circular machine-gun pit.

"The rain came down in torrents, so I was very glad to see a medical orderly arrive. Slowly we made our way back to the dressing station, which was a ruined farm building some quarter of a mile back. It was a poor sort of place ; there were no bandages, and they had had no food for twenty-four hours. The wounded were laid out in rows wherever there was room for them and, if they were lucky, they got a blanket. The medical orderly in charge was a Frenchman, who had been conscripted into the German Army, and he found me a blanket and a comparatively dry corner. Bullets periodically whistled through the shell-holes in the walls and rattled against the outside of the building. From time to time shells burst very close and lumps of plaster clattered to the ground. But nobody cared. The wounded and the orderlies were all quite as tired as I was, and many no doubt far more so. Sleep was all that mattered. Next morning a German soldier brought in a bottle of beer and a packet of twenty cigarettes. These were shared out among the wounded—German and British alike—and the beer passed around from man to man, each just taking a sip to quench our thirst. There is a certain camaraderie among the recently wounded, so that there is not the slightest feeling of animosity between men who were doing their damnedest to kill one another only a few hours before. In the dressing station there was also a Grenadier officer and one of the company commanders of the North Staffords, so I was able to piece together the details of the battle. The Germans had attacked with at least two infantry battalions and a certain number of tanks. One battalion had made a furious onslaught on the Grenadiers and the other on the North Staffords. As far as I could gather, the North Staffords had been more or less rolled up by the time our own little battle took place, so that we must have been fighting well inside the enemy's lines all the time, and probably reinforcements had been sent over to finish us off."

CHAPTER IX

The Lake

"B" ECHELON area was an unattractive stretch of marshy scrub-land, dotted with stumpy cork trees, an occasional clump of tall firs, and thickets of bushes. The previous inhabitants had been a few charcoal burners, who had been shanghaied on board a schooner by A.M.G.O.T. Scattered over this waste were the transport and administrative services of the Division. A precise area for every unit was no doubt neatly marked on a map in somebody's office; on the ground the rival quartermasters fought like colonial powers over a few yards of land. The lorries were parked under the trees, and the earth, down to the water-level, was scraped away by bull-dozers and heaped around them as protection against bomb and shell splinters. On the whole, the days in "B" Echelon were quiet. There were indeed some tragic losses from shelling, including Colonel David Wedderburn of the Scots Guards, but in general, the quartermasters, the cooks, the clerks, the cobblers, the armourers, the fitters and the varied crowd of "employed men" that every battalion collects, were able to do their work without interruption, except, of course, from their own side. It was at night that the fun began. German fighters and light bombers trailed overhead to attack the harbour or the gun lines, and they always had some anti-personnel bombs to drop on "B" Echelon. The area was the perfect target for bombing; it was so crowded that even a pebble was bound to damage somebody or something. The Germans apparently worked on this principle. The men in "B" Echelon replied by building elaborate "dugouts," using beams, doors and windows from the ruined houses of Anzio to support hillocks of earth and sand-bags. In these they slept comfortably enough while the bombs, "butterfly" or "bouncing," hopped around them.

"B" Echelon was no holiday camp, but that is what it seemed like to the companies. Everybody was in high good humour as they marched into the area in the early hours of the morning of the 13th. "Turn out, you jam-stealers! We've come to lap it up." The Battalion certainly needed a rest, and for three days they took it. There was work to be done, but it was work that any Guardsman can, and does, do half asleep—gun cleaning, kit inspection and replacement, and the ordinary fatigues. Besides this, every man had to answer his name at innumerable roll-calls. It was the first chance that Sergeant Kelly had of making an accurate "strength return" and he checked and rechecked "the bodies on the ground." The total was 520. Then he and his Orderly Room staff combed the graveyards and the field hospitals and made a list of 54 names for crosses, and 165 casualties, most of them already evacuated. There were 341 men missing. The Adjutant set up a dreadful tribunal to scrape the barrel of "B" Echelon. Every "employed" man was marched before him and required to explain exactly why it was essential that he should remain in "B" Echelon. The Regimental Sergeant-Major and the Orderly-Room Sergeant prosecuted; the man's immediate superior could, if he liked, defend, and the Adjutant was a very biased judge and jury, already inclined to the verdict "To a rifle section." The last of the reinforcements was absorbed, and out of the whole Battalion was squeezed two rifle companies, a combined No. 2 and 4 and a No. 1 and 3.

Colonel Scott at last had time to write to Regimental Headquarters. "There came with me into this place 794 men, and 286 followed from the Infantry Reinforcement Training Depot and the Central Reinforcement Unit, making a total of 1,080. Against this we have had 560 casualties, which leaves the Battalion at a nominal strength of 520. There are no more reinforcements available, and it is unlikely that any large number of wounded men will be well enough to return within two months. I understand that no draft from home is likely to come this month, and even if it did, it would be nowhere near the figure required. Both other battalions in the Brigade have approximately the same figure, but they have other battalions of their regiments in this sphere of fighting with whom they can, if the worst comes to the worst, amalgamate. Reorganization has not yet been settled with the Brigade Commander, who is temporarily Brigadier Erskine, Brigadier Murray having left the beach-head, but it looks as if we can muster only two weak rifle companies per battalion plus an equally weak Support Company. What the policy is, I do not know, but I am writing to the Lieutenant-Colonel personally and realize that the next step as to policy will have to come from the

Major-General. It is a tragedy that we have lost so many fine men, but nobody has anything but the highest possible praise for the bravery and brilliant fighting of the Battalion under the worst possible conditions. Of the figure ' Missing, 341,' a large amount must obviously be either killed or wounded, but since the enemy occupy the battlefield it is quite impossible for us to ascertain what wounded men fell into enemy hands or who were left dead on the field of battle. In officers, we are still pretty strong. In spite of 22 casualties (4 killed, 8 wounded, 11 missing), we still have 25 here and 7 in the I.R.T.D. Unfortunately, there are no men for them to command, so the normal predicament of shortage of officers in proportion to men is on this occasion reversed. Of the officers who embarked on the assault, the following are still with me: Gordon-Watson, S. Young, G. FitzGerald, Kennedy, Combe, D. FitzGerald, Collin, Quinn, Keigwin, Brand, Bland, J. Bell, D. Young, Boyd, McKinney the Q.M., Father Brookes and O'Neill the M.O."

To the Lieutenant-Colonel, Colonel Scott wrote: "I have given the figures of casualties up to date in an official letter. It is indeed tragic reading. I have commanded this Battalion exactly a year now, and during that period it has suffered 1,000 casualties one way or another. In my opinion the Battalion and the Brigade fought far better than I have ever seen them in a type of fighting which was unbelievably difficult, and although the result had none of the type of glory of the ' Bou ' (which, in fact, consisted of holding on like grim death to something you couldn't get off), I don't like to think what the position would be now if we had not been there. Our activities, so far, have been in four phases: The first, withstanding a heavy counter-attack on 26th February, just after we had got into position, casualties around 100, but the enemy seen off; the second, a two-battalion night attack on the 29th February/1st March against a main position, objectives obtained, casualties 150 roughly; third, a very heavy attack by three enemy divisions on the sector, night of 3rd/4th March—No. 3 Company overrun by about a battalion, and a lot of men never got back from the other companies, which were surrounded—approximately 250, mostly missing, as we have not been able to search the battleground; the fourth phase was when I had to send No. 1 Company to the North Staffords to help them out—on direct orders from above—and it was never heard of again. Then I had to send No. 4 Company, under command Scots Guards, and after having done absolutely brilliant work and covered the withdrawal of two Scots Guards companies, they were surrounded by tanks, and our tanks not being forthcoming, all survivors were made prisoners. Allowing for slightly wounded men returned to duty, that accounts for the casualties, except for a few losses in the last few days, including my great friend Sergeant O'Connell killed, and Tony Bell wounded. It is a horrible story and, as you can imagine, grey hairs are sprouting in all directions. It is pleasant to hear praise on all sides, and I feel that perhaps the sacrifice was not in vain, and that after we have won the war some of these magnificent chaps who are now prisoners will return to build up the Irish Guards. Thank God most of the highly trained personnel are intact. I lost my R.S.M. and three C.S.Ms. (Gilmore killed, Mercer wounded, Lynch missing), but all the rest are here, as are the complete Orderly Room staff, despite the fact that Corporal Cross, my shorthand clerk, fought a bloody rearguard action, capturing ten Germans to his own Remington. Rooney is acting R.S.M. as McLoughlin has gone home to England. I am trying to form two rifle companies and a Support Company, but the rifle companies will be weak, as there are only about 150 men available for them when one has taken off Support Company, Orderly Room, storemen, drivers, etc. Savill Young still commands Support Company (now on a small scale) with Desmond Young in charge of carriers, Boyd anti-tank, Wall machine-guns, and John Bell mortars. George FitzGerald, with Keigwin as his second-in-command, and Charlie Brand (the sole original platoon commander left) and Paul Harcourt as subalterns, commands one company, Kennedy (now a Major), with Simon White second-in-command, and Walters, Earls-Davies and Gordon-Shea, commands the other. With Simon Combe's H.Q. Company, that is the lot, so God knows what they will do with us. It would be crazy, I feel, to commit this Brigade, consisting of three battalions of one rifle company, plus support company, per battalion, into serious battle, as it would lose the only possible nucleus for future building up. If you lead the attack with Company Quartermaster-Sergeants and Orderly Room staff, when you have lost them, it is almost impossible to rebuild. Alex is coming this way today, and I hope to see him."

The whole Battalion hoped to see General Alexander ; above their own Commanding Officer, they discounted all commanders till they reached the "next Mick, the General himself." In him they had absolute confidence ; whatever he said and did was right. They knew that he could not, and did not, conduct the day-to-day fighting on this beach-head, for "he has divisions like we have sections," but they had the firm and comforting conviction that he always had his eye on the Battalion. The mercenary soldier tradition was very strong in the 1st Battalion. They accepted wounds and death, hunger and exposure as a normal part of the trade, and had the greatest contempt for troops who grumbled about casualties. "A good battle and bags of promotion" was one way of putting it; another was explained by C.S.M. Pestell to a bewildered German prisoner who asked him why he, an Irish neutral, was fighting for the English in filthy ditches. "Well, they fed me for seven years, so now I'm earning my keep." But equally strongly they held it was no part of their contract of service to be "messed about." Under the command of General Alexander, however remotely, they had the comforting feeling that there was always a good reason for what they were asked to do; the great Irish Guardsman would see them through. General Alexander visited the beach-head on the 14th, and made it his first concern, as he told the delighted Guardsmen, to come and see the Battalion as soon as he had landed. There were no heroic speeches, but you could almost feel the confidence and pride radiating from the Battalion as the General walked briskly round the area. He talked to old Guardsmen he remembered; he asked young Guardsmen for their opinion about the fighting and showed that he valued it; he explained his difficulties to section commanders and made them feel that they, too, could handle armies. He congratulated the Battalion on "a fine performance in a very tough slogging match," and that was enough.

There was, for the time being, a temporary pause in the slogging match, for both sides had fought each other, and themselves, to a standstill. The Allies had taken terrible punishment, but they had handed out even more, and the Germans halted on the line of the embankment to consolidate their gains and to bring up fresh troops. So the Battalion, in "B" Echelon, missed nothing except a few patrol skirmishes and a reorganization of the line. The whole of the 56th Division was shipped into the beach-head to join its advance brigade, the 168th, and relieved the 1st Division which went into reserve. The Allied line was held by three divisions—the 3rd U.S., on the right, the 45th U.S. in the centre, and the 56th British on the left. Two days' rest were enough for the Germans. On the 15th the reconnaissance pilots reported heavy traffic on the roads south from Rome. A prisoner from the 10th Parachute Regiment said that he himself had been part of this traffic, and added cheerfully that his battalion had a rumour of a big attack the following morning. The rumour was indeed well founded. At half-past six on the morning of the 16th the Germans launched three divisions against the centre of the beach-head. They proposed to smash their way straight down the main road to Anzio, a plan which was admirably simple and very nearly successful. The main weight of the attack fell on the 45th U.S. Division, forcing it slowly back. As their attack down the main road progressed the Germans "fanned out," that is, they brought up fresh troops on their right flank to attack and drive in the 56th British Division on the left (west). By midday Corps H.Q. were justifiably worried, particularly when they saw a special Order of the Day from Hitler, and they learnt from a captured Operation Order that the Germans had two more divisions, the 26th Panzer and the 29th Panzer Grenadiers, ready to exploit success. They ordered the 1st Division up to the Campo di Carne to hold the Fly-over bridge and the lateral road as a Corps defence line.

The Battalion kept track of the battle through scraps of information. " Ration Farm has gone," "The Caves have gone," " Carrier Farm has gone." When they saw Colonel Scott driving off to Brigade H.Q. they knew that the Battalion had been "blown for" and started preparing their kit. "It is rather a bore having to go up again after only two days out of it, but there it is," said Colonel Scott on his return. "On the north-east corner of the woods (Selva di Nettuno) there is a lake. We are to take up a position on the west of this lake to cover the front of the wood ; the Krauts are doing quite well, and if they get into the wood they will be down to the sea before anyone sees them again. The London Scottish will be immediately in front of us, and if anything goes wrong with them, we are to counter-attack. The 2nd Infantry Brigade are digging in round the Fly-over. We move now." The Battalion marched off leaving the "B" Echelon men digging trenches for a last-ditch stand. Major Gordon-Watson, as second-in-command, was left out of battle again, and in his frustration he could not decide whether he would prefer the enemy to break through and reach his zareba, or Colonel Scott to be wounded, only slightly.

"The Lake" was an indeterminate pond, spreading its ooze among the surrounding bushes and along the few existing paths. Even at midday it was cold ; everything dripped, and a thin mist lay on the ground. A broad "ride" ran westward from the pond just inside and parallel to the front of the wood ; the platoons halted at track-junctions along this ride, and the section commanders scattered into the thickets on either side to find hummocks which would give a foot or so of earth above the water level. South of the ride were the gun lines of two field regiments. The noise was shattering as they fired incessantly. At first the Gunners kindly warned the nearest sections, some of which were almost underneath the muzzles, but they soon forgot, leaving the Guardsmen to jump with surprise so often that "you'd have thought we had St. Vitus' dance." As the evening fell the German counter-battery artillery came into action and the rival guns fought a duel over the bodies of the Battalion, with the inevitable result. "We have had thirty casualties in three days ; it all adds up," wrote Colonel Scott on the 19th. It was a most depressing kind of addition. When men are killed in an assault, or beating off an enemy attack, or even when "sweating out" a heavy bombardment, their comrades know that they died to a purpose. But in a semi-reserve position, as the Battalion was then, there seems no reason why a particular shell should land on a particular trench ; the Germans would have been no wiser, and no worse off, if the shell had fallen a few yards to the north, south, east or west. The men who were killed in this way had, of course, died to just as much purpose as those who were shot in the heat of an attack—but it was not apparent at the time.

The position remained not quiet, but unchanged, till the night of the 18th. Till then, the Battalion spent its time building small stockades of tree trunks round its shallow trenches, roofing them with groundsheets to keep out the rain. Sergeant McConnell, of the pioneer platoon, was consulting engineer to the Battalion. He was called in to advise on so many dugouts or bunkers that he had no time to build one for himself. The little clearing in which Battalion H.Q. had established itself looked like a colony of moles, a jumble of untidy heaps of logs, sandbags and brushwood concealing damp excavations. The signallers' dugout was, as always, the neatest and the best constructed, though the residence shared by Colonel Scott and the Adjutant was the biggest and showiest. Major Young's "brolly" was the envy of all and kept him snug and dry. He dug a small deep hole and lowered himself carefully into it, pulling his umbrella down on top of it, like a big, black mushroom. Battalion H.Q. went to earth so thoroughly because the Germans continually—but it must have been fortuitously—dropped shells in the middle of it. The first of these shells killed Guardsman Gilbert just as he was setting off to lay a telephone line. Lieutenant Francis Collin, the Signals Officer, ran across to Gilbert and was wounded by the second shell. The Adjutant picked him up in turn and found him laughing. "My book ! " Small pieces of shrapnel had entered his thigh, but two large jagged chunks of metal were imbedded in the salacious novel in his pocket. Sergeant O'Sullivan—"Spike" to the whole Battalion—took charge of the Signals. Sergeant O'Sullivan combined a practical and tireless devotion to duty with a theoretical cynical pessimism. He took it for granted that all Staff were incompetent, that all troops except the Battalion would run away, and that every attack, except the Battalion's, would be a ghastly failure, but was cheerful about it. His one admission of any personal discomfort was later when, after three days and nights in the gullies without rest or sleep, he said, "I'm a little tired, but then, I'm an old man now." He and the Adjutant had their formula for cheering themselves up, and fell back on it once again. "It will all sort itself out in the end"; to which the established response was, "Have you heard, sir, the armour will go through at dawn?" Sergeant O'Sullivan was an old soldier and an old Signal Sergeant. Tucked among the stores he always had at least one wireless set which appeared on no list or G1098 Return. This set was now the most important to the Battalion; it was tuned on Radio Rome, where a young woman with a golden voice, in intervals of urging the beach-head forces to pack it in, gave the names of recent prisoners.

The Germans resumed their attacks down the main road on the 18th. While the daylight lasted the field guns held them off, smashing the infantry as they advanced across the open ground, and the Loyals on the Fly-over bridge polished off any persistent survivors. After dark, however, the German infantry reached the bridge and swarmed up and over the embankment. The Loyals, to the admiration of the Battalion, drove them back after fierce hand-to-hand fighting. In the pause, while the Germans re-formed, the Gordon Highlanders, on the left of the Loyals, moved two companies over to strengthen the Fly-over, and the Battalion sent its two companies up to fill the gap. The companies moved up through a German barrage of "unprecedented violence" as the War Diary describes it. The writer, Lieutenant James Quinn, had had some experience of barrages, so this one must have been bad. "There was nothing for the Battalion to do," continues the War Diary, "but to dig in as hard as possible, for the shelling had already taken toll of No. 2 Company. But once again the ground was very sodden, and it was impossible to dig down more than six inches without coming to water."

Only two men slept that night, and one of them nearly died as a result. An exhausted Guardsman stretched himself out in his shallow trench and did not notice the icy water seeping over him. His section commander found him next morning unconscious, rigid and a queer slate grey in colour. He looked like a three-day corpse ("which is what I feel like," said one man), but the doctors at C.C.S. took a pride in reviving him as the worst case of exposure they had seen. Sergeant Wylie, D.C.M., lay flat on his back, spread out his arms and legs, shut his eyes, and slept like a child through the shells and cold. He was a most remarkable man. He was neither stupid, insensitive nor unimaginative; he loved life and comfort as much as anybody else, but he had a control over his mind and his body that made him the perfect fighting soldier. He woke the next morning as fresh as a daisy, and as unconcerned. "What's the form today ?"

The failure of their attempt to seize the Fly-over by night had cooled the Germans' ardour ; the stream of accurate gun-fire that came with the morning light quenched it for several days. After that the 46th Royal Tank Regiment cleared the ground a few hundred yards north of the Fly-over to give the defenders "breathing space." The Battalion, having given the moral support that had been needed, returned to the Lake to meditate upon the future. It knew, more or less, what the Germans would do, for the Germans were logical and had a good supply of fresh troops. The break-through plan had failed, so they would—and did—abandon it and turn to infiltration. The desolate broken country west of the road was a maze of deep gullies into which whole battalions could disappear and reappear at will. They could—and did—feed fresh troops into these gullies and by constant pressure, ceaseless small attacks and isolated penetrations, gnaw through the left flank of the beach-head and open the way to the sea. A fence that will stand up to a bull will go down before rats. But the Battalion did not know what the Higher Authorities would do with the 24th Guards Brigade. The logical thing was to take it out of the beach-head and send it back to Naples to re-form and refit while there were still enough men left to re-form. This in fact, was the original decision, as announced by the new Brigade Commander, Brigadier Archer Clive. He came to see the Battalion at midday on the 21st, and told them that they would remain where they were until relieved in the near future. The Battalion were not surprised, and were not even suspicious.

At half-past one—which just gave the Brigadier time to get back to his headquarters—the Battalion received the order to relieve an American battalion in the gullies on the left of the main road and north-west of the Fly-over. "This change of plan has no operational significance and is only part of a tidying-up arrangement to get all Americans on the right side of the road, and all British on the left. The sector is very quiet, so you will have no trouble, and your weakness does not matter."

CHAPTER X

The Gullies

ABOUT a mile west of the fly-over bridge a track ran northwards from the Campo di Carne road to "Carrier Farm." After five hundred yards it crossed the end of a dank gully—the gully later known as the "Culvert"—and continued northwards past a farm called Pantoni by the Italians, but "White Cow Ration Farm" by the Battalion, because "there was a dead white cow at one end and a Sherman tank at the other, both of which looked as if they would supply food." The track ran on straight and level for another six hundred yards and then dipped sharply down into the valley of the Moletta River. Between the track and the main road sprawled a system of deep, overgrown gullies that was later called the "Boot." The plain was in fact a catchment area for the Moletta, and sooner or later all the gullies led to this valley. The Boot itself was laid askew across the plain. Starting near the Fly-over it ran diagonally north-west to within four hundred yards of "White Cow Farm" and then turned north to run parallel to the track till it debouched into the Moletta valley some five hundred yards east of the track. West of the track, beyond a slight rise, lay a somewhat smaller gully system already held by the Germans. "The general impression one got on the plain was of being on a peninsula with two bush-filled valleys forming a perfect approach for any enemy." On the other side of the Moletta valley rose the southern slope of "Carrier Farm" ridge, at this time still held by British and American troops. The slope was covered with scrub and patches of bright green grass grazed smooth by sheep and geese. Somewhere below ground level in this area lurked the 2nd Battalion of the U.S. 157th Regiment and an unknown number of Germans.

It was to be a blind relief. The best that the American R.H.Q. could offer was guides to meet the Battalion after dark. The maps were useless, they explained, for it was suicidal to move by day and impossible to see by night, with the result that they could not say exactly where their 2nd Battalion was. Colonel Scott thanked the Americans and, with his officers, went forward to the line of the Campo road. "The Americans had not exaggerated. It was impossible to go any farther as the Germans were shelling any movement, and the number of wrecked and abandoned vehicles left no doubt in our minds as to the accuracy of their observation." The plain stretched northwards, flat and featureless, except for a few battered houses and tanks, till it rose to meet the "Carrier Farm" ridge. It seemed to be utterly deserted.

The afternoon and evening passed quietly and a watery sun gave just enough warmth for sleep. "I think every man knew the intention as much as I did myself, and that is not saying much," wrote one officer. The Battalion was going back into the line, and that was all there was to it. The Quartermaster-Sergeants brought up dinners, and the Guardsmen saw by the amount of food dished out that it would be some time before they got another square meal. After some deliberation, Major Kennedy distributed his reserve of "smoked ham"—half an old pig he had killed and cooked in the caves.

As soon as the sun set that evening—the 21st February—the Battalion assembled on the "Supply Road." This was a new road planned by the Engineers to run through the woods from the sea to the Campo road, but so far it consisted of two white tapes threaded through the trees and bundles of brushwood and an odd load of rubble tipped into the deeper puddles. The Battalion floundered through thick, sticky mud, each man silently following the gloomy bulk of the man in front of him. It was already pitch dark and the only light was the unwelcome glare of a shell-burst. The American guides were waiting on the Campo road. "Are we glad to see you," they said, and started briskly down the road. The track was dotted with shell-holes and littered wreckage. The guides took to the ditch and the Battalion followed them in an obstacle race, until they reached a small bridge. The guides climbed back on to the track and pointed down into the darkness. "This is the command post. You'll find the Colonel down there." Colonel Scott and Battalion H.Q. slid down the steep side of the gully, clutching at the bushes, till they hit the bottom. The shells had begun to fall and the Americans were naturally eager to "pull out" quickly. Their method was commendably simple ; each man took what he could lay his hands on and left the rest—sub-machine guns, rifles, ammunition, rations, blankets, cigarettes, newspapers and a dead man. The dead man caused endless trouble, first to an American top sergeant, who was "broken" on the spot for refusing to carry him, and then to the Battalion which, after burying him as decently as possible, was involved in interminable correspondence with the U.S. War Department. The seven-foot-long blankets were a godsend, even though they had been used as linings for "fox-holes." The Battalion's task, as Colonel Scott already knew, was to protect the Campo road. All that the American commander could add was that the Germans had constantly tried to force a way down the gullies. There were "Krauts with burp-guns" all round them, he said, but the general policy was not to irritate individuals by shooting them. Even as they talked they could hear the staccato rattle of Schmeissers, as one by one the German standing patrols came out of their holes. This American colonel then formally gave the Battalion "anything they might find in the morning," wished them good night, shouted "Come on, fellows," and scrambled out of the gully.

No. 3 Company continued up the track to relieve the two forward American companies. No. 2 Company now came up to the bridge to meet fresh guides from the two rear American companies. There was a sudden shrieking rush of descending shells and a violent detonation, with lumps of concrete and earth falling like hail in the gully. Lieutenant Paul Harcourt was mortally wounded with a number of his platoon. Major George FitzGerald and Lance-Corporal Moriarty carried them down into the gully and laid them in a row in the culvert under the bridge. It was wet, but safe, and there they lay, and scores of men after them, while Dr. O'Neill bandaged them by the light of a torch. Lieutenant Harcourt could only speak in a whisper. "It is rather cold, isn't it ?" The medical orderlies put blankets, and he lapsed into unconsciousness muttering "There is no hurry." When the shelling stopped, No. 2 Company ran across the road into the open plain beyond, where the Americans were shouting directions. They tramped blindly through the dark until they reached the precipitous side of the Boot gully. In the pitch dark there was little they could do except post the two platoons round the "ankle" of the Boot, the joint where it turned north, and wait till the morning light. The German mortars had the gully neatly ranged, and slammed bombs into it. Their machine-gun posts had for days been skimming shots over the rim and they now opened steady fire to play their part in the German scheme, which was to keep the defenders down in the bottom where the mortars could pound them to pieces. Sergeant Gundel now commanded Lieutenant Harcourt's platoon. He had seen his own company—

No. 1—destroyed, but he was, if anything, invigorated by disaster. By nature gloomy, he became almost cheerful during these dreadful days. He also became even more militantly English than he had been in the Sergeants' Mess. "I may not come from Ireland, but I'm as good a —— Mick as you"—and he was. On this night, as always, he showed the rugged determination and stoical indifference to the worst the enemy could do that won him his D.C.M. He led his platoon—"Get a move on and keep quiet"—up the far side of the gully, and directed the Bren gunners on to the nearest Germans. The platoon swarmed up after him and, while he and the Bren gunners beat off the German patrols, the sections dug the trenches they were to hold for four days. Lieutenant C. Brand had to divide his platoon. Half of it, under Sergeant Wylie, D.C.M., stayed on top of the near (west) side of the gully ; the other half he led as far down the gully as they could go without losing themselves.

Meanwhile, No. 3 Company had passed Pantoni and found the American company commander on the right of the track "under a lone tree on the north slope facing Carrier Farm." A German machine-gunner in the valley was using the silhouette as a night aiming mark. The American said his tactics were to "dig in" and sit absolutely tight all day, as any movement was shelled. "He also mentioned," said Major Kennedy, "that one morning, when they woke up, they found a German platoon dug in only one hundred yards off where we then were. We were glad to hear that they had gone. I saw that he had three Browning machine-guns, and I told him I was going to keep them ; to this he agreed. The sniper in the valley was becoming increasingly brave and spraying bullets about the place, which I did not consider a good thing." Lieutenant Walters, who commanded the platoon scraped together out of No. 1 Company, had already come to the same conclusion. He sent out a section to deal with the sniper, while the rest of the Company sat down in the ditches. At that very moment every other sound was blotted out by the roar of aircraft. Major Kennedy and Sergeant O'Brien, commander of No. 13 Platoon, stopped talking to look up at two German fighter-bombers flying at high speed. "None of us thought anything of them, as they were over Anzio every night, and we naturally thought that these were no exception to the rule, except that they were flying low. It was not fear, but astonishment, tha struck me and Sergeant O'Brien as if we were dumb statues, when the area suddenly turned into a brilliant green mass, changing to orange and white as bomb after bomb hit the ground. I did not wait to get into a slit trench, but was pushed hard from behind,

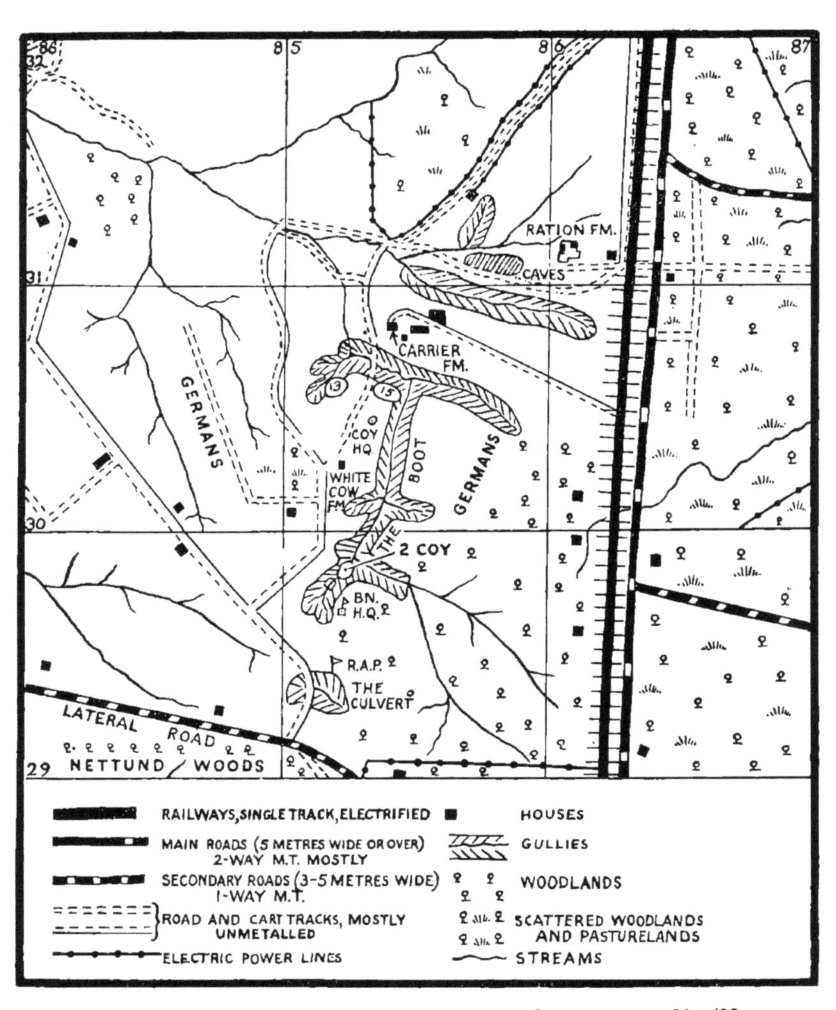

Positions occupied by the Battalion in the Gullies from 21st/22nd to 24th/25th February.

landing on top of two Americans, with Guardsman Gregg on top of me." The German pilots jettisoned their entire load of anti-personnel bombs slap on the Company. It was a cruel and crippling blow.

Battalion H.Q. heard the long crackling explosion as just another of the nasty noises of the night. They had enough worries already; No. 2 Company was not yet in position, the wirelesses were off net, the R.A.P. under the bridge was already full of wounded men, while the jeeps to evacuate the casualties and the carriers with the machine guns were stuck on the edge of the wood waiting for a lull in the shelling. But when the Adjutant heard somebody running down the track he knew with sickening certainty what the message was going to be. "Could we have the doctor, please? The Company's very bad. The bombs hit us." Along the road there was nothing but wounded men dragging themselves in from all sides. The stretcher-bearers, Guardsmen Britton, Fitzsimmons, Williamson, May and Short, carried the casualties down to "White Cow Farm" and dressed the wounds as best they could till Dr. O'Neill arrived. At first sight the casualties appeared to be huge and, in the dark, it looked as if nearly the whole Company lay on the ground. In fact, forty of the seventy wounded men belonged to other units—Americans and odd parties of British troops on their way to "Carrier Farm"—but that was little consolation for the sudden loss of thirty precious Guardsmen. The bombing of and the inevitable noise of collecting the wounded attracted the Germans. Schmeissers and Spandaus at close and longe range opened fire on the Company. "That's torn the lining out of the whole —— scheme," said one harassed man, but he was wrong. Guardsman Montgomery and Adamson raced up the road with a Bren gun to distract the Germans while Lieutenant Earls-Davies, Lieutenant Walters and Sergeant O'Brien sorted out their platoons and occupied makeshift positions. Lance-Sergeant R. H. Murphy engaged the nearest machine-gun posts, while Lieutenant Earls-Davies led No. 15 Platoon in a combined advance and mopping-up operation on the right of the track, till they reached the edge of the valley. Lieutenant Walters's platoon was reduced to fourteen men; Corporal Nash had been killed and six men wounded, including the veteran Sergeant Dunne—"Old Mickie." Three of these men, commanded by Guardsman White, went down to the bottom of the valley to protect the ford across the Moletta. Lieutenant Walters, Sergeant Kearney and the remaining ten men walked towards the junction of the Boot and the Moletta valley till they found an American platoon. "The American officer told us not to be surprised if we saw several Germans well behind us in the morning ; there generally were, he said, but they disappeared if they were fired on." Sergeant O'Brien brought No. 13 Platoon up on the left of the track to protect that flank and cover the valley. It was a remarkable achievement of a Company that had lost a third of its number in the middle of the night on strange ground under close fire. "I went round the men and they were full of confidence," said Major Kennedy, and it was largely due to him.

For three days and four nights the depleted Battalion held the gullies against continual attack. It was a savage, brutish troglodyte existence, in which there could be no sleep for anyone and no rest for any commander. The weather was almost the worst enemy, and the same torrential rain, which sent an icy flood swirling around our knees as we lurked in the gullies, would at times sweep away the earth that covered the poor torn bodies of casualties hastily buried in the Boot. Wallowing in a network of gullies, isolated by day and erratically supplied by night, soaked to the skin, stupefied by exhaustion and bombardment, surrounded by new and old corpses and yet persistently cheerful, the Guardsmen dug trenches and manned them till they were blown in and then dug new ones, beat off attacks, changed their positions, launched local attacks, stalked snipers, broke up patrols, evacuated the wounded, buried the dead and carried supplies. The bringing up of supplies every night was a recurrent nightmare. Carrying parties got lost, jeeps got bogged and, as the swearing troops heaved at them, down came the shells. "What I remember most," said one officer, "is the long strain of hanging on all day to hear the list of casualties every evening, to see the stretcher-bearers livid with fatigue, staggering past with their load, a dirty Red Cross flag held aloft as a precarious appeal."

The life was one of unremitting drudgery. As Gibbon says of the Roman legions, active valour may often be the present of Nature, but such patient diligence can be the fruit only of habit and discipline. Every single man did his duty and more than his duty. Guardsman Branthwaite, for instance, was wounded by shell-fire while carrying ammunition across to No. 2 Company. Four other Guardsmen were hit at the same time and were carried to the R.A.P., but Branthwaite could walk, and he knew the necessity of every round and every man who could fire a rifle. He brought the heavy box into the Company area, dumped it without a word and rejoined his section in their post. Twenty-four hours later, just before dawn on the 23rd, Lieutenant Brand told him to change to another post. The stiffening of the wound gave him away ; he could not move, and had to be lifted out of the slit trench. Such men are rare in the world, but the 1st Bn. Irish Guards was full of them.

No 2 Company and Battalion H.Q. held a firm bastion at the southern end of the gully system ; this was the key to the plain, and the Germans knew it. As a result, the fighting in this area was largely defensive, but a defence that involved frequent counter-attacks to clear the converging gullies and a running fight every night to bring up the rations. Sergeant C. Gundel, in particular, spent the days marking snipers and the nights crawling out to kill them—a routine which disheartened the Germans as much as it encouraged the Company. If a shot whistled close past a man's head he could always raise a laugh by shouting, "Take his name, Sergeant Gundel." No. 3 Company—a comprehensive title for the collection of men commanded by Major Kennedy—ranged the forward plain and gullies in a most offensive mood. Their role was to slaughter any small parties of Germans they found, and to disorganize any large formations. It was inevitably an expensive business, but the men who lost their lives saved the beach-head. They turned the gullies into a murderous maze in which men like Major Kennedy, M.C., Lance-Sergeant Murphy, M.M., Guardsman Montgomery, D.C.M., and Guardsman Adamson, D.C.M., hunted down Germans. Montgomery and Adamson were old soldiers and old friends, both Bren gunners, and two of the few survivors of No. 1 Company then serving with No. 3. Major Kennedy allotted them an outpost position to cover the relief of the Americans. They established themselves well forward of the Company with a Browning machine-gun and a box of grenades, and spent the night harrying German patrols. Just before dawn, Guardsman Adamson found more Browning ammunition and for the rest of the day they conducted a private war. They could be seen quite clearly as they moved from place to place, covering each other till they came to the final phase of each little operation, when under covering fire from Montgomery, Adamson closed in on the sniper or Spandau post and, not having the means or inclination to take prisoners, shot the Germans with a Tommy gun. In the afternoon Montgomery was wounded for the second time and had to drag himself back. Adamson continued operations alone for the last three hours of daylight. At dusk he came into Company H.Q. and asked a stretcher-bearer to dress what he called a slight wound on the side of his face. Before this could be done, he fainted. No one knew exactly when Adamson was wounded, but it is certain that, for some time, he must have been fighting in a state of pain which would have incapacitated a man of lesser physical and mental determination. "Guardsman Adamson's remarkable and persistent gallantry," wrote Colonel Scott, "his skill and his disregard of suffering, on top of a long and excellent record as a fighting man in Tunisia and Italy deserve, in my opinion, the immediate award of the D.C.M." He got it, and so did Guardsman Montgomery.

The story of the next three days is therefore the record of the courage and skill of individual officers and men, each continuously fighting their own personal battles, knowing them to be essential to the beach-head. The driving force behind the Battalion and the will that knit all these isolated actions into one battle came from Colonel Andrew Scott, D.S.O. Crammed into a slit trench cut like a bunk into the wall of the gully, or picking his way delicately through the slush and debris, Colonel Andrew kept a firm hand on everybody, even the irrepressible Kennedy. It looked so easy the way he did it, no fuss, no hurry, no gestures, just an endless round of visits and an impressive air of absolute confidence in the man he was talking to. Almost as essential to the Battalion was the support of the 19th Field Regiment. These remarkable gunners dropped shells wherever the Battalion asked for them ; they supported section attacks, they broke up large and small German assaults, they put defensive fire in front of ever-changing positions, and on several occasions they laid smoke to cover the withdrawal of one man.

About midnight, Major Kennedy slid into Battalion H.Q. "to see the boss," but what he wanted was some food and water and his share of the support weapons. His wireless, he explained, was suffering through the wet weather from condensed crystals in the mouthpiece and was, as usual, off net. There were no mortars and the machine guns had not yet arrived. While he was waiting for them, encouraging the wounded in the R.A.P. by describing the grand feeds they would soon be having in Dublin, the Germans attacked the Company and cut the track near "White Cow Farm." "This does not sound good." By the time the carriers arrived he had prepared both a plan and a speech to persuade Major H. L. S. Young to risk his machine-gun platoon. "I had a column of carriers formed up, myself in the leading vehicle, Guardsman Hamilton in the second, Lieutenant Wall in the third, with the M.G. platoon behind him. We set sail and eventually made ' White Cow Farm,' where I realized that there was definitely something amiss. Lieutenant Wall got his guns mounted on the first three carriers, one gun firing forward, slap up the road, and the guns on the next two carriers to fire to the left. I told him then to ' rev up ' the remaining carriers and make as much noise as possible while Hamilton, on the left, and I on the right made a wide sweep to find the exact position of the ambush. Everything took place as I had visualized it, and I heard the Germans digging and mounting some guns just by the road." Major Kennedy slipped round these Germans and found Company H.Q. where he had left them near the track, quietly refilling their magazines. C.S.M. Smilie told him that the Germans had attacked from the west on a broad front from "Carrier Farm" to "White Cow Farm." The weight of the attack had fallen on No. 13 Platoon, of which only Sergeant Dunne's section and Platoon H.Q. remained. The Germans had destroyed Corporal Breslin's section and Guardsman McCracken's section in the first sudden rush. There had also been the sound of brisk fighting in "Carrier Farm." "I expect we will have trouble from there before very long," he said in the same tone of voice he used of some recalcitrant Guardsman. In return, Major Kennedy told him "what to expect in the next few minutes, to man his guns and prepare to repel boarders." "I then slipped back to Lieutenant Wall. He drove forward till I fired on the first German post and then he turned on the heat. We did not waste much time and soon silenced some machine guns on the left and pushed on down the track." A post on the right, however, wrecked one of the carriers with a grenade, killed two of its crew and disappeared into the dark. The column reached Company H.Q. just as Lance-Sergeant Murphy marched in fourteen prisoners. "They were no trouble," he said. "A platoon of them started down the big gully, but we grenaded them out and captured these."

Lieutenant Wall mounted his Browning machine-guns round No. 13 Platoon H.Q. to replace the lost sections and to cover the left flank of the Company as well as the valley in front of them. Before the Guardsmen had finished digging the pits, heavy firing broke out from "Carrier Farm," directed vaguely in their direction. They waited for some minutes in the hope that it was some nervous British or American commander wasting ammunition, but no, the firing continued steadily and it sounded like high-rate heavy German guns. When they heard shots from the bottom of the valley and the crack of grenades they waited no longer and opened fire. A spasmodic duel followed, though the better-supplied Germans did most of the shooting. The skirmishing in the valley continued for about an hour, while Guardsman White and his men clung to the ford. It ended with a long burst, confused shouting and then silence. "More fortunate for us," reported Major Kennedy, "was the discovery of a German machine-gun post some twenty-five yards from the carrier wrecked in the ambush. We found it by capturing one of its crew who had wandered a little too far, and also by the fact that it opened fire on us, wounding Guardsman Mooney in the thigh, breaking his leg. One grenade put paid to it and, with the help of the prisoner, we got Mooney back to 'White Cow Farm.'" Mooney was carried back to the R.A.P. by six of the twenty prisoners. "I thought they would drop me whenever a shell fell near, but they stuck it well," he said. The escort returned to tell their comrades that they could give up any idea of breakfast; a carrier was bogged beside the Sherman tank in "White Cow Farm," blocking the track and there was now no time to hump the food and water.

The night was very cold and heavily wet with dew. The Guardsmen, waiting for dawn, improved the trenches and stamped about, flapping their arms in an effort to keep warm. "Dawn was more friendly than I expected it to be," said Major Kennedy. As soon as the ground mist cleared, C.S.M. Smilie turned Company H.Q. into "a miniature Stalingrad." He found a gravel pit dug into the side of a slight slope, moved out some dead Germans, and built a lean-to of sandbags. "Fortune was with us," he said, "for besides discovering a beautiful Springfield sniper rifle, we found another Browning machine gun, about three thousand rounds of ammunition and two boxes of American field rations. We also made a small filter to catch some water if it rained." Guardsman Bell, the Company's signaller, repaired his wireless set by transferring the innards of an American field telephone into the microphone. Major Kennedy started his running commentary on the local fighting. In No. 2 Company's area also dawn was quiet. As soon as it was light, the sentries saw a German walk leisurely and confidently towards them. He had a bottle in his hand. They let him come in, and then Lieutenant Brand formally captured him. The German was most indignant; he had come, he explained, on the usual errand, to exchange brandy for tinned meat. Sergeant-Major Pestell explained that the trade agreement was cancelled "as from now." The German spent an unhappy day deepening Major G. FitzGerald's trench and asking at intervals why Irishmen were in Italy at all. The failure of their agent's mission clearly annoyed his colleagues, for soon afterwards they started lobbing mortar-bombs into the gully.

The sun was up and the morning chill had passed. Guardsman Montgomery's gun was firing even faster than usual, and Major Kennedy found him "beating hell" out of some Germans who were trying to dig in on the slope below "Carrier Farm." "I could see a German tank on the road below the farm building with the crew drumming up in one of the long cow-sheds." C.S.M. Smilie was right; there was going to be trouble from Carrier Farm. Two more tanks nosed out of the farm and concentrated their fire on the machine-gun platoon's emplacements. Major Kennedy crawled towards No. 15 Platoon and shouted for Sergeant Murphy. Sergeant Murphy answered that there were some Germans down in the valley, but the platoon was O.K. "I did not shout any more, for I did not want to make a noise as I was going to disturb the Germans with other material." Once back in Company H.Q., he called for concentrations on Carrier Farm and the toe of the Boot. "It was difficult for me to direct the guns, as each time I wanted to see I had to go thirty yards, and each time I got back to the wireless I could scarcely make myself understood. I think it did succeed in keeping some German heads down." But there were too many heads, and they were on all sides. The tanks in Carrier Farm, untouched or replaced, increased their fire on the machine-gun platoon. They smashed two of the guns, wrecked all the carriers. A solid wedge of German infantry rose from the western gully and, under the cover of the pounding 88's, thrust themselves across the track behind the Company. Major Kennedy reported cheerfully that he was "now more or less surrounded."

Colonel Scott told him to concentrate the platoons and sit tight. Out went Major Kennedy on another of his devious and dangerous expeditions. He got within hailing distance of Sergeant Kearney, the left-hand man of Lieutenant Walters's platoon, and shouted "Close on Company H.Q." Then he crawled back till he reached the track and turned down it to visit Lieutenant Wall and Sergeant O'Brien. "The sides of the track were thick with dead bodies, both British and German, to the same extent as stooks covering a golden cornfield. I did not see a sign of No. 13 Platoon, but this did not worry me as the cover was high in their area, and the more concealed they kept the better they would be. I had hardly crawled a few yards across the road when I heard a moan from under a ground-sheet. I thought at first that it was one of our own fellows, but it turned out to be a German boy and, having gone so far, I decided that I would bring him to our own headquarters. First I tried crawling, but there were too many obstacles, so I walked and carried him. A Spandau opened fire, which was a foolish thing to do as we were able to pin-point it. Montgomery turned his gun round and left Adamson to make the Germans sorry they had fired, while he himself helped me to carry the German. The German raised the morale in Company H.Q. by wolfing our biscuits and saying that they had not seen food for days, added to which he was the first German (actually Czechoslovak) who had a watch which worked. This was 'borrowed' and given to Bell the signaller ; unfortunately it was not luminous so was no good at night."

It now uneasily occurred to them that it was high time Lieutenant Walters arrived. Guardsman Hunter went out with a sharp message from Major Kennedy. "My compliments, and get a move on." Hunter did not return, nor did he reach the platoon's position. After the war, Hunter excused his absence. "There was nobody about, but I saw an empty slit-trench with a Bren gun on top of it. This is funny, I thought, and I got into it. I saw a German walking about, so I pressed the trigger. A burst went off. I don't know whether I hit the Jerry. Next thing I heard was ' Nichts Mehr,' and saw a German just behind me with a Schmeisser in his hand. Why he let me get into the trench and fire I don't know, but maybe he was asleep in the bushes and I woke him up." After the same interval—that is, on repatriation from a prisoner-of-war camp—Lieutenant Walters explained his disappearance. "As dawn came I discovered that the Germans were dug in well behind our positions. There was no one, so far as I could see, between my platoon and the main road, about half a mile away. Sergeant Kearney passed me a message saying that we were to get back as best we could. I took the platoon, now consisting of ten men, down into the big gully on our right. We went up it, through the brushwood till I thought we had gone far enough to get behind the Germans who were behind us. Then I turned right up a bare little gully. Half-way up it towards the track we were fired on from the top behind us. A German section, with two Spandaus, overlooked us ; there was no cover, and that was the end."

The early part of the afternoon passed quietly. The Germans to the east of the Boot were subdued, and to the west there was no noticeable movement. At three o'clock precisely, the Germans, having massed in the western gully, attacked in mass strength. "We were lifted out of our slit trenches by a heavy barrage and all the west became alive." The machine-gunners and No. 13 Platoon fired like maniacs. Every round had been distributed. The Brens raced wildly ; rifle bolts grew stiff and unworkable with the expansion of heat. The Germans pressed on relentlessly with insidious energy, reckless of cost. No. 13 Platoon went out of action as they had come in, quickly and sharply. "Nor have they been heard of since." No. 13 Platoon was Major Kennedy's special pride, and he could not bear to say any more about it.

The position was now appallingly precarious. Guardsmen Abbot and Nicholson brought into action the reserve Browning gun from Company H.Q. and imposed a slight check on the Germans. No. 15 Platoon ran across and flung themselves down around Company H.Q.; the Bren groups joined the one Browning and temporarily sealed the left flank. The attack still persisted in a guerilla fashion, but there was a delusive slackening of tension. Half an hour later the intensity of the attack suddenly deepened. They thought at first that it was only a few Germans with machine-guns, but soon realized it was something bigger. A German company poured across the track and were within a hundred yards of Company H.Q. The Browning and the Bren guns hammered away at them, but they still came on. Major Kennedy screeched for defensive fire. "S.O.S. Right on top of us." C.S.M. Smilie was "doing good work with the 2-inch mortar to the Germans on the far side of the road, but he only had twelve bombs, so his pleasure was cut short." It was Lance-Sergeant Murphy who made the Germans falter. The Piat was standing forgotten. He picked it up, selected the most prominent German—a big blonde officer remarkably like C.S.M. Smilie—and plugged the bomb at his stomach. Everybody, including the German, watched the wavering flight of the bomb. It exploded and the officer disintegrated. There was seconds' silence; the Germans were aghast and Sergeant Murphy looked almost ashamed; then the sudden crash of shells. "The guns responded more accurately than I had dreamed possible, and I called for three minutes rapid and two minutes smoke. It would be hard to say what happened during that time, as I only caught glimpses of the Germans, but the concentration was dead on them, and about fifty yards in front of us. The smoke thickened and we attacked to round up those Germans who had not run or were dead. I do not think many were able to run. Lieutenant Earls-Davies brought in fourteen prisoners from as far as 'White Cow Farm,' I got three on our doorstep. The battle was hardly over when we saw about a company of Germans pouring out of 'Carrier Farm' and coming down the green grass towards us. It was on that green grass that most of them died, for they were caught flat in the fire of No. 15 Platoon's Bren guns under Corporal Doran, and by Abbot and Nicholson's Browning."

"The consolidation was a sad business," reported Major Kennedy. "We realized, then, our losses, the greatest being Guardsmen Montgomery and Hughes. Montgomery and Hughes are making their own way back, but the rest are helpless." The Adjutant, looking more like a haggard old crow than usual, took the list. In less than twenty-four hours No. 3 Company had been reduced to one weak platoon—twenty men left out of ninety. Guardsman Ryan, who had just run the gauntlet from the woods with a jeep load of medical stores, heard him say. "It's all right, John, we'll get them back somehow." He stepped forward. "I'll go and get the boys, sir." Two stretchers were clamped across the back of the jeep and a bandage tied to the windscreen to flutter as a pennant in the wind. Ryan carefully lit a cigarette, reversed the jeep out of its ditch, and slammed it up the track towards "White Cow Farm." Nobody really expected to see him again, but he reappeared, driving slowly this time, and waited only long enough for the two silent men to be lifted off the stretchers. He had parked the jeep in the farm and walked up the track till he found the Company. This was Ryan's occupation for the next two days. He ran a one-man ferry service back to the R.A.P. and then, since there was no ambulance available, from the R.A.P. to the Advance Dressing Station. There are many men walking round London, Dublin or Liverpool today who owe their lives entirely to Guardsman Ryan ; if they had had to lie out till nightfall they would have died. Ryan's conduct was also an example to the Germans. "Just before dark we saw a white flag. 'More prisoners,' we thought, but the glasses showed that it was a Red Cross party fulfilling a heavier task than we had to carry out ourselves. We let them be." No. 3 Company still had a subaltern officer left ; they were now to lose him. "Lieutenant Earls-Davies had to fall from the high ground above Company H.Q. straight down into it, getting concussion." Annoyance drowned the sympathy Major Kennedy no doubt felt. Lance-Sergeant Murphy took command of No. 15 Platoon ; it was little more than an honorary title.

It was now dusk, and with the dusk came a few hours' peace and silence. In the last light of the evening German aeroplanes showered leaflets inviting the Battalion to surrender. "It is not dishonourable for you to lay down arms in case you are facing nothing but certain death." The leaflets were addressed to "British Soldiers"—which annoyed the Battalion—and began with the admitted fact. "You are not facing Italians, but Germans." The attempt to divide the Allies was so crude that it might well have been conceived by our own "Bureau of Psychological Warfare," or whatever it was called. "Certainly the Yanks played you a nasty turn. They have staked all on one card. We shall see who has got the better trumps." The Guardsmen had their own explanation—the Germans drop a lot of paper in an area and come back a few hours later ; if it has all been tidied up, they know the Guards are there. The leaflets were in fact diligently collected. The two hours after the shower of leaflets were almost pleasant. It was quiet and not yet too dark to see ; a mist was just rising, but some crisp warmth from the day still lingered. Officers and men gathered in the bottom of the gullies for a talk before the business of the night began. They brewed black coffee in mess-tins over the flickering Tommy cookers, and passed the captured bottle of brandy from hand to hand.

The night began with an hour's shattering bombardment of the culvert. The little groups scattered to their trenches and watched the surrounding dark while the earth heaved around them. The Germans did not usually fire their heavy guns at night, but presumably they thought that the Irish Guards were due for relief about this time. Such an idea, if it existed, was confined to the Germans. The Battalion did not expect it, and the Division could not do it. Indeed, the only orders the Battalion got were the direct opposite. At half-past nine, when the shelling had slackened, Lieutenant Hood led the Brigade Commander into the culvert. Brigadier Archer Clive started smoothly by ordering Colonel Scott to "strengthen the Battalion's position." After Colonel Scott's question, "What with ?" the conversation flagged. Captain R. D. N. Young, Lieutenant J. MacMullen and six men, all that was left of the dismounted and gun-less carrier and anti-tank platoons, were already on their way up to join No. 3 Company. The Brigadier suggested that he himself might be able to squeeze a few more men out of the sick, halt and blind in "B" Echelon. He was certainly welcome to add his pressure to that of Major Gordon-Watson, who was even then assembling the last of the many "reinforcement platoons" under Lieutenant Chichester-Clarke. Otherwise, all that could be done to "strengthen the Battalion's position" was to treat the fifteen men of Battalion H.Q. as a company and to move it into the Boot. This would leave the bottom of the track unprotected, but would maintain a firmer grip on the all-important gully.

About this time an American private strayed into No. 3 Company. His whole "outfit," he said, was on the road along Carrier Farm ridge, but he could not get back to it as the shelling was too heavy for him. Major Kennedy looked at the shelling thoughtfully ; he would have liked the American battalion to join him, but decided to be satisfied and "highly gratified" with what he had. "This did not seem too bad a situation after all, for the road was a key feature and if Allied troops were on it, so much the better." News from nearer home then absorbed him. Corporal Donnan had gone back to

No. 15 Platoon's old positions to collect the blankets they had left behind in their hasty transfer that afternoon. He found Germans in the trenches and on the blankets. He tried to grenade them out, but they would not budge. "They were like a hive of angry hornets, so I decided to leave them till I had more than two men with which to attack them."

From behind the Battalion came every sound and sign of turmoil. Somebody was trying to move large numbers of troops and guns, and the Germans had caught them at it. Originally, it was probably "a reshuffle to simplify administration," a favourite occupation of all Staffs, but by now the German guns and bombers had clearly reduced it to an unholy mess. Somewhere in the middle of it were the "reinforcements" and the Quartermaster with his lorry of ammunition and rations. Eventually, Captain R. D. N. Young arrived alone, to say that the others would follow when they could. The main road would be blocked till dawn, and after, so Lieutenant McKinney had plunged down the coast road in the hope of finding a way round that way. Major Kennedy took Captain R. D. N. Young up to No. 3 Company, to put him in the picture as he said. "Things were fairly quiet except for the usual noises. The only thing of interest on the way was a new machine-gun post near 'White Cow Farm.' Having made sure that our wireless was working after a fashion, Captain Young went back for his men." The carrier and anti-tank platoon—Lieutenant MacMullen, Sergeant Alexander and five Guardsmen—did not arrive till after midnight. In the interval the "new machine-gun post" had moved itself and set a fixed line. Captain D. Young at the head of his little party walked straight into it and was killed instantly. Lieutenant MacMullen had hardly had time to take in what was happening, but he had always been taught to "lead on," and did so till they reached "White Cow Farm."

At two o'clock we "wrote off" the rations. Lieutenant H. McKinney had always been as punctual as a Quartermaster as he had been as Regimental Sergeant-Major. Guardsman Mills, who had made the journey so often that he knew the ground like the back of his hand, arrived from No. 2 Company to take first the most valuable party—the Commanding Officer and the signallers. "It is lucky you are small and your trench is big," said Colonel Scott to Major George FitzGerald as he squeezed in on top of him. The rest of Battalion H.Q. were ready to go and waiting for Guardsman Mills to return, when the Quartermaster's truck crept up the track. Lieutenant McKinney peered out of the cab suspiciously, and then apologized. The coast road was badly marked and, worse still, the Germans were very dozy, for they had let him get half-way to Rome before firing on him. He did not explain how they got back, but Corporal Broadbent, the storeman, told a friend that "Hughie had put a terrible rift on everybody." The stores were dumped in the bottom of the culvert. Drill-Sergeant Rooney, M.M., crammed the prisoners into the back of the lorry ; the Adjutant gave up his Service Dress cap for safe keeping, and the Quartermaster drove away. As the lorry turned into the Campo road an 88-mm. shell passed throught the cab and exploded in the back. Corporal Broadbent and all the Germans were killed. Drill-Sergeant Rooney alone was extricated alive, with a liver full of splinters. In the cab the driver was untouched, but the Quartermaster was blown through the roof and landed in a ditch, still clasping the Service Dress cap. Altogether it was a bad night for "Q." The "reinforcement platoon" passed the wreckage and were eager to describe it. "A proper shambles it was, bits of Kraut all over the place," said Sergeant Curry with gloomy satisfaction. Battalion H.Q. were impatient to be off and had no time to listen to the horrid details. They filed out of the culvert behind Guardsman Mills, every man carrying a box of ammunition or a jerrican of water, as well as all his own belongings. The rations had to be left behind, but two stone jars of rum and a sack of cigarettes were picked out and carefully escorted. Lieutenant Chichester-Clarke and his platoon sat in the old trenches waiting for a guide from No. 3 Company. "I'll send Gregg, a great little man," promised Major Kennedy.

The Germans were rampaging in the plain, firing at any sound they heard. Guardsman Mills set a brisk pace. Somewhere in transit the pack train of Battalion H.Q. got divided ; probably some overloaded man fell in a ditch, and when he got up could see no one in front of him. Lieutenant Quinn, bringing up the rear, halted his forlorn band in the middle of an unfriendly field to give the front half time to reach the Boot. Then Corporal Barrow, on the small wireless, whispered their misfortune to No. 2 Company's signaller. "Keep a good look-out," replied the Adjutant. "I'll fire a burst of tracer in the air. . . . How's that, now ?" Lieutenant Quinn missed the stream of tracer, but the Germans saw it and a sharp concentration of mortar bombs fell in the gully. "Did you see that mortar crump ?" asked the Adjutant. "That is where we are. I'll fire one more burst, but only one." This second burst had the same effect on the Germans, but when the smoke and flying mud cleared, the rear party jog-trotted happily into the Boot. Drill-Sergeant Kenny was bristling. "If I could lay my hand on the man who broke the column, I'd break his neck." With a flurry of spades, Battalion

H.Q. sank like moles into the scarred sides of the gully. No. 2 Company edged farther northwards, disturbing a number of Germans and taking three prisoners. When all were settled the rum was broached, to celebrate another dawn. Guardsman Gregg had an even more difficult time getting the reinforcement platoon up to No. 3 Company. Everywhere they turned they met fire and had to twist, double back and squirm through the screen of Germans. "They arrived none too soon, for dawn was just breaking and already the Germans on the other side of the track were warming their guns. We did the same, but we had not as much spare ammunition." At the same time, Lieutenant MacMullen, after a lonely search, found the Company, but alone. Sergeant Alexander and the five carrier men had to stay in "White Cow Farm."

By the first glimmer of light Lance-Sergeant Murphy started work on two of the German machine guns that had established themselves directly behind the Company. He led out an "assault section"—that is, one Bren gun and most of the surviving riflemen. He himself crept forward and grenaded the nearest post till the Germans tried to escape, when the section killed them. The process was repeated on the second post. This time he was wounded, but he got near enough to throw his grenades and force the Germans out of their posts. He then brought the section back and handed over to Lieutenant MacMullen. Just as the clear light came through the morning mist the look-outs shouted that the whole German Army was surrendering. There they were, in column of threes, on the other side of the track. "This, I thought, was too good to be true, but one never knows one's luck," said Major Kennedy, "and before I had time to see for myself, the Company was already leaping into action. For once the wireless worked on the first time of asking, and I reported the news. I did not wait for a reply, but went straight up to take charge of our new prize. Then I saw they were Americans under escort, about one hundred and thirty of them. Our leading troops crossed the road to meet a withering fire from the German reverse slope positions, in which Guardsman Ryan was wounded. We shouted at the Americans, but we were too late, for the Germans had already disarmed them, and I am afraid they thought we were more Germans as, when I first saw them, I shouted in German. The Germans lost no time in moving them off, and we only succeeded in getting five in. It was a big disappointment to us, as more would have been very useful." Certainly the big, blonde C.S.M. Smilie, wearing half-boots and a black leather jerkin looked very like a Storm Troop leader. Of the five Americans, two were killed later that day fighting in a section, and two were wounded. The fifth applied to join the Regiment.

Lieutenant Chichester-Clarke and Sergeant Curry of the reinforcement platoon did not last very long. They were both wounded by an 88-mm. shell as they took their first look at the ground. A troop of 88's, comfortably and commandingly installed in "Carrier Farm," sniped the Battalion all morning with unpleasant accuracy. The rest of the Germans devoted their attention to No. 2 Company in an effort to wear it down by a series of small attacks from the east. Between the attacks, they dropped shells into the gully. An artillery officer in direct wireless communication with his guns had accompanied the Battalion into the gullies. One of these shells wounded him, killed his signaller, and wrecked his set. Guardsmen Graham and Dawson, of Battalion H.Q., had dug two trenches into a shelf in the side of the gully. Dawson's trench looked safer, so Graham surrendered his to the gunners and moved in with Dawson for company. "No sooner was I in," he said, "than a shell knocked us sideways. My face was numb, and I did not like to touch it, so I asked Dawson if I had any face left. 'As much as before,' he replied. 'Is my arm all right?' It was. The gunners were dead and the officer hadn't much longer to go. I wouldn't like it to happen again."

The day wore on without any movement. "No doubt the Germans were licking their wounds." The unusual inactivity in his area, apart from the shelling, worried Major Kennedy. When one of the new Americans reported groaning from the road, he and Guardsman Hamilton went to have a look. "The view of the road and the country round it was even more confused than before for, to add to the British and German equipment, there were now American dead and dying." They found a wounded American sitting huddled up with a German guard over him. They brushed the German aside and then allowed him to help in putting their last shell dressings on the American's torn stomach. "Hamilton went off with a home-made Red Cross flag to get a stretcher. He returned with Ryan and told me that he had been taken to the German H.Q. where there were three German officers. They were parachutists, he thought, very smart and greatly distressed at the loss of their friends who had commanded the attack the previous night, a distress Hamilton could not share. Besides offering him some Chesterfield cigarettes, they also offered him armistice terms under which we were to surrender. He accepted a cigarette, but replied to the other offer by showing them his designations, which I am glad to say were always clean.

Hamilton and Ryan carried out a second evacuation after this, and although they were not official stretcher-bearers, the Germans gave Ryan a pass to drive his jeep, and one of the officers assisted in loading the stretcher on to the jeep."

There had previously been a little thin rain off and on, but in the early afternoon the clouds opened. The Guardsmen spread out groundsheets, and in no time had enough comparatively clean water to make a "brew." The water in the bottom of the gullies rose rapidly, swamping the low-lying slit trenches. To move along the gullies one had either to wade up to the knees or to scramble along the slippery banks clinging to bushes. The water oozed into the galleries cut in the gully walls, and the fine, hard earth soaked into mud. The damp got into the batteries of the No. 19 wireless set to Brigade, and ruined them. The Battalion's own small No. 18 set continued to work, but it was "screened" at the bottom of the gully and its range was limited. After this the Battalion had to work on a relay station. Captain S. H. Combe, from "B" Echelon, brought a spare set and a field telephone, and sat on the edge of the wood patiently passing messages to and from Brigade H.Q. and the gunners. Thus an urgent call from Major Kennedy for a "grand stonk on the place I call Alexander," had to be interpreted by the Adjutant—a task made more difficult by No. 3 Company's habit of firing a Bren beside the wireless just to show that they were in action—passed to Captain Combe and telephoned by him to the Gunners. But after a surprisingly short interval shells fell on the Germans in some obscure ditch. The first message from Captain Combe was also the best—the 2nd/6th Bn. The Queen's would attack that evening to clear the track and take over No. 3 Company's positions.

"That is just what we want ; a tank and a few more fellows could rout the Germans," said Major Kennedy when he heard the news from Colonel Scott. Finding things dull at home, he had come to call on Battalion H.Q. On the way he had found Lieutenant Walters's map-case, the sole trace of that unlucky officer and his men. In the Boot we were all glad to see him, particularly Sergeant O'Sullivan, who longed for just a few minutes' intelligent conversation about horses. Like everybody else, his eyes were red and his skin grey ; one trouser leg was cut to the knee and a loose bandage flapped as he walked, but otherwise he was the same John Kennedy who had bounced through England and Africa with unflagging energy. He was prepared, with his handful of men, to go on holding the forward positions for ever. If, however, the Queen's were really going to attack that night, there was a more important task, and that was to provide them with a secure base from which to operate. This duty also fitted Colonel Scott's dearest wish—to save the remnants of No. 3 Company. Sitting on the edge of his trench, Colonel Scott gave his orders slowly. If, after the Queen's attack had been confirmed, Kennedy thought there was a danger of his Company being heavily attacked, he was to withdraw to the south of "White Cow Farm," and hold the track for the Queen's. Major Kennedy, whose mind went back to Norway, gave this plan the code name of "Pothus Wood." He repeated his orders, shouted for his attendant Gregg, who was collecting cigarettes, and started down the Boot. "We thought we would go back this way for a change, although the gully was now a river bed about three feet deep in water. Fairly soon we came on a dead German. It reminded me that the gully was bound to be a pretty good target for 'stonks.' Continuing a bit farther, I definitely decided to take Lieutenant Brand's advice and go back the way we had come, for in the gully were nineteen Germans, some sitting, some standing, like rabbits outside a warren. Judging from the usual form, there were sure to be at least another twenty hidden in slit trenches. How lucky, I thought, were the ones in their trenches for, when I got back to my wireless, the others were going to get a severe 'caning.' The wireless did work, and the field gunners promised to deal with the Germans shortly. While waiting for this to happen, the mediums came on, and belted hell out of 'Carrier Farm.' The sun set in the west and darkness came on, bringing with it a hive of activity from the road. On our side the Micks, with their rifles and Brens cleaned, went up to their posts where, I am sorry to say, we had only one Browning left in action, and only two belts of ammunition for it."

At nine o'clock R.Q.M.S. Grey brought the ration lorry, a new one, up to the culvert with a load of ammunition, American picnic rations, new batteries for the No. 19 set, and more rum and cigarettes. A fatigue party from the Boot collected their share. As they staggered back across the plain they clashed with a German patrol. They fought it off and brought in all the stores with one exception—a bottle of whisky for Colonel Scott. The officer entrusted with this precious burden put it down in the grass, and then could not find it again. Colonel Scott's silence at the story was more dreadful than words; the other officers, who might reasonably have counted on a mouthful, were openly hostile. An insistent sniffing from a perpetual cold showed that Lieutenant G. Hood, the Brigade liaison officer, had somehow tagged on to the party. He bore a pencilled note from the Brigadier.

"2040 hrs., 23 Feb., 1944.

"My dear Andrew,

"I know your Battalion is practically worn out with two days and three nights fighting—and a very fine effort it has been, too. You *must* keep going till tomorrow night—*i.e.*, 20 hrs. I will then relieve you with the Grenadiers if a change-over of 24th Guards for another brigade does not take place, which I hope it will. Please keep it up for this final spasm. I hope tomorrow may be much easier as a result of tonight's clean-up by the 2/5 Queen's.

Yours,

ARCHER C."

Lieutenant Hood added that a company of Grenadiers would come up that night anyway, probably just before dawn. "The Queen's should be here quite soon, as I went to see them and carefully explained the way." He then disappeared into the dark. How he found his way about nobody quite knew, least of all himself, but he always turned up where he was wanted. About the same time Major Kennedy, with Guardsmen Gregg and Wilson, went out to look for the carrier men. There had been no sign of them all day except for an occasional burst of firing in "White Cow Farm." They found Sergeant Alexander and four of his five men by a small shed on the northern fringe of the farm-yard. The rest of the farm was now occupied by a strong German platoon. Each outburst of fire had represented a German attack which slowly herded them into one corner. "This meant that we were now surrounded more than we had previously been. I reported the situation to the Commanding Officer, who said that the Queen's were definitely going up tonight. This was all right as, but for the fact that we were short of ammunition, particularly grenades and machine-gun ammunition, had no flares and only three 2-inch mortar bombs, everyone was very well and quite happy. Sergeant Alexander and his four men went a long way to fill up the depleted sections." Major Kennedy was a man incapable of sarcasm—he genuinely meant what he said, he was quite happy, and counted five men a handsome reinforcement.

The night wore on and the only new troops on the scene were for the enemy. "Midnight came and passed, but there were still no signs of the Queen's. The Germans in ' White Cow Farm ' and in the whole area east of our positions became very noisy." Noise from the Germans meant only one thing—an attack—and at two o'clock in the morning of the 24th it came. Its first form was a straggling rush from the east against the Boot. No. 2 Company were waiting for it and "saw it off" with the steady, unhurried fire of men well used to such things. The attacks shifted north to No. 3 Company. The forward section commander reported first the sound of men assembling and then that he had been attacked. It was a small assault and the section weathered it, but it coincided with more noise from the west. This convinced Major Kennedy that it was time to withdraw. "If the Germans attacked and met thin air, they would gain nothing but a damn good shelling followed by a counter-attack from us." He came up on the air, asking permission to "apply Pothus Wood." The Adjutant had not been in Norway, so even though both of them were under fire at their respective wirelesses, Major Kennedy found time to give a brief description of that arctic operation. It was with relief that the Adjutant heard him turn to the present and announce his order of march. He and the admirable Guardsman Gregg were to lead, covered by C.S.M. Smylie with the walking wounded, three stretcher cases and the wireless formed the main party and, protecting the rear, were the remainder of the Company, fifteen men under Lieutenant MacMullen. And that was No. 3 Company of the 1st Bn. Irish Guards.

As the little column got close to "White Cow Farm" they smelt the Germans. Sure enough there they were, all asleep except for a machine-gunner on sentry. Gregg took the stretchers in a wide sweep past the farm and at the same time Corporal Donnan engaged the gun. "I went round to a flank to snipe the personnel," said Major Kennedy. "It was too big a target for one grenade. Corporal Donnan succeeded in baiting the machine-gunner and soon he was shooting wildly, making it easy to snipe his crew. To my amazement a house south-west of ' White Cow Farm ' then burst into action. At first I thought we had fallen into a trap, but I did not think this for long, for it was Bren fire. At last it was the Queen's." Hearing the sound of the attack on No. 2 Company, the Queen's had edged to the west and come up on the left of the track unobserved and missing the two lonely Guardsmen posted to meet them. Major Kennedy tore himself away from the Germans and walked up a little creek towards the house. He stood aside to let a German patrol go by and knocked off the last member of it. Farther up the creek he came on two wounded men of the Queen's who gave him their grenades, and he raced back to catch up the German patrol. The first grenade—"one I had carried about with me for many days"—did not go off, but the next two did. The wounded Queen's men received a prisoner each as a dividend on their investment. The nearest Queen's platoon commander was rightly suspicious of the strange figure that approached him out of the dark. "I had to satisfy him by light of his flares that I was not a German myself. Then I showed him some machine-gun posts which we dealt with, and he took me to his Commanding Officer." The Commanding Officer of the Queen's despatched two companies to occupy No. 3's old positions. Major Kennedy saw them clear "White Cow Farm" of its harassed garrison, and brought No. 3 back to the culvert.

The culvert was by now humming with activity. In the gully on one side of the road was a company of Grenadiers ; on the other was a machine-gun platoon from the Middlesex Regiment. On the road itself R.Q.M.S. Grey was quietly unloading more wireless batteries, ammunition and rum. "We sent the batteries across to Battalion H.Q., also the rum, leaving enough for ourselves, which rapidly recharged our own, dry batteries." Major Kennedy always assumed that Colonel Scott held supreme command over the gullies, and that he himself was his local deputy. Nobody disputed his position when he took charge, and he confirmed his dispositions with Colonel Scott. "It was too late to risk placing men in a position not previously prepared, which meant having to dig in daylight and under fire. Therefore I decided to keep the new company intact and use it for a counter-attack should the Queen's, who already had two companies in this area, be threatened. The machine-guns, I decided, would be best to consolidate after any counter-attack had been pushed home by us. When dawn finally broke, a quarter of an hour later, we were in a strong position on either side of the track." Battalion H.Q. and No. 2 Company felt much more comfortable ; for the first time their left flank and rear were secure.

On the 24th the shells fell steadily all day. About midday, Corporal Hislop started swearing, which was a sure sign that a code message was coming over the air. Bitter the memory of trying to decode it in the glutinous mud of the trench, and more bitter still was the realization that our key was out of date, for no one at Brigade H.Q. had remembered to send us the current one. At last we had it—the Duke of Wellington's would relieve us after nightfall. The Grenadiers slipped away to rejoin their battalion, which badly needed them. The day dragged by, and at last it was welcome pitch dark and raining. Battalion H.Q. trailed across to the culvert to meet the "Duke's." A slow file of men plodded up the track, led by Lieutenant Hood. He introduced them as "the Duke's," but the first six men denied it and gave the names of six different regiments till a sergeant said, "You're Duke's now," and then, apologetically. "They're new, sir, we only got them this morning." Their Commanding Officer, with a special conducting Guardsman, edged past a wrecked jeep into the culvert. "We plugged up the track," wrote Colonel Webb-Carter afterwards. "At regular intervals were the derelict carriers of the Irish Guards, all knocked out trying to bring up supplies. As we passed the last I heard an ominous whistle and dived into the ditch. The mortar shell burst on the track. 'It's about five hundred yards to go still, sir,' said the Guardsman quite unemotionally. He had remained in the perpendicular position and, feeling rather abashed, I climbed up and joined him on the track. It seemed an age, but at last we reached a small bridge over a little gully. Here was the R.A.P. and Andrew Scott's headquarters. That imperturbable officer—wrapped in a duffle coat—presented his usual robust and faintly Regency appearance. The little culvert was crammed. The R.A.P., where the doctor was treating a couple of recently wounded Guardsmen, occupied half the space—the rest contained the elements of both Battalion H.Q., Duke's signallers taking over from the Guards and my own officers trying to contact their opposite numbers. Andrew and I sat talking on a stretcher propped on empty ration boxes. The position was fluid in the extreme ; the Guardsmen were on top all right, but deathly tired." Two companies of "Duke's" piled into the culvert gully. There a wide selection of old slit trenches ran along the ruins. "Take your pick," said the Guardsmen. "There's nobody in any of them." "Now you get out of it, John, and give us some peace," said Colonel Scott.

Meanwhile the two other "Duke" companies reached the Boot. The disaster, the fear of which lurked behind every relief, befell us again that night. As the troops of both battalions were out in the open in the act of handing over the exiguous slit trenches, a concentration of 88-mm. shells and mortar bombs crashed into the Boot. The "Dukes" suffered most, as they had the most men, but the last-minute losses were heart-breaking for the Irish Guards. Sergeant Wylie, D.C.M., was killed—solid Jimmy Wylie, as brave as a lion and as patient and gentle as an ox, who had survived the worst of three campaigns and was looking forward to a fourth. Lance-Corporal Moriarty, D.C.M., could not leave the Boot while there were any men missing, but the sooner the rest of the Company were out of it the better.

The hand-over, which was bound, anyway, to be a sketchy proceeding, had to be hurried. A few officers and non-commissioned officers remained behind in the Boot and the Culvert to pass on what information they possessed to the distracted "Duke's" officers,

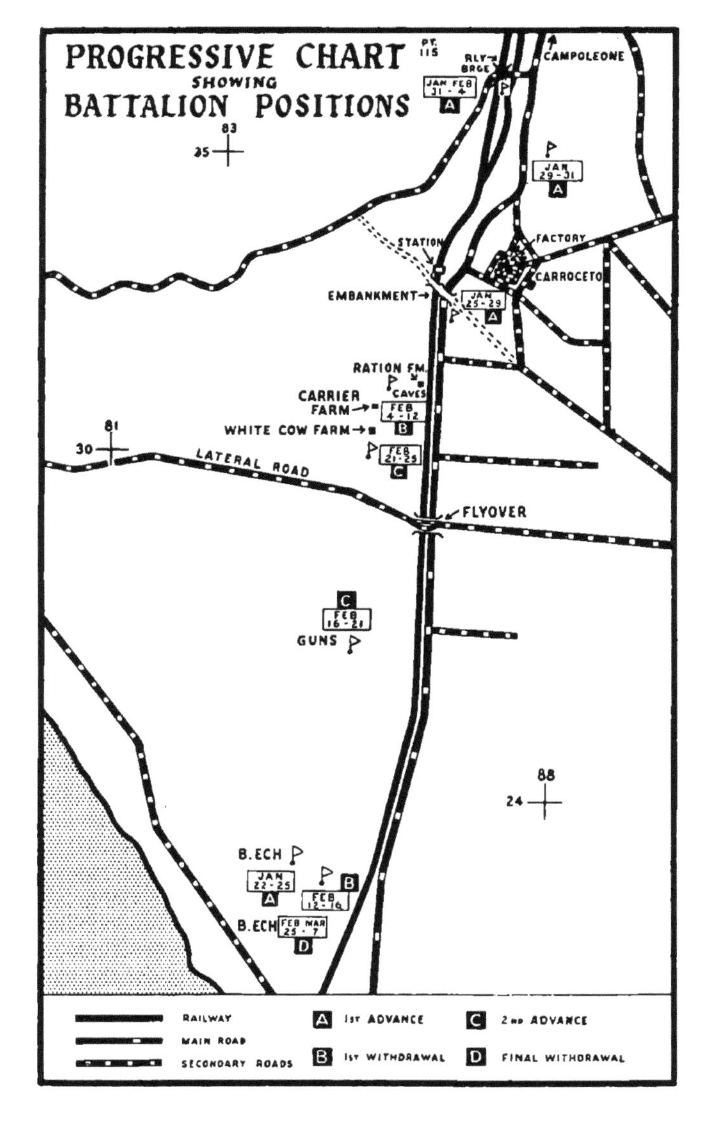
PROGRESSIVE CHART
SHOWING
BATTALION POSITIONS
PT. 115
RLY. BRGE
CAMPOLEONE
JAN FEB 31 - 4
A
83
35
JAN 29 - 31
A
STATION
FACTORY
CARROCETO
EMBANKMENT
JAN 25 - 29
A
RATION FM.
CAVES
CARRIER FARM
FEB 4 - 12
B
WHITE COW FARM
81
30
LATERAL ROAD
FEB 21 - 25
C
FLYOVER
C
FEB 16 - 21
GUNS
88
24
B.ECH
JAN 22 - 25
A
B
FEB 12 - 16
B.ECH
FEB MAR 25 - 7
D
RAILWAY
MAIN ROAD
SECONDARY ROADS
1ST ADVANCE
1ST WITHDRAWAL
2ND ADVANCE
FINAL WITHDRAWAL

pushing their men into position in the blackness and locating the wounded by the moans. "Andrew Scott had done all he could, and in a lull of shelling he moved off with his headquarters," said Lieut.-Colonel Webb-Carter. "He asked me to keep a particular eye on a Corporal Moriarty, who had not yet left the Boot, and who—Andrew said—had done particularly good work. At that moment, almost, the lifeless body of that gallant N.C.O. was toppling into an empty slit trench as, looking for a wounded man in the darkness, he was hit by a fragment of mortar shell. As the tall Guardsmen filed out, leaving us the heritage of death and desolation they had borne so long, a peculiar sense of isolation struck us. In all the long-drawn-out crucifixion of the beach-head, no positions saw such sublime self-sacrifice and such hideous slaughter as were perpetrated in the overgrown foliage that sprouted in the deep gullies."

"Flag up, pack up, go home." The Battalion marched in a daze back through the woods to "B" Echelon and lay where they dropped. At dawn the cooks brought mugs of boiling tea and buckets of bacon, but the men were still too tired to eat. In the evening, after a day's sleep in the dugouts and an hour cleaning weapons, they remembered they were hungry. The next day they remembered they were Guardsmen, and if they did not, they were reminded by Drill-Sergeant Kenny. The Battalion remained for another ten days in the beach-head. It was an exasperating time of constant alarms, but the now reduced and reinforced beach-head held firm and the Battalion was spared the final sacrifice. Orders arrived from Army Group H.Q. for the 24th Guards Brigade to re-form in Naples; they were cancelled locally by a local reluctance to part with any troops. On the 6th March a new brigade landed and the orders were reissued. Major-General P. Penney, C.B.E., D.S.O., M.C., came to say goodbye to the Battalion. "I can't let you go without saying how much I shall miss the Regiment, not only collectively, but individually. It has been a privilege and a sadness to have had your battalion in the 1st Division during these days, but their achievements, their unfailing response and their willing fighting spirit have been an inspiration. I regret your departure enormously, especially as I fear there is little chance of your rejoining us, but I am glad of the opportunity you will have of refitting and re-forming. I wish you all well, and I shall never forget what you have done and the sacrifices you have made."

The Battalion sailed from Anzio on the 7th March. It was a beautiful morning.

RETURN FROM ANZIO, 7TH MARCH, 1944.

L.S.T. "C."

Officers.

Major H. L. S. Young (O.C. Ship).
Captain S. A. H. White.
Lieut. J. F. Bell.
Lieut. M. McN. Boyd.
Lieut. Lord Plunket.
Commanding Officer.
Adjutant.
Rev. Father Brookes.
Lieut. W. F. Reynolds.

Other Ranks.

Support Company	88
H.Q. Company	
"Q" Staff	17
Servants	2
R.A.P.	1
(Sergt. Thorogood)	
Signals	25
Orderly Room Staff ...	8
(Including 2 D./Sergts.)	
Police	4
Officers' Mess Staff ...	3
M.T.—Drivers	10
Surplus	16

L.S.T. "D."

Officers.

2nd-in-Command.
(O.C. Ship).
Major G. P. M. FitzGerald.
Captain T. C. Keigwin.
Lieut. Hon. C. A. Brand.
Lieut. J. R. A. MacMullen.
Lieut. M. R. M. Aird.
Lieut. G. Gordon-Shee.
Lieut. G. V. Bland.
Lieut. J. C. F. Quinn.
Captain M. V. Dudley.
Medical Officer.

Other Ranks.

No. 2 Company	131
H.Q. Company	
Servants	1
Pioneers	12
R.A.P.	2
Intelligence	8
Coy. H.Q.	8
(C.S.M., C.Q.M.S., L./Cpl. Chandler, Gdsmn. Connolly, Kent and 3 Cooks)	
Despatch Riders ...	2
M.T. Drivers	9

Total : 20 officers, 247 other ranks.

EPILOGUE TO ITALY

The 1st Battalion never fought again. Briefly, it was shipped home to England to re-form with new recruits, but soon found itself providing drafts and training men for the 3rd Battalion in Normandy. The intake of the Regiment was never enough to maintain three battalions on active service. Once the reservoir of trained men stored in Hobb's Barracks from 1940 to 1943 was exhausted, one battalion had to be scrapped. The 1st Battalion stomached its pride, but it was not easy. The majority of officers and men were in time transferred to the 3rd Battalion. Major J. S. O. Haslewood, for instance, took over to Normandy a complete No. 4 Company which was first reconstituted in Italy.

For four weeks after its evacuation from Anzio the Battalion rested in the villages of Santa Agata dei due Golfe and Massalubrense perched on the top of the Sorrento peninsula. While the Great Men discussed the future of the Brigade of Guards in Italy—amalgamation, integration, reduction, abolition or reinforcement—the Battalion collected its wounded from every hospital in Southern Italy and Sicily. The bad cases were assembled in Naples General Hospital ; the men on the mend were posted to Sorrento convalescent camp and then, since there was very little difference, to Santa Agata. Vesuvius erupted soon after the Battalion's arrival, the grey lava dust turning the next day into night, blocking the roads and changing the green valleys into a landscape of the moon. "It's the end of the world—it would be just before Paddy's Day." Guardsman Graham's pessimistic forecast shows the Battalion's main interest at this time—St. Patrick's Day. The shamrock was flown from Ireland, and there was no question about who was to present it—it had to be General Alexander, Cassino or no Cassino. The Regimental Band was recaptured from the other side of Italy, calves and pigs were bought at exorbitant prices, droves of Italians were hired to clean and press the battle-dress, and the awards were approved in record time so that General Alexander could present them on the parade

The 17th of March was a perfect day. General Alexander wrote to Colonel Scott that evening. "I do so heartily congratulate you on having such a splendid battalion. It was a real joy to me to be with them today, and I thought they looked just fine. Smart, proud of themselves—in fact, just what one wishes and expects Guardsmen to look like. It must have impressed all the onlookers very much, like it did me. The Micks were always good (the best in the whole

1st Battalion Irish Guards

Palestine, 1938—Norway, 1940—North Africa, 1943—Anzio, 1944

Back Row.—Gdsn. P. McCarthy, Gdsn. R. Adamson, D.C.M., Gdsn. J. Lavery, Gdsn. P. O'Shea, D.C.M., Gdsn. J. Gethings, L./Sgt. C. Englishby, Gdsn. E. Davis, Gdsn. E. Rooney, Gdsn. E. Moore, L./Cpl. D. Murphy, L./Cpl. T. O'Connell, Gdsn. J. Ryan, M.M.

Middle Row.—Gdsn. W. Gormley, Gdsn. M. Lawton, Sgt. A. Hughes, M.M., Sgt. P. Hatche, Sgt. M. McCarthy, L./Sgt. C. Weir, M.M., L./Sgt. P. McNally, L./Cpl. R. Ashton, L./Sgt. D. Smith, L./Sgt. J. Sweeney, Gdsn. S. Robinson, Gdsn. G. Prentice.

Front Row.—L./Cpl. S. Carr, Sgt. R. McConnell, M.M., C.Q.M.S. W. Wallace, C.S.M. W. Pestell, D./Sgt. M. Moran, M.M., Major D. M. L. Gordon-Watson, M.C., R.S.M. W. Rooney, M.M., Major H. L. S. Young, D.S.O., C.S.M. G. Stone, Sgt. O'Sullivan, L./Sgt. P. Freeman, L./Cpl. G. Currie.

Face page 358

Brigade), but I really believe they were better today than ever they were or ever have been. I am only so sorry that I could not remain longer with you—go to High Mass and go round the company dinners, and then have lunch with you—but as you know I have this important and tricky battle of Cassino in full swing, and it must be won. This is my fifteenth St. Patrick's Day on parade with the Regiment and the fifth on active operations—not counting Constantinople and Gibraltar in 1922-4. Good luck to you all."

The companies marched straight off parade to monumental dinners. Lunch in the Officers' Mess was very late and very long, as was the evening in the Sergeants' Mess. A week later the officers gave a Grand Ball in their Mess, the Pensione Garoffalo in Santa Agata; the prolific Neapolitan nobility provided the partners. This was the Battalion's farewell party.

The 24th and the 201st Guards Brigades were amalgamated to form a new 24th. "24th Guards Brigade will receive 3rd Coldstream Guards complete and officers and men from 6th Guards and 2nd Scots Guards for their respective sister battalions. It will lose 1st Irish Guards." The Battalion handed over all its equipment and packed for immediate embarkation with a skeleton 201st Brigade. At the very last moment Colonel Andrew Scott was snatched away to command the 28th Infantry Brigade. General Oliver Leese, who had just succeeded to the command of the Eighth Army, was not going to let so outstanding and experienced a soldier escape him. Both Colonel Andrew and the Battalion were stunned; he had brought them through so much, and now he was not to bring them home. He said goodbye to the companies on the evening before the Battalion embarked, leaving them in a loneliness that took all the zest out of the return to England. The following June Brigadier Scott achieved what he and all the Battalion had so dearly wished to have together—an audience with His Holiness the Pope. The special blessing he received was for the 1st Battalion—"the Irish Guards who have fought so gallantly in this country."

On the 11th April the Battalion sailed from Naples in the *Capetown Castle*. Of the 926 men who left Ayr in February, 1943, 326 landed in Liverpool on the 22nd April, 1944. On the beach-head the Battalion lost 32 officers and 714 men, killed wounded and missing. It left behind it in the graveyards outside Anzio 7 officers and 66 men. The bodies of some of the missing dead, such as the gallant Charles Bartlet, were found after the war; the others are still missing. "Quis Separabit?" Wherever they lie, they are the 1st Battalion Irish Guards.

PART V

•

THE 2nd & 3rd BATTALIONS IN NORTH-WEST EUROPE

CHAPTER I

The 2nd Battalion

THE 2nd Battalion had not fully appreciated the delights of Duncombe Park and the Nissen way of life until, in early April, 1944, they moved to a tented camp on the Yorkshire wolds. During a miserable month mobilized austerity and security restraints crept in—the sure harbingers of D Day—and at the end of April an advance party was dispatched southwards in all the wrappings of secrecy. A week later the Battalion, stripped of "peace-time" kit, flowed by road and rail to the Divisional Concentration Area. A thoughtful staff had allotted to 5th Guards Brigade, Brighton and Hove, where the Battalion found very comfortable billets in and about Brunswick Square. None were sorry to have left Yorkshire with its memories of countless "stunts" and wintry encampments. "Brighton would be better," and it was—bow windows instead of bell tents ; the sun and the sea breeze ; London within the hour. Nor did the town itself lack anything for gaiety in food and drink or "boites de nuit." Leisure hours were spent in a Regency spirit : some admired Nash's art and "Prinny's" taste ; others dined long and well and attended "riots." "Very right and proper," said Captain H. FitzHerbert, remembering the Ball before Waterloo. There was even some work to do. Batches of new tanks arrived to be waterproofed before the end of May. The technical staff, under Captain Ronald Robertson, R.Q.M.S. Gerrard and T.Q.M.S. Coppen, had never a dull moment. Something was always going wrong, and they were the only people to keep the Battalion right. "Busy as a bee. Lost my E.M.E. Returns, returns, returns. Petrol, oil and water. No time for a tea party," answered Captain Robertson to the invitations of his friends.

The month passed quickly amid asbestos compound, exhaust manifolds and merry evenings. By June 1st the tanks were ready "in Christmas tree order, to be immersed up to the turret ring."

More and more aeroplanes flew overhead, and queer shapes—odds and ends of "Mulberry Harbour"—swam out at sea. On the 4th and 5th June Lieutenant M. Callender, an acute observer, reported the loading of barges and great bustle at Newhaven. "Significant," thought the strategists. Then the morning of the 6th brought news of the invasion, to the general excitement and relief. The years of waiting were over. For the 2nd and 3rd Battalions the shooting war had really begun. The question was, "When do we land?" At dinner time the Commanding Officer, Lieut.-Colonel Finlay, addressed all ranks in the mess-rooms. He stressed his complete confidence in their skill and courage, and warned them of the need for correct behaviour and sympathy towards the French people on the far side of the Channel. The personal messages from General Eisenhower and General Montgomery were handed out and eagerly read. The Battalion felt much more at ease.

Each squadron now set up a map of Normandy and every man, Commander-in-Chief for a few moments, fought chinagraph battles of his own, forming pivots, thrusting wedges and turning flanks. Much sympathy, too, was felt for the troops crossing in the landing craft as the wind blew hard and the sea ran choppy. On the 8th the Divisional Commander, Major-General A. Adair, D.S.O., M.C., addressed the whole of the 5th Armoured Brigade. After giving an outline of the battle to date, he told them how certain he and the other senior commanders were that the Division would prove itself the finest in any army. He reminded them of the qualities that had distinguished the Guards Division in the last war—calmness, accurate shooting and constant alertness. In this war the Division's morale had withstood the strain of four years' waiting and training, and the boredom of countless exercises, but now at last their chance was coming.

For the next ten days conflicting reports and gossip were as assiduously collected by the battalions as by the rest of England. Progress seemed good and hearts were high. They heard reliably that the Division would not be wanted immediately, since infantry now had priority over armour. Just to show that Drake was not the only person who could play games at times of invasion, the Battalion held a sports meeting and beat the 2nd Welsh Guards at cricket.

Orders were issued on the 16th to move early next morning to Fareham for embarkation. The 2nd Battalion said goodbye to Brighton and by the afternoon of the 17th were installed in a staging camp, A.14, some six miles from the coast. At first they were told to be ready to move in six hours and, despite reasonable incredulity, had to make frantic efforts to collect sea stores and fill in forms and labels of many colours before going to bed. Their incredulity was justified. The camp was still half full of other troops, and even had the storm not broken they could not have embarked for two days. In fact, of course, the worst storm for forty years upset all time-tables, smashed large numbers of landing-craft and did great damage to the beaches. At the Brigade's low level it meant another fortnight of bleak waiting. The camp staff did its best to make the Guardsmen comfortable and contented, but none the less it was not a happy time. They could eat strawberries bought in bulk by Major J. W. Madden ; they could watch the rain, or E.N.S.A., or go to sleep. Otherwise there was nothing. Even that last expedient of an Adjutant's wit, drill in the public highway, was prevented by the traffic. But, bored as they were, the 2nd Battalion counted themselves lucky in comparison with the 3rd Battalion, who were then pitching at sea.

At last the storm died down and the 2nd Battalion embarked in "those horrid little flat-bottomed affairs called 'Landing Craft Tanks.'" On 1st July, after a peaceful passage, it landed on the Arromanches beaches. None of the elaborate water-proofing was needed in the event, but the men did not complain of labour lost; rather they were relieved that their handiwork was not put to the salt-sea test. The landing craft lay off shore in the middle of a vast assembly of shipping until the tide was right and then put their load of tanks ashore whenever and wherever the naval commanders got a chance to beach. "We were put down on a very deserted piece of beach," wrote one troop commander, "with nothing in sight but some craft wrecked in last week's storm, and some odd khaki-clad beach-combers, British and American, who took no interest in us. Of the elaborate beach organization we had been promised, there was no sign and nobody to hand the disembarkation papers to, which I had carefully prepared in triplicate, having frequently been told that I would not be allowed to land on Norman soil without them. I grouped my charges conspicuously on the beach and, against all rules, started to de-waterproof them there and then, hoping that someone would soon come roaring up to tell me to get them to hell out of there. But no, and after half an hour I could temporize no longer and we drove off in single file for about half a mile down the beaches looking for a tracked vehicle exit. We got one in the end, but still not a sign there, so I set off inland by map, having only the vaguest idea where the Battalion was and being further handicapped by misinformation as to where they landed us from the two young officers of my craft. The ground there shelves noticeably for about eight hundred yards inland and gave a perfect defensive position for the Atlantic Wall. I saw a nasty looking anti-tank ditch, some wire, a good many live minefields (prominently and kindly marked by the Germans with a skull and cross-bones and 'Achtung Minen!'), several shattered, but by no means demolished, pill-boxes and a very large concrete bunker. The two things that struck me most were the thinness of 'The Wall' (barely half a mile thick at this point) and the comparatively small amount of devastation. Even houses right on the beach, though gutted and uninhabitable, still had four walls. Two fields of poppies slap in the middle of the forward slope were apparently intact, and everywhere there was more grass than shell holes. Inland destruction was very sporadic, little hamlets within a mile of the beach being seemingly untouched, and such villages as were hit having had only the odd house hit by a shell. Granted, I only saw one narrow strip, maybe a mile or less wide, and granted there'd been nearly a month to tidy up. Our little convoy drove along narrow roads crammed with traffic until I picked up the Guards Armoured Division's sign, and the rest was easy. Finally, having by-passed every single one of the laid down stages of invasion, I arrived in our squadron area."

Once in Normandy the 2nd Battalion had to endure another wait, and settled down at the village of St. Martin des Besaces three miles outside Bayeux on the Bayeux–Caen road. Brisk bartering started with the nearby farms—butter, milk and cheese against chocolate, cigarettes or, sometimes, just charm. It suited both sides. The farmers liked tobacco, the Guardsmen Camembert; and the Battalion learnt the art of haggling in the sharp school of Norman peasantry. It was impossible in the face of such plenty not to question the stories of "starving Europe." The Normans, at least, did not look under-fed. Captain Terence O'Neill, surely the most tolerant of men and quite a Francophil, was greatly irritated by a shopkeeper who told him that "Vraiment on n'a pas apercu l'occupation allemande."

The main recreation became "swanning" behind the lines, viewing the relics of earlier battles or even visiting the 3rd Battalion in their trenches. German Tiger and Panther tanks could be seen in their stark enormity, no longer just as photographs or models. The length of their guns caused some awed comment ("They stretch from here to Sunday week"), and the too frequent holes in Shermans' armour were anxiously inspected. All were glad to hear, though, that casualties among tank crews were very light, considering. The technical staff set out with more practical aims. Never the victims of false sentiment, they turned other's misfortunes to their advantage and stripped the hulks of any useful bogie, sprocket or machinery. " Call us carrion if you like," said T.Q.M.S. Coppen, "but our job is to collect spares, and you'll thank us yet." Which, of course, they did. The same staff, when a day of general swabbing was ordered, washed themselves in petrol rather than water—a fitter's privilege. The Battalion was also able to make some slight return to the Navy for their kindness in bringing them across the Channel, by taking parties of sailors from H.M.S. *Rodney* on battlefield tours. The sailors were very pleased to see the damage done by their own guns—including a Panther, reported to have been chased and hit on the move by 15-inch salvos.

But all was not unrelieved war. The social event of the season, a football match arranged by Captain J. R. Dupree and the M. le Maire of Bayeux, took place to celebrate the Fourteenth of July. The problem of finding a bi-lingual referee was solved by Captain J. R. Dupree volunteering for the task himself. In the blazing heat of the afternoon the Battalion team met Bayeux's best on the "Stade Municipale," and a great crowd of Guardsmen, other troops and civilians—"tout Bayeux" in its Sunday suits—came to cheer. The town band played national anthems with patriotic fervour ; M. le Maire and the Commanding Officer shook hands with the teams ; two little girls in white presented a bouquet of flowers to Sergeant Williams, the Battalion captain. After a good game, which the Battalion won 5—2, the two teams, referee and municipal officials withdrew to a further private celebration. That evening the first conference was held for Operation "Goodwood."

CHAPTER II

The 3rd Battalion

THE 3rd Battalion also left Yorkshire without regret. They had been glad to go there in the first place, because it meant joining the 32nd Brigade in the Guards Armoured Division, but they were now equally glad to move south with the Division. The countless reorganizations and the continual drain of men as reinforcements for the 1st Battalion still left their mark, for the Battalion still had one company composed of Scots Guards. The seaside resort allotted to them was Eastbourne—a most respectable town—where they waterproofed the vehicles, but could do little else to pass the time or to ease their impatience after the news of the invasion.

The 3rd Battalion left Eastbourne on 16th June, divided into a "marching party" and a "vehicle party." The marching party—the four rifle companies—embarked on the liner *Llangibby Castle* at Southampton on the 20th and swung at anchor off the Isle of Wight till the morning of the 23rd. The vehicle party—Battalion H.Q., Support Company and the transport, who naturally expected to travel in greater comfort—were crammed into an American liberty ship at Tilbury on the 19th and stayed in the mouth of the Thames for four days. Both parties landed near Arromanches on the 23rd, unmolested and dry-shod, and reunited "in pleasant orchards" outside Bayeux on the 25th. They found that, by the strange processes of the Army, the first reinforcements had already been in Normandy for nearly a week. This, for them, was nearly as galling as the story current in Eastbourne that a Guardsman had had a "next-of-kin" telegram from the War Office regretting to inform him that his wife, in the A.T.S., had been wounded in action.

The Battalion remained in this orchard for two days, "without a sign of the war," as Lieut.-Colonel J. O. E. Vandeleur wrote discontentedly. On the 28th, however, they approached the shot and shell. The whole 32nd Brigade moved up into the left-hand corner of the British salient west of Capriquet aerodrome. The Battalion was based on the village of La Gaule, two miles west of Capriquet, with its left-hand company at La Bayude farm, facing the Germans in the aerodrome. Taking the salient as a theatre, Colonel Vandeleur described the seating in this way. "The 3rd Battalion were in the dress circle, that is to say the village of Cheux was in the stalls with its farthest edge in the battle. The Battalion had its left-hand company—' X ' Company, Scots Guards—in the corner seats in contact with the enemy on Capriquet aerodrome. The remainder of the Battalion was tucked into the back seats of the dress circle behind the Welsh Guards in Cheux. The Coldstream Guards, with some rather cheap seats in the circle (outside edge), were holding the village of St. Morcellet." "A lasting impression of the time at La Gaule," he continued, "was the extraordinary way in which you suddenly left peaceful surroundings and discovered the battlefield. It was rather like walking on to a film set, the battle having skipped over the Bayeux area, having left no scars. Cheux looked as if somebody had pulled it down with a big rake. The whole place smelt of Camembert cheese and dead cows."

The Battalion spent nearly a fortnight round La Gaule, patrolling forward by night to the aerodrome and by day manning the slit trenches or resting in the ruined houses. The Germans kept a steady crump of shells and mortar bombs on the villages—nothing concentrated, but enough to keep the Battalion awake and to cause twelve casualties in as many days. The Battalion's main task was to make a "firm base" for a Canadian attack on the aerodrome, for they were still the audience in the theatre. They watched the Canadians attack on 4th July, saw the bombing of Caen by 460 Lancasters on the evening of the 7th and heard the artillery and naval barrage for the 1st Corps attack the following morning. "Interruption here for the most marvellous spectacle," wrote one officer in the middle of a letter. "A lovely turquoise evening with a grand sunset and hundreds of our four-engine Lancasters going in on a medium level attack on German positions to the south-east of us. I can see squadrons going in away to the east, wheeling over the target through the anti-aircraft fire and coming out right over our heads. It has been going on for twenty minutes, and I can see scores more away in the distance still coming in. Fighters are chasing busily about overhead, seeming not to have much to do, though one (nationality unknown) came spinning down ten miles away half an hour ago. We are near enough to see, with glasses, the actual bombs leaving the aircraft. Must go and watch again. It is getting a bit darker now, and they seem to have shifted their aim farther west. I can see at least sixty over me at a time coming out ; the stream seems endless." And the next day the writer concluded : "It was all a prelude to the attack on Caen, of which the latest news is excellent. Had I not slept so soundly this morning I should have heard the barrage."

Caen fell on the 9th and the British advanced to the banks of the River Orne. "Some of us," wrote another officer, "went to Caen, not to fight, but as camp-followers and vultures, and were much, to our embarrassment, greeted with flowers and 'Vive, vive!'" How long the 'écrasé' population of Caen will enjoy the honeymoon feeling is doubtful. Certainly their more fortunate neighbours have got over their exultation. They are polite, make profits, and will be glad to see us go, just like the people anywhere in England, except that they—the French—are polite."

The time had now come for the Battalion to leave the auditorium and take to the stage. On the 11th July the 32nd Brigade moved back to join the rest of the Guards Armoured Division at St. Martin des Entrees, just outside Bayeux. The 3rd Battalion found itself "another nice orchard," where it was able to sun itself in peace, and prepared to take a leading part in Operation "Goodwood."

EN ROUTE TO NORMANDY

NORMANDY. A GERMAN "PANTHER" TANK

Face page 370

CAEN

CHEUX

Face page 371

CHAPTER III

Cagny

2nd and 3rd Battalions

FOR some days the R.A.S.C. drivers, the clerks at ration dumps, and the Pay Corps Officers had all been saying that the Commander-in-Chief, General Montgomery, was planning an immediate break-out of the Normandy bridgehead. It was well known, they said, that the Germans were weak and demoralized and that now there was nothing to prevent the armoured divisions from driving on into France. Rear-area rumours swing wildly between the extremes; for the men well behind the line final victory or total disaster is always just round the corner. But even the greatest tangle of inaccuracy and invention cannot conceal the obvious truth, and this time, as often, the bush telegraph reported correctly the fundamental fact. There was going to be another attack. On the 14th began a series of conferences, out of which finally emerged Operation "Goodwood." During the night of the 17th, three Armoured Divisions, the 7th, the 11th and the Guards Armoured, moved across to the north-east corner of the bridgehead. Captain Terence O'Neill, Intelligence Officer at 5th Brigade H.Q., was sufficiently impressed to write in his laconic War Diary, "The switching of a Corps of three armoured divisions in the course of one night is a bold plan which should succeed—at least initially." Like all tipsters, Captain O'Neill was wise to hedge.

The plan was bold and comparatively simple. Beyond Caen stretches the flat rolling country known to the staff as the Great Caen Plain. To the partial eyes of the planners, the countryside looked conveniently like Salisbury Plain or the Yorkshire Wolds. It was "good tank going," and "devilish like the desert from the air," on which the armoured divisions could fight a proper tank battle, applying the methods they had learnt in training. There is in fact enough difference to make any comparison extremely dangerous.

There is, for instance, no tall standing corn on Salisbury Plain. Furthermore, the Caen Plain is enclosed by high ground on both flanks ; on the right a noticeable ridge runs from Bourgebus to Falaise and on the left a line of wooded hills runs south-east from Troarn through Argences to the River Dives. The country between is moderately flat and stretches in gentle rolls into the heart of Normandy. It was undoubtedly much more suitable for armoured warfare than the close "Bocage" country farther west. Once across the River Orne, which was only a question of crossing a bridge, where 6 Parachute Division and 51 Division already held a small bridgehead, there was no natural obstacle to prevent the tanks pouring down this funnel to Falaise. This was precisely the object of the operation. The three armoured divisions, one behind the other, in the order 11th, Guards Armoured and 7th, could advance through the 51st Division positions, fan out, and by sheer weight of metal overwhelm the German defences round Cagny and Bourgebus. The Guards Armoured would then swing left and capture Vimont, while the two other divisions continued down south to Falaise.

The enemy's strength in the area was estimated to be only one bad infantry division, the 12th Air Force Division, composed largely of Poles and Asiatics captured from the Russians. The Royal Air Force promised to bomb these Mongols—as the French called them—out of existence. "After that," the Battalions were told, "it will be money for old rope. You will get in amongst the German Mobile Bath Units and Bakehouses." There was known to be a German Tank School and Repair Shop at Vimont, so "the only tanks you will see will be up on blocks and a few wobbly Mark IVs."

Operation "Goodwood" did not succeed. The Corps managed to advance six miles on an eight-mile front and killed or captured several thousand Germans, but it did not break out of the bridgehead. From the very start of the attack things went wrong. The whole plan was laid down on too rigid a time-table. To achieve surprise the three Armoured divisions should have struck at once, or at any rate, rapidly one after the other, so that the full weight of the armour fell crushingly on the Germans. As it was, the Guards Armoured and the 7th Armoured Divisions stuck to their time-table, while the 11th Armoured, being the leading division, raced ahead and so was alone when it first hit the unexpectedly strong opposition. The wretched German Infantry and the few tanks and anti-tank guns north of Cagny were indeed shattered by the bombing, but the guns and troops on the ridge behind the village and on either flank escaped the full effect of the bombing and remained strong enough to halt the armoured brigade of the

11th Division. This check gave the Germans time to bring up the tanks and self-propelled guns which they had held in reserve out of harm's way. After the chance of a quick break-through was gone, the Guards Armoured and the 7th Divisions simply piled up on the 11th Division. The area round Caen became a confused mass of tanks shooting in all directions, most of them not really knowing what they were doing or supposed to be doing. It was an admirable position for the Germans. The little rises in the ground and the occasional hedges, combined with the standing corn, gave excellent cover from which the "Tigers" and "Panthers" of their heavy tank battalions could shoot up the steady stream of Shermans as they came across the open country.

Both battalions spent the days and nights of the 16th and 17th preparing for their first battle. They knew how much store was set by this battle and its success by everyone from the Prime Minister downwards. The officers attended conference after conference, pored over the rolls of maps and bundles of air photographs, repeated the orders to themselves so often that they knew them practically by heart and then briefed their squadrons and companies. The 2nd Battalion officers told their tank-crews just what Lieut.-Colonel C. K. Finlay told them, "We are to leave our present harbour area—St. Martin des Entrees—this evening, drive thirty miles east, halt about day-break to fill up with petrol, have breakfast and rest, cross bridges over the Orne about half-past ten and follow the 11th Armoured Division to Cagny, where they lead straight on and we turn left. Within the Guards Armoured Brigade, the 2nd Grenadiers will lead to Cagny, with the 1st Coldstream on the right and ourselves on the left behind them ; from Cagny the 1st Coldstream will lead to Vimont with ourselves in support. Within the Battalion, the order of march is No. 3 Squadron, No. 2 Squadron, H.Q. Squadron and No. 1 Squadron. The 3rd Battalion will be just behind us at the beginning and will come up to join us when we have taken Vimont."

The night march was long and tiresome. The 2nd Battalion started at eight o'clock on the evening of the 17th and took the whole night to cover the thirty miles between St. Martin des Entrees and the newly-built bridges over the Caen canal and the River Orne. They crawled along a rough tank track—called "Rat" route—already ground to powder by the passage of the 2nd Grenadiers and 1st Coldstream. Clouds of dust choked the crews and half-blinded the drivers, who had only white tapes and an occasional muffled light to guide them. Three tanks and three lorries got stuck in an unexpected bog by a little stream. The special recovery tanks and Captain Ronald

Robertson hauled them back on to the track and moved on again. The Armoured Brigade in one long column reached the River Orne before dawn and halted with the leading Grenadier tank four miles short of the bridges. The tanks of the 11th Division were ahead of them, hiding under the wrecked gliders that had been there since D Day. (No tank was to cross the River Orne until the bombing had started, in case the Germans should be alarmed. It was not explained what the Germans could do about it, anyway.) At four o'clock in the morning of the 18th, the 2nd Battalion switched off their engines and climbed wearily out of their tanks to "top up" with petrol.

The 3rd Battalion did not leave St. Martin till one o'clock in the morning. "Reveille" was at midnight for those who had the time to go to sleep. After a breakfast of sausages and tea, they strapped on their equipment and packed themselves into the large troop-carrying lorries. Sitting up stiffly, with their rifles between their knees and their heads nodding with sleep they bumped across a different, but equally dusty, track. "The men looked like harem women," said Lieut.-Colonel J. O. E. Vandeleur, "with handkerchiefs rolled over their faces to save themselves from choking." The 3rd Battalion was leading the 32nd Brigade, and so came up immediately behind the 2nd Battalion.

The day dawned bright and fine. The guns were already in action, and as the early sun dissolved the mists the R.A.F. began their work. For nearly an hour aircraft streamed overhead to bomb Colombelles, Cagny and every village and wood east of the River Orne. At first there was considerable anti-aircraft fire, but as the bombing went on it died away. This was the first heavy air bombardment the battalions had seen and, being also for their special benefit, it was something "quite new, heartening and never to be forgotten." The unfortunate French farmers and villagers whose homes and lives were ruined are not likely to forget it either. After a few minutes the battalions got tired of looking at the bombers ; if it was light enough to bomb it was light enough for fires. The tank crews, who live in luxury by infantry standards, got out their petrol stoves ; the Guardsmen of the 3rd Battalion scraped up dust, poured petrol over it and threw a lighted match at the soggy heap. Little groups gathered round the fires and stoves, boiling strong tea in brew-cans and frying bully-beef. "You will shave this morning just the same as any other morning," said the Regimental Sergeant-Major. Officers and men shed their equipment and propped broken bits of looking-glass up on the tank tracks or queued up by the driving mirrors of trucks. With sleeves rolled up and ragged towels draped down their backs they lathered and scraped their faces with cold water till they glowed red in the morning sun. "There, now I'm smart enough to meet the Germans." Very few men in either battalion had ever been in battle before. No matter how many battles you have fought, the hours spent waiting to go into the attack are always tense. No amount of experience can remove the tightening of the stomach, though a drink of tea often can. People naturally react in different ways. Sometimes—in fact, often—they are already so tired that they can think of nothing but sleep and no farther ahead than the next hour or so during which they will be able to close their eyes. If comparatively fresh—for no one has ever had enough sleep—some are studiously calm, carefully reading some book or talking of non-military things; others take an abnormal interest in passing details, another man's equipment, a solitary bird, the clouds overhead or the efforts of a driver to turn a truck; others, and these are very common, are unnaturally gay, joking heavily about everything, chiefly death and wounds. The lucky men are those who are busy with last-minute preparations and have no time to think of anything else. Officers and non-commissioned officers are the luckiest, for they have other men to think about and look after; a Guardsman has only himself. In the Irish Guards, and probably in the whole British Army, nobody has ever heard any heroics or noble sentiments before a battle or indeed at any other time.

"There is no need to hurry; we won't move for about four hours," said Lieut.-Colonel K. Finlay. Relying on the March Table the Brigade Commander, Brigadier N. Gwatkin, had worked out the time at which the 11th Armoured Division should debouch on the Caen Plain. He wanted to give the battalions time to rest and then move forward steadily, instead of jerking along with irritating halts. At half-past seven the 11th Armoured Division went off with a rush. They passed over the bridges and through the 51st Division's positions much more quickly then had been expected, and at once came on dazed German tank crews who had been caught out of their tanks, and quite willing to surrender. Encouraged by this, their reconnaissance regiment, the Northamptonshire Yeomanry, put their boots down on the accelerators of their fast Cromwell tanks and raced away.

Meanwhile, the 5th Guards Brigade was still taking it easy. The B.G.S. (Chief Staff Officer of the Corps) was standing on the bridge over the River Orne, expecting the Brigade to follow immediately on the tail of the 11th. When they did not appear he began pacing up and down, shouting "Where is the Guards Armoured?" "We've lost the Guards Armoured. Can't wait for them. Order up the 7th." Sitting on the bridge with a wireless was the 5th Brigade Liaison Officer, Lieutenant Philip Miéville. He was trying to get on to Brigade H.Q., but the air was choked with messages and it was some time before he could get through. The first the 2nd Battalion heard of this was when another brigade liaison officer, Lieutenant J. Yerburg, appeared on a motor-cycle and told Colonel Finlay, "Start moving at eight o'clock." The time was then 0815. Quarter of an hour later the Brigade moved slowly off towards the bridge called "York." The 2nd Battalion, led by No. 3 Squadron, crawled along behind the Coldstreamers. The orders were passed from squadron to squadron: "The Battalion is to get into positions south of the Caen–Troarn railway, where it will be available for future action when the Grenadiers have contained Cagny and the Coldstreamers are headed for Vimont." Just as they were moving off the first German shells fell round them, without causing any damage or alarm. At the bridges the Brigade met the armoured brigade of the 7th Division, also trying to cross. It took some time to get both brigades across, but once they did get going they went fast and soon caught up on the 11th Armoured Division. But it was too late—two hours too late—for surprise had been lost. Instead of three armoured brigades attacking with one blow, it was the first one, then a long pause and finally the two others. The 11th Armoured Division afterwards said that they could have got through if only there had been someone on their left. But as it happened, the Reconnaissance Regiment, the Northamptonshire Yeomanry, were quite alone when they hit the German anti-tank screen of guns and an hour ahead even of their own armoured brigade.

The R.A.F. had broken up the German defences in Cagny itself and immediately north of the village, knocking out some 75-mm. guns and some multi-barrel mortars—"Moaning Minnies"—the crews of which were easily captured. The defensive belt in the thick country to the east and south of Cagny, however, and in high ground to the west was intact. These first-class troops now moved up from reserve, where they had escaped the bombing, to deal with the attack. They halted the Northamptonshire Yeomanry and the 29th Armoured Brigade with heavy casualties. As the 5th Brigade moved forward they could see the row of burning tanks west of Cagny.

It was about midday when the 2nd Battalion passed out of the British minefield and debouched on the broad plain of La Butte de Hogue. They were greeted by heavy shelling and mortaring. "Just as well to get the baptism of fire over early," wrote Captain Alec Crichton, the Adjutant of the 2nd Battalion, and well known as a thinking man. They drove slowly on, passing through a sort of alley-way three miles wide between two lines of flaming villages, bombed to ruins by the R.A.F. Between the road and railway to Troarn and the village of Cagny the ground swells up to form an exposed ridge from which the open wheat-fields run straight down to Cagny. Due north of Cagny, beneath the rest of the slope, lies the farm La Prieurie—Priory Farm. The Grenadiers crossed the road, passed the farm, leaving it on their left hand, and climbed to the top of the ridge. As soon as they came over the rise and started to run down towards Cagny they lost half a squadron of tanks. The Coldstreamers behind them tried the other flank in an effort to get through the narrow gap of good going north-east of Cagny, towards Vimont, but again were shot at from both sides. The Brigadier then decided to try and work the Coldstreamers round from the west and south while the Grenadiers dealt with Cagny.

Meanwhile the 2nd Battalion had reached the line of the Caen–Troarn road and railway, and could see in front of them nine Grenadier tanks in a row all burning smokily. Sitting on the railway firing in the direction of Banneville, a village two miles down the road, was a squadron of the 11th Armoured which should have been four or five miles farther south. The Germans in Banneville were naturally doing all they could to break up the attack by striking the attackers in the flank and harassing their rear with constant shell fire. They brought their anti-tank guns well forward into the wooded country on the left flank, from which they could fire straight down the road. The leading squadron started to cross the railway just north of Priory Farm. They had to take it very slowly, so as not to strip off their tracks on the lines, and then negotiate a deep cutting and bank. It was here that the Irish Guards lost their first tank, Lieutenant Denis Liddle's, hit by an unlocated tank or gun which was probably shooting from Banneville. No one was hurt and the tank was recovered later. Lieutenant Wilfred Dodd's troop pushed on towards the Priory Farm, but on reaching a hedge between it and the railway Sergeant Ferguson's tank was hit and set on fire—"brewed up." Sergeant Ferguson, Guardsman Winslow and Guardsman Hunt were killed, Guardsman Bennet badly burnt and wounded, and Lance-Corporal O'Hara missing, believed wounded. A few minutes later, Lance-Sergeant McNally's 17-pdr. Sherman—a "Firefly" (the name given to the one Sherman armed with a 17-pdr. in each troop)—was also hit. This was awkward for Lieutenant

Dodd, as only a 17-pdr. could pierce the heavy German armour. He had seen the source of the trouble, three Panthers sitting in the edge of the Priory Farm's orchard. He tried shooting 75-mm. armour-piercing shot, but to no effect, and so asked for the loan of one of the other Fireflies in the squadron. When reminiscing afterwards Lieutenant W. Dodd always muttered, "I could have got those Panthers."

Captain Paul Stobart, farther back, also spotted these Panthers, but again could not get a kill with his 75-mm. Both he and Lieutenant Dodd offered to climb on the back of any Firefly and point out the target. He actually did mount Squadron Sergeant-Major Parke's Firefly, aimed his gun and claimed that a cloud of white smoke resulted from his first shots. No "kill," however, was found later in the area. The whole of the squadron was now under mortar fire and busily exchanging shots with the Panthers. Captain John Dupree's tank was hit on the rear side of the turret by a mortar bomb, which damaged the tank but hurt no one inside. A glancing shot scooped a sliver of armour out of the front of Captain Michael O'Cock's tank and broke a track. The crew wisely baled out and took refuge in old German slit trenches along the railway line before the tank was hit again. Captain O'Cock was very indignant, "That first shot was obviously aimed at Paul Stobart."

The Grenadiers sent back word that they could not get on any farther by their route. There was obviously no point in sending more tanks up after them to be picked off as they came over the skyline, so the Battalion wheeled right and moved down along the railway line in an attempt to get into the village from the north-west instead of from the north. Here they met complete confusion. They could see the Grenadiers and a few straggling Coldstreamers in front of them, and on their immediate right some tanks of the 29th Armoured Brigade, all milling about and firing in every direction. Being without any definite orders from Brigade H.Q., each squadron found a position of its own and spent the afternoon exchanging shots with German tanks and guns in the direction of Emiéville, a village on the left flank, a mile south of Banneville.

The Battalion spent the early afternoon in this unsatisfactory exchange of shots. "It is a typical first battle. We are much too late and nobody had any local objectives," was Captain Stobart's pronouncement. With his earnest manner and lecturing habits he was inevitably called "The Beak." There was always an intellectual or political review in his pocket, from which he quoted extensively, but compared unfavourably with a magazine which he himself had owned and edited, at a steady financial loss, before the war. He was as solemn as an owl and as brave as a lion. Only the fact that there was a battle on, and that he was right, saved him on this occasion from being shouted down as on all others.

The official explanation of the Battalion's present activities was that it was covering the left flank as far as Emiéville, while the 32nd Brigade in their lorries moved up to the line of the road. If you had told them that at the time, they would have replied vaguely, "Oh, really ?" "Progress was disappointingly slow," says the official report. The Divisional Commander was continually on the air ordering the Brigade Commander, "You must get on." The Grenadiers eventually got into Cagny, but the Coldstreamers, on their right, could make no headway towards Vimont. The country between Cagny and Vimont was thick and close, and every second hedge seemed to be strongly held. The battalions had all looked at the air photographs, so the type of country was no surprise to them, though the official report of the battle says that it was. The real surprise was the strength of the enemy. "You must get on" was being dinned into the Brigadier. As a last effort, he decided to try again on the left of the Grenadiers and turned to his reserve battalion, the Irish. The Grenadiers had taken Cagny, but were not able to do anything more. The Coldstreamers had had singularly little success ; their first push towards Vimont on the left of the Grenadiers —that is north of Cagny—had failed, and when they had been moved round to the south side of Cagny to attack on the right of the Grenadiers they had again been halted. About five o'clock in the afternoon—the officers had watches and the men had stomachs, so they knew roughly what time it was—the Brigadier ordered Colonel Finlay to attack Vimont. "Follow the pylons," he said. From Caen a line of electricity pylons ran south-east across the railway line through the Battalion's positions and then obliquely across country past Cagny and Frenouville to Vimont. These orders were passed on literally to the squadron and troop commanders ; all they knew was that they were to drive to Vimont as fast as they could along the line of the pylons. Major Giles Vandeleur, the Second-in-Command, was dissatisfied. "There is too much ' allez-allez ' about the whole thing."

Cagny itself is a long, straggling village with the houses, as in an Irish village, scattered along the side of the main road from Caen to Vimont. East of Cagny the ground rises gently up to the low ridge which runs from Emiéville southwards, dominating the left flank and hiding Vimont. Between Cagny and the top of the ridge the ground was open. The top, however, was festooned with thick hedges which merge into a strip of wood just where the road from Cagny passes by the village of Frenouville, a mile farther south-east. The German tanks and tractor-drawn 88-mm. guns were established along this ridge ; it was from here that they had been shooting the Grenadiers in the flank as they advanced due south towards Cagny. Infantry and more guns were concentrated at the southern end of Frenouville and the strip of wood ; and it was they who had halted the Coldstreamers.

The squadrons formed up in a line ahead—No. 2, No. 1, Battalion H.Q., and No. 3 Squadron. In every tank the words were repeated again and again—"Follow the pylons." Lieutenant Anthony Dorman's troop led the Battalion down the slope, passing some Grenadier tanks, to a ford across a small stream. Crossing the stream, No. 2 Squadron raced off to climb the ridge north of the road. Major Nial O'Neill led his squadron (No. 1) farther south and crossed the road in Cagny before he swung left and headed for Frenouville. Half-way up the slope the leading troop of No. 2 Squadron came under fire from the bulge in the ridge round Emiéville. Lieutenant Anthony Dorman drove hastily into a little hollow, traversing his gun to the left to cover that flank. The squadron veered off to the right, while he unhooked his binoculars and prepared for one of the long-range gun duels he had heard so much about on training. Beginning his formal "anticipatory fire order," "Seventy-five, traverse left, fire when . . ." he ended "straight ahead, let him have it ! " A German 88-mm. gun tractor was backing noisily out of the hedge just forward of the crest 300 yards away. With one shot the gunner destroyed it, and Lieutenant Dorman started his formal order once again. When No. 2 Squadron reached this hedge farther to the right, they halted to let No. 1 Squadron in the orchards south-east of Cagny come up level with them. Then, together, they plunged forward to fight their way into Frenouville. Major John Madden, No. 2 Squadron commander, only now noticed that his second troop was missing. "What has happened to John Gorman ?"

Lieutenant John Gorman had bogged his tank while crossing the stream and his troop had stayed with him. It was firmly stuck, and there was nothing to do but leave it there and transfer himself into "Ballyragget," one of his two other 75-mm. tanks. By the time he had cautiously negotiated the stream there was no sign of the rest of the squadron. He could get no reply to his wireless appeals—"the air was bedlam"—so, being a simple, straightforward young man, he put his head down and charged straight ahead. As he came up the hill he saw Lieutenant Dorman busily engaging the gun tractor and another gun. "Where are they ?" shouted Gorman. Dorman, interested only in Germans, waved towards the hill. Happy again, Gorman continued up the hill—if he did not find the squadron there at least he would be able to look round for them. Dorman watched him go, wondering what "Blockhead" Gorman was up to, but he soon thought of something else when he was wounded in the foot by a mortar bomb.

Lieutenant John Gorman, earnestly following the pylons, struck the lane from Cagny to Emiéville and swung cheerfully up it with his second tank just behind him. As he came over the brow he gave a wild cry "Gunner ! " Two hundred yards away were four German tanks—a Royal Tiger, an old-fashioned Tiger, a Panther and an old Mark IV—"having a conference they were, sitting in the middle of the field." The Germans were equally surprised and were all facing in the wrong direction. "Gun's jammed, sir." Guardsman Schole's voice was despairing. "Oh, Christmas, why ?" The nearest German tank was slowly traversing its massive gun. It was a Royal Tiger, the first seen on the Western Front. "Driver, ram ! " shouted Gorman, and Lance-Corporal Baron saw what he must do. "Ballyragget" crashed through the thin hedge and careered down the slope towards the Tiger. It slid down beside the long barrel of the 88-mm. and struck the Tiger at the rear of its right track. The muzzle of the 88 projected two feet beyond the Sherman, so Gorman and crew were like birds sitting on a sportsman's gun. The Tiger's crew jumped out with their hands up ; but the other Germans turned their attention to the second Sherman. Sergeant Harbinson, its commander, hadn't a chance. Three shots struck it as it came over the crest and it burst into flames. The driver, Lance-Corporal Watson, and operator, Guardsman Davis, were killed instantly, and the three others wounded and burnt. Guardsmen Melville and Walsh were able to climb out, but only Walsh had the strength to go back again into the blazing hull and extricate the dying Sergeant Harbinson.

This distraction gave Lieutenant Gorman and his crew a moment to get away from the tanks and run to a cornfield on the other side of the lane. "Corporal Baron." "Sir." "Melville." "Sir." "Scholes." "Sir." "Agnew"—there was no reply. The voices of the driver, co-driver and gunner all answered from the depths of the corn, but there was no sign of the operator. In a minute he came crashing through the corn to join them. Guardsman Agnew was the last man out of the tank. As he dropped to the ground he saw four men running for a ditch and promptly joined them. They were the German crew; after an exchange of cold stares, Agnew moved out to join his own side.

When Lieutenant John Gorman got an idea into his head he clung to it stubbornly. His present idea was to destroy those German tanks. "You stay here while I get a Firefly," and he slid away, leaving Lance-Corporal Baron and the Guardsmen lying in the cornfield. They lay there in the corn for some time and then began to crawl. They must have crawled in the wrong direction—which is easy enough to do when all you can see is a jungle of stalks—for they got caught in an artillery barrage. They continued to crawl till Melville and Scholes were both wounded by shell splinters. Corporal Baron beat down the bloodstained, shell-torn corn to make a rough bed and stayed to guard and tend his wounded friends until they were picked up by a passing tank. Lieutenant Gorman walked back alone to the orchards round Cagny. There he found what he wanted, his own 17-pdr. gun, which alone would penetrate the heavy armour of a Tiger or Panther. It looked undamaged, but there was no sign of life in or around it. He hammered on the hull. "Sergeant! Sergeant Workman!" A face popped out of the turret. "He's inside, sir. He is dead, sir." The solid shot that killed the Troop Sergeant had thrown his body back on top of the crew, but had left them and the tank undamaged. They lifted out the poor body and Lieutenant Gorman clambered in through the turret. It was no use trying to report to Squadron H.Q. — the air was full of voices all reporting "hornets"—so he returned on his "remount" to the battle.

Lieutenant Anthony Dorman had by now moved up to the ridge and was sitting there nursing his foot and directing the fire of his tank. In Wiltshire he had spent most of his time on training studying dippers and writing long letters to *The Field* describing the peculiar habits of these birds. But now, in Normandy, "Dipper" Dorman was busy watching "hornets"—the trade name for enemy tanks—and had little time for nature study. Gorman knew exactly where the "hornets" were. Covered by Dorman he moved cautiously forward, avoiding the lane this time and following the line of a thick hedge. The hedge reached up above the level of the turret, so he nosed the Firefly gently forward through it till he could just see the Germans. "Gunner." Five shots went high and wide, rocketing up into the sky. The gunner's hand was shaking and the sights were smeared with blood, but five misses in succession was too much. "Take it easy, boy, and have a go at the old Tiger." The gunner was years older than he, but Lieutenant John Gorman had the paternal manner of a policeman, for he had been reared in, and was going back to, the Royal Ulster Constabulary. The gunner took a deep breath and tried again. "Well done! Two hits on the turret; now put one into the new Tiger." Three seconds later both the disabled Tiger and the Sherman were burning brightly. The following day, and the following year, they were still there, to be seen by the curious. Lieutenant Gorman, like every other tank officer, had often been told that naval tactics applied to armour, but he was the only one who practised this theory literally. It was a remarkable sight—the Sherman jammed into the side of the Tiger, its turret only a few inches from the barrel of the 88-mm. gun. The German gunner had a power traverse to swing his heavy gun, and given another second he could have blown the Sherman to pieces, but he saw it just too late. In size there is not really much to choose between a Tiger and a Sherman, but at close quarters the Tiger completely overshadows the Sherman. It is indeed a few inches taller, but it is the length of the 88-mm. gun and the general impression of massive power that seem to crush the Sherman.

As too many Germans were now firing at him from all directions, Lieutenant Gorman reversed out of the hedge and turned back to look for Sergeant Harbinson and his crew. He found them by their burnt-out tank and carried them back to the Regimental Aid Post. In his search for the Regimental Aid Post, he found the tanks of Brigade H.Q. lined up in a wood by Cagny. "This made me feel I was very far back," he said. "It was a most confusing day."

After Colonel Finlay had launched the Battalion against Vimont he could exert little control over the attack, which dissolved into isolated games of hide-and-seek among the corn stacks and hedges. He was being blinded by the "fog of war"—the mass of conflicting details out of which he could not make a clear picture of the battle as a whole. He told the Adjutant, Captain A. Crichton, to lead him back to the Brigadier, but by the time Captain Crichton had found Brigade H.Q., parked in the middle of two divisional headquarters, all in the same field by Cagny, Colonel Finlay was thoroughly confused. The squadrons reported "hornets" everywhere. It was difficult to say exactly how many there were, but since at least the 503 Heavy Tank Regiment had been identified they were clearly "not a force to fool around with," as Colonel Finlay explained to the Brigadier. The leading squadrons, Nos. 1 and 2, had run up against a defensive screen of tanks and anti-tank guns concealed in the woods and hedges between Emiéville and Frenouville. "You must get on," said the Brigadier, and Colonel Finlay went off to try again.

The evening was drawing in, but there was still time for one more effort. No. 1 Squadron covered Frenouville and the 25-pdrs. shelled the cross-roads by the village, while No. 3 Squadron moved round the left flank with orders to "push on to the next bit of bocage." This order might mean practically anything, for from the forward crest of the ridge back to Vimont the frequent thick hedges, small fields and clumps of trees made the whole countryside "bocage," but the squadron took it to mean that they were to get on as far as they could. No. 3 Squadron came up into line on No. 2's left rear, and moved slowly forward. In the failing light the tanks were on top of each other before they fired. "I was brought up on indirect shooting at two miles range. None of this fifteen yards business," said Lieutenant Arther Cole. He and Captain Paul Stobart between them destroyed two anti-tank guns and their half-track towing vehicles. On the extreme left, Squadron Sergeant-Major Parkes and Lance-Sergeant Venables fought an engagement with a Panther and eventually destroyed it. On the right, No. 1 Squadron also moved forward. They got into the outskirts of Frenouville, but there they were halted, losing one tank in which Guardsmen Forbes and O'Sullivan were badly wounded. Lieutenant Michael Callender avenged the loss by killing a self-propelled 75-mm. gun and its crew, but the Germans maintained their lead and position by destroying Sergeant Andrew's Firefly. Since only a 17-pdr. could deal properly with the Germans Sergeant Andrews had pushed forward, but his tank was hit and he himself slightly wounded by an 88-mm. firing across from the wood on the left of the road. The same group of guns—for this 88-mm. was but one of a cluster—held up Nos. 2 and 3 Squadrons, knocking out Sergeant Robinson's tank when he tried to rush them. The "S.S. Krauts" who manned the tanks and guns were first-class troops holding a first-class position. "They knew their 'kit,'" as the Battalion said, and in their Tigers and Panthers had much better "kit" than the Shermans. In particular their gun-sights were excellent, a triumph of German technical skill, and gave them a great initial advantage. They could sit tight, tucked into a hedge or ditch, and wait for a Sherman to move, knowing that only a 17-pdr. could harm them, and confident that with their sights they could guarantee a hit with a gun that would penetrate and probably "brew up" any British or American tank.

At half-past nine, after night had closed on the battlefield, the Battalion received the order, "No further advance." This, being interpreted, meant that they withdrew to harbour in a tight triangle—or zareba, as the old Palestine and Africa soldiers insisted on calling it—just over the stream in the south-east outskirts of Cagny. The position at nightfall thus was that the three armoured battalions of the Division were established in and around Cagny, but that the Germans firmly held the left flank, and every attempt to go round Cagny on either side had failed. The Battalion now had time to count the score. Their total was one Royal Tiger and one Panther definitely destroyed, an ordinary Tiger and another Panther hit, but left in enemy hands, two 88-mm. and two 75-mm. anti-tank guns destroyed and one captured by Lieutenant Goodbody's reconnaissance troop in the Priory Farm. The Royal Tiger was the first seen in the West and the higher formations at first refused to believe in its existence. There was a lot of wreckage lying around Cagny, which the Battalion could not claim, as the R.A.F., gunners and 2nd Grenadiers had all contributed to it. The bag of prisoners was naturally small—eleven men, including one Feldwebel from the 125 Panzer Grenadier Regiment and the 503 S.S. Heavy Tank Battalion, both under command of the 21st Panzer Division. "Awful Krauts they were," said Lieutenant Eamon FitzGerald, who had to interrogate them, "stuffed with obscene postcards, and trying to ingratiate themselves. They said they all knew the war was now lost, so I said why did you try to kill us half an hour ago ? I don't care much for the smell either of Germans or of death. After searching the corpses for pay-books, I can understand Lady Macbeth's bad dreams, and as all the perfumes of Arabia were not available, it took half a bar of Naafi soap." One of the prisoners had on him a letter from his girl friend, a very indignant letter, because he had evidently told her that, after the war, an S.S. man would have as many women as fingers, and that she was very lucky to be one of them ; she took pains to point out that she was not that kind of girl.

It was a restless night for the 2nd Battalion, disturbed by mortaring, the difficulty of bringing up supplies and a stream of orders and counter-orders. The Battalion Medical Officer, Captain Ripman, had lost his vehicles by shelling during the day and was now reduced to his own feet, but he succeeded somehow in evacuating the casualties. The Battalion waited impatiently for petrol, ammunition and food. "Where the hell is Claud Hamilton ? I told him to bring F.2 Echelon up to Cagny at dusk." Colonel Kim Finlay was raging, and so was the Intelligence Officer, Lieutenant E. N. FitzGerald, when he was sent out to find the echelon. The dark plain was dotted with burning tanks and trucks. Lieutenant FitzGerald bumped across the tracks in his scout car towards a bright cluster of fires by Le Mesnil Fremental. As he guessed, it was the echelon. At four o'clock in the afternoon Captain The Lord Claud Hamilton, the commander, had been ordered off the track by Brigade H.Q. into a field, and sat there in company of the echelons of three armoured brigades in full view till the Germans could be bothered to shell the closely packed trucks. The drivers were only too glad to move up to the Battalion, though the tracks were abominable and the German snipers active. Leading the echelon into Cagny, Lieutenant FitzGerald met Lieut.-Colonel J. O. E. Vandeleur, the Commanding Officer of the 3rd Battalion, tramping around on his reconnaissance looking for someone to tell him something.

The 3rd Battalion had arrived in Cagny after a cross-country march in the pitch dark, led on a compass bearing by Colonel "Joe" Vandeleur. They had spent the morning and afternoon moving slowly forward in their T.C.Vs. behind the 2nd Battalion. The long line of trucks curled its way through the minefields, passing "flocks of hefty German prisoners looking damn surly." As they passed out of the old bridgehead, the first shells came down astride the track and everyone "sat very still with their fingers crossed." Captain Ian Grant, No. 1 Company commander, sitting inside the cab of his truck was wounded by splinters and died the following day. They moved on through increasingly heavy shelling and mortaring till they reached a wood short of the railway line, and there debussed. "The spectacle ahead of us was complete confusion—knocked-out tanks of the 11th Armoured Division in serried rows. The general directive was to shove on." Straight in front of them they could see the blazing ruin that had been Priory Farm, so, taking their 15-cwt. trucks with them, but leaving the troop-carriers in the wood, they marched towards the farm. "La Prieurie" was a solid stone farm-house based on the original buildings of a Benedictine priory founded in 1022. The barn, which was formerly the chapel, still has a magnificent Norman arch doorway. The priory was an off-shoot of Caen Abbey and, according to the old farmer's wife, is connected with Caen by an underground tunnel. The Battalion could have saved themselves a lot of trouble, she told them, if they had come by the tunnel, but she admitted that nobody had ever found it. The farm had been bombed and shelled into ruins and was burning fiercely. When the 3rd Battalion reached it, it was being shelled by both sides, British and German. "Open fields and thick hedgerows, smell of Camembert cheese, dead cows and plenty of dead Germans," was how it appeared to Colonel "Joe" Vandeleur. The Battalion started to dig themselves in among the fields and paddocks around the farm and hid the trucks under trees and alongside walls. It took the companies about an hour and a half's hard digging to get well

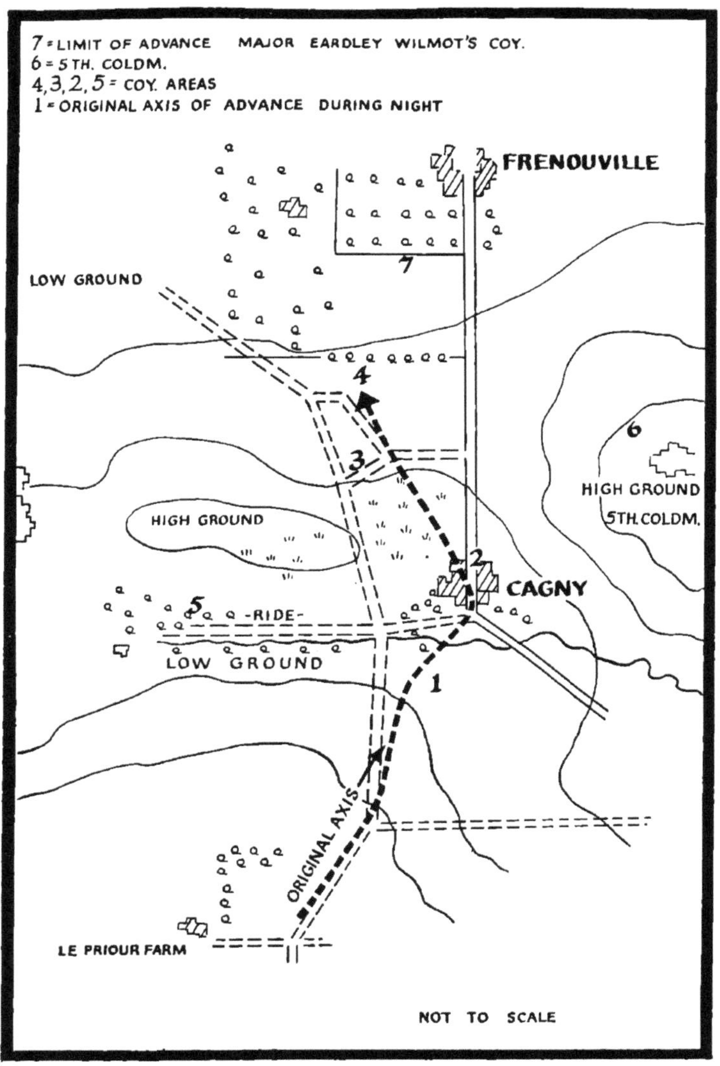
7 = LIMIT OF ADVANCE MAJOR EARDLEY WILMOT'S COY.
6 = 5TH. COLDM.
4, 3, 2, 5 = COY. AREAS
1 = ORIGINAL AXIS OF ADVANCE DURING NIGHT
FRENOUVILLE
7
LOW GROUND
4
6
3
HIGH GROUND
5TH. COLDM.
HIGH GROUND
2
CAGNY
5
-RIDE-
LOW GROUND
1
ORIGINAL AXIS
LE PRIOUR FARM
NOT TO SCALE

CAGNY

below the ground and then, of course, they were ordered to move.

It was after nine o'clock, and rapidly getting dark, when Colonel "Joe" Vandeleur "received a directive to move to a village called Frenouville, said to be in our hands and screened by the 2nd Battalion. At this time a sort of private battle was going on a few hundred yards to our left, and most of the 'overs' seemed to be coming to us. We had no idea of the situation ahead of us, but could hear Spandau fire." The Battalion formed up by companies in a large paddock and started out to Frenouville, leaving the trucks and carriers in the farm to be brought up later by the Adjutant, Captain Hugh Neilson. Major Anthony Eardley-Wilmot led off his company, No. 2, on a compass bearing, followed by No. 1 Company, now commanded by Captain Angus McCall. It was already pitch dark and nobody was quite sure of the direction, but they set their compasses on a fixed bearing for a night march and hoped for the best. The leading companies were well under way when the Battalion received a change of orders. It was impossible to recall Major Anthony Eardley-Wilmot; he and his company had already set out "at a lively pace and were not seen or heard of again until the next morning." The rear of No. 1 Company was retrieved, but the rest of it, with Captain Angus McCall, disappeared into the dark with No. 2. Colonel "Joe" Vandeleur collected the remaining company commanders behind a tank, propped his map up on it, and gave out the new orders. The gist of them was that the Battalion was now to move to Cagny first and then to Frenouville. "Never," he says, "was there more confusion at the start of an operation, and it steadily increased during the night. Everybody laughed when the tank drove off with the map." Colonel Joe retrieved his map, got out his compass, and led the way across country, with "X" Company—the Scots Guards Company—stumbling along behind him. When they reached Cagny they found "bomb craters as big as London buses, and stone walls surrounding the village like an old-fashioned fort; burst drains, stink of dead cattle and dead Germans everywhere. To further enliven proceedings some German fighters swept down in the moonlight with their cannons roaring. The place was like Dante's inferno. 'X' Company got all tied up in the pitch dark amongst the appalling ruins. To rectify the situation No. 4 Company, under Major Desmond Reid, passed through 'X' Company and gingerly worked their way through Cagny. Suddenly the whistle of bullets came straight down our only road, and it was fairly clear that Frenouville was held. The axis was changed on to a compass-bearing parallel to the road, and the whole Battalion marched forward in single file, like a lot of niggers going through the bush. We wound our way through standing corn for more than three hundred yards when the crack of Spandau and flash of small arms loomed straight ahead. Very lights and star-shells shot into the sky and every form of unpleasantness opened up on us, including those wicked old beasts, the 'Moaning Minnies.' To make things worse it was painfully obvious that our own troops, including some enthusiastic 2-inch mortar crews, were also shooting at us. However, luck came our way. We had inadvertently moved through a screen of our 2nd Battalion, who gave us some sound advice. It is not easy to cast a plan in the dark, so I spun a coin instead—heads, move forward in Wellington style, bayonet to bayonet; tails, consolidate where we were. Luckily it came down tails so, with the assistance of a drill-sergeant's pace-stick (metaphorical), we hatched out some form of defensive lay-out and dug like beavers. Many of us were so dog tired that we had lost all interest except sleep."

The headquarters of the two battalions, 2nd and 3rd, were together amongst the tombstones of Cagny cemetery. All night the Germans shelled Cagny and also Priory Farm where Captain Hugh Neilson, the 3rd Battalion Adjutant, was still waiting with the Battalion's transport. The doctor, Captain Thin, who had been left behind there, spent an uncomfortable night smoking under a jeep. "I suppose I slept a bit," he said, "but I was certainly woken at first light by some shells coming down, apparently from behind us. They fell closer and closer, and I got more and more frightened, and then, thank God, they lifted. At that very moment I was called over to Hugh Neilson's trench." A shell had fallen in the trench, killing Lance-Corporal Stock, an Orderly-Room clerk, and Guardsman Farrow, and wounding Captain Neilson. Anywhere seemed better than Priory Farm, so Lieutenant Eric Udal took the transport up to join the Battalion in Cagny.

"When dawn broke," wrote Colonel Joe, "the Battalion looked like a crowd at a football match, but by the mercy of Providence the leading elements were about three feet behind the reverse slope. Sergeant Kelly and his snipers were off at the crack of dawn, but met a nasty reception committee." The 2nd Battalion tanks, however, moved up to support the infantry, so the position, though exposed, was secure. No. 2 Company was still missing, and there was no news of it till Major Eardley-Wilmot rose out of a ditch to say that his company was sharing with the Germans the hedges short of Frenouville.

No. 2 Company had walked straight into the Germans. Major

Eardley-Wilmot had set his compass on a bearing that should take him to the main road opposite Frenouville, and his navigation was good. They crossed the open country in single file and then halted and closed up, while Sergeant Cooke took his section forward to find the way into the village. Just as Sergeant Cooke reached the hedge along the road a German light machine-gun opened fire. He emptied the magazine of his Sten gun in the direction of the flashes; the light machine-gun went on firing. "Section down," he shouted and rushed the post. He got the German machine-gunner by the throat and throttled the life out of him. Before he died the German bit Sergeant Cooke in the arm ; the bite went septic. Other Spandaus opened up and a storm of bullets swept over from the far side of the road. One bullet went straight through Captain Alec Hendry's boot without touching his foot. "That doesn't happen twice, sir," said a Guardsman, and Alec Hendry was left wondering what exactly he meant. It was painfully obvious that the company had walked accidentally into the middle of the Germans. The Guardsmen unhooked their entrenching tools and dug for dear life, well knowing that anybody that was not below ground before daylight was "for it." Squatting in their holes, with their chins on their knees, they waited for the dawn, while Major Eardley-Wilmot wondered how he was going to let Battalion H.Q. know where he was. The wireless-set was broken ; a runner would certainly lose his way in the dark and was almost equally certain to be killed in the light. Somebody had to go back, so as soon as it was light enough to see, Major Eardley-Wilmot crawled along the ditch back to Cagny. He found Colonel Joe, arranged for the gunners to shower smoke-shells all round his company, and crawled back to lead them back himself. He said himself that he had no idea what was happening, but that luckily neither had the Germans.

Major Eardley-Wilmot was recommended for an immediate Military Cross, but he did not live to receive the award, the first won by the 3rd Battalion.

Meanwhile, the two battalions were busy preparing for another attack on Vimont. Just before nine o'clock, when the attack was due to start, the Corps Commander ordered "No further advances," and told the Division to hold a firm base in the Cagny area "pending a further plan." This further plan did not involve either of the battalions. In the evening the 2nd Battalion handed over their positions to the 1st Armoured Coldstream and withdrew to a field between Priory Farm and the Cagny–Demouville road for a good night's rest. The 3rd Battalion remained where they were for the next four days. Their battle had now become a defensive one. They held Cagny while other battalions of the Guards Division and the 11th and 7th Divisions continued to attack to the south and west. They made some slight advances, capturing Le Poirier, Frenouville and Four Bourgebus, but any remaining hope of a great break-out was finally crushed when the weather broke on the afternoon of the 20th. In an hour the hot sunshine and blinding dust changed into torrential rain and clogging mud. The rain brought on a plague of mosquitoes. Soaking wet and bitten all over, the 3rd Battalion spent their days being constantly shelled, mortared and sniped, and their nights out on patrol. The only vehicles that could get through the sea of mud were the carriers, so the whole supply of food and ammunition and the evacuation of the wounded depended on Captain Desmond Kingsford and his carrier platoon. The constant shelling and patrolling made casualties inevitable ; during these days the 3rd Battalion lost 13 killed, 35 wounded and four men missing. Late at night on the 22nd the Battalion handed over Cagny and moved back to Faubourg de Vaucelles over tracks made almost impassable by the rain. By four o'clock the following morning most of them were back and stretched out in the mud, ready to sleep all day. "The one lesson we learnt at Cagny," said Colonel Joe, "was, needless to say, the old one of the futility of a night advance over unreconnoitred ground."

The 3rd Battalion spent three days at Vaucelles on a plateau just out of view of the Germans. Captain Angus McCall had somehow ruptured himself and had to be evacuated, so Captain D. Kingsford took over No. 1 Company, with Captain Peter Doyle as his second-in-command. Two new platoon commanders joined from the first reinforcements, Lieutenant Cyril Russell and Lieutenant Edward Ryder. The Battalion was occasionally shelled by day and usually bombed by night, but on the whole they were better placed than the 2nd Battalion round Mandeville.

The 2nd Battalion had remained in full view of the Germans ever since they left Cagny. They had first dug in amid oats and puddles in the middle of a heavy gun line ; the noise, though heartening, had made sleep very difficult. They then moved to an exposed forward slope, just south of Colombelles—a housing estate for the Caen factory workers. Admittedly there was little choice of harbour areas, but this one was peculiarly unpleasant. Most of the houses had been completely destroyed and the ground pitted with bomb-craters made by the R.A.F. before the earliest attack on Caen. The transport was shelled as it moved in, and Guardsman Griffin was mortally wounded. The tanks drove down into the craters, which gave some cover, but were so wide that they gave no great protection against the German mortars or anti-personnel fragmentation bombs. So for safety, the crews built parapets of mud round the tanks at the bottom of the craters. Here they lived, gloomily brewing tea, writing letters on sodden pieces of paper, and twice a day collecting vegetables from the allotments round the houses to put in their bully-beef stew. The nightly air-raids destroyed men and vehicles monotonously, while a plague of mosquitoes interrupted peaceful slumber. The Battalion was kept in this unpleasant area because the 2nd Canadian Corps was planning an attack and wanted the Guards Armoured Division to exploit its presumed success. Both battalions were kept on two hours' notice, which meant that they could not even go and call on each other. On the 25th the 2nd Battalion actually started off to join the Canadians, but the attack was held up and the Battalion spent the day sitting by the roadside till they were told to go home. The Germans then turned their full attention to the Canadians so that night the battalions got the best sleep that they had had so far. The next day the sun came out again ; the Americans began advancing in the west of the bridgehead. Everyone felt a little better, particularly as officers and men from the two battalions were at last able to exchange visits and compare reminiscences of "Dead Man's Gulch" at Cagny.

However, they soon got very bored with the battle panorama spread out before them, the odd burnt-out tank and the occasional shell. Lieutenant Chaine-Nickson was killed on the 27th by one of these occasional shells. "Michael Chaine-Nickson can ill be spared" says the War Diary. "He was a skilful officer." His troop buried him just by the road-side, and collected bunches of flowers to lay on his grave. After this Colonel Finlay got very worried about dispersion and ordered the officers to break up all "coffee housing" groups. "The last straw now is that the Officers' Mess truck has gone—the sole solace of a weary man." The writer ended his letter sadly. "It has now begun to rain again."

CHAPTER IV

Caumont

2nd and 3rd Battalions

THE Battle of Caumont and the Bocage started on 30th July. During the previous weeks, while the British and Canadians had been holding the Caen hinge and occupying the best of the German troops, the Americans had been landing their Third Army and preparing to break out on the other side of the bridgehead. To free more Americans for this drive southward and eastward into Brittany, the British extended their line to the west and took over the Caumont sector from the Americans. This mobile Third American Army, under the unique General Patton, went off with a rush. They captured Coutances at the base of the Cotentin peninsula on the 28th and drove rapidly south, leaving a long, exposed flank trailing behind them. The Germans, naturally, wished to stop this advance and began to move across westward from the Caen area to strike the Americans in the flank. At the moment they could easily drive across behind their own forward troops until they ran into the unprotected American supply trucks racing down the road from St. Lo. To prevent this the Allies had to break through the German defensive positions south and east of Caumont and force another salient southward between the exposed American flank and the approaching German armour. Two British corps and an American corps were therefore ordered to attack at once in the Caumont sector. On the 28th the Guards Armoured Division rejoined 8th Corps. They were told, on arrival, that there had never been much activity in the Caumont sector ; the German defensive position might be well organized, but it could only be held by second-rate troops. 8th Corps was to attack in the centre down the main road from Caumont through St. Martin des Besaces and Le Tourneur, with the other British corps on their left and the American corps on the right. Within 8th Corps, the 15th (Scottish) Division, supported by the 6th Guards Tank Brigade and the 11th Armoured Division, were to take St. Martin and the ridge on which it stands six miles south of Caumont on the first day, after which the Guards Armoured Division was to pass through St. Martin and capture Estry, Vassy and Condé-sur-Noireau while the 11th Armoured Division advanced on their right.

The country stretching south from Caumont is typical Normandy bocage. The literal translation of "bocage" is a "thicket" or a "copse," and originally the country was one big forest. Now, however, it is cut up into a close patchwork of fields, woods, orchards and farmhouses. The fields are small by the English standards and seem to have been dug out of the original earth, for each one is enclosed by steep banks on top of which grow thick hedges often eight feet high. If you stand on the high ground behind Caumont, you can see the country in a pattern of dark and light greens stretching southwards with a series of pronounced ridges. Innumerable streams run in all directions; on the hill-sides their banks were steep and wooded, but in the valley they spread themselves to form a narrow and treacherous marsh. The villages and farms scattered over the countryside were built of solid stone and had been standing for centuries; it took a lot of shelling to knock them down. The Germans had fortified some of these places to make local strong-points, but their main defences were carefully dug in the woods and hedgerows so that they could not be picked out of the general landscape. Through this tangle of woods, streams and fields the lanes and country roads threaded their tortuous way from farm to farm; sometimes they appeared in the open, but usually they were sunk below the level of the surrounding fields, barely wide enough to take an Army truck, but too wide for a tank to cross. The main road was the only one suitable for two-way traffic.

Cagny had shown that the original orthodox formation of an Armoured Division—one exclusively tank brigade and one infantry brigade—was quite unsuitable. The armoured brigade had outstripped the infantry, which had no chance to close up and influence the battle. "In this part of the world," wrote the Divisional Commander, Major-General A. Adair, D.S.O., M.C., "we were seldom likely to find ideal tank country, and somehow we had to evolve a system whereby the infantry was right up with the tanks." The system adopted was to unite the tank and infantry battalions to form "Bocage Battle Groups." The brigades were accordingly reorganized

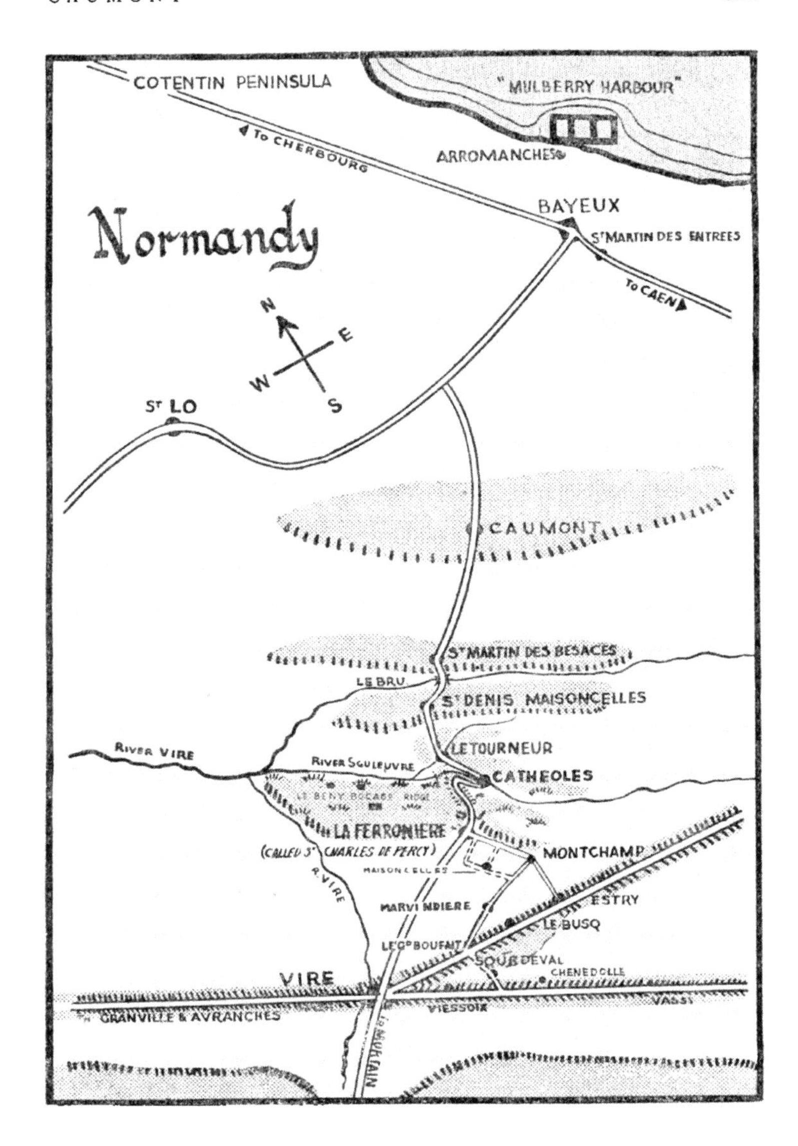
COTENTIN PENINSULA
"MULBERRY HARBOUR"
To CHERBOURG
ARROMANCHES
BAYEUX
Normandy
ST MARTIN DES ENTREES
To CAEN
N
E
W
S
ST LO
CAUMONT
ST MARTIN DES BESACES
LE BRU
ST DENIS MAISONCELLES
LE TOURNEUR
River VIRE
River Souleuvre
CATHEOLES
LA FERRONIERE
(CALLED ST CHARLES DE PERCY)
MONTCHAMP
R. VIRE
MARVINDIERE
ESTRY
LE BUSQ
SOURDEVAL
CHENEDOLLE
VIRE
GRANVILLE & AVRANCHES
VIESSOIX
VASSY
MORTAIN

so that the 5th Brigade consisted of two groups, one made up of the 1st Battalion and the 2nd (Armoured) Bn. Grenadier Guards, and the other of the 5th Bn. Coldstream and the 2nd (Armoured) Bn. Irish Guards, and the 32nd Brigade also consisted of two groups, one made up of the 1st (Armoured) Bn. Coldstream Guards and the 3rd Bn. Irish Guards, and the other of the 1st and 2nd (Reconnaissance) Welsh Guards. This is a rationalized account of a regrouping that was actually done in ninety flurried minutes on the main road to Caumont. The group in which the 2nd Battalion fought the Battle of the Bocage was based on the immediate convenience of the first of those ninety minutes, when the 5th Bn. Coldstream Guards happened to be in the next field to it. The two Irish Guards battalions, as a result, remained in different brigades and saw little of each other during the rest of the fighting in Normandy.

The British attack began at five to seven on the morning of 30th July. At about the same time the 2nd Battalion left the gloomy desolation of Colombelles and drove across to Bayeux to join the 3rd Battalion at St. Martin des Entrees, near the first harbour where they had landed four weeks before. Here they spent a pleasant, quiet afternoon, lying in the shade, waiting for orders and watching the sun turn the mud back again into dust. The news that evening was good. The first reports were exuberant—the Germans were said to be badly shaken and in full retreat, and all the Guards Division now had to do was "lead on." The later reports were more credible, but some of them satisfactory. After a day of hard fighting the Corps had broken through the Germans' defensive position on the ridge on either side of St. Martin. They had not, however, been able to take the village itself; this was a real nuisance, as St. Martin stands on the main road where it crosses the top of the ridge and dominates the approaches on either side. Even more of a nuisance was the failure of the corps on either flank to make any progress at all. Their failure meant that the 8th Corps was already in a narrow salient, with its left flank exposed to the attacks of the Germans moving over from Caen. Only some of these Germans, however, would be occupied; the rest could carry on slightly farther south on their way to cut off the Americans. When the British armour moved to attack at Cagny the German armour moved up to defend; when the British armour moved west to Caumont, so did the Germans, naturally enough. But the 9th S.S. Panzer, the 10th S.S. Panzer and the 21st Panzer Division did not take part in the attack on the U.S. Third Army; they were holding the line for the other divisions to move across.

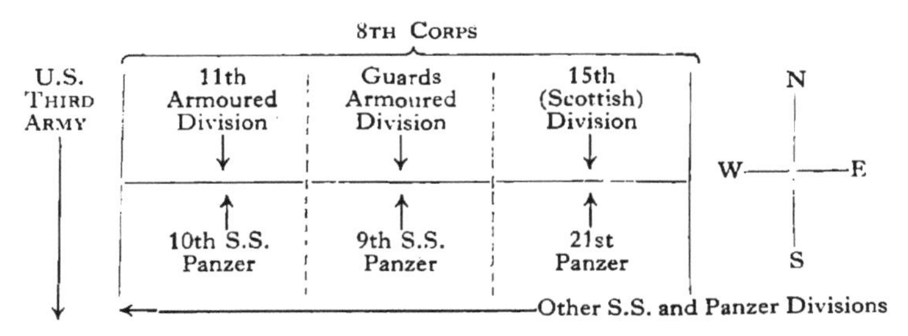

This was just what the Corps Commander had to prevent. He told the Scottish Division to organize a defensive flank and ordered the 11th Armoured to capture St. Martin des Besaces first thing the following morning. As soon as St. Martin was taken the Guards Division was to join the 11th, and the two divisions were to advance, "regardless of risk," and to slip in between the Germans and the Americans. The main object was to get to the important road junctions first.

The 2nd Battalion left Bayeux with the 5th Brigade at midnight. After a dusty, tiring drive they halted some miles short of Caumont at three o'clock in the morning, looking forward to a few hours' sleep and breakfast. No sooner had the crews dismounted than an 8th Corps staff officer appeared out of the dark with orders for the Brigade to move still nearer Caumont. They drove on another few miles through the night over a badly made and badly marked track. The tanks could grind their way across streams and hedges, but the heavy lorries of the supply echelon had to make a long circuit by road. After this hustled night journey the Battalion finally dismounted, got breakfast, and slept.

Captain Terence O'Neill's entries in the 5th Brigade War Diary were always brief and simple. "We spent the morning and afternoon waiting to move and then quite suddenly moved off in a hurry at tea-time, the 2nd Irish and the 5th Coldstream leading." It had taken the best part of the day to capture St. Martin des Besaces and to clear the road up to it. The Germans in and around the village had fought stubbornly to give their comrades time to organize new defensive positions to the immediate south. If no fresh Germans arrived in the area, the only troops they had to man these positions were the 752nd Grenadier Regiment. All German infantrymen were now called Grenadiers—much to the annoyance of the Grenadier Regiment of Foot Guards—and a German Grenadier regiment was roughly the equivalent of a British infantry brigade. This did not seem very formidable opposition, particularly as, in principle, the higher the number in the German Army the worse the unit, but the divisional Intelligence Staff were not convinced by their own optimism, and they added, "possibly intervening from the east will be the 21st Panzer Division"—the Brigade's antagonist at Cagny.

As soon as the 11th Armoured Division had taken St. Martin—and evidently before Terence O'Neill had finished his tea—the Divisional Commander ordered the 2nd Irish and the 5th Coldstream to advance together as a battle group. The 2nd Battalion had so far moved with the 5th Brigade as an "old-fashioned" armoured brigade. This was the first word they had of any change in organization. Lieut.-Colonel Michael Adeane, of the Coldstream battalion, being senior to Colonel Finlay, automatically took command of the group. It took the two Colonels and three hundred officers and non-commissioned officers an hour and a half to rearrange the two battalions. Out of the scrambling confusion of men, tanks and trucks, guns, carriers and motor-cycles, shouting officers, desperate Sergeants and patient Guardsmen, there emerged the Irish-Coldstream group, neatly formed up along the main road. No. 2 Squadron was leading with No. 4 Company, then came two infantry companies, followed by No. 3 and No. 1 Squadrons, and finally the reserve company of the Coldstream. Their objective for the night was a long, high ridge six miles south of St. Martin and the collection of houses scattered along the top of it called Beny Bocage.

Once before, at Cagny, the Germans had stopped a breakout by getting across the axis of advance farther back, and here they had chosen the Beny Bocage ridge as the most favourable position for a second line of defence. The ridge dominated the country between St. Martin and the main lateral Vassy–Vire road; its northern slopes fall steeply into the valley of the River Souleuvre; the one road over it winds through an easily defended gorge; it runs parallel to the main lateral road farther south, and is far enough—over six miles—in front of it to give full protection to the armoured divisions driving to the west. It was essential to the success of the whole Allied plan to stop this transfer of German armour, and it was therefore equally essential to rush the Beny Bocage ridge before the Germans had time to establish their line on its top. North of the main ridge there were two subsidiary positions on lesser ridges at which the Germans could stand and fight for time. Between St. Martin and Beny Bocage the road south is commanded by a series of enclosed heights. The country is cut by the River Souleuvre and its two tributaries. As soon as the main road leaves St. Martin it dips down into a valley, crosses the first tributary at the group of houses called Le Bru, and climbs up the first ridge. It crosses this ridge at the lowest part, skirting the two small hills—Point 192 and Point 238—which command the northern edge, and carries on for two miles across the broad wooded top till it drops down again to the valley of the second tributary at Le Tourneur. It climbs again to cross the second narrow ridge and then down again to Catheolles on the River Souleuvre. After Catheolles the road winds up a steep gorge and through thickly wooded defiles till it reaches the village of St. Charles de Percy at the southern end of the main ridge.

The battered little town of Caumont was choked with troops and vehicles, and the road beyond thick with barely moving traffic. The transport, supplies, reinforcements and wounded of three divisions were all trying to get to and from St. Martin at the same time on one narrow winding road. The group jerked their way forward through lorries, gun-tractors, ambulances, jeeps and marching troops. Progress was maddeningly slow. Outside St. Martin the group bumped into the tail of the 11th Armoured Division, when the traffic problem became "grotesque," as Colonel Finlay described it. The tanks had to halt ; the Coldstream infantry quite naturally had no desire to sit crowded in stationary lorries head to tail on a road that was liable to be shelled at any moment, so they "debussed" ; into the middle of them ran another convoy from the opposite direction. By the time the group had managed to get through St. Martin it was after nine o'clock. The summer evenings were long, but not long enough for tanks leaving St. Martin at that hour to reach Le Beny Bocage before dark, even if they met no opposition at all. The two hills—Points 238 and 192—offered a good base for the night, and Lieut.-Colonel Adeane reckoned that the group would reach the road beneath them just as the light was failing.

Major John Madden led No. 2 Squadron out of St. Martin and down through the forward Scottish positions. The German observers on Point 238 left the column alone till it was half-way down the hill, then they concentrated every gun they commanded. The road follows the easiest slope on both sides of the valley. As soon as the first shells exploded, No 2 Squadron and their infantry company crashed through the hedges and plunged straight down the valley towards the stream. The rest of the column continued steadily down the road, praying that No. 2 would be quick. No. 2 Squadron swung east to avoid the bridge at Le Bru, forded the stream and started to climb the ridge. The ground was broken and rough ; the tank drivers and commanders could not see more than a few yards in front of them, and they did not know where the Germans were except that they ought to be on top of the hill. The Squadron split into two half-squadrons. Major John Madden kept one half crawling up behind the Coldstream infantry, Captain Hugh Dormer led the other half round to the right to approach the hill from a flank. "The Coldstream company lost its way and reported that it was on the hill, when in fact it was some 800 yards short of it." The words of the War Diary sound hard, but they are not so meant. Everyone knows how easy it is for tired men to lose their way as they plod up a hill in the gathering dark. They had never seen the ground before, and now they could not see farther than the outline of the next hedge. At night every bump in the ground seems like a hill. The Coldstreamers were looking for a small hill, and they thought they had found it. Lieut.-Colonel Adeane got their wireless report as the rest of the group were approaching the other hill, Point 192. He congratulated the company and ordered them to dig in at once. No. 2 Squadron rejoined the Battalion.

In their steady thrust up the main road the group had met no opposition, except some heavy shelling which died away after they crossed the bridge at Le Bru. It was already dusk, so the tanks halted below Point 192 and a company went forward to secure the hill. The tank crews saw the silhouettes of the Coldstreamers on the crest and then heard the racing chatter of Spandau machine-guns. Tracer streamed over the hill into the dark sky. Lieut.-Colonel Adeane called a halt for the night ; they would attack those Germans in the morning, after patrols had found out their positions. The Coldstreamers dug trenches along the top of the hill, covering the crest, and the 2nd Battalion came up behind them. In the dark all the tanks crowded together in one steep, sloping field on the side of the hill just off the main road.

The crews stumbled through the long grass towards the hedges to find a comfortable spot to eat and sleep. On the other side of the road was a small stone farm-house. The old farmer came out to see what was happening ; tanks meant trouble, he complained, and the Battalion agreed. The following morning, however, when he saw that his house was not going to be damaged, he became very excited and patriotic and finally, in the afternoon, very drunk on cider. A year later, when the war was over, some of the Battalion went back to this spot ; they found that the old farmer and his neighbours had carefully marked the graves of the dead and regularly covered them with fresh flowers.

During the night the Coldstreamers sent out the routine patrols. They brought in the usual reports of German tanks and infantry moving about in the dark. Neither side discovered till the morning that they had slept within 200 yards of each other, divided only by the crest. The night was quiet and still. The only sight or sound was the crackle and glow of a fire just by Point 192 in front of the Coldstream company. It might be anything—a house, a haystack, or a tank. No. 2 Squadron checked over their tanks and found that Captain Hugh Dormer's was missing. He had not been heard on the wireless for some time, but there was nothing unusual in that, for he was second-in-command of the Squadron and would not normally speak in the routine calls. The other tanks in his half-squadron had not seen him, for in their attack he had been on the extreme right and some way ahead. Nobody felt any worry at first. When a battalion goes into harbour there is often a tank missing, but its crew usually walk in later demanding food and complaining about a breakdown or a "brew-up." As the night wore on and there was no sign of the missing crew the Squadron's thoughts turned to that fire, now only a faint glow. The following morning, on their way back to Point 192, they found Captain Hugh Dormer in the middle of a field and his burnt-out tank jammed up against the far hedge. It was clear what happened. To reach the top of the hill, Captain Dormer went round the side of an orchard and then, like everyone else, had lost his way. As his tank came over a small rise just clear of the orchard a concealed German tank put a shot straight into its bow. The driver and co-driver were killed, for their bodies were still in the tank. The engine was undamaged, so the tank plunged driverless across the field till it hit a tree. Even then the tracks were still working, and the tank dug itself deeper and deeper into the ground until it caught fire. He and the other two in the turret, the gunner and the operator, jumped clear of the tank and ran for the orchard. A machine-gunner cut down Captain Dormer and his companions captured the two Guardsmen. The Squadron buried "our Mr. Dormer, D.S.O." and marked his grave with his tank helmet and flowers. There was no sign of the other two men; they were later reported wounded and captured.

Captain Hugh Dormer held and avowed strong religious and political convictions. He devoted his whole mind to the war which, for him, was in every way a fight for civilization. During the training in Wiltshire he left the Battalion for several long periods. His brother officers did not know what he was doing, but guessed it was something connected with France and "cloak and dagger work." He returned, polite and uncommunicative. His friends did not like to question him, even when he was awarded the Distinguished Service Order for "undisclosed special services." After the war it was revealed that he had twice been dropped in France by parachute, had blown up a shale plant working for the Germans, and had made his way, on foot and hunted by blood-hounds, through France and over the Pyrenees. He returned eagerly to that most difficult and dangerous of all operations, regimental soldiering. Like so many of the best men in the country, he died gallantly but unobtrusively in a minor attack. And his diaries show that he had perhaps a feeling that, this time, he would not return from France.

The Battalion broke harbour at five o'clock the following morning, 1st August. The next stage on the road was the village of St. Denis Maisoncelles, about two miles farther on. No. 2 Squadron rejoined their Coldstream company half-way up Point 238. They reached the top with the loss of only one tank. A German shot came straight through the bank, leaving a neat tunnel, and struck the Pipe-Major's tank. The tank promptly went on fire and started to roll back down the hill out of control. In a direct line beneath it was the Regimental Aid Post ; the burning tank crashed through one hedge and bank and bore down on the group of wounded men. The doctor and his orderlies could not possibly shift the stretchers in time ; all they could do was hope that the one intervening bank would hold it. The tank hit the bank below a whitethorn tree, swayed and stopped. Pipe-Major Crozier was badly burnt and his thigh was smashed. The gunner, Guardsman Cuthbertson, was also horribly burnt, and had his foot hanging by a thread. When the stretcher-bearers got to the tank the Pipe-Major was hauling Cuthbertson under cover, and both of them were singing "The Mountains of Mourne." "There's the Micks for you," said the Battalion proudly.

Point 238 secured, the next task was to clear the ground overlooking the main road. At half-past six, No. 1 Squadron, under Major Nial O'Neill, and a company of Coldstreamers formed up in an orchard just above the harbour area. The orchard skirted the main road and was bounded by a sunken lane which joined the road at right angles. Their first objective was a group of farm buildings five hundred yards to the south. The infantry climbed through the deep overgrown lane and tramped across a field of turnips towards the farm. The tanks went out on to the road and waited there to give the infantry time to reach the hedge on the far side of the turnip field.

Lieutenant Michael Maconchy poked his gun muzzle over the wooden gate ; his troop sat behind him waiting the word to burst into the field. He pushed down the gate. The loud splintering of wood drowned the report of a German gun, but Sergeant Healey, in the second tank, saw a long flash from the sunken lane and his troop leader's tank burst into flames. Sergeant Healey swerved past the burning tank and raced for the hedge. He had almost reached it when he was hit, but in the front, not in the rear as he expected. The Tiger in the lane had left him to another gun, while it knocked the tracks off the third tank. In Michael Maconchy's tank he himself, Lance-Sergeant Riches and Guardsman Davidson were killed ; in Sergeant Healey's, the driver, Guardsman Barnett, was killed, but the rest of the crew got away. With no tank support, the Coldstreamers fell easy victims to the German infantry entrenched on the other side of the hedge. The survivors withdrew back to the orchard. No squadron leader likes seeing one of his troops destroyed before his eyes, and Major O'Neill was "hopping mad." He had been told that the sunken lane was clear, and indeed some of the infantry must have passed within ten yards of the Tiger. Now he was taking nobody's word, and crawled from hedge to hedge to see everything for himself. Besides the Tiger in the lane there were at least two anti-tank guns covering the flank, and about a company behind the hedge. He decided that a second attack would succeed if the sunken lane were properly cleared and a troop and Squadron H.Q. supported the infantry and leading tanks from the orchard. A Piat patrol went up the lane, but the German tank had gone. Meanwhile, reports about the enemy were pouring in. As Lieutenant Stephen Langton, the Signals Officer, said : "The reports on the air sounded as though a menagerie had escaped—Tigers, Panthers, Hornets and 'Crabs' everywhere, some dug in, some moving north, south, east and west. We gave up counting the brutes."

Lieutenant Cole's troop of No. 3 Squadron crossed the road to cover the west flank while a fresh Coldstream company moved up. Squadron Sergeant-Major Parkes, in his Firefly, covered the road itself where the "biggest Tiger ever" had been reported. Lieut.-Colonel Adeane ordered the infantry to attack as soon as they were ready. They were ready at ten o'clock. As the Coldstreamers climbed out of the lane into the root-field, both Lieut.-Colonel Adeane and the Company Commander were wounded by a sharp mortar concentration, which event caused some confusion though their loss was not really felt till later. The leading platoons, with Lieutenant Michael Carvill's troop in close support, and under covering fire from the orchard, reached the far hedge without much trouble. The Germans were waiting for them at the hedge. Machine-gunners beat the Coldstreamers back to the orchard with heavy casualties. Concealed guns knocked out two of the tanks, wounding Lieutenant Carvill. Before he was hit, however, Sergeant Cardus got his tank up to the hedge and destroyed a Mark IV on the other side. The Germans then turned their attention to the supporting tanks in the orchard and hit two of them—those of Captain Edward Tyler and Sergeant Mahoney, who was wounded. Lieutenant Patrick Pollock edged round the orchard till he could see the farm and the Germans moving about in it. He gave them ten rounds high explosive. No. 2 Squadron, meanwhile, was on Point 238 looking down over the battlefield, but the thick hedges prevented them seeing or helping No. 1 Squadron and the infantry. Here, as always, the main difficulty the Battalion had to overcome was the close country, the thick hedges and sunken lanes, which prevented deployment and limited vision to a hundred yards or less, with the result that two or three hidden guns or tanks could shoot up a whole troop before being spotted. The only news of the Germans came from a badly wounded prisoner from the 752nd Grenadier Regiment, who was brought in to the Battalion R.A.P. Most of his comrades were killed or wounded, he said—"Alles kaput," a phrase which became a German war-cry. The Battalion was happy to hear it, but was more interested in his statement that some fifty Panthers and Mark IV tanks of the 21st Panzer Division were supporting the German infantry in the area. There was something in his story, for shortly afterwards No. 2 Squadron saw about forty German tanks moving across their front.

At eleven o'clock the Battalion received a visit from Brigadier Norman Gwatkin, always a stimulating experience. He arrived the same time as a flight of German bullets, and alarmed everyone by giving his orders in the open. He liked the noise himself, and thought that everyone else did. He reckoned that the Germans were withdrawing, and ordered another attack immediately from Point 238 towards St. Denis Marconcelles, with the artillery support of five regiments of field and medium guns. Colonel Finlay, now in command of the group, ordered No. 2 Squadron and No. 4 Company Coldstream Guards to attack at one o'clock. The attack was completely successful, for the Germans had already left St. Denis Marconcelles. The Battalion moved up to join No. 2 Squadron in St. Denis. In the old enemy positions they found one Mark IV knocked out and about forty dead—most of them killed by Lieutenant

Patrick Pollock—to set off against their own seven destroyed tanks. The enemy tank came from the 2nd Bn. 3rd Panzer Regiment of 2nd Panzer Division. The Divisional Intelligence Staff thought over this information and told the Battalion the following day that this 2nd Battalion was possibly left behind in support of 752nd Grenadier Regiment—a deduction welcome though late. When the Battalion reached St. Denis, the Brigadier gave the order "No further advance," so they settled down in the village, refuelling and sorting the squadrons. They knew that the 32nd Guards Brigade was coming up to pass through them and would probably like to know where the Germans were, so Lieutenant Douglas Goodbody was ordered to take his reconnaissance troop and see how far he could go. The troop got about a mile, then the leading Honey tank, commanded by Lieutenant Charles Warren, was destroyed. There was a Panther lying in an orchard off the road, and it had probably never had as easy a victim in all the war. One shot smashed the flimsy little Honey. Lieutenant Charles Warren escaped with a wound and walked back ; the rest of the crew were not so lucky.

The enemy artillery had been active all the time from the south and west, and Brigade H.Q., just north of St. Martin, was heavily shelled all the afternoon. Captain Ronald Robertson went there hoping for a "cushy" tea and was never so frightened in his life. He swallowed a mugful of tea in a rocking Armoured Command vehicle and hastily returned to the front for peace. The Battalion was, of course, delighted to know that "Brigade was getting it proper."

The 3rd Battalion, meanwhile, had spent a peaceful night with the 32nd Brigade some miles north of Caumont. They had left their old Bayeux orchard the night before and, with the 1st Armoured Coldstream, had moved slowly up the roads in the rear of the Division. The weather was very hot and "the roads unbelievably dusty, so ' harem order ' was again the dress of the day." At five o'clock in the morning they were on the road again and drove down through Caumont to St. Martin des Besaces.

The Battalion halted short of it while Colonel "Joe" Vandeleur went forward to meet the Brigadier at the level crossing in the village. The 2nd Battalion and the 5th Coldstream were attacking the hills—Point 192 and Point 238—but even so, some Germans had the time to watch St. Martin and shelled Brigadier George Johnson and his Order Group as they walked up and down the main road. Amid the falling shells—one of which wounded the artillery commander—the Brigadier ordered the 3rd Battalion to pass through the 5th

Coldstream and 2nd Irish as soon as St. Denis Maisoncelles was captured.

It was a slow business getting the Battalion up to St. Denis through the congestion of traffic, the litter of destroyed vehicles and the continual shelling. However, this delay gave Colonel Joe and his company commanders, who went ahead, plenty of time to collect information from the 2nd Battalion. Lieutenant Charles Warren could tell them exactly where the nearest Germans were. In the bright sunlight they got a perfect view of their objective—the far edge of the ridge where the ground rose before it dropped down to the river. Here, at last, the Battalion had a chance of launching an attack well supported with armour over ground that had been carefully studied. The attack went in at six o'clock and was completely successful. Two companies advanced astride the road, No. 2 Company on the left, "X" Company on the right, each supported by two troops of 1st Coldstream tanks. The Germans met them both with light machine-gun fire and concentrated mortars on No. 2 Company, but the Guardsmen plodded steadily forward. The only Germans who held their ground were those in the orchards and the isolated buildings on the reverse slope. The Panther that Lieutenant Warren had met was still there, encouraging the Germans and killing Guardsmen. Lieutenant Burke of No. 2 Company was stalking it when, to his relief, he saw it pull out of the orchard and make off down the hill. After that the companies quickly disposed of the remaining Germans and called up the rest of the Battalion to join them. The local farmers came out of their cellars and were so friendly that they held up the consolidation of the position till an old woman had kissed every man in one platoon and an old man had produced cider for all.

As soon as the 3rd Battalion were firmly established, the 5th Brigade commander, Brigadier Norman Gwatkin, ordered the King's Company of the 1st (Motor) Grenadiers and Lieutenant Patrick McCorkell's troop of tanks to push on to Le Tourneur and seize the bridge. They reached Le Tourneur, but found it full of Germans. About half-past ten Lieutenant Patrick McCorkell wirelessed back that there were too many Germans for the Greandiers to deal with and that the Grenadier commander felt bound to extricate his company before it got swallowed up in the scattered houses and destroyed piecemeal. The Brigadier was away at a conference and, left to themselves, 5th Brigade H.Q. issued an extraordinary order. They told Colonel Finlay to find Colonel "Joe" Vandeleur of the 3rd Battalion—a battalion in another brigade—and persuade him to capture the bridge by three o'clock in the morning at the latest. It was pitch dark and obviously impossible for the tanks of the 2nd Battalion to do anything. Captain Eamon FitzGerald drove Colonel Finlay to the 3rd Battalion in his scout car; they arrived at Battalion H.Q. about midnight, to find the officers having their dinner. Colonel "Joe" Vandeleur had received no orders to capture any bridge and was at first very wary of the whole scheme. "What bridge? Whose orders? Which brigade?" and then "All right!" The forward companies had already sent patrols down to the line of the river and knew the ground, so Colonel Joe agreed to take on the task.

At two o'clock in the morning No. 2 Company, under Major Anthony Eardley-Wilmot, and "X" Company, Scots Guards, got out of their trenches and walked down the hill. An hour later they reported back that they held Le Tourneur and—more important—had captured the bridge intact. If the Germans had succeeded in blowing the bridge they would have held up the advance of the Division for at least a day. The 3rd Battalion were pleased with this second success. "People will probably remember very little of these two operations—the day and the night attack—because they went so easily and with little cost," said Colonel Joe, "but they were of considerable training value for further battles, and it was pleasant to get a chance to do our work tidily after the Cagny fiasco."

CHAPTER V

La Marvindiere

The 2nd Battalion

Day I.

COLONEL FINLAY got back to the 2nd Battalion at half-past five on the morning of the 2nd to find his Second-in-Command, Major Giles Vandeleur, giving out the orders for the day's advance. The objective was Vassy. The 2nd Welsh Guards were to lead the 5th Brigade on a centre line which split in two at Catheolles. The Grenadier group were to follow the Welsh as far as Catheolles, and there fork left through Montcharivel and Au Cornu to Vassy. The Irish and Coldstream were to drive straight on through Catheolles, St. Charles de Percy and Estry to Vassy.

Somewhere around Vassy the commander of the 21st Panzer Division was giving out similar orders, only in an opposite direction. The two divisions raced to meet each other. The Welsh and Grenadiers reached Catheolles first, but only just. As soon as they turned left after Catheolles they were held up by Germans on the ridge east of the main road. No allowance had been made for the Grenadiers being halted at this particular place. Their column was supposed to be clear of the main road by the time the Irish Guards reached Catheolles. Of course, they could not do it. Their transport was still blocking the main road while they attacked the ridge. The Germans held their ground firmly. The Irish Guards waited till the Brigadier would let them wait no longer and ordered them to scrape past the Grenadiers somehow.

To reach Catheolles the road turns right and runs obliquely down to the bottom of the valley through a deep defile. It was an ideal target for the German gunners and mortar men. They could drop their bombs neatly into the defile or bounce their high-velocity shells off the rock face. The leading squadron—No. 3—rattled down this "Mortar Gulch" till it came on the tail of the Grenadiers. There they had to halt ; their accompanying Coldstream infantry, hearing

Moving up to Marvindiere

2nd and 3rd Battalions, Holland

Face page 408

the sound of small-arms fire, jumped out of their trucks and stood in the middle of the mortar bursts looking round for someone to fight. The other companies and squadrons piled up behind them. The sharp explosions, the blue smoke and the pungent smell of the bomb-bursts filled the defile ; the shell splinters richocheted off the rocks and the monotonous yet urgent cries of "Stretcher-bearers !" echoed up and down the column. The Coldstream battalion lost their second Commanding Officer in two days.

The Germans had only succeeded in establishing themselves along the eastern flank of the position they had chosen, and were now being attacked by the Grenadiers. On the western flank the 11th Armoured Division had met little opposition and reached Le Beny Bocage without difficulty. As the need for cutting the main east-west roads was imperative, the Corps Commander ordered both the 11th and the Guards Armoured Divisions to push on and ignore the enemy on their flanks. The Corps was well ahead of the formations on its right and left. The further the two divisions advanced the deeper the salient they were making. Up till now the enemy they had encountered were rearguards, composed of local reserves and troops retrieved from the forward positions. From now on they met fresh troops moving up from the south and east. These troops were in fact first-class Panzer and S.S. divisions with a large number of heavy tanks, self-propelled guns and artillery. The Germans had been forestalled in their attempt to form an effective "Stop" on the strongest position in the locality, but they were still determined to protect the lateral roads. They quickly organized a series of subsidiary, but still very strong, positions on commanding ground. Using these positions as pivots, the Germans struck out at the British columns, trying to isolate one group from the other and cut their slender lines of communication and supply.

Major Giles Vandeleur straightened out the twisted column and, in the leading tank, ruthlessly pushed a way through the Grenadier trucks. The Coldstream infantry abandoned their trucks and climbed on the backs of the tanks. The persistent Grenadier attacks confined the Germans to the ridge south of Catheolles and east of the road. They completely screened the defile leading up and through the ridge to St. Charles de Percy. As the tanks, with their loads of Coldstreamers, passed through this defile the bullets of the Grenadiers' battle flew over their heads and an odd stray shell exploded in the road, but after Mortar Gulch this side of the valley seemed like the Wadi of Brotherly Love.

St. Charles de Percy is only a few houses round a cross-roads. On one of the houses was a large sign "La Feroninere." Captain Michael O'Cock solved the mystery afterwards. "This cross-roads, with houses, was always called St. Charles de Percy because of the way the map is printed, but it is really La Feroninere, which is not shown on the map. I don't think anyone ever went to the real St. Charles de Percy." The Battalion reached the cross-roads without difficulty and turned left to take a secondary road which led south-east to another Maisoncelles, Courtacon, Courteil, Montchamp and Estry. The first tank and the first shell arrived at the cross-roads at the same time, and from then on the shells fell regularly. Lieutenant Arthur Cole led the way towards Courteil. The second tank of his troop had just rounded the corner when its 75-mm. gun went off. The gun was, of course, loaded and ready for instant action; the blazing heat or constant shaking must have set off a defective charge. The shot struck the leading tank in the rear, killing three of the crew and wounding Lieutenant Arthur Cole. Arthur Cole did not consider himself much hurt, but later a piece of shell and his tobacco pouch were extracted from his left thigh. Just as that moment an 11th Division scout car came tearing down the road from Courteil. The officer in it explained excitedly that he had just been "on a great swan round the country." He and his corporal, in two cars, had started from the Beny Bocage and had driven at high speed in a circle through Beaulieu, Estry and Courteil. In Maisoncelles he saw two 88-mm. self-propelled guns. They saw him, too, missed him but got the corporal in the second car. Arthur Cole thanked the man kindly and advanced towards Maisoncelles. The 88's immediately opened fire, blowing large bits off the houses round the cross-roads to the alarm of No. 2 Squadron, who were just coming round it. No. 3 Squadron and their company considered by-passing Maisoncelles and Courteil, while No. 2 Squadron and another company prepared to clear the road. The hours passed in deliberation. At eight o'clock in the evening the Brigadier came up to see what was happening. He was justifiably angry when he discovered that two guns had held up the two battalions for nearly four hours. He ordered the group to get a move on and establish themselves on the high ground at Estry by nightfall. They could do this by by-passing Maisoncelles, Courteil and everything else, turning right (south) and striking across country.

Colonel Kim Finlay had had almost no sleep in forty-eight hours; he was obviously feeling the strain. The Brigadier ordered him to hand over the Battalion to the Second-in-Command, Major Giles Vandeleur, and go back to rest.

Major Giles Vandeleur told the Battalion their new line of advance, but he knew nothing more about the enemy than that Montchamp and the high ground to the north of it on the Grenadier front were held by the 21st Panzer Division. No mention had yet been made of the 9th Panzer Division or its possible arrival. The Coldstreamers once more mounted on tank-back and the tanks turned down a lane leading into the fields and headed well west of Courteil to reach Estry by way of the villages of Sieurnoux and La Marvindière. For two hours the tanks drove across the most difficult country they had yet encountered, but they saw no sign of the enemy except an odd sniper, to whom they gave a burst of Browning in passing. The frequent ditches and the blinding dust divided the Battalion into two parts, and as the advance continued at top speed the leading squadrons —No. 2 and No. 3—got farther and farther ahead of the others. The rear half lost direction. Lieutenant Duncan Lampard noticed that they were driving straight into the last rays of the setting sun. "Surely we should be going south, not west ?" The column turned left again. By ten o'clock it was getting too dark for the tanks to go ploughing blindly through enemy-held country. The leading squadrons, with their infantry companies clinging on their backs, had reached La Marvindière, while Battalion H.Q., No. 1 Squadron, the battery of self-propelled anti-tank guns and the reserve Coldstream companies had only reached Sieurnoix. Major Lord Willoughby d'Eresby, the commander of the Leicestershire Yeomanry battery, drove up to Major Giles Vandeleur's tank. They agreed that it was too late to try to reunite the Battalion group, so Major Giles Vandeleur ordered the two halves to harbour where they were.

Night I.

The leading squadrons spent a lonely night. The tanks always carried three days' rations on board, but the Coldstreamers had nothing. Out of common decency the crews shared their food with the hungry infantrymen. F.2 Echelon, the Battalion's forward supply column under Major Sir John Reynolds, found a lane which led them to Sieurnoux, but they could not get the petrol up till the following morning. After dark Major Lord Willoughby and Major the Marquess of Hartington, now commanding the Coldstream battalion, set out to try and find the leading companies and squadrons. After driving around many fields they met some of the 11th Division, who said the Germans were all round them. The expedition went on cautiously, but they could not find the leading troops.

Day II.

At dawn the following morning, the 3rd, the rear joined the forward half at La Marvindière. While the crew were eating, refuelling and loading ammunition, Brigadier Gwatkin appeared and ordered the group to press on as fast as possible to Estry and beyond, leaving only a minimum force to contain the enemy pockets. Estry, a village round an important cross-roads, had become a German strong-point. This was not known at the time, and all the information Divisional H.Q. offered was a mere guess that there might still be a few Germans there. The previous evening, while the Battalion had been racing south and had halted at La Marvindière, the German 9th Panzer Division had been moving north. During the night they occupied the village of Estry and the line of the road through Le Busq and Forques down to Vire along the top of the dominant ridge which protected the main Vassy–Vire road. The Battalion had no choice but to attack straight ahead from La Marvindière. The left flank was held by the Germans ; on the right the 11th Armoured Division could not get beyond Le Grand Bonfait, a farm just south of the Estry road, a mile down the lane which ran from Les Ecoublets to the road. The line of attack ran straight from the harbour area on the slope behind by La Marvindière, through the farm and orchard which stood on top of the rise, down into the dip on the other side and up the long slope to Estry. At nine o'clock No. 1 and No. 2 Squadrons moved into the orchard round the farm to fire on the line of the road along the far crext. No. 3 Squadron and a company of Coldstreamers advanced south to capture Le Busq first, fondly imagining it to be free of enemy. They crossed the lane in front of the farm and the little stream in the valley. So far, it looked as if there were really no Germans in Estry or Le Busq, and they worked their way slowly but unmolested up the long slope through thick hedges and orchards. The two squadrons round the farm sat watching them, ready to fire.

Colonel Finlay, who everyone thought had gone for at least a day, returned and took over command. At ten o'clock No. 3 Squadron was half-way up the slope up against a thick hedge ; they were still there at six o'clock in the evening. Behind the hedge ran a deep sunken lane. Lieutenant D. B. Liddle's troop nosed through the hedge. As the first tank got its bow through, it was hit at close range. This was the first sign of the Germans. Captain Paul Stobart, the Squadron's second-in-command, ever eager for German blood, dismounted and crawled through the lane. Along the crest he saw seven or eight Panthers and Tigers escorted by about a company of infantry. The Coldstreamers dug in by the sunken lane. They were comparatively safe here so long as they kept their heads down, for the lane was a complete tank obstacle which the tanks of neither side could cross, except at a few gaps, which both sides had fully covered. The Battalion could not as yet identify the enemy, but later they learnt it was the 9th S.S. Panzer Division, which had arrived at Estry at the same time as the Battalion reached La Marvindière. They spent the rest of the day playing hide-and-seek in and out of the hedges and orchards. The advantage of course lay with the Germans, for, as one officer records, "No matter what is said in Parliament, the German guns penetrate our armour, and our 75 mms. do not penetrate theirs."

Captain Stobart is one of the few men whose tank has been hit on the turret at a hundred yards' range by a Tiger without serious damage to the crew. He was easing his tank up to the crest to take a shot at one of the German tanks when a shot from another one, which he had not seen, hit his gun-mantlet, scooped out a large lump of armour and then glanced off, unseating the turret and Captain Stobart. Undaunted, he picked himself up and prepared to get his own back. He found a Coldstreamer armed with a Piat, and took him along to stalk the Tiger. When he got within fifty yards of the Tiger he turned to the Coldstreamer for the Piat. "Where are the bombs ?" "Oh, my number two on the gun carries them," was the reply, "and I don't know where he is." They had to go back for the bombs, and this time Major Patrick Whitefoord, M.C., came on the stalk as well, to act as "Number two on the gun." Paul Stobart took three shots at the Tiger. All the bombs hit the front plate, but the Tiger was not hurt. It was, however, irritated and immediately fired back, scattering the Piat party with a few rounds of high explosive. Still burning for revenge, Paul Stobart borrowed a rifle and returned to the hedge. He saw the same or a similar Tiger in the orchard, with its commander standing half out of the turret. His first shot went wide and was not noticed, but at the second the German officer slumped forward on the turret. Captain Stobart withdrew, his scores paid off.

No. 2 Squadron, meanwhile, had been supporting No. 3 Squadron from their left rear, steadily firing high explosive at the half-track vehicles and infantry coming westward along the main road from Estry. Captain John Dupree had the pleasure of seeing one ammunition carrier go up in flames. No. 1 Squadron was watching the rear and left flank. There was a little artillery support available, but not as much as usual. The Battalion's own battery, of the Leicestershire

Yeomanry, had unfortunately chosen the same field as the German Panthers for a harbour. The Germans won the resulting fight, destroying three self-propelled guns and most of the battery's transport. The Battalion knew that there were Germans on their left flank, and Germans in Montchamp and Point 187 behind them, but trustingly and, as it proved, unwisely they believed that the centre line was clear back to St. Charles de Percy. The lane from Sieurnoux which the echelon had used the previous night, was confidently stated to be protected by anti-tank guns, which was true, and free from enemy, which was untrue.

Major Sir John Reynolds, escorted by Lieutenant John Keatinge's troop, led out F.2 Echelon for a quiet drive back to replenish at "A" Echelon. Nothing happened until they got into the lane and then a German machine-gun opened up from an orchard. The two leading trucks burst into flames and blocked the lane. Farther down the lane the self-propelled anti-tank battery and a protective platoon from the 3rd Battalion (Lieutenant Thomas King-Harman's) were established on a little rise covering the stretch of country down to Sieurnoux, but they could not stop the German fire. Covered by the troop of tanks and some of the self-propelled anti-tank guns, Major Sir John Reynolds managed to get the rest of the troop reversed out, turned round and driven back to La Marvindière. The whole operation was difficult and dangerous, as the Germans could see and shoot the column the whole time. The 3rd Battalion platoon made sortie after sortie to destroy the German machine-guns. In the last of them Lieutenant Thomas King-Harman was killed charging a machine-gun post.

Night II.

The Battalion, joined by No. 3 Squadron, Welsh Guards, harboured in leaguer just south of La Marvindière. They had met early that morning for the Welsh squadron had harboured near the leading Irish squadrons the night before. Their Cromwell tanks had added to the general confusion during the night, for they were always reported as "Tigers," an understandable but disconcerting mistake. The night was quiet and undisturbed save for a few mortars and shells. The Coldstreamers sent out some reconnaissance patrols, but they found out very little that the Battalion did not know already.

After dark information began to come in about the progress of 11th Armoured Division on the Battalion's right flank. During the day their 29th Armoured Brigade had got a regiment across the Estry–Vire road. Their main force, however, was still north of the road, with its most easterly troops still in the orchards round Le Grand Bonfait. A liaison officer arrived from this brigade with the welcome news that they had cleared a good centre line back to St. Charles de Percy through Beaulieu. His brigadier kindly offered the use of this to the Battalion. In return he asked for instant warning of any intention to withdraw from the "La Marvindière feature," which he regarded as vital to his position. Colonel Finlay was delighted that someone besides the Germans thought La Marvindière important and promised that the Battalion would not leave it. The group made and kept close touch with the infantry of the 11th Division on the right of Le Grand Bonfait. From now on they were "in each other's pockets."

During the previous evening Brigadier Norman Gwatkin had been wounded in his scout car by a shell. The Brigadier was a sanguine man and spouted blood all over his companion, Lieutenant Philip Mieville. Lieutenant Mieville drove straight to the nearest field ambulance and accompanied the Brigadier into the reception tent. All he wanted to do was to wash off the blood and patch up a cut hand, but a meticulous clerk insisted on taking his name and next-of-kin. In the next casualty list appeared "Lieutenant P. Mieville—wounded, but remained at duty." Brigadier Gwatkin did not think much of his wounds and tried to hurry the medical orderly. "Come on. Don't take too long, I want to get back to my headquarters !" The orderly was used to dealing with difficult patients. "Now you stay here. You've —— had it for today." Colonel D. Greenacre, the second-in-command of the Brigade, took command.

The 2nd Battalion broke harbour at 5.30 on the 4th. The squadrons moved out to their previous positions, No. 3 forward towards the main road by Le Busq, No. 2 behind them on the left flank facing east, and No. 1 Squadron along the road from La Marvindière towards Montchamp, facing back to the north in what was thought to be reserve. The two battalions, Irish and Coldstream, thus formed a rough triangle, the transport, the fitters' half-tracks and the R.A.P. in the middle of the triangle, a sloping field just off the road to Montchamp. The Grenadier group was still at Catheolles busily beating off counter-attacks, but the 32nd Brigade had moved up during the previous evening and night. The 3rd Bn. Irish Guards had passed through St. Charles de Percy and were now fighting to clear Courteil and Montchamp behind the 2nd Battalion. The Germans sent up reinforcements to beat off the 3rd Battalion. A steady stream of German tanks and infantry filed past the 2nd Battalion's left flank on the way to Montchamp. No. 2 Squadron discouraged this traffic with high explosive and machine-gun fire, but the Germans only moved slightly over to the left and sent Panzer Grenadiers and self-propelled guns to silence the Squadron. Major John Madden's tank, "Dublin," was hit twice through the gearbox. Lieutenant Vivian Taylor and his crew spent most of the morning shooting little men who would stalk their tank with bombs and bazookas. Finally, he had to dismount his co-driver with a Browning to make them keep their proper distance. Lieutenant Denis Liddle, on the left of No. 3 Squadron, saw some Panzer Grenadiers digging in behind a hedge 160 yards from him. He lined up his troop and let the Germans have five rounds high explosive from each tank. No more digging was done. As F.2 Echelon had been unable to replenish during the previous day or night, supplies for the coming night would have to come up in "A" Echelon's vehicles on the 11th Armoured Division's centre line. "A" Echelon started on its way up to the Battalion at midday. Their journey was peaceful as far as Point 218, but as the column turned south down and towards Cavignaux, it was fired on by German tanks, and the leading scout car and lorry were destroyed. The remainder could do nothing but return back and wait till the area was cleared properly. These German tanks were firing from north to south—that is, from the rear of the Battalion. Though they were never physically on the road, they were able to shell it heavily and very accurately all the time.

In the afternoon the Germans went into reverse; they began to withdraw from Montchamp towards Le Busq. Most of them did not know, or had forgotten, that the 2nd Battalion was in the way. About half-past one Lieutenant Kevin Maguire, on the extreme east of No. 1 Squadron, reported movement on the road north of him. Soon afterwards an enemy scout came into view and was promptly shot. Captain Edward Tyler, who had taken over command of the Squadron for the day from Major Nial O'Neill, pushed two troops—Lieutenant John Keatinge's and Sergeant Brennan's—south of Lieutenant Maguire's to face east. The squadron of the Armoured Reconnaissance, Welsh Guards, moved up to close the gap between No. 1 and No. 2 Squadron. The other troop of No. 1 Squadron, Lieutenant Michael Callender's, was deployed by the houses of La Marvindière, watching north and south. At half-past two they heard the sound of German tanks behind them. Suddenly both Sergeant Brennan's and Lieutenant Keatinge's tanks were knocked out by a Panther some five hundred yards to the north-east. Lieutenant Keatinge was mortally wounded and Sergeant Brennan killed. Squadron H.Q. moved up to strengthen the threatened flank and exchanged shots with the Germans without damage to either side. Lieutenant Callender's troop then came under fire from the north. Again Squadron H.Q. moved to the dangerous area and lost another tank. They claimed hits on a Tiger, but later searches found no "dead" hulk. A troop of No. 2 Squadron now turned round and joined the battle at long range. Sergeant Murray's Firefly scored several hits on a Tiger, but was itself hit six times. The crew did not bale out until the fourth hole was made in the hull. Lieutenant Maguire then reported infantry moving south parallel to his position. The whole Squadron gave them one minute's concentrated rapid machine-gun fire and no more movement was seen in that area. Enemy Spandau squads began to infiltrate into the orchards east and north of them. In these orchards was a small stone store-house, an inviting little place. Captain Tyler, with the patience and ingenuity of the old sailor he was, had spent the early hours of the morning filling it with explosives and wiring the charges to his tank. One Spandau squad had the misfortune to choose this house as its nest. In the words of the signal log, "Enemy goes into house—house goes up."

Later in the afternoon the Germans began shelling the road and No. 1 Squadron's area. The fitters' half-track was hit, Lance-Corporal Morrell killed, and some trucks set on fire. Lieutenant Kevin Maguire had pushed his tank, "Ardagh," well into a hedge to cover the road from the north. A Mark IV tank came down from Montchamp along this road; it saw "Ardagh" first and put a shot right through the turret. Kevin Maguire was killed. "We never expected the turret to keep out anything," said his friends sadly. One of the other tanks destroyed the Mark IV; it was found the next day and identified as belonging to the 9th S.S. Panzer Regiment. The heavy mortaring and shelling spread over the whole Battalion area, causing casualties to the Coldstream as well as the Irish. A "Moaning Minnie" salvo landed just outside the R.A.P., wounding many, including Captain Alec Crichton, the Adjutant, and Lieutenant Douglas Goodbody. Alec Crichton got a piece of mortar bomb through his right thigh. The highest praise is due to the doctor, Captain H. A. Ripman, and his orderlies, who continued to treat casualties quite undismayed by the crash of mortars. By seven o'clock the evacuation of casualties had become a serious problem. The R.A.P. now contained about fifty wounded—some of them in urgent need of further treatment—and all the time the R.A.P. was under fire. A liaison officer, Lieutenant Fergusson-Cunninghame, Grenadier Guards, arrived in a scout car from Brigade H.Q. and at once offered to guide an ambulance convoy back if he was given half an hour to test the road for shell fire. Major Giles Vandeleur had six lorries unloaded, marked them with red or white crosses, and had the wounded lifted on board. The Casualty Clearing Post of the 29th Brigade, in answer to a wireless appeal, said they would have ambulances and beds ready—a considerable courtesy, as they had quite enough of their own wounded to occupy them. Lieutenant John Fergusson-Cunninghame reappeared, slightly winged by a spent bullet, but full of enthusiasm. With him as guide, and Major Giles Vandeleur in command, the lorries moved out of the field. They drove slowly and carefully, for there is a limit to the bumping a wounded man can stand. The Germans did not fire, except for a few bullets at the last lorry, which was half hidden by the dust kicked up by the rest of the convoy. All the casualties got back safely.

The road from Cagnivaux to La Marvindière was now guarded by Lieutenant Michael Callender's troop, but its entire length was regularly shelled and a long straight stretch was under direct German tank fire. Captain The Lord Claud Hamilton decided that he must get "A" Echelon up to the Battalion before nightfall, and ordered the lorries to "run the gauntlet." The blockade-runners carried out their orders cheerfully. They drove at full speed down the twisty road one at a time, and a Guardsman "policeman" turned them into the Battalion's area, otherwise they would have led on to the 9th S.S. car park. The gun traverse of the German tanks was no match for this simple manœuvre, and not one lorry was lost.

This shelling cost the Battalion its old gunner commander and great friend, Major Lord Willoughby d'Eresby. He was going back in his jeep to reorganize his damaged battery and try to get some guns up to support the Battalion. An 88-mm. fired at his jeep and he jumped out of it into the ditch beneath the hedge on the side of the lane. On the other side of the hedge was a Sherman ; to get at the 88-mm. it reversed through the hedge and ran over James Willoughby's legs. His feet were badly crushed, and he had to be evacuated the following morning. "We miss his company greatly, as he had trained with us for two years and been in all our battles. He knew his trade and always landed his shells in the right place." During the day No. 7 Self-Propelled Battery of the 21st Anti-Tank Regiment killed three Panthers, revenging the loss of the Leicestershire Yeomanry guns. Major "Dick" Taylor, the commander, himself destroyed one by firing through a house. He worked out the likely position of a tank in the courtyard and aimed accordingly. He was right—and the Germans were very surprised.

The day ended quietly enough. The fighting had been long, difficult and costly. The Germans had clearly bumped the Battalion by accident; but that was what the Battalion was there for. The eyes of the world were fixed on the spectacular American advances farther west. Nobody, except the Germans, paid much attention to the two British armoured divisions whose unexpected presence and unannounced deaths in obscure Norman orchards had made these advances possible. This day the Battalion lost four tanks and several casualties, including two officers killed, Lieutenants Kevin Maguire and John Keatinge. Only one destroyed German tank was found, the Mark IV. The German tanks, with their better guns and the advantage in ground, could do the Battalion more damage than it could do them, but their infantry certainly had a very uncomfortable afternoon. The casualties necessitated some reorganization. Captain Stephen Langton became Adjutant in place of Captain Alec Crichton and Lieutenant Charles Warren took over command of the Reconnaissance Troop from the wounded Lieutenant Douglas Goodbody. Just after dawn (5th) two German half-tracks rolled in through the gate and tried to harbour with the Battalion. They discovered their mistake when the leading vehicle got a 75-mm. shot through it. Captain Stephen Langton felt almost sorry for the crews as they were "put in the bag." "They were not so very far wrong—only a couple of fields." They came from 19th S.S. Panzer Grenadier Regiment of the 9th S.S. Panzer Division, which had been the Battalion's opponents for the past two days. One of the crew explained that they had orders to return to Estry and had met the Battalion unexpectedly on the way.

The 5th of August was uneventful, and passed chiefly in washing, eating and sleeping. Some shots were exchanged, and there was the usual shelling. A splinter penetrated Captain Robertson's small pack which he was using as a pillow at the time. To his great annoyance it wrecked his toothpaste. Estry was still firmly in German hands, but elsewhere the Germans had retired. At midday the 1st Motor Grenadiers did a "sweep" of the area behind La Marvindière but, as the 2nd Battalion told them before they started, the Germans had already gone, and they swept an empty space. Later, the Battalion's patrols watched the Germans withdrawing from Estry and Le Busq. Colonel Finlay and the new Commanding Officer of the 5th Coldstream, Lieut.-Colonel R. Hill, spent the day working out a plan to capture Le Busq the following afternoon. At the same time the 15th (S.) Division were preparing to launch a monster attack on Estry supported by flame-throwers, flail tanks to explode land-mines, and all the panoply of war. The two Colonels produced their plan, it was approved by the Brigade Commander, and at four o'clock the following afternoon—the 6th—No. 3 Squadron and the Coldstreamers attacked Le Busq. The other two squadrons moved up to support the attack with fire. Before they attacked they heard that the German armour had moved to Le Busq and the line of road running along the top of the ridge. The wireless reports were cheerful, "So far, no enemy noises heard and progressing well." "Attack going well, but under machine-gun fire and mortar fire. Nearly on objective." The right flank was quite easy: the left flank was covered by the houses of Le Busq. Lieutenant Wilfred Dodd's troop had to force its way through thick orchards to get right up to the houses and blast the Germans out of them. At five o'clock Major Patrick Whitefoord reported "Attack going well. Leading troops three to four hundred yards over the road, but in very close country, and advance slow and hampered by machine-gun and mortar fire."

The Germans had the far slope of the Estry–Busq ridge well covered. "Leading troops report," said Major Patrick Whitefoord, "that forward slopes are very unpleasant and under heavy machine-gun and mortar fire. They have withdrawn slightly, but can remain on the line of the main road." The Coldstreamers and Wilfred Dodd's troops cleared Le Busq. They found a burnt-out Panther on the edge of the village abandoned by the Germans after many efforts to recover it. The Germans knew every inch of Le Busq and poured shells into it from the woods to the east. Lieutenant Patrick McCorkell moved his troop across the road to protect the Coldstreamers. They got into the second field and shot high explosive and Browning into the woods, but it was blind shooting and the German fire continued. Major P. Whitefoord joined them and climbed up on his turret to look over the high hedge. A German machine-gunner saw his head and put a burst into the hedge below it. Patrick Whitefoord slid down into his tank with a bullet through his knee. A stream of abuse of the Germans and Normandy poured over the air as he "rang up" for a jeep to fetch him back to the R.A.P. Captain Micheal O'Cock took command of No. 3 Squadron. Lieutenant "Paddy" McCorkell kept his tank where it was, up against a thick hedge. He himself was standing in the turret directing the fire of his troop on to the muzzle-flashes of a battery of mortars. By the one unlucky chance in a thousand a mortar bomb fell straight down the turret and touched off the ammunition. The other tanks' crews heard a muffled explosion, then, very slowly, the Sherman rose straight in the air, the turret blew off and the hull turned an ungainly somersault. It landed on its back and lay there like a beetle, its tracks spinning in the air, till another explosion blew the whole suspension to the other side of the field. A blood-stained boot stuck out of the side—it came away in Mick O'Cock's hand. By the hedge where the tank had been there was a large smoking crater. Lying in the grass near the tank was the Troop Sergeant. He was walking across to talk to Lieutenant McCorkell when the tank blew up ; he had to be evacuated as "bomb happy."

Under the cover of the continual shelling the Germans brought up another infantry division. The Battalion was quite unperturbed by this, as it was no longer isolated. The 15th Division had failed to take Estry, but was containing it, and the 32nd Brigade, including the 3rd Battalion, had moved up to the village of Les Ecoublets on the left rear. On the right, however, the forward troops of the 11th Armoured Division were being heavily attacked by the 10th S.S. Panzer Division. It was the old story. Wherever either the 9th S.S. or the 10th S.S. Panzer Division appeared, the other soon followed like Mary and her little lamb. They were confirmed gate-crashers, always appearing uninvited and unwelcome.

After dark the Battalion went back to La Marvindière to eat, sleep and refuel. There was only need for one squadron to stay out with the infantry, and this time, as the other squadrons said, "it takes No. 2." The peace of the night was disturbed by the grinding of engines and tracks somewhere out in the dark quite close. The Germans had often moved to and from Estry by night and also had had a habit of creeping up by night, lying quiet and then taking a couple of quick shots at dawn. The Battalion listened carefully, trying to identify the type of tank from the engine noises ; they decided that it might be Churchills. Lieutenant Charles Warren went out to make sure, and discovered a bulldozer improving the road. "Things are looking up," he reported.

At six o'clock the next morning, the 7th, the squadrons moved out to their day positions and lay up camouflaged. No. 2 Squadron went back to Le Busq, No. 1 was a few hundred yards north-east of Le Grand Bonfait, with a troop in the orchards amongst the new Coldstream positions. Sergeant McManus, who was never worried by anything, moved his Firefly to the high ground north of the farm to protect the flank of No. 1 Squadron. He was at once engaged by three Mark IV's and an 88-mm. gun from a ridge 1,200 yards to his front. One of them soon scored a penetrating hit, but it was not until the tank had been hit twice again, and his driver and operator wounded, that he abandoned the tank. With the help of the un-wounded members of his crew he successfully evacuated the wounded. The Germans mortared the Battalion all day. A salvo of bombs landed on the slit trenches in which Major John Madden and his second-in-command, Captain John Dupree, were sitting and wounded them both, John Madden losing a leg.

The Battalion could not go on losing officers at this rate without getting some replacements. The casualties to date were :

	Officers.	*Men.*
Killed	6	29
Wounded	11	86
Missing		8
	17	123

All the reinforcements had been used up and the Battalion was still short of one Major, four Captains and three subalterns. Colonel Finlay began to make urgent demands for more officers. Head-quarters promised that bodies were being flown out from England at all speed, but meanwhile he demanded Captain Joe Savill from Brigade and made tentative enquiries about Major David Peel, Captain Will Berridge and Captain Patrick O'Donovan.

On the 8th everything was much the same as before, even the shelling. But an odd stray shell killed Lieutenant Denis Liddle, the second officer to be lost through sheer bad luck. In the afternoon the 15th (Scottish) Division, on the left of the Battalion, attacked Estry, but again unsuccessfully. No. 2 Squadron saw some Germans working round their left flank and had a good squadron shoot, putting an end to any movement in that area. In the evening the Battalion lost yet another officer whom it could ill afford. Captain Paul Stobart, while on an educational tour of his squadron with the day's news and his own views, was wounded by a mortar and had to be evacuated. Once more the officers were reshuffled amongst the squadrons. Battalion H.Q. was up to strength. Lieutenant Keith Briant took over H.Q. Troop from Lieutenant Duncan Lampard, and Lieutenant Neil Whitfield-Edwards was acting as Signal Officer. Lieutenant Whitfield-Edwards's only ambition in life was to be a troop leader and kill Germans. So far he had been foiled, but he was nearer to it now than he had ever been before, so he was happy. He was bitterly disappointed in England when he was sent to the Rein-forcements but, owing to the strange ways of the Army, had the satisfaction of landing in Normandy, as a reinforcement, before the

Battalion. Major Nial O'Neill still survived as Squadron Leader of No. 1 Squadron. He had Lieutenants Lampard and Quinan in his H.Q. Troop and Lieutenants Isitt, Osborne and Callender and Sergeant Cardus commanding troops. Edward Tyler, now a Major, succeeded Major Madden as Squadron Leader of No. 2. He had Captain Tylor in his headquarters as his second-in-command and, as troop leaders, Lieutenants Seth-Smith, Agnew, Gorman, and Sergeant Garland.

In No. 3 Squadron, Captain Michael O'Cock had S.S.M. Holly and Sergeant Upritchard in his headquarters, leaving his second-in-command, Lieutenant Wilfred Dodd, Lieutenant Keith Heatcote and Sergeant Mahony to command the three troops. He was not going to worry about a leader for the fourth troop till the tanks arrived to form it. Apart from these, there was Lieutenant John Swann in reserve with the Tank Delivery Squadron and the Irish Guards officers at Divisional H.Q. Colonel Finlay continued what he called his "Joe Savill policy" of demanding the return of these officers, but without result.

For the last two days the Battalion had been more or less stationary. There had been many rumours of a further advance and suggestions of a regrouping that would put the Battalion under the command of 32nd Brigade, but there was nothing definite until the 9th. That morning the Brigade Commander announced that the Guards Armoured Division was going to change places with the 11th Armoured Division. The object of the manœuvre was to put the Guards Division in a position to exploit the assumed success of an attack by the 3rd Division. The Battalion was ordered to relieve the 3rd Royal Tank Regiment at La Barbière on the right flank. Here it would come under command of the 32nd Guards Brigade, while its place in 5th Brigade was taken by the 1st Armoured Coldstream Guards. Colonel Finlay did not return from this Order Group. His health had completely broken down and he relinquished command of the Battalion to Major Giles Vandeleur. When Colonel Finlay returned to England he wrote a short account of the Battalion's actions. He ends with the sentence, "At 1200 hours Giles Vandeleur took over command of the Battalion from Kim Finlay."

During the afternoon the Battalion moved to La Barbière, leaving No. 3 Squadron behind to support the 5th Coldstream. They were looking forward to a rest, but without much conviction. Battalion H.Q. and No. 1 Squadron got the rest. For them that evening and the following day were quiet; they even got some post and papers and, a few of them, baths. But No. 2 Squadron had no sooner arrived at La Barbière than they had to turn round and drive up to the village of Le Bas Perrier to support the 1st Bn. Welsh Guards. Here they found No. 3 Squadron, who had moved up with the Coldstream. Together they spent the following day preparing to attack Chenedolle. The Division had been ordered to attack straight south to cut the main Vassy–Vire road. The Estry–Vire road runs along one ridge; the Vassy–Vire runs along another three miles south. Between the two stretches a broad, open valley, with the village of Chenedolle in the middle, protected by a long, high, isolated ridge. The 1st Welsh and 5th Coldstream, under 32nd Brigade, were to attack on the left over the ridge, with the 3rd Bn. Irish Guards and the Grenadiers, under 5th Brigade, on the right. The 32nd Brigade was well supported. As well as No. 2 and No. 3 Squadrons, it had the 3rd Bn. Scots Guards from the 6th Guards Tank Brigade in Churchill tanks, and a big concentration of guns. The unfortunate 3rd Battalion at Sourdeval got very little of this support; they were told they would not need any. The 1st Welsh and No. 2 Squadron moved to the village of Houssemagne so as to be on the extreme left of the Brigade front. They were quietly studying the Germans opposite them when a large propaganda van, dignified by the presence of the Divisional Intelligence Officer, Captain George Doughty, drove into their positions. The self-styled experts in psychological warfare proposed to address through loudspeakers and dishearten the Germans and their foreign troops. The dust raised by the van brought down an immediate "stonk" of shells, so the propagandists departed quickly to find a more receptive audience, leaving the less intellectual soldiers to suffer the result of their visit.

The Division attacked at eleven o'clock on the morning of the 11th August. The Germans resisted fiercely, and most strongly in the centre. The 3rd Battalion, as described later, had an appalling day. No. 2 Squadron, on the left flank, fought a most successful but costly action with the 1st Welsh Guards. Two troops, commanded by Captain Vivian Taylor, supported the Prince of Wales Company in their attack. The Welsh advanced through heavy shell and mortar fire to reach the long ridge which covered the village of Chenedolle. The tanks rolled slowly forward, keeping pace with the infantry, over the ridge, past Chenedolle and up the long spur towards the Vessy–Vire road. As they reached the top of the spur, Captain Taylor realized that there were not enough infantry to hold this ground unless they were given time to dig themselves into good positions. He ordered his tanks forward into the orchards on the top of the ridge. The Germans counter-attacked immediately; their anti-tank guns were already in position covering the crest. While these engaged the Shermans, infantry, Panthers and self-propelled guns worked through the orchards to get around Captain Taylor's force and strike the Welsh Guards. Captain Taylor's own tank was the first victim of the anti-tank guns. Sergeant Garland, one of the troop commanders, accelerated forward to engage the gun and give Captain Taylor and his crew a chance to escape. Captain Taylor jumped into the next tank and ordered his "remount" forward to help, in turn, Sergeant Garland. To get a shot at the anti-tank gun, Sergeant Garland had to move his tank into a most exposed position. Almost at once his tank was hit and crippled. Captain Taylor destroyed the anti-tank gun and moved on towards the orchards. Sergeant Garland and his crew stayed in their tank and kept up continual fire until they had shot away all their ammunition. Sergeant Garland then surrounded himself with smoke and ordered his crew to get away; he himself stayed behind to keep the smoke going until they were well away, and only then followed.

The troops were hotly engaged all the afternoon, fighting the Germans off the Welsh Guards. Captain Taylor's "remount" got bogged in an unexpected stream. By now the troops had lost six tanks out of eight in return for two Panthers and an assault gun, so one of the two survivors could not be abandoned. Captain Taylor and his crew stayed in their tank in close contact with the German infantry, who persisted in stalking them with the devilish "panzer-fausts." Well used to such things, he beat off all attacks on himself and the Welsh Guards till the Welsh Guards reported that they were firmly established. Then he brought his crew back safely through the Germans. Lieutenant Peter Agnew was one of the casualties in this action. His tank was hit and, as usual, went on fire. Though not wounded by the shot, he was badly burnt because he stayed inside to help out his crew. In any account of a tank battle with Sherman tanks the phrase "Hit and went on fire" recurs monotonously. If these tanks were hit anywhere in the hull they burst into flames, and in a minute were roaring furnaces. There are various suggested explanations : the system of stacking exposed ammunition round the body of the tank certainly cost a great many lives. The Germans, acute observers, called the Shermans "Tommy cookers."

No. 3 Squadron and the 5th Coldstream took Chenedolle. S.S.M. Parke's Firefly was hit at long range by a Panther, but no one was hurt. The inevitable shelling before dusk knocked off another officer, Lieutenant Willy Dodd. With six tanks destroyed, No. 2 Squadron was "thin on the ground," so it was relieved by No. 1 and came back to La Barbière for a day's rest.

The Guards Armoured Division now "froze" in its positions. Their offensive task was finished, and for a fortnight they sat still in the same area while attacks went in on their left and right. The Germans continued to shell steadily all the following days, but fortunately hit nobody. The Brigade had taken a great many prisoners, including Russians conscripted by the Germans. Captain Terence O'Neill kept a pet Mongol youth for a week, to dig trenches and carry his kit and maps. The Mongol, when first ordered to dig, thought it was his grave and started to cry. Captain O'Neill explained, by mime and gesture, that it was for life, not death, that he was digging. The Mongol then kissed him and dug the snuggest slit-trench ever seen for his deliverer. After a week Divisional H.Q. ordered Captain O'Neill to give up his Mongol "as a security measure."

The following day No. 2 Squadron moved to Sourdeval on the right to support the Household Cavalry, who had taken over the position from the 3rd Battalion. The squadron areas now were: No. 1 Squadron, with the 1st Welsh, north of Le Bas Perrier; No. 3 Squadron, with the 5th Coldstream, by Point 242, the Chenedolle position having been evacuated; and No. 2 Squadron, with the 2nd Household Cavalry Regiment. One troop of each squadron was dug in by bulldozers in the infantry forward positions. Battalion H.Q. now had only the echelons and itself to control—a simple task, not requiring much energy. The tired squadrons badly needed rest, but they could not get it. Though enemy activity was confined to the inevitable shelling, they were still in the line and could not really relax.

The long-promised reinforcements of officers arrived by air. To the Battalion came Major D. R. S. FitzGerald, who took over No. 3 Squadron; Captain Anthony Dorman returned from hospital; Lieutenant Harry Fitzherbert, Lieutenant Hugh McDermott, Tim Hallinin, Bill McFetridge, Alexander Faris and Joe Daly. Lieutenants David Radcliffe and Anthony Samuelson went to the Forward Tank Delivery Squadron. The officers were delighted to see their old friends. They promptly put them down on the duty roster and exchanged battle stories for home gossip.

The Guards Division was now being "pinched out of the line"—that is, the troops on either flank were advancing and the Germans retreating, leaving the Division behind in a quiet, if battered, countryside. The German counter-attack had failed and their whole 7th Army was in imminent danger of being encircled by the British and Canadians from the north and the Americans from the south. The

Germans now concentrated on keeping the two jaws of the trap apart at Falaise to give themselves a gap through which they could withdraw their troops. As General Eisenhower afterwards acknowledged, it was the unceasing British pressure which had prevented the Germans from massing their armour to launch an effective attack. The 8th Corps now stayed in reserve, while American, Canadian and other British troops completed the encirclement of the Germans by closing the Falaise gap. Unlike the newspaper correspondents, the Battalion knew that much of the German armour at least could escape before the gap was closed.

General Montgomery, accompanied by the Secretary of State for War, descended on No. 2 Squadron. Surrounded by the burnt-out hulks of Shermans, he made one of his rousing speeches to the stolid Guardsmen. Even though the Germans might escape through the Falaise gap, he hoped to destroy them west of the River Seine. After that, he said, they would "roll up the Buzz Bomb bases and see the cliffs of Dover from the coast of Calais. In the fighting to date we have defeated the Germans in battle; we have had no difficulty in dealing with German armour, once we had grasped the problems. . . . We have nothing to fear from the Tiger and the Panther tanks; they are unreliable mechanically, and the Panther is very vulnerable from the flanks. Our 17-pdr. will go right through them. Provided our tactics are good, we can defeat them without difficulty." For the ordinary tank commander, however, the basic and ineluctable problem was that every German tank could destroy Shermans, while only one Sherman out of four—the one Firefly, armed with a 17-pdr. gun—could penetrate the German armour. A lucky or very accurate shot from the ordinary 75-mm. gun could, of course, smash the German's suspension, but then, even Achilles had his heel. In the Normandy tank battles the Allies defeated the Germans because they could afford to lose six tanks to every one German. The 2nd Bn. Irish Guards lost 175 tanks in the whole campaign. Of the original sixty-one tanks the Battalion brought out to Normandy, only two survived the war, and each of these two had been twice hit and twice repaired.

The Battalion reverted to the command of 5th Brigade on the 16th. The squadrons returned to Battalion H.Q. and they all moved to a pleasant orchard near Le Queillet. "Rest and reorganize for four days," they were told, "after that anything may happen." Their life here was described as one of "ducks, hens and kip," but their pleasure was spoiled by the appalling stench of decomposing cows. They were in a rich dairy country previously abounding in fat milk cattle; it was now littered with rotting carcases, and the smell of death hung over the Battalion. It took the Royal Engineers three days to clear the Battalion's area, blowing "cow-graves" with explosives and pushing in the carcases with "bull-dozers." The more prominent dead cows were buried in time for an investiture by General Montgomery, who presented the Military Cross to Lieutenant J. R. Gorman and the Military Medal to Lance-Corporal Baron. To the Division he gave general congratulations on the success of their battle, which had made possible the spectacular success of the U.S. 3rd Army. The men who did not live to see this success were buried in a little cemetery near Le Queillet. The whole Battalion attended the official funeral of their friends.

To our great joy Brigadier Norman Gwatkin returned to command the 5th Brigade. He had a small becoming scar on his cheek and was temporarily paler, but otherwise just the same. The war had receded far enough for the Divisional H.Q. to give a Fete Champetre to celebrate the visit of the Major-General and the Brigade Major, Lieut.-General Sir Charles Lloyd and Colonel Tim Nugent. Finally, Major M. Gordon-Watson, M.C. (and two bars) arrived from England to be Second-in-Command. The Battalion welcomed him warmly, for he had commanded No. 2 Squadron for eighteen months at Tisbury, and the Watson "way of life" was well known. "His arrival," said one of his friends, "combined with the slaughter at Falaise, sealed the fate of the Germans in France. He compared the Bocage with Tunisia and Anzio, and found it rather wanting."

The Battalion spent the days repairing trucks and tanks, playing a little cricket, visiting the local farmers, suffering from a mild, but uncomfortable form of dysentery, and indulging in that perpetual vice of a mechanized army, "swanning." To "swan" is to get into a vehicle and drive round the countryside with or without a purpose. Truck loads of Guardsmen went on battlefield tours. "Devastation is still in belts only, and is pretty severe on every single building. Tilly, for instance, has no house remotely habitable, but is by no means flat. In general, I got the impression that a couple of hundred energetic tidier-ups could put right 90 per cent. of the non-household damage. Even in a well-wrecked village near Tilly, the runner beans in a cottage garden were neat and as undisturbed as ever."

Small parties of officers drove to Mont St. Michel or St. Pair, near Granville, for a bathe. The food was excellent and the views lovely. One of them wrote: "We had lunch beneath the Abbey at the 'original' and famous Mere Poulard, not one of the bogus imitations in the village, as the signpost told us." Mont St. Michel was full of U.S. rubbernecks asking when the curio shops would be open. Prices were very high, naturally, for the transatlantic liberators and tourists, but the food was good. At Rennes there was a little damage and few Americans, but plenty of Civil Affairs officers. The shops were fuller of good things than those in England. The married men began their purchases of scent and other luxuries to earn good marks at home.

On the 24th the Battalion received orders to move again next day. Major N. A. R. O'Neill, as Battalion Harbourer, went to the village of Cerisi Belle Etoile to choose a new harbour area. An accident on the way there left the Battalion with another gap to fill. His scout car went over a steep bank, threw him off and then landed almost on top of him, luckily only hitting his foot. His foot was badly crushed and bones were broken, which would take some two months to cure. The Battalion felt his loss greatly, as he was the only original Squadron Leader left. Brigade H.Q. now could hold on to Captain J. L. L. Savill no longer, and he arrived to join No. 1 Squadron.

The Battalion had to move once again; it was the same as any other, slow and uneventful, with the "wheels" going by road and the tanks separately by special track. The Battalion settled in amongst the fields and orchards round Cerisi Belle Etoile and began to "shoot in" the new tanks, especially the Fireflies. Here Major D. Peel, disgorged by the Forward Delivery Squadron, rejoined the Battalion to take command of No. 1 Squadron. The Battalion probably owed more to David Peel than to any other single man. He had been Adjutant during the long and often dreary period of training in Wiltshire. It is difficult for an Adjutant to be popular, for he is normally associated with drill parades and punishments, but David Peel was more than popular. He was loved and admired by every officer and man. The 2nd Battalion will for all time associate David Peel with its growth to maturity, and those who served with him will not easily forget his influence. He left the Battalion to reorganize the difficult and intricate Divisional Tank Delivery Squadron. On his ability rested the smooth running of the tank reserves in the Normandy battles.

After a week came new rumours of another move to battle. Paris had fallen, but more important now than Paris were the obscure forests and villages in which the S.S. troops stood to fight. The order to move came suddenly over the telephone from Corps H.Q. to Divisional H.Q. "Put the tanks on transporters and prepare to move to L'Aigle tomorrow, 28th August." L'Aigle was seventy miles away. There the Division would come under command of

30th Corps, cross the Seine and advance on Amiens and on to Antwerp. It was an almost unbelievable order. The Battalion knew the Germans had been beaten in Normandy, but they did not yet realize how complete was their rout. When, eventually, the Germans decided to withdraw behind the Seine they conducted their retreat with great skill, but they had left it too late. They managed to extricate more troops than the Allies hoped, but even so their losses were enormous. They lost some 400,000 men, half of them prisoners, 1,300 tanks and 2,000 guns. Even more disastrous for them, they had lost the chance of holding the line of the Seine.

At eight o'clock on the morning of the 28th August the tanks were sitting on their transporters ready to move ; they did not move till the afternoon. The Battalion occupied the morning by giving a demonstration of a "Rhino." It was a great success, and the Corps Commander and other exalted spectators were delighted. A set of iron prongs, something like a snow-plough, was attached to the front of Sergeant Cardus's tank to convert it into a "Rhino." Sergeant Cardus then drove his tank at a typical Bocage bank and pierced it at high speed ; he even crossed a sunken lane that was supposed to show what a "Rhino" could not do. The attachments were, in fact, excellent, and it was a pity they arrived too late. The Battalion carried a lorry load of them till Christmas, and then dumped them in Holland, as they were no use for canals.

Major Gordon-Watson and an advance party went ahead to find a parking place for the Battalion near L'Aigle. They found some suitable fields by the side of the main road, surrounded by large dry barns and owned by a most hospitable farmer. "He invited four officers to dinner," said Major Gordon-Watson. There is another description of the same event : "Watson forced his way into a farmhouse and insisted on the farmer having himself and us to dinner there and got ' la patronne ' to kill a duck for the occasion. Then he made her drink some Thermos compo tea—several hours old—and finally kissed her exuberantly after 'un grand Calvados,' of which there is still a bottle or two left in every farmhouse."

The tank transporters had a terrible journey ; they arrived at four o'clock in the morning, some three hours late. Four of the tanks had been left behind ditched on the road. Everybody washed and breakfasted, and the tank crews took some hours' sleep before continuing their march. The provisional orders were that, on the far side of the Seine, the Guards Division was to lead on the right, with 11th Armoured Division on the left, and 8th Armoured Brigade, 43rd Division and 50th Division in reserve. Enemy opposition between the Seine and the Somme was reported to be very light—no guns or mortars, and only one Tiger—but previous experience had taught the Battalion how to interpret the optimism of the Higher Command. At midday they continued their journey. They reached Pacy, forty miles away, at midnight, unloaded from the transporters and crossed the Seine on pontoons erected near Vernon. They moved into a harbour area in Stouen la Chappelle, and by two o'clock in the morning the whole of the Battalion was asleep. The supply echelon caught up with them the following morning, the 30th, and the tanks refuelled. At midday the Brigadier gave out the orders for the advance to Amiens ; the Battalion was in Brigade reserve behind the 2nd Grenadiers. They moved off at three o'clock in the pelting rain, drove through enthusiastic crowds till they reached some fields just beyond Gisors. This was the first time the Battalion experienced the joys of a triumphal march. The local population lined the streets, cheering and throwing fruit and flowers and sometimes bottles. But much better was to come. The worries of the Technical Adjutant, Captain R. Robertson, over bogies and engines also began now and were to grow steadily more and more severe.

CHAPTER VI

Sourdeval

3rd Battalion

AFTER the rest of the Division had passed through them at dawn on the 2nd, the 3rd Battalion had spent a quiet day, troubled only by snipers. After seven men had been wounded, patrols swept the area and brought in a few snipers from III/752nd Grenadier Regiment of the 326th Division. Nothing more happened till the following afternoon, the 3rd, when they were ordered forward to St. Charles de Percy. There was no transport available, so the Battalion had to slog along the main road. It was a hot, dusty and unsavoury march, for the road was littered with dead horses. At Catheolles they came under enemy observation, so the companies took to the ditches. They were constantly shelled and frequently machine-gunned as they wound their way up the circling road. They reached St. Charles de Percy just before dark, and there Colonel Joe was told that he must capture Montchamp and Maisoncelles that night.

The Battalion had learnt their lesson at Cagny and now moved forward cautiously on a narrow front from one limited objective to another, making each a firm base for the next move. No. 1 Company, under Major D. Kingsford, led on the right of the road to the first objective, the village of Courteil. A mile down the road they ran straight into the Germans and came under heavy fire which wounded Lieutenant Owen Hickey. "Try the left," ordered Colonel Joe. They tried it, but the fire was just as heavy and they could not get on, With the Battalion H.Q. was a squadron leader of the 1st Coldstream. Major Batt, a gallant and able officer, who was killed the next day. This officer led one of his troops up the road to join No. 1 Company, and together they made a third attack. This did the trick, as Colonel Joe said, and No. 4 Company passed through No. 1 Company to capture the next objective, a farmhouse and orchard half-way to

Maisoncelles. It was now pitch dark ; the country on either side of the road consisted of small fields, thick hedgerows and deep cuttings which might—and, in fact, did—hold swarms of Germans. Colonel Joe decided to have "a good look ahead before going for Maisoncelles." As this meant waiting for the light next morning, the companies dug in where they were.

The Germans counter-attacked before dawn, while it was still dark. They launched their troops towards St. Charles de Percy, parallel to the road, and skirting the two leading companies. Battalion H.Q., in a field just outside St. Charles, bore the weight of the attack and beat it off noisily. The Germans almost certainly ran into Battalion H.Q. by mistake, as they were trying to pass in front of and through it rather than attack it. The result was "we wondered what the hell they were playing at, or if their leading troops really knew their task." They must have been very alarmed when they heard Colonel Joe bellowing "MOW them down ! "—not that most of them could understand any European language. Many of the prisoners who were brought in afterwards were "Tartars, who looked as if they ought to be wearing pigtails." Captain Eric Udal spent a long time interrogating one unhappy man with a pick-handle and in German, till the man thought of one intelligible word—"Russki ! " The whole of Battalion H.Q. followed Colonel Joe's advice. He himself was delightedly firing the gun mounted on his scout car ; Captain Bruce, with some clerks and signallers, climbed trees and loosed off every form of weapon at whatever they thought was a German, and others were belting away with German machine-guns they had collected in the course of the day. The distinctive note and high rate of fire of these Spandaus coming from the middle of Battalion H.Q. confused the Germans, who ran towards them only to be shot down.

That day (the 4th), the 3rd Battalion widened its positions southward. The forward companies were under constant small-arms fire from the Germans who were dug in not more than a hundred yards in front of them. No. 2 Company were ordered to send two platoons a mile south to join and protect the Armoured Brigade's battery of self-propelled anti-tank guns who were operating on the fields and tracks east of Beaulieu. Captain Ellison Woods had just arrived to take command of the Company and this was his first action. He walked to a gateway to take a look at the fields and was killed by a sniper. Captain A. Hendry took over command and the Company reached a low hill (Point 176) where they were joined by the self-propelled battery. Here they fought a separate battle for forty-eight hours, during which Lieutenant T. King-Harman was killed gallantly charging a Spandau. The rest of the Battalion remained all day in their positions, losing four men killed and nineteen men wounded, chiefly by shell-fire. In the late afternoon a small carrier force was sent to help Lieutenant King-Harman's platoon, which was being constantly attacked. Lance-Corporal Brennan, of this force, destroyed one machine-gun himself, but was wounded in the leg in the process. His single-handed success was remarkable ; even more remarkable was his long crawl back through the fields to the platoon.

On the next day, the 5th, the Battalion made a "full dress" attack with proper artillery support. No. 4 Company took Courteil before lunch. Then a combat group, consisting of the "X" Company, Scots Guards, a troop of Coldstream tanks and two anti-tank guns, pushed through Courteil to take the village of Maisoncelles six hundred yards to the south-east. This was not a task that had been set the Battalion, but knowing that the 2nd Battalion at La Marvindière had been attacked all day by Germans from this area, Colonel Joe decided to learn a little more about his right flank before going on to Montchamp. "X" Company met the Germans at Maisoncelles and, after a brisk encounter, cleared the area to within twenty yards of the cross-roads. They captured a German tank intact ; the drive had seized up, and the crew were too busy repairing it to notice the Guardsmen. "We were most interested in the thing, which is undoubtedly formidable and has a gun stretching from here to Sunday week." The Germans reacted immediately by firing everything they had at the Company. The Battalion had apparently touched a sensitive spot, so Colonel Joe built up the defence round this point by adding two 17-pdr. anti-tank guns, the mortar platoon, under Captain Dick Ingleby, and the remaining platoon of No. 2 Company. Just after nightfall one Panther tank, one Mark IV, two Mark III's, a couple of motor-cyclists and a captured petrol lorry, with the 2nd Battalion signs still on it, drove out of a wood on the right and sailed along a track fifty yards in front of the position. The crew of the 17-pdr. were lying by the guns, resting after a long day. In a blur of movement they were on their guns, the layer let fly at ten yards' range, and up went the Panther. "Heads down ! " shouted the gunners to the infantry, and they fired every field piece they had. "The German tanks' crews seemed to go crazy," says a witness and, "much to our astonishment, all four tanks blew up or were abandoned by their crews." The phrase "to our astonishment" is a little hard on the gun crews ; the tanks were inspected next day and they all had shot holes and dead Germans in them. The German

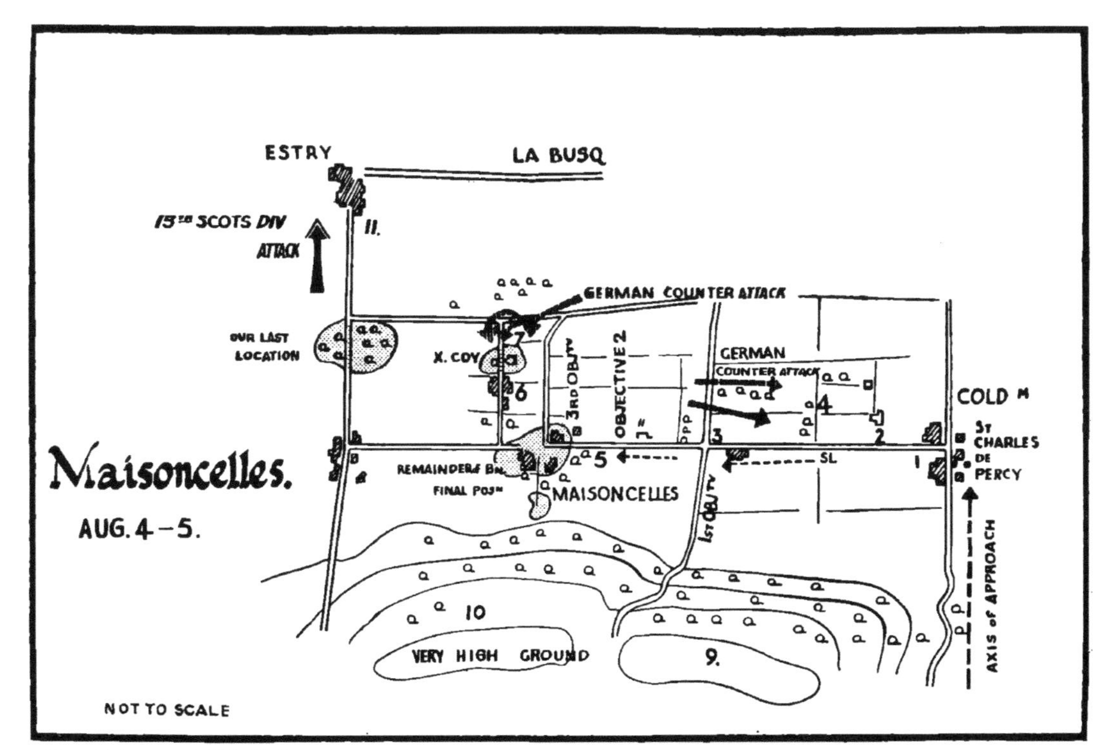

Very high ground (10) (9), heavily wooded, was not clear on night of attack and areas (2), (4), (3) heavily shelled under observation from (9). Areas (2), (4), (3), (5) small fields, big banks, thick hedges, big trees. No visibility except towards (9) and (10), very narrow lane at (6), and orchard surrounding three farm buildings. Germans tried to break back at (7). This is where "X" Company knocked out four tanks and captured one.

force must have been an independent battle group, for immediately after the tanks were destroyed a company of infantry appeared from nowhere and attacked the forward platoons. Once again the gunners let fly with everything they had; the Bren guns joined in, and Captain Ingleby's mortars showered down bombs. The Germans were "seen off" and "X" Company were, as they proudly said, the talk of the town.

The Battalion sat in these positions all the next day, exchanging shots with the Germans in Montchamp. During the night (6th/7th) patrols went out to investigate Montchamp and find the Welsh Guards who were said to be somewhere in the area. They found neither Germans nor Welsh Guards, so at dawn No. 1 Company moved into Montchamp. The village itself was clear of Germans but full of booby-traps. After Corporal Potter had been killed, the companies waited outside the village while the pioneer platoon gingerly searched for mines and booby-traps. Captain D. Compton and his pioneers cleared the houses and streets with such professional skill that they were congratulated by the Royal Engineers.

The Battalion's next task was to clear the area between Montchamp and Estry and hold it while the 15th (Scottish) Division prepared to attack Estry. Already Crocodiles—flame-throwing Churchill tanks—and flails were moving up the road to Montchamp. No. 1 Company pressed on to Pont a' L'Ecrivain, then "X" Company led the way to Les Ecoublets and there the Battalion halted. By now the Germans had withdrawn to Estry and Le Busq, so that the Battalion had to deal only with road-blocks and the anti-personnel mines scattered on the road and in the ditches.

The 15th (Scottish) Division attacked Estry the next day, the 8th. The Scotsmen were held up and streams of their casualties poured into the Battalion's R.A.P. The Germans retaliated on the Scots by heavily shelling and mortaring the Irish Guards. A salvo from the abominable multiple-mortars (the "Moaning Minnies" or "Green Line buses") killed Sergeant English and his carrier section. The steady "crumping" all day inevitably caused other casualties. This was unpleasant, but there was much worse to come. The Battalion was ordered to take over the tip of the 11th Armoured Division's salient. This position was at present held by a composite battalion of the Monmouthshires and the Norfolks—a composite battalion because they had lost so many men there that they had to amalgamate to form one weak battalion. Its name was Sourdeval.

At midday on the 9th Colonel Joe and the company commanders went over to look at Sourdeval. To get there they had to wind their way over dusty roads, with elbow-like turns, in full view of the German observation posts. The small group of houses called Sourdeval lies on the northern slope of a razor-back ridge. Just below the crest of the ridge the Norfolks and Monmouths had dug their positions. The approaches and the whole area were overlooked by the high ground on the left and were under constant shell and machine-gun fire. "There seemed to be a deathly stillness all round this unpleasant place, and never before had we seen such a shambles of burnt-out vehicles and shelled orchards. This was our new home, and it smelt terrible—a new brand of Camembert this time, more ripe than ever." Another officer said more simply, "The stink of corpses was sickening." The Germans had attacked several times recently and had done great execution amongst the defenders.

The Battalion was not looking forward to the journey, as any dust on the road was bound to bring down heavy shell-fire. It was with relief that they heard they were not going to move till after dark. The graveyard of burnt vehicles in the orchard round Battalion H.Q. showed Colonel Joe the folly of bringing up right forward any more transport than was operationally necessary. He divided the transport into three groups—"F" (for fighting), "F.2" and "A." "F" was the actual vehicles the Battalion always needed, the carriers, jeeps, the wireless rear-link truck, and the Commanding Officer's scout car. "F.2" was the vehicles necessary to maintain the Battalion in battle, such as petrol, ammunition, signal stores and the like. The remainder of the vehicles were grouped in "A" Echelon and left well behind. The companies moved quietly into the positions at midnight. "We tidied up the defences a bit, and felt quite secure doing some useful patrolling and really getting to know a lot about the Germans in front of us." These Germans started shelling at dawn and continued all day. Captain D. G. Kingsford was killed; he was asleep in his slit trench, exhausted after a night of constant work, too tired to hear the shell that hit a tree above his trench. Captains David Compton and Geoff Jeffries, and seventeen Guardsmen were wounded by shell splinters or machine-gun bullets.

Early that evening the Germans attacked the two forward companies, Nos. 1 and 4. The Guardsmen beat them off easily.

After dark Captain Udal and his intelligence section found several dead bodies in front of the companies. These Germans carried no means of identification, but Eric Udal gave his opinion that they were paratroopers. He was right; the 10th S.S. Panzer Division had been reinforced in this particular sector by battalions from the combined 3rd and 5th Parachute Division. Lieutenant Kingan led a strong patrol from No. 4 Company over the Sourdeval ridge down the slope through the German positions to the bottom of the valley to the stream and bridge by La Jarriere. He found that the bridge was strongly held and that it was impossible to get across the river to the houses on the other side.

Late that night the Battalion was ordered to attack the following morning and cut the main road running east from Vassy to Vire. This attack was to be "en cadre," with the Grenadier attack on the right directed on Viesseux, and an attack on Chenedolle on the left by the 5th Coldstream and 1st Welsh, supported by the 2nd Irish and the 6th Guards Tank Brigade. The Battalion, therefore, was the centre of a divisional effort directed southwards, but the Welsh and Coldstream attack on the left was considered the main effort and was given the maximum support. The Battalion got only a squadron of 1st Coldstream tanks and one field battery. When Colonel Joe protested three times, Brigade H.Q. stated that unfortunately no more support was available and the attack must take place with the support available as part of the major plan. The Battalion knew very well what lay ahead of them. The patrols could hardly move before being engaged; they had contacted the German posts all along the line of the stream in the valley below the ridge. They knew that German paratroopers were dug in along the embanked road behind the stream and had fortified the two large farmhouses on either side of La Jarriere. They could see the high ground on the left flank and knew that the Germans had heavy tanks and anti-tank guns on it. The only cover was over to the right on the axis of the Grenadiers. The only course open to the Battalion was a head-on attack under the most unfavourable circumstances possible, supported by only one field battery with a limited amount of smoke and their own 3-inch mortars. Finally, in case anyone remained under any delusion, the Germans attacked early on the morning of the 11th. The Battalion beat off this attack only just in time to start their own.

The Battalion attacked at nine o'clock on the morning of 11th August. The vista in front of them was appalling. From the top of Sourdeval ridge the open fields of ripe corn sloped down to the stream in the bottom of the valley. Beyond the stream the ground rose again steadily for five hundred yards up to the line of the main road. A man on this rise could see a mouse move on the forward slope opposite him. On the left flank the Germans entrenched on the high ground could sweep the cornfields with enfilade fire. The Battalion, therefore, had to cross the crest of the ridge, walk down the forward slope with no protecting support, straight into the

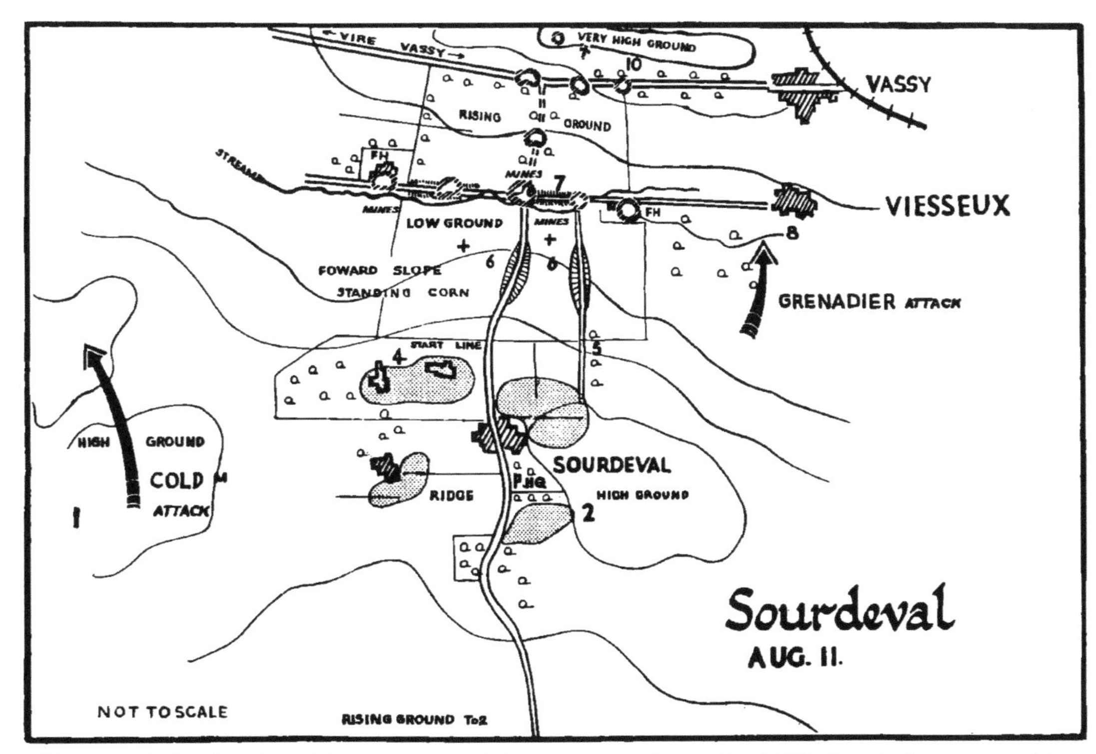

High ground (1), originally held by enemy, overlooked approaches to Sourdeval and O.Ps. brought fire on approaching vehicles. This danger passed after Coldstream attack. The high ground at (10) road and forward slope between (7) and (10) just visible from (4) and (5). (6) equals gentle forward slope in full view of enemy positions located by patrols. Track (6) deep cutting where most casualties occurred, the stream *not* an obstacle.

faces of the paratroopers and their Spandaus, completely under the view of German observers and the fire of their tanks and guns on the high ground to the front and flank. Being fully aware of what they were taking on, Colonel Joe chose an intermediate objective, the line of the stream at La Jarriere. From Sourdeval a narrow lane ran down through the fields to La Jarriere. No. 2 Company, under Major Anthony Eardley-Wilmot, advanced on the left of this lane, and No. 4 under Major Desmond Reid on the right, each company supported by a troop of Coldstream tanks.

"To cut a tragic story short, the moment the leading companies crossed the crest of the ridge they came under devastating fire, the ground being scythed by the Spandaus and ceaselessly crumped by heavy German artillery." The German guns and tanks on the far slope could not miss the Coldstream tanks as soon as they appeared over the crest, and promptly destroyed them. The companies pressed on. For a long hour the two companies walked straight down the hill, pushing through the corn or plodding through root fields. Spandaus, firing straight up the lane and its hedges, drove the Guardsmen away from even this slight cover. Strung out in open order, they advanced steadily through the fire. "The men were splendid, advancing steadily," said Colonel Joe, "and nothing could be done to support them because the bulk of the Brigade's fire-power had been retained for the attack on Chenedolle." There was no cover and the fire came from all sides, so there was no point in going fast or slow, to the left or to the right. They fixed their eyes on the stream ahead of them and ignored the fire. Each man talked occasionally to the man five yards on either side of him till one or the other, or both, or he himself or all three, were hit. The sharp crack of the sniper's rifle punctuated the clatter of machine-guns and the steady thump of mortar bombs. Snipers picked off anyone who showed signs of commanding. Amongst others, they shot Lieutenant Lord Edward Fitzmaurice through the head. Mortar bombs wounded Major Desmond Reid and Lieutenant Kingan, both grievously, and Lieutenant Ryder slightly. The wounded lay where they fell or, if they could, crawled to the shelter of the standing corn. The burning phosphorus of the mortar bombs fired the dry stalks. The companies choked and coughed their way through a swirl of smoke and flame. The wounded watched the flames creep on to them. Some dragged themselves painfully out of the corn back to the open root fields. The stretcher-bearers shed their equipment and worked frantically to shift the unconscious till they, too, dropped wounded in the corn. Lieutenant Pat Bourke crawled back up the ditch along the lane. He knew the ditch was covered by a Spandau, but it was the only way to get back to two helpless men. He was killed before he got there.

At ten o'clock the companies reached the line of the stream. Three-quarters of their strength lay on the slope behind them—33 men killed and 72 wounded. The surviving officers, Major A. Eardley-Wilmot, Lieutenant Harvey-Kelly and Lieutenant Brian Wilson led the charge. The Guardsmen rushed the trenches along the stream. At last they could get at a solid enemy. On the right flank a blast of fire killed Major Eardley-Wilmot and swept away the leading wave. Lance-Corporal Bolton, a mortar-section commander, picked up a Bren from a dead gunner's hand and walked on steadily and firmly, firing from the hip—three paces forward, fire long bursts, change magazine, three paces forward. With this remarkable support his friends on either side came on again. All along the line the Guardsmen jumped into the trenches, slaughtered the paratroopers with cold rage and pitched their bodies out of the trenches. The first men to get to close grips were C.S.M. Larkin and Guardsman J. Cullen. C.S.M. Larkin's body was found on top of a trench with two dead Germans underneath him. There were four Germans in the trench. Guardsman J. Cullen killed the other two and then turned on three Germans who were throwing grenades at his section. Cullen was an old and wise soldier; he threw back a grenade to cover himself, shot the Germans and installed his section in the comparative safety of the trenches. The main road still lay ahead, five hundred yards up the bare slope. "It was obviously impossible to continue with the next phase over the same axis of advance, so the attack was called off."

The shattered companies sat in their captured trenches stolidly enduring the constant shelling. They could not get forward, and they were not going to go back. The two other companies, who had waited on the top of Sourdeval ridge to pass through the leading companies as soon as they reached the stream, could now do nothing. They went forward in small parties with stretchers to bring in the wounded. The stretcher-bearers hoisted crude Red Cross flags. The Germans continued firing, but the stretcher-bearers worked on devotedly. Colonel Joe was now determined on two things—the wounded, many of whom were badly burnt, must be collected, and Nos. 2 and 4 Companies, who were losing more casualties, must be withdrawn. There was only one answer—smoke—and at half-past three Brigade H.Q. gave permission to use it, "provided it did not interfere with other operations." The artillery battery said it would take them an hour to prepare enough smoke shells. While they were waiting, Captain Drew, of the Scots Guards, volunteered to go forward, destroy a particularly troublesome German machine-gun post on the left flank, and shout the orders to the companies to withdraw when the smoke came down. Two Scots Guardsmen went with him. First one companion was wounded, then the other, his soldier servant, was killed, then Captain Drew himself got three bullets through the calf of the leg, but he got there and he killed the Germans.

The smoke came down at half-past four. Captain Drew, in spite of his wounds, went forward again to meet and guide the Guardsmen. The Germans sent infantry round the right flank to cut off the withdrawal. Guardsman J. Greenan with a Bren gun headed them off till all his comrades of No. 4 Company were away, and then walked slowly back, turning every now and then to discourage the Germans from following him. Every man who could be spared from the reserve companies was sent out into the smoke to search the corn. The doctor warned the casualty clearing station by wireless, "Wounded casualties amount to eighty-one ; there may be more, but that is all that is known now." As a final touch three Scots Guardsmen were killed when a mine they were fusing exploded. The Battalion counted its losses and "felt very bitter." The remnants of No. 2 and No. 4 Companies were amalgamated into one company called No. 2, and were commanded for the day by Lieutenant Edward Rawlence, normally the Transport Officer, but now the only available officer. The Company contained two platoons, one of the survivors of No. 4 under Lieutenant John Stanley-Clarke, who had been "left out of battle," and the other survivors of No. 2 under Lieutenant William Harvey-Kelly, the only company officer untouched. Lieutenant Brian Wilson had been wounded early in the attack ; he had stayed on his feet all day, but now he collapsed. Captain Alec Hendry, who had also fortunately been "left out of battle," later took over the Company.

The following day was quiet. Search parties found and buried the dead where they lay, marking the shallow graves with broken rifles and steel helmets. The next day, the 13th, the Germans withdrew and the Battalion handed over "this horrible place" to the dismounted troopers of the 2nd Household Cavalry Regiment. "Both our predecessors, the 11th Armoured, and ourselves had taken a packet in this beastly place, and we were glad to leave it."

The Battalion moved to Le Busq. Around their new positions lay the wreckage of the 2nd Battalion's fighting, many hulks of Shermans and an odd German tank. Here they were "mildly in contact" with the enemy, but they spent most of their time resting, refitting and washing. After all their casualties the Battalion could only muster three weak companies, so a field company of Royal Engineers came up to act as the fourth company. The Sappers were delighted at the idea of fighting as infantry, but there was no call for them to do so. The fighting in Normandy was over. "It got quite hilarious during our stay in Le Busq. We heard all about Falaise ; we got the news of the landing in the South of France. What had originally been a front-line position became a sort of gipsy encampment, and we all smartened up and completely revived from that horrid Sourdeval." The Battalion were still on "compo" rations, but from the surrounding farms they were able to get butter and cheese, new potatoes and peas. There was also plenty of cider. Breakfast was ruined one morning when the sleepy cooks made the Battalion's tea with their own private store of cider.

Reinforcements arrived in driblets : First two subalterns, Lieutenants R. C. Taylor and M. Aird, and ten Guardsmen from the Reinforcement Holding Unit, then Major G. E. Fisher-Rowe to take over No. 1 Company from Lieutenant Peter Doyle, and, finally, Major J. S. O. Haslewood and the complete No. 4 Company from the 1st Battalion—"all veterans, and it was grand to see them," said Colonel Joe. In the Reinforcement Camp was another complete company commanded by Captain M. V. Dudley. They were trying to get up to the Battalion ; the Battalion was pleading to have them sent up immediately, but it was days before they arrived. On the 19th a short memorial service was held for the dead, and their names were read out. After the name Major Anthony Eardley-Wilmot, Colonel Joe was able to put the letters M.C.—that morning his award for Cagny had been announced.

Here "X" Company, Scots Guards, left the Battalion to join the 1st Bn. Welsh Guards. The Scots Company Commander wrote to his Lieutenant-Colonel : "Everyone was very doleful when we left the Irish Guards, as we got on so splendidly with them and they treated us wonderfully. They gave us a party when we left, and not one could doubt they were as sorry to see us go as we were to leave. Colonel Joe has always treated us as something special (better than we deserved) and gave us a great send-off, and is also sending a card to every man in the Company. So far, we have given him nothing but three cheers which were the loudest and heartiest I ever heard." The farewell party for the Scots Guards was the best and longest given in Normandy since the days of William the Conqueror. The central piece was "a barbecue roast ox, surmounted by flowers, washed down with whisky, rum and Naafi beer, all to the sound of the pipes and gramophone records played through a naval loud-hailer."

On the 23rd the Battalion moved to Montilly, "an even nicer place, where we lived in orchards, ate dozens of apples, drank a lot of Calvados apple brandy, got terrible headaches, had a children's party, a divisional milling competition and a concert from the Life Guards' Band—we had completely forgotten there was a war on." The children's party was an enormous success. The Battalion asked the Mayor and priest of the village to send thirty children. They must have found that they could not refuse any child if they wished to continue living in the same village as their parents, for the entire juvenile population—110 children—descended on the Battalion, all of them very hungry. The Quartermaster, Lieutenant Hastings, was hard put to it to fill these voracious boys and girls, but he somehow produced enough sandwiches, cakes, sweets and prunes. The children ran races ; the pipers played, and the despatch-riders gave a trick motor-cycle display, jeered by their friends and cheered by the children. The parents walked solemnly round the Battalion area dressed in their stiff Sunday best, trying to tell embarrassed Guardsmen how grateful they were. The Battalion now understood why most of the French they had seen so far were so well dressed—the French always put on their best clothes to be liberated.

On the 29th the Battalion left Montilly just after midnight and drove steadily till they crossed the Seine on the morning of the 30th at Vernon. "Then came the ride to Brussels," says Colonel Joe. "A lovely drive through magnificent country, most interesting scenes of the German retreat, but no fighting."

CHAPTER VII

The Liberation of Brussels

2nd and 3rd Battalions

ON the 28th August the commander of 30th Corps, General Horrocks, had asked Major-General Adair how long it would take the Guards Armoured Division to reach the Seine. He wanted to get the Corps up to the River Somme as soon as possible. The 43rd Division was already on the far bank of the River Seine, and the 11th Armoured Division and the 8th Armoured Brigade were in process of crossing. General Alan replied that as the Guards Division was still one hundred miles away, the earliest that it could concentrate north of the Seine was the night of the 30th August. "Then we will start tomorrow," said General Horrocks, "11th Armoured Division directed on Amiens, 8th Armoured Brigade on Beauvais. You will come up as soon as you can, moving by night if necessary, pass through the 8th Brigade and seize the crossing over the River Somme at Corbie." By nightfall on the 30th August the Guards Division was assembled on the north bank of the Seine.

The Division was up early the next day to take full advantage of the German rout. At two o'clock in the morning, in the pouring rain, the 2nd Battalion started off again. By ten o'clock, after a difficult drive over a tortuous route, they reached Beauvais. The local F.F.I. had collected a number of prisoners from the woods, and wanted more. "Beaucoup Boches," they shouted, pointing in all directions at once. Even Captain H. C. Fitzherbert and "F.2" column were invited to clear a wood with a 3-ton lorry. Beyond thanking them politely—"Merci, m'sieu, merci, nous avons assez de Boches"—the Battalion paid no attention. There was no need to. The German troops were streaming along the roads, sometimes ahead and sometimes behind the Division, trying to get back anyhow to the Fatherland. They stole farm carts, bicycles and even perambulators, to relieve the weariness of their feet.

Through cheering crowds and a hail of unripe fruit the Battalion drove on through Breteuil, Morieuil, Sourdon, and Villers Bretonneux. In silence they passed the cemeteries of the last war. "Same enemy, same ground"—it sounded like a sort of fire order. At Fouilloy Major David Peel led the Battalion across the River Somme. They harboured for the night on the high ground north of the river.

Meanwhile, the 11th Armoured Division on the left had captured Amiens. There they picked up the German Army Commander. His information was sadly out of date; he was looking for some divisions with which to hold the line of the Somme, and carrying a map with divisional sectors nicely drawn in and a fine set of orders for a ferocious battle.

The next morning, the 1st September, the advance continued. The Coldstreamers found Arras deserted except for a few snipers and one General von Grolmann. From all sides reports came in that the Germans were retreating in disorder. For the 2nd Battalion—still in 5th Brigade reserve—the day was much the same as the two previous ones. Their original orders had been to halt in Arras, but when, at half-past five, they drove in tired and dusty and thinking only of tea, they were given a company of the 5th Coldstream and told to occupy Douai before dark. In an hour their report came back. "Nothing to worry about. All O.K." On the way they had met only one German, an unusually disagreeable officer, whose car was packed with looted brandy and cigars, and whom the French were very eager to lynch. They drove into Douai over a Class 9 bridge—to the disgust of the Royal Engineers, who had always maintained that nothing less than a Class 30 could bear an armoured battalion. In the town the Battalion got the warmest welcome so far. The crowds filled the streets cheering wildly, blocking the way of the tanks and generally behaving more like devotees of the Juggernaut than stolid burghers of Artois. Helped by the F.F.I., who were numerous and partially organized, the Battalion rounded up some four hundred prisoners, including three women whose misfortune touched Captain Fitzherbert's chivalrous heart. These were marched off to the Town Hall for imprisonment, being heartily booed by the crowds on the way. They came from six different divisions and a variety of static units. Unfortunately there was amongst them no paymaster, to the great disappointment of the Battalion, who knew that the 2nd Grenadiers had captured one with 600,000 francs. Altogether, the F.F.I. north of the Seine were useful to the division, as they were always willing to take over disarmed prisoners, who would otherwise have been, as always, an intolerable nuisance.

Battalion H.Q. stayed in the main square in a cafe, where the proprietor, though patriotic, did not forget to present a large bill. The squadrons, each to be joined later by a platoon of infantry, went out to guard the three main roads leading out of the town to Arras, Lille and Cambrai. Meanwhile, Captain E. N. Fitzgerald was busy on the telephone in the Sub-Prefecture. He rang up the Mayor of Lille and, in his best Parisian French, enquired about the Germans' progress. There was an S.S. regiment there, he was told, but they and all the other Germans were retreating fast and making no attempt to defend the city. Later in the evening the Commanding Officer paid a ceremonial visit to the Town Hall and was greeted with speeches and toasts by the Mayor and Sub-Prefect. This enjoyable ceremony was interrupted by the news that an enemy column had bumped into No. 3 Squadron. A battle group of the 10th S.S. Division, on their way from Albert to Valenciennes, had taken the wrong road, as the F.F.I. had altered all the signposts. In this encounter the Germans lost six of their precious lorries and a dozen men, but Lieutenant J. A. P. Swann, a troop commander, was killed and Sergeant A. Muse, a tank commander, was taken prisoner.

"We were in position with our tanks at a cross-roads and waiting for the infantry to arrive," said Sergeant Muse. "Just as it was getting dark a truck load of German infantry came up to our position and a platoon of Coldstreamers arrived at the same moment. About ten minutes later, while the Coldstreamers were still getting into position, I heard something moving up the road to my right. It sounded like a tank, but we could see nothing. After another ten minutes I judged it was within fifty yards of me. We fired armour-piercing, high explosive and, on seeing figures running about, Browning. Sparks flew off something, but I still did not know what it was. Lieutenant Swann asked me what I was firing at, and I told him. He said that one of our tanks was moving about up the other road and sent me to find out what it was doing. Half-way to that tank, I was hit by a grenade which injured my legs, left shoulder and eardrum. I went on and found that the tank was only moving into the shade, as the moon was very bright. Then I heard Lieutenant Swann calling me. As I was going back I heard a shot fired and saw Lieutenant Swann fall to the ground. He was dead. I went on round to the left-hand side of my tank, intending to get inside, as I could not see my crew anywhere. I saw three people standing on the left of my tank. Thinking they might be Germans, I turned round to go back again. One of them shouted 'Come back !' Now, thinking that they were Coldstreamers, I went over to them and was taken prisoner.

"As our tanks had moved up and were firing Brownings down the road, the Germans began to withdraw. I could now see that their transport was mostly horse drawn. They cleared the dead horses out of the way, collected their dead and wounded, put them on the carts and went back the way they must have come. The German wounded, and myself, were fixed up with torn shirts and bandages. The medical officer apologized to me for not having any medical kit of any kind with him. I now joined my tank crew, who were also prisoners. We walked on until about seven o'clock the next morning, when we rested until 0930 hours. Neither the Germans nor ourselves had anything to eat. The column consisted of S.S. and other German soldiers, Poles, Russians and Czechs. An English-speaking guard, the soldier who had called me over, asked me what I thought of V.1. I told him it was not too bad at all, but he claimed that London was no more, and that Southern England did not exist—the Fuehrer had said so. I then asked him why they were withdrawing so fast, and he said it was the same as us in 1940. We retreated and built up our arms and pushed them back. They were going to do the same. I reminded him of the strip of water between us in 1940. He replied they could easily hold us while their armaments were being made ; he was convinced Germany would win—in the end.

"We went on again and halted again at 0500 hours the next morning, a march of nineteen and a half hours. We then set off again at 0800 hours. We still had nothing to eat. At about midday we reached Tournai, where the Germans were taking food from the warehouse and the column was shot up by Typhoons. We were put in a glasshouse just off the road, where we were left until about 1800 hours. We were then left with three guards, as the rest of the column had left. Later an officer put us in M.T. and we caught up the rest of the column. Every vehicle in the M.T. column had a Red Cross. Guns had branches stuck in parallel to the gun, and a sheet with a Red Cross spread over them. Only one vehicle was a real ambulance. We then walked till 0400 hours, when we reached a S.S. H.Q. in a big house. We were put in a barn and our boots removed. The next morning the German column pulled out in a hurry and left us with three guards.

"We started walking until we came to the cross-roads in Angiers. There a civilian told us that an American car had just gone over the cross-roads. The German, who understood English, told the others about this and they all got jittery. Seeing this, I told them that they were now our prisoners. They agreed, and said we either go free or go with them. I said we would go free and have their rifles and take them with us. As we were taking their rifles a German staff car came over the cross-roads and opened fire on us. We jumped into a ditch, ran into a house and through into the woods at the back. The three Germans escaped in the confusion. Some Belgians arrived and we asked them to stop the next English vehicle they saw. In five or six hours they stopped a Household Cavalry scout car. We climbed on board it and set off to find our Battalion. On the way we came upon two German trucks parked across the road, which fired on us. As we were crowded in the car, we could not fire back. Three of us jumped into the ditch and the driver said he would go on, mop up the enemy and return. He did not return, so we made our own way to a place called Tollembeek. There the Maquis put us up for the night and the next day took me to a civilian hospital at Ninove."

To return to the Battalion and the 1st September. The 2nd Bn. "A" Echelon also had its share of cheers, prisoners and the joys of liberation. The commander, Major Sir John Reynolds, and a crate of champagne joined the Battalion in Douai late at night ; both were welcome.

The 3rd Battalion, in the 32nd Brigade, now in reserve, left Froissy that morning and reached Arras just as it was getting dark. Having already cheered the 2nd Battalion, the inhabitants turned out again to cheer the 3rd. Battalion H.Q. descended on a large country house outside the town. Their approach up the drive, the crashing of trees and the grinding destruction of gates and posts brought out the owner. He was in tears, but of joy, not, as the drivers thought, of rage. He was delighted to have the Signal Office set up in his drawing room, and produced his wife and daughters, beds, food, wine and, finally, since he scorned the effeminate Calvados of Normandy, bottles of a home-made applejack that brought to the eyes tears of yet another kind. The following day the 3rd Battalion moved into the northern outskirts of Douai. The 2nd Battalion was still there, still being cheered by the indefatigable crowds. Some more prisoners were taken and a few collaborators unearthed by the F.F.I. The Major, Sub-Prefect and the Town Council, headed by the town band, marched in state to Battalion H.Q. While the band played "God Save the King" and "La Marseillaise," these civic worthies exchanged speeches and toasts with Lieut.-Colonel Giles Vandeleur. On the pavement outside a crowd of townspeople collected, all anxious to join in the toasts. In the early afternoon the Battalion moved out to join the 3rd Battalion. They drove into the village of Waziers, two miles up the main road to Brussels. The civilians, as usual, cheered wildly and swarmed over the tanks. The F.F.I. were called in to control the crowd. As usual, they failed to do this, but they pointed out an alleged collaborator's house, very suitable for a Battalion H.Q. Battalion H.Q. promptly installed themselves for a comfortable bath and dinner. Major Sir John Reynolds had the first bath and took most of the hot water ; the discontent of those who followed was later submerged in champagne, politically tainted by collaboration, but otherwise excellent.

In the afternoon the battalions of the Division were redistributed among the two brigades to form four regimental groups, each consisting of an armoured battalion and an infantry battalion of the same regiment. The fighting in Normandy had proved that the old rigid organization of one purely armoured brigade and one infantry brigade, occasionally assisting each other, was no longer desirable or practicable. The tanks and the infantry must work together as one composite force. The grouping at Caumont had been haphazard, as in the stress of the time it had to be. The 2nd Armoured Bn. Irish Guards had formed a group with the 5th Bn. Coldstream Guards, for instance, simply because they happened to be harbouring in adjacent fields. Similarly the 3rd Bn. Irish Guards got the support of whatever tanks chanced to be available. Now, however, a motherly Divisional Staff arranged a series of suitable regimental matches. The armoured battalion of each of the four regiments—Grenadiers, Coldstream, Irish and Welsh—was joined to its opposite infantry number to form a battle group. For the moment the Grenadier and Coldstream groups were under command of 5th Brigade, and the Irish and Welsh groups were under command of 32nd Brigade.

These groups might, and often did, change from one brigade to the other to suit the needs of the moment, but from now until the end of the war the Division fought on the basis of regimental union.

The Irish Group was born at six o'clock on the evening of 2nd September. Few unions can have had such a splendid result ; the two battalions worked in perfect accord and mutual trust. Each knew that it could depend absolutely on the other, and that either would take any risk to help the other. The tedious theoretical volumes preaching "Infantry and Tank Co-operation" reduced themselves to the practical fact that "the Micks muck in." The first day of the Group's life made history, and its first orders are a classic of this kind. Lieut.-Colonel J. O. E. Vandeleur, of the 3rd Battalion, as senior officer and therefore Group Commander, summoned the officers of both battalions to his H.Q. "Enemy information—one word, Chaos. Our intentions: The Irish Guards will dine in Brussels tomorrow night." The Divisional Commander's orders had been even briefer. "The Division will capture Brussels." The plan was straightforward. The main road was allotted to 32nd Brigade, the secondary roads to 5th Brigade. The distance to be covered was ninety-two miles, and it was to be covered "at all possible speed," with a squadron of the 2nd Household Cavalry Regiment leading on each centre line as pace-makers.

There was not much sleep for anyone that night. Both battalions were up and ready to move by half-past four the following morning. It was dark and very cold as the column slowly ground its way forward to the start line for the great race to Brussels. In the dim light before dawn the 3rd Battalion medical officer, Captain Thin, peered at the children of the industrial villages for signs of starvation, and found them.

At six o'clock the Household Cavalry Regiment Squadron and the Welsh Group passed through the Irish, and a few minutes later they were off. To begin with, the Irish Group bumped slowly along bad cross-country tracks and roads, with some long halts while the Welsh Guards fought to clear the route. But soon they crossed the frontier into Belgium and hit the main road. Then the whips were out; every driver became a Jehu, flogging his vehicle faster and ever faster. On, on, on they drove, *ventre à terre*, through Tournai, Ath, Enghien and Hal. Captain E. Rawlence, the 3rd Battalion transport officer, had a terrible day racing up and down the column in a jeep, keeping it closed up, repairing breakdowns and changing trailers from one overloaded truck to another. The 2nd Battalion had no mechanical trouble; for years they had been preparing their tanks for a day like this. Through the Belgian villages roared "St. Patrick," "Ulster," "Leinster," and "Connaught," "Achill," "Bantry," "Cloneen" and sixty-seven other Irish villages and towns. The rattle of tank tracks on the cobbled streets brought the astonished inhabitants out of their houses to wave flags and cheer wildly. Contrary to expectation, the Belgians were more demonstrative than the French, and more practical; they established plum, apple, pear "points," and lobbed bottles of "Lion d'Or" beer into the vehicles. Some stray American armoured cars appeared from the side roads; they cheered the Group and the Group cheered them. The sun shone hotly, and but for the dust everybody enjoyed themselves enormously. Opposition was by-passed or ignored. In Engiennce, for instance, there was a brisk battle in progress between several hundred Germans and the local detachment of the Armée

Blanche, the underground army. These Belgian irregulars could not understand why the passing tanks and troops would not stop to help them, and shook their heads sadly at the shouts of "Nous allons a Bruxelles ! " Each party thought their own battle the most important. The 32nd Brigade won the race to Brussels. They reached the southern suburbs just as the light was failing. The Welsh drove straight into the centre of the city ; the Irish turned right at the Café des Sports in the southern outskirts and circled round the city by Alsemberg to the eastern suburbs to cut the Germans' main escape roads. It was getting dark as they passed through Alsemberg and "map-reading was mighty difficult." Progress was slow but exhilarating, for the streets were choked with enthusiastic crowds who cheered each tank and truck as it passed, shouting "Thank you ! Thank you ! " A hail of hydrangeas and unripe apples whistled through the air. The column pushed its way slowly through the crowds, and by nine o'clock reached the gate of Brussels' great park, the Bois de la Cambre. Major D. R. S. Fitzgerald, leading the column, missed the main entrance, but the following squadrons and companies turned in through the gates and plunged into the maze of avenues, lanes, rides and prospects. The main avenue through the park was covered by two German 20-mms. firing from the racecourse at the other end, but Colonel Joe thought so little of this opposition that he told Major D. R. S. Fitzgerald to rejoin the column at the racecourse. Lieutenant C. Warren and his reconnaissance troop took to the paths through the trees and quickly shifted these Germans. Other Germans camped in the park tried to make a stand. Spandaus opened up from rhododendron bushes and bamboo clumps, and outraged German shouts rang through the woods. The 3rd Battalion Guardsmen jumped off the trucks and dived into the bushes to get at these troublesome creatures ; the tanks wheeled into the rides and groves, charging ornamental temples and riddling Germans and statues alike. It took longer to reassemble the column than it did to dispose of the enemy. In the dark, every bit of the park looked the same. The air was full of demands for direction and guidance. "Where are you ? I am by a pond." "So am I. How many ponds are there ?" "There are a lot of men running about these woods." "Don't shoot, it's the 3rd Battalion." More by good luck than anything else the group eventually emerged at the far end of the park in some sort of order.

The Irish Guards now learnt what liberation really meant. The street lamps had been turned on, the shops were lit up and lights hung from every window. Deliriously happy Belgians crowded round the tanks and trucks, laughing and weeping, some of them shouting the only English words they knew, "Goodbye Tommy!" Men and women, young and old, they showered flowers, fruit and kisses on the Guardsmen. They climbed on to the trucks and thrust bottles into the turrets or poured champagne, brandy and ice-cream into the outstretched mess-tins. Anyone in an open car was hauled out and smothered with embraces. Major Gordon-Watson, M.C., kissed everyone he could see, greybeards included, and openly wept. So did they all. Officers and men were so tired that they could hardly stand or talk; they just took in a dazed impression of overwhelming joy. This outpouring of gratitude showed that the men who were left behind in Normandy would always be remembered by those they had died to free. This one night made up for the long, dreary years of training.

Colonel J. O. E. Vandeleur proposed to hold the east of Brussels with three strong points, one on the main road to Louvain at Woluwe, near the airport, held by No. 1 Squadron and No. 1 Company, another held by No. 3 Squadron and No. 2 Company on the other road to Louvain on a cross-roads in the Foret de Soignes, and between them the "central keep" as he called it, formed by the rest of the Group in the main square of the suburb of Auderghem. Captain Joe Savill was taking no more chances on map-reading by night and detailed a small Boy Scout to lead No. 1 Squadron to Woluwe. In a city of happy people, that Belgian boy was probably the happiest.

It was nearly midnight by the time the Group reached the main square in Auderghem. The square was full of people, many in pyjamas and nightdresses. The cafés were open and bands turned out to play on the pavements. As the tanks and trucks drew up, the Belgians descended on them in an avalanche. The police tried to form a cordon, but soon gave up the attempt and joined in themselves. For hours on end the Belgians stood and cheered and wept. They brought all the food and drink from the precious stores they had hoarded and loaded them on the Guardsmen, apologizing all the time that they had not anything better to give. No kindness was too great. When they heard that the Irish wanted billets they vied for the honour of giving up their own beds so that their "chers liberateurs" could sleep in comfort. They struggled to get their hands on any Guardsman to drag him off to their houses. One old lady captured two officers, fiercely defended her prizes, and took them to supper. Once inside her house, she burst into tears because she had not had time to warm the wine.

But before the Group could comfortably settle down to enjoy the

Belgians' hospitality, they first had to clear the area of Germans. This was soon done. Prisoners—always such a nuisance—began coming in almost at once, mostly from the Chateau Dietrich, a former Luftwaffe headquarters, some five hundred yards away. Patrols searched the lanes and gardens, pulling Germans out of ditches. The only casualty was Captain A. E. Dorman. Lieutenant Mahaffy mistook him for a German and shot him through the leg, much to his annoyance. There was spasmodic firing throughout the night, chiefly at Woluwe, where No. 1 Squadron and No. 1 Company also came in for some mortaring from the airport, which was still held by the Germans. In Anderghem there were very few bullets, except Lieutenant Mahaffy's. When all was "peaceful," though noisy, and the Guardsmen settled down for what remained of the night, the officers of both battalions sat down to dine in the largest café in the square—in accordance with Colonel Joe's operation order in Douai. During dinner someone complained that the Germans were holding a house just down the road. Colonel "Joe" Vandeleur described what followed: "Everybody was having much too good a time to be disturbed so a combined Officers' Mess party went off to deal with the matter, assisted by a Honey tank. We shot the place up and found some miserable little Huns in full marching order—the clerical staff of the Luftwaffe headquarters—praying in slit-trenches. They were fixed up quickly and we returned to dinner. The night was uproarious," he continued, "and we could not get any work done on our tanks and vehicles."

Dawn was just as uproarious; the enthusiasm and generosity showed no signs of flagging. At least one officer breakfasted off whisky—not because he liked it, but because a kindly Belgian had kept a bottle for "the day" and wanted to see it drunk. It would have been churlish to refuse. More prisoners left behind in the general rout straggled in, showing little sign of resistance. No. 3 Squadron caught four officers trying to escape, one of whom the people recognized as a leading Gestapo agent. It was with some difficulty and reluctance that his escort, Sergeant McRory, saved him from being lynched on the spot. Even so, he was kicked vigorously and spat on, much to the discomfort of Sergeant McRory, who got some of the "overs." Captain Stephen Langton marched a batch of two hundred prisoners down through the city to the control cage. On the way there the crowds hissed and booed and spat to their hearts' content; one moment they would kiss the Guardsmen, the next kick the Germans. These Germans had an unusually large escort because so many officers and men wanted to see the centre of the city.

Some of them fulfilled a life-time's ambition and drove a tram, others went to laugh at Division H.Q. in the centre of the main boulevard. At Division H.Q. the streets and pavements were littered with maps and papers, which harassed clerks were trying to collect and sort. During the night they had set one of their Armoured Command vehicles on fire, to the delight of the Brussels fire brigade, who left the burning Palais de Justice and swept down to rescue their liberators. It was the Intelligence Office that was destroyed ; some saw the work of Nemesis in the flames.

"*From :* O.C. No. 9 Command Pay Officer.

"*To :* O.C. —th Bn. Irish Guards.

"Monsieur Jules Schmitt, of 22 Av. Theo Vanpe, Audergham, Bruxelles, called at the office of the Deputy Paymaster-in-Chief, Rear H.Q., 21st Army Group, and deposited with him 20,000 Belgian francs with the following note :—

" 'Payment of the sum of 20,000 Belgian francs (20.000 fr. b.) to the benefit of the relatives of killed soldiers of No. 2 Squadron British Irish Guards.'

"For information, please refer to gentlemen, Captain V. Taylor, or Lieutenant Samuelson, or their Major (I forget his name)."

All day long the crowds cheered and celebrated their liberation indefatigably. Group H.Q., in the biggest café in the central square, was perpetually surrounded by an enormous crowd, whose enthusiasm prevented any work. The local "Armée Blanche" were called in to clear the street, with orders that no one must come into the Battalion's area. The immediate result of their activity was that a Belgian band marched up the street and began to play "Tipperary." In a few minutes the entire population was dancing wildly. Though the battalions were too busy to allow official "walking-out," both officers and men made many useful friends and later stayed for days and nights, and had innumerable free drinks and dinners on the strength of the "3rd September." Major John Haslewood, whose natural acumen had been sharpened by the practice of the law, turned his professional experience of human nature and its weaker points to good advantage. He found a rich collaborator who, as he had foreseen, filled him with food and drink for months afterwards as a form of restitution and insurance.

Major David Peel and Sir John Reynolds brought up "A" Echelon with its, and their, comforts to join the Battalions. It was not long before these two shrewd business-men sought out comfortable lodgings and a Belgian girl to cook the rations. They had not forgotten to add little extra luxuries to their store during the triumphal drive. The echelons were the battalions' travelling supply points, storehouses and workshops. The 3rd Battalion's echelon was a comparatively simple affair—a string of lorries carrying petrol, ammunition and rations. The 2nd Battalion, being armoured, had more complicated needs. Its echelon was divided into three parts—"F.2," which kept up as close as possible with the squadrons, "A," which, in theory at least, travelled a safe distance from them, and "Cushy B." "F.2" was made up of about twenty-five assorted vehicles, armoured and unarmoured, fitters' half-tracks, the unwieldy square wireless truck, known as the "gin palace," used to relay messages back to Divisional H.Q., petrol, ammunition and ration trucks, with a few tanks for protection. Behind them travelled "A" Echelon, fifty trucks carrying much the same sort of thing, but in bulk, which was broken up and passed on to "F.2" Echelon when that had lowered its stocks by supplying the squadrons. And, farthest back of all, came "B" Echelon, carrying the Battalion's baggage. Though they occasionally changed about, as a general rule Captain H. FitzHerbert commanded "F.2," Sir John Reynolds "A," and Captain The Lord Claud Hamilton "B."

Harry FitzHerbert had left his family firm of stockbrokers in Dublin at the outbreak of war to join the Regiment. On arriving in Normandy in August, he had taken over his old command, "F.2," which he guided with the greatest skill from the Seine to the Rhine. "Harry and his boys" never failed the fighting squadrons; they always arrived where they were needed. His immediate superior was Jack Reynolds, the pivot of "A" Echelon, who had served in the 1914-18 war as a subaltern and returned as a subaltern to this. He fought with the 2nd Battalion at the Hook of Holland and Boulogne in 1940, and from 1942 onwards had commanded H.Q. Squadron. He was recognized both from his ability and his kindness to be the outstanding personality of the Battalion. Years on the Liverpool Cotton Exchange had given him a quick eye, a clear mind and a lively sense of the benefits that attend prosperity. Thus, though a firm believer in discipline, he knew the value of welfare, and throughout the campaign succeeded, with the help of Guardsman Parker, in combining efficiency with comfort. His echelon was the best organized and best cared for in the Division; his Mess a haven of sanity after the bedlam of battle. Here, over a meal eaten at ease, news and reminiscences could be compared and checked. Such was the nature of the host, that all extra luxuries were gladly shared, and even gossip was tempered by charity.

The third of the Echelon Graces, Captain The Lord Claud Hamilton, had been inclined by the youthful study of criminal law towards a somewhat pessimistic view of human affairs. His gloomy reflections on the world were, however, often illuminated by an epigram, and he was heard to confess off the record that life in "B" Echelon could sometimes be almost enjoyable. Since his real delight was to hear of heavy German losses, he found recent events quite to his liking.

Up and down the echelons, across North-West Europe, hurried the tireless figure of Captain and Quartermaster Jack Keating. There can have been no better Quartermaster in the Brigade of Guards. He had been with the Battalion since its formation in August, 1939, and knew every man and everything in it. Though always busy, he made time to solve the innumerable problems brought to his office. He was equally attentive to all down to the newly-joined reinforcement. He knew by instinct and experience what would be needed next—Belgian currency, extra rations, more battledresses. He was never asked for a thing and found without. His energy was matched only by his patience, and his repartee with its native kindliness made him justly loved. The Battalion well realized how fortunate it was in being so served.

Men in the squadrons and companies automatically referred to service in the echelons as a "cushy old job" and "dead steady." But this was by no means true. In theory the echelons should not go into battle, in practice they often did. In the breakout over the Escaut Canal, for instance, "F.2" Echelon was just as exposed to the German fire as any other part of the Group. A Sherman tank goes on fire remarkably easily, but not quite so easily as a petrol truck or ammunition lorry. If you want any examples of brave men you need look no farther than the drivers of these vehicles who drove slowly up an exposed road with shells and incendiary bullets whistling all round them. For sheer hard work and self-help in the long, swift advances the echelons could not be beaten. They drove for hours on end, often fifty miles behind the battalions, and not really knowing what was happening or where the battalions were, but somehow they always picked up the track. The battalions had very few Ordnance maps, as the map point was still west of the River Seine, but the echelons had none. Major Reynolds had one quarter-inch-to-the-mile map for the whole of "A" Echelon, while Captain FitzHerbert, undaunted, led "F.2" Echelon on a motoring guide to

North-West Europe, which he had taken off a German prisoner. He found it, he said, very useful as it showed roughly the position of the main cities, roads and canals.

No. 1 Squadron and No. 1 Company, meanwhile, had missed most of the joys of liberation, being out in the village of Woluwe on the northern road to Louvain. Instead of flowers and kisses from grateful Belgians, they were receiving mortar bombs and shells from the Germans on the aerodrome. Major E. Fisher-Rowe had always disliked Germans; he did so now even more for showing such unfair discrimination, and said so loudly. "Polish them off," said Colonel Joe, "it will be excellent training for the new men in your Company." Supported by a Field Regiment and the tanks of No. 1 Squadron, the Company had "a grand little field day," watched by an admiring audience from both battalions. The tanks and spectators moved round to the side of the aerodrome, from which they could clearly see the German ground staff running about trying to blow up their equipment. The tanks had a morning of skilful and accurate shooting, destroying six 88-mm. guns and chasing the crews up and down the runways with high explosive. "Much better than Kirkcudbright Ranges," said the gunners. After this it was a walk-over for the Company, with no casualties. In fact, an enjoyable time was had by all—except the Germans. As the prisoners were being brought in an obscure 88-mm. gun began firing for no particular reason. "Jairmany calling!" remarked an embittered German officer in the accents of Joyce. Everyone laughed, and then, remembering that he was a prisoner, told him to shut his trap.

In the afternoon there was another private battle. Seven German tanks and about two hundred infantry at Waterloo were alleged to be willing to surrender to British troops, but meanwhile were taking it out of the local Armée Blanche, who had unwisely disclosed themselves. Colonel Joe, in Wellington's footsteps, led off a small force—Lieutenant Stanley-Clarke's platoon and Lieutenant MacFetridge's troop of tanks—to deal with Blucher's descendants. These men had to cancel their afternoon engagements. Only Guardsman Lacey kept his, as he had been invited out to luncheon and could not be found. The rest of the battalions settled down for the afternoon to get some long-overdue sleep—except Captain R. Robinson, the Technical Adjutant, who tore himself away from the sprockets, tappets, firing pins and the thousand other intricate mechanisms he was inspecting and repairing, not to get some sleep, which he badly needed, but to go into Brussels to buy sticky cakes.

The special force drove cheerfully into Waterloo, leaving behind them the revelry by day. Lieutenant MacFetridge, in the leading tank, picked up a Belgian guide outside Waterloo station and drove on, making the obvious jokes. Almost immediately he was "brewed up" by a Panther tank, which showed no signs of surrender. A moment later Colonel Joe drove up in his scout car ; that also was "brewed up." The platoon came under fire and lost two killed and seven wounded. There were no more jokes, and the tanks set to work to destroy the Panther, which they did, while the platoon extricated themselves from the ambush, for such it was. The second battle of Waterloo, though the casualties were lighter, was not as successful as the first. Lieutenant MacFetridge walked back to Auderghem repeating his lesson to himself, "Don't believe what you hear of the Germans." The reverse at Waterloo, however, worried nobody. The news everywhere else was good. The 11th Armoured Division were in the suburbs of Antwerp and the Household Cavalry had reached Louvain and Malines. Another uproarious night left the battalions too exhausted to stand the noise much longer, so they moved into the grounds of the Chateau Dietrich and shut the gates behind them. "Protective leaguer against the Belgian girls," Colonel Joe called it. The Chateau stood well back from the main road in the middle of ornamental gardens, stables, outhouses and gardeners' cottages. Its real name was the Chateau Val Duchesse, a royal palace and museum, but it had acquired its present sinister name from having been the German Air Force headquarters. The Germans, as always, had left the place in a filthy state, but they had surrounded it with thick barbed wire for the particular purpose of keeping out Belgians and, being obviously good billets, the Group gladly accepted it when it was offered them by the local Major. At the front door Colonel Joe stopped short. "Gelignite !" he said. "I smell gelignite," and refused to allow occupation till the cellars had been meticulously searched.

A terrific, almost hysterical outburst of cheering brought the Irish Guards out from their barbed-wire enclosure. "Peace ! Peace !" The rumour had swept round and the city was delirious with delight. "Antwerp has fallen. The Germans have surrendered." The Mayor, in full regalia, made a stirring speech thanking God and the Irish Guards for giving them liberty and peace. The Irish Guards looked at each other awkwardly ; they had been in the Army too long to believe rumours, particularly one like this, which sounded a real "cakey bar." But the Belgians were so certain and so happy that it was difficult to disbelieve or disillusion them, and the younger soldiers, at any rate, gladly gave up the effort. The older soldiers reserved judgment, and so were not surprised when the Group was ordered to prepare to move the following morning. This order crushed the rumour, and everyone now said that the order was only to be expected because they had just made the Chateau fit for human habitation and were looking forward to forty-eight hours' rest. "A pity," said one officer. "In our chateau we would have been better off than the Welsh Guards in their club house at Waterloo Golf Course."

CHAPTER VIII

The Escaut Canal

2nd and 3rd Battalions

AS everything was ready for the next advance, there was no reason to stop "walking out." Many badges and emblems were given to the local girls in return for their favours. The men were now running short of "cigarettes pour Papa" and "chocolat pour Bebe," but were still ready with smiles and embraces. After dinner, the usual time for orders, Colonel Joe outlined the next day's programme—an advance through Louvain, already held by the Grenadiers, across the Albert Canal to Beeringen, through Hechtel and on into Holland to Eindhoven. A nice day's run, and in case anyone was wondering about the Germans, the Intelligence assured the commanders that there would only be slight opposition and that would be confined to the canals and bridges. Everyone went to bed full of optimism.

Two hours before the battalions were due to start, Brigade H.Q., who had got the news the previous day, told them that a "Champagne Point" had been opened in Brussels. The civic authorities had handed over to their gallant liberators a warehouse full of drink, said to be worth a million pounds, reserved for the German Army. Major D. A. Peel collected twenty-eight cases of champagne and a large variety of wines and liqueurs for the 2nd Battalion, which he distributed among the squadrons. Major D. H. FitzGerald, the Second-in-Command, collected two lorry-loads for the 3rd Battalion. The huge remaining stocks were later seized by N.A.A.F.I. and Army Group and were never seen again.

The Irish Group moved off at half-past ten on the 6th September. The route was lined by cheering crowds who, as before, heaped piles of fruit and flowers upon the Guardsmen. They followed the Welsh Guards through Louvain and drove on without incident till lunch-time. They ate their haversack lunches and brewed tea in the fields outside Diest. Over the wireless came many reports of German tanks to the left and right, but beyond swinging half the guns in one direction and half in the other, they paid no attention and went on quietly eating their stale sandwiches. After lunch they ignored requests of the inhabitants of Diest to deal with the local Germans, and prepared to drive the fifteen miles to Beeringen.

The Welsh Guards reached the Albert Canal at four o'clock. They found that, of the large bridge marked on the maps to carry the road across to Beeringen, only the skeleton existed, and the subsidiary bridge had already been blown by the Germans. The far bank, however, seemed to be clear of the enemy and the Sappers were sent for to build a bridge as soon as possible. Meanwhile, the Irish Group halted short of the village of Puel, two miles from the canal. The 2nd Battalion spent an uncomfortable night in a farm-house, but the 3rd Battalion spent an even more uncomfortable one in the pelting rain. It was miserable, cold, wet and dark. The battalions dined on rain-water and bully-beef and then tried to find somewhere dry to sleep till two o'clock. By three o'clock, long before dawn, the battalions were back in their tanks and trucks, as ordered, ready to move. They waited there till midday, when the 3rd Battalion moved forward towards Beeringen.

The town of Beeringen lies on the north side of the Albert Canal in low flat country below the level of the canal. Between the canal and the town is a stretch of swamp about five hundred yards wide, through which meanders a small stream. During the night the Sappers had built a Bailey across the piers of the incomplete bridge, and at dawn the Welsh Group crossed. The town itself is small, with narrow straight streets, and is entirely dominated by the large coal-mine on its north-west outskirts. Anyone standing on the slag-heap can look straight down into the streets on to the canal and bridge and farther down along the road to Diest. There were plenty of Germans in the town, as the Welsh Guards found when they entered it. They left a squadron and a company to clear it, and with the rest pushed on to Hechtel. There they met strong opposition and had to prepare a full-scale attack. For this they needed artillery, and the Irish Guards had to wait while the guns drove up from Louvain, crossed the bridge and by-passed Beeringen. At midday the 3rd Battalion eventually started and found their old friend "X" Company, Scots Guards, now with the Welsh Guards, in the centre of the town. The 2nd Battalion followed and the whole Group moved into the town. No. 2 Squadron and No. 3 Company held the bridge area, No. 1 Squadron and No. 1 Company the east end of the town, No. 2 Squadron and No. 2

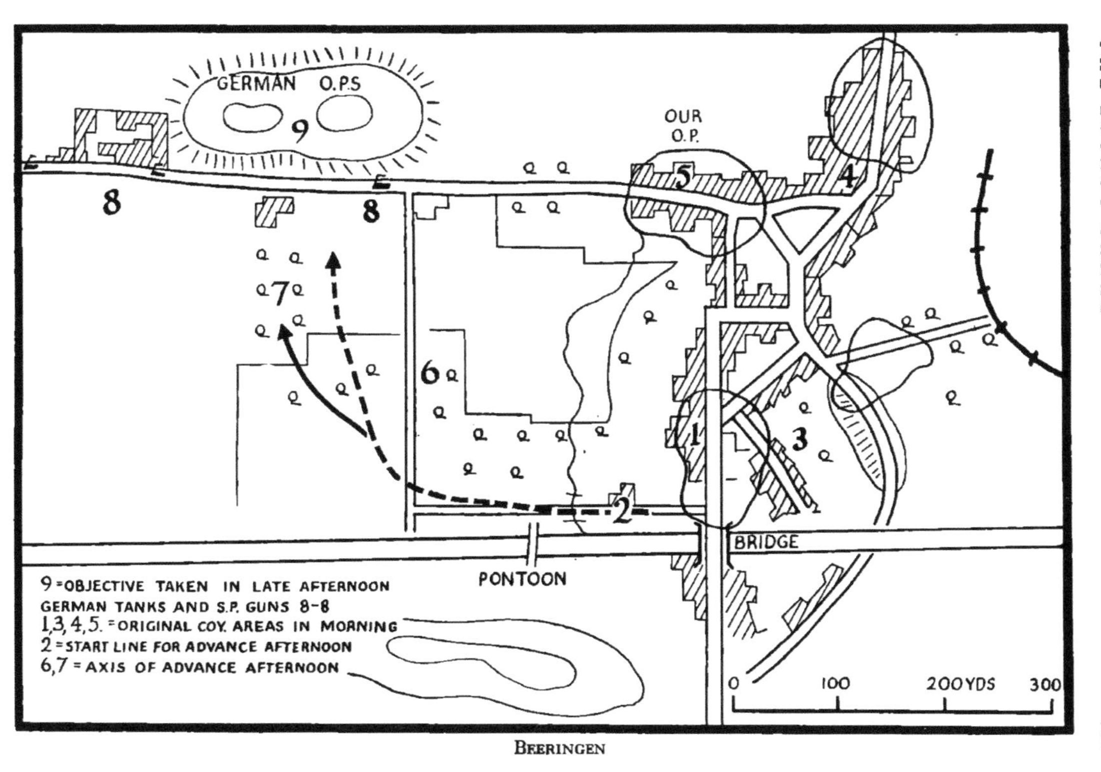
GERMAN O.P.S
OUR O.P.
BRIDGE
PONTOON
0
100
200YDS
300
9 = OBJECTIVE TAKEN IN LATE AFTERNOON
GERMAN TANKS AND S.P. GUNS 8-8
1,3,4,5 = ORIGINAL COY. AREAS IN MORNING
2 = START LINE FOR ADVANCE AFTERNOON
6,7 = AXIS OF ADVANCE AFTERNOON

BEERINGEN

Company the northern end, and No. 4 Company dug into the marshes and cemetery south of the town.

As No. 1 Company was working its way up the main road to the outskirts of the town it lost some men to German machine-gunners hiding in houses. Major E. Fisher-Rowe could not stand for that sort of thing, and promptly and swiftly liquidated these Germans. From Normandy up till now the war had been totally unreal. No. 4 Company, which had arrived out from the 1st Battalion in August, had not yet lost a single man. This afternoon they suffered their first of many casualties. Guardsman E. Breslin—a fine red-headed Mick—was killed by a shell which landed in his slit trench beside him. The German shelling was most accurate and unpleasant. The edge of the town had not been cleared up, and there were German tanks milling about up and down the road leading to the coal-mine. Six self-propelled guns in the fields north of the town kept shooting into the streets. These self-propelled guns were part of 559th Heavy Tank Battalion, with which the Group was to have dealings as far as Eindhoven, where the last survivor was destroyed. They knocked out a scout car and caused several casualties. Captain R. Bruce and Sergeant Johns had been killed earlier in the morning while reconnoitring the eastern outskirts of the town, by a shell which exploded on a wall above their heads. During the afternoon two more officers were hit—Lieutenant Lord Plunkett and Captain Simon White, "the Knocker," who was very badly wounded in the stomach. Simon White had worked hard for the Regiment, and had spent endless dreary months in reinforcement camps in Africa and Italy waiting for a chance to fight with the 1st Battalion and to satisfy on the Germans his passion for blowing up things.

No. 2 Squadron passed some hours shooting up German infantry between the town and the coal-mine, while No. 1 Squadron, trying to work its way up the main road, lost a tank to a troublesome self-propelled gun sitting in the middle of the road. The shelling continued. It all seemed to come from high-velocity guns, so Colonel Joe suspected, as did everyone else, that the fire of the S.Ps. and tanks was being observed and directed from the towering slag-heap. The casualties were heaviest in proportion amongst officers, as often happens, because they had to walk about the town on various reconnaissances. Five officers in all were lost, including the Gunner battery commander, Major Eames. Before he was wounded, however, Major Eames found an observation post in the top window of a convent, from which there was a perfect view of the slag-heap and the road running past it and the mine works beyond. Colonel Joe could see at least three German tanks and self-propelled guns moving up and down the road right under his nose, seldom bothering to conceal themselves. By mid-afternoon, Colonel Joe had got tired of being shelled and decided to capture the mine works and slag-heap.

"Before launching our attack," he said, "we decided to do a bit of pot-shot shooting with the mediums in the hope of getting some direct hits on to the tanks and S.P. guns, or at least frighten them into moving off from our axis. This shooting was a treat to watch, and two German tanks went up in a sheet of flame and the rest cleared off like lamp-lighters." He ordered No. 3 Company, under Major M. Dudley, and a weak squadron of tanks, No. 3, under Major D. R. S. FitzGerald, to attack round the left flank. To do so they would have to cross the swamp and get over the stream. The swamp was open, with several hard tracks running across it; the stream, however, was too deep and muddy to be forded. The only crossing-place Major Dudley could find was a small wooden bridge, which was still held by a German section. As soon as the Germans saw No. 3 Company tramping slowly across the marsh they turned their Spandau machine-guns on to them and forced them into the pot-holes. Lance-Sergeant Roberts, the leading section commander, crawled forward through the mud. The German warrant officer in charge of the bridge was an active and over-enthusiastic commander, so Lance-Sergeant Roberts shot him first and then the machine-gunner. The section joined Sergeant Roberts, and together they captured the bridge, taking the remaining eleven Germans prisoner.

It took some time for two regiments of field guns to lay a smoke-screen to cover the tanks as they moved up to the stream. This smoke screen was entirely wasted, as the bridge collapsed under the first tank. There was another delay while the tanks looked for another crossing-place, and more smoke shells were got ready. The tanks at last found an old disused railway bridge, and at six o'clock the attack went in again. The leading tank, Lieutenant H. H. MacDermott's, was knocked out on the far side of the bridge, but the rest of the Squadron got across and joined the infantry who had waded through the stream. Lieutenant H. H. MacDermott, a careful man, did not at all mind being "brewed up," but he did think that the observers in the convent window, who could see the S.Ps., might have warned him in time. "Such a waste of tanks." The Company and Squadron shot up some lorries and a platoon of German infantry and reached the coal-mine without much difficulty. After this the tanks became separated from the infantry and the succeeding phase became rather disjointed, the infantry swinging left towards the mine's offices, and the tanks heading towards the slag-heap. Meanwhile, Nos. 2 and 3 Squadrons, and of course the ubiquitous Major Gordon-Watson, concentrated their fire on an S.P. on the road, and destroyed it, and then moved up to consolidate the position. Just as No. 3 Squadron was drawing into harbour it lost another tank, knocked out by a self-propelled gun farther up the road. The attack had considerable success, and from now on the shelling diminished. The Company had not enough men to clear completely the large mine area, and since no reinforcements could be spared from the town, had to be satisfied with a limited consolidation. It was a relief to be free of the constant shelling, for already the 3rd Battalion alone had lost eight Guardsmen killed and sixteen wounded.

That evening the battalions first heard of the "Big Plan." The Brigade Major gave them a rough outline of this operation by which the 2nd British and the 1st U.S. Armies were to advance into Germany and "pinch out" the Ruhr. The 2nd British Army was to attack north-east towards Munster, while the 1st U.S. struck through the Maastricht gap. The Guards Armoured Division was warned that it would lead the advance to Arnhem, assisted by the 1st British Airborne Division, which would be dropped round Grave to seize the bridge over the River Maas. There was to be no advance into Germany until two corps were across the Rhine and ready to attack. The officers listened to this proposal with reservations. The timings, the swing to the east after Arnhem, and the use of only one airborne division were all based on the assumption that the Germans were retreating rapidly—"pulling out" as fast as they could, with no fight left in them. The leading troops, officers and men, knew this assumption to be rash and untrue, even as they heard the plan. The Germans did not want—as they never have wanted—any fighting in Germany, and were determined to hold on to Holland, where they had their V.2 bases. The days of easy advances—the "promenades militaires" —were already over. The battalions knew this, and the planning staff soon learnt it.

Meanwhile, the American attack on Liége was driving the Germans back northwards towards Louvain and Hasselt. As far as the British were concerned this German withdrawal constituted an armoured threat to their rear. 5th Brigade, which had been following the 32nd, moved down south to head off this quite involuntary threat and to shepherd the Germans away from the 2nd Army's lines of communication.

At Beeringen, activity started at daybreak of the 8th, when No. 3

Squadron began exchanging shots with Germans to the north. In an unfortunate concentration of mortar-fire Captain R. B. H. Ingleby, the mortar platoon commander, Captain G. A. Jeffries and Lieutenant M. Aird were all wounded, leaving the 3rd Battalion now very short of officers. A stray bomb from the same concentration wounded Lieutenant T. E. Hallinan, a troop commander of No. 1 Squadron. The Germans made no attempt to counter-attack, but their self-propelled guns were still active ; one cunning gun stalked No. 3 Squadron's leading troop and "brewed up" two tanks, one behind the other, in quick succession.

The main road runs north from Beeringen through Beverloo to Bourg Leopold, the Belgian Aldershot, where it turns east to Hechtel and then north again to the Escaut Canal at "de Groote Barrier" and on to Eindhoven. An alternative road leads to Hechtel by the east, through the village of Helchteren, up which the Welsh Guards had advanced. This group split into two and was now fighting outside both Helchteren and Hechtel. The 5th Brigade was ordered to clear the main road and 32nd Brigade to continue up the eastern road. Accordingly the Coldstream Group of the 5th Brigade attacked through the Irish on the morning of the 8th September, with Bourg Leopold as their objective. Although they suffered eighty casualties in a series of attacks, at nightfall they were still held up by a German strong-point in the village of Heppel, two miles north of Beeringen. They took the village the next morning, but did not capture Bourg Leopold till two days later.

On the right flank, where the Welsh Guards could not deal with both Helchteren and Hechtel, the Irish were ordered to clear Helchteren. About midday, they started to hand over Beeringen to a mixture of Free Belgians and 11th Armoured Division—that is the official description of what they did. "But actually," says an officer, "we just cleared out." The town and the roads were jammed with the transport of the 5th Division moving up to enlarge the bridgehead, and it was dusk before the Irish Guards reached the outskirts of Helchteren and met the Welsh Guards. A squadron and a company of Welsh Guards held the town, but there was still an unknown quantity of Germans lurking in the houses and woods outside, and a company of them were holding a windmill overlooking the town from the east.

"The customers are pretty tough," but beyond this warning the Welsh Guards could give little information. The customers really were unpleasant—a mixture of German parachutists and Dutch traitors enrolled in the S.S. There was nothing for it but a "night clearing." It was too late and too dark to make a reconnaissance or to try anything more complicated than Colonel Joe's "simple little plan," of a sweep on either side of the town, the two bands of sweepers to meet at the windmill on the far side.

It was a pitch-dark night, and as the tanks and troops moved forward the only light came from burning houses and haystacks. "The sweeps were noisy, with the Besas blazing at suspected enemy posts," says the 3rd Battalion War Diary. The night was certainly noisy, but the "Besas" were Brownings, and half the time the suspected enemy were 3rd Battalion infantry who had lost the tanks in the dark. For some reason the 3rd Battalion obstinately called the tanks' machine guns "Besas," although it was a year since the 2nd Battalion had exchanged its British Crusader tanks, armed with Besa machine guns, for American Shermans mounting Browning guns. There was no difficulty in taking over the town itself from the Welsh Guards, who rejoined the rest of their group outside Hechtel. Captain M. A. Callender and Major A. Hendry, however, spent most of the night trying to clear the woods on the south-east and lost a number of casualties and one tank to a bazooka. Major E. Fisher-Rowe, on the north side, decided that it was too dark to see anything, even a windmill, and kept his company in the town till daylight. During the night Lance-Sergeant Radcliffe, the medical sergeant of the 2nd Battalion, was killed while searching the woods for the wounded. He was a man of outstanding character and courage. Not just this time, but always, he found his way to the thick of the battle, suddenly appearing out of a hole in the ground with his haversack over his shoulder or, as on this occasion, working his way up dark ditches to find some man "missing, believed wounded."

Irish Guards and Germans took a few hours' rest till it was light enough to see over the sights and then began again to kill each other inside and outside the town. No. 4 Company and No. 2 Squadron combed the middle of the town before breakfast and discovered a dozen snipers—"hefty S.S. men who looked first-class soldiers, and were determined to give no information." These Germans were from a battle group about one thousand strong which had been ordered to hold the Albert Canal but, having arrived too late for that, had dug in round Helchteren ; but that did not matter very much to them, as they still held Hechtel, the main road between it and Helchteren, and "the conspicuous windmill," and were fighting stubbornly in the surrounding woods.

After breakfast, about eight o'clock, Major Fisher-Rowe arranged with Captain J. L. L. Savill, commanding No. 1 Squadron while

Major D. Peel was "left out of the battle," to attack the windmill immediately. Captain Joe Savill left Captain M. A. Callender and a troop with No. 2 Company, and moved the rest of his tanks up to the main cross-roads in the village to meet the company. As soon as the Guardsmen got out of their trenches down came a stream of mortar bombs, bursting among the tanks and platoons. The Germans always handled their mortars with great skill, but this was one of their most successful shoots. Captain J. Savill was badly wounded in the eye and leg, Lieutenant J. B. Osborne, a troop commander, was slightly wounded, and Sergeant Cardus, the other troop commander, who had just taken over from Lieutenant T. Hallinan, dangerously wounded in the head by a mortar bomb which had landed on his turret. Somewhat discouraged, Major E. Fisher-Rowe started to prepare the attack all over again, when Colonel Joe told him to call it off as the Group was about to move.

Captain Savill next saw Sergeant Cardus in the neighbouring bed of a Brussels hospital. "He was making no sense at all. The doctor was holding up his hand and asking how many fingers he could see, but Sergeant Cardus did not know what the doctor was talking about." "Smoky" Joe Savill could not see too well, either, for he had lost his right eye. However, they were both "put on the road again"—as the mechanically minded Battalion described it—Sergeant Cardus with a steel plate in his skull and a French Croix de Guerre, and Captain Savill with a glass eye and a Belgian Croix de Guerre. In a couple of months Captain Savill returned, as good as new, to the Division to take charge of the Forward Delivery Squadron, and later, when the Belgians asked the Commanding Officer to recommend somebody for the Order of Leopold, he recommended Joe Savill, who is now a Chevalier, Second Class, and can travel free on Belgian trains, second class.

The Germans in the woods round No. 1 Company had kept Major Hendry and Captain M. Callender busy all night, sniping and machine-gunning. The difficulty was to find these troublesome Germans ; once found, the tanks could deal with them quite easily. Not being able to see properly from his tank, Captain Callender got out and walked forward into the wood. He found the Germans ; a machine-gunner shot his arms to pieces with a burst of Spandau, leaving his right hand attached loosely to his wrist. Hereafter, Michael Callender became an interesting surgical case. He spent the next eighteen months going in and out of operating theatres as keen surgeons cut strips of skin off his back to see if they could re-attach the hand to his wrist, and in the end, fortunately, they succeeded. Before being carried away he was able to direct the field-guns on to the enemy, and no more trouble came from that quarter.

The whole area was full of Germans: the 315th Infantry Regiment, the 677th Panzer S.S. Regiment and two more S.S. regiments in the immediate vicinity, with the 714th and the 2nd Panzer Regiments farther back. The Welsh Guards, at Hechtel, had met Panthers and the Coldstreamers were fighting with parachutists outside Bourg Leopold. One prisoner gave a piece of information that the battalions stored up for future reference—two Panzer regiments, formerly at Antwerp, had installed themselves at Valkenswaard on the main road to Eindhoven.

At 1100 hours the Irish Group handed the cross-roads over to the Fife and Forfar Yeomanry and set out to move north by a sand track to join the Welsh Group at Hechtel. On the way round, No. 2 Squadron spotted some enemy infantry creeping along a ditch and gave them ten minutes' Browning and high explosive. This brought out a unique prisoner, a deep-sea diver. He had been hauled out of his natural element, given a rifle and sent to the front, and was still protesting against such treatment. The battalions spent a quiet afternoon in some woods while the Welsh Guards were having a very unpleasant time in Hechtel. The Germans were so obviously determined to hold Hechtel that the Brigadier decided to spend no more time and effort, but to by-pass it. He ordered the Welsh Group to remain where they were, containing the thousand-odd Germans, and told the Irish Group to go round the right flank the following morning, clear Exel, a village two miles to the north-east, continue on to the main north road and then drive straight to the Escaut Canal. "From the look of the map there does not seem to be any serious obstacle."

It had started to rain in the later afternoon and was raining hard when Colonel Joe and the officers went forward to a Welsh Guards' observation post to see what the ground was really like. The Brigadier had chosen an axis of advance off the map which showed flat open ground, but "to our horror," says Colonel Joe, "we discovered that the appearance of the ground over which we were to attack bore little relation to the map." The alleged open ground was in reality a dreary expanse of sand-dunes, rapidly turning soggy in the pouring rain, and covered with thick plantations of firs and pines. To console himself, Colonel Joe took "one or two pot-shots" at the only thing he could see clearly—a couple of Germans running about near a café on the outskirts of Hechtel. All that could be decided was a forming-up area on the edge of the sand-dunes and the general axis of advance—a compass bearing of 45 degrees. Of the enemy dispositions and the ground ahead they knew and could see nothing, so the proposed advance was as much an exploration as an attack. During the night Colonel Joe thought it all over, and decided that it would be wiser to launch only one squadron and one company, in case the country proved as unsuitable for tanks as it looked. It was a most worrying night, for he knew the Welsh Guards were having a hard time but could do little to help them.

The next morning, the 10th, the battalions formed up in battle groups and drove two miles into the sand-dunes, with the infantry riding on the tank-backs. This was the first time that the 3rd Battalion rode into battle on the 2nd Battalion tanks. It became from now on the regular mode of travel near the front and was known in wireless jargon as "mounting heavy friends." The artillery shelled a number of places, chosen off the map, in which there might be Germans, and then Major J. Haslewood's No. 4 Company and Major E. G. Tyler's No. 2 Squadron started off towards the Bourg Leopold road, which ran straight across the line of advance. They were to establish a firm base there from which the Group could launch an attack on Exel. The rest of the battalions waited behind cover ready to follow and listening-in to the wireless conversations and reports.

Lieutenant C. B. Tottenham took a compass bearing and led No. 1 troop into the pinewoods. Behind came a platoon of No. 4 Company, then Lieutenant S. Daly's troop and Sergeant Garland's, each with its attendant infantry. For half an hour they moved slowly forward through the pines and sand-dunes. The tanks battered their way through the trees, slithering and churning in the soggy sand. One of No. 1 Troop's three tanks got hopelessly bogged, leaving Lieutenant Tottenham with only two, his own and that of his troop sergeant, Sergeant Fitzsimmons. Neither the tank nor the infantry commanders could see more than twenty yards through the trees. They could hear the crashing of undergrowth and the shouts of section leaders, but they lost sight and touch of each other. The only opposition, so far, was sniping and an occasional Spandau burst; the infantry dealt with that. Lieutenant Tottenham and Sergeant Fitzsimmons struggled on till they reached the far side of the wood. As Lieutenant Tottenham's tank broke out from the line of woods it was hit. A shot from an anti-tank gun dug in near the road jammed the turret. Another gun actually in the wood took two quick shots at Sergeant Fitzsimmons' tank, but missed. Sergeant Fitzsimmons gunner did not miss; he blew the gun to pieces with high explosive and finished off the crew with the Browning. Sergeant Fitzsimmons moved quickly forward to the edge of the wood and destroyed the other gun near the road. This "kill" gave Lieutenant Tottenham and his crew a chance to get away from their useless tank. The Guardsmen found their way back to Squadron H.Q. Charles Tottenham took over from Sergeant Fitzsimmons the command of the one remaining tank. He saw three German Mark IVs trundling along the road, advanced out of the wood, engaged the middle tank, and destroyed it. Yet another anti-tank gun opened fire and drove him back to the cover of the trees. But the wood was no longer peaceful : scores of hidden German infantry came to life to hold back No. 4 Company and fire bazookas at the tanks.

No. 4 Company fought their way slowly forward, clearing Spandau posts as they went. The Germans were all from the Hermann Goering Training Regiment, who were holding Hechtel, with the usual orders from Hitler himself to fight to the last man and the last round. They surrendered just the same. Guardsman Flynn marched in three terrified prisoners, threatening them with the spout of his empty 2-inch mortar. Meanwhile, Lieutenant J. Gorman and Lieutenant Daly and his troop were crashing round the wood trying to join Lieutenant Tottenham. They could not find him at first, and Lieutenant Tottenham had to fire red Very lights to show them—and incidentally the Germans—where he was. Lieutenant Gorman arrived first ; Lieutenant Daly veered off on the way to machine-gun the crew of a German anti-tank gun and to destroy some German machine-guns. The whole Squadron eventually joined Lieutenant Tottenham ; he was immensely relieved to see them, for he had held the position alone for over half an hour. Lieutenant Charles Tottenham was later awarded the Military Cross. The Company came up and the whole group formed a "strong-point" covering the road. Between their position in the copse and the road ran a marshy stream, unmarked on any map. A patrol reported that, in their opinion, the tanks could not cross this stream ; there was already a stray tank there inextricably bogged. Another patrol went out to try to find a crossing farther south. It had to run down the exposed slope in the face of heavy machine-gun fire, and though the tanks gave all the support they could, it was under fire the whole way and the whole time. More German anti-tank guns and machine-gun teams moved up from the rear and right flank. Lieutenant Tottenham caught an anti-tank gun in an open ride, knocked it out and dispersed the crew.

By now it was midday ; there was no sign of the patrol and time was pressing. Sergeant Barnes was ordered to try crossing the stream at full speed in his Honey tank. Before he had gone more than one hundred yards the Honey was hit by an anti-tank gun which, in its turn, was promptly destroyed with its crew by twenty rounds high explosive from Lieutenant Gorman, M.C. But no sooner was one gun silenced than another started and Spandau fire intensified. Weighing up the difficulties, Major Tyler and Major Haslewood reported to Battalion H.Q. that, quite apart from the Germans, the rough country and the marshy stream made this route impossible as an axis of advance for an armoured group.

On the other flank, 5th Brigade, after a slightly sticky start, was lucky enough to find a disused railway track across an old artillery range, which was the only sure passage across the otherwise treacherous ground. The Grenadier Group drove down this and got a patrol into Exel. Lieut.-Colonel "Joe" Vandeleur heard this news just after he got Major Haslewood's report. He therefore suggested to 32nd Brigade H.Q. that he should change over to the left centre line. Divisional H.Q. agreed and granted the Irish Group priority over all traffic. Colonel Vandeleur ordered the 4 Company/2 Squadron battle group to return and join the end of the column. The group accordingly began to withdraw at three o'clock, when Lieutenant Gorman destroyed a self-propelled gun with a Parthian shot. They were able to tow back two of the damaged tanks, but the third was so badly bogged in the marshy ground that they had to strip and abandon it. Finally, the infantry patrol returned, after spending three hours under fire, and the battle group rejoined the battalions complete.

The Irish Group moved slowly up the disused railway line and then along a track carved in the rough country till they reached the main road at about five o'clock. It was a tedious drive, but they could go no faster as the line and track had already been torn to ribbons by the Grenadiers and Coldstreamers. "The going was appalling," said an officer, "at every bump and turn everyone was shot several feet into the air." The Group re-formed in the order No. 1 Squadron (Major D. Peel) and No. 2 Company (Captain A. Hendry), combined H.Q., No. 3 Squadron and No. 3 Company, No. 2 Squadron and No. 4 Company, still together, and finally, No. 1 Company in reserve riding on the Armoured Recovery vehicles, Honeys and any odd vehicle. By this time their Brigade H.Q. was some fifteen miles away and out of wireless range. They knew where they had to go. They passed through the Grenadiers and Coldstreamers, crossed the main road and, by six o'clock, were installed in Exel. There were no

Germans there, and altogether it looked a most suitable village in which to spend the night.

Meanwhile, the 2nd Household Cavalry Regiment had been exploring the countryside. In an advance the Household Cavalry in their scout cars operated on the flanks, and often well in front of the Division. They had an admirable habit of suddenly appearing out of a side road or racing straight down the road from the direction of the Germans with a fund of invaluable information and an unquenchable desire to help. If anyone wanted to know "whether Jerry was up the road" the answer was "Ask the 2nd Household Cavalry to go and see." Above all, they could always be relied on somehow and somewhere to find a way round any obstacle, natural or unnatural.

This evening the Household Cavalry found something splendid—a fine new unmapped German-built military road running from Exel due north to Overpelt and then turning left to the Escaut Canal at De Groote Barrier. "The angle appealed to me," said Colonel Joe, "I prefer an oblique approach to dead ahead." The Grenadiers were already moving up the main north road towards the canal, so Colonel Joe decided there and then "to have a crack and beat the Grenadiers to it." The Group covered the eight miles to De Groote Barrier at top speed. Near Overpelt, where a transverse road from Lommel joins the military road, the leading troop ran straight into a large black Mercedes staff car, going hell-for-leather. They shot the car and its contents, a smartly dressed officer, to bits with the added pleasure of knowing that they were evidently not expected from this direction. In Overpelt they found a Household Cavalry car waiting for them with the news that the road ahead was clear, certainly as far as a factory just south of the bridge. A Household Cavalry patrol in this factory reported that the bridge was still intact, but that it was prepared for demolition and strongly held by 88 mm. guns. A troop of Honey tanks raced ahead to join the Household Cavalry in the factory; from there they wirelessed back that the bridge was still standing, and that there were at least two 88s on the north bank. No. 1 Squadron and No. 2 Company followed as fast as they could in the gathering dusk and reached the factory just before the light failed.

The Meuse–Escaut Canal is a major water obstacle which cut straight across the 2nd Army's line of advance. It was the first good line on which the Germans could make a stand, and they were certain to hold it if given enough time to collect their forces. If this bridge at De Groote Barrier could be captured intact it would save days of

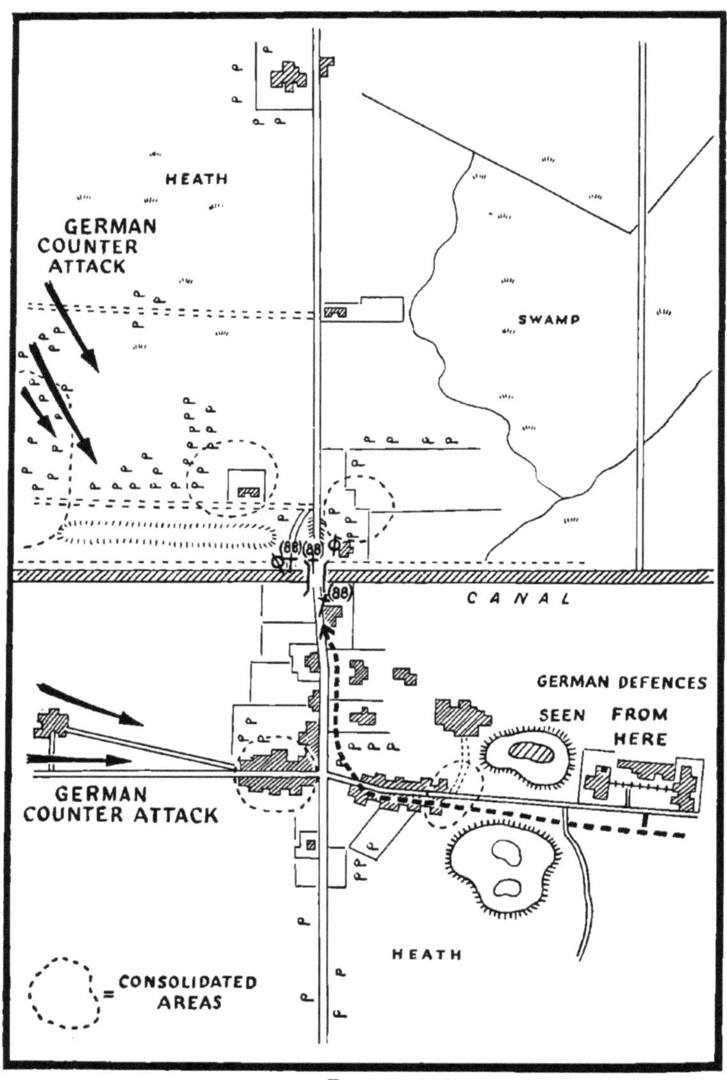
HEATH
GERMAN
COUNTER
ATTACK
SWAMP
(88)
(88)
(88)
CANAL
GERMAN DEFENCES
SEEN FROM
HERE
GERMAN
COUNTER ATTACK
HEATH
= CONSOLIDATED
AREAS

Escaut

preparation, a large-scale assault crossing and a number of lives. The Irish Group were now so far ahead that they were out of wireless touch and beyond artillery range, so they would have to depend entirely on their own resources and surprise. Major David Peel, the commander of the leading battle group, moved his squadron up to the factory gates, de-bussed the infantry company and climbed a slag-heap to have a good look round. The light was all in his favour and he could get a good view of the bridge and its approaches. Colonel Joe followed him up. "Obviously boldness is the thing," he said. "We will rush the bridge." Major Peel, who would have to do the actual rushing, studied the ground even more closely. The military road from Overpelt crosses the main north road some four hundred yards south of the bridge and carries on westward parallel to the canal to the village of Lommel. Half-way between this cross-roads and the bridge there is a "jink" in the road. Now a gun cannot fire round corners, as Colonel Joe acutely remarked, so the defenders must be either on or near the north end of the bridge, where there certainly were at least two guns, or in the houses and gardens around the cross-roads.

Theoretically, the Germans should be holding the cross-roads which commanded the approaches to the bridge. There was no sign of them ; but to make sure, Lieutenant D. Lampard's troop and Lieutenant John Stanley-Clarke's platoon patrolled slowly forwards. The other ranks of the Squadron kept up heavy and steady machine-gun and high explosive fire on the bridge and the cross-roads to discourage the Germans. Thus covered, Lieutenant Duncan Lampard halted short of the cross-roads, which he found clear of enemy and took another look at the bridge. He was just in time to catch a tractor towing an 88-mm. gun across the bridge. It did not reach the other bank ; a couple of high-explosive shells knocked the gun and tractor to one side of the bridge.

Major David Peel came up on foot with Captain A. Hendry. "Now Duncan," they said, "it is up to you and John. Rush the bridge however you like, and we will follow up behind you." It had taken the Germans a long time to realize what was happening, but the fate of the tractor-drawn 88 woke them up and they started shooting at the tanks. Lieutenant Lampard moved his troop up to the cross-roads, put his own tank and Sergeant Steer's in among the houses on the near side, and sent Lance-Sergeant McGurren over the far side. As Lance-Sergeant McGurren crossed the road another 88-mm. gun fired at his, missed and got a heavy burst of Browning in return. The fourth tank of the troop jammed its turret

3rd Battalion. Six-pounder anti-tank gun detachment. Nijmegen Bridge. Morning after crossing

Escaut Canal Bridge, North Bank. A German 88-mm. gun in the foreground

Face page 476

and had to withdraw from the action. The rear and left were now secure, so Lieutenant Lampard dismounted to talk to Lieutenant Stanley-Clarke and make a simple plan. His troop, they decided, would cover the platoon up to the "jink" in the main road. When the infantry got there they were to fire a green Very light as a signal for the other eleven tanks of the Squadron to fire only on the bridge. When the platoon had got as near to the bridge as they could and were ready for the final assault, they were to fire a red Very light as a signal for the Squadron to stop shooting and the troop to charge. The 88-mm. and its tractor blocked part of the bridge, but that could not be helped.

It was after eight o'clock when the waiting crews saw the Very light burst green at the top of its slow arc. Something or somebody had set fire to a large brick house on the right of the bridge. Whatever was inside it, it burnt remarkably well and the flames lit up the bridge and banks like a theatre set. For two minutes every gunner kept his right foot hard down on the firing button that controlled his Browning. All co-drivers who could see, and some who could not, fired their pull guns. The red Very light went up and Lieutenant Lampard's troop charged. Lance-Sergeant McGurren's tank hit the corner of a house and the engine stalled. Sergeant McGurren swopped shots with an 88-mm. while the driver wrestled with the engine. In the second tank Sergeant Steer shouted to his driver. Corporal Kettleborough swung past Sergeant McGurren and drove straight for the bridge, where the 88's tractor had now been set on fire by the shooting. The tank crashed through the flames and explosions. Corporal Barrett, Lieutenant Lampard's driver, kept his tank hard on its tail, followed by Sergeant McGurren.

Colonel Joe was dancing with excitement on the top of a slag-heap. "It's the drivers who've done it—the man behind the wheel ! " The platoon led by Lieutenant Stanley-Clarke and Corporal Helliwell ran across behind the tanks, sprayed by Spandau fire, and flung themselves into the ditches. An excited German surrendered, shouting "Well done, well done !" They had got the bridge. The Squadron and Company swept across to join them. The first to follow was a Sapper officer, Captain Hutton, with a party of four Guardsmen of No. 2 Company—Guardsmen H. Trimble, C. Mollard, E. Colthorpe and K. Fielding, who had been detailed as "You, you, you and you." They climbed over the side of the bridge and cut the cables. The machine-gun bullets were drumming into the wooden beams, but they worked steadily till they had removed the detonators from the charges in the piers. No. 3 Squadron and

No. 3 Company went over to reinforce the original group and took up a position in a wood on the left of the road, just over the canal. The H.Q. and the reserve squadron and companies formed a "hedgehog" round the cross-roads south of the bridge. Two prisoners were captured from the infantry that had been supposed to protect the 88s. The unhappy men complained that they were not ready, and had been expecting their own tanks, not British ones. The fate of the 88-mm. on the bridge and the Browning and high-explosive fire first put them off their aim and then made them move to a safer place. The sergeant in charge of the demolition squad had made a stirring speech earlier in the day : "The bridge must and will be blown. Every man fights to the last round"—but he himself was one of the first to leave, forgetting to press the switch.

Brigade H.Q. was out of wireless touch, but just after midnight Colonel "Joe" Vandeleur was able to report straight back to Division through a Household Cavalry car, "Bridge captured intact ; situation in hand, all fighting has now subsided." At first the Staff could not believe the news and demanded confirmation by independent witnesses. An hour later the Sapper reported he had "deloused" the bridge by removing the initiating mechanisms, and would remove the main charges the following morning. "The bridge is in good condition," he said, "and about Class 40." The Group expected a counter-attack, but nothing came—not even a shell or mortar bomb. The only stir was the arrival, in the middle of the night, of Captain H. FitzHerbert with petrol and ammunition for the tanks. "I really thought I ought to join you," he said, and had found his own way by instinct and broken Flemish.

The Commander of 5th Brigade, having been told that he could enlarge the bridgehead as much as he liked, ordered his two groups, the Grenadier and Coldstream, to cross over at first light. The Corps Commander, however, cancelled this order, so that at dawn on the 11th the bridge area was held only by the Irish Guards with two companies and two squadrons north of the canal and the rest south. The Germans had done nothing at all during the night, and the morning, too, started quietly. No sound came from the dank mist that lay over the countryside. The first report that reached Battalion H.Q. was a routine message from the Air Force, "Bomb-line today, Belgian–Dutch frontier." The second report was a warning that there were six German self-propelled guns and a company of infantry somewhere round the village of De Luyken. This did not affect the Group, and they went on having their breakfasts.

Suddenly the mist was broken by fire. "Tanks attacking down the canal!" shouted the sentries. Already one self-propelled gun was firing into the reconnaissance troop and another was hurling shots down the road. The first two shells crashed into the Honeys of the reconnaissance troop, killing seven men and wounding several others, including Lieutenant B. C. P. Warren. Captain R. S. Langton, the Adjutant, and Sergeant Wright ran over with a stretcher, but the first man Sergeant Wright brought back was Captain Langton himself, slightly wounded by another shot. The crew of the 3rd Battalion anti-tank gun covering Battalion H.Q. sprang to their gun. The commander had opened his mouth to shout "Fire!" when a Gunner officer standing by him said, "Hold it, it may be one of ours." He had no time to say anything more, for a high-explosive shell wrecked the gun and killed him and also two of the crew. The other anti-tank guns opened fire immediately. R.S.M. Grant, standing in front of one of them, had no time to get out of the way and was badly burnt by the muzzle flash. Major Peel, standing in the doorway of Battalion H.Q., saw the German self-propelled gun in a field some five hundred yards away. He climbed into the C.O.'s tank, "St. Patrick," and took aim. He hit it four times and set it on fire, though a "Firefly" of No. 1 Squadron, shooting from the far side of the canal, claimed half the credit. The other Germans withdrew to the cover of the gardens whence they had come. The Reconnaissance Troop made a dash for the cover of the canal embankment but, for all their speed, two of them were hit on the way. The Germans now launched a determined attack. A company of mixed S.S. and ordinary infantry, supported by the self-propelled guns, advanced along the canal. With them was a section of Engineers whose orders, as a prisoner said afterwards, were to blow up the bridge when it had been recaptured. The infantry were quickly "seen off" by the 3rd Battalion, but the self-propelled guns were less vulnerable and more enterprising.

Major Peel handed over "St. Patrick" to Lieutenant Briant and went forward to observe for Major Gordon-Watson in "Ulster." He walked from garden to garden looking for the nearest German self-propelled gun. Unfortunately, it saw him first and fired a high-explosive shell, which wounded him mortally. Lieutenant Briant drove "St. Patrick" forward, but again the Germans were too quick, and "St. Patrick" and the Commanding Officer's kit went up in flames.

Meanwhile, Captain E. E. Rawlence, the 3rd Battalion M.T. Officer, was lying semi-conscious in an ambulance. He was still concussed from a collision on a motor-cycle the day before, but the noise of firing brought him from his stretcher. He borrowed a Piat and, without telling anybody, started out to stalk the self-propelled gun. He did not come back. A bullet or a splinter must have hit the Piat bomb he was carrying, for he was killed instantly. The German attack petered out to a failure and they withdrew to De Luyken, where they were later caught by a Grenadier column working up from the south.

In the middle of the attack a Dutch woman, who claimed to be a nurse from Amsterdam, attached herself to the 2nd Battalion. As soon as anyone had time to think of it she was arrested as a spy and sent to Brigade H.Q. like all such prizes.

After the German withdrawal, Major John Haslewood took his company on patrol to the village of Lommel where he encountered the inhabitants with cries of "Pas de danger." Soon after he left, part of the village was destroyed by shell-fire. A second patrol was sent out, and it too shouted "Pas de danger" ; this time the villagers dived into their cellars.

By midday all was quiet—even in Lommel—and remained so for the rest of the day. Two companies of Coldstreamers moved up to reinforce the bridgehead, and a motor company of the 1st Grenadiers passed through to hold an outpost position a mile up the road. A steady flow of prisoners and deserters was driven into the Group's arms by the steady advance of the troops in their rear. After the capture of Hechtel and Bourg Leopold—at last reported clear by the 8th Armoured Brigade—the Germans evidently decided to withdraw all their troops to the north of the Escaut Canal. Typhoons caught large bodies of infantry and tanks crossing a bridge west of Lommel and destroyed both them and the bridge. The 2nd Battalion spent most of the day wirelessing back urgent demands for Father Cox, the Catholic chaplain, to bury the dead, and for Major D. R. S. FitzGerald to replace Major Peel. David Peel died of his wounds during the afternoon. His death was one of the severest losses of the campaign, and the news of it threw gloom over the whole Battalion. It seemed too hard that he had been killed the day after his great success, which won him a Military Cross and the Battalion a spectacular triumph.

Everyone slept well and undisturbed. The next morning there was no sign of the Germans, though the 3rd Battalion sent out patrols to investigate the numerous stories of Germans still south of the canal. Later in the afternoon the Dutch police reported that there were German tanks in the area and that they had seen Germans with bazookas digging trenches along the road to the north. The only

Germans the Group saw, however, were a small party building a road-block on the Belgian-Dutch frontier. Lieutenant Lampard's troop put an end to their labours. Otherwise it was a quiet day, devoted to rest, reorganization and congratulations. The Corps Commander himself, Lieut.-General Horrocks, came up to congratulate the Group. Standing on the captured bridge, now rechristened and signposted "Joe's Bridge," he told them that their exploit had saved days for the 2nd Army and had enabled him to bring forward the date of the next great advance. The capture of Brussels had been good ; the bridge was excellent. And now the Regiment would have the great honour of leading the next advance. This last remark took the gilt off the gingerbread, but his audience cheered up when they heard that there would be "no move for the Guards Division before the 16th."

The Germans came back to the attack the following morning—the 13th—but not yet on a large scale. The 3rd Battalion was pestered by patrols and the tanks fought a number of small skirmishes. Civilians passing through the bridgehead were bursting with stories of German activity. Dutchmen from Valkenswaard, up the road, said that the town was full of troops, about 8,000, including Todt Organization workers. As the bridgehead across the Escaut Canal was an essential spring-board for the next big attack, the Divisional Commander reinforced and enlarged it. The two reserve companies of the 3rd Battalion crossed over, and the whole Battalion took up new positions in the woods on the left flank. The 32nd Guards Brigade moved in on the right flank. The 2nd Battalion was relieved by 15th/19th Hussars and drove back two miles to the disused railway station at Overpelt. Here they repaired the tanks and reorganized the squadrons. Captain M. P. O'Cock replaced Major D. Peel as leader of No. 1 Squadron, with the revived Captain Langton as his second-in-command. Captain J. V. D. Taylor became Adjutant.

The less fortunate and more tired 3rd Battalion remained in the bridgehead for more fighting. Early on the morning of the 14th the Germans launched two battalions in a heavily supported counter-attack. The weight of it fell on No. 3 Company on the left flank. Waves of Germans seeped through the thick woods and scrub, firing bazookas as they came and setting up Spandaus beneath the trees. They surrounded first the forward section and then the whole of Lieutenant H. Kennard's platoon; the fighting degenerated into savage slaughter among the bushes. Humphrey Kennard was killed leaping from bush to bush. In such fighting weight of numbers was bound to prevail, and the platoon would inevitably be swamped if it were not reinforced or extricated. Captain Michael Dudley, the Company Commander, wanted to send up a tank, but the platoon was half a mile away from Company H.Q., and the tank crew did not know the way through the tangled, enemy-infested wood. Guardsman Moynihan, the Company runner, said he knew the best way. Walking through the rides, he led the tank up to the platoon, reported back to Captain Dudley, and then returned again to withdraw the platoon. He brought back the survivors without losing a single man on the journey.

The fighting continued all day, and all day the wood and the bridge were heavily shelled and mortared. During the afternoon the Company launched an attack to regain the lost ground. The Guardsmen scrambled through the undergrowth, shooting and grenading their way forward. Sergeant McElroy led his platoon, shouting encouragement to his section commanders and bayoneting the Germans. A bullet struck him in the foot, but he charged on, leaving a trail of blood on the dead leaves. They retook the position and threw the Germans out of their old trenches. When Captain Dudley came up to see the platoon he found Sergeant McElroy hobbling around, a boot on one foot and a shell dressing on the other. Captain Dudley took him back protesting to Company H.Q. and told him to go to the R.A.P. Sergeant McElroy went down the path, but turned back into the wood, and was back with his platoon when Captain Dudley returned there. This time he had to be forcibly evacuated with a reliable guard.

Meanwhile the German fire was intensifying. The Battalion expected another attack, but the barrage turned out to be a cover for the enemy's withdrawal. The Germans had given up the effort to retake the Escaut bridge. In the attack and counter-attack the Battalion lost 7 men killed, 23 wounded, and 5 missing—bad enough, of course, but much lighter than might have been expected in beating off two German battalions. The following morning they handed over their positions to a battalion of Hampshires from 50th Division, and moved back out of the bridgehead to join the 2nd Battalion at Overpelt to rest, reorganize and study the plans for Operation "Market Garden."

IRISH GUARDS BATTLE GROUP
(2nd Battalion and 3rd Battalion)

Normal Order of March
(Varied in detail, but not in principle.)

"A" Coy./Sqdn. Battle Group.

One troop tanks.
One troop tanks carrying one infantry platoon.
A detachment of Royal Engineers.
Company and Squadron H.Qs. and Artillery Forward Observation Officer.
Third troop and Squadron H.Q. troop carrying infantry platoons.
Two 3-inch mortars.
Two 6-pdr. anti-tank guns.
A section of carriers (for administrative purposes).
Detachment of Pioneer Platoon.

"R" (for Reconnaissance) Group.

Officers commanding 3rd and 2nd (Armoured) Battalions.
Representatives of the supporting arms.
Honey tanks.
Rear link and Command wireless trucks.

"O" (Order) Group.

O.C. Support Company.
Officers commanding Specialist Platoons.
O.C. "B" Battle Group.
Pioneer Platoon (less one detachment).
One troop 17-pdr. anti-tank battery.
A section of carriers.
Two detachments 3-inch mortars.
Two detachments 6-pdr. anti-tank platoons.
2nd (Armoured) Battalion Regimental Aid Post.

"B" Battle Group.

Squadron tanks.
Infantry company in lorries.
Artillery Forward Observation Officer.
Detachment Royal Engineers.
Two 3-inch mortars.
Section of carriers.
Detachment Pioneer Platoon.
Two detachments 6-pdr. anti-tank platoons.

"C" Battle Group.

Squadron tanks.
Infantry company in lorries.

Reserve Group.

Fourth infantry company in lorries.
Main Battalion H.Q.
Troop 17-pdr. anti-tank guns (towed).
3rd Battalion Regimental Aid Post.
Section of the Field Ambulance.
"A" Echelon, 3rd Battalion.
Medium M.G. Platoon.
"F" Echelon, 2nd Battalion.

CHAPTER IX

"Market Garden," Phase I—The Advance to Nijmegen

2nd and 3rd Battalions

BY the 11th September the advance from the Seine had come to a halt along the general line of the Meuse–Escaut Canal. Beyond it to the north lay a network of canals and rivers. The German High Command had been sacrificing rearguards in a fight for time to concentrate fresh troops along the Rivers Maas, Waal and Neder Rijn (or Lek), and every additional day was of immense value to them. To finish the war quickly it was essential to prevent the Germans from establishing a firm line along any one of these water obstacles. A further attack had, of course, always been intended after due preparations and "administrative build-up," but now the preparations were cut short and the operation advanced in date six days. The main problem was supply. The capture of Antwerp had in no way shortened the lines of communication, since the German guns on the island of Walcheren still prevented ships sailing up the River Scheldt. It was not until the Marines and Commandos had captured Walcheren and cleared both banks of the Scheldt estuary that the Allies were able to use the docks at Antwerp.

Meanwhile, the 2nd Army was being supplied from the dumps at Bayeux and the Channel Ports four hundred miles away. The R.A.F. had spent years carefully battering the French and Belgian railways, and the havoc it had caused would take months to repair. For the time being, therefore, the forward troops had to be maintained by road. The Army's transport was already severely strained by this long haul. Whether it could meet the new heavy demands that a large-scale attack would put on it was a risk, but a risk that the Army Commander was prepared to take. It was not the only risk involved in this unique operation. "Market Garden" entailed the deployment of three corps—30th, 8th and 12th—and the biggest airborne drop ever yet attempted. The 2nd British Army proposed to get across the series of canals and rivers to its front and then to swing first west to the sea, thus cutting communications between Germany and the Low Countries and, later, having outflanked the Siegfried Line, to attack east towards the Ruhr. The main striking force was 30th Corps which, led by the Guards Armoured Division, was to advance in the centre, with the 8th and 12th Corps echeloned back on either flank. Across the axis of advance lay six major water obstacles—the Wilhelmina Canal, the Zuid Wilhelm Varts Canal, the River Maas, the Maas–Waal Canal, the Waal, and the Lower Rhine. Airborne troops, under Lieut.-General F. A. M. Browning, undertook to capture the bridges across these obstacles. The 101st U.S. Airborne Division was to drop between Eindhoven and Grave and help the advance of 30th Corps so far as the River Maas by seizing the bridges and cross-roads on the axis. The 82nd U.S. Airborne Division would drop in the area of Grave and Nijmegen to capture the bridges over the Rivers Maas and Waal. These two bridges were all-important. The canals could be spanned by Bailey bridging; the Maas and the Waal could not. Farthest north of all, the 1st British Airborne Division was to drop west of Arnhem to capture the bridge across the Lover Rhine.

The bridges were all intact so far, but there could be no guarantee that they would still be standing when, or if, the airborne troops captured them. Basing their calculations on the gloomiest possibility—that all the bridges would be destroyed—the Royal Engineers assembled 9,000 sappers and the whole resources of the Army Group's bridge column. To carry the necessary bridging equipment and ferries, the Engineers might need as many as 5,000 vehicles, a slow and vulnerable group which would have to be protected by fighting troops. Add to this another large vulnerable group, the 2,000 vehicles belonging to the Airborne Forces' administrative tail, remembering that the Corps already had some 12,000 vehicles of its own, any one of which might be wanted at any time, and you get some idea of the traffic problem. For this vast column there would be only one road on which there would be at least six serious bottle-necks—the bridge areas. On the whole, it would be much easier for a rich man to get into heaven. The country to the north of the Escaut Canal was ideal for defence—flat, heavily wooded and very marshy, making it nearly impossible for the tanks even to leave the roads. The plan for the Guards Armoured Division was simple enough—straight up the main road, through Eindhoven, Graves and Nijmegen, meet the 1st British Airborne Division on Arnhem Bridge, and then to push on to Nunspeet on the Zuider Zee and wait there for the rest of the 2nd Army to catch up. On a quarter-inch map covered with axes and concentration areas, arrows and circles in gay and varied colours, it looked a very neat plan, but what it really amounted to was that one armoured division was to advance over a hundred miles on a one-tank front. No one was surprised to read in a later report: "The enemy was in considerably greater strength than had been anticipated, and but for the weight of the support and the magnificent fighting qualities of the breaking-out troops, the attempted junction with the airborne troops might well have been delayed for a number of days."

The Corps Commander, Lieut.-General Horrocks, decided to open the attack with waves of rocket-firing Typhoons and as many guns as possible. Relying upon this weight of metal, the armour and infantry of the Guards Armoured Division would "punch a hole" in the German defences and advance at top speed. The 43rd Division was to follow up, while the 50th Division held the existing bridgehead as a firm base. The time programme was optimistic—the break-out to be completed by the capture of Valkenswaard, half-way to Eindhoven, on the afternoon of D Day, and the whole operation to be completed by the capture of the final objectives on the following day. The Divisional Commander chose the 5th Brigade to lead the advance; the Brigade Commander chose the Irish Guards Group; Colonel J. O. E. Vandeleur chose No. 3 Squadron; Major D. R. S. Fitzgerald chose Lieutenant Heathcote's troop; Lieutenant Heathcote chose himself to lead the 2nd Army.

The Irish Guards Group had now assembled round Overpelt and Neerpelt under the command of 5th Armoured Brigade. The 2nd Battalion had had several days' rest and received new tanks and men. While the unfortunate 3rd Battalion was fighting in the damp woods across the canal, they were entertaining the Divisional and Brigade Commanders to dinner. Colonel "Joe" Vandeleur had been invited, but he could not come as the Germans attacked him at tea-time. The stationmaster's wife was a great help to the Mess. She lent them all her linen in return for permission to display the portrait of King Leopold and a promise from the Medical Officer to deliver her pregnant daughter.

The 3rd Battalion badly needed a rest and more men—it got neither. The reinforcements were lost somewhere between Regimental H.Q. and the Escaut, spending days in cattle-trucks and transit camps. The Battalion had to be reorganized on a basis of three rifle companies. No. 3 Company was temporarily disbanded; Major M. Dudley, Captain D. Gilliat and Company H.Q. were "left out of battle," and the rest of the Company lent to the other rifle companies. As a consolation they were told that a three-company organization was an advantage to the infantry when working with an armoured battalion, which has only three squadrons. The Battalion group normally fought in company-squadron groups. The men of the three companies could be carried into battle on the tanks of the attached squadron—one section per tank—but the fourth company had to be lifted in soft-skinned vehicles. In the coming operation it might be very dangerous to have an odd company trailing behind the rest of the group. In actual fact this is just what happened—the third company being lorry-borne. It did not really matter, as behind the lorry-borne infantry came Captain FitzHerbert with the petrol trucks, and he did not mind. There was always a "soft," not to say inflammable, tail "jogging up the centre line."

On Saturday afternoon, the 16th, the Brigade Commander gave his orders to the Irish Group. Weather permitting, the leading tank was to pass through the forward positions at 1435 hours the following afternoon. Enemy opposition immediately to the front was estimated at three battalions with some anti-tank guns. In support there would be ten Field Regiments, three Medium and one Heavy Regiment and eleven squadrons of Typhoons available on call. At first the field guns, then the mediums and heavies, would fire a barrage, lifting at two hundred yards a minute, to cover the group through the difficult wooded country as far as a small bridge south of Valkenswaard. No one knew the capacity of this bridge, so a bulldozer was provided to make a rough crossing if necessary by pushing in the banks of the stream. During the airborne drop the Typhoons would be grounded so as not to interfere with the fighter escort of the gliders and troop planes. As soon as the drop was over, the Typhoons would take to the air to support the Irish Group. An R.A.F. squadron leader, in direct wireless communication with the pilots, would be with the Group and could direct all the Typhoons on to any target he was given. The Germans were not expected to put many aircraft into the sky and would anyway concentrate against the airborne forces. The troops were therefore ordered not to fire on any aircraft for the first two hours. Even if they were being attacked by their own aircraft the troops were not to fire in retaliation, as that would only confirm the pilot's belief that he was attacking Germans, and he would bring up his friends to help.

During the afternoon the bulldozer on a tank transporter and three R.A.F. officers with a wireless control car joined the Group. A "contact man" from the 101st U.S. Airborne Division also appeared.

He was a Sergeant with a wireless set which had a maximum range of ten miles. The 101st U.S. Airborne Division had fought on the Anzio beach-head alongside the 1st Battalion. Major Gordon-Watson, who can remember every single thing he ever did, led off the American for a good talk about the old days. Major Dudley had also been on the beach-head, but he did not get a chance to say a word.

The Company Quartermaster-Sergeants handed out the N.A.A.F.I. rations of cigarettes and chocolate, but no beer. The men made simple macabre jokes, as always before an attack. "You are keeping the beer until tomorrow night" ; "We don't want to waste these cigarettes, Mick. You had better not draw yours."

Later in the evening Lieut.-Colonel J. O. E. Vandeleur, as Group Commander, gave out his orders. No. 3 Squadron was to lead without infantry. Its main task was to reach the bridge south of Valkenswaard and hold it for the rest of the Group to pass through. The Royal Engineers' reconnaissance party and the bulldozer would travel with Squadron H.Q. Then would come No. 1 Squadron with No. 1 Company on tank-back, combined with Battalion H.Q. with the R.A.F. officers and the American sergeant, followed by No. 2 Squadron carrying No. 4 Company and, finally, No. 2 Company in lorries. There was nothing more to do now than wait and talk over the plan. "Two hundred yards a minute is about seven miles an hour—much too fast, I think." "A bulldozer on a transporter! You can imagine what that thing will look like about sixth place in the attacking column."

The morning of 17th September dawned bright and fine with a slight wind, a perfect day for airborne operations. At midday the battalions heard that the "Market" part of "Market Garden" was going according to plan ; the Airborne Corps was on its way from England. There was plenty of time to dish out dinners, hang air recognition strips on the tanks and trucks and to form up ready to move. The leading squadron, No. 3 Squadron, crossed Joe's Bridge at a quarter to two. At the same time Lieut.-General Horrocks and Major-General Adair climbed up to the roof of a large factory, from which they could get a grandstand view of "the greatest breakout in history." At two o'clock the preparatory and counter-battery bombardment came down. In the clear blue sky the gigantic air armada was just visible. The word went round the battalions, "H is 1435." At 1425 more guns joined in to harass the enemy. At half-past two the heavy mortars of 50th Division began firing on the few known enemy positions. Two minutes later 240 field guns fired their first shot. This was the signal for the leading troop commander to move his troop up through the 50th Division's forward positions. At 1435 hours Lieutenant Keith Heathcote, in the leading tank, shouted "Driver—Advance!" No. 3 Squadron drove straight up the main road, keeping close up to the barrage. As there were no air photographs no one had located exactly—"pin-pointed"—the enemy positions. The gunners were firing a narrow rolling barrage into the woods along the roadside "where Jerry ought to be," and the tanks advanced in the hope that the Germans would run away or surrender. The Typhoons were circling overhead in a "cab rank," waiting to be whistled up by their link on the ground. The clouds of dust made it difficult to see the actual shell-bursts, so that several times Lieutenant Heathcote got involved in the barrage. Behind the Irish Guards a battalion of the Devons and an armoured regiment, the 15th/19th Hussars, followed up on either side of the road to clear the woods and hedges.

For ten minutes all went well. The exalted spectators on the factory roof rubbed their hands as they watched the Irish Guards pouring up the road and when they saw the tanks cross the Belgian–Dutch frontier where the road changed from macadam to concrete. When they turned to look again the road was covered with burning tanks. "Oh, my God, they won't get through!" Infantry in the ditches, and anti-tank guns from the wood, had struck down the rear of No. 3 and the head of No. 1 Squadron. Nine tanks were knocked out in two minutes. The gunner in Sergeant Capewell's tank put a belt of Browning bullets into a "bazooka boy," and so saved the front half of No. 3 Squadron which, like a mutilated lizard, went careering on until Major M. O'Cock's wireless cries of "Hi! you've lost your tail," brought them to a halt. Major M. O'Cock, No. 1 Squadron commander, goggled with fascination as one tank after another in quick succession went up in flames. First the tenth in front of him, then the ninth, and so on till, with a shock, he realized that the tank just in front of him had been hit and that it was his turn next. He could not go forward, he could not go back, he could not cross the deep ditches to leave the road; there was nothing he could do except wait for it. It never came. A few tanks farther back, Captains E. N. Fitzgerald and E. Udal agreed that it was just as well that Colonel "Joe" Vandeleur had decided this time not to put his Headquarters immediately behind the leading squadron.

Before the tanks had halted the 3rd Battalion infantry were off them and into the ditches. The tanks edged into what cover they could find along the road, spraying the hedges and woods with Browning and firing high explosive at any suspicious place. Lance-Sergeant

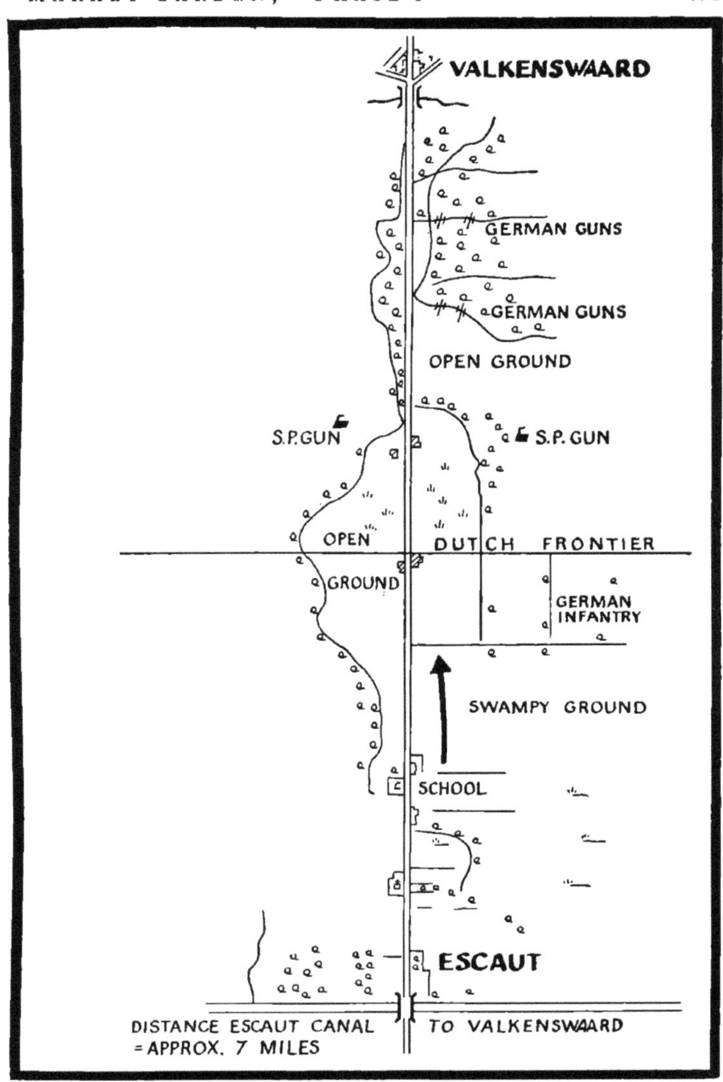

BREAK-OUT TO VALKENSWAARD

Cowan, No. 2 Squadron, saw a German self-propelled gun tucked up against a roadside cottage. In all probability the crew were just getting Major O'Cock's tank in the sights. With one shot Sergeant Cowan knocked it out and then induced the crew to climb on the back of his tank and point out their friends' positions, which they gladly did in return, as they thought, for their lives. Meanwhile, Colonel "Joe" Vandeleur had called in the Typhoons to help. The R.A.F. officers, in their wireless car, were just behind his Headquarters. They knew what was wanted, and they knew exactly what the Typhoons could do. Speaking to the pilots in their own professional jargon, they directed them straight on to the targets. After their taste of ground warfare all the R.A.F. officers asked to go back to flying duties as being much safer and quieter. In the next hour the Typhoons flew two hundred and thirty sorties—a record in ground support. The tanks, as arranged, fired red smoke at the enemy positions to give the pilots an aiming mark, and burnt yellow smoke abundantly and eagerly to mark themselves. The pilots' aim was sure, and there were no mistakes. The Typhoons came cutting in from every angle at zero feet, bombarding with rockets the enemy positions within a hundred yards of the road. It was frightening enough for the battalions, and how much more for the Germans who took the rockets. The din was appalling—tanks, trucks, planes, shells and rockets, machine-guns all roaring and blazing. Colonel "Joe" Vandeleur seemed to enjoy it. Though continually shot at, he stood by his scout car with Colonel Giles Vandeleur and gave orders to gunners, airmen, company commanders and German prisoners.

At 1510 hours Major Denis FitzGerald, on the rear link wireless truck, reported to Brigade H.Q., "Air support very good—using it now." and held out the microphone so that the staff could hear the swish of the rockets. It was the immediate close support of the Typhoons that enabled the advance to continue. "It was all very thrilling," said Colonel Joe, "especially as the bazooka boys and the parachutists were hopping about the hedges all around us." But the 3rd Battalion had had quite enough of these Germans and were glad to get the order to put an end to them. They attacked outwards from the road on either flank. Two companies of the German 6th Parachute Regiment, with self-propelled guns in support, held the left of the road, while Battle Group Hoffman held the right. Most of these were new recruits, but many were good, experienced fighters who had survived Normandy and the retreat, and had to be dug violently out of their trenches. An unknown, but enterprising, Guardsman killed

Hoffman himself. The Typhoons shot the infantry into their objectives, the rockets landing two hundred yards in front of them. "I have never seen Guardsmen so angry, nor officers. The Krauts got rough treatment that day," said an officer afterwards.

The rockets and the ugly mood of the 3rd Battalion had an excellent effect. Germans came running out of trenches, trembling with fright, and were sent doubling down the road in very quick time. All were still doubling when they passed Divisional H.Q., a mile the other side of the canal. In all, about 250 prisoners reached the "cage"—some a little short of breath, as one despatch-rider, acting as an escort, made his party travel at motor-cycle speed. The Medical Officer, Captain Ripman, who as always went where the bullets were thickest, enrolled other Germans as unwilling stretcher-bearers.

Into the midst of the confusion, amid the rockets, shells, tanks and Germans, drove a large saloon car. It was the *Times* Staff photographer, as imperturbable as *The Times* ought to be. Everyone found a moment to pose for him themselves, and chose suitable prisoners to stand in attitudes of despair or defiance. After him came a newsreel camera man. Captain E. R. Udal saw him taking pictures from the roof of his car and, being a kindly man, advised him to come down or else he might be shot. Down he came. The stream of prisoners was unabated. One Unter-Offizier said that he had once owned nine 7.62 Russian anti-tank guns, but now had none working. As for the crews, "Alles tot, alles tot." Only four of these guns were found, but no more fired so, presumably, he spoke the truth. He could not decide which were the worse, the rockets or the Brownings, and was sent weeping down the road.

The advance could now continue. During the fighting the artillery barrage had gone plodding remorsely on and had far outstripped the troops. The medium guns—which alone had the necessary range—began all over again. They were down to their last reserves of ammunition, the rest being still west of the Seine. No 3 Squadron withdrew five hundred yards so as to get a flying start past the shattered hulls of the knocked-out tanks. The bulldozer transporter got stuck across the road trying to turn round, and it was half an hour before the column could start. But this half-hour was useful. The Typhoons put in a concentrated attack on some 88-mm. guns they had seen well in front. No. 4 Company were fully occupied making haversack rations out of food found on a German truck. There was no trouble on this stretch of road. About half-past five the leading troop reached the bridge south of Valkenswaard. Their report that the bridge, though only a temporary structure, was intact and fit to carry tanks was welcome, as no one was looking forward to spending part of the night in the woods with the bazooka boys. No. 1 Company found a long roll of cloth, which it would have been a pity to leave to rot; No. 3 Squadron were more warlike and took four 88-mms. from their unnerved German crews. Lieutenant B. C. Isitt, thinking it rash to leave such dangerous things as 88s lying about, tried to destroy them, but only succeeded in firing one into the middle of the Group H.Q. The German infantry in the woods round the bridge were not as pusillanimous as the 88-mm. crews. Their snipers were particularly active, one of them wounding Lieutenant Cyril Russell. Both Colonel Vandeleurs had bursts of Spandau machine-gun fire just beside them, but no Germans came so near the mark as Lieutenant Isitt.

The reshuffle of the groups and the crossing of the bridge took a considerable time. No. 2 Squadron and No. 4 Company approached Valkenswaard very cautiously, while a battery put concentrations down on likely points of resistance. It was already dark; the only light came from houses set on fire by shelling. "We finally battered our way into the place expecting to find it a complete shambles. Well, it more or less was, with three or four really big fires burning, the streets strewn with debris, some Germans still firing, and other Germans milling about trying to find their way back to Germany. Yet all the inhabitants stood about in the streets yelling themselves hoarse and getting in the way of the fighting. It just did not make sense. The rest of the Group came up and harboured around the central square, blocking all roads. Some thirty prisoners of all sorts were taken, including two bicycle scouts just back from Eindhoven, who reported to the 2nd Battalion instead of their own commander, and were lodged for the night under the municipal bandstand. A German half-track later drove in—a welcome addition to the 3rd Battalion's transport, and more useful than the horse-drawn platoon truck they had already captured.

A Dutch civilian, an agreeable and informative man, reported to Headquarters from the Resistance in Eindhoven. The 2nd Battalion christened him "Dutch George," took him on strength, and gave him a seat in a Honey tank, with which he was well pleased. He might not have been so pleased had he known that the Honey tank is the most dangerous known form of transport. A little later the Mayor's clerk came running into Headquarters with a message telephoned by the German Commander in Eindhoven to his subordinate, who was supposed to be still holding Valkenswaard. This unknown officer was told to defend the town to the last man, with the assurance that reinforcements were on the way. By arrangement with the girl in the Post Office, Captain E. N. Fitzgerald kept contact with her counterpart in Eindhoven until early next morning, when the line was cut. All she could say, though, was that the Germans were still in Eindhoven and that she had not seen anything of the American airborne forces.

The day's fighting cost the 2nd Battalion nine tanks, with eight men, including S.S.M. Parkes, killed and several wounded, including Lieutenant D. Lampard and Lieutenant J. B. P. Quinan ; the 3rd Battalion lost seven killed and nineteen wounded. In the little cemetery outside the town are buried S.S.M. Parkes, Lance-Sergeant J. Walters, Guardsmen McD. Ackers, M. Delaney, W. Moore, J. Johnson, N. Malton and T. Watson.

At nine o'clock Division sent out a situation report, "Air droppings appear to have been successful. News is still mainly from enemy sources, for we are not properly in communication with our own troops. The Air Force report that all the bridges on the main axis were intact at 1500 hrs., but have no later report." Later in the evening more news came through. The 1st British Airborne was close up to and holding the northern end of the Arnhem bridge. The 82nd U.S. Division had captured intact the Grave bridge and those over the Maas-Waal canal, but had not yet reached the southern approach to Nijmegen bridge. The 101st U.S. Division had captured all its objectives between Eindhoven and Grave. There was no definite news about the bridge over the Waal and the lower Rhine. The Intelligence spent the day in a state of indignant surprise : one German regiment after another appeared which had no right to be there. Divisional H.Q. was heavily mortared during the night ; the news gave general pleasure.

The Group prepared to move again early the following morning in the same order of march, except that a squadron of the Household Cavalry would lead. They then went to sleep. While they slept, two German despatch-riders wheeled their motor-cycles out of a backyard and made a successful dash for safety. At 0600 hrs. on the 18th the battalions were ready to move off behind the Household Cavalry squadron. A battalion of Dorsets from 50th Division was due to take over Valkenswaard, but did not arrive till 0900 hrs. The 2nd Battalion were very worried about twenty wounded men they had put in a large house. There was no food for them, and urgent appeals were sent back to Division. Dutch civilians were anxiously reporting Germans everywhere in large numbers. There were particularly convincing reports of a Panther tank and two S.Ps. in Aalst—a village four miles up the road, half-way to Eindhoven. Captain E. N. Fitzgerald rang up the station-master of Aalst, who confirmed their presence by the village church.

The Group, led by No. 2 Squadron, advanced straight up the road towards Aalst. The German tanks moved down to meet them, while their infantry made full use of the wooded country which lined each side of the road. The tanks had no option but to drive straight ahead. Just south of Aalst, Lance-Sergeant Cowan saw an S.P. and promptly knocked it out. The Group swept on through the village and beyond it. Two miles to the north they came to a full stop at the bridge crossing the little River Dommel. The leading scout car had just got across the bridge when a shot whistled over; it reversed at high speed. There were four 88-mm. guns covering the bridge and infantry in houses on a side road covering the line of the river. At first the Group thought they would repeat on a small scale the Escaut exploit, but these Germans showed more spirit than their comrades and stuck to their guns, firing on any tank that edged too far forward. Near the guns, Spandau teams behind a concrete wall kept off the 3rd Battalion infantry. Rockets would soon demolish the concrete emplacements, but when Colonel "Joe" Vandeleur asked for air support the answer was "No Typhoons available yet today." The only thing to do now was to keep the Germans occupied by tank and artillery fire and to try a way round a flank. No. 1 Squadron and No. 1 Company set out to find a bridge on a side road to the west, and then to get back on the main road behind the Germans, while No. 2 Squadron engaged the 88s. Aalst is a dormitory town for Eindhoven, and the Germans curiously did nothing to stop the Dutch continuing their normal habits beyond firing an odd shot at them as they came and went. Amongst these "commuters" was the managing director of the Phillips Electrical Works. Every morning and evening on his way to and from the factory he had watched the Germans siting their guns and digging defences along the road. He left Eindhoven that afternoon with the stream of civilians and came running through the woods to Major J. Haslewood. After he had recovered his breath—which took some time, as he was an elderly man—he sat down and drew a sketch map of the German positions, marking little crosses on either side of the road to show the gun-pits. His map later proved to be absolutely accurate. At the time it was confirmed by a German map which had been found on the destroyed self-propelled gun, so it was with double confidence that the Irish set the gunners to work.

At two o'clock the Group wirelessed to Divisional H.Q.: "For your information, U.S. Airborne telephone number is Zon 244." The professor's son had told Major Haslewood that the telephone in the doctor's house was still connected to Eindhoven. Major Haslewood and Captain E. R. Udal rang up the exchange who put them through to a doctor's house in Zon. The doctor in Zon, when he had finished saying "Wonderful! Welcome!" brought an American officer to the telephone. "This is the best call I've ever had," he said. They had a long conversation, exchanging information about their positions. Unfortunately, said the American, the bridge over the Wilhelmina Canal had been blown—blown just when they were in sight of it after landing—but the approaches were easy for rebuilding. Major Haslewood then put a Royal Engineers officer on the telephone and the American told him just what materials would be needed for a new bridge—a unique example of advance Sapper reconnaissance.

During the afternoon the Grenadiers hunted for a way round the German defences farther to the left, but without success. Everywhere they tried they met either Germans or dykes, or bridges too weak to bear tanks. No. 1 Squadron and No. 1 Company, under Major E. Fisher-Rowe, were out on the same search nearer in, while the rest of the Group kept the Germans in front fully occupied and entertained a flock of War Correspondents with hair-raising stories. Suddenly all the shooting stopped. No. 1 Squadron and No. 1 Company had found a way round the Germans by crossing the stream and railway at Gestel. Major E. Fisher-Rowe wirelessed back that the only obstruction now was the crowds. At the same time a German surrendered to No. 2 Squadron and said that Eindhoven had fallen. He and his friends had been ordered to withdraw, which they had gladly done, but he himself had been left behind in the general scramble.

"All aboard and motor on!" The Group passed through the line of 88s, now deserted and pitted with shrapnel, and entered Eindhoven amid the cheers of the Dutch and Americans. It was a very satisfactory reception—orange banners and flags, flowers and fruit everywhere. Nobody paid any attention to the Germans who were still holding Geldrop. The Group wound its way through the crowd and drove on at top speed to the Wilhemina Canal. The crowds were fading away, usually a sure sign that there were Germans ahead, but the Group met no one till they came on American parachutists at the destroyed bridge at Zon. Colonel "Joe" Vandeleur crossed by raft to see the enthusiastic American regimental commander in the village school. The Americans, armed to the teeth and grinning from ear to ear, guaranteed the safety of their bridgehead, so the Irish settled down for the night south of the canal. Two squadrons and two companies lined the canal banks ; the rest of the tanks harboured along the side of the road and the infantry gathered round a windmill. No. 4 Company set fire to a pigsty—an accident which gave them roast pork for supper.

During the day, 12th Corps, on the left, and 8th Corps, on the right, had both attacked across the Escaut Canal. In spite of these diversions the Germans had launched a series of attacks throughout the day on the original bridgehead and the axis of advance in an attempt to cut off the Division.

After dark the road was cleared and the Sappers set to work to build a bridge in record time. They worked all night and had a bridge up by six o'clock the next morning. On the whole, the information about the bridges in front was good. The 82nd U.S. Division were still holding the Grave bridge, and reported that they also held the bridges over the Maas–Waal Canal and were fighting three hundred yards south of the Nijmegen bridge. Arnhem was an exception to their good news. "The position is obscure." Bad weather and the intense bombardment constantly interrupted communications between Arnhem and Airborne Corps H.Q. As far as was known the 1st British Airborne Division was established north and north-west of Arnhem, but the enemy, consisting of S.S. troops with tanks and self-propelled guns, was holding the town itself. Civilians passing through said that some of the men of the 1st Parachute Brigade were still holding out near the north end of Arnhem bridge. This was only a rumour ; all that was definitely known was that the Airborne had so far taken nine hundred prisoners, but that their own casualties were beginning to mount up. They had received no fresh supplies, for bad visibility and the heavy enemy "flak" had caused the containers to be dropped on the enemy.

At six o'clock on the 19th the Household Cavalry and Grenadier Group passed across the Sapper bridge to capture Nijmegen. Lieut.-General Browning, the commander of the airborne operation, explained that he had captured the high ground south of the River Waal, but had not enough troops to capture Nijmegen itself as well. He could do one or the other, but not both and, in his opinion, the high ground was the more important of the two. This day the Irish Group were in reserve. They did not start till nearly ten o'clock, by which time the Grenadiers had already crossed the River Maas by the Grave bridge. To capture this bridge intact was a remarkable achievement by the American paratroopers. It is one of the longest in Europe and towers above the broad Maas and its marshy banks. The Irish Guards drove hard and fast all morning, passing through St. Oedenrode, Uden and Grave. The Germans had only succeeded in blowing one bridge, and that a small one, otherwise there was no sign of them anywhere, except as prisoners. All the way the battalions were greeted by cheering crowds and Americans, who were as glad to see them as they were to see the Americans. By Grave bridge the 3rd Battalion met the 504th Parachute Regiment, who had once been under the command of the 1st Battalion in Italy. An excited American ran along the trucks shouting "Where is Major Kennedy? I am Captain Kennedy, and I want my Irish friend, Major Kennedy." He had to be told that his friend, Major John Kennedy, was still with the 1st Battalion in Scotland.

There are two bridges over the River Waal at Nijmegen—a road bridge, six hundred yards long and one hundred feet above the water, and, downstream from it, a railway bridge. Both were still intact, though known to be prepared for demolition. The Dutch Resistance gave rather confused information, but they were emphatic about two things: That the German demolition control centre was in the Post Office, and that the road bridge could not be blown anywhere because a youth called Van something had cut the leads from the Post Office to the bridge, or alternatively, that the "Underground" had removed all the explosive charges from the bridge. This story was rather doubtful. Why should the Germans blow the bridges from the wrong side, and did they never inspect or test their preparations? But however doubtful, the story could not be ignored. The Grenadiers drove straight into the town to join the American paratroopers who were locked in battle with a detachment of the 9th S.S. Division and assorted "flak" troops. They made a gallant effort to rush the road bridge, but failed, for the approaches were guarded by forts, concrete pill-boxes in the middle of the roundabout, and well-sited 88-mms. After fighting all afternoon they captured the Post Office; there was nothing in it but civilians in the cellars and dead Germans behind the counters. As it grew dark the German shelling of the town intensified. In the flickering light of burning houses and trams the Grenadiers fought in the streets and on the roof-tops. The Germans were certainly holding the town in considerably greater strength than had been anticipated. The fighting died down for the night with the Germans still in firm possession of the approaches to the bridges. During the night more German troops—S.S. from Arnhem—crossed the river and occupied an old fort just south of the road bridge. The Irish Group had halted at the village of Maldon on the outskirts of Nijmegen. There they were to stay till the Grenadiers had cleared the town, and "get as much rest as you can," said the Divisional Commander. The rain poured down, drenching the troops and washing out any celebrations.

The other two corps engaged in "Market Garden," the 8th and 12th, had made only very limited advances on the flanks of 30th Corps. As a result the Guards Armoured Division had two wide-open flanks. Its axis was being continually attacked by the enemy—a battalion, supported by tanks, at a time—and these attacks were sure to continue until the two flanking corps made better progress. Late in the evening the Germans launched a heavy attack on the Zon bridge area, but it was beaten off by British tanks and American infantry. On the right flank, in particular, "the situation was causing some anxiety," as the Germans were building up their strength in the Reichwald Forest. Besides trying to cut off the Guards Division, the Germans were fighting hard to eliminate the 1st British Airborne Division. "The failure of the communications prevented any assessment of the true situation at Arnhem," says the official report. All that was known was that the Airborne were still near the northern end of the bridge over the River Lek, but they were not holding it, and the houses they occupied in the town were being steadily reduced by Tiger tanks. Their situation was indeed precarious. They should have been joined during the day by the Polish Parachute Brigade but, as a final touch, the weather turned against them and the "drop" had to be postponed. This bad weather severely limited all air activity; only 73 sorties could be flown in the whole day as compared with the 550 of the first afternoon. A message at midnight from the Airborne read: "Position not too good. Re-supply in enemy hands. Expedite assistance as soon as possible." When the Corps Commander, Lieut.-General Horrocks, met Lieut.-General Browning, they agreed that the overriding necessity was to relieve the Airborne. Since the Germans holding the Nijmegen bridge could not be rushed from the front, they must be taken from the rear.

In the early hours of the 20th the commanders of the Guards Division and the 82nd U.S. Division met and agreed that the paratroopers of 504th Regimental Combat team should cross the river west of the town below the railway bridge. The only available boats were the Guards Division assault boats—a type the Americans had never seen before. The Divisional Commander wanted to provide British crews, but the Americans would not hear of it. Just give them a little instruction first, they said, and they would paddle across somehow.

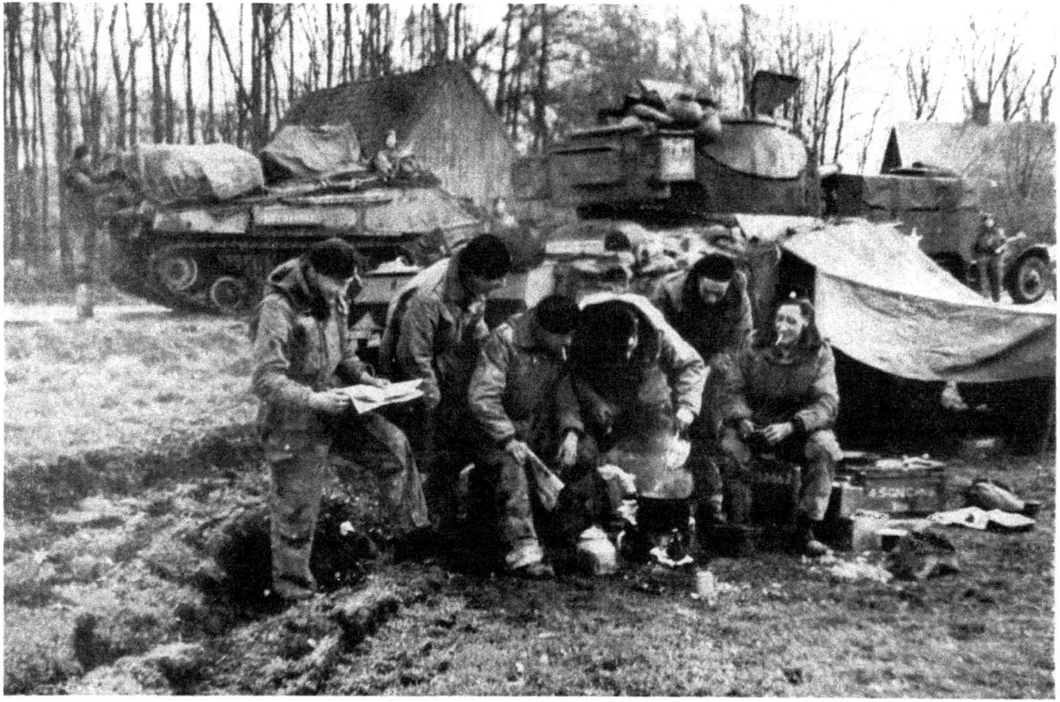

2nd Battalion—A Halt and "Brew" near Zon

At first light the Grenadiers took up again their task of clearing the town, house by house, towards the bridges. Since only our 2nd Battalion would be engaged, Colonel Giles Vandeleur went to the Free Dutch H.Q. to meet Colonel Tucker, the commander of the U.S. 504th Regiment Combat Team. The first thing to be done was to clear the area south of the River Waal between the railway and the Waal–Maas canal. The chief features of this area were the high embankments of the river, the marshy ground behind them, a muddy open basin where the canal flows into the river, a large factory and an even larger and taller power house. During the morning Colonel Giles and Colonel Tucker led the Dutchmen and Americans out to clear the area. They met so little opposition from unenthusiastic groups of aged German reservists, that the two Colonels got well ahead of their troops, reached the river bank and took a good look round uninterrupted except by a few shells. Parallel to the river runs a road along which straggle the suburb and gardens of Hees. At midday No. 2 and No. 3 Squadrons moved up to Hees, and halted there while Colonel Giles took Major E. Tyler and Major D. R. S. FitzGerald and the troop commanders forward on foot to choose fire positions for the tanks. The timings had to be calculated exactly as the whole area was more or less under German observation and was already under spasmodic shell fire. Colonel Tucker had first chosen the canal mouth as a good and secluded launching place for the boats, but his engineers said that the launching must be done higher upstream, otherwise the current—never less than three knots—would sweep the boats too far downstream. In other words, the parachutists must launch their boats in full view of the Germans. What this meant was clearly shown when a lorry from the bridging section foolishly came down the road parallel to the river. In an instant the number of boats available was reduced from thirty-two to twenty-six and the number of lorries by one. Colonel Tucker was to assemble his troops in the area of the power house about 1,500 yards downstream from the railway bridge, to cross the river under the cover of smoke and then, once on the far bank, to swing right-handed (*i.e.*, eastwards) to capture the old fort which dominated the northern approaches to the bridges. When this fort was captured the Grenadiers, who should by that time have secured the southern approaches, were to try again to rush the bridges with tanks.

The assault was due to start at three o'clock precisely. At half-past two the tanks moved slowly up to the river, reaching their positions just before three. No. 2 Squadron lined the embankment near the Power House and No. 3 Squadron hid behind rubble heaps on the waste land round the factory. No. 2 Squadron had by far the better field of fire, but was itself completely exposed to the Germans on the far bank. Colonel Giles Vandeleur went up to the American Command Post on the ninth floor of the Power House to watch the assault and direct the fire of the tanks. There were a hundred guns in all supporting the operation ; at five minutes to three they put down a smoke screen along the far bank and then lifted to fire concentrations farther back. Under cover of this smoke the Americans carried their boats down to the water's edge and then gathered round to watch Major Thomas, R.E., demonstrate how to use them. The squadrons covered this little demonstration by pouring H.E. and S.A. into the opposite bank. The boats, each loaded with fourteen men instead of the usual ten, hit the water about five past three. The wind had by then blown large gaps in the smoke, so the tanks fired more smoke to thicken up the screen. The Germans replied with heavy shell-fire on the bank—"As heavy as I ever want to meet again," said Captain E. N. Fitzgerald, who was sitting on the bank with a wireless set passing on fire orders to the tanks.

The Americans carried out the assault with the greatest courage and resource. They were heavily burdened with L.M.Gs. and ammunition and packed so tight that they could hardly move. When a boat was hit, the survivors unhesitatingly struck out for the far bank. Half-way across the river they came under close machine-gun and rifle fire from the bank and flanking fire from the railway bridge. Fortunately the German 88-mm. and 20-mm. guns had been sited for anti-aircraft work and so, not being able to depress their barrels low enough to fire into the river, concentrated on the Irish Guards' tanks. Only half the leading wave of Americans reached the far bank. They charged up the steep embankment, supported by the tanks' fire, and secured a small bridgehead of a couple of hundred yards. Out of the twenty-six boats which had set out only ten returned, the remainder having been sunk or swamped. The Americans ferried over more men and equipment as fast as they could—each boat took twenty-five minutes to cross and return—and then began to fight their way upstream towards the bridges. No praise is too high for their courage, especially that of the second and third waves, who stood on the bank watching the fate of the first. The squadrons were able to shoot the Americans right into their objectives. The old fort—the "Huis van Holland"—which was holding up the advance, got particular attention—even armour-piercing shot to keep the defenders' heads down. Colonel Tucker had told the tanks to shoot anywhere, any time at anything. His troops, he said, would fire amber Very lights if the fire was coming too close to them. No Very lights ever went up, not necessarily because the Irish Guards' shooting was so good—though, of course, it was—but because all the Very cartridges had got wet in the crossing.

At four o'clock Major Tyler saw figures moving on the railway bridge and reported that he could distinguish American uniforms or, maybe, German. Being over-excited, he said a different thing every minute, and so did every other tank commander. In fact, no one could possibly tell at that distance, through the smoke and girders. Unfortunately, Colonel Tucker had already crossed the river to join his troops, and his staff could not say exactly where the leading troops were, so for safety's sake the tanks held their fire from this most inviting target. Many obvious Germans, however, presented themselves to view and duly "had it" (in the Regiment the much-abused phrase "had it" was only used for death). In the midst of the fighting a horse-drawn cart appeared on the far side, moving slowly along the dyke road seven hundred yards away. God alone knows why. A tank gunner was ordered to engage it. Being a groom in civilian life he took very careful aim and with one shot demolished the wagon. The horse continued on its way alone.

By now the squadrons were short of ammunition ; some of the Brownings got so hot that they "ran away"—that is, they could not stop firing. Major D. M. L. Gordon-Watson, M.C., ordered Sir John Reynolds, Bart., to unload the kit and comforts from his jeep and trailer and send it full of high explosive and ·300 to No. 2 Squadron. No protests or evasions availed, and the precious and specially caparisoned jeep with its explosive burden accomplished and survived the mission.

Communications between the two banks of the river were not good, but at five o'clock the American Command Post said that their troops controlled the northern end of both bridges. This information proved to be false but fortunate. The Grenadiers had by this time captured the fort which guarded the southern end of the road bridge. They had seen no Americans at the northern end of the road bridge and were frankly incredulous of the statement that a flag with a white star had been hoisted there. They could see a fire burning, but no flag. The Grenadiers moved a squadron of tanks up to the roundabout and prepared to rush the bridge. In the failing light, just after seven o'clock, the Grenadiers crossed the bridge. There were no Americans about, and there had never been a flag anywhere, but there were Germans everywhere and 88-mm. guns covering the northern end. They spent an uncomfortable half-hour looking for the Americans until they found them about a mile farther on in the village of Lent, where the railway crosses the main road. The action was a brilliant achievement. Between them the Grenadiers and the Americans had captured intact one of the most important bridges in Europe. The support of the 2nd Battalion had been invaluable to the Americans. "You Guards," they said, "stand high in our estimation." When it was over, No. 3 Squadron went back to Maldon, but No. 2 Squadron stayed beside the Power House to guard and be entertained by the American Command Post. Their only loss for the day had been one tank hit on the turret by a shell.

As soon as the Grenadiers had taken the bridge the 3rd Battalion sent No. 2 and No. 4 Companies across to join the Americans. The Battalion had moved up into Nijmegen while the Grenadier tanks were preparing to rush the bridge. Normally the Grenadiers would have been supported by their own infantry battalion, but it would have taken half the night to reassemble the Grenadier infantry from their scattered houses and cellars. Major D. H. FitzGerald was in temporary command as Colonel Joe had, in his own words, "a violent bilious attack and was tucked up in bed." Sporadic fighting continued far into the night on both banks and on the bridge itself. Germans in the girders sniped the Sappers who were removing the demolition charges. The Guardsmen shot these snipers down like rooks, all except those who had lashed themselves to the iron-work. Nobody had time to remove the bodies, and for days they hung there. The Sappers themselves took eighty prisoners, one of whom volunteered to save them trouble and show them everything. The span the Germans had chosen to blow was 250 feet long—too wide to be bridged by a Bailey. The German led the Sapper officer on to a specially constructed cat walk, and there, right across the whole width of the bridge were the charges, securely fastened, and painted green like the girders. Everything had been prepared in minute detail. Each charge had its serial number and had been specially made to fit into the various shaped girders, even the bars of the handrails each had a charge attached.

Having lost the road bridge, the Germans let the railway bridge go too. The approaches had been weakened by shell-fire and blocked by disabled tanks, but the Grenadiers made their way across it without meeting opposition. The Germans seemed to have no unified command, but fought separately in little parties. The S.S. and young troops fought savagely, but the "old men" all ran away or surrendered when the S.Ss.' backs were turned.

The two companies had a busy and rather uncomfortable night, sweeping in so many prisoners that they did not know what to do with them. At first they crammed the Germans into the little chambers in the side of the railway bridge, but these soon overflowed, and the prisoners complained bitterly about the bad housing conditions. No. 4 Company appealed for help. "We have three hundred prisoners, and more are coming in. Can the Grenadiers please take some ?" "Send some back to us," replied Battalion H.Q., "there is plenty of room in the classrooms." Battalion H.Q. and the other companies were comfortably and securely lodged in a large school south of the river. Battalion H.Q. was particularly secure as it was in the deepest cellar. The top storey of the school looked like the set for a third-class spy film. The self-styled chief of the Nijmegen Underground Movement claimed to be in wireless communication with his counter-part in Arnhem. He rejected the offers of the Battalion signallers to help him, and produced an extraordinary home-made wireless set. His lieutenants, whose uniforms were also home-made, carefully carried the machine to a top-storey window facing Arnhem. Dutch and Irish waited while "underground engineers" connected wires, turned knobs, dismantled and reassembled the parts in a different order. Nothing happened ; the set maintained a stolid Dutch silence. The interpreters offered advice and consolation to their compatriots and optimistic progress reports to the Irish Guards. Still nothing happened. The Dutchmen were armed with another piece of practically home-made machinery—Sten guns. These are easier to operate than a wireless set ; a bump or a shake will set them off just as well as pressing the trigger. Sure enough, one went off and wounded an interpreter. "Regrettable," said Major Denis FitzGerald, "Interpreters are essential in Holland and Belgium, as no one else can speak their language, but we have plenty of reserves." Both Battalions had collected a number of interpreters, who now masqueraded as Irish Guardsmen with carefully prepared A.B. 64s—the soldier's pay-book—in case they were captured. The Germans, it was hoped, would not notice that No. 2710001 Guardsman Heinsius, P., could hardly have come from County Cork.

Information about the British Airborne trickled in from more orthodox sources. Refugees reported that only a few parachutists were still fighting in Arnhem itself. The Germans had recaptured the whole of the town and were now fiercely attacking the Airborne's remaining positions. An officer of the Airborne Engineers, who had swum the River Lek and walked through the enemy lines, confirmed these reports. The resources of the Airborne Division were stretched to the uttermost, he said, and if it was to remain intact as a fighting force, it must be relieved within the next twenty-four hours. There was only one way to reach Arnhem in time, and only one formation available who could possibly do it. At midday on the 21st the Irish Group was ordered to break out of the bridgehead and advance up the main road to Arnhem.

About ten miles east of Nijmegen the River Rhine divides into two streams. The southern stream, from now on called the River Waal, flows due west through Nijmegen to the sea. The northern stream, the River Lek, or Northern Rhine, flows north-west to Arnhem some fifteen miles north of Nijmegen, and then turns west to the sea. The strip of land between the two rivers was known as the "Island." The chemical formula for the Island is that of a patent medicine—90 per cent. water. It was surrounded by water, based on water, criss-crossed by innumerable waterways, below water-level and completely flat, so that if the rivers burst their dykes it was also under water. The soil was rich with river mud, excellent for fruit trees, which the Dutch farmers planted industriously, lining the main road to Arnhem with orchards. This road was embanked high above the surrounding fields and cut off from them by a deep drainage ditch on either side.

When the 2nd Battalion returned to Nijmegen later in the winter they met an instructor at the Dutch Staff College who spoke good English with a sprinkling of Army jargon. He showed great professional interest in the plan of attack on Arnhem, which the officers explained to him as well as they could. The Dutchman nodded gravely and then put a broad finger on the map. "You see the main road." The Battalion had seen only too much of the main road. "You see the side roads." The officers had not seen the side roads. "Well, I did my training at Arnhem. Every year this attack was set as a problem in the Colonel's promotion examination. It was the sack for those who went straight up the main road. If the officer decided to go left flank he got a Brigade. The attack up the main road is not on—certainly not with tanks." One look at the country was enough to tell both battalions that it was unsuitable, if not impossible, for tanks. But so had been the country north of the Escaut Canal. Here, as there, everything depended on three factors: one constant, the fighting qualities of the Irish Group, and two fluctuating, the strength of the opposition and the support. Anyway, Colonel "Joe" Vandeleur, unlike the Dutch officer, was fighting a battle, not a Staff College exercise, and had his orders which were based on the principle that whatever the difficulties and casualties, it was imperative to reach the Airborne, and the main road was the only one available to the Group.

Just before dawn No. 1 Squadron had crossed the bridge and joined No. 4 Company. They saw no enemy, but knew there were plenty about for they were shelled and mortared all morning. The Americans, who were actually in contact with the Germans to the north and east, could not give much information either, except that the Germans seemed to be well established round Elst, a town half-way to Arnhem. A deserter from these Germans said that they had been ordered not to attack but to dig in and hold the road. The best information came from a captured map. The railway line to Arnhem runs parallel to the road a mile to the right-hand side. Half-way to Elst is Bessen station, connected with the main road by a low thickly hedged lane. On the map the station and lane were covered with the German conventional signs for anti-tank and anti-aircraft guns and the whole area was dotted with infantry positions. The optimism of the Intelligence was as firm as ever ; the opposition would be slight, they said, and would anyway be disorganized by the Polish Parachute Brigade, who were to be dropped round Elst that afternoon.

Colonel "Joe" Vandeleur, now recovered from his bilious attack, demanded all available artillery and Typhoon support. This did not amount to very much. The advance to Nijmegen had been so rapid that the majority of the guns had not yet caught up and there was no large reserve of ammunition. No more artillery could be brought up at short notice, as the road to the south was both threatened by the enemy and fully occupied by the 43rd Division moving up to Nijmegen. Worse still, there were as yet no advance landing grounds for the Tactical Air Force. Colonel Joe had to be content with a call on a limited number of Typhoons and the support of only one of the Division's Field Regiments, as the other one had gone south with the Coldstream Group to protect the supply route.

CHAPTER X

"Market Garden," Phase II—The Attempt to reach Arnhem

2nd and 3rd Battalions

WITHIN an hour the Irish Group was lined up along the main road. No. 1 Squadron, without infantry, was in Lent, with its leading troop, Lieutenant T. Samuelson's, under the railway bridge which was the Grenadiers' forward outpost. Down the road stretched first No. 2 Squadron, carrying No. 2 Company on tank-back, and then No. 3 Squadron with the rest of the 3rd Battalion, whose tail was in Nijmegen. An artillery concentration was ordered on the German positions marked on the captured map, but opinions differed as to where it came down, except for about twenty shells that definitely fell in the wrong place. At half-past one the Group advanced. For ten minutes and two miles all went well, though the column was driving along an open road raised six feet above the surrounding countryside. The leading column reached a solitary farm surrounded by an orchard, an island in the bare open ground stretching south from the suspected enemy positions. They could see in front of them a line of trees at right-angles to the main road. Behind those trees ran the side road to Bessen. That was where the captured map marked the enemy guns. The map was right. Inside a minute the three tanks of the leading troop were in flames. The leading rifle company, No. 2, under Major Hendry, dived straight off the tanks on which they had been riding into the ditches on either side. The column piled up behind the leading tank, so that the vehicles were packed head to tail in silhouette along the road. For some reason or other no armour-piercing shot was fired at the column. The Germans had seven French 75-mm. guns which, as the Irish discovered later, could fire only high-explosive shells. The three leading Shermans were probably destroyed by one or two Tigers, whose tracks the Irish saw later. No one can understand why the Tigers did not knock off the remaining forty-nine tanks in a row.

But they did not. German infantry in the ditches with Spandaus and "squeeze guns" kept firing down the middle and sides of the road —very noisy and uncomfortable for Captain R. S. Langton in the leading tank. The wounded crews of the leading troop were lying by their tanks in the middle of the road and could not be reached. The infantry companies found cover in the ditches and orchards. By great good fortune only one shell landed in the ditches, but that one caused fifteen casualties. On the other hand, the tanks and trucks stood up like coconuts at a cockshy for the German gunners to knock down. The deep ditches which saved the infantry were a curse to the tanks. Since they could not get off the road, the 2nd Battalion was forced to fight on a one-tank front. Only the leading tank, if it was not hit, could fire forward ; a few of the others—about seven—could fire to the flank at the houses and railway station, but most of them were masked by the orchards along the road. Both sides of the road were orchard, orchard all the way. Colonel "Joe" Vandeleur made every effort to get the Typhoon support which had been promised, but first the control set broke down and then a second set was sent forward, which also broke down, so there was no communication with aircraft. "The tanks lacked vital support at a critical moment of the battle," said the official report, as if it was the sort of thing that might happen to anyone.

A few minutes after the leading troop had been destroyed, Colonel Giles Vandeleur and Captain Eamon Fitzgerald drove up in a scout car to Captain Langton's tank, now the leading element of the 2nd Army. The Germans greeted them with a hail of fire. It was easy enough to locate the Germans, particularly as everyone already knew where to look. It was intensely irritating for the observers in the ditches, under the smooth, bare tree-trunks, to be able to see the Krauts and yet to be unable to guide with accuracy the fire of the tanks, masked as they were by the bushy-topped trees. Colonel Giles decided that the tanks would obviously be murdered if they tried to attack, and that only the infantry had a chance. He crawled away down the ditch to report to his cousin, Colonel Joe. The only available artillery support was one regiment of field guns. Few as they were, they would be better than nothing. The Group was first disappointed and then very angry that no sound came from their guns. It was an hour before the first shells landed, but it was difficult to observe effects. The 3-inch mortar platoon under Lieutenant J. Compton and Sergeant Moran, however, opened fire inside ten minutes. The enemy gunners were active, and from a quarter to three o'clock until dark a steady stream of shells and mortar bombs came down on the line of the road.

At half-past three Major J. Haslewood, the Company Commander detailed for the infantry attack, rattled up the road in a carrier, being nearly killed *en route*. He joined Captain E. Fitzgerald in the ditch by Captain Langton's tank and peered over the flat and singularly uninviting countryside. It was out of the question to bring his company up the ditch and strike right to the railway station; not a single Guardsman would have survived the walk across four hundred yards of open country. He reported to Colonel Joe that an attack, to succeed, would have to go up both sides together, with the tanks supporting on the road and the guns pouring shells into the German positions. Colonel Joe fully agreed, but he could not get the artillery support. He ordered Major Haslewood to take his company and No. 3 Squadron and try to work round the right flank by the railway line. At the same time the Welsh Group were trying to loop round the left flank, but could make no progress and were engaged in heavy fighting a mile to the west.

About five o'clock the Brigade Commander, Brigadier Norman Gwatkin, came up and urged Colonel Joe to try everything possible. He was already doing so. The feeble shelling of the enemy positions did nothing to "loosen" the situation. The anti-tank guns could not be "pin-pointed," as anyone who went forward immediately came under heavy fire. The whole roadside was one long orchard, full of machine-gunners. No. 4 Company and No. 3 Squadron cleared the orchards towards the railway, but as soon as they debouched on the open ground the tanks were accurately engaged and the infantry pinned down by machine-gun fire. It was an impasse. The attack never got under way. At seven o'clock, as night was falling, the Irish Group were told to make no more efforts as a whole division, the 43rd, was being brought up to clear the road. The Group withdrew a thousand yards to harbour. They had done their best and suffered heavily, but on such ground, and without air or artillery support, two battalions could not break such strong defences. The 3rd Battalion had lost Lieutenants Wilson and Gordon-Shea wounded and now had only two platoon commanders left, Lieutenants Mahaffy and Harvey-Kelly. Rupert Mahaffy, sitting in a ditch, told Major Haslewood with gloomy satisfaction that, out of all the platoon commanders who had landed in Normandy, he was the sole survivor. The Medical Sergeant in his half-track ambulance made a gallant effort to reach the wounded up the road, but the Germans forced him back with bazooka fire. The wounded lay out till it was dark enough to send out patrols.

There was still little news of the Airborne Division. As far as was known they were holding an area of about a mile by half a mile round Hartestein, between the Lower Rhine and the high ground to the north. They were again short of food and ammunition, as most of the containers dropped by parachute missed that much-contracted perimeter. They were now completely cut off, as the Germans had recaptured all Arnhem and the ferry at Hevedorp. In the late afternoon the Polish Parachute Brigade had been dropped north of Elst. Heavy enemy "flak" forced the aircraft to drop them much too near the enemy positions. The unfortunate Poles suffered heavily before they were able to collect themselves in the area from which they were supposed to cross the river. The Germans were determined to prevent help reaching the Airborne. Not only did they strengthen and hold their position in front of the Guards Division, but they also launched continued attacks along the lines of communication. During the day they actually succeeded in cutting the road at Veghel. In the confusion of battle it was some time before this was noticed. When it was, the Corps Commander ordered the R.A.F. to "ground-strafe" on recognition within the bomb line. This unusual procedure was successful, and the road was reopened with only one British vehicle shot up by mistake.

With the Germans firmly established in and around Arnhem the original Corps plan of seizing Arnhem Bridge and sweeping on to the Zuider Zee was obviously no longer possible. The first thing to do now was to secure a firm bridgehead across the Lower Rhine. The Corps Commander therefore ordered the 43rd Division to attack through the Irish Guards the following morning and to join the Airborne on the banks of the Lower Rhine. Until this was done the Guards Division was to hold its present position; once it had been done, it was to pass through and capture Apeldoorn. The difficulty in this plan, even supposing the 43rd Division reached the southern bank, was that the bridgehead held by the Airborne on the north bank was getting steadily smaller and the whole river was under German control, so that a large-scale assault crossing was inevitable.

During the night Major E. Fisher-Rowe took out a strong fighting patrol to find and destroy the German anti-tank guns near Bessen station and to collect information for the 43rd Division. A thick damp fog lay over the fields, blinding sentries and chilling the men to the bones. The patrols reached the station, but they could see nothing—neither could the Germans. The Spandau posts blazed off belts of ammunition at the figures looming in the mist. No one was hit, but the Group was no better off for information. The stretcher-bearers, however, were able to tip-toe up the road and bring back the wounded from the destroyed tanks. This fog lasted all night. Under cover of it a squadron of the Household Cavalry got up to the bank of the Lower Rhine and joined the Polish paratroopers. There they remained all the following day sending back a stream of information and directing the artillery on to targets passed to them by isolated paratroopers in Arnhem. A German steamer towing three barges gave them their best target. Soon they signalled back, "Steamer damaged—three barges sunk." Divisional H.Q. replied "Congratulations on brilliant naval action. Splice the mainbrace." They did—with Rhine water.

Early next morning the gunners and the 4th Bn. Wiltshire Regiment of the 129th Brigade began their preparations for an attack through the Irish Group. Colonel Joe showed them the enemy line and strongly advised the commanding officer (who had asked for advice) to avoid the east side of the road and to launch his attack towards the orchards just west of where the side road joins the main road. He also promised to support them with a squadron. The attack began about midday after a heavy artillery preparation, to which the Germans replied by showering shells on the Group. The Irish were very angry at getting the shells clearly meant for the 4th Wiltshires. The pioneer truck, loaded with explosives, was hit; the flames set fire to the thatched roof of the house occupied by Headquarters and turned them out of doors. Six men were killed and twenty-one wounded, including Captain G. S. Corbett, who was hit in the eye by a shell-splinter. Some of the shells landed on Brigade H.Q., one of them wounding Captain Terence O'Neill. Caught in his truck at lunch-time, Captain O'Neill was hit on his sciatic nerve and removed to England.

The 4th Wiltshires met strong opposition. What exactly happened is unknown, but at nightfall their leading companies were still only some hundred yards ahead of the leading troop. This troop, Lieutenant J. Daly's, lost a Firefly in their efforts to support the attack. Lieutenant Daly's continual shooting made him most unpopular with the 3rd Battalion company. They had been shelled and machine-gunned all morning, and the company commander roundly abused him for drawing the Germans' fire. At four o'clock Lieutenant W. C. T. MacFetridge led his troop into the orchard east of the road in a second attempt to help forward the 4th Wiltshires. Almost immediately his tank was hit by a Panther, and he himself was killed. Captain R. S. Langton brought up another Firefly to avenge him. He personally took a shot at the Panther and forced it to withdraw, but not until it had hit and damaged another tank. During the night the 5th Bn. Wiltshires, of the same Brigade, tried a night attack along the railway. Just after the 4th Wiltshires began their attack the Germans, with tanks, lorried infantry and guns, cut the Corps' lines of communication well to the south between Uden and Grave. In the early afternoon the Germans also started shelling St. Oedenrode and it looked as if they were preparing to launch a general co-ordinated attack. The 32nd Guards Brigade were sent back to Grave to guard against this, and no further traffic came up the road for the rest of the day. The Germans could continue to threaten and often cut the road until 8th and 12th Corps could come up on the flanks. So far, 12th Corps was only level with Eindhoven and 8th Corps had not yet reached Helmond. The Airborne were heavily attacked all day, and their effective strength was estimated to be now only 1,200 men. It was at last possible to give them heavy and continual artillery support, but even with this they had not the strength to regain the ferry at Hevedorp. During the night, however, a relief column of 4th/7th Dragoons and a battalion of the Dorsets with "ducks" managed to slip through the enemy and reached the Poles on the bank of the Lower Rhine. The banks were steep, the "ducks" difficult to launch and the whole southern bank under heavy machine-gun fire. None the less they completed the task—a most gallant action, causing them heavy casualties.

The following morning, the 23rd, more of 130th Brigade on the left flank reached the Lower Rhine. It was an immense relief. There now seemed to be a good chance of making an assault crossing to join the Airborne. There was much to be done first; ammunition, bridging equipment and, above all, more infantry had to be brought up. The official report kept on emphasizing the need for more infantry, repeating, almost monotonously, that the country was quite unsuitable for deploying armour against determined, or indeed any, resistance. To get more infantry up it was necessary first to clear the road. At dawn the 32nd Brigade and the 101st U.S. Airborne Division began to clear the axis south-west from Uden, and by the afternoon they had driven the Germans off the road. Traffic began to flow through once more though subject to occasional interruptions from enemy shelling, bazooka-ing and small-arms fire. Sergeant McRory, limping up the road in a lame tank, stopped to help a battalion of the 101st Division. The Americans were most appreciative of the number of Krauts he killed for them, and sent a letter of thanks to the Battalion, referring to him as "Our Boy." Even the Forward Delivery Squadron was engaged. Lieutenant A. G.

de las Casas, also on his way up the road, tried to drive some Germans from a wood near Uden and was "brewed up" in a tank he should have delivered intact to the 2nd Battalion. The Coldstream Group were still fighting south of the River Waal to clear the bank east of Nijmegen. They crossed the German frontier east of Beek and were thus the first British troops, other than H.Q. British Airborne Corps, to enter Germany. The Welsh Guards, however, were held up and the 43rd Division were making very little progress towards Elst.

Meanwhile, the Irish Group remained where it was to hold the road and support 129th Brigade if necessary. As opposed to the brisk fighting in the rear, they had a quiet day, save for a few mortar bombs, suffering mostly from the steady pouring rain. The weather cleared slightly in the evening, which caused an outburst of air activity. The battalions had not seen so many German aeroplanes since the early Normandy days, all on their way to bomb Nijmegen Bridge. Captain R. Robertson, driving across, was very nearly hit the same time as the bridge. S.S.M. Holly put his truck into one of the bomb holes and hung suspended above the water. The brief spell of flying weather came too late in the day to help the Airborne, which meant that all the craft had to be used for ferrying not men, but the ammunition and food of which they were acutely short. Two hundred and fifty Poles, however, did manage to cross during the night. The next morning, the 24th, the 129th Brigade cleared Bessen and the main road as far as Elst. Since the Irish Group's role was still to protect the road until Arnhem was cleared, this gave them a chance to inspect the German positions which had held them up. There still remained eleven 75-mm. anti-aircraft guns sited for anti-tank defence, the tracks and empty shell cases of at least one Tiger—the wide deep marks of which can be easily identified—and two 88-mm. guns. There were also the trenches, dirt and debris of infantry dug in along the little road—about three hundred men with about as many machine-guns to judge by the cartridge cases. All were practically as the Irish Guards had said and the captured map had shown.

Colonel "Joe" Vandeleur was the man best placed to pass judgment on the operation. These are his reflections: "Looking back, I am of the opinion that the axis was totally unsuitable for armoured movement, owing to the high embankments denying deployment from the roads. A better axis did in fact exist to the west, but a long way round. This was the one used by 214th Brigade of 43rd Division, who succeeded in reaching the river and extricating some of the Airborne during a gallant night's fighting." It was also the Dutch Staff College's "school solution" to the problem of attacking Arnhem

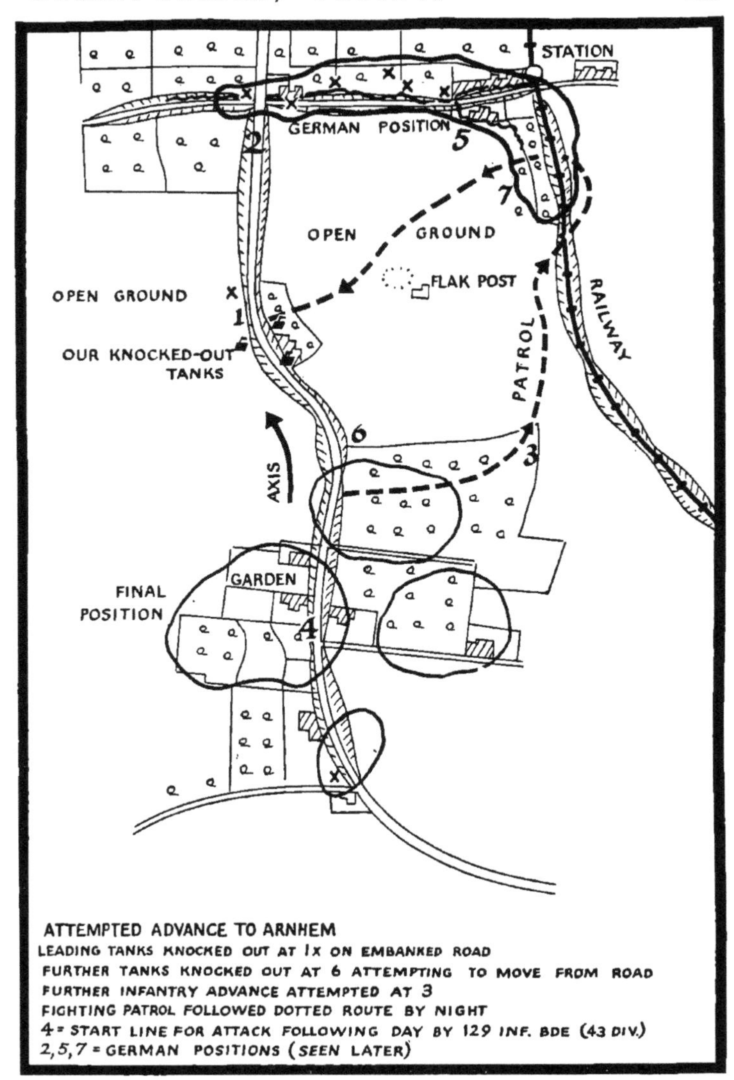

Attempted Advance to Arnhem

from the south. "Our bitterest regret," continued Colonel Joe, "was that the air tentacle was not working, for with even moderate support from the Tiffies (Typhoons) we might have broken through to Elst, if not farther." He then described the German strength and position. "It was lucky that the Germans did not hold the fire of their anti-tank guns until more of our column had passed the little farm and orchard. Had they done so, no vehicle could have escaped destruction on that main road which was so narrow and steeply embanked. It is easy to be wise after the event, but the whole affair was most disappointing, and we would have liked to be able to claim success in reaching the hard-pressed Airborne Division."

The Airborne were certainly hard pressed, their casualties were heavy and their positions were being steadily blown to pieces by concentrated tank fire. From statements made by German prisoners it was clear that the 1st Parachute Brigade had ceased to exist as a formation. The Germans, fighting harder than ever, were bringing down more tanks and infantry to stop the relieving columns and, at the end of a day's fighting, were still holding Elst in front and Bemmel on the right flank. In the afternoon they again cut the main road south of Veghel and stopped all traffic. This time the attack came from the west and was made by the 6th German Parachute Regiment, which had been by-passed in the original drive to Nijmegen. During the afternoon the 69th Brigade came up on the right to attack Dammel. At the same time the 8th Armoured Brigade came up to support the 43rd Division, thus relieving the Irish Group. The two Battalion H.Qs. moved back to the area of Ousterhout. The squadrons and companies billeted themselves in farms near the main road ; the two Battalion H.Qs. moved into the Huis Ousterhout, a large Dutch mansion, cream-coloured with green shutters and a red roof, which both sides had forgotten to destroy. It had been a German H.Q. and still bore traces of their filth, but it was soon cleaned and turned to better uses.

The next few days were peaceful for the Irish Guards, who were even able to do some drill on the road. They were now in 30th Corps reserve and did not expect to be committed to action again until a bridgehead had been secured over the Lower Rhine. Huis Ousterhout became a social centre, rivalled only by F.2 Echelon's establishment at Nijmegen, a house taken over from the late German commander, where Major Sir John Reynolds organized hot baths and comfort. After days of discomfort, hunger and sleeplessness, they keenly appreciated the humble joys of sleeping on a real bed—even if the blankets were dirty—and of eating food off a table. "It is all a fool's paradise," wrote one happy officer, "but it is worth it." During these days the Irish got no mail or rations, as the road behind them had once again been cut—this time for forty-eight hours—by the 107th Panzer Brigade. They fed on rations collected from a large German food dump at Oss, captured by Captain P. A. C. O'Donovan and his Divisional H.Q. troop. A meticulous foreman—inevitably called the Wizard of Oss—insisted on a signature for every withdrawal. He did not mind whether it was German or British, so long as it was a signature. The Germans, meanwhile, ate British rations and read the Guardsmen's letters somewhere between Veghel and Uden.

After tasting German hard rations the Guardsmen changed their opinion of British "compo packs." The Oss dump was said to contain enough meat and bread to feed the whole of the 2nd Army for two months ; the meat and bread would have been a welcome change from bully and biscuits. Fortunately local purchase and "free enterprise" eked out the meals ; vegetables and fruit, particularly apples, pears, potatoes, tomatoes and onions were plentiful and excellent. When, for instance, Lieutenant K. R. Briant bought a wounded but wholesome calf, a whole company had stew. No. 2 Squadron and No. 4 Company amassed enough food to have a gala dinner celebrating their joint victories. The other squadrons and companies asked them what victories they had to celebrate, on the assumption that only those who had stayed in the rear the whole time could have collected so much food and drink. Just before the road was cut the long-awaited reinforcements arrived—four officers (Lieutenants Billy Reynolds, Peter Mounsey, Dennis Galloway and Geoffrey Warnock) and seventeen men from the 3rd Battalion, and new tanks and crews for the 2nd Battalion.

Operation "Market Garden" was officially closed when, on the morning of 25th September, the decision was taken to withdraw the Airborne that night. Casualties and shortage of supplies made their position untenable. Each effort to ferry supplies and reinforcements across the Lower Rhine was a major operation, since the Germans dominated the narrow crossing-place. This German domination made the small area the Airborne still held unsuitable for development into a Corps bridgehead, particularly as it would also be impossible to build and maintain a bridge in that area. The previous night (24th/25th) the 4th Bn. Dorsetshire Regiment had forced a crossing of the Lower Rhine and joined the Airborne. During the following night (25th/26th) 163 men of the Airborne Division, 160 Polish paratroopers and 75 Dorset men were ferried back over the river. One hundred and eighty men of the Dorsets were left on the north bank still fighting to cover the withdrawal. Every man who crossed the Lower Rhine knew that he was being used to save the Airborne. The rain came pouring down, making the damp country even damper. The Irish Guardsmen lay in their little farms that night, wet, cold and occasionally shelled, but when they thought of the Dorsets they knew that, for once, they were lucky. Officers and Guardsmen went to visit the Airborne wounded in hospital. As always in any military operation, those who had fought and suffered most were the quietest and most appreciative. The paratroopers who had fought (not the Airborne Corps' "seaborne tail") were remarkably cheerful and not a bit annoyed ; they just said, "What a pity, with more luck we'd have massacred the Huns, but all the supplies dropped in the wrong place or did not drop at all, so *rien à faire*." "We all felt pretty terrible about the unfortunate Airborne," said a Guardsman. "Everything combined to stop our reaching them, but we tried so hard and got so near."

CHAPTER XI

Aam and the Defence of the Nijmegen Bridgehead

2nd and 3rd Battalions

THE Corps front on the Island was now a rough semi-circle; the 43rd Division held from Elst west and the 50th Division from Elst east. The main enemy counter-attacks were expected from the south-east through the Reichwald Forest against the American divisions farther south, and, from the north-east, against the 50th Division. Meanwhile, the Germans continued bombing and shelling the Nijmegen bridges, much to the discomfort of F.2 Echelon in the "town house." It was clear that the opposition had grown too strong for the 2nd Army to continue the advance on the original plan. Accordingly, a new plan was produced to push the Germans out of range of Nijmegen and to secure a good defence line behind which to prepare for a further advance, this time north-eastwards. One of the 50th Division brigades—the 69th—was therefore ordered to extend the bridgehead eastwards as far as the transverse canal, the Weteringe Linge, and the village of Halderen, from which the Germans could observe the bridges. It did not have much success, and was only just able to hold on to its own positions while waiting for reinforcements. Since it now considered itself hard-pressed and over-stretched, the Welsh Guards Group had been sent to hold Aam, a village two miles east of Elst.

On the 28th September the 3rd Battalion and No. 2 Squadron were ordered to relieve the 1st Bn. Welsh Guards. The company commanders, muttering "This is a bore; really, it is somebody else's turn by now," drove over at lunch-time and found the Welsh Guards living in peace. There was no shelling, which seemed to them "very peculiar, as Elst was being pounded into ruins." The Dutch women and children were all walking about "looking quite gay." Aam is, or was, an undistinguished and uninviting group of farms and brick houses on a rough road two miles to the east of the main Arnhem road. Around it stretch the flat, sodden fields, small orchards and dripping woods. It looks, and is, a dreary countryside. Through Aam, from north to south, runs the broad raised causeway of an unfinished military road from Arnhem to Nijmegen. A thousand yards north of Aam, just south of the Weteringe Linge canal, the Dutch, or Germans, had built an embankment and bridge to carry over the unfinished "autobahn" another also unbuilt road. "X" Company Scots Guards, now serving with the Welsh, held a forward position on this embankment. Major Stuart-Fotheringham, the Company Commander, had no complaints about the Germans—in fact, they had allowed him to shoot duck. Half-way between the embankment and Aam village was another company position dug in among the orchards and hen-houses on the right of the causeway, watching the right (east) flank. The other two companies were in the orchards and farmyards on the line of the side road. During the afternoon No. 2 Company occupied the rear position on the left. No. 1 and No. 4 Companies waited till nightfall. There was no fourth company, so the rear right-hand position had to be left unoccupied. Captain A. E. Dorman sent one troop of No. 2 Squadron up to No. 1 Company behind the embankment, the second to No. 4 Company and kept the third back round Battalion H.Q. in Aam. The Battalion could not see the Germans, but the Germans showed that they could see the Battalion. As soon as it was dark they heavily mortared No. 4 Company, killing five men and wounding five more. Patrols searched the ground in front but could find no Germans; they did, however, find a battalion of Green Howards on the south-eastern flank. Farther south, the Germans were remarkably enterprising. Sailors in special rubber suits swam down the River Waal and blew up both the Nijmegen bridges. "After we had taken the bridges," says one letter, "the Germans sent little men in swim-suits with torpedoes and blew up both of them, which makes the bridge defences look rather silly. It also makes traffic rather difficult, as tanks don't swim unless carefully prepared. Corps H.Q. has now blown for the Navy." The railway bridge was permanently destroyed and it took a day to repair the road bridge.

The following day was quiet enough; there was a certain amount of shelling, but otherwise no interference. The Germans for the time being were busy digging and building a defensive line from the Lower Rhine to the River Waal to contain the eastern flank of the Allied bridgehead. During the afternoon the two remaining squadrons of the 2nd Battalion relieved the 2nd Bn. Welsh Guards, who had been supporting the infantry of the 69th Brigade on the

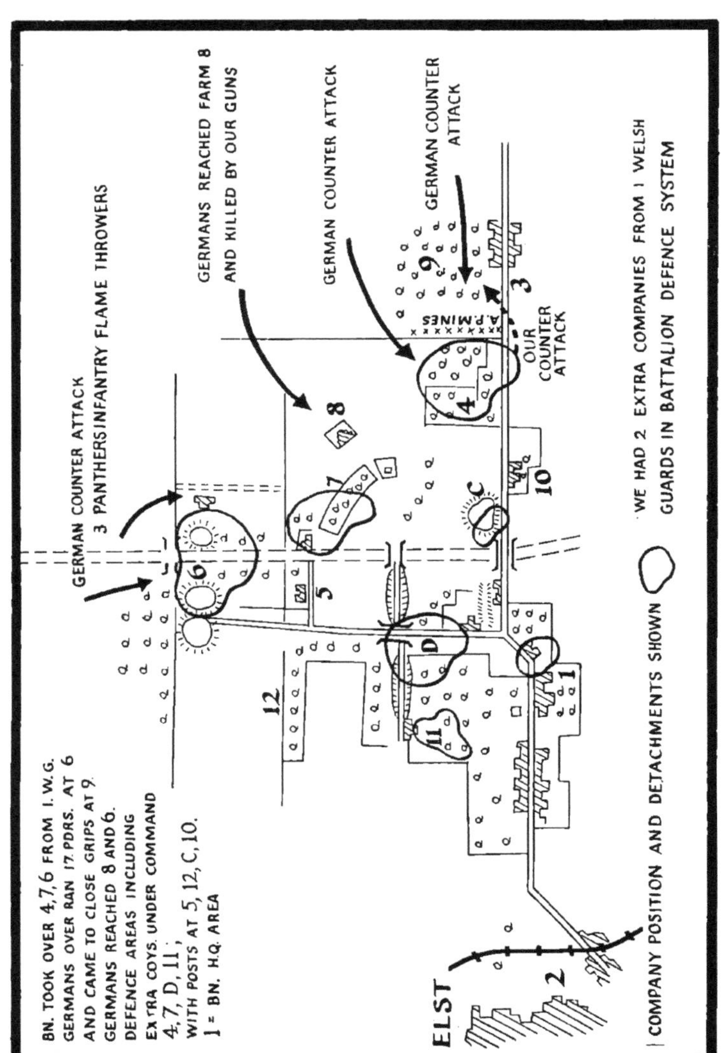
BN. TOOK OVER 4,7,6 FROM 1. W.G.
GERMANS OVER RAN 17 PDRS. AT 6
AND CAME TO CLOSE GRIPS AT 9.
GERMANS REACHED 8 AND 6.
DEFENCE AREAS INCLUDING
EXTRA COYS. UNDER COMMAND
4, 7, D, 11;
WITH POSTS AT 5, 12, C, 10.
1 = BN. H.Q. AREA
GERMAN COUNTER ATTACK
3 PANTHERS INFANTRY FLAME THROWERS
GERMANS REACHED FARM 8
AND KILLED BY OUR GUNS
GERMAN COUNTER ATTACK
GERMAN COUNTER
ATTACK
A.P. MINES
OUR
COUNTER
ATTACK
ELST
1
2
3
4
5
6
7
8
9
10
11
12
C
D
COMPANY POSITION AND DETACHMENTS SHOWN
WE HAD 2 EXTRA COMPANIES FROM 1 WELSH
GUARDS IN BATTALION DEFENCE SYSTEM
AAM

right flank. No. 3 Squadron, now commanded by Captain D. F. Radcliffe, had one troop with the 7th Green Howards in an orchard south-west of Heuvel, one troop on the cross-roads in Bemmel in support of the 5th East Yorks, and his Squadron H.Q. and reserve troop on the road between Ressen and Bemmel. No. 1 Squadron, under Captain R. S. Langton, remained in reserve at Ousterhout. The next day, the 30th, brought more reports of German activity and threats, so No. 1 Squadron moved up to strengthen the line. They took over the orchard and Bemmel cross-roads from the troops of No. 3 Squadron, who rejoined the rest of their squadron on the Bemmel–Ressen road. The days had been quiet enough, but the Germans shelled regularly at dawn and dusk and spasmodically through the nights. The 3rd Battalion, not having the protection of steel plate, naturally suffered most from this fire, particularly as their men were often working out in the open under a bright moon laying defensive mine belts. That afternoon German shelling intensified; most of it fell on No. 4 Company, wounding Lieutenant John Blake, but enough landed round Battalion H.Q.'s farmhouse to make them evacuate the top room and set themselves up in the cellars. A batch of reinforcements at last arrived—six officers and 155 Guardsmen. Out of these a complete new No. 3 Company was formed and given to Captain M. Dudley to hold the right-hand rear positions.

At five o'clock on Sunday morning, 1st October, German patrols approached the right flank. "This was the beginning of a strenuous day." It was also the beginning of a concerted German effort to clear the Island and drive the British Army back over the River Waal. The German patrols withdrew, ordered a heavy concentration of mortar and shell-fire on Nos. 3 and 4 Companies and then came on again. The companies beat them off before breakfast time. The Germans, however, remained in the copses round the Battalion. "Situation in hand," reported Colonel Joe to Brigade H.Q., "but it will be difficult to dislodge the enemy unless we have more infantry." Then "everything started at once." The Germans launched a violent attack on the 69th Brigade and heavily shelled the right flank of the Battalion to keep it quiet. They concentrated first on the Green Howards on the right of No. 4 Company. Of No. 1 Squadron, which was supporting the 69th Brigade, only Lieutenant B. de las Casas's troop was engaged. It was hidden in the orchard at Vergert and had some difficulty in keeping touch with the infantry. Four Tigers and accompanying infantry drove the forward Green Howard company out of Heuvel and were about to turn their attention on Lieutenant de las Casas when one of the Tigers got bogged and the others gave up the attack to drag it out of the mud. Lieutenant de las Casas fired at them with his 75-mm., but saw the shots bounce off. The German tanks did not even bother to reply. He then tried Browning and finally dismounted in disgust, borrowed a rifle and took pot-shots at the tank commanders. Luckily the Germans had great trouble in extricating their friend and, when finally successful, withdrew to Heuvel, camouflaged themselves carefully and took a rest.

Though thus deserted, the German infantry pressed on and by eleven o'clock had worked round the flanks of No. 4 Company. One detachment occupied an orchard opposite No. 3 ; it was heavily shelled and mortared, but after each "stonk" bravely fired back. Lieutenants J. Daly and C. Tottenham took their tanks forward to "stop this nonsense." The Germans "reacted favourably" to the continuous Browning fire and high-velocity shells ; about forty frightened men came out with their hands up. There was no telling how many had been left there dead. Lieutenant J. Daly then drove down a track south-eastwards to find and make contact with Lieutenant de las Casas. Some four hundred yards along he came across a German company hiding in the ditches on either side of the road. The Germans, though quite anxious to surrender, were naturally unwilling to get out of the ditches under fire. Lieutenant J. L. E. Daly had no infantry with him to pull them out. Finally they reached a compromise. Lieutenant Daly ceased fire, and about fifty Germans came out and ran down the road towards the 3rd Battalion. These prisoners came from every regiment in the 9th S.S. Panzer Division. One Spandau machine-gun, however, still kept firing at Lieutenant Daly from a little orchard. He could not silence it with his Browning, so he dismounted to stalk it with his revolver. The Spandau got him first, in the knee, and though he was able to continue for the rest of the day, he had to be evacuated that night. His troop continued its patrol, but could not find Lieutenant de las Casas, who was busy with his Tigers, and then returned to the 3rd Battalion.

The Germans now turned their full attention to the Irish Guards. They brought up self-propelled guns and tanks to harass No. 1 and No. 2 Companies on the left flank while they shovelled in a series of small attacks against No. 3 and No. 4 Companies. They kept the pressure constant by bringing up fighting groups in lorries, dropping them about a thousand yards away and sending them forward under mortar support. The shelling increased steadily, spreading over the whole area. Lieutenant Samuelson was one of the many wounded by splinters. "Casualties began to pour into the Aid Post at an unpleasant rate." A 17-pdr. anti-tank gun knocked out one self-propelled gun, and the field and medium guns kept the other quiet, but they could not stop the shelling. At midday the German gunners found Battalion H.Q., hit it and set it on fire. A direct hit killed the attached battery commander and his staff and wrecked all the wireless sets. Then the Aid Post got two direct hits and had to be moved. It was already crowded by civilian refugees, including one woman about to give birth. The Dutch women and children, who had once "looked quite gay" pointed to the trucks and pleaded to be evacuated. "It is out of the question," said Colonel Joe, "the road is under constant drum-fire." The refugees were crowded into cellars until there was a chance to hustle them across the fields during the occasional lulls in the shelling.

There was a brief pause at one o'clock and an encouraging visit from Brigadier Gwatkin, who always liked to smell powder. Two more small parties of reinforcements arrived. As there was no time to distribute them amongst the companies, they were given positions of their own to hold on either side of the road beside No. 3 Company. With this added strength the Battalion waited for the Germans to attack again. They had not long to wait. "By tea-time the situation around No. 3 Company on the extreme right flank had got rather ugly, as the German infantry were piling up their attacks." The "new boys" fought like veterans and beat the Germans out of the orchards and down the road in savage hand-to-hand fighting. The 153rd Field Regiment (Leicestershire Yeomanry) gave the Battalion magnificent support. "Their S.O.S. shoots over No. 4 Company and their defensive fire shoots in front of No. 3 were executed with pin-point accuracy. The Battalion was literally astounded by the speed, accuracy and intensity of their fire. To the gunners must go the credit for breaking up the German attacks before they got really threatening." Another mark was scored up in the huge general debt of the infantryman to the field gunner.

Once the momentum of the German attack was broken the Battalion began to put in short-jab counter-attacks to gain more room to employ the guns in front of No. 3 Company. "It was a great moment when the Germans started to wave the white flag." Their last attack of the day ended in a spectacular disaster. Between and forward of No. 3 Company and No. 4 Company was a large isolated barn, unoccupied, but so placed that the companies could cover every side of it. The Germans sent a strong company to capture it. The Battalion watched them install themselves and call up their friends. Two troops of No. 2 Squadron sidled forward, the field gunners and mortar men prepared a pile of shells. When the Germans were snugly settled the Battalion let fly with the complete field regiment, the mortars and the tanks' 75s and machine-guns. "That was the end of the Germans in the barn ; those that were left gave themselves up to No. 4 Company." The other Germans retaliated by heavily shelling No. 4 Company and setting fire to Company H.Q. Major Haslewood and his dog, "Boxer," had to take to a drain. "Boxer" was a Schnautzer hound, formerly the property of a German officer. Having once been wounded it was an expert at predicting the flight of a shell. This shelling killed Guardsman Fox, who had survived North Africa and Italy ; he was hungry and thirsty, and hoisted himself out of his trench for a moment to pick an apple.

When the day ended the Battalion's positions were all tight and firm and they had collected ninety-nine prisoners. The Germans had spent a singularly profitless day against the Battalion. The Battalion, on the other hand, had received its latest and most valuable reinforcement at the height of the battle. Into the harassed Headquarters, which was noticeably shuddering as its house crumbled under direct hits, stalked Major John Kennedy. He was wearing a cap-comforter and a blue sailor's jersey with an American carbine slung over his shoulder. "I have come," he said. He looked as if he had come straight from the gullies of Anzio. He had left his draft in England to take its normal course, probably lasting three months, jumped into a friend's aeroplane at Northolt and lorry-hopped through Belgium and Holland. "Never was a man more welcome," said Colonel Joe. "His battle record was second to none in the Regiment. He was one of those rare persons who really enjoyed war. It did us all good to see him."

The afternoon attacks had been made by infantry of the 116th Panzer Division supported by the tanks of 9th Battle Group Frunsberg (9th and 10th S.S.) and 108th Panzer Brigade, though the prisoners taken looked very much the same sorry lot as before. Their orders, they said, were to capture Aam and press on to Elst. Until they were cut short, the ordinary infantry all swept into bitter complaints about their monstrous treatment by the S.S., who forced them into battle from the safety of slit trenches. The Irish Guards had no sympathy to spare and, anyway, were very annoyed to find the 9th and 10th S.S. Divisions knocking about again after they thought they had finished them off in Normandy.

Divisional H.Q. warned the two battalions that the Germans were likely to renew their attacks the following morning as this was clearly a concentrated effort to eliminate the Nijmegen bridgehead.

As soon as it was dark all battalions in the line relieved the units that had been the most exposed during the day. No. 2 Company, under Captain A. Hendry, changed places with No. 1 Company on the embankment, putting Lieutenant Harvey-Kelly's platoon on the left of the bridge and Lieutenant Galloway's on the right. The Somerset Light Infantry, on the left flank, and the 3rd Battalion both sent out "contact patrols," but they did not meet, since the Germans were sitting in between. The enemy infantry and armour closed in under cover of darkness. At midnight eight Panther tanks drove down the causeway, halted about a hundred yards in front of No. 2 Company and switched off their engines. "It is extraordinary how quiet these machines are, and we were surprised that they could approach us over this sodden ground." A Panther rolled over the forward section of the left-hand platoon. Lieutenant William Harvey-Kelly "hopped out of his hole" and put a Piat bomb into the tank. After this, the others kept their distance for the night.

On the right, meanwhile, No. 3 Squadron sent Lieutenant W. Clark's and Sergeant Denver's troops to relieve Lieutenant de las Casas, who had had an eventful day, and the East Yorks relieved the Green Howards and occupied the same positions. Lieutenant Clark and Sergeant Denver reached Vergert before dawn and found two platoons of the East Yorks in twin orchards either side of a ditch. "When we arrived," said Lieutenant Clark, "Basil de las Casas told us there had been some mortaring, but otherwise nothing. His Tiger visitors had 'fallen themselves out.' There was no sign of any infantry in the southern orchard, but all the guns and even a Bren carrier were there. Two men emerged from a dug-out to say that all their friends had gone the night before. About half-past seven a harassed infantry officer rang up to say that the Germans had driven his platoons out of the northern orchard. I decided to attack with my troop, leaving the other troop to cover the south orchard. A scratch infantry section of two officers, the R.S.M., the C.S.M. and about five sergeants and men followed our tanks up to a house on the edge of the road. The infantry were fired on from a bush in the ditch, which the tanks immediately sprayed with Browning. We then set off up the road at about 20 m.p.h., the hull gunner firing into both ditches and the turret gunner shooting at the enemy after we had passed. This machine-gun fire actually caused a bazooka man to miss us at six-to-seven-foot range. Another bazooka man was hit at twenty yards' range by my hull gunner before he could fire. We came back to the start of our run via the south orchard and finished off the ditches with high explosive. All this had enabled the infantry section to get across to the north orchard, whither we followed them to give support and got a view of the open ground beyond it. We managed to get across the ditch and shot our way to the north-east edge of the orchard where we caught some enemy infantry in the ditches. Sergeant Denver's troop then joined me, and together we put high explosive and Browning into the houses, barns and woods to our right front. The enemy unfortunately replied with mortars and we were forced to withdraw. Sergeant Denver was wounded almost at once, and I sent his tank back. My own tank got bogged in the ditch between the orchards, so I sent the crew to cover and went to get my Troop Sergeant's tank to tow it out. Mortar fire was heavy and accurate. Guardsman Holland was killed while trying to attach the tow rope, and both tanks were hit by mortar bombs several times. As one tank was obviously not enough to pull mine out, I and my crew mounted the Sergeant's tank and we all returned to the south orchard. The mortar and shell fire continued until the afternoon, but the Germans did not attack again."

On the 3rd Battalion front the Germans shelled and mortared all night, and at dawn (2nd October) they fell on No. 2 Company. In their effort to get to Nijmegen bridge they brought up everything they had and carefully stage-managed their attack. Squads of "man-pack" flame-throwers advanced towards the embankment, squirting streams of burning oil. Just behind them came ten tanks, firing steadily to protect them, and behind each tank filed a section of fifteen men. Farther back were more infantry in open formation. Captain Hendry called for the guns ; the response was quick, but before the first shells landed the flame-throwers and tanks were on the two forward platoons. The right-hand platoon was burnt and shot out of its trenches ; it fell back on No. 4 Company and there re-formed. The tanks swung round, destroyed the 17-pdr. anti-tank guns and pressed on to encircle the embankment. It looked for a moment as if they were going to have a clear run through to Battalion H.Q. Lieutenant Harvey-Kelly's platoon, however, held its position and attracted the attention of the Germans while Captain A. Hendry withdrew the third platoon and Company H.Q. to a position level with No. 4 Company. The Company wireless set perversely "went dis," that is, refused to work, so Captain Hendry sent C.S.M. French back to Battalion H.Q. to report the situation and ask for heavy artillery fire on the embankment. This fire came down on the embankment before Lieutenant Harvey-Kelly had withdrawn his platoon. He found it quite intolerable, and the German prisoners fully agreed. Four of the Panthers attacked straight down the road to help their infantry forward; Lieutenant Tottenham's troop moved up to meet them. Sergeant Kerry's Firefly hit and halted the leader before being itself knocked out by the second. The medium and field gunners were by now pouring shells into, behind and around the embankment. They hit and set on fire the maimed Panther and forced the others to withdraw.

The German infantry switched their attacks on to No. 4 and No. 3 Companies, but they were beaten back by the Bren gunners. Their losses were very heavy as they advanced in close formation across open ground with the apparent intention of swamping the companies. The Corps Commander wirelessed a message of congratulations to the Battalion, telling them that they must at all costs hold the German attack. This the Battalion had already done. The concentration of artillery, tanks, mortar and small-arms fire was too much for the Germans and they withdrew about midday. The German guns and mortars, however, continued to shell the area all afternoon. "They were said to have disposed of about 150 guns in this sector," said Colonel Joe. "It certainly felt like it." They put another eight rounds straight into Battalion H.Q.'s house, which was now known as "Stonk Hall."

By mid-afternoon the German attempt to clear the Island had definitely failed. A token of the severity of the fighting was the loss suffered by No. 4 Company alone—more than sixty men in two days. The Irish Guards had done their task; their position was made even more secure than before by the addition of "X" Company, Scots Guards. Pleasure was added to satisfaction when Colonel Joe was told that the Irish was to be relieved by the Coldstream Group. The 3rd Battalion transport went back to find billets for the Battalion in Hoogbrek, and the 2nd Battalion harbour parties found some farm-houses near Alverna, south of Nijmegen. There was no common medium of language, but it was remarkable what results were achieved by signs and gesticulations or even by a Dutch liaison officer. The Coldstreamers took over the Irish positions after dark and the battalions drove away, while the Germans, hearing the noise of the hand-over, put down a last spiteful concentration.

The 3rd Battalion crossed the River Waal by a pontoon bridge during an air-raid. The Nijmegen main bridge was floodlit with a blue searchlight and bombs were crashing in the water on the other side of it. The anti-aircraft tracer shells in the sky reflected in the river and reminded at least one old Etonian of the 4th June fireworks display. "The whole effect," he says, "was quite lovely." "The river was an incredible sight," said another officer. "The broken bridges standing gaunt like a surrealist picture in the blue glare. What a nocturne ! "

Many "pets" accompanied the battalions on their withdrawal. "It would be cruel," said Major Haslewood, as his C.Q.M.S. nursed a wounded porker, "to leave the poor thing to suffer in a lonely sty. Bring it along on a stretcher till we find it a home." One of the 2nd Battalion scout car drivers also took pity on a piglet, propped it up on the seat of his car with its head and trotters sticking out of the roof, and drove back. A military policeman—an ex-Coldstreamer—noticed this peculiar pair on the bridge and asked what the passenger was supposed to be. "A young Grenadier," answered the driver, with admirable presence of mind, and was immediately allowed to proceed. Both battalions went to bed as soon as they got into their billets and slept the clock round. The Germans never renewed their attacks, even though the bridgehead on the Island was the main threat to their defensive plans. Perhaps they did not realize that the Irish Group had been withdrawn.

CHAPTER XII

The Winter

2nd and 3rd Battalions

ALONG the whole line from the sea to Switzerland the war now resolved itself into slow, hard fighting until the failure of the German Ardennes attack in December and the opening of the Allied offensive in February. General Eisenhower writes in his report: "My decision to concentrate our efforts in this attempt—("Market Garden")—to thrust into the heart of Germany before the enemy could consolidate his defences along the Rhine resulted in a delay in opening Antwerp and in making the port available as our main supply base. I took the full responsibility for this, and I believe that the possible and actual results warranted the calculated risks involved. Had our forces not pushed north and east to hold the line of the Maas and the Waal well north of Antwerp, the port itself would have been in constant danger not only of a blow possibly synchronized with the later break-through in the Eifel, but from independent attacks launched at close range from Holland."

For nearly a fortnight after the end of "Market Garden" both battalions remained in billets, the 2nd Battalion near Alverna, the 3rd Battalion at Hoogbrek, "a dull, flat place, and very wet." They both needed the rest to refit and to train their new men. The Adjutants and Company Clerks began their heart-breaking task of accounting for every man, casualty or reinforcement over the past month. It was nearly a week before the lists and the bodies could be made to tally. The first twenty-four-hour leave parties set off for Brussels with great alacrity, even though the journey took over four hours each way over roads packed with the traffic of two corps. These first parties, on their return, told stories that spurred others to go in spite of the difficulties over money and food. The Belgian Government had introduced some anti-profiteer regulations, with the result that some officers found themselves with only notes of 100 francs and over, which no one would accept, and were unable to get any food except ice cream, cake and fruit. Captain Harry FitzHerbert, for instance, had peche melba, plum tart and brandy for breakfast. Accommodation, too, was difficult, as Army Group H.Q. had commandeered the best hotels as officers' and other ranks' rest centres. There was always, however, plenty to drink. But the city of Brussels and Divisional H.Q. between them solved the problem. The city gave the Hotel Anspach as "a token of thanks to their liberators," and the Division turned it into a Guards Division Officers' Club, called the "Eye Club," after the Divisional sign, the ever-open eye. For the next two years the "Eye Club" was the centre of the officers' continental activities. There were also officers' and other ranks' clubs in Nijmegen and Grave, which were grievously overcrowded, since, by now, both 30th and 12th Corps were concentrated between Grave and the Island. The Nijmegen clubs, however, were soon shut; the town and bridges were under spasmodic shell-fire, and Higher Authority judged the area too dangerous for "recreational purposes." Much worse, though, was the Town Major of Nijmegen, who drove the 2nd Battalion from their "Town House," insisting that the civilian owners should return from a country retreat to be shelled in their own house. This left a serious gap in the 2nd Battalion's comforts organization, but Sir John Reynolds was not going to be defeated by a mere Town Major. He found a new "Town House." A Dutch family, van Heiningen, put rooms in their house at the disposal of the Battalion in return for fuel for bath water. "This foresight," says the War Diary, "may serve us well if we have to return to the mud of the front." Otherwise the battalions played football matches against each other and did some serious training, shooting off vast quantities of ammunition in field firing exercises. They spent much time, too, trying to work out their "demob numbers." The demobilization scheme, based on age and service, had just been issued. "I can't manage it at all," wrote one man in despair, "but my number does not seem to be very high up on the list. Some of the young things look like being in for ever."

On the 11th October H.M. The King inspected contingents from all the battalions of the Division in Grave Barracks. Three days later the Corps Commander, Lieut.-General Horrocks, called all the officers and sergeants of the 5th Brigade to the Divisional Club in Grave, and there reviewed the actions from the Escaut Canal to Nijmegen Bridge. The audience went away impressed and pleased—"laudati a viro laudato." The break out from the Escaut Canal, he said, ranked as one of the most spectacular in history; he need only give an order to the Guards Armoured Division to know that it would be carried out. For the future he was very confident. The German attacks on the Island, in the Reichwald, and against the centre line had all failed with heavy losses. Future operations now depended entirely on the clearing of Antwerp port, the only way of obtaining sufficient supplies for the final thrust into Germany which would bring victory. After the failure of the attempt to rush Arnhem and so outflank the Siegfried Line, General Eisenhower had ordered the 21st Army Group to open the port of Antwerp "as a matter of first priority."

The city of Antwerp had been captured on 4th September, but it was useless as a port so long as the Germans held the mouth of the River Scheldt. British and Canadian troops began to clear the river banks. During the month of October and the beginning of November they forced the Leopold Canal and landed on the islands of North Beveland, South Beveland and Walcheren. By the 9th November the west branch of the Scheldt was clear. The channel was swept of mines, and the first ship unloaded in Antwerp on the 26th November. Meanwhile, in the centre of the 21st Army Group, steady progress was made towards the Lower Maas across flood and dyke. By the 10th November the Allies held an unbroken line along the left bank of the Maas to beyond Grave, north of which they held the Nijmegen bridgehead across the River Waal.

The Corps Commander warned the Brigade that these operations would involve a readjustment of the front and that, as a result, it would have to go back into the line or at least into support. Fortunately it was only into support; the 3rd Battalion took over the protection of the Nijmegen bridges and the river line; the 2nd Battalion relieved the 13th/18th Hussars in support of the 82nd U.S. Airborne Division, which was holding the "Swamp" front along the south bank of the Waal by Groosbeek, east of Nijmegen.

The 3rd Battalion moved into Nijmegen on 17th October to protect the bridges. The great bridge was still standing, and the railway bridge had been replaced by a pontoon. It was essential to keep these open as they were the only means of communication with the troops fighting on the Island. It was a "most peculiar task, but amusing, and a change from normal land operations," wrote Colonel "Joe" Vandeleur. "You will remember, from your reading of the war news, that some brave German frogmen swam down the river while we were fighting on the Island and destroyed the railway bridge and did their best to destroy the road bridge. All sorts of expedients were expected of the enemy, such as

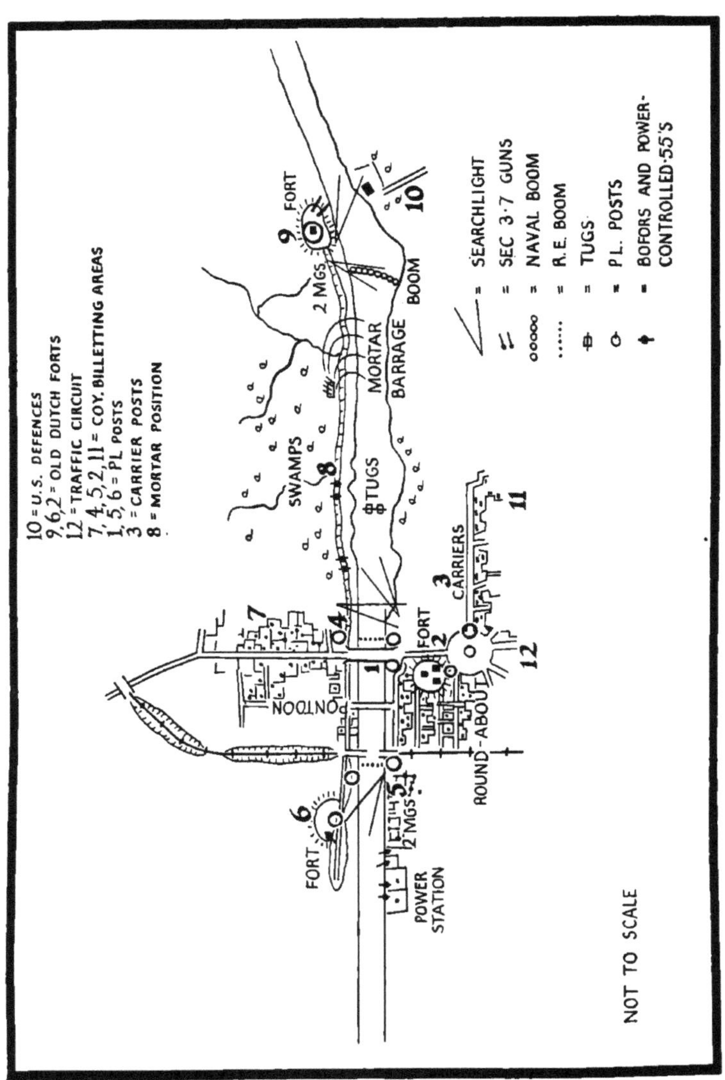
10 = U.S. DEFENCES
9, 6, 2 = OLD DUTCH FORTS
12 = TRAFFIC CIRCUIT
7, 4, 5, 2, 11 = COY. BILLETTING AREAS
1, 5, 6 = PL POSTS
3 = CARRIER POSTS
8 = MORTAR POSITION
FORT
2 MGS
MORTAR
BARRAGE
BOOM
SWAMPS
TUGS
CARRIERS
FORT
PONTOON
ROUND-ABOUT
FORT
2 MGS
POWER STATION
= SEARCHLIGHT
= SEC 3·7 GUNS
= NAVAL BOOM
= R.E. BOOM
= TUGS
= P.L. POSTS
= BOFORS AND POWER-CONTROLLED·55'S
NOT TO SCALE

Nijmegen

midget submarines, parachutists and log-rafts, besides ordinary shelling and bombing."

The road bridge was a favourite target for the German long-range guns, so a smoke screen was kept going to hide it and straw mats were hung along it to conceal the volume of traffic. The Garrison Commander of Nijmegen had a dual command, anti-aircraft and ground defence. The guns protecting the water-line had a similar dual purpose. "On closer examination," Colonel Joe found this plan unsatisfactory and suggested that the command be split so that he would be in sole charge of the ground defence without any reference to the Garrison Commander. When "this was readily agreed to," Colonel Joe formed a Defence Committee with himself as chairman. The naval member was the commander in charge of a great boom, specially brought over from Dover, and of the tugs to sweep the channel. Another most important member was a sturdy Dutch woman, the famous "Tugboat Annie," hostess of a waterside inn, whose task it was to keep the Dutch tugmasters in good humour, for however heavy the shelling or bombing, they had to be ready to put out into the river at any moment. Tugboat Annie "played her part splendidly," and certainly deserves well of her country. The other members were the commanders of the assorted defence units. The Battalion had under its command Engineers to maintain the bridges and two small booms, military police to control the traffic, pioneers to operate the smoke generators, machine-gunners to sweep the water-line, batteries of 3-inch mortars to fire fixed barrages on to the water, and a large body of Gunners to man the heavy and light anti-aircraft guns which would "engage enemy craft and large floating objects" and to operate the searchlights sweeping the booms and the channel by night.

Two companies at a time were on duty, ready to "engage with small-arms every floating object, large or small." On foggy nights—that meant most nights—a platoon went out in tugs and moored just short of the naval boom. Life was not comfortable. The guard duties were heavy, but continued shelling by long-range guns and the occasional air-raids prevented boredom. The regular midnight "stonk" caused two casualties. Major M. Dudley was one night driving a jeep full of Guardsmen as fast as he could over the bridge, to get home before the shells. A bump at the end of the bridge lifted the front wheels off the ground, the weight of four Guardsmen in the back seat kept them in the air, and the jeep skidded on the back wheels off the wet road and fell on to a concrete machine gun post. Lieutenant Patrick Higgins and his servant, farther up the river bank, heard the crash and ran down the dyke-road towards the shouts. It was midnight, and the first shells came down. There was a ditch on one side of the dyke-road, but on the other a sheer drop down to a lower road. Patrick Higgins jumped to the wrong side, fell twenty feet on to the cobbles, broke both legs and several ribs, and lay there for an hour before his servant could find him. Trickles of brandy from his broken hip-flask ran out from under him. "This gave the stretcher-bearers a completely wrong idea of the whole incident," he said. " 'He's bleeding badly,' said one of them as they picked me up. 'Oh, no, he's not; it's drink.' But I felt too cold and sick to bother." In the jeep, the only person who had to be sent to hospital was Major Dudley. His place of commander of No. 3 Company was taken by Major John Kennedy, who regarded the accident as a providential arrangement to give him the Company in which he had always served. The other casualty was Lieutenant P. Sarsfield-Hall, unluckily killed one morning on the road outside Battalion H.Q. A German jet-propelled aeroplane streaked over the river and dropped a bomb beside him. The detention room later got a direct hit which "released the occupants, sending them to hospital instead of prison." Even so, the platoons paraded every morning for drill and P.T. in the streets, with the sentry's ear cocked for the sound of shells. "In many ways we had a lot of fun," said one man. "The Battalion ran its own night club in a large cellar. The band was excellent, and the Dutch girls danced with great verve. The band leader got wounded one day, but stuck to his fiddle." At the end of the month the Battalion handed over the defences to the 1st Bn. Welsh Guards and went to Maldon for four days, theoretically in a counter-attack role, in reality to build rifle ranges. While it was away the Germans put two large haystacks into the river upstream, which floated down, gathering weight as they went, bounced off the groynes and tore to pieces the naval boom and the two smaller booms. They also dropped parachute mines which badly damaged the pontoon bridge —"a trick we had not thought of." The Battalion took over the defences again from the Welsh Guards, and on the 12th November, after a lot more ammunition had been shot away at flotsam and jetsam, finally relinquished the bridges to the Canadian Corps. That night the Battalion drove to Grevenbicht, whence they moved south-east on the 14th with the whole Guards Armoured Division, to a sector of the winter defence line north of Sittard.

On the day that the 3rd Battalion took over Nijmegen bridges, the 17th October, the 2nd Battalion moved up to the River Waal by Groosbeek to support the 82nd U.S. Airborne Division—the

"Transatlantic Skymen," as the Battalion called them in a home-made wireless code. Major-General Gavin, the American commander—a most considerate and helpful man—told them what he wanted done. Their main task was to help repel any German attacks ; the secondary one was "to irritate the goddam Krauts" by sniping with high explosive. The phrase "God damn" was no longer current in the British Army, though four hundred years ago it was so popular that Joan of Arc and Francois Villon called the English soldiers "les godoms." Other words, shorter and cruder, had taken its place. It was curious to find it as popular as ever with Americans. Though the best they ever called the Germans was "goddam Krauts," the word was not necessarily perjorative, and could be used affectionately, as in "goddam jeep" or "goddam cigarettes." The only problem was how to get a squadron up to the river bank to support a parachutist battalion in almost inaccessible positions among the riverside factories. The ground was marshy and cut by dykes, the roads narrow with very bad corners and the whole area under enemy observation. The Battalion drove to Dekkers Wald, south of Nijmegen, and camped in the woods near the American Divisional H.Q. After dark two troops of No. 2 Squadron made the perilous journey forward along the bund (dyked-road) running by the river bank.

The next day began the great game of knocking down factory chimneys. Lieutenant P. A. Cuffe's troop, which had the best stand, enjoyed themselves immensely. Sometimes the Germans shot back, but that upset the Americans more than the Irish Guards. It was gratifying to see the accuracy and effect of 75-mm. and 17-pdr. high explosive, though some of the chimneys stood up well to the battering.

Nos. 1 and 3 Squadrons, by careful search, found billets for all their men. The civilians were most obliging and the area had more and better houses than Alverna. H.Q. Squadron, however, was in the open for some time, as Major Sir John Reynolds's effort to evict a mixture of Americans and R.A.S.C. from a large convent dormitory was defeated by the 30th Corps billeting officer. Finally, he had some wagons and some coaches towed up a railway and halted on a siding in the woods. The Guardsmen installed themselves comfortably in third-class carriages and goods wagons. On the 23rd Major-General Gavin said he no longer required any close tank support, so No. 2 Squadron came back from the river bank. They spent the whole of the next day removing the mud from their tanks. Corps H.Q., having nothing better to do, then ordered the Battalion to send two officers out on patrol with the Americans to see whether the ground of Kranenberg was suitable for tanks. They said they wanted this information before making any plans for an attack on the Reichwald and Cleves—an example of foresight which filled the Battalion with suspicion. Lieutenant M. D. M. Seth-Smith was detailed to go out with a patrol from the 504th Parachute Regiment on the night of the 27th, and Lieutenant B. de las Casas with one from the 325th Glider Regiment on the night of the 28th.

Meanwhile the Quartermaster, Captain J. Keating, was busy, arranging a children's party. He invited "one hundred pairs children, Dutch," to parade at 1600 hrs. on the 27th in the school hall and found a baker who made some sweet cakes from the Battalion's flour and sugar. He was also organizing an all ranks' dance in Nijmegen Winter Gardens for the same evening. Two hundred children arrived for the tea, bringing their own knife, fork, cup and plate. A vast amount of food—hard biscuits, sugar cakes and chocolate—was distributed, as quickly consumed and washed down by numerous mugs of strong tea, which some of the children later regretted. Then fruit and spam sandwiches. After the eating, clowns, gymnasts and singers performed for half an hour, much to the children's delight. Some, of course, cried, others had to be evacuated in a hurry, but most enjoyed themselves and sang "God Save the King" and the Dutch National Anthem lustily at the end. The fathers of the Battalion, such as Captain FitzHerbert, Captain Keating and Sergeant Flynn had a great opportunity to show their knowledge of children's appetites and habits.

In spite of the shortage of women, both battalions thoroughly enjoyed the Quartermaster's ball that evening. "No wonder Henry the Eighth called Anne of Cleves a Flemish mare," wrote one man afterwards. "He should have seen some of the Nijmegen forms. Not that the Guardsmen were discouraged ; they were prepared to face anything." For the dancers it was a perfect night, being still and brightly moonlit. For the patrollers it was downright bad. Lieutenant Seth-Smith's patrol was seen and fired on as soon as it reached the German outpost line. After five hours' dodging right and left it had to return without having got any farther. Lieutenant B. de las Casas' patrol, the following night, was also held up on the outpost line. There was too much moon and too many German sentries. Anyway, the ground in question could be studied perfectly well from an observation post in the Glider Regiment's lines.

Leave to Brussels and Antwerp was the main preoccupation. By the end of the month most of the officers and men had spent forty-eight hours in comfort amid "the delights of a Continental city."

Majors Michael Gordon-Watson, M.C., and Sir John Reynolds set out with a limousine and a lorry to explore the Reims area. They returned in four days with twenty-eight cases of champagne. In their tour they called on all the famous firms, and any purchases were preceded by frequent and heavy tasting of the best bottles. The Intelligence officers of the Division all went down to Maastricht and Aachen to visit the U.S. corps that broke through the Siegfried Line, a feat of which they were inordinately proud. "The line," wrote Captain E. Fitzgerald, "consists only of a row of pill-boxes. But the Americans did magnificently, and say that they could get to Cologne tomorrow, were there enough men and ammunition to follow up. This is probably true, as the ground is open and rolling like the Wolds. I saw and spoke to some civilians trekking out of Aachen. They doffed their caps and grinned and, on questioning, made all the right answers, ending—as any Frenchman might—by 'der Schweinhund Hitler' and the throat-cutting gesture. I almost expected them to say 'Cigarette pour papa.'"

About this time the Germans gave up any attempt at a "black out" in the Rhine and Rhur valley. Captain Eric Hopton, hot from Paris, said that this "light up" was taken at S.H.A.E.F. as the first sign of German civilian surrender. "I hope so," he added, "for the Germans fighting near Antwerp are doing too well altogether."

The month, which opened with heavy fighting, passed as a whole very quietly. Much useful training was done. Trade tests were passed, and the reinforcements, which included two old friends, Captains P. Jeffreys and F. Mennim, assimilated. There had been time, too, for inter-Allied entertainment. Among the officers of the 82nd U.S. Division who came to dinner Major Sir John Reynolds found a business colleague from the Chicago Ring, and Major Gordon-Watson met the inevitable "old hand from Anzio." During this period the 2nd Battalion lost Captain Ronald Robertson, who had to be sent back to England with a damaged knee. "Little Ron" had been Technical Adjutant, in charge of maintenance and repair, as long as anyone could remember, and never in all those years had he run short of spares, resource or patience. On the Battalion's long marches and in battle he could always help a broken-down crew with a new part, a tow or a cup of tea. However overworked he and his staff might be, no one was ever left stranded or forgotten. The Battalion was not to see him again till July, 1945, when he returned as Chief Instructor at the Divisional College in Bonn. His assistant, Lieutenant J. Yerburgh, took his place as Technical Adjutant and fully lived up to the master's high standard.

But it was now getting very cold, and the Dutch pointed gloomily to the profusion of nuts as the sure sign of a hard winter. Everyone watched with dismay the fine days passing and the enemy building up his forces. "Perhaps," says the War Diary, "the next month will bring the last battle and victory." This is Captain E. N. Fitzgerald's last entry in the Battalion War Diary. On the 6th November he became Intelligence Officer at 5th Brigade H.Q.

On the 12th the 2nd Battalion was also relieved by the Canadians and moved south. The new Corps sector stretched from Maesyck to Geilenkirchen in the Maastricht appendix of Holland and, up till now, had been in the sector of the 9th U.S. Army. It was to be held by the Guards Armoured Division on the left and the 43rd Division on the right. At first, however, the Guards Armoured Division was ordered to take over the Sittard–Gangelt area, while the U.S. Cavalry regiments remained on the left flank up to Maesyck, thus leaving the 43rd Division free to attack Geilenkirchen. After this attack the 43rd Division was to take over all their allotted sector, from Geilenkirchen to Hongen, and the Guards Division to extend to Maesyck, 5th Brigade relieving the U.S. Cavalry regiments. "The sector was said to be quiet—almost of Arcadian simplicity—though of course the Germans might attack any day, especially as the Corps was the hinge of an attack on the right by the 9th and 1st U.S. Armies towards the Rhine." On the left the 8th and 13th British Corps were first to clear the Venlo pocket, and then all three corps would advance in company with the U.S. Armies to the Rhine, "where we might expect to spend Christmas." The Brigade Commander ended the conference at which he gave these orders with a few general points of discipline. "Smoking in tanks and by drivers of all W.D. vehicles will cease forthwith, except when actually in the firing zone. V.D. is too prevalent throughout the 21st Army Group, though not, of course, in the 5th Guards Brigade."

The 2nd Battalion started at seven o'clock in the morning and drove south in filthy weather over terrible roads. After a brisk drive over many bridges and canals the Battalion at last reached a pontoon bridge over the River Maas (Meuse), just north of Maastricht. A strong current was swamping the pontoons and rocking the bridge, but the leading tank drove firmly on to it. Battalion H.Q. and six tanks of No. 1 Squadron got across before the pontoons sank. The rest waited on the wrong side for the bridge to be repaired ; but when, one after the other, the pontoons all sank and the bridge was swept away, they had to retrace their steps and cross by a proper bridge at Maastricht. The whole Battalion eventually reached

Geleen by half-past eleven that night. "The civilians showed signs of pleasure at our arrival—even a little cheering. Officers and men spent most of the time dodging cups of soup pressed on them by their hosts." Geleen is a coal town based on the Maurits mine, the largest in Europe. It was a gloomy place, but seemed prosperous, and was certainly comfortable. The Battalion was boarded out in twos and threes with the families living round the main square. Next morning the sergeants-in-waiting, going round at reveille, got the same greeting at every house. "You cruel man, you must not wake the soldiers ; they are tired. Have a cup of coffee." When the squadron officers came to "see breakfasts up" there was no one there but the cooks and hundreds of small boys with mess-tins chanting the names of Guardsmen. The Guardsmen themselves were still between the sheets and had sent their hosts' children to collect their breakfast. If Geleen had only been in London it would have been as good a station as Wellington Barracks, for the Adjutant had a huge square for drill, and Lieutenant P. Mieville (who had a keen nose for such things) found thirty baths in the pithead.

The first day was spent visiting the American cavalry light tank squadrons, which had such alluring code-names as "Cupid" and "Jasmine." The 3rd Battalion, at Grevenbicht, sent reconnaissance parties to the 125th U.S. Squadron. "The sector was very quiet, and the Americans were very rash in the manner in which they conducted us round their dispositions. We could not lose face by being cautious, but we were astonished that the Germans did not shoot at us. There seemed to be a sort of 'live and let live' atmosphere." Colonel Joe put two companies in Nieuwstadt, one company in Holtum, and kept the fourth in reserve with Battalion H.Q. at Born. Honey tanks of the 2nd Battalion covered the gap between Nieustadt and Holtum. On the left of the 3rd Battalion came the 744th U.S. Light Tank Squadron, and on the right the 32nd Guards Brigade. The 2nd Battalion remained in reserve in Geleen, sating themselves with food and sleep.

On the evening of the 14th Lieut.-Colonel J. O. E. Vandeleur was ordered to take command of 129th Brigade of the 43rd Division the following morning. It was an inevitable loss—no Battalion could hope to keep so distinguished a Commanding Officer. All the same, it was difficult to imagine the 3rd Battalion without Colonel Joe ; the two were synonymous. He had commanded it since its formation, trained it in England, brought it to France and led it through Normandy, Belgium and Holland to the borders of Germany. The loss was more personal to the 3rd Battalion, but the 2nd Battalion, too, felt it had lost a remarkable leader. "He had commanded the Irish Guards Group," says the War Diary soberly, "with great success from Douai to Nijmegen, capturing a well-known bridge on the way." Colonel Joe's parting recollections were "of the magnificent fighting qualities of the Irish Guards, and of the debt he owed them for their unswerving loyalty and gallantry." "In hunting parlance," he wrote, "it was like riding a patent safety, guaranteed to be in at the kill, however hard the going. In fighting it is the heart of the men that counts as much as the equipment and planning. That quality, heart, was never lacking." He never lacked it himself. Brigadier J. O. E. Vandeleur, D.S.O., commanded the 129th Infantry Brigade for the rest of the war, then commanded the 32nd Guards Brigade, and finally, in August, 1946, succeeded Colonel C. A. Montagu-Douglas-Scott, D.S.O., as the Lieutenant-Colonel Commanding the Regiment.

Lieut.-Colonel T. W. Gimson arrived the following night—the 15th—to take over command from Major Ivo Reid, now Second-in-Command since Major D. H. FitzGerald had gone as a G.I. on the staff of 30th Corps H.Q. Colonel Tom Gimson had commanded the 1st Battalion way back in the Sanderstead days of 1942. An excellent and most popular Commanding Officer, he had been forcibly extracted from the 1st Battalion and sent to the Staff College to teach other men how to be Brigadiers. When released from this job, he was sent to Headquarters, Combined Operations, to help plan the invasion of France. When the remnants of the 1st Battalion arrived home from Italy without a Commanding Officer, he took them over and began to re-form the Battalion in Hawick. All the war he had been fretting for an active command, and now at last he had got it. But he was a man dogged by bad luck ; before the 3rd Battalion went into action again he was struck down by phlebitis and evacuated to England.

The take-over on the 15th went smoothly and, for once, according to the orders issued. As the 3rd Battalion were moving in, however, the Germans did shoot at them—one shell. This one shell killed Lieutenant Robin O'Kelly and Sergeant Mathews of the Intelligence Section and wounded Lieutenants Paddy Mathews and Shane Jameson. "Journalists tell us that Hitler is missing," wrote an officer at this time, "but the majority of the Krauts are still very much with us, though they are quiet. Gossip from the *Times* correspondent says that Christmas will see an armistice. But it seems certain that Antwerp and all that will bring black arrows back on the map and white crosses on the ground." This optimism in Higher

Formations, caused by the advances of the Americans and French in the south, was succeeded by the inevitable wave of pessimism. The Allies were halted by the mud and by Germans dug in behind the swamps. The days passed in shelling and patrolling. Every morning the Germans sent over a few shells, every afternoon Corps and Divisional H.Q. suggested that the Germans might be withdrawing, every night patrols paddled across the river in small rubber boats and found the Germans still there.

On the 21st, in driving rain, the 2nd Battalion relieved the 744th U.S. Light Tank Squadron along the river bank on the left of the 3rd Battalion. They exchanged farewell dinners with these Americans who were as pleasant and agreeable to work with as their Airborne Divisions farther north. No. 1 Squadron occupied Buchten and Gebroek, No. 2 Squadron Roosteren, and No. 3 Squadron and Battalion H.Q. the village of Papenhoven. "The new area is on the whole good and quiet," says the War Diary, "but not suitable for tanks to hold alone." The two squadrons in the line brought up only one troop of tanks; the remaining crews dismounted, leaving their empty tanks behind in Papenhoven, and became, to their great disgust, temporary infantry. It was an ideal defensive position, but very uncomfortable: every trench filled with water as soon as it was dug. The rain came pouring down, turning the fields into lakes and the roads into muddy canals. "What we need now," wrote an officer, "is a detachment of naval personnel, for the troops have to be supplied and relieved by boat." But human beings can get used to anything. One officer wrote afterwards that he missed the "lap-lap of flood-water." The level of the River Maas rose daily, swamping the bridges and closing them to traffic every few hours. The Dutch said it was the greatest flood in twenty years, but the Battalion remarked that wherever it went it was always the worst storm, flood, famine, plague or harvest—according to the season—of the century. The agitated Burgomeister of Roosteren reported that the flood banks were collapsing and asked for sandbags. The local militiamen, inspired by the old Dutch tradition that the dyke must be saved, rowed out with these across the mines and booby-traps scattered in "lease-lend" profusion by the Americans, and repaired the banks. "The American mines were a great nuisance to us," complains the War Diary incidentally, "and the only casualties they have caused have been to our own side and a few unfortunate cows."

It was a dull, wet period with nothing to relieve the monotony and discomfort but the arrival of a squadron of the R.A.F. Regiment and a flying bomb. The R.A.F. Regiment took over part of the line and allowed the dismounted crews of one squadron to get out of the trenches back into their tanks. The flying bomb landed near 5th Brigade H.Q., upsetting the calm of the "G" Office. Since the German 176th Division opposite them had few guns, little ammunition and less aggression, the Squadron filled in the empty days by "indirect shoots." The tanks floundered through the mud to a spot alleged to correspond to a point marked on Major Gordon-Watson's map, and there elevated and turned the guns in accordance with a system worked out by some keen Artillery officers. They bombarded the church towers of Echt, Dieteren and Susteren and the factory chimneys near Asterberg, all probable observation points in a flat country. Even if it did no particular harm to the Germans it kept the tank gunners in practice. The 2nd Battalion's only casualty in this period was Sergeant Ludlow, the M.T. Sergeant—"Twenty to Four," as he had been called in Norway and long before. The Battalion's water-truck driver was Guardsman Foley, a fine old soldier, who had never failed to deliver the Battalion's water in battle and to miss the target on the ranges. On guard over the vehicle park one night, Foley scored his only hit ; he shot Sergeant Ludlow in the leg when he forgot to answer the challenge. "Can I do anything for you ?" asked the doctor who, like everybody else in the Battalion, was going to miss an old friend. Sergeant Ludlow replied solemnly, "Just tell Sir John"—an impressive pause—"that all is well."

The month ended in plans, possibilities and cancellations. The Brigade were told to be ready to hand their sector over to the 22nd Armoured Brigade "this day, next day, some day, never." The troublesome point was how the 22nd Brigade were going to get up to them, as the only bridges left standing were at Maastricht, over which the whole traffic of the 9th U.S. Army had to pass. Everything was vague and varied from day to day, but the two Irish Guards battalions were told that, whatever happened, they would be relieved very soon. The 3rd Battalion handed over to the 1st Battalion of the Rifle Brigade on the night of 1st December, and went back to Limbricht and Einighausen. On the 2nd, the 2nd Battalion handed over to the 8th Hussars and returned to Geleen. In their absence troops, tanks and vehicles of all kinds, from Crocodiles to American scooters, had poured into the town. The Adjutant, Captain V. Taylor, took no chances. "Send ahead strong harbour parties," he ordered, "to make sure of securing accommodation."

On 1st December the Commander-in-Chief, Field Marshal Montgomery, arrived at Divisional H.Q. to present more medals—a Bar to the D.S.O. for Colonel Joe, a D.S.O. for Colonel Giles Vandeleur, Military Crosses for Major David Peel (posthumous), Captains E. Tyler and E. N. FitzGerald and Lieutenants Duncan Lampard and Charles Tottenham. After the presentation he reviewed the campaign. It had put 1,500,000 Germans out of action and freed the occupied countries far quicker than even the Prime Minister had expected. The achievements of the Division, he said, were in the highest traditions of the Brigade of Guards and the Army. Only very well-trained troops could have done the rush from the Seine to the Rhine, capturing on the way Brussels and the Escaut and Nijmegen bridges. He then explained the scheme for leave to England. The qualification was six months' unbroken presence with the armies, and the turns to go would be decided in the most impartial way—by lot. Three thousand men a day would be sent, in as much comfort as possible, with kind ladies distributing cups of tea all the way. Every man would get a week at home, with another for travelling. This meant that 40,000 men would be away from their units at the same time, but the Army would be able to stand that number.

After one day's rest in Limbricht the 3rd Battalion were ordered to relieve the 1st Grenadiers in the Gangelt sector of the line. They left Limbricht on the afternoon of the 4th and waited in the woods by Gangelt until dark. The relief itself was uneventful but slow, and it was after midnight before the last company changed over. There they remained, doing a little patrolling and capturing an odd prisoner, till they in turn were relieved on the 7th by the Durham Light Infantry and went back to Raath, a village near Geleen. The 2nd Battalion, meanwhile, had been doing "nothing of importance except fitting End-connections—a device which clips on to the outside of the tracks to increase their area by about 40 per cent and so help the tanks through the mud." It was very cold and "very bloody."

In Geelen and Raath the two battalions, which had been operating separately, came together again to form a group for a new offensive—Operation "Shears." "Shears" remained Top Secret and nebulous till the 10th, when the Brigadier gave the orders to the battalion commanders and the representatives of all the "animals" in support, the Crocodiles, Buffalos, Avres, Flails. "Largely speaking, the plan was to drive the enemy beyond the River Roer." The date of the attack depended entirely on the weather ; the plan needed frost and only rain was falling. After Major Gregory Hood, of the 2nd Grenadiers, who was detailed to test the ground daily, had bogged five tanks in one morning on the highest ridge he could find, the attack was postponed till the 15th. Amendments poured in, but as the rain still poured down, they were of little interest. On the 13th "Shears" was cancelled for good and all, and a great mass of papers gladly torn up. During this period there were many changes and cross-postings of officers. Major D. M. L. Gordon-Watson, M.C., left the 2nd Battalion to go to the Staff College and was replaced as Second-in-Command by Major J. S. O. Haslewood of the 3rd Battalion, who handed over his No. 4 Company to Major M. Dudley, now recovered from his car smash. Major H. L. S. Young, D.S.O., arrived from England to become Brigade Major of the 5th Brigade, and Major B. O. P. Eugster, M.C., replaced Major I. Reid as Second-in-Command of the 3rd Battalion.

On the 15th the air and the telephone were full of rumours of possible moves, but nothing actually happened for forty-eight hours ; then the 3rd Battalion went back to Gangelt and the 2nd Battalion to Bree in support of the 32nd Guards Brigade. It was a simple and quiet move, and once in their trenches and billets the battalions were able to give their full attention to the German attack on the American 1st Army south of Malmedy. Late on the night of the 16th, Divisional H.Q. had sent out this message : "A big German offensive has started in the Ardennes in the Malmedy direction, and is employing two armoured and seven already identified infantry divisions, three of which were already in the line and the other six specially brought up. Americans have captured an Operation Order by Rundstedt saying the attack was to start today (16th). 2nd Army H.Q. have no indications as to the enemy intentions, but it is thought that possibly Liége may be the objective. It is clearly a big thing." On the 17th all that the battalions knew was that "the Germans, attacking with the major part of their reserve in the West, have taken the Americans by surprise and made a deep penetration westwards." The news remained vague, but it was clear that the situation might become serious unless the German penetration could be prevented from becoming a break-through. The next two days brought a record batch of orders and their inevitable cancellations. Sometimes the battalions received the cancellations first. Christmas Day was postponed, by order, to the 30th December, then reverted to the normal 25th, and finally postponed indefinitely—"very difficult for Santa Claus's march-tables." The Germans sent over batches of Christmas cards, some bloodthirsty, some vulgar, all ungrammatical. The cards were delivered by shells that tore each card to ribbons on landing, but they were carefully pieced together as they provided a little amusement ; and anything funny was rare in Holland. Interest centred on the Ardennes offensive, which continued to make headway westwards, though held firmly to the north by the tenacious defence of Monschau, Malmedy and Stavelot, and to the south at Bastogne and Echternach. The evening of the 19th was enlivened by reports of parachutists, gliders and Krauts of every shape and size, but a quiet night was passed by all except the duty officers.

The battalions now began to feel the repercussions. The 30th Corps, consisting of the Guards Armoured, the 43rd, 51st and 53rd Divisions and the 29th Armoured Brigade, was ordered to concentrate as a reserve south and east of Brussels and destroy any enemy trying to cross the River Meuse. While this plan was being made, the Division had been ordered to move on the 20th from Sittard to a training area near Louvain. When they reached Hasselt, *en route*, as they thought, to Louvain, the columns were diverted, the 32nd Brigade to Tirlemont, the 5th Brigade to St. Trond. Considering that the diversion took place in the middle of the night and that nobody knew where he or anyone else was going, it was most creditable that the Brigade was sorted out and in its assigned locations by midday on the 21st. The Division was made responsible for the safety of the River Meuse from Namur to Huy. The "Great Men" now thought that the main battle would be fought out east of the Meuse, for the Americans were regaining control and the German plan of a quick break-through to Liége had clearly failed. But even so, some Germans might still try to cross the river, and the two Irish Guards battalions were held back as a counter-attack force in the villages of Landen and Attenhoven, three miles south of St. Trond. The 1st U.S. Army ordered that no information was to be given to any British soldier except on a corps level. This order was obeyed, and the battalions could only learn that the position was already much better, thanks to the gallantry of the U.S. Airborne divisions. When they extracted information that the 101st U.S. Airborne Division was still holding Bastogne after very heavy fighting, they were delighted to know that their old companions at Nijmegen were thrashing the Germans again. The battalions imposed a curfew on Landen and Attenhoven and patrolled the main road from Tirlemont to St. Trond. They did not want to do this, and asked every day if they could lift both the curfew and the patrols, but were always put off with vague reports of "Jerry up the road, parachutists dropping with sulphuric acid and poisoned sweets, and saboteurs in Allied uniforms."

With the news the weather improved. The thick mist which had lasted for days—and under cover of which the Germans had launched their offensive—lifted and let the clear sun shine through. Though cold, it was fine, and "everybody took brisk walks in the fields, a pleasant change from the dull aspect of Holland." Both battalions, in fact, liked Landen. Many men afterwards returned there for leave—the highest tribute to the hospitality of the inhabitants. Two years later the 2nd Battalion put a stained glass memorial window in the local church. After their first alarm—"rather a windy few days for them"—the locals recovered their confidence, especially when the Allied Air Forces, grounded by the bad weather, took to the air again. The news was still of hard fighting in the Ardennes. "In the north the Germans had withdrawn their armoured forces, presumably to allow the infantry to take over as the tanks could not clear a route to Liége. General Patton's Army had made slight progress northwards and had joined up with the Airborne garrison in Bastogne. The Germans, however, still held a strong infantry flank in this area, and had shifted their main drive to their 5th Panzer Army and will probably reinforce towards Givet, Namur and Dinant. The Panzer Lehr Division is doing well round St. Hubert, and they will probably exploit this success. They have in reserve the 9th Panzer and 3rd Panzer Grenadier Divisions."

The Quartermasters, Lieutenants Keating and Hastings, and the cooks were busy preparing for Christmas gaiety. Christmas Day was bright. At eleven o'clock there was a special High Mass, with a choir of school children dressed in hideous white frocks. Then the two battalions sat down together to dinners. The companies and squadrons had turned schoolrooms into temporary messes. The pioneers covered the desks with boards and found a bottomless store of lanterns and garlands. "Christmas dinners always seem to get larger every year, and this year's wallop of tinned turkey, roast pork, roast beef, boiled potatoes, fried potatoes, peas, cabbage, brussels sprouts and plum puddings had to be seen to be believed. The tables groaned under the beer, cigars, cigarettes and chocolate ration."

Boxing Day morning was quiet, and so welcome to tender heads. But it was time for another of the sudden urgent inconvenient moves beloved by Higher Formations. In the middle of dinner—of all times —the 3rd Battalion were ordered to take over the river line from Huy to Vise. "Brigadier Norman Gwatkin and Lieut.-Colonel John Hornung, M.C., and Captain E. Hopton from Divisional H.Q. were dining with us," wrote Major B. O. P. Eugster, M.C. "At half-past ten Savill Young came in with a face of mournful pleasure to inform us that we were to move down the line of the Meuse." Colonel Tom Gimson gave out his orders after midnight, and Lieutenant

Seth-Smith's reconnaissance troop of Honey tanks led the Battalion out of Landen at dawn on the 27th. Battalion H.Q. settled in the village of Momalle, some ten miles back from Liége, with the companies strung out along twenty miles of the river. "In fact, to go all round the companies meant a drive of one hundred miles and took about seven hours, and we were guarding the bridges used by two American armies." However, it was quite comfortable, and the Guardsmen enjoyed looking at the shining black pans of the U.S. truck drivers. They could also watch the aircraft overhead during this "the best day in the air since Falaise." The 2nd Battalion, more fortunate, remained in Landen, gathering a crop of orders and forecasts. The Division was warned to move farther south at the end of the month to relieve the Americans at Dinant. This "warning order," however, was little more than a high-grade rumour, and was immediately succeeded by another that the battalions would stay in Landen for another two weeks—"but no one believed in probabilities any more."

The 3rd Battalion spent only a day on the bridges before they were relieved by the Engineers of 30th Corps. When the Engineers heard the Battalion was already on the Meuse, they rang up late at night and suggested that the Battalion should remain there for another forty-eight hours and hand the bridges over to the Americans. The suggestion was not accepted. The 3rd Battalion returned to Attenhoven and Landen on the 30th. Their old hosts gave them an enthusiastic welcome, being apparently convinced that their soldiers, the Irish Guards, had swept back the German offensive single-handed, a conviction that the Guardsmen saw no point in dispelling. New Year's Eve was gay, despite the black frost and bitter snow. There were the usual celebrations in the evening, everybody wishing everybody else a happy and, at last, a peaceful New Year.

"January, 1945, was spent in an almost 'Yorkshire' routine of training and can be described most adequately as uneventful." It was the first time the battalions had had a chance to draw a long breath since the landing in Normandy.

CHAPTER XIII

"Veritable"

2nd and 3rd Battalions

WHILE the Americans were slowly pushing the Germans out of the Ardennes, the Guards Armoured Division, with most of 21st Army Group, enjoyed their first real rest since Normandy. For once they were able to watch the war progressing cleanly and quietly in chinagraph across the map. As a further consolation, the Home Leave scheme started almost according to plan. In true democratic fashion lots were drawn, and the lucky few who got the first places actually went. A fortnight later they returned with news from England and reports of the damage done by Vs. 1 and 2 in London, which up to now had been the German prisoners' favourite topic of conversation. Some of the stories made the journey sound like a major test of human endurance, but no man's eagerness to take his turn was damped, and even the newly-joined reinforcements began to reckon when their day would come, months ahead.

Conferences, training and entertainments made time pass quickly. Everyone was cheerful in spite of the cold and the "Pirbright look" of the country with its fir trees and sandy heath. "We made a great mistake in capturing Bourg Leopold last September," wrote an officer. "It has been refurbished as a battle range, and some old Belgian Army T.E.W.Ts. have been translated for our benefit. They suit the ground, you know. The Battalions have been graciously allotted several days 'for really hard field training—the proper stuff.' And now we return as tyros to the scene of former victory, with knob of the bolt, two, three, and all that. It is so cold, too; the tea freezes in the containers. But then, others are winter-sporting in the Ardennes." Many of the afternoons were occupied with demonstrations of the latest engines of destruction. A Sapper team, versed in flame-throwing and allied arts, performed tricks of which any Indian fakir would have been proud, to the delight of Major John

Kennedy, who had not seen such a display of arson since he had set fire to a hillside in Tunisia. Lieutenant John Gorman, M.C., was billed on another day to lecture on "Cats' Eyes," a delicate mechanism which allegedly enabled tank drivers to see in the dark but, being otherwise engaged, he forgot to return from Brussels until the next evening. The device, in fact, was never used, so an explanation would have been superfluous in any case. Of the many conferences held, one deserves perhaps a special mention. A strongly worded directive straight from Rear H.Q., 21st Army Group, ordered the fighting troops "to surrender at once all W.D. vehicles held surplus to War Establishment and all civilian cars without exception." Now it is well known that no respectable battalion can possibly exist on its bare W.E., which would have left the 2nd Battalion with not more than a hundred 3-ton lorries and the 3rd Battalion not even mobile. In the course of the advance some vehicles had inevitably been lost and others—such as a limousine for Sir John Reynolds and a lorry for Major Ivo Reid's kit—had taken their place in the column. These got in no one's way and carried essential stores. Brigade H.Q. was no mean offender itself, but it had to call a conference to execute or discuss the order. There was remarkable unanimity among the Battalion's representatives. All were glad to take the opportunity of emphasizing how grossly their battalions were under War Establishment despite repeated demands to Division for replacements. If by any chance, they explained, there did happen to be one or two oddities in their column, that was only because something had to carry the load of the truck lent to the Quartermaster to replace something blown up in Normandy. The battalions kept their extras, but were asked, please, to paint them khaki.

But social life occupied most of the days. Visits to Brussels were easy and as frequent as finance allowed. A lucky few even went to Paris on business or compassionate grounds. Landen and Athenhoven, too, did their best to be gay with parties, dances and the village hospitality.

In the middle of January Lieut.-Colonel Tom Gimson was crippled by severe phlebitis while on a duty visit to England. To the great disappointment of both battalions he had to give up his command. Lieut.-Colonel D. H. FitzGerald was posted back to join the 3rd Battalion as Commanding Officer, but since he could not be spared from 30th Corps H.Q. for some weeks, Major Basil Eugster, M.C., acted in his stead. Lieut.-Colonel Giles Vandeleur thus became commander of the Irish Guards Group.

By the 25th January, 12th Corps, which had relieved the Division in the Geleen-Geilinkirchen sector, had driven the Germans back across the River Roer from Julich to Roermond. The ground was now ready for Operation "Veritable" a grand offensive by the 21st Army Group to clear the Germans from the left (west) bank of the Rhine.

The concentration of troops began immediately. On 5th February the Guards Armoured Division followed the rest of 30th Corps north to Tilburg. Being the Headquarters of the 1st Canadian Army, Tilburg was liberally furnished with cinemas, canteens and comforts, and, being Dutch, it had plenty of schools and solid bourgeois houses. The inhabitants were as ill-favoured as their compatriots at Nijmegen or Geleen, but as hospitable, and they did their best to make the Guardsmen welcome. "Much better than the burghers are the oysters and whitebait which come from just down the river—tasty and plentiful. It's a relief to find that something good comes out of all this water. While we are taking our ease here the unfortunate infantry divisions are sitting up to their necks in mud outside Nijmegen, waiting for the word ' go.' They say it will be a bigger attack even than Alamein, though of course the desert gang, true to form, deny that anything could be comparable to that achievement. It's a pity there are none of the Duce's legions on this front, only German parachutists."

Operation "Veritable" was planned in the grand manner. It was to be executed by two converging offensives between the River Rhine and the River Meuse. The 1st Canadian Army, reinforced by the 30th British Corps, would attack south-east from Nijmegen through the Reichwald and very shortly afterwards the 9th U.S. Army, still under Field-Marshal Montgomery's command, would cross the River Roer at Julich and swing north-east to join the 1st Canadian Army at Wesel. The 1st Canadian Army had under command the 2nd Canadian Corps and the 30th British Corps, comprising in all six infantry divisions, two armoured divisions, three armoured brigades, more than one thousand guns and innumerable technical troops, with very strong R.A.F. support. The plan for the northern attack had been drawn up in outline as far back as the previous October, when Lieutenants Seth-Smith and de las Casas had done their moonlight patrols. It was simple enough. The assault infantry divisions, Canadians on the right, British on the left, were to "punch a hole" in the enemy defences, after which the armoured divisions were to "pour through" past Goch and Cleve and end up, if possible, on the far side of the Rhine bridge at Wesel, where they would meet the Americans.

It looked very pretty on the map, but the maps did not fully allow for the weather, the ground or the Germans. In fact, Operation "Veritable" saw some of the most severe fighting of the whole campaign. Though it was apparent at the time that the co-ordinated attack by 9th U.S. Army in the south would be delayed for some days by floods and administrative difficulties, the 1st Canadian Army's attack started as scheduled on the 8th February, after a heavy air bombardment and artillery barrage. By the end of the first day everyone realized that the battle would be slow and hard. The Germans were fighting well, had more guns than usual and moved up strong armoured and parachutist reinforcements. Worse still was the going. Continual rain and floods had wrecked the roads and turned the countryside into a quagmire. A certain amount of damp had been allowed for—a great deal more was met. The Canadian troops, who were attacking along the River Waal in what was officially called "The Swamp," had been given "Ducks" and "Alligators" and every other sort of amphibian, and were thus the best off. They had expected to have to paddle and were wearing their waders. The British troops on the other hand, in the Reichwald and south of it, had hoped to move all their impedimenta of war down the roads and forest paths. These, however, gave way underneath the leading troops. The tanks, guns and lorries piled up nose to tail; the traffic jams lasted for miles and days, and the supply of the forward troops became almost impossible. On such roads it would be days—possibly weeks—before the Guards Armoured Division could get near the front, much less make an "armoured dash for the Wesel bridge." The rain poured down ceaselessly. The two battalions in the snug billets of Tilburg felt much sympathy for the less fortunate infantry divisions "up there in the mud." The offensive degenerated into a series of short advances against a skilful and stubborn defence, which depleted and exhausted the original infantry divisions. On the 11th, 30th Corps H.Q. ordered the 32nd Guards Brigade to re-form as an infantry brigade in Corps reserve. "So while the 2nd Battalion lapped up oysters and did indifferent foot drill in Tilburg," wrote an officer of the 3rd Battalion, "we drove to a dirty barracks in Nijmegen. The town had not improved in our absence. After two nights there, it was as we knew it would be, in spite of all the promises that we would not be used as spare infantry for odd jobs." The Brigade moved first to the wrecked village of Graesbeck and there, at midnight, received orders to capture the village of Hommersum on the Dutch-German border.

On the morning of the 14th the Brigade advanced through the

15th (Scottish) Division at Gennep and got its first view of Hommersum—"a beastly place it looked and was." By the afternoon the 1st Bn. Welsh Guards and the 2nd Bn. Coldstream Guards had captured the intermediate objectives, from which the 3rd Battalion was to attack Hommersum itself. At five o'clock in the afternoon the 3rd Battalion advanced with the support of 7th Field, 5th Medium and 3rd Heavy Regiments of Artillery. "The guns did capital execution and put the Germans out of business." They reached the village with very few casualties and collected fifty wet and frightened prisoners out of the battered houses. "At first the ground was 'good old Pirbright'—sand and heather—but for the last stretch it became a bog. We had been warned that the water might be up to our waists and that possibly no vehicles could get through. But luckily it was not quite as bad as that—only knee deep—and the carriers reached us with hottish breakfasts next morning."

For two days the Battalion sat round Hommersum looking out across the sodden fields. The slit trenches filled with water, but incessant German bombardment kept the Battalion below ground and water level. The shelling was as heavy as any that the Battalion had experienced and caused thirty-five casualties. The discomfort reached the standards of the 1914-1918 war, and the old 1st Battalion men admitted that it was nearly as bad as the Anzio beachhead.

On the 15th the Battalion made two small attacks on some troublesome German posts to clear the right flank of a Coldstream advance. Lieutenants Richard Tenison and Basil Berkeley were both wounded in the first attack. In the second, Lance-Sergeant Noone was wounded in the leg and could not be rescued before the barrage for the Coldstream came down all about him. He crawled into a hole from which he later emerged cheerful and "none the worse for a noisy afternoon." The Coldstreamers reached their objective without difficulty, and two days later—the 17th—the Welsh Guards passed through the Battalion to capture another village, a mile and a half to the east. Thus the 3rd Battalion found itself in reserve. Now, at last, the Guardsmen could spread themselves above ground in the wrecked houses. The Quartermaster, Lieutenant R. Hastings, brought up the mobile baths, fresh clothing, a home mail and the Naafi rations. Visitors came too. "General Alan Adair and Brigadier George Johnson," writes a freshly washed officer, "have just been around the Battalion and are very pleased with what we've done. Brigadier Norman Gwatkin came as well, to see if there were any shells about. He finds it very dull in Tilburg."

On the 21st February the Division was ordered to reassemble in Nijmegen. Unfortunately somebody decided that there was just time for the 3rd Battalion to tidy up the sector before handing over. The offending area was a scattered group of houses centred on the village Terporten-Vrij (some 2,100 yards ahead of the present front nlie). Any Germans that might have been there were officially stated to have been washed away by the River Niers when it burst its banks. The only possible lines of advance were the two parallel tracks that did duty for roads in this part of Germany. Accordingly, Major B. Eugster, M.C., ordered No. 1 Company, on the right, to occupy a chateau supposedly empty of Germans. The attack began at 1 p.m. after an early lunch. For the first mile or so the tracks held firm and there was little sign of opposition. "Then it started proper." The forward companies ran into mud and mines, and the few carriers that were not blown up got bogged. When the companies were well stuck, the Germans unleashed their guns and mortars. "There was a great deal of noise and H.E., which was not surprising, as three German battalions were holding the area. We had made a sort of salient—stuck our necks out in fact—and now we got it from both sides. To add to our worries the wireless sets got wrecked, and messages had to be sent, if at all, by runner. Worst of all was a break-down in the Gunners' net, which left the Battalion virtually without artillery support; this put us at a mighty disadvantage to the Germans."

The companies, however, pushed on and rushed the German posts. "The closer you got to the infantry," said one man, "the safer it was, as their gunners didn't try to follow." They chased the Germans from ditch to ditch and house to house. A bazooka bombarded No. 3 Company from a house on the right flank. Sergeant Macarthy and his section stormed in the front door, killed the team and led on through the back yard. When the leading platoon of No. 3 Company reached the chateau, they found it held by a battalion. Major John Kennedy gathered up the platoon and swept it through the defences. "How he did it," wrote Captain Kennard, "beats me. They came under every sort of fire from bazookas upwards. As he reached the chateau at the head of the platoon, Germans streamed out of the back door and hopped into trenches. 'Come on, lads!' he shouted, 'we've got them now, and running to the trenches in front of anyone else he walked up and down killing the Krauts with his revolver. He soon used up his ammunition, and was about to jump into a trench when a single shot got him from the flank. He was killed at once."

On the left No. 1 Company also came under heavy fire. The village was held by another German battalion manning good defensive positions. Lieutenant Claud Proby, a recent arrival from England and in his first serious action, led the first platoon in a series of attacks on the enemy's forward posts. Once they were cleared the Company advanced across the final stretch of open ground towards the village. Here it was caught without cover and without artillery support. One look at the ground ahead and another at the Guardsmen lying squeezed into the mud were enough to show that it would take a properly supported battalion to "tidy up" the village alone. Major Edward Fisher-Rowe had been in every action from Normandy onwards, and he was not afraid to make a decision. He ordered No. 1 Company to withdraw to the nearest cover. He saw them started and then turned back to pick up the casualties. He and a Guardsman lifted a badly wounded man on to an old gate and carried it down the track. He was killed by a burst of Spandau in the head. Lieutenant C. Proby and Sergeant Grant, the two forward platoon commanders, completed the withdrawal. Lieutenant Proby was twice wounded, but waited till the Guardsmen were entrenched before he obeyed the order to return to the R.A.P. Sergeant Grant brought up the rear, covering his men with Bren gun fire "to make sure the Germans kept their proper distance."

Meanwhile, No. 3 Company was fighting in the middle of the German trenches, connected to the Battalion only by the thin line of the track. Major Kennedy was dead and all the platoon commanders were wounded, leaving Captain Colin Kennard, D.S.O., the only officer in the company. The men were scattered in little groups fighting private battles, and the ground between them was swept by German fire. Captain Kennard started to concentrate the Company, but the orders had to be passed by word of mouth, and it was a slow process. Major Eugster sent a runner with the order "withdraw in conformity with No. 1 Company." It was almost as difficult to leave the chateau as it had been to get there. Captain Kennard and C.S.M. Black between them extricated the remains of the Company. Captain Kennard assembled and established the Company in a position forward of the Battalion, while the C.S.M. undertook the evacuation of the wounded. Although wounded himself, C.S.M. Black personally rescued twelve wounded men from an open field. The medical staff and carrier platoon drove up and down the track regardless of mines and the shelling to bring their friends back to the R.A.P.

Night was falling and the sorely tried Nos. 1 and 3 Companies settled down in their new trenches. Brigade H.Q., having now digested Major Eugster's report of the battle, the unexpected opposition and the heavy casualties, ordered the Battalion to return to its original position behind 1st Welsh and 5th Coldstream Guards. This final move was constantly shelled by the Germans, but at 10 p.m. the men sank wearily to sleep in the billets they had left twelve hours before. The Battalion suffered some 175 casualties in this attack. "No doubt great damage was done to the Germans," wrote an officer, "but that hardly offset our own losses. The whole thing was much too like Sourdeval last summer—the leading companies well-nigh destroyed. We can't afford to lose people like John and Edward and so many first-class N.C.Os. and Guardsmen. John had been in fourteen full-scale attacks with the 1st Battalion and ourselves, and Edward in everything from Normandy onwards. Both knew their job thoroughly, were loved by their companies and never thought of their own safety. We all know our loss."

Some days later, when the British line had been advanced beyond Goch, the Battalion recovered the bodies of Major John Kennedy and Edward Fisher-Rowe and twenty-five Guardsmen, and buried them in a little churchyard just inside Holland. In John Kennedy the Regiment lost one of its finest officers and best-loved men. "Sticky Kennedy, the Mad Mullah," or "His Reverence," was an institution and has become a legend. To his friends of all ranks who had grown up with him in the Army, his death at this late stage of the war was a cruel blow. He had survived so much, risked so much and given so much. His comrades of the old 1st Battalion will always remember him, a tall figure in a cap-comforter and leather jerkin, with a carbine over his shoulder, striding indefatigably round his company positions, so full of eagerness that the words fell over each other out of his mouth. There were no subtleties about John Kennedy. He was so transparently honest that it did not occur to him to deceive anybody and he never saw any reason for being unkind. The world is a poorer and duller place without him; in his own favourite words of praise he was a "great man."

After a harassed night and a hasty breakfast the 3rd Battalion returned to Nijmegen to rejoin the Division. The 3rd Battalion would not have been human if they had not hoped for a little rest and comfort, but there was no time for it. The Division already had its orders to take over part of the line east of the Reichwald the following day. When the poor are in trouble they rely on their neighbours, and the 3rd Battalion had good friends in Nijmegen. The 2nd Battalion and the 1st Coldstream Guards had the billets ready to step into, with hot baths round the corner and dinners already cooked. They did the housekeeping and all the dreary chores that are necessary to keep a barrack-room fit for habitation, while the 3rd Battalion made the most of their twenty-four hours.

On the 23rd both battalions, organized once more in a Regimental Group, under the command of 5th Brigade, drove into Germany. The journey took nearly twenty-four hours. The tanks crawled down a disused railway line, rocking backwards and forwards over the sleepers, while the trucks and troop-carriers struggled through the mud, traffic and military policemen—all inextricably confused. "But most depressing was the universal wreckage, looking its worst in the rain. It comes as rather a shock—town after town destroyed. We have not seen anything like it since Normandy, which we had almost forgotten. But we'll get used to it as we go on through this wretched land, for we are well into Germany now." The 2nd Battalion, still fresh from Tilburg, where they had been able to paint their machines, found the shattered farms rather low-class billets. Brigade H.Q. had to rough it in a cellar with a pile of turnips and an old goat, which Major Savill Young christened "Nulli Secundus." But the 3rd Battalion were quite content with their position in reserve. "The sector is cushy as they go around here. Some tired Krauts, who know their proper station, and what's good for them, are sitting around Uden waiting for the next shell. For our side is packed with guns, which fire all day and night. It's very encouraging, but there are two drawbacks—one the noise, and the other the number of gunners who want our billets."

Once settled down, the 3rd Battalion was brought up to strength again by a new company of reinforcements under Captain Barney de Boulay. Though at continual short notice to move, the battalions, to their pleasant surprise, were left in peace for another ten days while the battle was carried on by others on both flanks. The 9th U.S. Army started its long-delayed attack across the River Roer and advanced rapidly northwards. The 1st Canadian Army, meanwhile, was gradually reducing the Wesel bridgehead by pushing up two main axes, the Kleve–Calcen–Xanten road on the left and the Goch–Kevalaer–Geldern road on the right. The 2nd Canadian Corps attacked Calcen and Udem, and the 30th British Corps fought its way through woods and villages towards Kevalaer. The German infantry and tanks put up some resistance, but it was the "going" rather than the Germans that was the effective enemy. The surface of the roads was so bad as to be an obstacle in itself, but the tanks and often the infantry were rigidly confined to them, as the surrounding countryside was a quagmire. As a result, only a very small proportion of the available troops could be used at any one time.

The Guards battalions heard of their next task on the 1st March. The Division, with 5th Guards Brigade in the lead, was to drive through Goch to Kevalaer, turn east between the 3rd Division and 52nd Division, and then advance past the village of Kapellen to the high ground around Bonninghardt on the main cross-roads south of Wesel. After several postponements due to traffic jams and German demolitions, the Group started at half-past one in the morning of the 4th March. It was one of the worst of its many night drives. Snow, rain and incalculable halts combined to fray tempers and make progress dreary and slow. Every cross-roads, culvert or bridge had been blown by the retreating Germans, but the Sappers worked tirelessly on one crater after another, and by the afternoon had opened the Kevalaer–Kapellen road. The Group was then ordered to meet a brigade of the 3rd Division in Kapellen and to continue the advance.

The Group reached Kapellen without difficulty, but could find out little about the confused fighting that was going on in the woods and lanes beyond the town. Colonel Giles Vandeleur decided, therefore, to keep well to the right (or south) of the 3rd Division and to capture as a first objective the village of Hamb, two miles from Kapellen. The light was failing as the attack began. Hamb itself was unoccupied, but when the leading infantry and tanks emerged from it heavy shell and mortar fire came down on them. As it was already dusk the infantry halted to dig in. Lieutenant N. Whitfield, however, who was in command of the forward troop, chafed at darkness and delay and led his tanks onwards for the final assault. Unfortunately, tanks move clumsily in the night; they all got bogged at once and the crews spent the next six hours wearily extricating their machines.

During the night the heartening news arrived that patrols from the 9th Army had met the 52nd Division at Geldern. Otherwise Hamb was uncomfortable. The German gun-fire, increasing in weight and accuracy, took a steady toll of casualties. Colonel Giles Vandeleur realized that unless the Group deprived the Germans of their observation posts on the high ground commanding Hamb before daybreak, it would be under continual and well-directed fire and would suffer heavily in a daylight attack. He therefore ordered No. 2 Company to secure a foothold on the high ground before dawn by capturing a copse some eight hundred yards ahead. Captain Alec

Hendry detailed Lieutenant O'Grady's platoon for this task, giving him the support of the undaunted Lieutenant N. Whitfield. Lieutenant Whitfield, who knew the ground yard by yard from his nocturnal adventures, was delighted to have another chance of killing Germans at close quarters, and at six o'clock on the 5th March he led the way up the lane. The small force met stiff opposition at once, but luckily the German anti-tank and machine gunners could not take proper aim in the dark. Lieutenant N. Whitfield and Lieutenant O'Grady reached the copse with three tanks and nine men and cleared out the enemy. The remainder of the squadron-company group moved up to reinforce them, but it was halted on the forward edge of the village and along the lane by heavy concentrated fire. It was by now daylight and the German gunners could see their targets. Seven tanks were knocked out in quick succession by self-propelled guns and the infantry suffered considerable casualties on the open ground in front of Hamb. Both Captain Alec Hendry and Captain Will Berridge were wounded. The nine men and the three tanks held the copse all morning against constant attack. In order to carry on the advance the Brigade Commander ordered the Grenadiers, reinforced for the occasion by 5th Coldstream Guards, to work around the left flank, attack across the Irish front and capture the high wooded ground west of Bonninghardt. This attack, beginning at midday, with great artillery support, was skilfully executed and was completely successful. The Germans, already dismayed by the O'Grady-Whitfield thrust, were in no mood to offer resistance unto death—despite Hitler's order that the Wesel bridgehead was to be held. Two hundred and fifty prisoners, all young parachutists, were chased back to Kapellen where they spent the night in a ruined church formed up in column of sixes. The Irish "copse" party withdrew in glory to eat and sleep in Hamb.

Next morning, the 6th March, the 32nd Brigade passed through to capture Bonninghardt. The Irish Guards did no more fighting west of the Rhine. A rested officer wrote: "After ' l'affaire Hamb,' which cost us some seventy casualties, life was pure peace. Even the rain and shells stopped." The advance had now reached what the strategists called "a major phase line, where certain re-groupings are necessitated." On the 10th March—a month after the start of "Veritable"—the Germans finally withdrew and blew up the Wesel bridge. "I'm afraid we wasted our time in Tilburg last February studying means of capturing the bridge intact by an armoured dash," continued the same officer. "Things look cheerful enough now,

Russians rolling on and the Americans well across the Rhine at Remagen. They say the German armour is going south, so most of it will be facing the Americans for a change and not us, when we start again on the other side. We really rather enjoy this place—living in comfortable farms well stocked with food, fowl and animals. The Guardsmen eat vastly ; each company and squadron has its own abattoir, and the truck drivers are dumping military loads to make room for hen coops. The German civilians give no trouble and are confined together into the less-habitable houses. The better houses are occupied by the victorious troops and the foreign slave workers. These polyglot creatures have changed places with their former masters and now do nothing but sleep between orgies. They are mostly Polish and Ukranian, with a dash of Dutch and Belgian, and are delighted to share their pleasures with their gallant liberators. The girls are very buxom and tough, but that does not seem to put anyone off. Luckily these ' displaced persons ' are the concern of Military Government, and not us. A batch of them have just been collected and told that they are to go home at once. The poor wretches danced and sang for joy, kissing the Military Government officers who broke the news. In fact, of course, they are only going as far as a camp near Einghoven where they will have plenty of time for disillusionment. Tomorrow we return to Gemey for a long rest. Everyone says the end of the war is only a matter of weeks now, but Hitler, like another more admirable ruler, is an unconscionable time a-dying."

The battalions were given widely separate billets in the Divisional rest area. The 2nd Battalion settled down in well-found houses and schools in the undamaged part of Nijmegen ; the 3rd Battalion, the victims in their own eyes of unfair discrimination, shared out between the companies a few battered farms lying in the desolate waste between Ottersum and the Reichwald. Their first act was to set two of their houses on fire—Battalion H.Q. Officers' Mess and No. 3 Company H.Q. Valuable stores were saved only just in time, the drink in one case and Captain Colin Kennard in the other. The battalions had nothing to do except "reorganize—a word that covered anything from sleep to foot drill. Brussels leave began again, and for those who sought after official pleasures E.N.S.A. parties did their creaking best."

St. Patrick's Day was celebrated with the customary enthusiasm. In the morning a ceremonial parade was held for the presentation of shamrock and then the Guardsmen turned expectantly to the traditional dinners. They were not diasppointed. It was almost too easy, said the Quartermaster, to post calves, sheep and geese from German farmyards to company cookhouses. After an enormous meal and the necessary interval for digestive repose, those who could face more went to a gala ball in the Nijmegen Winter Gardens. Neither the place nor the people had changed much since the Battalions' first dance the previous October, but a gay evening was had by all, Guardsmen and Dutch girls alike. Many, finding dancing difficult, preferred the pleasures of battle chat. Reminiscences, especially of personal achievement, flowed freely, and it took a good man to cap an Anzio story.

CHAPTER XIV

Across the Rhine

2nd and 3rd Battalions

WHILE the 21st Army Group was re-forming to cross the Rhine in the north, the American Armies in the south, led by General Patton, cleared the left bank of the river down to the Swiss frontier and enlarged their bridgehead to a length of twenty miles and a depth of ten. Hitler's refusal to allow a withdrawal behind the "water obstacle" until it was too late cost the Germans enormous losses in men and material. Their defeat west of the Rhine was as disastrous to them as the Falaise Pocket west of the Seine, and had the same result, a precipitous retreat. Though some units still fought on with their old skill and courage, henceforward the German Army in the West was, as a whole, ill-equipped, disorganized and defeated. Their commander, Field-Marshal Model, anticipating his failure, committed suicide ; his successor, Field-Marshal Kesselring, introduced himself to his staff as the new "V3" hot from success on the Italian front. They all knew the end was very near.

The Allied plan for ending the war was simple enough ; to isolate the Ruhr and then drive into the heart of Germany. On 9th March Field-Marshal Montgomery issued his orders for crossing the Rhine north of the Ruhr. "My intention," he wrote in his despatches, "was to secure a bridgehead prior to developing operations to isolate the Ruhr and to thrust into the heart of Germany. In outline, my plan was to cross the Rhine on a front of two armies between Rheinberg and Rees, using Ninth American Army on the right and Second Army on the left. The principal initial objective was the important communication centre of Wesel. I intended that the bridgehead should extend to the south sufficiently far to cover Wesel from enemy ground action and to the north to include bridge sites at Emmerich ; the depth of the bridgehead was to be made sufficient to provide room to form up major forces for the drive to the east

2ND BATTALION TANKS IN GERMANY

2ND AND 3RD BATTALIONS ADVANCE INTO GERMANY

and north-east. I gave 24th March as target date for the operation. The battle of the Rhineland was not completed until 10th March, so that the time available for preparing to assault across the greatest water obstacle in Western Europe was extremely short. The all-important factor was to follow up the enemy as quickly as possible. . . . The width of the Rhine on our front was between four and five hundred yards, but at high water it was liable to increase to between seven and twelve hundred yards. . . . The course of the river was controlled by a highly developed system of dykes ; the main dyke was generally sixty feet wide at the base and some ten to sixteen feet high and formed a formidable obstacle. Although our operations in February had been severely handicapped by flooding, the waters were subsiding rapidly and the ground was drying remarkably quickly. The Ninth United States Army comprised XIII, XVI and XIX Corps, with a total of three armoured and nine infantry divisions. In addition to 8, 12 and 30 Corps, Second Army included for the initial stages of the operation 2 Canadian Corps and XVIII United States Airborne Corps ; the latter comprised 6th British and 17th American airborne divisions. The total forces in Second Army were four armoured, two airborne and eight infantry divisions, five independent armoured brigades, one Commando brigade, and one independent infantry brigade. 79th Armoured Division was in support of the operation with all its resources of specialized armour and amphibious devices. A tremendous weight of day and night heavy bombers, medium bombers and Allied tactical forces was made available in support of the operation."

The main assault to secure a crossing for the Second Army was to be made at Rees by the 15th (Scottish) Division and the 51st (Highland) Division, while the Commando Brigade, under Brigadier Derek Mills Roberts, D.S.O., M.C. (late of the 1st Battalion) made a private attack on Wesel to disrupt the German defence and join the airborne corps which was due to land north of the town. The Guards Armoured Division was given its customary role of "breaking out of the bridgehead." The whole operation bore the code name of "Plunder."

The road from Nijmegen to the front was packed day and night with convoys of sappers, building materials, guns—everything needed for the attack. Even fragments of the Royal Navy sailed past on lorry-back followed by a dutiful flight of sea-gulls. The river bank was shrouded in smoke to mask the Germans keeping the watch on the Rhine, and behind this sooty curtain the largest flock of sappers and pioneers in history hurried about, digging, levelling and coughing as they got the bridge sites ready for the climax of their campaign. They measured the stream, they analysed the mud, they tested the dykes, they were very happy. The gunners, too, were looking forward to a good shoot; they had plenty of shells and plenty of targets and few worries, for the Germans had no guns to spare for counter-battery work. The assaulting infantry, for their part, sat waiting in their billets, eyeing maps and photographs and intelligence summaries, and wondered what it would be like on the way across and on the far side. Brigadier Mills-Roberts drove around with an eager look marshalling his Commandos and scheming death for the odd two hundred Germans in Wesel.

The Battalions meanwhile were taking it easy in billets. The sun shone and the food was good, thanks to the hens and pigs which accompanied the Guardsmen out of their last battle. The Division was not expected to cross the Rhine till D+3 so they had time to eat, sleep, think and watch the world go by. The Guardsmen found themselves more comfortable among the Dutch families than anywhere else in Europe. They liked the clean tables with shining oilcloth, the solid food, the stuffy homely atmosphere of the kitchens, the very loud laughter at everybody's jokes and the language which they could understand because it was all they expected a foreign language to be. The Dutch understood, too, how much a man needs sleep and they had wonderful feather beds. Meanwhile some of the Battalions went to visit Castra Velera, the Roman camp from which Varus, also a successful general from the East, had set out in 9 B.C. on the great expedition which ended in disaster in the German forests. It was then that the Emperor Augustus beat his head against the wall and muttered "Varus, Varus, give me back my legions."

The assault began on the night of 23rd/24th March, after a heavy bombardment from the air and artillery. By daylight both the British and Americans secured their crossings, Brigadier Derek Mills Roberts took Wesel and the airborne troops were on the ground beyond the town. Work started on the bridges. Considering that their last line of defence had now been breached, the German reaction was not strong. Their harassing fire caused casualties among the sappers working in the open on the bridge sites and ferries, but they made no attempt to counter-attack. Most of their best troops had already been sent down to the Remagen front and the complete breakdown of the transport system prevented a concentration of reserves. The stoutest resistance came from the remnants of three parachute divisions who fought tenaciously to the north and east of Rees and carried out a well-planned system of demolitions along our line of advance. By 28th March the bridges were ready and two more infantry divisions had crossed to extend the bridgehead. The 6th Guards Tank Brigade drove over to join the XXVII Airborne Corps near Wesel and disappeared in the direction of Munster with a swarm of Americans and 6th Airborne on their backs. The Guards Armoured Division was now ordered to cross, to pass through 51st (Highland) Division near Isselburg and advance north-east along the Bocholt–Enschede road, and from there onwards "to crack about in the plains of North Germany."

"We are now packing to cross the Rhine," wrote an officer on 29th March. "We expect to have rather better luck this time than we had last September. Major D. R. S. Fitzgerald still has No. 1 Squadron, Eddie Tyler No. 2 and Mick O'Cock No. 3, while Major Sir John presides over 'A' Echelon and John Haslewood does the billeting as second-in-command. But the 3rd Battalion, as you know, has suffered heavily lately. Chris Dodd and Colin Kennard have succeeded Edward Fisher-Rowe and John Kennedy as Commanders of Nos. 1 and 3 Companies. Barney du Boulay, fresh from England, has taken over No. 2 and Michael Dudley has returned to command No. 4. Billy Reynolds, emulating his big brother, leads the Support Group, and Ivo Reid makes a dead-steady rear link. Our orders are to capture Bremen and Hamburg. No doubt we will. Anyway, we are getting a good start. The Rhine bridge at Rees is the sapper's dream—a 1,000 yards of Bailey and pontoon, and no gaps!

"*PS.*—We have just received a Psychological Warfare unit, complete with loudspeaker and 'ghost voice,' and two Army photographers. Nothing can stop us now."

At five o'clock on the morning of 30th March the two battalions drove across the Rhine into the bridgehead held by the 51st Division. In a sense the whole war, nearly five years of it, had been leading up to this moment. In the grey light they rattled across the dirty dismal-looking river almost without looking at it.

The Irish Group remained in reserve while the Grenadier Group led the Brigade up the main road to Aalten and Enschede. Once past the 51st Division front line, the Grenadiers ran into a series of demolitions and road-blocks manned by a few unhappy Germans. They cleared them without much delay until, about midday, they came on nine large craters in the road in front of Aalten. Then the Brigadier ordered the Grenadiers to advance on foot, and the Irish Group made its way through woods up to the inevitable canal just south of Aalten where the bridge was as inevitably blown. There was nothing to do but sort the eighty-odd prisoners they had taken *en route* and wait till the Grenadiers took Aalten at dusk and the sappers could come up and build a bridge. They were now back again in Dutch territory, and from far away over the level country they could see the sign of welcome—orange streamers flapping from the sails of the windmills. In one of the frontier villages, Dinxperloo, the Dutch cheered and sang on one side of the road while the Germans sulked on the other. The Dutch welcomed them as they once welcomed William the Silent: "They could not have done more had he been an angel from heaven."

The next morning the Grenadiers continued the advance, the Irish Group falling in behind Brigade Headquarters as soon as their bridge was built. The Brigade entered Groenlo in the early afternoon. The population cheered and wept and broke into a large dump of gin. The local resistance leader in his orange arm-band came out of a Klompenfabrik and gave a hundred bottles to the Brigade. "Echte oude Genever," he said, "Proper pre-war strength." The resistance movement relieved the battalions of all worries about prisoners and rounded up straggling Germans as well as many scoundrels, or persons said to be scoundrels. In all about 120 prisoners were taken that day mostly from the 8th Parachute Division and its satellites. Leaving behind the gin and orange arm-bands and the dancing inhabitants of Groenlo, the Brigade crossed two more craters and reached Eibergen. The Grenadiers cleared this town by a night attack, the sappers built the bridge across one more river in this network of land and water, and the Irish Group prepared to take the lead.

As soon as it was light on the 1st April the Irish Group drove up the road through Haksbergen to Enschede. "In this town are many manufactures," said the interpreter, "this is the Dutch Manchester." There was a sigh from nearly a hundred Manchester Micks, who would have given anything to see the approaches to London Road station in the rain.

The Germans were expected to defend Enschede and soon it was clear that they were going to. The bridge into the town was blown and the leading squadron came under brisk fire from a railway embankment. The Brigadier ordered the Irish Group to by-pass the town on the right and to cut off the German retreat. No. 3 Squadron and No. 4 Company cleared the embankment with some casualties and the loss of two tanks. The whole Group, harassed by 88-mm. shells, skirted the town, and by nightfall it was in the rear of the Germans astride the north-east exits. During the night the 32nd Brigade attacked the town from the west and it sounded as if somebody was having a rough time. It must have been the Germans, for in the early hours of the morning a company of them, looking for a way out, blundered into No. 14 Platoon, commanded by Lieutenant Dominic Sarsfield. The Germans withdrew slightly and then returned to batter a way out for themselves and their friends through No. 3 Company. After an hour's confused fighting the Germans gave up their attempt, leaving behind 15 dead, 17 wounded and 25 prisoners. No. 3 Company lost three men killed and thirteen wounded, including Lieutenant Sarsfield.

There was not much left of the night ; towards dawn the officers walked round the bivouacs—"No fraternizing after the next town. We're going back into Germany."

The next morning the Irish Group led the advance on through Oldenzaal and then turned eastwards for Germany. They met the first obstacle, a huge crater, just on the frontier at Depoppe on the Oldenzaal-Bentheim road. No. 3 Company entered the customs post to declare themselves and found the beds still warm and breakfast on the stove. The telephone was still ringing, and one of the Guardsmen answered it. "Wer da ?" asked a voice. "This is your old chum Mick." It took four hours of bulldozing and tipping to fill in the crater ; the rubble they used came from the first house in Germany blown down specially for the purpose. While this was being done No. 4 Company advanced up the road towards the hill on which stood the small country town of Gildenhaus. Parties of Germans were roaming the country on both sides of the road. Some of them gave themselves up and others fired machine-guns from a safe distance, but when No. 4 Company, followed later by No. 3 Squadron/2 Company group, started to climb the slope to Gildenhaus they met serious soldiers from the 8th Parachute Division. No. 2 Squadron/1 Company group turned right off the road to take Gildenhaus from the flank.

A troop of Honey tanks, commanded by Captain H. C. H. Fitzherbert, raced ahead of No. 2 Squadron along the tracks through woods and fields. The Germans did not or could not stop them till they were into Gildenhaus. There, at close quarters in the streets, they destroyed the Honeys with bazookas and killed Harry Fitzherbert. The leading troop, commanded by Lieutenant Peter Cuffe, was ambushed in a narrow lane outside the town by a squad of paratroopers. Lieutenant Cuffe's tank was hit by a bazooka bomb and he himself was fatally wounded. The same bomb destroyed the hull Browning, but Guardsman J. J. O'Shea, the driver, kept the "bazooka boys" off with pistol shots, while Sergeant McComish in the second tank deliberately ditched himself so as to clear the lane. O'Shea then extricated his tank and returned to the squadron, but the grinding passage of a mutilated tank was too much for a small wooden bridge over a stream and it collapsed behind him. Lieutenant Brian Russell's platoon crossed the stream, ran through the woods past houses hung with sheets and napkins, and joined the two isolated tanks. Sergeant McComish had been keeping the Germans quiet with H.E.; the infantry arrived when he had only two rounds left and just when the Germans were bringing a self-propelled gun into action. With the platoon to protect them, the third tank of the troop tried to tow Sergeant McComish out of the ditch. The S.P. got them both. A German light gun company, withdrawing through the wood into Gildenhaus, then agreed to take a hand in the fight, although as a prisoner said later, it had really nothing to do with it. With both tanks already in flames, there was no longer anything to protect, so Lieutenant Russell ordered his sections to withdraw. As he did so he was killed. Sergeant Cleaton took command, gave one section a good start and then slowly retreated with the other two. The first section got back to its company headquarters an hour later, sniped all the way from the houses with the white flags. Five men in the other two sections were killed and as many wounded before they ran out of ammunition. The Germans marched off the Guardsmen, taking their wounded with them in wheelbarrows and farm-carts. Sergeant Cleaton promptly knocked his escort over the head and got away; the others escaped later, and all the wounded were eventually recovered from a captured hospital.

So long as they remained with the Paratroopers they were treated well, but as soon as they got into the hands of the Volkssturm—the German Home Guard—their life was made a misery. They all remembered Guardsman Kelly weighed down by equipment belonging to wounded men and pushing a stretcher-wheelbarrow into the bargain—

"Like the black sheep of old
I'll return to the fold . . ."

his voice trailed cheerfully on in front of them.

When Harry Fitzherbert, a neat stockbroker from Dublin, presented himself to Regimental Headquarters in 1939 they said he was too old for active service, and they said so again in 1944. It nearly broke his heart when the 2nd Battalion left him behind in England, but he got out to Normandy in time to lead "B" Echelon across France and

Belgium. He still did not think he was far enough forward, and nothing would do him but the Reconnaissance Troop. The Battalion called him "The oldest living officer" or "The Old Man of the Reichwald" and the squadrons fought for the pleasure of having him attached to their Mess. As the commander of the Reconnaissance Troop he could always seize the fleeting opportunity, and he died as he probably would have preferred to die—behind the enemy line, all guns firing. For the 2nd Battalion John Reynolds wrote of him, "It can be the lot of few to be so missed by those they leave behind."

The main group meanwhile forced its way up the main road, No. 1 Squadron leading. "We were in a merciless frame of mind when we arrived at Gildenhaus," wrote Lieutenant N. Whitfield. "Typhoons raked a hill to the right and then No. 1 Squadron went in. The leading tank was knocked out at the far end of the town by an 88-mm. Its troop brewed up every house they could see. No. 3 Troop followed and continued the good work, but one tank went just too far and was also hit." By now it was getting dark. Colonel Vandeleur withdrew the tanks, turned the Typhoons on to the village and then sent in Nos. 2 and 4 Companies. The Germans fought resolutely, but the Guardsmen were very angry and laid about them vigorously by the light of the burning houses. A downpour of rain damped the flames and the companies with their prisoners spent the night in the sodden ruins of Gildenhaus.

First thing the next morning, 3rd April, the Grenadier Group passed through to attack Bentheim. The Irish Group remained round Gildenhaus for two days, routing prisoners out of the surrounding woods. "It was most interesting to walk round the town—or what remained of it," wrote an officer. "The place was on high ground with a view for miles over the country we had traversed. All our movements must have been observed practically from the time we crossed the Dutch frontier. In addition the trenches and earthworks were so extensive and elaborate that it was clear that the town had been prepared as a 'hedgehog' defensive position. Concrete had been skilfully and extravagantly employed." The Battalions ate, slept and read the letters which had accumulated in the past week. The ration trucks ran backwards and forwards unmolested until one of the 3rd Battalion trucks went up on a mine. Sergeant Breen and Sergeant Francis, the Post Sergeant, were killed in the explosion. Meanwhile, the 32nd Brigade, on another axis of advance, had reached and crossed the River Ems at Lingen some twenty miles to the north. This axis promised to be more suitable for tanks, so the Divisional Commander ordered the 5th Brigade to join the 32nd. On the 5th April the group handed over its motley collection of prisoners to infantry of the 51st Division and drove to Nordhorn. Here, in "a pleasant and quite undamaged village," they spent another day of rest and "an evening of great optimism in which Bremen was set as the goal for the next day's advance—a calculation from which the factor ' enemy ' has been omitted."

On the morning of the 7th the Irish Group crossed the River Ems and the Dortmund–Ems Canal, and led the 5th Brigade through Lingen up the road to the village of Thuine on the edge of the bridgehead held by the 32nd Brigade. No. 3 Company took over the village from the Coldstream and the rest of the group advanced up the road. The Germans opened fire immediately, shelling the road and mortaring the village. A bomb fell on No. 3 Company's headquarters, wounding five men and killing a Guardsman and C.S.M. Beresford. The group pushed slowly up the road against the usual opposition of self-propelled guns, infantry and road-blocks. The Group H.Q. noticed with interest that they were being "bracketed" by a battery of 105-mm. guns. After shells had fallen "plus" and "minus" they all took refuge beneath tanks. The two commanding officers sheltered beneath the same tank, but it was Colonel Giles Vandeleur, the farthest under, who was slightly wounded by the next shell. Group H.Q. was moved to a safer place where Colonel Dennis Fitzgerald took command of the group and Major John Haslewood succeeded to the 2nd Battalion.

The centre of the local resistance was the little village of Lohe, three miles up the road from Thuine and held by troops of the 7th Parachute Division. No. 2 Squadron and No. 4 Company attacked and cleared it that evening. No. 3 Squadron and No. 2 Company went round through a pine forest to cut the road behind Freren, the next village. This they did successfully, leaving, as they said, "a trail of brewed-up houses in their wake." No. 4 Company pushed on to capture the nearby village of Venslage before dark. Here it found a hospital in which were Lance-Sergeant Gannon and several other wounded prisoners from the 2nd Battalion. During the night No. 2 Company captured a German pedalling unsteadily towards Freren. When hauled off his bicycle, he said that he was a shoemaker attached to a company in that village and had a message for them to withdraw. His company must have acted on their own initiative, for there was nobody in Freren the following morning. From Freren No. 1 Squadron/3 Company group led the way up the road west to Furstenau. After about three miles they came on the German rearguards entrenched in the woods by the side of the road. No. 3 Company drove back these Germans under cover of tank fire, but a little farther on, about a mile and a half short of Furstenau, they found a strong defensive position covering the road. The Germans were at last determined to make a stand. While No. 1 Squadron and No. 3 Company engaged the Germans straight in front of them, No. 3 Squadron and No. 2 Company turned off the road into the woods to attack the village from the north. They ploughed through the woods towards a road that ran north from Furstenau to Vechtel. As the leading tank emerged on to the road, it was hit by an H.E. shell, which wounded Sergeant McManus, and then by an A.P. which "brewed-up" the tank. Another troop came up and they got across the road, but in doing so they lost another tank, Sergeant Capewell's. The infantry joined the tanks, and there they sat overlooking Furstenau, but being shelled every time they moved. Between them and the village ran a railway line along which the Germans had dug positions to meet just such an attack as the Irish Group were preparing to make. The noise of the carriers crashing through the trees with the company's rations kept the German gunners awake and active. When the noise and the shelling died down, No. 4 Company and No. 2 Squadron quietly replaced No. 2 Company and edged forward. Before doing anything violent the group made an appeal to reason ; they sent a policeman up the main west road into the village to invite the Germans to surrender. Furstenau was held by the battle-group Grossdeutschland, who did not accept the invitation or return the policeman. At eight o'clock Colonel Fitzgerald ordered the guns to open fire on the railway embankment, and Major Michael Dudley led No. 4 Company in to the attack from the north. The Grossdeutschland were seasoned troops ; they held their fire till the Company was well ahead of its supporting tanks and close to the embankment. The leading sections were swept away by machine-gun bursts. Major Michael Dudley plunged ahead and was shot dead by a sniper. The reserve platoon gathered up the Guardsmen in front of it and scrambled up the embankment. A bullet struck the crown on C.S.M. Black's sleeve and glanced off it—the first time, as one man said, that a crown has done anybody any good. The Company had been reading in the newspapers that all resistance had practically ceased in Germany. Some of them had the latest papers stuck in their trousers pockets as they clung to the railway line, waiting for the tanks to come up. Major Edward Tyler, the Commander of No. 2 Squadron, dismounted from his tank and took charge of the Company. He sent one troop across the railway and then led the platoons forward to join it. By nine o'clock they had taken Furstenau and two hundred prisoners.

The Irish Group moved a few miles to the village of Vechtel the following day, but it could not continue its drive to Bremen till a bridge had been built across the Hase Canal.

Counting the first day in Furstenau, the Irish Group spent the next three days reorganizing itself, collecting prisoners and sorting "displaced persons." It was their first real encounter with D.Ps. Frenchmen, Italians, Dutch, Poles and men and women of every shape and size from Eastern Europe came trotting down the road asking the way to go home. The battalions passed them on to a Camp in Freren, where they were assured that they could see anywhere from sunny Calabria to the snow-clad Caucasus within a very few days. The Military Government official at Brigade H.Q. could think of only one way of disciplining these D.Ps. as well as the Nazis and civilians, which was to "freeze" their bank accounts. "This universal sanction," said the War Diary mildly, "had no great effect on the illiterate and penniless slaves who had never heard of a bank, and connected freezing only with the steppes they had left some years ago." The prisoners were put to useful work, cutting hair, painting signs and doing all the fatigues while the Guardsmen, for a change, looked on as if they were sergeants; the local women were each given a bar of soap and a bale of clothes and told to get on with the washing. The 2nd Battalion needed to repair and replace some tanks, which it could do, but the losses of the infantry battalion were irreplaceable. The 3rd Battalion had in effect lost a platoon at Gildenhaus and another at Furstenau, and it now had to return to the three-company organization it had used before when short of men. No. 1 Company was "suspended." Maior C. Dodd went to No. 4 Company, taking with him Lieutenant Willy Moore's platoon, and the only other platoon, Lieutenant Brian McGrath's, was kept at Battalion H.Q. as a reserve and defence.

The bridges across the Hase Canal were ready on the morning of the 12th, and the 5th Brigade crossed into Loningen. The Irish Group led the way eastwards up the road to Essen. The Intelligence Staff at Corps H.Q. had told them that the enemy was now out of contact and retreating fast. The Group, however, soon made contact again in Essen and Hammelte. The leading tank was blown up on a mine ; after that, No. 1 Squadron advanced slowly, with No. 3 Company clearing the woods on either side of the road. "The country, as usual, was most unsuitable for tanks, being all bog and forest, with sandy tracks which soon gave way under heavy traffic." The Household Cavalry scout cars took a quick look at Essen and reported it to be strongly held by S.S. troops and guns. This information was correct, as No. 3 Squadron found when it approached the village. The infantry riding on the backs of the tanks hastily took to the woods, and the Squadron settled down "to exercise our fire-power on Essen," as they put it. The Brigade Commander, and everybody else, saw no point in "bumping the enemy head on," when it should be quite easy to by-pass Essen. It was quite easy. By nightfall the Group was in the village of Hemmelte behind Essen. Before leaving Hemmelte the following morning, No. 2 Company and No. 3 Squadron attacked Warnstedt, where there were some Germans who had had the temerity to shell the Group during the night. The Company was promised some flame-throwers—to make a quick job of the village—but the contraptions would not work, so the Guardsmen had to set fire to the village by hand. The Germans inside destroyed three tanks before the place became too hot for them. From Warnstedt the Group advanced through Sevelten and Coppelen to Emstek. There was some opposition from odd groups of infantry, but Colonel John Haslewood had got tired of the delays and forced the pace by leading the way in his scout-car. The road into Emstek was mined and two tanks went up. It was dusk when the Group approached the village and the tank commanders were, as usual, standing up in the turrets. There was no sign of life till a sniper shot Lieutenant J. O'Brien. There must have been a squad of musketry instructors in the village, for then a score of marksmen opened fire from the houses, picking Guardsmen off the tanks. The reply was inevitable. "Brew the place up." No. 3 Company filed through the burning houses to the next village, Dratum, which offered no resistance, and there the Group spent the night. The next morning the 3rd Battalion moved into Buhren and the 2nd into Hagstedt, chiefly because they were comfortable villages, and the Division was to have three days' rest while 21st Army Group decided what to do next.

"We were warned that we would join VIII Corps and cross the Elbe and drive to Hamburg or Lubeck. A change of orders came on the 16th April. We were now to join XII Corps, which was about one hundred and fifty miles away somewhere between the River Weser and the River Elbe. We would find out what to do when we got there." After two days' steady driving through Vechta, Diepholz, Neunburg and Rethem, the 5th Brigade reached Soutau, west of Bremen and south of the Bremen–Hamburg autobahn. The Brigade was warned to be up and ready at 0430 hrs. on the 19th for a quick advance to "the Great White Way," as the Staff insisted on calling the autobahn, but it was midday before it got the order to move. The Grenadiers led the way to Tostedt along a road liberally decorated with the Red Rat signs of the 7th Armoured Division, and there branched left to capture the village of Sittensen, by the side of the autobahn. The opposition was paltry and they crossed the autobahn without any difficulty. The Irish Group followed comfortably into Sittensen and spent the night in the farm-houses round the village. "The farms are on the whole better stocked than the majority in England," remarked the War Diary in passing. "Eggs and chickens are plentiful, and the cupboards are stacked with bottled fruit." During the night the Grossdeutschland Regiment arrived in Zeven, a small town north of the autobahn and on the road to Bremerwörde. This was the road the Brigade wished to take, but the Brigadier decided to put off an attack on Zeven till he could get the guns then busily supporting the 32nd Brigade. To harass the enemy, however, he ordered the Irish Group to send a company and squadron to Elsdorf and Wistedt just across the autobahn.

No. 1 Squadron and No. 3 Company moved into Elsdorf and sent a troop and a platoon to occupy Wistedt, two kilometres to the west. They passed a pleasant evening shooting at transport flushed from Rotenburg by the 32nd Brigade, but the night was disturbed by the sound of troop movements closing in on them. The 15th Panzer Grenadier Division was retiring from Bremen. The morning of the 21st April began with heavy rain. At first light the troop of tanks in Wistedt moved out of the centre of the little village to cover the roads leading into it. In front of the village rose a small hill, thick with trees and silent in the rain. Daylight came, the sections "stood down" and began to think seriously of breakfast. Out of the wood rolled two self-propelled guns ; their first shots hit the tank posted as a sentry on the road. Behind the self-propelled guns came a company of infantry. The tank went on fire as soon as it was hit, and the crew baled out. Guardsman E. Charlton, the driver, stopped to look at the German infantry running down the road. He climbed on to the burning tank, unhooked the Browning machine gun from the turret and jumped back into the road to meet the Germans. He faced them four-square, firing steadily. A bullet struck his left arm ; he moved to a gate in the hedge and supported his arm on the top bar, still firing. His left arm was hit again, and he propped the Browning on the gate, firing and loading it with one hand. A final burst of fire shattered his right arm, and Charlton collapsed by the gate, the Browning on top of him. The Germans swept over him, but Charlton had ruined for them the effect of their sudden attack ; the platoon and the other tanks had recovered themselves. The Germans

GUARDSMAN E. CHARLTON, V.C.

Face page 574

carried Charlton away, but he was already dying, and there was nothing they could do for him except bury him with the honour he deserved. A German officer who took part in the attack was later sent from a prison camp to the 2nd Battalion to show them Charlton's grave, as he had talked so much about the bravery of an Irish Guardsman.

The Germans surrounded Wistedt and pressed home their attack. The 17-pounder Sherman was hit on the cupola, and the commander killed, as it came forward to join the troop. Guardsman Mendes, from the troop leader's tank, went back to fetch it and drove it up himself to cover the battered sections. He held the Germans off till it was hit again and he was ordered to "bale out," as it was on fire. At the same time the second tank in the troop was destroyed and the German infantry swept into Wistedt. One tank and five men broke out of the circle covered by the indomitable Mendes, now fighting on foot with a borrowed Bren gun. Elsdorf was attacked at the same time by the 104th Panzer Grenadier Regiment supported by eight self-propelled guns. The weight of this attack fell on the platoon and troop commanded by Lieutenant Geraghty, who was killed in the opening exchange of fire. Captain Stephen Langton, who was on the Second-in-Command's routine tour of inspection, took charge. Standing on the back of one of the tanks he tried to manœuvre it into position to engage the S.Ps. The tank was hit by a bazooka, so he tried another one, this time with more success, as a Guardsman had taken the precaution of killing the "bazooka boy." No. 3 Squadron and No. 2 Company raced down the autobahn from Sittensen and caught five S.Ps. coming from the opposite direction. The two 17-pounder Shermans opened fire and the S.Ps. withdrew in a cloud of smoke. At eight o'clock the Germans called off the attack on Elsdorff, leaving thirty prisoners behind them, and retired to their stronghold, Zeven.

Zeven was taken on the 24th by the Grenadiers and the Coldstream. Till then the Irish Group remained in Elsdorf, being shelled by the Germans and twice bombed, once by the Germans and once by the Americans. Neither the shelling nor the bombing caused serious casualties, but they reduced Elsdorf to a heap of ruins. "In the execution of the 21st Army Group operations in the north," says the Supreme Commander's report, "the resistance encountered by the British Second Army in its attacks towards Bremen and Hamburg was persistent." Following the fall of Bremen on the 26th April, however, the situation changed. The main Allied effort was now transferred to the sector of VIII Corps, which launched an attack across the Elbe at Lauenberg. The Germans still resisted spasmodically, and were even more industrious in laying mines. In its advance northwards towards Cuxhaven the Division entered the German Naval Area, and came on sea-mines buried in the roads, and bridges blown up by torpedoes.

On the 27th, while the rest of the Division moved north, the Irish Group cleared the town of Ostereistedt. "Easter Egg" town, as the battalions rightly or wrongly translated it, was briskly defended, and the 2nd Battalion lost four tanks before Captain D. Radcliffe with two troops got into it from the rear. "We met some very nasty mines which did not go up under the first vehicle, but when the third or fourth crossed them." On entering the town a German gun put an H.E. shell straight into the turret of the leading tank. The commander was killed, the operator and gunner badly wounded, the co-driver knocked unconscious and the tank itself set on fire. Guardsman Egan, the driver, got them all out of the tank before the ammunition exploded.

The group reioined the 5th Brigade at Seedorf, north of Zeven. The Grenadiers had gone ahead to relieve a concentration camp at Sandbostel, some miles off the main road. No. 3 Company went up to help, but found the Grenadiers held up by a river and senseless opposition by the German garrison. Sandbostel camp housed 6,000 political prisoners and 16,000 prisoners of war in separate compounds. The prisoners of war waved and cheered, but the only sign from the political side was a thick column of smoke. Right up to the last minute the Germans were killing their starving, diseased victims. The next morning, the 29th, the Irish Group advanced to Hasedorf, farther north, but a small party of Irish Guards entered Sandbostel with the Grenadiers. "The prisoner-of-war section was in moderately good condition," wrote an officer, "but the political cage was even worse than reports had described. The scenes were disgusting and as bad as those photographed and publicized from Belsen and Buchenwald. One hut, in which the smell would have felled an ox, was filled with distinguished Frenchmen, dead and dying. As we came in an emaciated scarecrow in a bunk by the door raised himself on his elbow and said in precise English, 'Well, gentlemen, what do you think of conditions in this camp ?' and burst into mad laughter. Even the commandant of the German guards looked a bit ashamed, but of course he said it was nothing to do with him, it was the wicked S.S., and he was a harmless and unwilling spectator—all the usual 'Nicht Nazi' nonsense."

The war and the fighting petered out. By the end of April the German High Command, such as it was, had concentrated all their efforts on holding back the Russians. North-West Germany was clearly lost to them, and they now made no serious attempt to check the British advance. The local units were left to their own initiative which, in most cases, meant wholesale surrender. But there were still units and individual die-hards prepared to snipe and "bazooka" the advancing columns, and the demolition squads were still acting on their old orders. From Hasedorf the Irish Group sent a company and squadron to Bremerwörde; it collected a large batch of prisoners from a Marine division, but saw the bridge across the River Osle blown up as it approached. It is difficult to see what the Germans gained. The only people to be inconvenienced were the citizens of Bremerwörde; the Division just continued its advance northwards on the east of the River Osle, leaving the 51st Division to enter Bremerwörde at their leisure.

On 2nd May the Irish Group reached Estorf and Ohlendorf, and both surrendered to Colonel John Haslewood in a scout-car. The advance was like an exercise in an area in which there were an unknown number of homicidal maniacs. The villages *en route* sent their mayors to surrender, the stray battalions, "battle-groups" depots and camps sent delegates as soon as the battalions approached or surrounded them, but every now and then, out of a hedge or a wood, came a sudden burst of fire. Lieutenant Sebastian Hogg was killed by one machine-gun burst fired from a hill-top into his platoon. A company cook was killed and others wounded by an odd shell hitting a barn. And there were always and everywhere the mines.

The Group halted at Estorf. There was a vague river-line in front of it, and this was the reason given by the Division for checking the advance. The battalions could think of another reason—the war was over. On 2nd May the German armies in Italy capitulated. The newspapers and wireless bulletins were full of the comings and goings of Count Bernadotte, and there were rumours from both sides that members of the German High Command were at Field-Marshal Montgomery's H.Q. And all the time Germans wandered in to the companies in increasing numbers. "Where are you from?" "We are from the north." "What are you doing here?" "We don't know, but we are not going to fire another shot."

On 4th May Division announced the unconditional surrender of all the German armed forces in North-West Germany, to take effect at 0800 hrs. on 5th May, 1945. That eight o'clock passed almost unnoticed. Everyone had already taken it for granted that the war was over, and they knew they were right when they got orders to dress in their best to impress the German civilians.

The war was over. The 2nd Battalion "handed in" their tanks and became infantry once again, the Division moved down to the Rhine around Cologne, and as the months went by first the 3rd Battalion was disbanded and then the 2nd, until there was left only the 1st Battalion Irish Guards—the home and symbol of all the men of all three battalions who fought in Norway, Boulogne, North Africa, France, Belgium, Holland and Germany. The men who died cannot be forgotten by their comrades. At every reunion, at every Sergeants' Mess party, the talk inevitably swings to the old days and old friends.

"Up the Micks!"

St. Patrick's Day, 1944. Massalubrense (Cape Sorrento)

2nd Battalion Tanks prior to Farewell to Armour Parade, June, 1945

ROLL OF HONOUR

DECORATIONS

AND AWARDS

NORWAY

1st Bn. Irish Guards

KILLED OR DIED OF WOUNDS

Number.	*Rank.*	*Name.*
10398	Major	C. L. J. Bowen.
27656	Captain	J. R. Durham-Mathews.
15271	Lieut.-Colonel	W. D. Faulkner, M.C.
33666	Major	V. V. Gilbert-Denham.
18189	Major	T. A. Hackett-Pain.
67054/2	Lieutenant	F. R. A. Lewin.
49895	Captain	Hon. B. A. O'Neill.
2717086	Guardsman	Corbett, J.
2718507	Guardsman	Donnelly, M.
2717810	Guardsman	Draper, E.
2718736	Guardsman	Elliott, J.
2717964	Guardsman	Jordon, N.
2718831	Guardsman	McClelland, A.
2718911	Guardsman	McLoughlin, D.
2718899	Guardsman	Rankin, W.
2695829	Guardsman	Rigby, W.
2716210	Guardsman	Sliney, E.
2717070	Guardsman	Smith, H.
2717983	Lance-Sergeant	Taylor, S.
2717801	Guardsman	Tierney, J.

WOUNDED ...	Officers	5
	Other Ranks	23

DECORATIONS

Bar to Military Cross.

63088	Major	D. M. L. Gordon-Watson, M.C.
65413	Captain	B. O. P. Eugster, M.C.

Military Cross.

2715069	R.S.M.	Stack, J.

Distinguished Conduct Medal.

2718517	Sergeant	Johnston, W.
2719527	Guardsman	Wylie, J.
2717837	Guardsman	O'Shea, M.
2716776	Guardsman	Callaghan, T.

Military Medal.

2718134	Drummer	Hughes, A.

Twelve Mentioned in Despatches.

HOOK OF HOLLAND

2ND BN. IRISH GUARDS

KILLED OR DIED OF WOUNDS

Number.	*Rank.*	*Name.*
2717655	Guardsman	Bolger, T.
2717202	Guardsman	Burke, J.
2717392	Lance-Corporal	Carroll, P.
6654626	Guardsman	Hayes, J.
2719871	Guardsman	Murphy, T.
2719674	Guardsman	McWalter, J.
2717456	Lance-Sergeant	Parker, L.
2717586	Guardsman	Power, T.
2716746	Guardsman	Stewart, J.
2718967	Lance-Corporal	Stewart, G.
2719968	Guardsman	Wiggins, G.

WOUNDED ... Officers ... ... Nil
Other Ranks 12

BOULOGNE

2ND BN. IRISH GUARDS

KILLED OR DIED OF WOUNDS

Number.	*Rank.*	*Name.*
71093	Lieutenant	H. L. S. Leveson.
67903	Lieutenant	D. W. S. P. Reynolds.
2718195	Sergeant	Alberts, W.
2719682	Guardsman	Barbour, J.
2719766	Guardsman	Chattington, F.
2719056	Guardsman	Clark, A.
2719734	Guardsman	Creasey, T.
2719884	Guardsman	Dobson, J.
2717608	Lance-Corporal	Foley, T.
2717576	Guardsman	Freeman, F.
2718618	Sergeant	Houston, S.
2716657	Guardsman	Kearns, P.
2717913	Lance-Corporal	Kelly, C.
2719742	Guardsman	King, G.
2718087	Lance-Corporal	Lynam, J.
2719816	Guardsman	Myers, J.
2719255	Guardsman	McDermott, D.
2720006	Guardsman	O'Flynn, B.
2719194	Guardsman	Phillips, J.
2719902	Guardsman	Price, F.
2717246	Guardsman	Quigley, R.
2719462	Guardsman	Rapson, P.
2719308	Guardsman	Turish, A.
2719183	Guardsman	Walsh, E.
2719466	Guardsman	Williams, J.

WOUNDED ... Officers 1
Other Ranks 14

HOOK OF HOLLAND AND BOULOGNE

DECORATIONS

Number.	*Rank.*	*Name.*
Distinguished Service Order.		
13865	Lieut.-Colonel	J. C. Haydon, O.B.E.
Military Cross.		
45462	Captain	H. S. Phillpotts.
37264	Captain	C. R. McCausland.
62427	Captain	J. D. Hurnung.
Distinguished Conduct Medal.		
2717907	Sergeant	Gilchrist, W.
Military Medal.		
2716755	Sergeant	Carragher, M.
2718862	Lance-Corporal	Burke, I.
2717551	Lance-Corporal	Mawhinney, T.

Twelve Mentioned in Despatches.

NORTH AFRICA

1st Bn. Irish Guards

KILLED OR DIED OF WOUNDS

Number.	*Rank.*	*Name.*
102077	Major	S. J. R. Bucknill.
233195	Lieutenant	M. J. Eugster.
69552	Captain	J. B. Fitzgerald.
7351	Captain	G. B. Ismay.
165051	Lieutenant	F. A. Mahaffy.
156080	Lieutenant	D. G. Madden (M.I.D.*)
165064	Lieutenant	J. J. Nunn (M.I.D.*)
219073	Lieutenant	J. G. A. Pym.
165066	Lieutenant	A. W. T. Rochford.
2720817	Guardsman	Allcock, F.
2717914	Guardsman	Barry, J.
2723087	Guardsman	Battey, E.
2721164	Guardsman	Beck, C.
2720899	Guardsman	Bird, N.
2722335	Guardsman	Blackburn, R.
4615494	Lance-Corporal	Buckley, F.
2718002	Lance-Sergeant	Burriss, A.
2719989	Guardsman	Bradshaw, R.
2719497	Guardsman	Brady, J.
2720433	Sergeant	Brighouse, T.
2720432	Guardsman	Brockbank, G.
2720901	Guardsman	Brocklebank, A
2722364	Guardsman	Brooks, W.
2721207	Lance-Corporal	Brough, S.
2722831	Guardsman	Campbell, W.
2718725	Lance-Sergeant	Carr, H.
2719269	Guardsman	Caton, N.

* Mentioned in Despatches

Number.	*Rank.*	*Name.*
2722399	Guardsman	Chambers, J.
2722679	Guardsman	Collis, E.
2723130	Lance-Corporal	Connors, J.
2720246	Guardsman	Corkan, J.
2719215	Guardsman	Daly, J.
2721077	Guardsman	Dempsey, M.
2722930	Guardsman	Ditchfield, F.
2719137	Guardsman	Drake, S.
2722908	Guardsman	Drean, S.
2721128	Lance-Corporal	Duckworth, A.
2717825	Lance-Corporal	Duffy, P.
3384137	Guardsman	Dunne, T.
2718368	Guardsman	Edwards, E.
2718836	Guardsman	Elliott, E.
2721272	Corporal	Elliott, R.
2719553	Guardsman	Furey, M.
2720911	Guardsman	Green, H.
2721719	Guardsman	Harrop, H.
2721781	Guardsman	Hall, J.
2721897	Guardsman	Handley, C.
2717743	Guardsman	Harris, O.
2721001	Guardsman	Harris, J.
2722466	Guardsman	Harris, S.
2722402	Lance-Sergeant	Henderson, R.
2717841	Guardsman	Hennessy, J.
2721366	Guardsman	Hesketh, W.
2721468	Lance-Sergeant	Higginson, M.
2718441	Lance-Sergeant	Hoggett, T.
2719690	Guardsman	Horsley, J.
2721282	Lance-Corporal	Howden, C.
864622	Guardsman	Hoyle, J.
2716825	Guardsman	Hurley, J.
2722258	Guardsman	Jackson, H.
2720915	Guardsman	Johnson, H.
2721589	Guardsman	Keady, M.
2718550	Guardsman	Kelly, E.
2718103	Guardsman	Kelly, B.
2720970	Guardsman	King, R.
2721739	Lance-Sergeant	Kinnane, M.
2718799	C.S.M.	Kinnane, M.
2721566	Lance-Sergeant	Kitney, G.
2717927	Lance-Sergeant	Landers, J.
2717036	Guardsman	Leavy, J.
2719312	Guardsman	Lewis, N.
2721137	Lance-Corporal	Lewis, S.
2718792	Guardsman	Lewins, R.
2722901	Lance-Corporal	Lockley, R.
2717341	Sergeant	Long, W.
2720274	Guardsman	Lumley, D.
2719655	Guardsman	Magee, H.
2718338	Lance-Sergeant	Maguire, T.
2718689	Guardsman	Mairs, W.
2716873	C.S.M.	Malone, R.
2720377	Guardsman	Manley, J.
2721694	Guardsman	Mann, C.
2717958	Sergeant	Marr, J.

Number.	*Rank.*	*Name.*
2717551	Sergeant	Mawhinney, T. (M.M.).
2722055	Guardsman	Maule, H.
2718459	Guardsman	Megaw, T.
2719746	Guardsman	Mellish, L.
2718163	Sergeant	Middleton, J.
2721037	Guardsman	Mitchell, K.
2721240	Guardsman	Moloughney, J.
6409581	Guardsman	Mulligan, T.
2716837	Guardsman	Murphy, J.
2719026	Guardsman	Murphy, H.
2717646	Lance-Sergeant	Murray, W.
2717933	Lance-Sergeant	McCarthy, A.
2722921	Guardsman	McCluskey, J.
2718357	Guardsman	McKimm, S.
2719325	Guardsman	McKimm, N.
2716913	Lance-Sergeant	O'Connor, D.
2718058	Sergeant	O'Donnell, A.
2720811	Guardsman	O'Shea, J.
2716292	R.S.M.	Peilow, B.
2718717	Guardsman	Reddington, P.
2722642	Guardsman	Reid, G.
2720860	Guardsman	Rice, J.
2720578	Guardsman	Rickman, G.
2718348	Guardsman	Ridge, P.
2718758	Guardsman	Roberts, B.
2719803	Guardsman	Rompen, L.
2721292	Guardsman	Rosendale, C.
2722664	Guardsman	Rowley, A.
2718203	Guardsman	Ryder, J.
2723057	Guardsman	Savage, R.
2717709	Sergeant	Somers, J.
2722704	Lance-Sergeant	Sparks, F.
2718803	Lance-Sergeant	Teeling, G.
2572167	Guardsman	Thurlow, J.
2719086	Guardsman	Tweed, R.
2720441	Guardsman	Vare, R.
2720735	Guardsman	Vause, C.
7019405	Guardsman	Walker, J.
2721242	Guardsman	Walsh, W.
2721396	Lance-Sergeant	Warhurst, L.
2722912	Guardsman	Whitfield, W.
2720442	Guardsman	Wolfendale, J.

WOUNDED ... Officers 16
Other Ranks 229

DECORATIONS

Victoria Cross.

2722925	Lance-Corporal	Kenneally, J.

Distinguished Service Order.

31921	Lieut.-Colonel	C. A. Montagu-Douglas-Scott.
138640	Captain	C. D. Kennard.

Military Cross.

121345	Captain	O. S. Chesterton.
138638	Captain	D. J. L. Fitzgerald.

Number.	*Rank.*	*Name.*
Distinguished Conduct Medal.		
2718820	Sergeant	Lynch, D
2721511	Lance-Sergeant	Ashton, A.
2720987	Guardsman	Nicholson, J.
2718628	Guardsman	Horan, S.
Military Medal.		
2718877	C.Q.M.S.	Mercer, P.
2721745	Lance-Sergeant	Maher, E.
2721484	Lance-Sergeant	Pearson, T.
2720564	Lance-Sergeant	Banks, G.
2721689	Guardsman	Hayman, H.
2717731	Guardsman	Hickey, D
2721385	Guardsman	Hollingworth, J.

Twenty-four Mentioned in Despatches.

ITALY

1st Bn. Irish Guards

KILLED OR DIED OF WOUNDS

Number.	*Rank.*	*Name.*
174882	Lieutenant	C. J. W. Bartlet.
156083	Lieutenant	P. C. Da Costa.
87530	Lieutenant	H. J. Gillow.
228331	Lieutenant	D. W. Hall.
228330	Lieutenant	A. P. Harcourt (M.I.D.*)
247102	Lieutenant	C. M. Musgrave.
228333	Lieutenant	Hon. S. E. T. Preston (M.I.D.*)
137409	Captain	R. N. D. Young (M.I.D.*)
2720952	Guardsman	Angell, W.
2721511	Lance-Sergeant	Ashton, A. (D.C.M.)
2718668	Guardsman	Ayre, D.
2722272	Guardsman	Barker, S.
2717130	Guardsman	Bandtock, G.
2720456	Guardsman	Barrett, M.
2722147	Guardsman	Barton, D.
2723424	Guardsman	Battersby, J.
2720068	Guardsman	Beesley, J.
2720339	Guardsman	Bennett, W.
2720503	Guardsman	Betts, A.
2721267	Guardsman	Booth, J.
2718680	Lance-Corporal	Borland, T.
2722124	Guardsman	Bradley, J.
2720540	Guardsman	Bradshaw, A.
2722808	Guardsman	Brannan, T.
2720379	Lance-Corporal	Broadbent, S.
2721665	Guardsman	Brooks, V.
2716885	Guardsman	Brennan, M.

* Mentioned in Despatches.

Number.	*Rank.*	*Name.*
2718797	Guardsman	Burke, E.
2720673	Guardsman	Byrne, F.
2721609	Guardsman	Byrne, W.
2719390	Guardsman	Cain, D.
2720319	Guardsman	Callaghan, T.
2722791	Lance-Sergeant	Cartlidge, F. (M.I.D*)
2721806	Guardsman	Colbeck, H.
1875581	Guardsman	Connor, J.
2721334	Guardsman	Coogan, W.
2719942	Guardsman	Coomber, V.
2721808	Guardsman	Corlett, W.
2721586	Guardsman	Corrigan, O.
2720295	Lance-Corporal	Crawford, T.
2722128	Guardsman	Dalton, E.
2721614	Guardsman	Darcy, C.
2720721	Guardsman	Darlow, W.
2721560	Guardsman	Day, F.
2722712	Lance-Corporal	Dempsey, T.
2717367	Guardsman	Devaney, J.
2720446	Guardsman	Dickens, G.
2723037	Guardsman	Dinsmore, J.
2718647	Guardsman	Dolan, T.
2722197	Guardsman	Dowling, E.
2717078	Guardsman	Downey, J.
2717006	Guardsman	Duggan, J.
2718380	Guardsman	Duffy, J.
2716910	Sergeant	Dunne, P.
2723080	Guardsman	Farrell, E.
2721815	Guardsman	Findlow, H.
2718838	Lance-Corporal	Foran, D.
2720909	Guardsman	Geering, S.
2718921	Guardsman	Gibson, W.
2720508	Guardsman	Gilbert, A.
2718644	C.S.M.	Gilmore, G.
2718653	Guardsman	Graham, C.
2721522	Guardsman	Gyte, F.
2719489	Guardsman	Hall, R.
2717279	Sergeant	Harlow, H.
2720323	Lance-Corporal	Hargreaves, G.
2717206	Lance-Corporal	Harris, P.
2720839	Lance-Corporal	Harrison, R.
2718238	Lance-Corporal	Hennessy, A.
2722345	Guardsman	Hewitt, R.
2721856	Guardsman	Hitchin, F.
4855664	Lance-Corporal	Holwell, G.
2722640	Guardsman	Hope, W.
2720727	Guardsman	Hoten, W.
2719874	Guardsman	Houghton, W
2719891	Guardsman	Hughes, S.
2719239	Guardsman	Irvine, J.
2722971	Lance-Corporal	Johnston, W.
2718981	Guardsman	Johnston, J.
2717567	Guardsman	Kelly, E.
2717831	Guardsman	Kelly, J.
2720402	Guardsman	Kidd, A.

* Mentioned in Despatches.

Number.	*Rank.*	*Name.*
2718770	Guardsman	Maloney, T.
2718881	Guardsman	Manly, P.
2720848	Guardsman	Marchington, A.
2720191	Guardsman	Melia, J.
2722391	Guardsman	Miller, G.
2722825	Guardsman	Millne, J.
2721823	Guardsman	Moores, M.
2721290	Guardsman	Moran, M.
2718497	Lance-Corporal	Moriarty, M. (D.C.M.).
2718878	Lance-Sergeant	Murphy, G.
2721590	Guardsman	Murphy, W.
2722117	Guardsman	Murray, J.
2718566	Guardsman	McCracken, M.
2717766	Lance-Sergeant	McDermott, W.
2721480	Guardsman	McGale, J.
2718572	Guardsman	McNamara, P.
2718492	Guardsman	O'Beirne, E.
2721861	Guardsman	O'Brien, P.
2719569	Lance-Sergeant	O'Connell, R.
2716792	Lance-Corporal	O'Donnell, J.
2723120	Guardsman	O'Neill, J.
2722478	Guardsman	O'Reilly, L.
2722661	Guardsman	Peters, W.
2718328	Guardsman	Pollock, W.
2721040	Guardsman	Porter, S.
2716882	Sergeant	Quinn, J. (M.I.D.*).
2717303	Lance-Corporal	Quinn, T.
2723016	Guardsman	Rance, J.
2720474	Guardsman	Redmond, G.
2721043	Guardsman	Rowson, N.
2722016	Guardsman	Rush, C.
2721295	Guardsman	Sheffield, C.
2718369	Guardsman	Smith, J.
2720698	Guardsman	Stevens, W.
2720447	Guardsman	Stubbs, F.
2721222	Guardsman	Sumner, R.
14220910	Guardsman	Taylor, H.
2720801	Lance-Corporal	Thompson, R.
2722120	Guardsman	Upton, M.
2722604	Lance-Corporal	Walsh, W.
2722482	Guardsman	Warner, V.
2722241	Guardsman	Welsh, J.
2721397	Guardsman	West, A.
2721306	Guardsman	Williamson, H.
2719338	Lance-Corporal	Woods, A.
2718063	Lance-Sergeant	Wyles, M.
2719527	Sergeant	Wylie, J. (D.C.M., M.I.D.).

* Mentioned in Despatches.

WOUNDED ... Officers 16
Other Ranks 211

DECORATIONS

Distinguished Service Order.

67098 Major H. L. S. Young.

Second Bar to M.C.

63088 Major D. M. L. Gordon-Watson, M.C. and Bar.

Number.	*Rank.*	*Name.*
Military Cross.		
73091	Major	G. P. M. Fitzgerald.
94576	Major	D. M. Kennedy.
186929	Captain	T. C. Keigwin.
99560	Captain	S. H. Combe.
156081	Lieutenant	A. N. Bell.
219070	Lieutenant	J. C. Crewe.
Distinguished Conduct Medal.		
2718336	Sergeant	Dunne, J.
2717328	Sergeant	Gundel, C.
2718497	Lance-Corporal	Moriarty, M.
2718746	Guardsman	Montgomery, W.
2718510	Guardsman	Adamson, R.
2717158	Sergeant	Headon, T.
Military Medal.		
2719505	Corporal	D'arcy, J.
2718472	C.S.M.	Moran, M.
2718419	Sergeant	McConnell, R.
2718341	Lance-Sergeant	Weir, C.
2722392	Lance-Sergeant	Murphy, R.
2718785	Lance-Corporal	O'Brien, M.
2722217	Lance-Corporal	Cross, A.
3312196	Guardsman	Taylor, H.
2721837	Guardsman	Branthwaite, J.
2718210	Guardsman	Ryan, J.
2721127	Lance-Corporal	Dodd, A.
2720247	Lance-Corporal	Fahy, J.
2719854	Lance-Sergeant	Wright, E.
2717223	Guardsman	English, D.
2721319	Guardsman	French, W.
2719186	Guardsman	Kerr, J.
2719743	Guardsman	Lee, E.

Nineteen Mentioned in Despatches.

NORMANDY

2nd Bn. Irish Guards

KILLED OR DIED OF WOUNDS

Number.	*Rank.*	*Name.*
233957	Lieutenant	M. H. Chaine-Nickson.
104106	Captain	H. E. J. Dormer, D.S.O.
278673	Lieutenant	J. C. F. Keatinge.
226183	Lieutenant	D. B. Liddle.
165062	Lieutenant	M. K. Maconchy.
243516	Lieutenant	J. K. Maguire.
258178	Lieutenant	F. D. P. McCorkell.
2719213	Corporal	Atkinson, F.
2720993	Guardsman	Baghurst, A.
2722743	Lance-Corporal	Baker, L.
2722715	Guardsman	Barnett, A.

Number.	*Rank.*	*Name.*
2721400	Guardsman	Beckett, S.
2719937	Sergeant	Brennan, M.
2719764	Lance-Corporal	Brill, G.
6096248	Guardsman	Coltan, T.
2719429	Lance-Corporal	Concannon, P.
4206579	Guardsman	Cullen, T.
2719685	Guardsman	Davies, W. (M.I.D.*).
2721186	Guardsman	Davidson, E.
2722167	Guardsman	Drinkill, E.
2720188	Lance-Sergeant	Ferguson, A.
2722984	Guardsman	Gerrard, T.
2721859	Guardsman	Griffin, W.
2719491	Lance-Sergeant	Harbinson, H.
2720252	Guardsman	Hill, H.
2723557	Guardsman	Holley, F.
2720207	Guardsman	Hunt, C.
2721386	Guardsman	Jayes, A.
2719660	Sergeant	Jennings, G.
2718214	Lance-Sergeant	Kelly, J.
2720785	Guardsman	Kershaw, A.
2719991	Guardsman	Kibble, G.
2723499	Guardsman	Lally, C.
2720845	Lance-Corporal	Lawton, H.
2722931	Guardsman	Mahon, F.
2723397	Lance-Corporal	Moore, D.
2721288	Lance-Corporal	Morrell, H.
2722769	Guardsman	Moss, C.
2719972	Guardsman	McManus, D.
2723305	Guardsman	Oliver, J.
2720684	Guardsman	Phillips, T.
2721934	Guardsman	Ramsden, H.
2719097	Lance-Sergeant	Riches, R.
2719071	Sergeant	Robinson, G.
2722320	Guardsman	Roddis, E.
2723372	Guardsman	Shepperson, E.
2721254	Guardsman	Stansfield, J.
2720535	Guardsman	Swallow, F.
2722795	Guardsman	Tierney, W.
2723385	Guardsman	Trippier, J.
2723296	Guardsman	Vinall, L.
2721048	Lance-Corporal	Watson, H.
2722383	Lance-Sergeant	Warriner, B.
2718695	Guardsman	Whitney, B.
2720416	Lance-Corporal	Williamson, C.
2722964	Guardsman	Winrow, J.
2719530	Lance-Sergeant	Wood, R.
2719982	Lance-Sergeant	Workman, G.

* Mentioned in Despatches

WOUNDED ...	Officers	15
	Other Ranks	96

NORMANDY

3RD BN. IRISH GUARDS

KILLED OR DIED OF WOUNDS

Number.	*Rank.*	*Name.*
295058	Lieutenant	P. O. D. Bourke.
104182	Major	A. R. Eardley-Wilmot, M.C.
253926	Lieutenant	Lord E. N. Fitzmaurice.
108939	Captain	I. D. R. Grant.
121551	Captain	D. G. Kingsford, M.C.
200112	Lieutenant	T. E. Stafford-King-Harman.
149144	Captain	E. M. Woods.
2719151	Guardsman	Allen, W.
2723353	Guardsman	Anderson, E.
2722999	Guardsman	Ambrose, R.
14514367	Guardsman	Aspinall, G.
2721250	Lance-Corporal	Bamford, H.
2723812	Guardsman	Barlow, R.
2722611	Guardsman	Briggs, J.
2723648	Lance-Corporal	Britton, G.
2722123	Guardsman	Borsbey, J.
2722034	Guardsman	Buckingham, D.
2724032	Guardsman	Byrne, J.
2717181	Guardsman	Conroy, J. (M.I.D.*).
2722104	Lance-Sergeant	Cooke, M.
2720741	Sergeant	Douglas, W.
2723623	Guardsman	Dingwall, D.
2721894	Sergeant	English, T.
2723836	Guardsman	Eager, G.
2718941	Lance-Sergeant	England, T.
2719380	Lance-Corporal	Elliott, E.
2722649	Guardsman	Farrow, A.
2723795	Guardsman	Ferguson, G.
2723874	Guardsman	Fitt, G.
2723585	Guardsman	Fogarty, J.
2719790	Guardsman	Fraser, E.
2721431	Lance-Sergeant	Graham, A.
2720708	Guardsman	Harvey, L.
2718887	Guardsman	Hennessy, J.
2723954	Guardsman	Hesketh, G.
2720624	Sergeant	Hopper, H.
2721509	Guardsman	Hunter, W.
2720361	Guardsman	Hulmes, H.
2721588	Guardsman	Jordan, M.
2721820	Guardsman	Jones, J.
2722562	Guardsman	Kirkpatrick, E.
2717614	C.S.M.	Larkin, D.
2724051	Guardsman	Lindsay, B.
2722514	Guardsman	Liptrot, A.
2723657	Guardsman	Madden, H.
2722878	Guardsman	Maher, P.

* Mentioned in Despatches

Number.	*Rank.*	*Name.*
2722056	Lance-Sergeant	Mears, R.
2721196	Guardsman	Mitchell, F.
2722781	Lance-Corporal	McCarthy-Phillips, P.
2723871	Guardsman	McCallan, P.
2720234	Lance-Corporal	McEwan, J.
2722785	Guardsman	McKibbin, R.
2722080	Guardsman	McLoughlin, G.
2717277	Sergeant	Oulsnam, J.
2723994	Guardsman	O'Hanlon, J.
2724063	Guardsman	Potts, A.
2723906	Guardsman	Price, E.
2724079	Guardsman	Quinn, M.
2717332	Lance-Corporal	Raynard, W.
2724138	Guardsman	Sloan, G.
14220908	Guardsman	Smith, H.
2720228	Lance-Corporal	Stock, D.
2716637	Guardsman	Stokes, M.
2724014	Guardsman	Tyrrell, T.
2721769	Guardsman	Warriner, A.
2719513	Guardsman	Watt, R.
2721961	Guardsman	Weinstein, M.
2721800	Guardsman	Whitby, F.
2720865	Lance-Corporal	Whittaker, R.
2723802	Guardsman	Williams, D.
2722670	Guardsman	Williams, A.
2719388	Lance-Corporal	Williams, R.
2721323	Guardsman	Wimbridge, L.
2721704	Guardsman	Wrigley, H.

WOUNDED ...	Officers	6
	Other Ranks	182

BELGIUM AND HOLLAND

2nd Bn. Irish Guards

KILLED OR DIED OF WOUNDS

Number.	*Rank.*	*Name.*
268994	Lieutenant	W. C. T. MacFetridge.
132247	Major	D. A. Peel, M.C.
273380	Lieutenant	J. A. P. Swann.
2723046	Guardsman	Ackers, W.
2719101	Guardsman	Apperley, B.
2721989	Guardsman	Arnold, B.
2722520	Guardsman	Bell, J.
2723094	Lance-Corporal	Black, J.
2723282	Guardsman	Boston, C.
2721182	Lance-Sergeant	Casey, C.
2720079	Lance-Sergeant	Cashion, E.
2721100	Guardsman	Chambers, W.
2719127	Guardsman	Clarke, T.
2723669	Guardsman	Clisby, R.
2723337	Guardsman	Cole, J.

Number.	*Rank.*	*Name.*
2723031	Guardsman	Connery, P.
6985004	Lance-Corporal	Crozier, D.
2722792	Guardsman	Deehan, T.
2723363	Guardsman	Dunford, C.
2718741	Guardsman	Fanning, M.
2722415	Lance-Sergeant	Farmer, T.
2723100	Guardsman	Fearnyough, J.
2719596	Guardsman	Fernandez, M.
2723676	Guardsman	Greenall, H.
2720871	Lance-Sergeant	Hall, F.
2719974	Lance-Corporal	Hall, W.
2723111	Guardsman	Heyes, J.
2723771	Guardsman	Holland, D.
2723560	Guardsman	Hughes, W.
2723581	Guardsman	Johnson, J.
2723368	Guardsman	Letchford, H.
2722690	Guardsman	Loder, O.
2720350	Lance-Sergeant	Mather, E.
2719160	Lance-Corporal	Modler, J.
7020985	Guardsman	Moore, W.
2720055	Guardsman	Murphy, A.
2718054	Guardsman	McGovern, T.
2721140	Guardsman	Nay, D.
2721589	Guardsman	Neal, H.
2722947	Lance-Corporal	O'Connor, E.
2720233	Lance-Sergeant	O'Neill, T.
2717391	S.S.M.	Parkes, W.
2723224	Guardsman	Pegg, T.
2723067	Guardsman	Plant, L.
2723227	Guardsman	Pratt, P.
2720359	Guardsman	Quinn, O.
2720304	Lance-Sergeant	Ratcliffe, J. (M.I.D.*).
2723711	Guardsman	Rice, T.
2723635	Guardsman	Robinson, R.
2720108	Guardsman	Simcock, W.
2723252	Guardsman	Thomas, T.
2722995	Lance-Corporal	Walker, E.
2721799	Guardsman	Waterhouse, R.
2723656	Guardsman	Watters, W.
2720300	Lance-Sergeant	Wildman, E.
2723582	Guardsman	Wood, J.
2723212	Guardsman	Young, W.

* Mentioned in Despatches.

WOUNDED ... Officers 18
Other Ranks 100

BELGIUM AND HOLLAND

3RD BN. IRISH GUARDS

KILLED OR DIED OF WOUNDS

Number.	*Rank.*	*Name.*
172774	Captain	W. R. R. S. Bruce.
106178	Major	G. E. Fisher-Rowe.
253922	Lieutenant	H. O. C. Kennard.
94576	Major	D. M. Kennedy, M.C.
307921	Lieutenant	R. P. O'Kelly.
219069	Captain	E. E. Rawlence (M.I.D.*).
228328	Lieutenant	P. G. E. Sarsfield-Hall.
2724119	Guardsman	Allois, A.
2724407	Guardsman	Allbutt, L.
2718779	Sergeant	Allen, R.
2721176	Sergeant	Ashton, J.
2722895	Guardsman	Ashworth, W.
2721832	Lance-Sergeant	Ball, K.
2721917	Guardsman	Barlow, J.
2722072	Guardsman	Barry, G.
2724789	Guardsman	Begley, J.
2719254	Lance-Corporal	Bent, H.
14664830	Lance-Corporal	Boggis, B.
2721313	Lance-Sergeant	Boswell, T.
2721083	Guardsman	Boland, M.
2724349	Guardsman	Bracegirdle, H.
2716778	Sergeant	Breen, T.
2721333	Guardsman	Breslin, E.
2718263	Guardsman	Broderick, F.
2724382	Guardsman	Brown, A.
14692029	Guardsman	Brown, A.
2722829	Guardsman	Burton, J.
2722126	Guardsman	Carruthers, J.
2720772	Lance-Sergeant	Cole, E.
2723341	Lance-Corporal	Connor, T.
2721108	Lance-Sergeant	Davidson, T.
2723677	Guardsman	Dee, M.
2723495	Guardsman	Dee, P.
2723025	Lance-Corporal	Delaney, M.
2724791	Guardsman	Devine, R.
2723804	Guardsman	Dobson, F.
2724294	Guardsman	Donnelly, J.
2724254	Guardsman	Downey, W.
2718840	Corporal	Doyle, J.
14441956	Guardsman	Doyle, W.
14436399	Guardsman	Doyle, J.
2719614	Lance-Sergeant	Dunn, J.
2718093	Sergeant	Dunne, M. (M.I.D.* twice).
2719918	Guardsman	Follis, A.
2722131	Guardsman	Foster, W.
2724354	Guardsman	Forry, J.
2722593	Guardsman	Fox, R.
2719622	Guardsman	Frain, A.

* Mentioned in Despatches.

Number.	*Rank.*	*Name.*
2719797	Lance-Sergeant	Francis, F.
2723527	Guardsman	Gale, J.
2724458	Guardsman	Giles, G.
14679953	Guardsman	Gilham, L.
2717800	Lance-Corporal	Gilmore, G.
2724101	Guardsman	Gilmore, L.
2721896	Lance-Sergeant	Grayston, C.
2722509	Guardsman	Green, E.
2723975	Guardsman	Greenhill, A.
2723878	Guardsman	Grogan, M.
2719061	Guardsman	Hemmingway, T.
2720683	Guardsman	Henderson, C.
2720527	Guardsman	Hewitt, J.
14673282	Guardsman	Holmes, R.
2720034	Lance-Corporal	Houghton, W.
2719554	Sergeant	Houlahan, J.
2724279	Guardsman	Hubbard, E.
2717595	Guardsman	Hutchman, L.
2724336	Guardsman	Ifould, J.
2720945	Sergeant	Johns, T.
2717050	Lance-Corporal	Kane, J.
2722891	Guardsman	Keatinge, W.
14581944	Guardsman	Keen, L.
2719839	Guardsman	Kelly, C.
2723969	Lance-Corporal	Kenny, E.
2722363	Guardsman	Kent, F.
2723066	Lance-Corporal	Lally, J.
2723768	Lance-Corporal	Layde, R.
2720484	Guardsman	Le Ber, W.
2722513	Lance-Corporal	Lees, A.
2721106	Lance-Sergeant	Lennon, J.
2723420	Guardsman	Lynch, J.
2717698	Sergeant	Lyons, J.
2718372	Guardsman	Mallon, N.
2722006	Guardsman	Marler, C.
2723405	Guardsman	Mather, T.
2721847	Sergeant	Matthews, T.
14678822	Guardsman	Maxwell, W.
2719049	Guardsman	Medley, P.
2722057	Lance-Corporal	Miller, S.
2718447	Guardsman	Mogey, J.
2723687	Guardsman	Mollard, C.
2719793	Guardsman	Moore, G.
2719817	Sergeant	Moran, P.
2724801	Guardsman	Moriarty, A.
2724301	Guardsman	Mulcahy, G.
2723538	Lance-Corporal	Murray, J.
2722988	Corporal	Myers, G.
2723725	Guardsman	McCormack, N
2720351	Lance-Sergeant	McKibbin, W.
2722803	Corporal	McSorley, M.
2719914	Guardsman	North, E.
2723438	Guardsman	Ormond, J.
2722863	Guardsman	Owtram, R. (M.I.D.*)
2723823	Lance-Corporal	O'Neill, J.

* Mentioned in Despatches.

Number.	*Rank.*	*Name.*
14681745	Guardsman	Parsons, A.
14680268	Guardsman	Pavey, E.
14677526	Guardsman	Pemberton, P.
2724283	Guardsman	Penfold, J.
2720550	Guardsman	Pennington, T.
2717309	Guardsman	Perry, J.
2724202	Guardsman	Pook, W.
2722319	Lance-Sergeant	Potter, J.
2723465	Lance-Corporal	Porter, F.
2719534	Sergeant	Prendergast, J.
2722012	Lance-Sergeant	Prior, R.
2719998	Lance-Sergeant	Proe, J.
2721321	Guardsman	Rendell, V.
2720044	Lance-Sergeant	Richardson, C.
14690376	Guardsman	Rouen, A.
2720320	Guardsman	Rourke, W.
2720546	Guardsman	Sampey, T.
2723413	Guardsman	Shaw, S.
2723125	Guardsman	Shaw, S.
2723868	Guardsman	Shearer, E.
2723525	Guardsman	Simpson, W.
2722516	Guardsman	Singleton, F.
2724018	Guardsman	Smith, S.
2722871	Guardsman	Smith, S.
2720492	Guardsman	Sparling, P.
2723891	Guardsman	Stone, R.
2723810	Lance-Corporal	Stevenson, J.
14665889	Lance-Corporal	Stephenson, T.
14693730	Guardsman	Thistleton, M.
2723262	Guardsman	Thornley, J.
2721301	Guardsman	Todd, C.
2724288	Guardsman	Torr, S.
2724368	Guardsman	Towers, J.
2719613	Lance-Sergeant	Unsworth, T.
2616031	Guardsman	Varley, R.
14669019	Guardsman	Venn, T.
2724097	Guardsman	Wade, R.
2718774	Guardsman	Walker, P.
2718987	Guardsman	Walker, G.
2724056	Guardsman	Wallace, M.
2718606	Lance-Sergeant	Watters, J.
2720212	Guardsman	Watts, A.
2724057	Guardsman	Watson, T.
2721019	Guardsman	Wheatley, R.
2722121	Lance-Corporal	White, H.
2718183	Lance-Sergeant	Williams, W.
2722238	Lance-Corporal	Willshaw, J.

WOUNDED ...	Officers	28
	Other Ranks	413

GERMANY

2ND BN. IRISH GUARDS

KILLED OR DIED OF WOUNDS

Number.	*Rank.*	*Name.*
324096	Lieutenant	P. A. Cuffe.
139211	Captain	H. C. H. Fitzherbert.
240008	Lieutenant	J. C. O'Brien.
2721519	Lance-Sergeant	Baldwin, H.
2722582	Guardsman	Berry, A.
2722614	Guardsman	Charlton, E. (V.C.)
2724239	Guardsman	Cox, G.
2720722	Lance-Corporal	Doades, G.
2723692	Lance-Corporal	Eppleston, D.
2723922	Guardsman	Farrington, J.
2723314	Guardsman	Higgs, J.
2724234	Guardsman	Hughes, E.
2723366	Lance-Corporal	Iceton, D.
2720100	Lance-Sergeant	Kenwright, G.
2718842	S.S.M.	McRory, J. (M.M.).
2722853	Guardsman	McNulty, D.
2723693	Guardsman	Ritchie, A.
2721748	Lance-Corporal	Sullivan, D.
2719322	Lance-Corporal	Taylor, T.
2720462	Guardsman	Trickett, W.
2723386	Lance-Corporal	Unwin, R.
2724017	Guardsman	Welch, M.

WOUNDED ...	Officers	3
	Other Ranks	43

GERMANY

3RD BN. IRISH GUARDS

KILLED OR DIED OF WOUNDS

Number.	*Rank.*	*Name.*
93020	Major	M. V. Dudley.
330864	Lieutenant	A. Geraghty.
260227	Lieutenant	W. H. J. Hogg
278612	Lieutenant	B. B. Russell.
2724774	Guardsman	Albon, M.
2720765	Guardsman	Arkwright, J.
2720827	C.S.M.	Beresford, W.
2724739	Guardsman	Bridge, S.
2720609	Lance-Sergeant	Booth, S.
2721681	Guardsman	Bowers, F.
14581915	Guardsman	Buckland, R.
2721125	Guardsman	Cartledge, S.

Number.	*Rank.*	*Name.*
13111455	Lance-Sergeant	Cassin, J. (M.I.D.*).
2724872	Guardsman	Catling, R.
2724351	Guardsman	Charlesworth, K.
2724529	Guardsman	Clancy, R.
2721593	Lance-Sergeant	Corkrum, T.
2723744	Lance-Corporal	Downey, R.
2724353	Guardsman	Dawson, S.
2724794	Guardsman	Fee, J.
2724198	Lance-Corporal	Ford, R.
2724703	Lance-Corporal	Game, T.
2721562	Guardsman	Glendinning, N.
2724041	Guardsman	Greetham, G.
2723501	Guardsman	Guest, R.
2720971	Sergeant	Harrigan, J.
2724219	Guardsman	Harrison, F.
2723837	Guardsman	Hooker, E.
2724948	Guardsman	Johnson, W.
2724306	Guardsman	Lloyd, T.
14784080	Guardsman	Marsh, E.
2724335	Guardsman	McCarthy, C.
2720423	Guardsman	McAneny, P.
2724765	Guardsman	Oakam, F.
2718553	Lance-Corporal	O'Brien, R.
2721502	Guardsman	Pearce, W.
2723861	Guardsman	Pooley, D.
2724366	Guardsman	Roberts, R.
2719612	Guardsman	Robertson, A.
2724463	Guardsman	Rossiter, R.
2722987	Guardsman	Rotchford, T.
2724181	Guardsman	Skinner, C.
2723011	Sergeant	Stacey, J.
2722018	Guardsman	Stimpson, D.
2723535	Lance-Corporal	Vernede, J.
2724624	Guardsman	Wells, W.

* Mentioned in Despatches.

WOUNDED ...	Officers	2
	Other Ranks	106

NORTH-WEST EUROPE

2ND BN. IRISH GUARDS

DECORATIONS

Number.	*Rank.*	*Name.*
Victoria Cross.		
2722614	Guardsman	Charlton, E.
Distinguished Service Order.		
104106	Captain	H. E. J. Dormer.
52724	Lieut.-Colonel	G. A. M. Vandeleur.
Bar to M.C.		
108251	Major	E. G. Tyler, M.C.

Number.	Rank.	Name.
Military Cross.		
132247	Major	D. A. Peel.
224215	Captain	J. V. D. Taylor.
267573	Lieutenant	D. Lampard.
278682	Lieutenant	C. B. Tottenham.
225172	Lieutenant	J. R. Gorman
108251	Major	E. G. Tyler.
138639	Lieutenant	E. N. Fitzgerald.
243515	Lieutenant	W. E. Dodd.
276105	Lieutenant	J. B. P. Quinan.
268986	Lieutenant	G. N. R. Whitfield.
102707	Major	J. S. O. Haslewood.
124478	Major	M. J. P. O'Cock.
156060	Major	R. S. Langton.
Distinguished Conduct Medal.		
2723989	Guardsman	Mendes, J.
Bar to M.M.		
2717019	Lance-Sergeant	O'Donnell, J. (M.M.).
Military Medal.		
2716684	Sergeant	McManus, J.
2721275	Sergeant	Garland, S.
2719886	Sergeant	Fitzsimmons, M.
2720932	Sergeant	Steers, F.
6977185	Lance-Sergeant	McGurren, T.
2719063	Lance-Sergeant	Wright, T.
2722698	Lance-Corporal	Barnett, H.
2721637	Guardsman	Mealey, W.
2722656	Guardsman	Kettleborough, C.
2722581	Lance-Corporal	Baron, J.
2718842	Sergeant	McRory, J.
2719381	Sergeant	Gallagher, H.
2721082	Guardsman	O'Roarty, O.
2716785	Sergeant	Murray, J.
2721063	Sergeant	McComish, S.
2717019	Lance-Sergeant	O'Donnell, J.
2718123	Guardsman	Flynn, J.
Croix De Guerre.		
254296	Captain	H. J. Ripman (R.A.M.C. attd.).
2720019	Sergeant	Cardus, J.

26 Mentioned in Despatches.

NORTH-WEST EUROPE

3RD BN. IRISH GUARDS

DECORATIONS

Number.	Rank.	Name.
Bar to D.S.O.		
28140	Lieut.-Colonel	J. O. E. Vandeleur, D.S.O.

Number.	*Rank.*	*Name.*
Distinguished Service Order.		
28140	Lieut.-Colonel	J. O. E. Vandeleur.
65413	Major	B. O. P. Eugster, M.C.
50869	Lieut.-Colonel	D. H. Fitzgerald.
Military Cross.		
237623	Lieutenant	J. O. Stanley-Clarke.
121551	Captain	D. G. Kingsford.
104182	Major	A. R. Eardley-Wilmot.
307919	Lieutenant	W. Moore.
314053	Lieutenant	R. H. S. O'Grady.
269231	Lieutenant	J. R. A. MacMullen.
121346	Major	A. P. Dodd.
Distinguished Conduct Medal.		
2716645	Sergeant	McElroy, A.
2719057	Lance-Sergeant	Helliwell, F.
Military Medal.		
2721107	Corporal	Bolton, M.
2722539	Corporal	Roberts, J.
2718043	Guardsman	Cullen, J.
2717358	Guardsman	Grenan, J.
2717753	Guardsman	Moynihan, P.
2721687	Guardsman	Fielding, K.
2723650	Guardsman	Trimble, H.
2723687	Guardsman	Mollard, C.
2723977	Guardsman	Colthorpe, E.
2722896	Lance-Corporal	Brennan, R.
2721092	Corporal	Veale, P.
2721185	Guardsman	Critchley, J.
2721916	Lance-Sergeant	Atkinson, J.
2717572	W.O.II	Black, J.
2719257	Sergeant	Byrne, P.
2721585	Lance-Sergeant	Wilkinson, R.
2717080	Sergeant	McClean, M.
2718440	Sergeant	Grant, J.
2717873	W.O.II	Ritchie, J.
2722375	Sergeant	Cain, J.
Croix De Guerre.		
228326	Captain	J. A. H. Hendry
2716900	Lance-Corporal	Russell, R.

17 Mentioned in Despatches.

HOME

KILLED BY ENEMY ACTION

Number.	*Rank.*	*Name.*
63033	Major	J. Gilliat.
2719737	Guardsman	Gibson, G.
2719948	Guardsman	Haller. F.
2720194	Lance-Sergeant	Livermore, P.
3764247	Bandsman	Mather, H.
2717504	P.S.M.	Morrow, J.

Number.	Rank.	Name.
2719641	Guardsman	Murray, G.
2721457	Guardsman	O'Boyle, J.
2719749	Guardsman	Pizzala, F.
2722011	Guardsman	Phillips, L.
2720001	Guardsman	Quinn, B.
2719229	Guardsman	Waddington, R.
2720116	Guardsman	Wilkinson, J.

WOUNDED ... Officers ... ... Nil
Other Ranks 21

OTHER THEATRES (E.R.E.)

KILLED OR DIED OF WOUNDS

Number.	Rank.	Name and Unit.
	Lieut.-Colonel	E. O. Kellett, D.S.O., M.P., Notts Yeomanry, North Africa.
2721868	Guardsman	Abbott, H., 5 Guards Brigade, Belgium and Holland.
2720542	Guardsman	Geoghan, G., 5 Guards Brigade, Normandy.
2719054	Lance-Sergeant	O'Dowd, C., M.M., S.S.U., Italy.
2719627	Guardsman	Tobin, C., S.S.U., Italy.

WOUNDED ... Officers 4
Other Ranks 14

DECORATIONS

Number.	Rank.	Name.
Bar to D.S.O.		
69334	Brigadier	D. Mills-Roberts, D.S.O., M.C.
13865	T./Brigadier	J. C. Haydon, D.S.O., O.B.E.
31921	A./Brigadier	C. A. Montagu-Douglas-Scott, D.S.O.
Distinguished Service Order.		
17944	Brigadier	G. L. Verney, M.V.O.
	Colonel	H. F. d'A. S. Law, M.C.
	Lieut.-Colonel	E. O. Kellett, M.P.
69334	Lieut.-Colonel	D. Mills-Roberts, M.C.
Military Cross.		
262296	Lieutenant	T. E. Miller, M.M.
69334	Major	D. Mills-Roberts.
132243	Captain	T. B. Langton.
101405	Rev. Father	J. R. Brookes.
106849	Captain	A. D. F. O'Neill (M.I.D.*).
Military Medal.		
2723216	Guardsman	Egan, W.
2720127	Corporal	Conby, M.
2720347	Sergeant	Henderson, P.
2716586	Lance-Sergeant	O'Reilly, J.
2719054	Lance-Sergeant	O'Dowd, C.
2716717	Lance-Sergeant	Walsh, E.

24 Mentioned in Despatches.

* Mentioned in Despatches.

INDEX

Milton Keynes UK
Ingram Content Group UK Ltd.
UKHW022009090823
426617UK00006B/129